THE PRIVATIZATION OF PEACEKEEPING

Private military and security companies (PMSCs) have been used in every peace operation since 1990, and reliance on them is increasing at a time when peace operations themselves are becoming ever more complex. This book provides an essential foundation for the emerging debate on the use of PMSCs in this context. It clarifies key issues such as whether their use complies with the principles of peacekeeping, outlines the implications of the status of private contractors as non-combatants under international humanitarian law and identifies potential problems in holding states and international organizations responsible for their unlawful acts. Written as a clarion call for greater transparency, this book aims to inform the discussion to ensure that international lawyers and policy makers ask the right questions and take the necessary steps so that states and international organizations respect the law when endeavouring to keep peace in an increasingly privatized world.

LINDSEY CAMERON is a legal advisor in the Legal Division of the International Committee of the Red Cross. Prior to joining the ICRC, she worked as a researcher in the Faculty of Law at the University of Geneva. She has also worked for the UN High Commissioner for Refugees in the Balkans and at the Court of Appeal for Ontario in Canada.

Disclaimer: This book was entirely researched and written independently of the author's work in the Legal Division of the ICRC. The opinions expressed herein are her own and do not necessarily correspond to those held by the ICRC or its Legal Division.

THE PRIVATIZATION OF PEACEKEEPING

Exploring Limits and Responsibility under International Law

LINDSEY CAMERON

CAMBRIDGE
UNIVERSITY PRESS

CAMBRIDGE
UNIVERSITY PRESS

University Printing House, Cambridge CB2 8BS, United Kingdom

One Liberty Plaza, 20th Floor, New York, NY 10006, USA

477 Williamstown Road, Port Melbourne, VIC 3207, Australia

4843/24, 2nd Floor, Ansari Road, Daryaganj, Delhi – 110002, India

79 Anson Road, #06-04/06, Singapore 079906

Cambridge University Press is part of the University of Cambridge.

It furthers the University's mission by disseminating knowledge in the pursuit of education, learning and research at the highest international levels of excellence.

www.cambridge.org
Information on this title: www.cambridge.org/9781107172302
DOI: 10.1017/9781316771594

First published 2017

Printed in the United Kingdom by Clays, St Ives plc

A catalogue record for this publication is available from the British Library

ISBN 978-1-107-17230-2 Hardback

For my family

CONTENTS

FOREWORD

This book deals with an issue that is becoming more and more important in practice: the need for UN peace forces is increasing, but the willingness of powerful states – and even of traditional contributors such as Canada, Sweden, Finland and Austria – with well-trained armed forces to put their streamlined armed forces at the disposal of the UN is decreasing. The forces of those who actually contribute the great majority of troops are often not sufficiently equipped and trained and raise in some cases serious concerns about their respect of international humanitarian law (IHL) and human rights. It is therefore tempting to use professionals hired, trained and equipped by the private sector, quickly available to the UN as long as it is willing and able to pay, not constrained by national interests (and national caveats) that must be taken into account. This idea, however, seems contrary to the basic axiom that developed over the last 300 years: that war is not a private business, but a monopoly of the Westphalian state that must be implemented through its official agents. This axiom equally permeates both contemporary IHL and the law and the practice of peace operations.

The international law applicable to private military and security companies (PMSCs) involved in peace operations is itself of practical importance. In addition, the analysis required to determine the international law applicable to them provides a testing ground for crucial conceptual *de lege lata* questions and *de lege ferenda* dilemmas in several fields of public international law. The three central legal issues Lindsey Cameron deals with are, first, the status, rights and obligations of PMSC personnel involved in peace operations, for the clarification of which the distinction between self-defence and direct participation in hostilities is central under both IHL and the law of peacekeeping. Second, related to the first question, but comprising many more aspects, the limitations to the use of PMSC personnel in peace operations are discussed. Third, the responsibility of states, the UN and other international organizations for wrongful acts of such 'private' personnel is discussed.

xi

The elegant and pragmatic structure of the book is not preestablished Cartesian, but rather resembles an English garden, perfectly adapted to the landscape, in this case international reality and the different legal issues, which cannot be clinically separated but interact.

This research successfully cumulates the complexity of applying IHL (simultaneously) to two actors for which it was not made, but to whom it applies and for whom it offers, as Dr Cameron shows, solutions: PMSCs and peace forces. Particularly interesting and challenging is that she had to face the exponential difficulty of having to define self-defence for persons who belong both to PMSCs and to peace forces. For both categories, the concept is different than for individuals, which already is a concept not defined by international law. PMSCs use self-defence and defence of others not as a defence in an exceptional situation, but as a preplanned object of their business. Peace forces have always used the term in a wider sense than the criminal law defence. Political reasons make 'self-defence' easier to accept for states and public opinion than law enforcement or even peace enforcement by the UN, which it often constitutes in reality. For both, the distinction between this ill-defined concept of self-defence and direct participation in hostilities is crucial, because the latter makes PMSC staff who are most often civilians lose protection as civilians by IHL and international criminal law and because the PMSC industry for the time being stresses that their staff are not meant to directly participate in hostilities, ignoring that the mere guarding of a military objective constitutes direct participation in hostilities. On this crucial issue, Dr Cameron suggests a better, more nuanced and practical interpretation of the term 'self-defence' than anything I have read before and after this book. Her line is in my view also much more appropriate, at least for PMSCs, than that suggested by the ICRC in its *Interpretive Guidance on the Notion of Direct Participation in Hostilities* (which considers that the absence of belligerent nexus is the decisive criterion). I agree that if persons and objects PMSCs defend are not protected against attacks in IHL (e.g., if persons are combatants or civilians directly participating in hostilities or objects are military objectives), guarding or defending them against attacks constitutes direct participation in hostilities and not criminal law defence of others. This is always the case when the attacker is a person belonging to a party to the conflict, even if he or she does not benefit from or has lost combatant status. The unlawful status of the attacker does not trigger the right to self-defence of a civilian for the benefit of combatants, including peace forces when they are combatants. If the person attacked – and under the domestic legislation of some states even if the object attacked – is civilian, criminal law self-defence may justify a use of force, even against combatants. The analysis is complicated by the fact that individual PMSC staff will often not know the facts that determine the legality of conduct in a certain situation. Therefore, Dr. Cameron is right to suggest that the use of force by PMSCs belonging to peace forces in defence of others and of property should be admitted only restrictively and only against direct attacks, not against the taking of control, arrest or capture, a distinction most often forgotten in scholarly writings.

Apart from these central problems for her subject, Cameron equally deals in small masterpieces of conciseness and accuracy with many preliminary issues she must tackle before dealing with the central issues.

The author totally masters such diverse branches as IHL, *ius ad bellum*, UN law, the law on the responsibility of states and international organizations and, perhaps most important, the facts. Her style and her nuanced way of arguing are marked by Anglo-Saxon pragmatism. Factors in favor and against certain arguments are balanced and solutions are often followed by a reality check. They are then applied in very well chosen hypothetical examples. Dr Cameron does not justify, as do many others who write about PMSCs, her preconceived ideological ideas, but genuinely enquires into what international law has to say about certain questions, which is often (but not always) not a black-and-white answer, but useful thoughts are always offered to the reader.

Marco Sassòli
Professor and Director of the Department of Public International Law
and International Organization at the University of Geneva

ACKNOWLEDGEMENTS

My deepest thanks go, first and foremost, to Professor Marco Sassòli. His unparalleled knowledge of international humanitarian law and general international law, combined with his attention to detail and dedication to his students, made him a thesis supervisor of which most students can only dream. Professor Sassòli's profound humanity, sense of humour, and integrity have influenced and shaped my approach to scholarship and the law as much as the vast knowledge he has shared with me over the years we worked together at the University of Geneva.

My research on private military and security companies began in a course taught by Professor Yves Sandoz, whose exceptional kindness, humanitarianism, and unique experience in shaping international law inspired and encouraged me. Warm thanks also go to Professors Laurence Boisson de Chazournes, Nigel White and Nicolas Michel for having adjudicated the defence of my PhD, from which this book arose.

This work was done in an entirely personal capacity and represents my views alone. That being said, I warmly thank my colleagues in the legal division of the International Committee of the Red Cross, from whom I have learned a great deal over the years. Very special thanks go to Jean-Marie Henckaerts, Bruno Demeyere, Eve Lahaye, Iris Müller, Heike Niebergall-Lackner, Helen Obregon and Marie-Louise Tougas. Warm thanks are also due to Knut Dörmann and Laurent Colassis for giving me academic freedom.

In addition, this work would never have seen the light of day had it not been for the friendship and encouragement of Professor Julia Grignon. In a similar vein, I thank very warmly Elizabeth Spicer at Cambridge University Press for her patient support and guidance with this project.

I am eternally grateful to Serge for his patience, good humour, wisdom, unfailing encouragement and partnership, which make it all possible. This book is for Jules and Margot, in the hope that you will live in a better and more peaceful world.

ABBREVIATIONS

AJIL	*American Journal of International Law*
AMISOM	African Union Mission in Somalia
AP I	Protocol (I) Additional to the Geneva Conventions of 1949, and relating to the protection of victims of international armed conflicts of 8 June 1977
AP II	Protocol (II) Additional to the Geneva Conventions of 1949, and relating to the protection of victims of non-international armed conflicts of 8 June 1977
ASR	Articles on State Responsibility of the International Law Commission, 2001
AU	African Union
CENTCOM	United States Central Command
CIHL	customary international humanitarian law
CIVPOL	civilian police (in peace operations)
CRS	Congressional Research Service (US)
DARIO	Draft Articles on the Responsibility of International Organizations of the International Law Commission, 2011
DFID	Department for International Development (UK)
DFS	Department of Field Support (UN)
DoD	Department of Defense (US)
DPKO	Department of Peacekeeping Operations (UN)
DRC	Democratic Republic of the Congo
ECHR	European Convention on Human Rights
ECOWAS	Economic Community of West African States
ECtHR	European Court of Human Rights
EJIL	*European Journal of International Law*
EU	European Union
FARDC	Forces armées de la République démocratique du Congo
GC I	Geneva Convention (I) for the amelioration of the condition of the wounded and sick in armed forces in the field of 12 August 1949

GC II	Geneva Convention (II) for the amelioration of the condition of wounded, sick and shipwrecked members of armed forces at sea of 12 August 1949
GC III	Geneva Convention (III) relative to the treatment of prisoners of war of 12 August 1949
GC IV	Geneva Convention (IV) relative to the protection of civilian persons in time of war of 12 August 1949
HPCR	Program on Humanitarian Policy and Conflict Research (Harvard)
HRC	Human Rights Committee; Human Rights Council
IACHR	Inter-American Court of Human Rights
ICC	International Criminal Court
ICCPR	International Covenant on Civil and Political Rights, 1966
ICJ	International Court of Justice
ICRC	International Committee of the Red Cross
ICTR	International Criminal Tribunal for Rwanda
ICTY	International Criminal Tribunal for the Former Yugoslavia
IED	improvised explosive device
IHL	international humanitarian law
IHRL	international human rights law
ILC	International Law Commission
INTERFET	International Force for East Timor
IOLR	*International Organizations Law Review*
IPTF	International Police Task Force
IRRC	*International Review of the Red Cross*
JICJ	*Journal of International Criminal Justice*
KFOR	Kosovo Force
MINURCAT	United Nations Mission in the Central African Republic and Chad
MINUSTAH	United Nations Stabilization Mission in Haiti
MONUC	Mission des Nations Unies en République démocratique du Congo
MONUSCO	United Nations Organization Stabilization Mission in the DR Congo
MPRI	Military and Professional Resources, Inc.
NATO	North Atlantic Treaty Organization
NGO	non-governmental organization
NYUJILP	*New York University Journal of International Law and Politics*
OAU	Organization of African Unity
OLA	Office of Legal Affairs (UN)
OMP	opération de maintien de la paix (peacekeeping operation)
ONU	Organisation des nations unies
ONUC	Opération des Nations Unies au Congo
ONUCI	Opération des Nations Unies en Côte d'Ivoire
OSCE	Organization for Security and Co-operation in Europe
PMSC	private military and/or security company

POW	prisoner of war
PSC	private security company
RCADI	Recueil des cours – Académie de droit international de La Haye
RUF	Revolutionary United Front
SOFA	Status of Forces Agreement
SOMA	Status of Mission Agreement
SRSG	Special Representative of the Secretary-General
UAE	United Arab Emirates
UK	United Kingdom
UN	United Nations
UNAMA	United Nations Assistance Mission in Afghanistan
UNAMI	United Nations Assistance Mission for Iraq
UNAMID	African Union–United Nations hybrid operation in Darfur
UNAMSIL	United Nations Mission in Sierra Leone
UNESCO	United Nations Educational, Scientific and Cultural Organization
UNEF	United Nations Emergency Force
UNFICYP	United Nations Peacekeeping Force in Cyprus
UNGA	United Nations General Assembly
UNIFIL	United Nations Interim Force in Lebanon
UNHCR	United Nations High Commissioner for Refugees
UNMEE	United Nations Mission in Ethiopia and Eritrea
UNMIK	United Nations Mission in Kosovo
UNMIS	United Nations Mission in Sudan
UNMOGIP	United Nations Military Observer Group in India and Pakistan
UNOSOM II	United Nations Operation in Somalia II
UNPOL	United Nations Police
UNPROFOR	United Nations Protection Force
UNSC	United Nations Security Council
UNSG	United Nations Secretary-General
UNTAET	United Nations Transitional Administration in East Timor
UNTSO	United Nations Truce Supervision Organization
US	United States of America
USAID	United States Agency for International Development
YB	yearbook
ZäoRV	Zeitschrift für ausländisches öffentliches Recht und Völkerrecht

~

Introduction

The proliferation of private military and security companies (PMSCs) in the past decade, and especially the extensive recent use of them by major military powers in the conflicts in Iraq and Afghanistan, has led to impassioned debate and controversy. In many respects, the use of private contractors in armed conflict is not a new phenomenon. In fact, some of the earliest treaties governing armed conflicts provided prisoner-of-war status for 'sutlers' and 'contractors' 'who follow an army without directly belonging to it'.[1] Sutlers and contractors provided catering and basic logistical support for armed forces. However, the sheer number of these traditional contractors and the expansion of their roles to include security provision, combined with cases in which states contracted companies to fight for them around the turn of the twenty-first century, has changed the playing field.[2]

Much of the debate has to do with the ethics and wisdom of their use. Political scientists are particularly concerned by what they perceive as the weakening of the state monopoly over the use of armed force, long considered the hallmark of modern statehood. What are the implications for states and for international society? Should PMSCs be used at all? If so, how? On one hand, some see PMSCs as potential saviours, invoking the alleged success of a PMSC in halting conflict in Sierra Leone in 2000, which they contrast sharply to the almost criminal inaction of the international community during the genocide in Rwanda in 1994.[3] Such

---

[1] Hague Convention (II) with Respect to the Laws and Customs of War on Land and Its Annex: Regulations Concerning the Laws and Customs of War on Land. The Hague (29 July 1899) Article 13.

[2] On behalf of the United States alone, there were more than 210,000 private military and/or security contractors in Iraq and Afghanistan in 2010. See US Commission on Wartime Contracting, Final Report to Congress 'Transforming Wartime Contracting: Controlling Costs, Reducing Risks' (August 2011), 2.

[3] In particular, Doug Brooks, 'Messiahs or Mercenaries? The Future of International Private Military Services' (2000) 7 *Intl Peacekeeping* 129–144 at 131 and 134; see also Oldrich Bures,

commentators – including some with strong ties to the industry – argue that PMSCs could be used as the peacekeepers of the future and have argued for the acceptance of their use in Darfur, for example.[4] On the other hand, others characterize virtually all PMSCs as mercenaries and argue they should be banned altogether, pointing to an alleged greater propensity for violence or to their ostensible impunity. Indeed, it took seven years to successfully prosecute Blackwater guards for the Nisour Square massacre, and no PMSC personnel have been prosecuted for involvement in the abuses in Abu Ghraib prison, nor for their acknowledged role in relation to the trafficking of women in Bosnia in the 1990s.[5]

'Private Military Companies: A Second Best Peacekeeping Option?' (2005) 12 *Intl Peacekeeping* 533–546 at 543.

[4] See, e.g., Malcolm Patterson, 'A Corporate Alternative to United Nations *ad hoc* Military Deployments' (2008) 13 *J Conflict and Security L* 215–231; Patterson, *Privatising Peace: A Corporate Adjunct to United Nations Peacekeeping and Humanitarian Operations* (Palgrave Macmillan, 2009); F. Fountain, 'A Call for "Mercy-naries": Private Forces for International Policing' (2004) 13 *Michigan State UJ Intl L* 227–261; Bures, 'A Second Best Peacekeeping Option?'; Victor-Yves Ghebali, 'The United Nations and the Dilemma of Outsourcing Peacekeeping Operations', in Alan Bryden and Marina Caparini, *Private Actors and Security Governance* (Geneva: DCAF, 2006), pp. 213–230; James Pattison, 'Outsourcing the Responsibility to Protect: Humanitarian Intervention and Private Military and Security Companies' (2010) 2 *Intl Theory* 1–31; Leslie Hough, 'A Study of Peacekeeping, Peace-Enforcement and Private Military Companies in Sierra Leone', 16.4 *African Security Review*, Institute for Security Studies, 8–21; Margaret Gichanga, 'Fusing Privatisation of Security with Peace and Security Initiatives' (2010) ISS Paper 219; K. Charles and C. Cloete, 'Outsourcing United Nations Peacekeeping Roles and Support Functions' (2009) *South African J Industrial Engineering* 1–13. See also M. Gichanga, M. Roberts and S. Gumedze, 'Conference Report: The Involvement of the Private Security Sector in Peacekeeping Missions', Institute for Security Studies, Nairobi Office, 21–22 July 2010. For industry lobbying, see M. Boot, 'Darfur Solution: Send in the Mercenaries', *Los Angeles Times*, 31 May 2006, p. B13; Christopher Rochester, 'White Paper: A Private Alternative to a Standing United Nations Peacekeeping Force' (Peace Operations Institute, 2007); Doug Brooks, 'Private Military Service Providers: Africa's Welcome Pariahs', in Laurent Bachelor (ed), *Nouveaux Mondes – Guerres d'Afrique* (spring 2002), pp. 69–86. For an article explicitly opposing such use of PMSCs, see A. Leander and R. van Munster, 'Private Security Contractors in the Debate About Darfur: Reflecting and Reinforcing Neo-Liberal Governmentality' (2007) 21 *Intl Relations* 201–216.

[5] Enrique Ballasteros, 'Report of the Special Rapporteur', UN Doc E/CN.4/1999/11 (13 January 1999), wanted them banned. See also Sarah Percy, 'Morality and Regulation', in Simon Chesterman and Chia Lehnardt, *From Mercenaries to Market* (Oxford University Press, 2007), pp. 24–28. On the difficulty in prosecuting those involved in sex trafficking in Bosnia, see Margaret Maffai, 'Accountability for Private Military and Security Company Employees That Engage in Sex Trafficking and Related Abuses While Under Contract with the United States Overseas' (2008–2009) 26 *Wisconsin Intl L J* 1095–1139. Maffai does not argue that PMSCs should be banned.

Many focus on the changes needed at international and national levels in order to control and regulate the existing industry.[6]

The use of private military and security companies in peace operations has garnered far less attention to date than their use in armed conflicts and other situations more generally. Perhaps this is not surprising, as the roles of PMSCs in peace operations have often been confined to more traditional activities of civilians accompanying armed forces. Peace operations are also not often seen as 'armed conflicts', such that there may appear to be less cause for concern. Recently, however, the United Nations has clearly reported its use of private security guards in peace operations.[7] Moreover, the Secretary-General has acknowledged that the UN relies on private security guards in situations to which international humanitarian law applies, stating, 'The use of armed private security companies has enabled operations in situations in which there was a mandated need for the United Nations system to carry out its work, such as in complex emergency situations and post-conflict or conflict areas.'[8] Indeed, in 2013, the UN spent more than $30 million on private security in special political missions and peace operations; for 2014, more than $40 million was budgeted.[9] In addition, one state contributes its civilian police to UN and other peace operations via PMSCs. This state of affairs raises new and interesting questions relating to the use of force in peace operations – but it is far from the only use of PMSCs in that context. Indeed, private

---

[6] One of the key papers that set the tone for debates in regulating the industry is by Caroline Holmqvist, 'Private Security Companies: The Case for Regulation' (SIPRI Policy Paper No. 9, 2005); see also Human Rights First, 'Private Security Contractors at War: Ending the Culture of Impunity' (2008).

[7] Report of the Secretary-General, 'Use of Private Security', UN Doc A/67/539 (22 October 2012), para. 3: 'The United Nations has long used private security companies, mostly involving unarmed local contractors to secure premises for the protection of United Nations personnel and/or assets against criminal activities. In recent years, however, faced with demands from Member States to carry out mandates and programmes in high-risk environments, in addition to increased evidence that the United Nations is a specific target in some such environments, organizations of the United Nations system have, as a last resort, contracted armed private security companies to protect United Nations personnel, premises and assets.' See also 'Report of the Working Group on the Use of Mercenaries as a Means of Violating Human Rights and Impeding the Exercise of the Right of Peoples to Self-Determination', UN Doc A/69/338 (21 August 2014).

[8] Ibid.

[9] UN Advisory Committee on Administrative and Budgetary Questions, 'Reports on the Department of Safety and Security and on the Use of Private Security', UN Doc A/67/624 (7 December 2012), Annexes I and II. The special political missions include UNAMA, the UN Assistance Mission in Afghanistan.

military and security companies have been used in every peace operation since 1990. Reliance on them is increasing at a time when peace operations themselves are becoming ever more complex. Indeed, even the UN Working Group on the use of mercenaries, in its recent study on the UN use of PMSCs in peace operations, did not advocate for abolishing their use but merely suggested 'ways and means to ensure an efficient selection and vetting process when employing private security companies.'[10] For these reasons and others, the laws governing their use merit careful study.

This increased use of PMSCs in UN peace operations comes at a time when the fundamental principles of peacekeeping themselves are perceived to be under threat. In particular, the more 'robust' mandates given to some operations has led to concern that the principle on the need for a limited use of force is not respected by the UN Security Council in establishing mandates.[11] At the same time, the UN is contemplating moving beyond its 'how to stay' approach toward a 'how to deliver' approach, in an international climate in which staff security is a constant concern.[12] In its 2015 Report, the High-Level Panel acknowledged that 'Missions without a military component face a particular security challenge, and the Panel supports . . . the use of properly vetted private security contractors where they are a necessary option.'[13] The role that PMSCs might play thus remains an open question.

The essential research questions for this study are: may private military and security companies be used in peace operations, especially in situations in which there is on-going armed conflict? If so, for what? What law governs their actions? Who is responsible for their acts and omissions in violation of international law?

---

[10] 'Report of the Working Group on the Use of Mercenaries as a Means of Violating Human Rights and Impeding the Exercise of the Right of Peoples to Self-Determination', UN Doc A/69/338 (21 August 2014), para. 3.

[11] For example, see 'Letter Dated 1 June 2014 from the Permanent Representative of the Russian Federation to the United Nations Addressed to the Secretary-General', UN Doc S/2014/384, 2014.

[12] UN Chief Executives Board for Coordination, 'Conclusions of the High-Level Committee on Management at Its Twenty-seventh Session' (Venice, 3 and 4 April 2014), UN Doc CEB/2014/3 (21 May 2014), para. 23.

[13] 'Report of the High-Level Independent Panel on Peace Operations on Uniting Our Strengths for Peace: Politics, Partnership and People' (17 June 2015), UN Doc A/70/95; S/2015/446, para. 300. This option is listed last, after small military or police contingents, or a guard force.

Part I provides a detailed overview of the use of PMSCs in peace operations, including the known existing policies governing their use. It sets the stage on a factual level for the legal analysis in the subsequent parts. Part II sets out the legal framework governing UN peace operations. It examines whether the use of PMSCs by the UN in various roles, including potentially as the peacekeeping force, would comply with that general legal framework. Furthermore, it investigates whether their use complies with the principles of peacekeeping.

Moving from a general international law framework to an analysis focused on international humanitarian law, Part III looks at one of the key limits on the use of PMSCs, which is that they may not be used in roles in which they are likely to take a direct part in hostilities. It especially looks at the link between direct participation in hostilities and the use of force in self-defence. While this discussion has ramifications for their use in 'normal' armed conflict situations, the complex legal framework surrounding the use of force in self-defence in UN peace operations calls for a separate analysis.

Finally, Part IV widens the scope again to look at the responsibility of international organizations, and especially the UN, for the actions of PMSCs in peace operations. This analysis not only encompasses actions in relation to the use of force, but extends to potential responsibility for any of the acts of PMSCs.

One of the central themes of this book is that in fact, in some cases, PMSC personnel may already be acting as peacekeepers, in the traditional sense of the word. Regulations on the use of force permitted for private security contractors strongly resemble the rules established for peacekeepers in traditional peace operations, in which force was limited to self-defence and defence of the mandate, and in which mandates were far less robust than they are today. This has implications on at least two levels. First, the debate must move beyond whether PMSCs may be used as peacekeepers in traditional operations and focus on the implications of that being the reality. Second, the implications of the use of PMSCs as security guards (and in other roles) in peace operations with a robust mandate and which are likely to become party to an existing armed conflict must be examined and understood to ensure that they are regulated effectively.

This study uses the term 'private military and/or security companies/contractors' as used in the Montreux Document, to mean that they are

> private business entities that provide military and/or security services, irrespective of how they describe themselves. Military and security services include, in particular, armed guarding and protection of persons and objects, such as convoys, buildings and other places; maintenance and operation of weapons systems; prisoner detention; and advice to or training of local forces and security personnel.[14]

Given the fact that the actions of contractors hired to provide other services to troop contingents may also be implicated in important ways in actions (or omissions) that may have a significant impact on individuals in states where a peace operation is being carried out, this study does not hesitate to take a broad view of contractors. This approach allows it to include, for example, the company contracted to carry out waste management for the Nepali forces in Haiti linked to the cholera epidemic.

As for the term 'peace operations', this book adopts the approach of the High-Level Independent Panel on Peace Operations of 2015. These

> range from special envoys and mediators; political missions, including peacebuilding missions; regional preventive diplomacy offices; observations missions, including both ceasefire and electoral missions; to small, technical-specialist missions such as electoral support missions; multidisciplinary operations both large and small drawing on civilian, military and police personnel to support peace process implementation, and that have included even transitional authorities with governance functions; as well as advance missions for planning.[15]

Where the discussion refers only to peace operations under UN command and control, and subject to the traditional principles of peacekeeping, that will be made clear. While it is acknowledged that the loose categories of 'peace enforcement' and 'peacekeeping' often denote different types of operations that may carry relevant implications in practice, the premise here is that such categories and any legal limitations (or lack thereof) that they may be understood to entail give rise at most to a rebuttable presumption. Moreover, while the legal framework regarding the use of force may be relevant when it comes to an assessment of direct participation in hostilities and PMSC activity, any number of activities carried out by PMSCs in any kind of peace operation may give rise to situations where rights and responsibility are in play.

---

[14] Montreux Document, para. 9(a).

[15] 'Report of the High-Level Independent Panel on Peace Operations on Uniting Our Strengths for Peace: Politics, Partnership and People' (17 June 2015), UN Doc A/70/95; S/2015/446, para. 18.

PART I

UN Use of PMSCs

Peacekeeping is not a soldier's job, but only a soldier can do it.[1]

Private military and security companies or contractors have been involved in every peace operation since 1990, in roles other than as the military component of the peacekeeping force.[2] There are different levels at which PMSCs are implicated. On the most 'innocuous' level, they perform the same kind of support and logistics functions as they do in relation to deployments of armed forces in more traditional conflict situations. In addition to that, they are increasingly tapped to perform security functions for peace operations.[3] Moving further up the scale in some ways, the United States uses PMSCs to contract and deploy civilian police contingents to peace operations. Although they are less controversial than the use of PMSCs as a military contingent in peace operations, even these roles are not without legal ramifications.

Much of the writing advocating for or abhorring recourse to PMSCs as peacekeepers centres on the military component of peace operations – and, in particular, on a United Nations force authorized to use robust force in order to protect civilians. Indeed, there have been recent proposals to use PMSCs as a military force in peace operations and PMSCs themselves are clamouring for such a role.[4] This is not surprising: one of the main

---

[1] Charles C. Moskos identifies this phrase as 'the unofficial motto of the United Nations soldier': *Peace Soldiers: The Sociology of a United Nations Military Force* (Chicago and London: University of Chicago Press, 1976), p. 139.

[2] Deborah Avant observes that '[e]very multi-lateral peace operation conducted by the UN since 1990 included the presence of PSCs'. D Avant, *The Market for Force* (Cambridge: Cambridge University Press, 2001), p. 7.

[3] Lou Pingeot, *Dangerous Partnership* (Global Policy Forum and Rosa Luxemburg Foundation, 2012).

[4] See, e.g., Malcolm Patterson, 'A Corporate Alternative to United Nations *ad hoc* Military Deployments' (2008) 13 *Journal of Conflict and Security Law* 215–231; Patterson, *Privatising Peace: A Corporate Adjunct to United Nations Peacekeeping and Humanitarian Operations* (Palgrave Macmillan, 2009); Doug Brooks, 'Messiahs or Mercenaries? The Future

7

concerns with the development of the doctrine of 'robust' peacekeeping is that it may require many more boots on the ground than traditional peacekeeping, i.e., many more forces than UN peace operations are usually able to muster, with a strong military capacity.[5] While some argue that a doctrine of robust peacekeeping must be developed that takes into account the anticipated continuation of 'very severe resource limitations',[6] others seem to believe that PMSCs could ably fill the gap.[7] Consequently, the legal framework of that potential scenario merits careful study.

of International Private Military Services' (2000) 7 *International Peacekeeping* 129–144; F. Fountain, 'A Call for "Mercy-naries": Private Forces for International Policing' (2004) 13 *Michigan State University Journal of International Law* 227–261; Oldrich Bures, 'Private Military Companies: A Second Best Peacekeeping Option?' (2005) 12 *International Peacekeeping* 533–546; Victor-Yves Ghebali, 'The United Nations and the Dilemma of Outsourcing Peacekeeping Operations', in Alan Bryden and Marina Caparini (eds.), *Private Actors and Security Governance* (Geneva: DCAF 2006), pp. 213–230; James Pattison, 'Outsourcing the Responsibility to Protect: Humanitarian Intervention and Private Military and Security Companies' (2010) 2 *International Theory* 1–31; Leslie Hough, 'A Study of Peacekeeping, Peace-Enforcement and Private Military Companies in Sierra Leone' 16.4 *African Security Review* (Institute for Security Studies), pp. 8–21; Margaret Gichanga, 'Fusing Privatisation of Security with Peace and Security Initiatives' (2010), Institute for Security Studies Paper 219; K. Charles and C. Cloete, 'Outsourcing United Nations Peacekeeping Roles and Support Functions' (2009) *South African J Industrial Engineering* 1–13. See also M. Gichanga, M. Roberts and S. Gumedze, 'Conference Report: The Involvement of the Private Security Sector in Peacekeeping Missions', Institute for Security Studies, Nairobi Office, 21–22 July 2010. For a surprisingly ambivalent position, see Alex J. Bellamy and Paul D. Williams, *Understanding Peacekeeping*, 2nd edn (Cambridge: Polity Press, 2010), pp. 321–336, especially at 336. *Contra*, A. Leander and R. van Munster, 'Private Security Contractors in the Debate about Darfur: Reflecting and Re-inforcing Neo-Liberal Governmentality' (2007) 21 *International Relations* 201–216. For industry lobbying, see M. Boot, 'Darfur Solution: Send in the Mercenaries', *Los Angeles Times*, 31 May 2006, p. B13; Christopher Rochester, 'White Paper: A Private Alternative to a Standing United Nations Peacekeeping Force' (Peace Operations Institute 2007); Doug Brooks, 'Private Military Service Providers: Africa's Welcome Pariahs', in Laurent Bachelor (ed.), *Nouveaux Mondes – Guerres d'Afrique* (Spring 2002) 69–86. In his evidence before the UK Select Committee on Foreign Affairs, Tim Spicer also recommended the creation of a peace enforcement force of PMSCs for interim use: Select Committee on Foreign Affairs, Examination of Witness (Lt Col T Spicer OBE) 11 June 2002, Response to Mr Pope, paras 3–4.

[5] See generally, however, James Sloan, *The Militarisation of Peacekeeping in the Twenty-first Century* (Oxford: Hart, 2011), who argues that militarization is not the solution for peacekeeping. On the other hand, see the statement by the UN Security Council President exhorting states to ensure the UN will meet the demand for peacekeepers (in terms of both personnel and logistics) in the face of the surging demand for such operations: S/PRST/2004/16 (17 May 2004).

[6] Richard Gowan and Benjamin Tortolani, 'Robust Peacekeeping and Its Limitations', in Bruce Jones (ed.), *Robust Peacekeeping: The Politics of Force* (Centre for International Cooperation, 2009).

[7] See above, note 4.

Peacekeeping, in its original incarnation, involved the deployment of interposition forces to monitor the implementation of a peace agreement or ceasefire, predominantly following international armed conflicts. Since then, and in particular since the end of the Cold War, peace operations are frequently deployed in situations of ongoing non-international armed conflicts and are mandated with a broad variety of tasks. Indeed, today, the term 'peace operations' is generally preceded by the adjectives 'complex', 'multi-disciplinary' or 'multi-dimensional'.[8] In addition to monitoring ceasefires, they can be tasked with monitoring elections, carrying out disarmament and demobilization and reintegration, supporting security sector reform, demining, helping to strengthen rule of law institutions, protecting civilians, assisting the delivery of humanitarian aid and even being put in charge of the entire civilian administration of the territory in which they are deployed.[9] Despite the fact that they are deployed with considerable frequency and endowed with such complex mandates,[10] some important questions remain concerning the legal framework governing the personnel of peace operations.

Peace operations have also gone through a long period of intense doctrinal development over the past fifteen years. This development began with the Report of the Panel on United Nations Peace Operations of 2000 – better known as the Brahimi Report – and largely culminated in the Capstone Doctrine, issued in 2008, although it remains ongoing.[11] While some of these reforms have produced structural changes within the UN

[8] It should be noted, however, that already in 1960, ONUC was a complex peace operation on many levels. See E.M. Miller, 'Legal Aspects of the United Nations Action in the Congo' (1961) 55 *AJIL* 1–28, written by Oscar Schachter under a pseudonym due to mounting criticism of the UN operation and concern that it would inflame further criticism as he was the director of the UN legal division at the time. See L.F. Damrosch, 'Oscar Schachter (1915–2003)' (2004) 98 *AJIL* 35–41 at 37. On the evolution of peace operations, see *inter alia* James Cockayne and David Malone, 'The Ralph Bunche Centennial: Peace Operations Then and Now' (2005) 11 *Global Governance* 331–350.

[9] In UNSC Res 2086 (2013), the UN Security Council lists (non-exhaustively) the types of activities or tasks with which a multidimensional peace operation can be mandated (para. 8). For examples of international territorial administration missions, see UNSC Res 1272 (1999) (UN Transitional Administration in East Timor) and UNSC Res 1244 (1999) (UN Mission in Kosovo).

[10] As of the time of writing, there have been a total of 67 UN peace operations deployed.

[11] 'Report of the Panel on United Nations Peace Operations', UN Doc A/55/305 – S/2000/809 (21 August 2000) (Brahimi Report). See also the follow-up report by the Secretary-General on the implementation of the Brahimi Report: UN Doc A/55/502 (20 October 2000). For the Capstone Doctrine, see United Nations Department of Peacekeeping Operations and Department of Field Support, 'United Nations Peacekeeping Operations: Principles and Guidelines' (18 January 2008) (Capstone Doctrine).

peacekeeping department,[12] they have also led to new doctrines. One of the key concepts that has emerged is the protection of civilians in peace operations.[13] Since 1999, peace operations have frequently been mandated to protect civilians, and developing ways to operationalize and implement the protection of civilians is a priority for the United Nations.[14] Despite the prominence of the concept, however, the UN has not yet defined it,[15] although the Secretary-General has stated that 'the protection of civilians is a legal concept based on international humanitarian, human rights and refugee law', distinguishing it from the responsibility to protect, which is a 'political concept'.[16]

The concept of the protection of civilians has also been used in UN authorized 'peace enforcement' operations such as that in Libya in

---

[12] In particular, the Department of Field Support has been created.

[13] UN Secretary-General, 'In Larger Freedom: Towards Development, Security and Human Rights For All', UN Doc A/59/2005 (21 March 2005); Report of the High-Level Panel on Threats, Challenges and Change, 'A More Secure World: Our Shared Responsibility' (2004). Key resolutions of the UN Security Council affirming the role of peacekeeping in protecting civilians are UNSC Res 1674 (2006) and UNSC Res 1894 (2009). For the UN Secretary-General's thematic reports on the protection of civilians, see UN Doc S/1999/957 (8 September 1999); UN Doc S/2001/331 (30 March 2001); UN Doc S/2002/1300 (26 November 2002); UN Doc S/2004/431 (28 May 2004); UN Doc S/2005/740 (28 November 2005); UN Doc S/2007/643 (28 October 2007); UN Doc S/2009/277 (29 May 2009); UN Doc S/2010/579 (11 November 2010); UN Doc S/2012/376 (22 May 2012). See also Victoria Holt, Glyn Taylor and Max Kelly, *Protecting Civilians in the Context of UN Peacekeeping Operations* (Independent study jointly commissioned by the Department of Peacekeeping Operations and the Office for the Coordination of Humanitarian Affairs, 2009). An important aspect of peace operations that has undergone doctrinal and practical development is the role of women and a gender perspective in peacekeeping, including the deployment of female peacekeepers, especially pursuant to UNSC Res 1325 (2000). This issue and its relationship to PMSCs is beyond the scope of this study.

[14] See the section on 'Protection of Civilians by United Nations Peacekeeping and Other Missions' in UN Secretary-General, 'Report on the Protection of Civilians in Armed Conflict', UN Doc S/2012/376 (22 May 2012) paras 47–56. UNSC Res 1894 (2009) requests the Secretary-General (in consultation) to develop an operational concept. See UN Doc S/Res/1894 (2009) para. 22. See also paras 23–24. The first peacekeeping operation to receive a protection of civilian's mandate was UNAMSIL in 1999: UN Doc S/Res/1267 (1999).

[15] Damian Lilly, 'The Changing Nature of the Protection of Civilians in International Peace Operations' (2012) 19 *International Peacekeeping* 628–639 at 630.

[16] UN Secretary-General, 'Report on the Protection of Civilians in Armed Conflict', UN Doc S/2012/376 (22 May 2012) para. 21. He goes on to state that 'The protection of civilians relates to violations of international humanitarian and human rights law in situations of armed conflict. The responsibility to protect is limited to violations that constitute war crimes or crimes against humanity or that would be considered acts of genocide or ethnic cleansing. Crimes against humanity, genocide and ethnic cleansing may occur in situations that do not meet the threshold of armed conflict.' Ibid.

2011.[17] In the past, peacekeeping has often been distinguished from peace enforcement based on the crude yardstick that peacekeeping operations are under UN command and control and rely on a lesser use of force, whereas peace enforcement operations are authorized by the UN Security Council but carried out by states or other organizations (such as NATO).[18] However, the UNSC has recently created an 'Intervention Brigade' – that is, an enforcement operation tasked with protecting civilians and 'neutralising armed groups'[19] – within a UN commanded and controlled peace operation,[20] thus muddying the waters in many regards.[21] From the purely legal perspective of the application of IHL, the United Nations' foray into peace enforcement in its own operations does not change the existing legal framework. No matter whether force is authorized for the protection of civilians – or for any other reason – in a UN commanded and controlled peace operation or in a peace operation carried out by a state, group of states, or regional organization, international humanitarian law will apply based on the facts on the ground.[22]

---

[17] UNSC Res 1973 (2011). The interpretation of the resolution authorizing that operation was very controversial, with some countries insisting that the use of force by NATO against Libya went far beyond what they understood they had accepted. UN Secretary-General, 'Report on the Protection of Civilians in Armed Conflict', UN Doc S/2012/376 (22 May 2012) para. 19.

[18] Lilly, 'Changing Nature', 628–639.

[19] UNSC Res 2098 (2013) paras 12(a) and 12(b). The existing force also has the task of protecting civilians in the mandate but has not carried out operations independently of government forces in actions against organized armed groups.

[20] UNSC Res 2098 (2013). See UN Secretary-General, 'Special Report of the Secretary-General on the Democratic Republic of the Congo and the Great Lakes Region', UN Doc S/2013/119 (27 February 2013), recommending the establishment of the intervention brigade, paras 60ff.

[21] Resolution 2098 was adopted unanimously, with no abstentions, but some states expressed concerns with the enforcement action. In addition, they emphasized the exceptional nature of the brigade (enshrined in the text of the resolution in para. 9), reiterated that it did not set a precedent for UN peacekeeping, and reaffirmed the importance and continued relevance of the fundamental principles of peacekeeping. See, e.g., the statements of Guatemala, Argentina, Pakistan, China. Procès verbale: UN Doc S/PV.6943 (28 March 2013).

[22] See below, Chapter 10, on the use of force in peace operations. In this light, it is relevant to point out that Brazil has introduced the concept of 'responsibility while protecting', which articulates that 'the authorization for the use of force must be limited in its legal, operational and temporal elements and the scope of military action must abide by the letter and the spirit of the mandate conferred by the Security Council or the General Assembly, and be carried out in strict conformity with international law, in particular international humanitarian law and the law of armed conflict'. Brazil presented the concept in a letter to the Secretary-General, UN Doc S/2011/701 (11 November 2011), para. 11(d). The UN Secretary-General has cited this with approval, in addition to citing his own recommendation 'that the Council systematically call for compliance with international humanitarian

The complexity of modern peace operations and the increasing tendency to mandate a robust use of force to protect civilians are important to bear in mind when considering the use of PMSCs in peace operations. Chapter 1 will outline the existing framework of UN policies and regulations for the contractors – including PMSCs – currently used by the UN and by states participating in UN peace operations. Chapter 2 looks at whether the UN or states have articulated an opinion (be it legal or political) as to whether PMSCs could be used as the military component of the force. While that aspect may be the most controversial, in light of questions as to whether existing frameworks limit the roles for which they can be used, as well as the issue of respect for unlawful acts, the use of PMSCs in a broad range of roles merits careful consideration.

law by peacekeeping and other missions authorized to use force'. UN Secretary-General, 'Report on the Protection of Civilians in Armed Conflict', UN Doc S/2012/376 (22 May 2012) para. 20 (citing his report of 28 October 2007 (UN Doc S/2007/643). See para. 25 of that report.

1

Contracting by the UN

Policy and Practice

Existing UN policies and procedures indicate a reliance on PMSC (or 'contractor') activity in peace operations. This chapter will demonstrate that a certain amount of PMSC activity, in certain roles, is tolerated and provided for in UN policy and doctrine.

Initially, UN peacekeeping operations were staffed virtually exclusively with military personnel. As the number and size of operations began expanding at the end of the Cold War (precisely the moment at which states started to reduce their large standing armies), the UN General Assembly and the Secretariat began exploring alternative ways to staff peace operations. The possibility to use civilian personnel contributed by governments was first discussed in detail in 1989;[1] shortly thereafter, the use of civilian contractors was assessed as well.[2] The first report by the UN Secretary-General examining the use of civilian contractors in UN peacekeeping operations affirmed,

---

[1] Report of the Secretary-General, 'Administrative and Budgetary Aspects of the Financing of United Nations Peace-Keeping Operations', UN Doc A/44/605 + Add.1 and 2 (11 October 1989), especially at paras 28–35 and 55. That report recommended pursuing 'other measures' to enable quick start-up and staffing of operations, including 'Development of documented proposals by Governments in connection with the offering of specialized civilian personnel and equipment for peace-keeping operations' (para. 55(b)(i)).

[2] Report of the Secretary-General, 'Use of Civilian Personnel in Peace-Keeping Operations', UN Doc A/45/502 (18 September 1990) (hereafter UNSG, 'Use of Civilian Personnel'). This position espoused in this document also paved the way for more extensive use of civilian police (who are civilians) in peace operations. Civilian police had been used occasionally from ONUC in 1960 onwards but their use became more common after 1989. See Annika Hansen, *From Congo to Kosovo: Civilian Police in Peace Operations* (Oxford University Press: International Institute for Strategic Studies, 2002). See also Erwin Schmidl, 'Police Functions in Peace Operations: An Historical Overview', in Robert Oakley, Michael Dziedzic and Eliot Goldberg (eds.), *Policing the New World Disorder: Peace Operations and Public Security* (University Press of the Pacific, 1998), pp. 19–40, for a concise history of law enforcement in military operations.

It should be stressed at the outset that certain civilian functions, tasks and services in a peace-keeping operation can only be performed by United Nations staff members. When peace-keeping operations are set up, the Security Council and the General Assembly entrust to the Secretary-General overall responsibility and authority in all operational and administrative areas. This overall responsibility and authority cannot be delegated to non-United Nations personnel. As a result *the core civilian functions of a peace-keeping operation, including the political direction and administration of an operation in the field in all its facets, must be performed by United Nations staff members.*[3]

This restriction applied even to civilian personnel provided by governments, not only to contractor personnel. The reasoning for the restriction was grounded in a need to have experience in UN practices and its approach to peacekeeping.[4] On the other hand, the report asserted that 'almost any of the normal logistics, technical and supply-support functions required in peace-keeping operations could be performed by civilian personnel, whether provided by Governments or through commercial contractual relations, if the Secretary-General, taking into account the operational and political circumstances of the mission and the relative costs of civilian and military personnel, judges that this is the most cost-effective way of meeting the mission's requirements.'[5]

The report went on to list 'tasks and services that could be provided by either military or civilian personnel':

(a) Medical services, including hospitals and clinics;
(b) Operation and maintenance of fixed-wing aircraft and helicopters;
(c) Operation and maintenance of truck and bus transport;
(d) Catering and mess services;
(e) Construction of major camp infrastructure;
(f) Camp operation and maintenance;
(g) Installation and support of communications systems;
(h) Plant engineering and construction services for projects, such as:
    (i)   Water supply and storage systems;
    (ii) Sewage treatment plants;
    (iii) Electric power generation plant and reticulation systems;
    (iv) Airfields and heliports;
    (v)   Roads and tracks;
    (vi) Hard surfacing

---

[3] UNSG, 'Use of Civilian Personnel', ibid., para. 2. Emphasis added.
[4] Ibid.   [5] Ibid., para. 4.

(i) Professional consulting services in civil engineering, electrical engineering, architecture, etc.;

(j) Services of highly qualified technicians, such as radio technicians, radio operators, riggers, electricians, generator mechanics, vehicle mechanics and heating and air conditioning technicians.[6]

The report discusses other civilian personnel in peace operations, including UN Civilian Police and election monitors. In regard to CIVPOL, it states, 'While it may be argued that police are technically uniformed personnel and not civilians, it has been considered useful to preserve the distinction between police serving in a non-military capacity and the more usual Military Police units found in United Nations peace-keeping operations.'[7] The report goes on to affirm that '[a]lmost all the tasks and services discussed in this report, as well as other logistics functions required by a peace-keeping operation, could also be undertaken by civilian contractors.'[8] While this statement follows the discussion of CIVPOL and election staff, it would seem that the report does not mean to anticipate the use of contractors for those roles, since they are not 'tasks and services' and because they are of a different nature than the kinds of activities enumerated as candidates for outsourcing.

That early policy, in which contractor support was an element, but not the main focus, was created specifically in relation to peace operations. In the late 1990s, concerned with the way outsourcing in general was occurring across the UN system, the Office of Internal Oversight and the Joint Inspection Unit prepared reports that formed the basis for a UN-wide outsourcing policy.[9] Those reports also canvassed practice during peace operations and thus can be deemed to also be geared and applicable to such operations.[10] The Secretary-General adopted a policy on outsourcing in 1999, which was endorsed by a resolution of the General Assembly

---

[6] Ibid., para. 5.

[7] Ibid., para. 6. Hence the use of the term CIVPOL (sometimes also UNPOL).

[8] Ibid., para. 9.

[9] 'Report of the Office of Internal Oversight Services on the Review of Outsourcing Practices at the United Nations' (Programme Budget for the Biennum 1996–1997, annex) UN Doc A/51/804 (21 February 1997); 'Review of the Efficiency of the Administrative and Financial Functioning of the United Nations', Note by the Secretary-General transmitting to the General Assembly the report by the Joint Inspection Unit, 'The Challenge of Outsourcing for the United Nations System' (JIU/REP/97/5), UN Doc A/52/338 (5 September 1997).

[10] For example, practice in UNMIH (Haiti) and the former Yugoslavia were considered in the reports listed in the footnote above. In canvassing practice implementing the resolution, however, the Secretary-General does not list the UN DPKO as one of the bodies from

in 2000 and in subsequent years.[11] In particular, General Assembly Resolution 55/232 sets out cumulative criteria that must be satisfied in order for an activity to be considered appropriate for outsourcing. In addition to cost-effectiveness and efficiency, the cumulative criteria include:

(b) Safety and security: activities that could compromise the safety and security of delegations, staff and visitors may not be considered for outsourcing;

(c) Maintaining the international character of the Organization: outsourcing may be considered for activities where the international character of the Organization is not compromised;

(d) Maintaining the integrity of procedures and processes: outsourcing may not be considered if it will result in any breach of established procedures and processes.[12]

One may query whether the fact that one instrument is a report of the Secretary-General and the other is a General Assembly Resolution has implications for the hierarchy or bindingness, and whether both form part of the internal law of the institution. For the purposes of this study, which does not seek to address whether the UN has exceeded its own legal framework in regard to contractors, the question is not relevant. The key point is to endeavour to determine how the UN has interpreted the limits of its own policies and illustrate how it has relied on contractors in a number of roles.[13] Interestingly, despite recommendations by the Joint Inspection

which comments were elicited. See Report of the Secretary-General, 'Outsourcing Practices', UN Doc A/57/185, para. 2. However, in the 2004 report, practice from a number of peace operations was listed.

[11] Report of the Secretary-General, 'Outsourcing Practices', UN Doc A/53/818 (4 February 1999); UNGA Res 54/256 'Outsourcing Practices in the United Nations' (27 April 2000) UN Doc A/RES/54/256 (endorsing the report and requesting a more elaborate policy); UNGA Res 55/232 'Outsourcing Practices' (23 December 2000) UN Doc A/Res/55/232, adopted without a vote; UNGA Res 58/276 'Outsourcing Practices' (23 December 2003), UN Doc A/Res/58/276; UNGA Res 59/289 'Outsourcing Practices' (13 April 2005), UN Doc A/Res/59/289.

[12] UNGA Res 55/232 'Outsourcing Practices' (23 December 2000) UN Doc A/Res/55/232, para. 4. Note that 4(a) relates to true cost effectiveness. All three parameters have been reiterated in subsequent resolutions. See, for example, UNGA Res 59/289 'Outsourcing Practices' (15 April 2005) UN Doc A/Res/59/289 (adopted without a vote).

[13] It is worth recalling that Oscar Schachter understood the creation of international law by the UN in a broad sense, emanating not only from the main political organs. He pointed to the lack of attention that had been paid to the development of law by the UN and said, 'A further explanation of this fact is that these legal decisions and opinions are scattered throughout records of meetings, secretariat memoranda, press releases, and other miscellaneous documents. Moreover, legal questions are usually presented in the context of policy or administrative problems and are often considered as incidental questions by the organs

Unit and its inclusion in the Secretary-General's policy, there is no specific element in the General Assembly's Resolution prohibiting the outsourcing of 'core functions' – which is perhaps a notion that could, if developed, be analogous to the concept of core state activities.[14] The Secretary-General considers that both his policy and the UNGA Resolution must guide outsourcing;[15] however, the notion of 'core functions' has not been elaborated on in any public policy known to this author. These policies and the recently adopted policy on UN contracting of private security guards will be discussed in Section 1.3 below.

1.1   Traditional Roles of PMSCs in Peacekeeping

1.1.1   Airlift, Logistics, Catering, Supply

The list quoted above corresponds to the actual role of many PMSCs in peace operations today, such as providing airlift and logistical support. Indeed, the 1990 report of the Secretary-General setting out the policy affirmed that the UN had become increasingly reliant on contractors, in particular for airlift, vehicle maintenance, catering and transportation.[16] Thus, air support was one of the first services supplied by contractors for UN peace operations. As more regional organizations become involved in carrying out UN-mandated (but not UN-commanded and -controlled) peace operations, recourse to PMSCs for airlift support – i.e., flying troops and equipment into and around the mission – becomes indispensable.

whose main functions are not primarily legal. Nevertheless, it is clear that these legal decisions are adding, bit by bit, to the body of international law.' Oscar Schachter, 'The Development of International Law Through the Legal Opinions of the United Nations Secretariat' (1948) 5 *BYBIL* 91–133 at 91.

14 Report of the Secretary-General, 'Outsourcing Practices', UN Doc A/53/818 (4 February 1999), para. 6(a); 'Review of the Efficiency of the Administrative and Financial Functioning of the United Nations', Note by the Secretary-General transmitting to the General Assembly the report by the Joint Inspection Unit, 'The Challenge of Outsourcing for the United Nations System' (JIU/REP/97/5), UN Doc A/52/338 (5 September 1997), paras 37–38.

15 Report of the Secretary-General, 'Outsourcing Practices', UN Doc A/57/185 (2 July 2002), para. 2.

16 UNSG, 'Use of Civilian Personnel', para. 9: 'the United Nations has in recent years made increasing use of civilian contractors. For instance, they provide or have recently provided fixed-wing air services to the United Nations Military Observer Group in India and Pakistan (UNMOGIP), the United Nations Good Offices Mission in Afghanistan and Pakistan (UNGOMAP), the United Nations Iran-Iraq Military Observer Group (UNIIMOG) and UNTAG [United Nations Transition Assistance Group in Namibia], helicopter air services to the United Nations Observer Group in Central America (ONUCA), vehicle maintenance to UNTAG and ONUCA and catering and bus transportation services to UNTAG.'

Indeed, the United States is reportedly the only country that can supply its own airlift; most other states rely on contractors.[17] PMSCs have provided airlift for the ECOWAS operation in Sierra Leone[18] as well as for the UN force that followed the Australian-led INTERFET operation in East Timor.[19] According to the contractor that provided air support in Sierra Leone, 'ICI was contracted by the [US Department of State] to provide 2 helicopters and crew. All flight taskings originate[d] directly from the U.S. Embassy in Sierra Leone. Area of operations include[d] Sierra Leone and Guinea.'[20] The air support it conducted included transporting personnel, food and other items and providing 'limited heli-borne surveillance to facilitate the monitoring of any movement of armed rebels'.[21] The latter task is an important example: in some circumstances, that kind of activity may constitute reconnaissance operations that in fact amount to direct participation in hostilities.[22] Furthermore, this activity can be central to the capacity of a peace operation to achieve its goals. For example, in the Democratic Republic of Congo, a PMSC 'developed airfields for MONUC and assisted with air traffic control in the country'. According to Durch and Berkman, the sheer size of the territory of the DRC 'and its paltry road

---

[17] See William Durch and Tobias Berkman, *Who Should Keep the Peace? Providing Security for Twenty-first Century Peace Operations* (Henry Stimson Center, 2006), pp. 77ff.

[18] ICI of Oregon, www.icioregon.com/SierraLeone.htm (accessed 1 October 2011).

[19] Durch and Berkman, *Who Should Keep the Peace?*, p. 77.

[20] ICI of Oregon, www.icioregon.com/SierraLeone2.htm (accessed 1 October 2011).

[21] Ibid.

[22] For example, a mandate 'to observe and report in a timely manner on the position of armed movements and groups', as was given to MONUC in 2004–2005 could well involve a participation in hostilities, depending on to whom the mission was to report and how the information would be used. See, for example, UNSC Res 1565 (2004), para. 4(h). The resolution fails to specify to whom MONUC is to report. Daphna Shraga observes that such reconnaissance missions have not been interpreted by the Security Council or President as entailing the direct participation in hostilities of the force, but even she leaves the question open. See Daphna Shraga, 'The Secretary-General's Bulletin on the Observance by United Nations Forces of International Humanitarian Law: A Decade Later' (2009) 39 *Israel Yearbook on Human Rights* 357–377, 364–366, especially 365.

In addition, contractors are currently supplying the airlift capacity for AMISOM, the African Union operation in Somalia. 'Report of the Monitoring Group on Somalia and Eritrea Pursuant to Security Council Resolution 1916 (2010)', UN Doc S/2011/433 (18 July 2011), annex 6.1, p. 256, note 3. The report notes, 'DynCorp International, AECOM and Pacific Architects & Engineers (PAE, a Lockheed Martin company) have signed in September 2009 a five-years contract with the US Department of State Africa Peacekeeping Program (AFRICAP) which includes provision of logistics support, construction, military training and advising, maritime security capacity building, equipment procurement, operational deployment for peacekeeping troops, aerial surveillance and conference facilitation; in 2010, Dyncorp, in Somalia since February 2007 when AMISOM landed first in Mogadishu, was replaced by PAE and AECOM.'

network [meant that] MONUC is probably more reliant on air transport than any previous UN mission.'[23] For its part, the Special Committee on Peacekeeping Operations affirmed that it 'supports the practice of contracting private companies for the provision of required capabilities' in respect of 'strategic lift'.[24]

The use of private contractors for airlift to peace operations, while apparently indispensable and widely accepted, is not, however, without problems – aside from the potential for direct participation in hostilities referred to above. A SIPRI report from 2009 states that 'UN missions have continued to contract aviation services from companies that have been named in UN Security Council reports for wholly illicit arms movement and have been recommended by the UN for a complete aviation ban. For example, UN peacekeeping missions in Sudan have continued to use aircraft operated by Badr Airlines even after the UN Security Council recommended an aviation ban be imposed on the carrier in response to arms embargo violations.'[25] The report lists a number of other companies involved in similar violations that also provide airlift services for UN peace operations and other UN missions.[26] It goes on to state that

> [i]n most cases, those air cargo carriers featuring in UN and other arms trafficking-related reports are contracted into humanitarian aid, peace support, stability operations and defence logistics supply chains by 'middlemen' – air charter and brokering companies, which issue tenders and subcontract on behalf of their clients. Government departments, UN agencies, NGOs and defence contractors tend to use a relatively small number of air charter companies, *most of which are also listed in open sources as using the services of air cargo carriers documented in UN and other arms trafficking-related reports.*[27]

In light of this example, it should be noted that experts on peace operations have pointed to the fact that peace operations can be an enabling factor for organized crime.[28]

---

[23] Durch and Berkman, *Who Should Keep the Peace?*, p. 83.

[24] Report of the Special Committee on Peacekeeping Operations, 'Comprehensive Review of the Whole Question of Peacekeeping Operations in All Their Aspects', UN Doc A/57/767 (28 March 2003) para. 96.

[25] Hugh Griffiths and Mark Bromley, 'Air Transport and Destabilizing Commodity Flows', SIPRI Policy Paper 24 (May 2009) 25.

[26] Ibid., 25–28.   [27] Ibid., 29. Emphasis added.

[28] James Cockayne and Daniel Pfister, 'Peace Operations and Organised Crime' (Geneva Centre for Security Policy and IPI, 2008), 25. See also the special issue of *International Peacekeeping* on peace operations and organized crime: (2009) 16 *International Peacekeeping* 4–168.

When it comes to logistics support, as the UN Secretary-General's report quoted above indicates, private military and security companies have long been providing essential support services for peace operations. There are many other examples in addition to those listed by the Secretary-General: for instance, food and catering are provided by private contractors for the United Nations Interim Force in Lebanon;[29] in Côte d'Ivoire, for a short time the American PMSC Pacific Architects & Engineers provided logistical support, including food and fuel supply, 'transport, medical and communications support, and some self-sustainment support' for the United Nations Operation in Côte d'Ivoire (ONUCI).[30] In the United Nations Transitional Administration in East Timor, DynCorp 'provided transport, logistics, and communications services'.[31] Pacific Architects and Engineers also constructed base camps in Darfur and Chad.[32] In addition, companies hire individual contractors to fill specific posts. For example, DynCorp International was awarded a contract from UNOPS to field individuals to manage air operations in Somalia, including to 'act as the principal liaison between AMISOM and UNSOA [the UN Support office for AMISOM] in Mogadishu',[33] as well as engineers and supply officers.

In terms of supplying UN peacekeeping operations, on a more technical level, the Working Group on Contingent-Owned Equipment provides an option for 'dry lease' of troops/police (meaning they are supplied without necessary equipment) in its 2008 manual, which anticipates heavy reliance on contractor support. The manual gives five ways of

---

[29] Office of Legal Affairs, 'Interoffice memorandum to the Chief, Procurement Operations Service, Procurement Division, concerning a request for reimbursement of value added tax (VAT) charges from the United nations Interim Force in Lebanon (UNIFIL)', (2009) UN Juridicial YB (Part Two, Chapter VI) 411–414 (19 March 2009).

[30] See 'First Report of the Secretary-General on the United Nations Operation in Côte d'Ivoire', UN Doc S/2004/443 (2 June 2004) at para. 65; and 'Second Report of the Secretary-General on the United Nations Operation in Côte d'Ivoire', UN Doc S/2004/697 (27 August 2004) at para. 56 (indicating that 'the contractual and logistics support arrangements with Pacific Architects and Engineers for the former ECOMICI contingents have been discontinued and memorandums of understanding between the United Nations, France and Belgium are being developed to ensure continuity of support to those contingents'). PAE had been providing support to the ECOWAS troops in Côte d'Ivoire before they were replaced (and rehatted in part) by the UN operation.

[31] Durch and Berkman, *Who Should Keep the Peace?*, p. 83.

[32] See the website of Pacific Architects and Engineers, PAE, 'Foreign Assistance and Global Stability', www.paegroup.com/capabilities-operations-foreign-aid (accessed 1 October 2011).

[33] Partial post description as advertised on DynCorp International's website, www.dyncorprecruiting.com/ext/detail.asp?dynBLU21095 (accessed 1 October 2011).

providing troops/police, two of which are 'wet lease', meaning the contributing state or another participating state provides the necessary major and minor logistics equipment, means of maintaining it and maintenance personnel. One of the three 'dry lease' options, on the other hand, anticipates that the troop/police contributor provides major equipment and the UN hires a contractor to maintain it; and in terms of logistics, that the troop/police contributor provides major equipment and a contractor provides minor equipment, maintenance personnel, workshop and spare parts, etc.[34] Major equipment is not defined in concrete terms but as 'major items directly related to the unit mission as mutually determined by the United Nations and the troop/police contributor'.[35] Minor equipment, on the other hand, 'means equipment in support of contingents, such as catering, accommodation, non-specialist communication and engineering and other mission-related activities'. It includes equipment that supports major equipment as well as individuals.[36]

One of the keys to successful peacekeeping operations that has been identified is that troop/police contingents should be self-sustaining. In that regard, states will be reimbursed by the United Nations also for minor equipment necessary for self-sustenance including when it is provided by contractors.[37] Either the UN or the contributing state may use PMSCs in support of the operation.[38] In specifically setting this policy down in the manual, the UN at least tacitly underlines its acceptance and approval of the use of PMSCs in this capacity.

Private military and security companies are also heavily relied on to support non-UN peace operations. In addition to those providing logistical support and equipment for the ECOWAS operations, for example, the Monitoring Group on Somalia and Eritrea identified a number of PMSCs active in Somalia, Puntland and Somaliland.[39] In other non-UN missions

---

[34] See 'Manual on Policies and Procedures Concerning the Reimbursement and Control of Contingent-Owned Equipment of Troop/Police Contributors Participating in Peacekeeping Missions' (hereafter COE Manual), chapter 2, annex B, paras 25–31. The manual sets out how such arrangements will be reimbursed.

[35] Ibid., chapter 2, annex A at para. 21.   [36] Ibid., para. 22.

[37] Ibid., chapter 3, annex B, para. 5 and elsewhere in the manual.

[38] Østensen characterizes these options as 'direct versus indirect UN use of PMSCs'. See Åse Gilje Østensen, *UN Use of Private Military and Security Companies: Practices and Policies* (Geneva: DCAF, 2011), p. 12.

[39] 'Report of the Monitoring Group on Somalia and Eritrea Pursuant to Security Council Resolution 1916 (2010)', UN Doc S/2011/433 (18 July 2011), annex 6.1, p 256, para. 7. In addition to those contracted by local actors, it found that 'AECOM, Dyncorp, OSPREA logistics and PAE [were] contracted by the US Department of State to equip, deploy and train

such as the AU mission in Darfur, PMSCs 'prepared bases, set up logistics systems, and provided housing, office equipment, transport and communications gear'.[40]

Logistical services such as waste disposal for peacekeeping forces may seem rather prosaic and the outsourcing of them inconsequential or, at the very least, uncontroversial. The fact that even such services and the way they are provided can have a very significant impact on a peace operation (and its potential for success) is, however, illustrated by the outbreak of a cholera epidemic in Haiti in 2010. An independent report on the outbreak that killed 4,500 Haitians concluded that improper and insufficient waste handling by the contractor for MINUSTAH in relation to a Nepalese contingent contributed to the contamination of the river that led to the epidemic.[41] The framework for the potential responsibility of international organizations in relation to such actions by contractors will be addressed in Chapter 13.

A further example, from the UN Mission in Ethiopia and Eritrea (UNMEE), indicates that this type of logistics outsourcing, although generally beneficial for the local economy, carries potential risks for the success of a peace operation. In 2008, local Eritrean contractors who were under contract to supply food for UNMEE suddenly indicated that they would not be delivering the next week's food rations because 'they had "no vehicles to do business for UNMEE"'. UNMEE personnel in Eritrea had only two days' emergency rations left at that time. The contractor, whose stance was likely influenced by the overall obstructionism of Eritrea towards the mission, subsequently delivered the rations when the UN Department of Field Support put pressure on Eritrean diplomats at the

---

AMISOM, [and] Agility and RA International [were] contracted by the United Nations in support of AMISOM'. Another report of the Monitoring Group indicates that 'Dyncorp provides logistical support to AMISOM. Its facilities and personnel were specifically targeted during the suicide attack on 17 September 2009 at AMISOM force headquarters.' 'Report of the Monitoring Group on Somalia Pursuant to Security Council Resolution 1853 (2008)', UN Doc S/2010/91 (10 March 2010) 58, para. 222.

[40] Durch and Berkman, *Who Should Keep the Peace?*, p. 84.

[41] See Alejando Cravioto, Claudio Lanata, Daniele Lantagne and G. Balakrish Nair, 'Final Report of the Independent Panel of Experts on the Cholera Outbreak in Haiti' (undated, 2011), www.un.org/News/dh/infocus/haiti/UN-cholera-report-final.pdf (accessed 28 September 2011). This report was commissioned by UN Secretary-General Ban Ki-moon. The report indicates that although investigators were aware of allegations that the contractor had dumped faeces directly into the river tributary system (rather than into the septic pits), they were unable to confirm such allegations independently. See p. 23 of the report.

UN.[42] Admittedly, companies that are contracted to supply food rations to peace operations may or may not necessarily be 'PMSCs' (as opposed to local food suppliers or commercial contractors), but the example serves to show that all forms of outsourcing can leave peace operations subject to additional pressures from potential 'spoilers'.

Logistics contractors may also be used by other UN agencies in areas where peace operations and humanitarian operations are occurring, including when the UN determines that the personal safety risk for UN staff would be too high. This means that such contractors are also especially exposed to high-risk situations. For example, in Darfur in the first quarter of 2008 alone, twenty-six truck drivers contracted or subcontracted by the World Food Programme disappeared.[43] This may also raise questions for the UN regarding the moral responsibility for outsourcing such risk vis-à-vis the contractors themselves, as opposed to the responsibility of the UN for the actions of contractors towards third parties.[44]

A further activity of this nature is demining, albeit not listed in the 1990 contractor policy report above. According to Durch and Berkman, '[a] number of firms conduct most of the UN's demining efforts'.[45] In fact, PMSCs are described as 'implementing partners' for the UN Mine Action Service.[46] A US report states that civilian contractors have cleared four times as many as the UNIFIL teams in Lebanon.[47] In other contexts, PMSCs provide technical expertise to peace operations relating to 'counter-improvised explosive device capabilities'.[48] PMSCs also are involved in 'training managers and quality controllers of demining

---

[42] See UN Secretary-General, 'Special Report of the Secretary-General on the United Nations Mission in Ethiopia and Eritrea', UN Doc S/2008/145 (3 March 2008) para. 14.

[43] 'Towards a Culture of Security and Accountability: The Report of the Independent Panel on Safety and Security of UN Personnel and Premises Worldwide' (9 June 2008) 57, para. 212 (Lakhdar Brahimi, Chair), www.un.org/News/dh/infocus/terrorism/PanelOnSafetyReport.pdf (accessed 13 November 2011).

[44] Ibid., para. 213. According to Brahimi, the UN transfers risk to contractors 'in environments where it cannot operate' and must confront the ethics of that moral dilemma head-on. Ibid., para 14.

[45] Durch and Berkman, Who Should Keep the Peace?, p. 83. They cite, in particular, RONCO in Sudan.

[46] Østensen, UN Use of PMSCs, pp. 34–35.

[47] See 'United States Participation in the United Nations 2007', p. 17, www.state.gov/documents/organization/121905.pdf (accessed 19 September 2011).

[48] 'Report of the Monitoring Group on Somalia Pursuant to Security Council Resolution 1853 (2008)', UN Doc S/2010/91 (10 March 2010) 58, para. 221. They have also been contracted to remove IEDs for the UN Mission in Nepal. See Østensen, UN Use of PMSCs, p. 35.

programmes'.[49] Demining has also been conducted by other private out-
fits, such as non-government organizations (NGOs), in peace operations. In Western Sahara, for example, a UK-based NGO called Land-
mine Action UK clears the mines in the Frente POLISARIO-controlled
areas west of the Berm.[50] This example serves as a reminder that PMSCs
are not the only non-government actor contracted to provide important
support and expertise to peace operations. Depending on the context,
demining can involve participating in hostilities; however, most often in
peace operations it will not. It can, however, raise important questions of
responsibility.[51]

1.1.2   Acting as Observers, Monitoring, Training

In addition to these activities, it is worthy of note that PMSCs have long
been conducting activities in peace operations that are not listed in the
Secretary-General's report, such as acting as an observer force, carrying
out intelligence work, and training both new forces and peacekeepers.
Some of these activities may pre-date the UN General Assembly Resolution (2000) on outsourcing; others have occurred after its adoption. Thus
far it appears that many of these uses of PMSCs occur in peace operations
that are not under UN command and control, such that the policies on
outsourcing do not formally apply to them.

For example, the United States' contribution to the OSCE's Kosovo Verification Mission were PMSCs contracted by DynCorp.[52] On the ground,

---

[49] Østensen, *UN Use of PMSCs*.

[50] UN Secretary-General, 'Report of the Secretary-General on the Situation Concerning
Western Sahara', UN Doc S/2011/249 (1 April 2011), para. 62.

[51] See, e.g., *Behrami and Behrami v. France* and *Saramati v. France, Germany and Norway* (App
nos 71424/01 and 78166/01) Decision on Admissibility (GC) ECHR 31 May 2007.

[52] That mission was mandated to monitor 'compliance by all parties in Kosovo with UN Security Council Resolution 1199, and report instances of progress and/or non-compliance to
the OSCE Permanent Council, the United Nations Security Council and other organizations', and was specifically tasked to 'verify the maintenance of the cease-fire by all elements', and was mandated to 'verify the level of cooperation and support provided by the FRY and its
vant FRY/Serbian military/police headquarters in Kosovo regarding movements of forces';
'maintain liaison with FRY authorities about border control activities' and 'visit border
control units and accompany them as they perform their normal policing roles'. It was
also mandated to 'verify the level of cooperation and support provided by the FRY and its
entities to the humanitarian organizations' especially in regard to issuing visas, 'expedited
customs clearance for humanitarian shipments' and radio frequencies, and it could 'make
such representations as it deems necessary to resolve problems it observes'. The terms of the
mandate were contained in an agreement signed by the Chairman in Office of the OSCE
and the Foreign Minister of the FRY (CIO.GAL/65/98). The decision to establish the mission was taken by Permanent Council of the OSCE on 25 October 1998, Decision 263. See

the mission spent most of its time and energy snuffing out low-level cease-fire violations and was unable to conduct many detailed investigations.[53] The head of the mission was a US citizen but was an ambassador in the US diplomatic service, not a contractor employee. Private contractor personnel have been used in other observer missions as well, for example in the Sinai Field Mission in the 1980s[54] and more recently as the Civilian Protection Monitoring Team in Sudan in 2002–2004.[55] The Civilian Protection Monitoring Team was created by an agreement in 2002 between the Sudanese Government in Khartoum and the Sudan People's Liberation Movement, funded largely by the United States,[56] and 'commanded by [a] retired US brigadier general'.[57] As such, it was a sui generis enterprise with a mandate 'to decide when an alleged incident ... warrants investigation' and given concomitant powers to 'decide the most effective means to investigate alleged incidents', including the power to 'conduct an on-the-ground visit' in the absence of either party to the conflict. The monitors were also tasked with issuing reports and recommendations, which would be made public.[58] Other than specifying that the chief of the mission must be 'a person of proven international stature with experience in field operations and the investigation of military incidents or the violations of laws and customs of war', the agreement did not stipulate any particular required status for the mission personnel. It appears to have been entirely run and operated by a private company.[59]

OSCE, PC.DEC/263, 25 October 1998, 193rd Plenary Meeting, PC Journal No. 193, Agenda item 1 (www.osce.org/pc/20595, accessed 1 October 2011). Terms of mandate available at www.ess.uwe.ac.uk/kosovo/Kosovo-Documents3.htm (accessed 1 October 2011).

[53] See 'Report of the Secretary-General Prepared Pursuant to Resolutions 1160 (1998), 1199 (1998) and 1203 (1998) of the Security Council', UN Doc S/1999/99 (30 January 1999) especially annex I. For another description, see Brigadier-General J.R. Michel Maisonneuve, 'The OSCE Kosovo Verification Mission' (spring 2000) Canadian Military Journal 49–54.

[54] Durch and Berkman, Who Should Keep the Peace?, p. 10.

[55] Staffed by US PMSC Pacific Architects and Engineers (PAE): Durch and Berkman, ibid., p. 61. See also the company website, www.paegroup.com/capabilities-operations-foreign-aid (accessed 1 October 2011).

[56] 'Agreement Between the Government of the Republic of Sudan and the Sudan People's Liberation Movement to Protect Non-Combatant Civilians and Civilian Facilities from Military Attack' (31 March 2002), www.ecosonline.org/reports/2002/Agreementbetweenthegovernementandsplm.pdf (accessed 1 October 2011) (hereafter Sudan-SPLM Agreement 2002).

[57] Agence France Presse, 'Civilian Protection Monitoring Team to Begin Operations in Sudan', 25 September 2002, http://reliefweb.int/node/110233 (accessed 1 October 2011).

[58] Sudan-SPLM Agreement 2002, Article 2(3) and 2(4).

[59] The company was Pacific Architects and Engineers (PAE); on its website it affirms that its 'experience in peacekeeping operations ranges from human rights monitoring in Sudan to providing personnel and logistical support for international aid missions'. Available at

Thus, PMSCs have operated as ceasefire monitors and investigators in different international and non-international armed conflict situations. While these roles may not necessarily involve a use of force – but in the case of Kosovo involved extensive negotiation with the parties to the conflict to cease their uses of force – they do entail investigative and reporting authority. It should be pointed out, however, that the agreements in question do not provide these observers or verifiers with specific judicial powers to subpoena witnesses or otherwise compel testimony in regard to the incidents and events they are mandated to investigate.

Furthermore, private military and security companies are involved in many different components of training in peace operations, including training state forces in anticipation of their eventual inclusion in peacekeeping forces.[60] There are also PMSCs that provide training to UN peacekeeping forces.[61] More commonly, however, PMSCs provide training for new police and armed forces for the host states of peace operations. For example, DynCorp was awarded 'a $35 million contract to recruit and train a new 4,000-man Liberian army, while UN forces keep the peace'.[62] A company called Bancroft Global Development is contracted by AMISOM to train Transitional Federal Government soldiers in Somalia, 'from infantry tactics to administration and accountability' and also trains the presidential guard in charge of security for the Transitional Federal Government President.[63] As will be seen in Part III, training often does not entail a direct participation in hostilities, but, depending on the circumstances and the 'curriculum' of the training, it can.[64] In peace operations in which there may be ongoing armed conflict between government forces and organized armed groups, training of government forces by PMSCs

www.paegroup.com/capabilities-operations-foreign-aid (accessed 1 October 2011). The CMPT reports are available at www.ecosonline.org/ (accessed 1 October 2011).

[60] See Daniel Karis, 'A Comparative Study of Two Peacekeeping Training Programs: The African Crisis Response Initiative (ACRI) and the African Contingency Operations Training Assistance Program (ACOTA)', thesis (2009), www.peaceopstraining.org/theses/karis .pdf, who indicates that both programmes were delivered at least in part by PMSCs. The UN Secretary-General's 'Report on the Progress of Training in Peacekeeping', UN Doc A/65/644 (21 December 2010), does not explicitly mention of the involvement of PMSCs in peacekeeper training; however, it should be noted that member states are responsible for predeployment training of military personnel whereas the UN Secretariat is responsible for training civilian personnel. See UNSG Report, ibid., para. 47.

[61] One of these is Black Bear Consulting, a Canadian PMSC.

[62] Durch and Berkman, *Who Should Keep the Peace?*, p. 83.

[63] 'Report of the Monitoring Group on Somalia and Eritrea Pursuant to Security Council Resolution 1916 (2010)', UN Doc S/2011/433 (18 July 2011) annex 6.1, 259, paras 26–27.

[64] Chapter 8, notes 55–58 and accompanying text.

must be carefully limited if it is not to involve a direct participation in hostilities by the PMSC. Moreover, such activities raise questions as to necessary oversight and potential responsibility.

PMSCs have also been involved in planning and strategy for the design and structure of peace operations themselves. According to one account, the head of Black Bear Consulting

> is one of the United Nations' chief military consultants for peacekeeping operations. During the 1990s, whenever the U.N. was examining a new operation, [Brigadier General Ian] Douglas [the head of Black Bear] was one of the contractors who would fly out to the region, make a military assessment, and provide the Security Council with deployment options. Douglas has conducted these services in Sierra Leone, Angola, Uganda, Rwanda, Zaire (Democratic Republic of Congo), and many other global trouble spots.[65]

The above examples illustrate activities of PMSCs that are largely in line with early and current UN policies.[66] There are, however, a number of other areas in which PMSCs are active in UN peacekeeping that hover at the margins of what the policies clearly allow. Foremost among these is the use of PMSCs as civilian police and for conducting intelligence.

1.2 PMSC Activities at the Margins of the Policies – CIVPOL, Intelligence

It is an open secret that the United States uses PMSCs to provide its civilian police (CIVPOL) contributions to peace operations. A US Congressional Research Service Report for Congress on UN Peacekeeping describes it thus: 'The United States currently contracts with outside firms to provide U.S. civilian police, either active duty on a leave of absence, former, or retired. They are hired for a year at a time and paid by the contractor.'[67] PMSCs have deployed civilian police on behalf of the United

---

[65] James R. Davis, *Fortune's Warriors: Private Armies and the New World Order* (Vancouver: Douglas & McIntyre, 2002), p. 31.

[66] See Report of the Secretary-General, 'Use of Civilian Personnel'.

[67] Marjorie Ann Browne, 'United Nations Peacekeeping: Issues for Congress' CRS Report (updated 13 November 2008) 18 (footnote omitted); Marjorie Ann Browne, 'United Nations Peacekeeping: Issues for Congress' CRS Report (13 August 2010) 18. The companies involved advertise their role on their websites, and the website of the US agency responsible indicates on its own website that it uses PMSCs to recruit and deploy CIVPOL. The Bureau of International Narcotics and Law Enforcement in the Department of State oversees the Civilian Police programme; www.state.gov/j/inl/civ/ (accessed 28 March 2016).

States in UN peace operations in Haiti, Liberia, Kosovo and Sudan.[68] Here, one should recall that in Kosovo, CIVPOL was endowed with the capacity to conduct 'executive policing' – that is, to use force, detain and arrest people. The United States explains its recourse to private contractors to recruit, deploy and manage its CIVPOL as necessary in light of the fact that it does not have a federal police force from which it can draw police.

As the UN Security Council meetings with troop and police contributing countries are held in camera, there is no public record of a state objecting to the United States sending contractors in this role in that context.[69] The Secretary-General's report on contracting discussed above does not specifically prohibit the use of civilian contractors as CIVPOL, but a fair reading leads to the conclusion that it does not explicitly anticipate it either.[70]

Private military and security contractors have also supplied intelligence services for UN peace operations.[71] Two South African firms 'provided local intelligence to UNTAET in East Timor'[72] and the UN contracted a PMSC 'to provide intelligence on the UNITA rebels' guns-for-gems trade in Angola'.[73] In addition, in the context of enforcing sanctions against Iraq, the UN hired a private company to carry out surveillance

---

[68] See www.state.gov/j/inl/civ/ (accessed 28 March 2016). According to a job description on DynCorp's recruiting website, DynCorp 'provides a U.S. contingent of up to 15 law enforcement, judicial, and corrections advisors who are part of the U.N. Mission in Sudan (UNMIS)'. According to the description of the posts on DynCorp's website, 'UNMIS includes more than 600 officers from 44 countries. The mission is focused on re-building Sudan's security infrastructure. Law enforcement specialists train, equip, and mentor the Sudanese police force in democratic principles; judicial advisors help restore the justice system; and corrections advisors work with local counterparts to help modernize the prison system. The deputy program manager is based in Juba, and there are DI advisors in Juba, Khartoum, Malakal, and Wau.' www.dyncorprecruiting.com/ext/progs.asp (accessed 1 October 2011).

[69] See also the discussion on host state consent, Chapter 4, Section 4.2.

[70] See above, note 2 and accompanying text.

[71] It is widely reported that PMSCs conduct a significant amount of intelligence work for the United States. See Simon Chesterman, '"We Can't Spy . . . If We Can't Buy!": The Privatization of Intelligence and the Limits of Outsourcing of "Inherently Governmental Functions"' (2008) 19 *EJIL* 1055–1074. Two reporters from the *Washington Post* conducted a two-year investigation into outsourcing of intelligence: Dana Priest and William Arkin, 'National Security, Inc.' (part of 'Top Secret America') (20 July 2010), http://projects.washingtonpost.com/top-secret-america/articles/national-security-inc/ (accessed 3 October 2011).

[72] Durch and Berkman, *Who Should Keep the Peace?*, p. 83; Peter Singer, *Corporate Warriors* (Cornell University Press, 2003), p. 183.

[73] Singer, *Corporate Warriors*, p. 182.

of arms sites.[74] Bellamy and Williams point out that 'many states have consistently balked at the creation of a centralized intelligence-gathering capacity ... in spite of the fact that complex peace operations are very difficult to undertake effectively without good intelligence.'[75] They therefore (perhaps too glibly) conclude that the fact that PMSCs can be contracted to provide such 'services' and 'capabilities' means that 'concerns of UN members about centralized intelligence structures can be bypassed.'[76] Intelligence can be at the core of operations and can involve direct participation in hostilities (in particular reconnaissance operations, but also others).[77]

1.3 Security Services

The provision of security services is quickly becoming the most controversial role in terms of existing functions of PMSCs.[78] Indeed, over time, UN peace operations have begun to embrace a wider variety of PMSC activities, including those offering armed protection services. For example, the UN Assistance Mission in Afghanistan contracted Nepalese security guards to protect its compounds.[79] In April 2011, when a mob attacked the UN compound in Mazar-i-Sharif, four Nepalese guards were killed trying to defend it. According to a news report, 'UN officials said the Gurkhas ... were believed to have killed a number of assailants before they were overcome,'[80] which suggests they were armed and authorized to use force in self-defence. In his report on UNAMA, the UN Secretary-General referred to them as 'international guards' (rather than private security

---

[74] Ibid.   [75] Bellamy and Williams, *Understanding Peacekeeping*, p. 326.   [76] Ibid.

[77] As Sean Watts explains, 'the more valuable and integrated the intelligence contribution is to the targeting process, the greater the likelihood the intelligence gatherer is taking a direct part in hostilities, and therefore is subject to evaluation for combatant status.' 'Combatant Status and Computer Network Attack' (2010) 50 *Virginia Journal International Law* 391–447 at 427.

[78] The UN Working Group on mercenaries has also studied the issue: 'UN Working Group on Mercenaries to Launch Study on the Use of Private Military and Security Companies by the UN' (18 March 2013), www.ohchr.org/EN/NewsEvents/Pages/DisplayNews.aspx?NewsID=13154&LangID=E. See also the report by Lou Pingeot, 'Dangerous Partnership: Private Military Companies and the UN', Global Policy Forum (July 2012).

[79] Four Nepalese guards were killed in April 2011 when a mob attacked the UN compound in Mazar-i-Sharif.

[80] AFP, 'Armed Afghan Mob Kill Gurkhas, UN Staff' *Sydney Morning Herald*, 2 April 2011, http://news.smh.com.au/breaking-news-world/armed-afghan-mob-kill-gurkhas-un-staff-20110402-1cs6j.html (accessed 1 October 2011).

guards).[81] For his part, Staffan de Mistura, the Special Representative of the Secretary-General for UNAMA, stated, 'Some people called them contractors. For us they are colleagues. They've been risking their lives for us... And they've been dying with us, and for us.'[82]

Although the contracting of the private security guards for UNAMA was perceived as sufficiently unusual as to be newsworthy, even prior to the killing of guards by a mob,[83] various UN agencies have used private security guards, including in other peace operations.[84] For example, Defense Systems Ltd, a British PMSC, 'provided local security guards to UN peacekeeping operations in Angola'.[85] Moreover, the use of security guards in peace operations did not begin with modern PMSCs: already in the early 1990s, the UN hired local private guards to protect its staff and assets in increasingly volatile peacekeeping environments.[86] However, the UN Secretary-General observed that that practice 'has not always been successful and has sometimes compounded the problem'.[87] In Iraq in the 1990s, the UN had also created a unit of armed guards composed of personnel contributed by states (United Nations Guards Contingent in Iraq), but that was not a peace operation force run through the UN Department of Peacekeeping Operations; rather, it was created and deployed based on an agreement between the UN Relief Coordinator in Iraq and Iraq's

---

[81] Report of the Secretary-General, 'The Situation in Afghanistan and Its Implications for International Peace and Security', UN Doc A/65/873 – S/2011/381 (23 June 2011) para. 4.

[82] UN News Service, 'In Afghanistan, UN Staff Remember the 'Quiet Heroes' Killed in Mob Attack' (5 April 2011), www.un.org/apps/news/story.asp?NewsID=38013&Cr= afghan&Cr1=# (accessed 10 April 2011).

[83] Colum Lynch, 'U.N. Embraces Private Military Contractors' Foreign Policy (17 January 2010), http://turtlebay.foreignpolicy.com/posts/2010/01/17/un_embraces_private_ military_contractors (accessed 20 January 2010).

[84] Abby Stoddard, Adele Harmer and Victoria DiDomenico, 'Private Security Providers and Services in Humanitarian Operations' (2008) Humanitarian Policy Group Reports Issue 27, 8–13; Durch and Berkman, Who Should Keep the Peace?, pp. 83–84, report that 'DSL... provides personnel and property security for both the United Nations Children's Fund (UNICEF) and the World Food Program.'

[85] Durch and Berkman, Who Should Keep the Peace?, p. 83.

[86] Report of the Secretary-General, 'Security of United Nations Operations', UN Doc A/48/349 – S/26358 (27 August 1993) para. 22. See also the 'Report of the Independent Panel on the Safety and Security of UN Personnel in Iraq' (20 October 2003) 7, 11, 12, referring to 'locally recruited unarmed UN security guards', whose main role was to inspect traffic and perform night watch duties. Security for UNAMI was also provided to some extent by the presence of US forces in the area. Available at www.un.org/News/dh/iraq/ safety-security-un-personnel-iraq.pdf (accessed 13 November 2011).

[87] Report of the Secretary-General, 'Security of United Nations Operations', UN Doc A/48/349 – S/26358 (27 August 1993), para. 22.

foreign minister and funded through voluntary contributions.[88] This practice has recently been revived, and a static UN guard force was established in Somalia and one was planned for Libya.[89] PMSCs were used as convoy security in Somalia and their use as static guard forces was contemplated by the UN Secretary-General but was not pursued due to UNGA Resolution 67/254, which requires that PMSCs be used only as a 'last resort'.[90]

Furthermore, it is important to recall that many security guards may be subcontracted by other firms that are contracted by the peace operation itself. For example, in Somalia, the logistics company (Supreme) that was contracted by the United Nations Support Office for AMISOM (UNSOA) to provide fuel for AMISOM subcontracted a Dubai-based private security company to guard its compound. The security company (Compass) provides security and support both for Supreme (the UN contractor) and for the local supplier that Supreme subcontracted to supply the fuel.[91]

This brief overview suggests that security in peace operations beyond that provided by the troop and police contingents has been characterized by ad hoc solutions. An examination of the policies and resolutions on security contracting will show that the UN approach to contracting for security services has evolved over the years from an absence of a public position, through an apparent semi-ban on private security, to open acceptance of the practice.

First of all, the 1990 Secretary-General's report did not mention security services as an example of an activity that could be performed by contractors. However, UN General Assembly Resolution 55/232 of 2000 stipulated that services could not be outsourced if there was a risk to the safety or security of delegations, staff or visitors. At one point, it was apparently considered that the policies and UNGA resolutions on outsourcing prohibited the outsourcing of security services. This interpretation is evident in the fact that, in his 2002 report pursuant to UNGA Resolution 55/232

---

[88] Ibid., para. 23.

[89] 'Letter Dated 14 October 2013 from the Secretary-General Addressed to the President of the Security Council' (14 October 2013), UN Doc S/2013/606, p. 5.

[90] Report of the Secretary-General, 'Estimates in Respect of Special Political Missions, Good Offices and Other Political Initiatives Authorized by the General Assembly and/or the Security Council. Thematic Cluster III: United Nations Support Mission in Libya' (16 April 2014), UN Doc A/68/327/Add. 12, para. 11.

[91] 'Report of the Monitoring Group on Somalia and Eritrea Pursuant to Security Council Resolution 1916 (2010)', UN Doc S/2011/433 (18 July 2011) annex 6.1, p. 262, paras 36–38. In terms of 'support', the private security company 'coordinates' the local militia of the local supplier in order to secure the compound.

on outsourcing, the Secretary-General stated that 'in those offices where the provision of security personnel was outsourced, the offices concerned have already initiated action to seek a budgetary allocation to replace contracted security personnel with staff members of the Organization so that the outsourced activities, which may compromise the safety and security of the delegations, staff and visitors, will be phased out in due course.'[92] However, within two years, that approach had been revised to one merely requiring 'approval of a designated official in accordance with the Secretary-General's outsourcing practices' in order to outsource the provision of guard services.[93] Much of the contracting for security services listed in the report was in the context of peace operations. The last element of the quotation above is revealing: there was no official change in policy nor in the terms of the General Assembly resolutions relating to outsourcing. The acceptance of security outsourcing was instead grounded in an unwritten practice.

Indeed, the UN openly contracts with PMSCs to provide security, and new policies clearly indicate a tolerance of it as they seek to regulate it. In this regard, a number of bodies have called for greater regulation on security contracting within the UN system, including a Working Group of the Human Rights Council, which has recommended that

> United Nations departments, offices, organizations, programmes and funds establish an effective selection and vetting system and guidelines containing relevant criteria aimed at regulating and monitoring the activities of private security/military companies working under their respective authorities. They should also ensure that the guidelines comply with human rights standards and international humanitarian law.[94]

This recommendation, coming from the Working Group within the UN that is most actively involved with the treatment of PMSCs under international law, clearly shows that current internal UN policy does not prohibit the contracting of PMSCs for security services. In addition, the Special Committee on Peacekeeping Operations requested the UN Secretariat to develop a 'thorough policy for screening and verification before hiring

---

[92] Report of the Secretary-General, 'Outsourcing Practices', UN Doc A/57/185 (2 July 2002) para. 3. However, outside analysts Stoddard et al., 'Private Security Providers' at 24, considered the language to be 'ambiguous at best'.

[93] Report of the Secretary-General, 'Outsourcing Practices', UN Doc A/59/227 (11 August 2004) 13.

[94] Human Rights Council, 'Report of the Working Group on the Use of Mercenaries as a Means of Violating Human Rights and Impeding the Exercise of the Right of People to Self-Determination' (9 January 2008), UN Doc A/HRC/7/7, para. 60.

local security personnel, which includes, inter alia, background checks on any criminal and human rights violations of the candidates, as well as links to security companies'.[95]

In response to this request, the UN has recently adopted a policy on hiring armed private security guards in peacekeeping operations. The existence of a policy is, in itself, prima facie evidence that the use of armed contractors in that role fits within the legal framework of peace operations in the UN's view. The policy that was adopted sets parameters for when armed private security companies (PSCs) may be used and the objective for their use. It sets out conditions regarding a security assessment, selection criteria and screening requirements, and outlines a requirement to develop rules on the use of force. The policy also sets out lines of responsibility for training as well as management and oversight of the companies and contracts. The key conditions set down in the policy underline the fact that recourse to armed security guards is supposed to be exceptional and establish the permitted purposes for which they may be used. Specifically, the policy states,

2. On an exceptional basis to meet its obligations, the United Nations Security Management System may use private companies to provide armed security services when threat conditions and programme need warrant it.[96]

3. The fundamental principle in guiding when to use armed security services from a private security company is that this may be considered only when there is no possible provision of adequate and appropriate armed security from the host Government, alternate member State(s), or internal United Nations system resources . . . [97]

In other words, armed PMSCs are to be used as a last resort. The policy goes on to say:

8. The objective of armed security services from a private security company is to provide a visible deterrent to potential attackers and an armed response to repel any attack in a manner consistent with the

---

[95] 'Report of the Special Committee on Peacekeeping Operations', 2010 substantive session (22 February–19 March 2010), UN Doc A/64/19, para. 41. See also Elke Krahmann, 'The UN Guidelines on the Use of Armed Guards: Recommendations for Improvement' (2014) 16 *International Community Law Review* 475–491.

[96] UN Department of Safety and Security, 'Chapter IV: Security Management, Section I – Armed Private Security Companies', in UNSMS Security Policy Manual (November 2012) para. 2.

[97] Ibid., para. 3.

United Nations 'Use of Force Policy', the respective host country legislation and international law.

9. Armed security services from a private security company may not be contracted, except on an exceptional basis and then only for the following purposes:

   a. To protect United Nations personnel, premises and property.

   b. To provide mobile protection for United Nations personnel and property.[98]

This policy permits an astonishingly broad use of force. Despite all of the limitations apparently set down, the fact that it provides that armed private security guards may use 'an armed response to repel any attack' can be far-reaching. Indeed, it is striking that this authorization of force in self-defence is arguably the same as that foreseen for the first peacekeeping forces.[99] It is worth emphasizing here that the new policy states that the objective of using private security guards can include the use of force 'to repel any attack'. The first peacekeeping forces were 'entitled to respond with force to an attack with arms, including attempts to use force to make them withdraw from positions which they occupy under orders from the Commander, acting under the authority of the Assembly and within the scope of its resolutions'.[100] The emphasis is on a prohibition to initiate the use of force.

For the sake of completeness, it is worth mentioning that there are also sets of 'non-binding guidelines' for the UN, established by the UN Inter-Agency Standing Committee, on contracting security guards.[101] UN assistance convoys may use armed PMSC guards only if their use is approved by the UN Security Coordinator (now UN Department of Safety and Security, or UNDSS). Finally, where private security companies are contracted to provide security services in the context of a peace operation without being integrated as CIVPOL or UNPOL, there may be additional limitations on the capacity to use them in law enforcement roles. In UNMIK, for example, the Special Representative of the Secretary-General issued

---

[98] Ibid., paras 8 and 9.   [99] See Chapter 10.

[100] UN Secretary General, 'Summary Study of the Experience Derived from the Establishment and Operation of the Force', UN Doc A/3943 (9 October 1958) paras 179–189, especially para. 179 (hereafter UNSG, 'Summary Study').

[101] UN Inter-Agency Standing Committee, 'Use of Military or Armed Escorts for Humanitarian Convoys: Discussion Paper and Non-binding Guidelines' (14 September 2001) (as approved by IASC and UN Office of Legal Affairs). Additional UN guidelines are found in UN IASC (and Office for the Coordination of Humanitarian Affairs) 'Civil-Military Guidelines and Reference for Complex Emergencies', 2008.

a regulation on the licensing of security service providers. That regulation stipulated, 'As the primary role of the international security guard is deterrence, no license holder, security guard or other employee of a license holder may conduct investigations into criminal matters or conduct law enforcement functions.'[102]

The use of private security contractors in peace operations, as an activity that implies a use of force – even if only in self-defence – is bound to pose some of the most significant challenges to the legal framework, much as the same is true for security contractors in 'regular' situations of armed conflict.

1.4 Conclusion

This review of UN policy on contracting in peacekeeping operations, coupled with the examples of practice, shows that existing UN policies and regulations certainly allow for and seek to accommodate the use of contractors in UN peace operations in terms of military support roles. Although PMSCs have not yet been officially engaged as the military force for a peace operation, they have been involved in virtually every other aspect of such operations, from building bases, supplying food, transporting peacekeepers to and within mission areas to carrying out training, policing and security functions.

The policies on the use of contractors highlighted above contain certain limitations that relate to the potential use of contractors as a peacekeeping force. In particular, the first report by the Secretary-General on the use of contractors affirmed that 'Th[e] overall responsibility and authority [in all operational and administrative areas of a peacekeeping mission] cannot be delegated to non-United Nations personnel.'[103] This limitation must be taken into account when considering the possibility that the UN may delegate the conduct of a peace operation to a PMSC. In addition, it is worth noting that nothing in the reports or policies indicates that it is a priori permitted or foreseen that civilian contractors could take on the role of a peacekeeping force. Rather, the policies might best be seen as setting out the parameters of an exception to the usual framework to allow for the inclusion of civilian contractors in certain, limited roles. The UN General Assembly resolution on outsourcing that prohibits contracting

---

[102] UNMIK, 'On Licensing of Security Services Providers in Kosovo and the Regulation of their Employees', 25 May 2000, Regulation No. 2000/33, section 5.
[103] UNSG, 'Use of Civilian Personnel', para. 2.

out services in such a way as to compromise the international character of the organization would result in a breach of 'established procedures' or that could compromise safety or security could be interpreted to mean that outsourcing the conduct of operations is prohibited. However, in my view such a conclusion would depend on the precise circumstances and the facts of the situation; it is not possible to construe the wording of the resolution as a blanket prohibition.

It is useful to spend a moment analyzing the legal value of the various policy and regulatory instruments addressing the use of contractors in peace operations (and, in the case of security providers, more broadly) within the UN. These instruments range from reports by the UN Secretary-General to 'policies' adopted for supplying peace operations in the DPKO to General Assembly resolutions and, finally, to the recently adopted policy on contracting security providers. When it comes to international organizations, it is a perennial question as to which of its internal decisions comprise part of the law of the organization – and, as such, are binding on the organization.[104] There is no set rule applicable to all organizations. For the United Nations, Sands and Klein assert that 'the legal consequences of any particular act falls to be determined principally by reference to the constituent instrument of the organisation, but also by reference to obligations arising outside the organisation, including general international law.'[105] However, they note that some acts will not be provided for in the constituent instrument, such that it may be difficult to determine their 'normative status'.[106] Schermers and Blokker note, 'Virtually no provisions have been adopted concerning the form that internal rules have to take. Any decision by a competent organ creates binding internal rules, provided that the intention to do so is sufficiently clear; in general, no requirements exist as to motivation or as to the procedure to be followed.'[107]

---

[104] According to Articles 2(b) and 10(2) of the ILC's Draft articles on the responsibility of international organizations (2011), the 'rules of the organization' 'means, in particular, the constituent instruments, decisions, resolutions and other acts of the international organization adopted in accordance with those instruments, and established practice of the organization'; however, one may question whether an action not in accordance with such rules that is not 'towards its members' constitutes a breach of an obligation.

[105] Philippe Sands and Pierre Klein, *Bowett's Law of International Institutions*, 6th edn (London: Sweet and Maxwell, 2009), p. 460, para. 14-032.

[106] Ibid., para. 14-031, citing the UNSG Bulletin on IHL. See also the comments by Oscar Schachter in note 13, above.

[107] Henry Schermers and Niels Blokker, *International Institutional Law*, 5th revised edn (Martinus Nijhoff, 2011), p. 758, para. 1202. 'The constitution can only regulate the functioning of an international organization in general terms, with the result that more detailed

According to this, then, any of these policies may, in theory, constitute decisions that form part of the internal legal order of the United Nations and govern its actions. However, the discussion above shows that on many occasions, the use of PMSCs by the UN appears to go beyond what the policies themselves allow. Moreover, the UN Secretary-General overrode the initial prevailing interpretation of General Assembly Resolution 55/232 with no formalities. In this regard, an observation by Schermers and Blokker is sobering: 'In practice, however, the legal basis of internal rules is not of any great importance. As long as they are not disputed, even illegal decisions are as effective as any other. Conforti mentions a number of UN decisions that were taken contrary to specific Charter provisions, but were nonetheless executed as they were not challenged.'[108] This observation leads ineluctably to the statement of Sands and Klein above, that one must test the decisions or policies of international organizations against general international law.[109]

Below, in Part III, I contend that uses of force by PMSCs to repel attacks may amount to a direct participation in hostilities in situations where the peacekeeping force has become a party to a conflict.[110] The policy on the use of private security guards described above clearly condones the use of guards in such circumstances. Is that policy commensurate with international law? Put another way, does it contravene international law for the UN to contract security guards and permit them to use force in circumstances in which that use of force may lead them to directly participate in hostilities? Elsewhere, I have postulated an argument that governments have an obligation to use government forces in armed conflicts, including in non-international armed conflicts.[111] What forces may or must the UN use?

---

provisions must be made by the organization itself. The power of international organizations to make rules for their own legal order is generally recognized, and flows from the existence of the organization. Every organization requires internal rules, and these rules can be derived from no other legal order. The resulting law is part of a separate legal order, which is dependent on the organization's own constitution, but independent of any other legal order.' Ibid., para. 1196.

[108] Ibid., para. 1197, footnote omitted. The examples given were 'the division of Security Council seats, package deals on membership, and the readmittance of Indonesia and Syria as members'.

[109] One can presume, however, that the policies will be followed unless states contest their legality.

[110] See Chapter 10.

[111] See Lindsey Cameron, 'The Use of Private Military and Security Companies in Armed Conflicts and Certain Peace Operations: Legal Limits and Responsibility', PhD thesis (2015) University of Geneva, chapter 3, notes 275–293 and accompanying text.

In my view, the answer to these questions must be dealt with according to the same framework and analysis as that below (in Part II) regarding PMSCs as peacekeepers in that in essence, it amounts to the same role. Certainly, the scope for the use of force authorized for the protection of civilians under Chapter VII mandates has the potential to be much broader than that which is prescribed here. The use of force in more limited self-defence/defence of property circumstances may be anticipated to be more circumspect.[112] Nevertheless, in theory, the result is the same. Admittedly, peacekeeping involves much more than using force and showing force – but as we have seen, PMSCs are also deeply involved in other aspects of peacekeeping, such as training police and armed forces. To some extent, this type of activity – engagement as a peacekeeping force – is a kind of final frontier that warrants special scrutiny.

---

[112] See Christopher Penny, '"Drop That or I'll Shoot . . . Maybe": International Law and the Use of Deadly Force to Defend Property in UN Peace Operations' (2007) 14 *International Peacekeeping* 353–367.

Survey of Existing Opinion and Practice on the Possibility of PMSCs as the Military Component of a UN Peace Operation

In the survey that follows, I attempt to discern whether the UN or states express an opinion as to whether they consider the use of PMSCs as the military contingent of the peace operation to be a lawful possibility. As practice, one can point to the supplying of UN CIVPOL via PMSCs by the United States.[1] This section seeks to provide the fullest possible overview of the various positions in order to develop a sense as to whether there is any emerging norm on this issue.

2.1   The UN Position on PMSCs in Peacekeeping

The discussion above has shown that PMSCs are deeply involved in peacekeeping in many roles. When it comes to the possibility of using PMSCs to staff the military component of peacekeeping forces, however, although some policies would appear to go against it, there does not appear to be a settled UN position on the issue. Although the UN Department of Peacekeeping Operations (DPKO) reportedly considered contracting a PMSC to conduct peace enforcement in eastern DRC in 1996, it rejected the option.[2] Public reports of recent UN–state discussions on reforming and improving peacekeeping – as expressed in the 'New Horizons' policy document – do not canvass the possibility of outsourcing entire operations.[3] In addition, the use of PMSCs or the 'private sector'

---

[1] See above, Chapter 1, Section 1.2.

[2] Bures, 'A Second-Best Peacekeeping Option?', 539. Singer, *Corporate Warriors*, p. 185. Also in Singer, 'Peacekeepers, Inc.' (Brookings, 2003), available at www.brookings.edu/articles/peacekeepers-inc/.

[3] UN DPKO–DFS, 'A New Partnership Agenda: Charting a New Horizon for UN Peacekeeping' (non-paper) (July 2009) (hereafter, DPKO-DFS, 'New Horizon').

was not raised beyond logistical support roles in Security Council discussions of that and other reports.[4]

The possibility was raised at least at one point in the process, however. Prior to drafting the New Horizons non-paper, the DPKO and DFS commissioned external studies on how to improve relations with troop- and police-contributing states and how to streamline the establishment of peace forces. One of the studies commissioned by the DPKO, completed by the Center on International Cooperation, specifically canvasses the possibility of deploying PMSCs as peace forces. It states, '[W]ere PMSCs to be deployed under direct UN command, without an intervening national authority, the accountability issues would be serious indeed.'[5] On the other hand, it does not identify any legal impediments to the UN establishing a force in such a way. In addition, the report's authors argue that 'one other model perhaps worthy of exploration is the use of PMSCs by national contingents', noting that 'this has been done before in non-UN contexts', citing the Kosovo Verification Mission of the OSCE.[6] In particular, the authors imagine the use of PMSCs 'as either a "first responder" or a force multiplier *within a national command structure and under their authority and accountability*', acknowledging that there may be 'ethical and financial objections' but foreseeing no legal impediments.[7] Furthermore, the report enigmatically states that the question whether to use PMSCs in peace operations 'has been in the margins of the Security Council's informal consultations on peacekeeping this year', suggesting that the substance of corridor-speak is not represented in official minutes of meetings, but leaving a great deal to the imagination in terms of the tenor and contours of such discussions.[8]

The High-Level Panel Report of 2015 recommends the development of a standing force capable of rapid deployment at the outset of an operation

---

[4] See UNSC Verbatim Record (31 July 2009) UN Doc S/PV/6178 and S/PV/6178. Resumption 1.

[5] B. Jones, R. Gowan and J. Sherman, 'Building on Brahimi: Peacekeeping in an Era of Strategic Uncertainty' (Center on International Cooperation, April 2009), 22.

[6] Ibid.   [7] Ibid. Emphasis in original.

[8] Ibid., at 22. Emphasis in original. In contrast, Åse Gilje Østensen reports that an 'anonymous UN Department of Safety and Security source' stated that proposals for a UN PMSC peace force have not been 'treated with much credence in the UN, nor seriously studied as a potentially viable solution to many of the issues facing peacekeeping operations' (Østensen's words). Åse Gilje Østensen, 'In the Business of Peace: The Political Influence of Private Military and Security Companies on UN Peacekeeping' (2013) 20 *International Peacekeeping* 33–47 at 45, note 14.

(or the rehatting of existing forces).[9] That report does not mention PMSCs for such a role; however, academics have pointed to the fact that the idea of a standing force is not new but has never been implemented and have suggested that PMSCs be used to fill the gap.[10]

In terms of whether the existing policies on outsourcing discussed above would restrict the capacity of the organization to engage a PMSC in the military component of a peace force, probably the strongest hindrance is the admonition that 'core functions' should not be outsourced. The policy outlined by the Secretary-General in 1999 was 'limited to the provision of non-core support-type activities or services'. In addition, the Secretary-General agreed with the Joint Inspection Unit that '[u]sing core activities and services as the criterion for determining what can and cannot be outsourced has an inherent logic.'[11] The reports beg the question, however, as to what is a 'core' activity. Acting as the military component in a peacekeeping operation would seem to be a 'core' activity of the UN; however, it is important to recall that that activity is already 'outsourced' in the sense that the UN has to rely on states to perform such roles since it does not have its own armed forces. It is not a question here of the UN either providing its own peacekeepers or hiring a private company to provide them, but rather to whom it may outsource the provision of peacekeepers – only to states? Or also to private companies?

In this regard, it is worth noting that the Draft Convention on Private Military and Security Companies of the UN Working Group on mercenaries includes an article that would prohibit the 'delegation and/or outsourcing of inherently State functions' and is open to international organizations as parties.[12] Judging by the Draft Convention, the UN Working Group on mercenaries supports an interpretation that the use of armed force may be outsourced only to states. The Draft Convention defines

---

[9] 'Report of the High-Level Independent Panel on Peace Operations on Uniting Our Strengths for Peace: Politics, Partnership and People' (17 June 2015), UN Doc A/70/95; S/2015/446, especially at paras 39(b) and 95.

[10] J. Genser and C. Garvie, 'Contracting for Stability: The Potential Use of Private Military Contractors as a Rapid-Reaction Force' (2015) 16 *CJIL* 439–481.

[11] Report of the Secretary-General, 'Outsourcing Practices', UN Doc A/53/818 (4 February 1999), paras 6–7.

[12] Report of the Working Group on the use of mercenaries as a means of violating human rights and impeding the exercise of the right of peoples to self-determination, annex, 'Draft of a Possible Convention on Private Military and Security Companies (PMSCs) for Consideration and Action by the Human Rights Council', UN Doc A/HRC/15/25 (5 July 2010), Articles 9 and 3.

inherently state functions as 'functions which are consistent with the principle of the State monopoly on the legitimate use of force and that a State cannot outsource or delegate to PMSCs under any circumstances...'.[13] The construction of the argument is somewhat convoluted, however. The Draft Convention prohibits the outsourcing of certain uses of force by states or international organizations, since references to 'State parties' 'shall apply to intergovernmental organizations within the limits of their competence'.[14] Given the fact that peace operations inevitably involve a delegation of the use of force to states, this article cannot be read as prohibiting that delegation in itself. Rather, it must mean that, if ratified by them, intergovernmental organizations would only be able to delegate the use of force to states.

Aside from this, and given the fact that the Draft Convention is still far from being adopted as positive law, the core function test does not help to clarify whether there is a constraint on using PMSCs in peacekeeping roles beyond those outlined above.

In addition to those policies, which may be taken collectively as a rather ambiguous expression of UN opinion on the matter, UN practice in regard to using PMSCs in peacekeeping is relevant. In addition to that identified above – and in particular, the recent practice relating to security guards – there is the extensive use of contractors by the UN in UNPROFOR (which occurred prior to the development of general UN policies on outsourcing). According to one report, one company

> maintained for UNPROFOR a strength of 425 international staff from 24 nations, including planning officers, quality assurance, architects, civil, mechanical and electrical engineers, plant operators, drivers, communicators, computer programmers and network installers, facility and camp managers in addition to traditional... personnel including security officers assigned to crime prevention, crime detection, close protection and border security duties.[15]

It goes on to note that the services performed became more diverse as the mission continued, in particular including armoured personnel

---

[13] Ibid., Article 2(i).

[14] Ibid., Article 3(2). Article 9 stipulates that '[e]ach [intergovernmental organization] shall... specifically prohibit the outsourcing to PMSCs of functions which are defined as inherently [intergovernmental organization] functions, including direct participation in hostilities, waging war and/or combat operations ...'

[15] UK Select Committee on Foreign Affairs, Minutes of Evidence, 13 June 2002, Appendix 6: Memorandum from ArmorGroup Services Limited. Available at www.publications.parliament.uk/pa/cm200102/cmselect/cmfaff/922/2061318.htm, para. 75.

carrier drivers who drove fuel, rations and ammunition to UN bases, 'sometimes under small-arms and artillery fire'.[16]

In April 2013, the UN General Assembly adopted a resolution on special subjects relating to the budget in which it '*Notes* that the United Nations finds it necessary, as an exceptional measure, to use armed security services from private security companies to secure the premises and personnel of the Organization' and '*Stresses* that such services should be used as a last resort to enable United Nations activities in high-risk environments only when a United Nations security risk assessment concludes that other alternatives, including protection by the host country, support from the Member States concerned or internal United Nations system resources are inadequate'.[17] The Secretary-General has indicated that he has heard the General Assembly on this point. In the fall of 2013, when three UN missions were in need of additional security, the Secretary-General indicated his intention to establish UN Guard Units, staffed by contingents contributed by states in a manner similar to peace operations forces. The tasks of the guard unit would include providing 'perimeter security and access control for United Nations facilities and installations ... It would act as a deterrent against possible attacks by extremist elements ... The guard unit would also be able to relocate United Nations personnel under imminent threat of physical violence to safer locations.' Remarkably, in two of the letters signalling his intent to establish such forces – on the confirmation by the Security Council that 'these arrangements are acceptable' – he pointedly indicated that he had also considered the possibility of using a private security company to perform the same tasks, but did not do so in order to comply with the General Assembly's resolution.[18] In a third letter, the Secretary-General recommended the creation of a static UN guard force within UNSOM (the peacekeeping mission in Somalia), tasked with securing the UN compound in Mogadishu and providing convoy security for UN movements and personnel. Noting the time lag for receiving contingents for such a force, however, he simply stated that, 'pending the readiness of this dedicated force, the United Nations would continue to

---

[16] Ibid., para. 77.

[17] UN General Assembly, 'Special Subjects Relating to the Programme Budget for the Biennium 2012–2013', UN Doc A/RES/67/254 (12 April 2013), paras V. 10 and V. 11.

[18] UN Secretary-General, 'Letter Dated 21 November 2013 from the Secretary-General Addressed to the President of the Security Council', 27 November 2013, UN Doc S/2013/704 (for UNSMIL). See also similar letter dated 29 October 2013 (BINUCA), UN Doc S/2013/636.

rely on the current arrangement with private contractors.'[19] One may surmise that this arrangement meets the requirement of the UNGA Resolution as a situation of 'last resort'.

The identifiable practice and policies of the UN in relation to contracting PMSCs to provide significant assistance with peacekeeping (in qualitative terms) demonstrates an evolution over time to a broadening of the types of roles and activities private actors may assume. The recent practice of the Secretary-General and the UN General Assembly resolution suggest that the organization does not speak with one voice on the matter. While respecting the wishes of the UN General Assembly, the Secretary-General nevertheless reiterates the possibility of recourse to PMSCs as a guard or security force when necessary.

2.2   Views of the United Kingdom

The United Kingdom has extensively and publicly considered the viability of using PMSCs in peace operations as the peacekeeping force itself, providing an opportunity to explore the issue from the perspective of a state. The UK Government's 2002 Green Paper, entitled 'Private Military Companies: Options for Regulation', endorsed the notion that the UN could use PMSCs to recruit and manage its peace operations forces. The paper goes so far as to essentially equate some national troop contingents with mercenaries, the epithet generally reserved for PMSCs, saying, 'In one sense the United Nations already employs some mercenary forces. It is clear that at least some countries who contribute to UN peacekeeping do so for largely financial reasons.'[20] The paper asserts that such states often send poorly trained and badly equipped forces, which the UN has little choice but to accept. It goes on to hypothesize that a 'private company which had an interest in continuing business for the UN could be held to much higher standards – and these would include standards on behaviour and human rights as well as efficiency in carrying out agreed tasks.'[21] Aside from the fact that the authors of the Green Paper appear to believe that commercial contracts provide better opportunities for enforcement of international

---

[19] UN Secretary-General, 'Letter Dated 14 October 2013 from the Secretary-General Addressed to the President of the Security Council', 14 October 2013, UN Doc 2013/606.

[20] UK, Green Paper, Return to an Address of the Honourable the House of Commons dated 12th February 2002 for a Paper, entitled: 'Private Military Companies: Options for Regulation', HC 577, available at www.official-documents.gov.uk/document/hc0102/hc05/0577/0577.pdf (accessed 17 October 2011) para. 58 (UK Green Paper).

[21] Ibid.

law norms – and completely fail to consider whether and how such norms would even bind such personnel, other than through the contract[22] – the report is strikingly pejorative and undiplomatic vis-à-vis other troop contributing states. Furthermore, the drafters of the Green Paper argued:

> It is at least possible that if the tasks of UNAMSIL were put out to tender, private companies would be able to do the job more cheaply and more effectively. It is also possible that such forces might be available more quickly to the UN and that they would be more willing to integrate under a UN command than is the case with such national contingents.[23]

The House of Commons Foreign Affairs Committee that studied and reported on the Green Paper was quite sympathetic to these arguments. It acknowledged the 'extensive support' PMSCs 'already provide' to the UN and other organizations in the form of 'security guarding, logistic support, and de-mining' and opined, 'These are legitimate activities, and the use of PMCs in this area of UN and other intergovernmental organisations' work is relatively uncontroversial.'[24] It characterized PMSC involvement in peacekeeping and peace enforcement as 'more problematic' but asserted that 'the idea of hiring PMCs to do the job has obvious appeal' in light of the failure to protect Rwandans and perpetual problems in mobilizing and deploying peacekeepers.[25] It acknowledged evidence that 'some UN member states, particularly those from the developing world, are likely to be highly suspicious of proposals to increase the role of PMCs in UN peace operations.'[26] Furthermore, it observed that contributing forces to the UN can be a source of income for some states and surmised that '[s]ome member states might dispute the expenditure of UN funds on private military companies rather than on the current practice, which helps to support their national armed forces.'[27] It also conceded that PMSCs may exaggerate their own capacity – but, perhaps due to the bias that the Rwanda scenario evokes, it did not question the ability to use force as a solution.[28] Finally, it stated:

---

[22] Indeed, if the contract binds the company, its specific terms do not necessarily bind each individual hired by that company. Those would have to be reiterated in the employment contract between the company and the employee. One may object, however, that this way of making international legal standards binding on PMSCs is somehow qualitatively different from that through public law.

[23] UK Green Paper (above, note 156), para. 59. UNAMSIL was the United Nations Mission in Sierra Leone.

[24] UK House of Commons, Foreign Affairs Committee, Ninth Report, Session 2001–2002, para. 85.

[25] Ibid., paras 85–89.   [26] Ibid., para. 92.   [27] Ibid., paras 92–93.   [28] Ibid., para. 94.

If the Government concludes that private military companies should not be permitted to engage in combat activities, this would probably rule out their employment for the high intensity, peace enforcement end of UN interventions. However, if regulation of the private military sector resulted in the development of a transparent, trusted industry in the United Kingdom, further commercial involvement at the low intensity end of UN peace operations might become increasingly acceptable to member states. If this helped to increase the speed and efficiency of UN reactions, to ensure the enforcement of UN Security Council resolutions, and to prevent further atrocities such as those committed in Rwanda and the Balkans in the 1990s, then such regulation should be welcomed.[29]

Thus, the Foreign Affairs Committee imagined that PMSCs could act as interposition forces in a peace operation that (in its view) would not require or lead to the forces being engaged as combatants. As such, it perceived increased PMSC involvement in peace operations as a 'potential benefit of a regulated private military sector'.

For its part, the UK Secretary of State for Foreign and Commonwealth Affairs subsequently received the committee's report in a generally positive light.[30] Specifically in response to the committee's recommendation that the government 'consider carefully whether the greater use of PMCs in UK humanitarian and peace support operations might help to reduce military over-stretch', it stated, however,

The Government sees no difficulty of principle in private companies offering support to humanitarian or peacekeeping missions directly to the UN or to other international bodies ... But when the UN formally requests the Government to contribute to such operations, it does so in the expectation that the front-line tasks will be undertaken by the UK's Armed Forces, with their known skills and experience. The Government would therefore not consider it appropriate for the UK to agree to undertake such tasks and then, as it were, to sub contract them to private companies. If the existence of other commitments meant that the Armed Forces were not able to undertake new peacekeeping or other humanitarian operations themselves, the Government considers that it would be preferable to decline the mission at the outset.[31]

---

[29] Ibid., para. 95.

[30] See also the comments by then Foreign Secretary Jack Straw reported in Nigel D. White, 'Institutional Responsibility for Private Military and Security Companies', in F. Francioni and N. Ronzitti (eds.), *War by Contract* (Oxford: Oxford University Press, 2011), pp. 381–395 at pp. 381–382.

[31] UK, Secretary of State for Foreign and Commonwealth Affairs, 'Ninth Report of the Foreign Affairs Committee: Private Military Companies. Session 2001–2002, Response of the Secretary of State for Foreign and Commonwealth Affairs' October 2002, Cm 5642, p. 4.

This represents the only formal, public statement by a government on the feasibility of sending a PMSC as a national contingent in a peace operation known to the author. It is worth pointing out that the obstacle to sending such a force as identified by the UK Government is that it would not be 'appropriate' to essentially mislead the UN as to the quality of the forces being offered. One may consider, however, that the question of what is 'appropriate' is in fact a kind of oblique allusion to comity in international law.[32] However, other UK government actors displayed considerable openness to the idea, without exhibiting a sense that recourse to such forces would somehow impinge on a general obligation of behaviour or expectation owed to other states.

2.3   Views of a French Parliamentary Commission

In 2012, a French Parliamentary Commission published a report recommending that France introduce legislation and a regulatory scheme for PMSCs.[33] The authors of the report referred to the Brahimi Report's recommendation to have the capacity to deploy a force within thirty days and commented, 'Même s'il convient d'en étudier l'importance ou le rôle exact, on voit bien que le deploiement d'[PMSC] peut être d'un apport utile pour envoyer des capacités en avant-garde.'[34] The report went on to say,

> À plus forte raison, elles pourraient jouer un rôle utile pour consolider les moyens déployés dans les zones en crises. Les OMP de l'ONU sont parfois critiquées pour le manque de savoir-faire, voire de savoir-être, de certains contingents. Les États disposant des armées les plus modernes et les mieux formées sont généralement réticents à mettre des contingents à disposition de l'ONU, la prise en charge de l'organisation ne suffisant pas à compenser les soldes des soldats. Par ailleurs, le commandement et les règles

---

[32] The doctrine of comity may more frequently be invoked in private international law; nevertheless, it captures the notion of deference to the interests of other states and subjects of international law that is clearly present in the sentiment expressed in the Secretary of State's words. For a brief overview of comity, see Gary Born, 'International Comity and U.S. Federal Common Law' (1990) 84 *American Society of International Law Proceedings* 326–332, especially at 326–327.

[33] Christian Ménard and Jean-Claude Viollet, 'Rapport d'information sur les sociétés militaires privées', 14 February 2012 (No. 4350). Interestingly, the impetus for such legislation is a concern that existing French laws (and in particular the 2003 law on mercenaries) may be overly dissuasive for the industry and that France will miss out on the significant economic boon the industry commands.

[34] Ibid.

d'engagement ne correspondant pas forcément aux attentes des Gouverne-
ments, les États occidentaux ont réduit le format de leurs armées, dont les
spécialistes sont devenus d'autant plus précieux.[35]

The debate in the National Assembly was generally supportive of the recommendation to introduce new legislation involving a strict regulatory
scheme for PMSCs but no comment was made in response to the potential
use of PMSCs in peace operations. It is therefore difficult to gauge French
opinion on this point, beyond noting that it did not raise objections when
stated in such a vague manner.

There is thus not yet a clear norm that one can identify through the
practices and expressed opinions of states or the UN on this matter. The
statements of the UK and France regarding a hypothetical use of PMSCs in
peace operations reveal a certain level of ambiguity in terms of the potential lawfulness of such a practice. On the other hand, one can point to the
practice of the United States of recruiting and sending UN CIVPOL via
a PMSC, coupled with an absence of states or international organizations
protesting publicly against that practice, as evidence that PMSC peacekeepers are tolerated in at least some roles.[36]

2.4   Conclusion

It is clear that current UN policies permit and seek to accommodate the
use of PMSCs in certain roles in peace operations, such as logistics support and catering. The gradations in levels or types of accepted activity of
PMSCs can best be seen in the detailed policies. Moreover, this is commensurate with their current roles in UN peace operations. The objective

---

[35] Ibid. ('... they could play a useful role in consolidating the resources deployed to crisis
zones. UN peace operations are sometimes criticized for the lack of know-how, or even
of ethics (savoir-être), of some contingents. States with the most modern and best-trained
armed forces are generally reticent to put them at the disposal of the UN, as the management by the UN is insufficient to cover the salaries of the soldiers. In addition, the command
and the rules of engagement do not necessarily correspond to the expectations of Governments, western States having decreased the size of their armies, in which specialists have
become that much more valuable') (author's translation).

[36] The ICRC Study on customary IHL identified 'Practice establishing the existence of a rule
that allows certain conduct' via an empirical study of 'States undertaking such action,
together with the absence of protests by other States'. See Jean-Marie Henckaerts and Louise
Doswald-Beck, *Customary International Humanitarian Law*, 2 vols. (Cambridge: Cambridge University Press, 2005), vol. 1 at xl. It demands a great deal of states, however, to
require that they protest any and all activity of other states as a means of finding the existence of a permissive rule.

for the rest of this study is to determine whether that policy and practice is in harmony with the general international legal framework and to discern the limits to the use of PMSCs in the peacekeeping context. I submit that, for the most part, the more traditional PMSC-type roles (e.g., logistics support) are in keeping with the general principles of peacekeeping and therefore do not need to be tested against it. They nevertheless need to be tested against the general international legal framework – especially when it comes to PMSCs providing security for peace operations in hostile environments. Moreover, those specific policies may provide some indication as to the possibility of using PMSCs as peacekeepers in the sense of the actual force. Finally, no matter in which capacity PMSCs are used in peace operations, it is essential to clarify with whom responsibility lies for any wrongful conduct and to underline that in any case, obligations of due diligence remain.

Part II will analyze the legal framework governing UN peace operations in an effort to determine whether it presents any legal impediments to using PMSCs as civilian police and as peacekeepers. A subsequent part will examine whether PMSCs active in peace operations in other roles, such as security guards, might (voluntarily or not) directly participate in hostilities and will assess the ramifications of that potential scenario. In my view, the fact that security guards contracted by the UN or in peace operations may, according to UN policy, use force according to the same strictures as the first peacekeeping force – but in a context in which the rest of the force may have been drawn into armed conflict based on a broad mandate – means that, in essence, the UN has already accepted PMSC 'peacekeepers' in roles akin to that of a military contingent. Although that role is now a very narrow aspect of what twenty-first-century peacekeeping entails, it is nevertheless the most controversial task when one imagines the outsourcing of peacekeeping.

PART II

The Legal Framework of UN Peace Operations and the Use of PMSCs

Private military and security companies are widely used in peace operations and peace operations themselves are deployed in fluid and complex situations. In light of this, a more complete picture of the legal framework governing the use, obligations and responsibility of contractors in these operations is in order.[1] This part examines the legal framework for peace operations in an effort to determine whether there are inherent limitations on the lawfulness of using PMSCs in various roles in peace operations, with a focus on the military contingent, the civilian police and security guards.

The legal framework for peace operations is generally agreed to be comprised of the UN Security Council mandate establishing the operation, the various agreements for the contribution of troops and police between member states and the UN, the status of forces agreement with the host state and, last but not least, the principles of peacekeeping – consent, impartiality and a limited use of force. Chapter 3 canvasses the basic legal framework, while Chapter 4 delves into the principles of peacekeeping in

---

[1] No other comprehensive study on the matter exists. Only a few articles deal with PMSCs in UN peace operations from a legal perspective: Mirko Sossai, 'The Privatisation of 'the Core Business of UN Peacekeeping Operations': Any Legal Limit?' (2014) 16 *International Community Law Review* 405–422; Chia Lehnardt, 'Peacekeeping', in Simon Chesterman and Angelina Fischer (eds.), *Private Security, Public Order: The Outsourcing of Public Services and Its Limits* (Oxford: Oxford University Press, 2009), pp. 205–221; Russell Buchan, Henry Jones and Nigel White, 'The Externalization of Peacekeeping: Policy, Responsibility, and Accountability' (2011) 15 *Journal of International Peacekeeping* 281–315; and Matija Kovač, 'Legal Issues Arising from the Possible Inclusion of Private Military Companies in UN Peacekeeping' (2009) 13 *Max Planck Yearbook of United Nations Law* 307–374. While Kovač's article does cover PMSCs as a peacekeeping force, it does not cover other contractors. See also Chia Lehnardt's thesis, *Private Militärfirmen und völkerrechtliche Verantwortlichkeit* (Tübigen: Mohr Siebeck, 2011). For an empirical study of the use of PMSCs in UN peace operations, see Åsa Gilje Østensen, *UN Use of Private Military and Security Companies: Practices and Policies* (Geneva: DCAF, 2011); see also Østensen, 'Implementers or Governors? The Expanding Role for Private Military and Security Companies Within the Peace Operations Network' (2014) 16 *ICLR* 423–442.

light of PMSCs in peace operations. Having determined that nothing a priori in the general legal framework would prohibit the UN from recourse to PMSCs in various roles, Chapter 5 looks specifically at the possible ways in which a private military or security company might be incorporated as the military force in a peace operation to discern potential legal limits to such action. Chapter 6 explores the law applicable to peace operations and outlines some areas of concern.

3

The Legal Basis for Peacekeeping/Peace Operations

The starting point for any discussion of the legal framework of UN peace operations is that the power to undertake or create such operations is not written anywhere in the UN Charter. Instead, the legal basis for peace-keeping is most commonly considered to be located in the implied powers of the organization.[1] One scholar argues that it can be construed as a provisional measure under Article 40,[2] whereas Christine Gray argues that 'the debate seems to be without practical significance.'[3] Nonetheless, it does mean that the specific rules on peace operations are not set down in the Charter; rather, they have evolved through peacekeeping doctrine over the past six decades.[4] Most UN peacekeeping operations are established via a Security Council resolution – sometimes under Chapter VII (or in

[1] On implied powers of the UN, see *Reparations for Injuries Suffered in the Service of the United Nations* (Advisory Opinion) [1949] ICJ Rep 174; on the acceptance of peacekeeping as a proper exercise of such implied powers, see *Certain Expenses of the United Nations* (Advisory Opinion) [1962] ICJ Rep 151. See also A. Orakhelashvili, 'The Legal Basis for Peacekeeping' (2003) 43 *Vanderbilt JIL* 485; on peacekeeping as an implied power or an inherent power, Hilaire McCoubrey and Nigel White, *The Blue Helmets: Legal Regulation of United Nations Military Operations* (Aldershot: Dartmouth, 1996), pp. 39–59.

[2] Hitoshi Nasu, *International Law on Peacekeeping: A Study of Article 40 of the UN Charter* (Martinus Nijhoff, 2009).

[3] Christine Gray, *International Law and the Use of Force*, 3rd edn (Oxford: Oxford University Press, 2008), p. 262.

[4] See UN Secretary General, 'Summary Study of the Experience Derived from the Establishment and Operation of the Force', UN Doc A/3943 (9 October 1958) (UNSG 'Summary Study'); UN Secretary General, 'An Agenda for Peace: Preventive Diplomacy, Peacemaking and Peace-keeping' (17 June 1992), UN Docs S/24111 – A/47/277; UN Secretary-General, 'Supplement to An Agenda for Peace: Position Paper of the Secretary-General on the Occasion of the 50th Anniversary of the United Nations' (3 January 1995), UN Doc A/50/60–S/1995/1; 'Report of the Panel on United Nations Peace Operations', UN Doc A/55/305–S/2000/809 (21 August 2000) (hereafter Brahimi Report). See also the follow-up report by the Secretary-General on the implementation of the Brahimi Report: UN Doc A/55/502 (20 October 2000); United Nations Department of Peacekeeping Operations and Department of Field Support, 'United Nations Peacekeeping Operations: Principles and Guidelines' (18 January 2008) (hereafter Capstone Doctrine).

part), but often no chapter or article is specified. The General Assembly can also establish peace operations using the Uniting for Peace Resolution, but has rarely done so.[5] In contrast to these, the enforcement actions the UN was supposed to undertake using forces under Article 43 of the Charter have instead been conducted by states, regional organizations or coalitions of states under an authorization by the UN Security Council.[6]

There is, thus, no single treaty provision against which to measure the possibility to use PMSCs as a troop contingent and in other roles in UN peace operations. On one hand, the principles of peacekeeping – consent, impartiality and a 'restricted' use of force – play an integral role in ensuring the legality of any peace operation that is not established under Chapter VII of the UN Charter. On the other hand, the mandate itself, the Status of Forces Agreement between the UN and the host state and the agreements between the UN and troop- and police-contributing states may contribute to the technical legal basis for the presence of the force in a state.

It is also important to understand the legal basis for police deployments considering that the one context in which PMSCs are contracted by a state to recruit, deploy and manage peacekeepers is in relation to UN Civilian Police.[7] By and large, police deployments within UN peace operations occur according to the same framework that governs military and civilian deployment for the rest of the operation.[8] The specific rules governing the

---

[5] Uniting for Peace, UNGA Res 377(V) (3 November 1950). Although the very first peace operation (UNEF) was established using the mechanisms set up in this resolution, it has not been used since then to establish a peace operation. It is not within the powers of the General Assembly to establish an enforcement operation, however. See *Certain Expenses of the United Nations* (Advisory Opinion) [1962] ICJ Rep 151 at 166 and 170–172. One other peace operation besides UNEF was established on the basis of a UN General Assembly resolution: the United Nations Security Force in West New Guinea in 1962; see UNGA Res 1752(XVII) (21 September 1962). That resolution was based on an agreement between Indonesia and the Netherlands and was not adopted using the Uniting for Peace procedure. In Congo in 1960, the UN General Assembly adopted a resolution under Uniting for Peace in support of the existing peace operation that had been set up by the Security Council. See UNGA Res 1474 (ES-IV) (19 September 1960). The resolution requested states to comply with the Security Council resolution in financing and supporting the mission with forces.

[6] In general, for example, the UNSC authorizations to use force against Iraq in 1991 and against Korea in 1950 are excluded from what can be considered 'peace operations' as they amount to 'enforcement action or war'. For Libya in 2011, some consider UNSC Res 1973 (2011) to have authorized a use of force; others considered that the force used to enforce the no-fly zone went far beyond the terms of the resolution.

[7] See, in particular, Marjorie Ann Browne, 'United Nations Peacekeeping: Issues for Congress', CRS Report (updated 13 November 2008) 18; Marjorie Ann Browne, 'United Nations Peacekeeping: Issues for Congress', CRS Report (13 August 2010) 18.

[8] Edmund Primosch argues that the common tasks carried out by UN CIVPOL – monitoring local police, supervising IDP and refugee voluntary return, investigating complaints against

force itself will flow from a combination of the UN Security Council resolution setting the mandate of the operation, international law, the law of the police contributing state and the host state's laws.[9]

While there is no black letter rule prohibiting the use of PMSCs in peace operations – in particular as the troop contingent itself – the use of PMSCs must be able to conform to all aspects of this framework if their use is to be contemplated. All of these principles, policies and internal directives must also be set against the backdrop of general international law, including international human rights law, and in particular international humanitarian law when it applies in UN peace operations. This rather nebulous framework thus sets the stage for the method that will be used in this part to test the possibility to use PMSCs as the military or police contingent in peace operations.

3.1   Agreements Governing Troop and Police Contributions

This brief overview outlining how UN peacekeeping operations are established and staffed provides context for the ways in which private military and security personnel may be engaged in an operation.

---

local police when necessary, training local police, assisting humanitarian aid agencies and helping to ensure safe and neutral elections – 'can be regarded as appropriate action in order to attain the common ends of UN members' and therefore is a lawful action under the UN Charter. See his 'The Roles of United Nations Civilian Police (UNCIVPOL) Within United Nations Peace-Keeping Operations' (1994) 43 *ICLQ* 425–431 at 429.

[9] See James Watson, Mark Fitzpatrick and James Ellis, 'The Legal Basis for Bilateral and Multilateral Police Deployments' (2011) 15 *Journal of International Peacekeeping* 7–38, passim. One issue that may raise specific questions in terms of the laws that govern deployed CIVPOL is the emergence of 'executive' policing, wherein CIVPOL are mandated to carry out policing functions such as arrest, detention and investigation, including the use of force in law enforcement in peace operations. Renata Dwan argues that although CIVPOL have been mandated to carry out such tasks in international territorial administrations, this function is unlikely to be commonly used because it is highly invasive of sovereignty, it is complex (i.e., not always feasible), and simply because it is qualitatively so vastly different from the usual way in which UN CIVPOL are used. See Renata Dwan, 'Introduction', in Renata Dwan (ed.), *Executive Policing: Enforcing the Law in Peace Operations* (SIPRI Research Report No. 16, Oxford University Press, 2002), pp. 1–4. The DPKO does not seem to view it as impossible that CIVPOL will be mandated to conduct interim law enforcement, stating only that such powers 'have historically been given' in the context of territorial administration missions. See UN DPKO, 'What the UN Police Do in the Field', on the DPKO website: www.un.org/en/peacekeeping/sites/police/work.shtml (accessed 14 November 2011). The legal framework governing their use of force in any case is set out in UN DPKO/DFS, 'Policy (Revised): Formed Police Units in United Nations Peacekeeping Operations' (1 March 2010) 7–10. See also Bruce Oswald, Helen Durham and Adrian Bates, *Documents on the Law of UN Peace Operations* (Oxford: Oxford University Press, 2010), pp. 8–11.

First, the UN Secretary-General usually presents a report to the Security Council outlining the proposed mandate, functions, composition and deployment of the mission. The Security Council then adopts a resolution establishing the operation on the basis of that report. The Secretary-General sets about staffing and equipping the mission, from the troop and police contingents to the civilians. In early peace operations, some states eagerly offered their national armed forces for the Secretary-General to include in the peacekeeping force.[10] As a general rule, however, the Secretary-General approaches states to request contributions of troop or police contingents. They are integrated into the force as follows:

> Armed military peacekeepers that are contributed by their States are deployed as a contingent and commanded by a contingent commander usually from their State. Consequently, military members serving as part of national contingents are under operational control of the [UN Force Commander], but remain part of their respective national armed forces and under national command. Thus, there is no direct contractual relationship between contingent members and the UN.[11]

This description helps to illustrate the usual relationship between states and the UN during a UN peace operation and provides a backdrop against which to consider the potential role or place of contractors in such missions.

Military personnel are also provided to missions by states on an individual basis. These tend to be military observers, who are seconded to the UN by their sending state. In this capacity, they are 'experts on mission'[12] and they must sign 'an undertaking which requires them to comply with all relevant UN rules, regulations, and directives'.[13]

Individual civilian police are likewise seconded by their sending states to the operation. As Oswald et al. indicate, 'they are under the operational control of the [Police Commander]' rather than under national command, but 'it is usual for police personnel to also have to report back to their national Governments'.[14] They also sign individual undertakings requiring compliance with the rules as outlined above.

Recruiting civilian police to serve in UN peace operations has long been a challenge. As Schmidl points out, states do not keep extra units of law

---

[10] Robert Siekmann, *National Contingents in United Nations Peace-Keeping Forces* (Dordrecht: Martinus Nijhoff, 1991), pp. 21–23.

[11] Oswald et al., *Documents*, p. 6.

[12] UN Model SOFA, 'Draft Model Status-of-Forces Agreement Between the United Nations and Host Countries', Annex to the Report of the Secretary-General, UN Doc A/45/594 (9 October 1990), para. 26.

[13] Oswald et al., *Documents*, p. 6.   [14] Ibid.

enforcement personnel for extra-territorial deployment, unlike military forces.[15] Consequently, it was rare that an entire unit could be sent. In the late 1990s, Schmidl observed that 'police officers, even from one country, usually are drawn from a wide array of police forces and have highly diverse backgrounds'.[16] The UN DPKO has worked to change this tendency, developing a policy on Formed Police Units, the deployment of which has grown drastically.[17] Formed Police Units are 'cohesive mobile police units, providing support to United Nations operations and ensuring the safety and security of United Nations personnel and missions, primarily in public order management'.[18] Thus, police may also be provided to a mission as a Formed Police Unit, in which case they are deployed on a similar basis as troop contingents, with a national commander being responsible for discipline.[19] However, they are subject to a memorandum of understanding (MOU) between their sending state and the UN and they also sign individual undertakings.[20] The DPKO also created the 'Standing Police Capacity', a pool of twenty-five professional police officers based at the UN logistics base in Italy who can be deployed rapidly at the start-up phase of a new mission.[21]

As Part I illustrated, in addition to these contributions from state forces, the UN relies on contractors in order to staff peace operations.

3.2 Status of Forces Agreements

Status of forces agreements between the United Nations and the host state in which the peace operation is operating also form part of the legal framework. In addition to the policies described above, the work of

---

[15] Erwin Schmidl, 'Police Functions in Peace Operations: An Historical Overview', in Robert Oakley, Michael Dziedzic and Eliot Goldberg (eds.), *Policing the New World Disorder: Peace Operations and Public Security* (University Press of the Pacific, 1998), pp. 19–40.

[16] Ibid.

[17] UN DPKO/DFS, 'Policy (Revised): Formed Police Units in United Nations Peacekeeping Operations' (1 March 2010, revised 1 March 2013) 3, para. 6.

[18] Ibid., para. 8. [19] Ibid.

[20] Ibid. at 4, para. 9, and the 'Manual on Policies and Procedures Concerning the Reimbursement and Control of Contingent-Owned Equipment of Troop/Police Contributors Participating in Peacekeeping Missions' (hereafter COE Manual).

[21] See 'Standing Police Capacity' on the website of the UN Department of Peacekeeping Operations: www.un.org/en/peacekeeping/sites/police/capacity.shtml (accessed 14 November 2011). The High-Level Panel on Threats, Challenges and Change had advocated the creation of a capacity of 50–100 officers, which was endorsed by the UN General Assembly, but in the end UN member states have approved only 25. Ibid. The central role and diverse functions Civilian Police are increasingly mandated to perform is highlighted in UNSC Res 2185 (2014).

the UN Office of Legal Affairs regarding Status of Forces Agreements (SOFA) and contractors provides evidence of UN tolerance of PMSCs in peace operations and further illustrates the potential limitations on their use.

Beginning in 1995, on request by the DPKO, the UN Office of Legal Affairs began drafting clauses to include in Status of Forces/Status of Mission Agreements (SOFAs or SOMAs) with respect to contractors. The OLA took this initiative in response to some of the difficulties experienced by contractors. In fact, the Assistant Secretary-General for Peacekeeping Operations requested the views of the OLA as to whether 'privileges and immunities provided for under the [Convention on Privileges and Immunities of the United Nations] could be extended' to contractors.[22] The OLA characterized the functions performed by contractors as 'commercial in nature and rang[ing] from the procurement of goods and the supply of services to construction and catering services'. As such, they did not benefit from the status of experts on mission as a group as a whole. The OLA offered no opinion as to whether more important functions could be outsourced to contractors (such that contractors entrusted with such functions could benefit from the status of experts on mission), thereby leaving open the possibility that contractors could be tasked with 'specific and important' functions.[23]

The OLA then indicated to the Assistant Secretary-General for Peacekeeping Operations that it was developing a set of clauses with respect to contractors that could be proposed for inclusion in SOFAs or SOMAs. It warned, however, that 'the willingness of this Office to consider extending such facilities to the Contractors would not of itself result in their obtaining them since Governments have in the past expressed reservations on including the Contractors in the SOFAs/SOMAs.'[24] The contractor 'facilities' the OLA mentioned refer in particular to

> freedom of movement for the proper performance of the services; prompt issuance of necessary visas; exemption from immigration restrictions and alien registration; prompt issuance of licences or permits, as necessary, for required services, including for imports and for the operation of aircraft

[22] UN Office of Legal Affairs, 'Privileges and Immunities and Facilities for Contractors Supplying Goods and Services in Support of United Nations Peacekeeping Operations' (1995), UN Juridical YB (Part Two, Chapter VI) 407–408 (23 June 1995) (hereafter OLA, 'Privileges and Immunities for Contractors').

[23] One may also query the relevance of the categorization 'commercial' to distinguish 'specific and important' functions.

[24] OLA, 'Privileges and Immunities for Contractors', 408.

and vessels; repatriation in time of international crisis; right to import for the exclusive and official use of the United Nations, without any restriction, and free of tax or duties, supplies, equipment and other materials.[25]

As such, the host state may set limits on what contractors may or may not do through the terms it agrees to or refuses in the SOFA. In the absence of a mission-specific SOFA, there appears to be no basis in the Model SOFA to presume a host state can be deemed to have accepted the inclusion of PMSCs in the operation.[26] Theoretically, a host state could insist on a clause prohibiting the use of private security contractors in a SOFA, or prohibiting PMSCs from carrying out any number of other specified activities. It may also seriously impede the use of contractors simply by denying them certain facilities or immunities, rendering the execution of their tasks virtually impossible. Dieter Fleck argues that the role of PMSCs should be provided for in the SOFA, which should also 'provide for cooperative solutions of contentious issues' that may arise in relation to them.[27]

Nothing, thus, in the legal basis for peace operations or in the basic documents establishing them would appear, prima facie, to prohibit the use of PMSCs in various roles. As these provide no blanket prohibition, the possibility of using them would depend on the specific terms of the agreements.

[25] Ibid. For an example of a SOMA incorporating essentially all of these terms for contractors, see 'Exchange of Letters Constituting an Agreement Between the United Nations and Sierra Leone on the Status of the United Nations Observer Mission in Sierra Leone' (1998), UN Juridical YB (Part I) 46–48 (29 July 1998).

[26] But see below, Chapter 4, Section 4.2, on consent, in relation to this issue and to specific restrictions on which a host state may insist, with greater or lesser success.

[27] Dieter Fleck, 'The Legal Status of Personnel Involved in United Nations Peace Operations' (2013) 95 *International Review of the Red Cross* 613–636 at 634.

4

Principles of Peacekeeping

The following pages will consider whether the established rules on traditional peacekeeping operations (i.e., those based on the consent of the host state, although possibly also under a Resolution adopted under Chapter VII of the UN Charter[1]) allow the UN Security Council or UN Secretary-General to accept a PMSC as the sole and complete contribution of a state to a peace operation. The same analysis would apply where the PMSC would form a 'guard force' and may be relevant where the PMSC constitutes only part of a state's contribution to the operation. Throughout this discussion, the analysis is carried out on the assumption that the peace operation is lawful in every other respect – for example, if it has been created under Article 39 of the UN Charter, that that article has been properly invoked.

The general principles on peacekeeping, arguably as much as the specific rules on delegation and the creation of subsidiary organs in UN law, influence the overall assessment of the viability of the exclusive use of PMSC forces in peace operations. They are: the requirement of the consent of the host state to the operation (especially when it is not established under Chapter VII of the UN Charter), the requirement that the force

---

[1] Many contemporary operations are based on both consent and Chapter VII. See United Nations Department of Peacekeeping Operations and Department of Field Support, 'United Nations Peacekeeping Operations: Principles and Guidelines' (18 January 2008) (hereafter Capstone Doctrine), pp. 31–35, for how the UN reconciles the need for both bases. The Chapter VII resolution is generally thought to broaden the mandate of the operation to use more force than in a mission without a Chapter VII resolution but is not indispensable for the use of force up to and including in defence of the mandate, which goes beyond classical peacekeeping rules that limited the use of force to that only in self-defence. For example, the operation in Kosovo is considered to be based on the Military Technical Agreement concluded with Milosevic as well as UNSC Res 1244 (10 June 1999) UN Doc S/RES/1244 (1999). Only rarely has the Security Council specifically stated that it is *not* adopting the enabling Resolution under Chapter VII. See, for example, UNSC Res 1495 (2003) with regard to MINURSO and the situation in Western Sahara.

be impartial and conduct itself with impartiality, and the principle that the use of force be restricted to only that required in self-defence.[2] These principles were set down by former UN Secretary-General Dag Hammarskjøld at the time of the creation of the first peace operation and have remained touchstones of legality and legitimacy ever since, despite the fact that they have not been interpreted in a consistent manner over the years.[3] Indeed, peace operations and the principles underpinning them have been stretched and pulled in every direction since their inception. One may, therefore, legitimately question whether such elastic principles can impose constraints on the resort to PMSCs in UN peace operations. As is shown below, in certain circumstances the peacekeeping principles in fact ensure the respect of basic legal obligations. Arguably, in peace operations established under a resolution adopted under Chapter VII of the Charter, these principles may not constitute a legal requirement in order for a peace operation to be lawful. Nevertheless, recent UN doctrine affirms their vital role in peacekeeping and they are reiterated in the preamble of UN Security Council Resolutions on peacekeeping.[4] Private military and security company involvement in peace operations as a principal component of the force itself would thus have to be able to comply with these principles in order to be a feasible option. There are, arguably, two other relevant principles as well: Marrack Goulding identifies five principles of UN peacekeeping, the first of which is that they must be UN operations and

---

[2] See UN Secretary General, 'Summary Study of the Experience Derived from the Establishment and Operation of the Force', UN Doc A/3943 (9 October 1958) (UNSG 'Summary Study'); UN Secretary General, 'An Agenda for Peace: Preventive Diplomacy, Peacemaking and Peace-keeping' (17 June 1992), UN Docs S/24111 – A/47/277; UN Secretary-General, 'Supplement to An Agenda for Peace: Position Paper of the Secretary-General on the Occasion of the 50th Anniversary of the United Nations' (3 January 1995), UN Doc A/50/60–S/1995/1; 'Report of the Panel on United Nations Peace Operations', UN Doc A/55/305–S/2000/809 (21 August 2000) (hereafter Brahimi Report) Capstone Doctrine.
[3] For insistence that the principles are quasi-constitutional, M. Goulding, 'The Evolution of United Nations Peacekeeping' (1993) 69 *International Peacekeeping* 453. See, however, UNSG 'Agenda for Peace' (above, note 2), which defined peace operations in part as being conducted '*hitherto* with the consent of all parties' (emphasis added) for an example of the fluctuation in application of the principles (para. 20). In addition, a number of states reaffirmed their commitment to the principles of peacekeeping in the explanation of the vote adopting UNSC Res 2098 (2013). See UN Doc S.PV/6943 (28 March 2013). See also their reaffirmation in 'Report of the High-Level Independent Panel on Peace Operations on Uniting Our Strengths for Peace: Politics, Partnership and People' (17 June 2015), UN Doc A/70/95; S/2015/446, paras 124–129.
[4] Brahimi Report, para. 48; Capstone Doctrine, pp. 31–35. 'Report of the High-Level Independent Panel on Peace Operations on Uniting Our Strengths for Peace: Politics, Partnership and People' (17 June 2015), UN Doc A/70/95; S/2015/446, paras 124–130.

the fifth is that the forces must be supplied by states.[5] This analysis will begin with Goulding's first principle.

4.1 The Operation Must Be Under UN Command and Control

According to Goulding, in order to be a UN operation, a peace operation must be (1) established by a UN organ, (2) under UN command and control, and (3) financed by UN member states as 'expenses of the organization'. It is the second element that particularly concerns this analysis. Indeed, a number of factors support the notion that it is not simply the fact that a peace operation acts under a mandate adopted via a Security Council resolution that makes it a UN peace operation. One indicator is the fact that the UN Convention on the Safety of United Nations and Associated Personnel provides that an operation is not a UN operation unless it is under UN command and control.[6] Furthermore, Corinna Kuhl indicates that peace enforcement is distinguishable from peacekeeping solely on the basis that UN-*authorized* operations are not UN peacekeeping, whereas UN-commanded and -controlled operations are – apparently regardless of the degree to which they respect the other peacekeeping principles.[7] Indeed, this requirement is in line with the policy discussed above that states that the 'overall responsibility and authority cannot be delegated to non-United Nations personnel' and that 'the political direction and administration of an operation in the field in all its facets, must be performed by United Nations staff members'.[8]

This 'principle' (if it may be considered as such) entails that no operation may be completely outsourced to a PMSC, by whatever means, if the UN does not retain command and control over the operation, and still remain a UN peace operation. The UN could retain command and

---

[5] Goulding, 'Evolution of UN Peacekeeping', 453–454.

[6] UN Convention on the Safety of United Nations and Associated Personnel, New York, 9 December 1994, in force 15 January 1999, 2051 UNTS 363, Article 1(c)(i).

[7] Corinna Kuhl, 'The Evolution of Peace Operations, from Interposition to Integrated Missions', in Gian Luca Beruto (ed.), *International Humanitarian Law, Human Rights and Peace Operations* (31st Round Table, San Remo 2008), pp. 70–76 at pp. 70–71. Kuhl was, at the time of writing, Chief of the UN DPKO Peacekeeping Best Practices Section. Alexander Orakhelashvili argues, however, that 'there is no indication in the Charter of any presumption in favour of, let alone requirement for, UN command and control over these forces.' See his *Collective Security* (Oxford: Oxford University Press, 2011), p. 323. In fact, he argues that 'UN forces have never been subjected to exclusive UN command and control' due to the dual state-UN command system they are under (p. 327). He argues that the UN consequently does not have 'effective control' over its peacekeeping forces.

[8] Report of the Secretary-General, 'Use of Civilian Personnel in Peace-Keeping Operations', UN Doc A/45/502 (18 September 1990) para. 2.

control by placing the PMSC contingents under a UN-appointed commander, for example. It is submitted, furthermore, that it would not be sufficient that the UN retain 'overall' control over such an operation, but that it must exercise command and control in the day-to-day functioning of the mission.[9]

Of course, this requirement is relevant only for UN peacekeeping. As peacekeeping is undertaken more and more by regional organizations (based on a UN mandate), this requirement cannot be taken as a principle of peacekeeping in general but may be highly relevant for determining which operations may constitute UN peacekeeping.

4.2 Consent

As traditional peace operations were established without a Chapter VII resolution, respect for Article 2(7) of the Charter necessitated the existence of consent on the part of the host state(s) in order to establish a force on its territory.[10] In his *Agenda for Peace* in 1992, then Secretary-General Boutros Boutros-Ghali indicated a sea change in peacekeeping by describing peace operations as '*hitherto*' with the consent of the parties. The insertion of that simple word indicated a willingness to deploy peace operations in the absence of the consent of the parties, perceiving that as both lawful and legitimate.[11] Only three years later, however, in his *Supplement to an Agenda for Peace*, the 'hitherto' had disappeared in the wake of the spectacular failure of peace operations that had not been established with the consent of the parties (and that had not respected the other cardinal principles of peacekeeping either).[12]

Aside from that rather brief hiatus, this principle has remained integral to peacekeeping doctrine even with the advent of Chapter VII resolutions

---

[9] *Pace* European Court of Human Rights in *Behrami and Behrami v. France* and *Saramati v. France, Germany and Norway* (App nos 71412/01 and 78166/01) ECHR 2 May 2007.

[10] Article 2(7) of the UN Charter in effect prohibits the UN from intervening in 'matters which are essentially within the domestic jurisdiction of any state' in the absence of a Security Council Resolution adopted under Chapter VII of the Charter. For a fascinating discussion of the differing interpretations of former Secretaries-General Dag Hammerskjold and U Thant as to the UN's legal obligation to withdraw UNEF from Egypt on Egypt's withdrawal of consent to the presence of the operation, see Jack Garvey, 'United Nations Peacekeeping and Host-State Consent' (1970) 64 *AJIL* 241–269.

[11] UNSG 'Agenda for Peace', para. 20 (definition of peacekeeping: '*Peace-keeping* is the deployment of a United Nations presence in the field, hitherto with the consent of all the parties concerned, normally involving United Nations military and/or police personnel and frequently civilians as well. Peace-keeping is a technique that expands the possibilities for both the prevention of conflict and the making of peace').

[12] UNSG 'Supplement to Agenda for Peace', paras 33–36.

accompanying host state agreements, even if only as a practical necessity for the success of the operation. The requirement of host-state consent for legal reasons in traditional (i.e., Chapter VI½) peace operations (so as not to contravene Article 2(7) of the Charter) jives with – but is not identical to – the consent sought by the Department of Peacekeeping Operations (DPKO) in order to ensure the success of its operations.[13] The DPKO seeks the 'consent of the main parties' to the conflict as an essential element to the ability of the operation to function and implement its mandate.[14] In this sense, for the DPKO it may be not only the host state (with which a status of forces agreement, or SOFA, would be negotiated and signed) whose consent is relevant, but also non-state parties to a conflict with sufficient capacity to impede the freedom of movement of the mission.[15] Furthermore, there is a palpable concern that an absence of consent by the main parties may lead to UN forces 'being drawn towards enforcement action',[16] presumably via a use of force against a party in an attempt to implement the mandate. For the DPKO, consent is thus a guarantor of impartiality and should act as a damper on the use of force by peacekeepers, thereby underpinning the other two essential tenets of peace operations.

Arguably, however, on a purely legal level, the requirement that a host state consent to the force remains necessary to ensure that the UN respects Article 2(7) of the Charter.[17] Ray Murphy observes that consent

---

[13] Capstone Doctrine, 34. See also 'Report of the High-Level Independent Panel on Peace Operations on Uniting Our Strengths for Peace: Politics, Partnership and People' (17 June 2015), UN Doc A/70/95; S/2015/446, para. 127, stating, 'Clearly the consent of the Government is fundamental for the deployment of a mission, and that should be reinforced.'

[14] Capstone Doctrine, 32. The Special Court for Sierra Leone stated, 'In non-international armed conflicts, this consent is obtained from the warring parties, not out of legal obligation, but rather to ensure the effectiveness of the peacekeeping operation.' *Prosecutor v. Sesay, Kallon, Gbao* (Case No. SCSL-04-15-T) Trial Judgment (2 March 2009), para. 226. Thus, that court considers that the view of non-state parties does not affect the 'sovereignty' concern when it comes to Article 2(7) of the UN Charter. Eric David takes a different view, arguing that the UN General Assembly prohibits intervention into states 'sans distinguer si l'intervention se fait en faveur du gouvernement ou d'une partie de la population; l'un et l'autre étant par définition des elements constitutifs de l'Etat et le droit international ne privilégiant ni l'un ni l'autre en cas de guerre civile, il est logique que l'un et l'autre aient un droit égal à pretender représenter l'Etat...' *Principes de droit des conflits armés*, 4th edn (Brussels: Bruylant, 2008), para. 1.107. McCoubrey and White, *The Blue Helmets*, pp. 69–71, indicate some of the nefarious effects of failing to gain the consent of all parties to the conflict.

[15] Capstone Doctrine, p. 32. [16] Ibid.

[17] Garvey notes that Hammarskjöld was enigmatic or paradoxical when it came to consent and what its withdrawal would entail. As Garvey puts it, 'Hammarskjold at one and the same time says that Egypt was obligated not to withdraw her consent until the tasks [in the

'confers the legitimacy required for a lawful presence' of a peacekeeping force but argues that '[i]n fact, the legality of a peacekeeping force on any country's territory should be guaranteed' in a Status of Forces Agreement (SOFA) between the UN and the host state.[18] While it is true that the SOFA is important, Murphy himself notes that some peacekeeping forces deployed for as long as twenty years without having signed a SOFA.[19] This suggests that consent itself plays a role in the lawfulness of an operation beyond its (crucial) contribution to helping to establish the legitimacy of the operation. At the same time, as indicated below, 'robust' peace operations involve a willingness to continue to implement a mandate at the outer limits of consent. A recent report of the UN Secretary-General says openly that UNAMID and MONUSCO 'have experienced challenges in the implementation of their mandates' due to spoilers, but which have been 'compounded' by '[l]imited consent by host Governments'.[20]

Consent is increasingly under pressure in peace operations.[21] It may be the case that host states do not formally withdraw their consent to an operation as a whole, but they impose restrictions making it difficult or impossible for the mission to continue to carry out its functions. In practice, if host states do not truly consent to the members of a peacekeeping force, they may impede the deployment of those participants by refusing to issue visas or by stalling the provision of such documents. For example, this occurred when Eritrea, which had never signed a SOFA for UNMEE, imposed visa and fuel restrictions and expelled mission staff members, forcing the Security Council to terminate the mission.[22] That may have been a case of general obstructionism with respect to the mission as a whole, but the tactic remains the same.

mandate] had been completed, but that "Egypt constitutionally had an undisputed right to request the withdrawal of the troops, even if initial consent had been given".' Garvey, 'UN Peacekeeping and Consent', 249, citing Hammarskjøld's own aide-memoire on the understanding he had with Nasser regarding UNEF, in 6 ILM 581 at 596 (1967). According to Hammarskjøld, withdrawal of consent would lead only to an obligation to negotiate, not to an immediate requirement that the force leave the country; ibid., 253.

[18] Ray Murphy, *UN Peacekeeping in Lebanon, Somalia and Kosovo: Operational and Legal Issues in Practice* (Cambridge: Cambridge University Press, 2007), p. 7.

[19] Ibid, p. 110.

[20] UN Secretary-General, 'Implementation of the Recommendations of the Special Committee on Peacekeeping Operations', UN Doc A/65/680 (4 January 2011), para. 3.

[21] Ian Johnstone, 'Managing Consent in Contemporary Peacekeeping Operations' (2011) 18 *Journal of International Peacekeeping* 168–182, 179.

[22] UN Secretary-General, 'Special Report of the Secretary-General on the United Nations Mission in Ethiopia and Eritrea', UN Doc S/2008/226 (7 April 2008). See also UNSC Res 1827 (2008).

What is relevant here is the scope and contours of a host state's consent to the deployment of a peace operation on its soil.[23] That is to say, does the principle of consent affect whether a PMSC could be used as a military force in a peace operation? To what degree does consent affect the Secretary-General's freedom of choice in the composition of the peace force? In the past[24] as well as very recently,[25] some host states have attempted to block a particular state from participating in a peace operation on their territory or attempted to limit the deployment (in geographical or functional terms) of certain contingents. Other states have argued that a host state's views on the contingents that form part of the operation on its territory must be taken into account in determining the composition of the force on the grounds that consent as a legal basis for the operation goes not just to the existence of the mission but to all aspects of the operation.[26] For this study, the question when it comes to PMSCs as a contingent of a peace force (or as the entire force) is whether the UN is legally bound by a host state's objection to the composition of the force on its territory.

4.2.1 Host States May Have a de facto, but Not de jure, Veto

UN doctrine does not accept that consent legally requires that a host state agree to the composition of the force, but the host state's consent to the composition of the force will play an important role in the UN's decision-making. Here, it is worth quoting at length from the foundational document on the principles of peacekeeping:

---

[23] One of the principal concerns regarding the scope of consent is in relation to the freedom of movement a UN operation has once deployed on the territory. However, it is well known that the first peace operation, UNEF I, withdrew from Egypt in 1967 when Egypt withdrew its consent.

[24] See Siekmann, *National Contingents*, pp. 64–77, for a discussion of the resistance of host states to the inclusion of troops from certain countries in the force.

[25] Recently, DRC objected to Indian troops forming part of MONUC. See F. Wild, 'Congo Accuses Some UN Peacekeepers of Complicity in Conflict', Bloomberg, 27 November 2008. As of 2011, however, Indian forces continue to compose part of MONUSCO. See www.un.org/en/peacekeeping/missions/monusco/facts.shtml (accessed 28 March 2011). In addition, Eritrea and Sudan attempted to block 'Western forces' from deploying on their territory. See Richard Gowan and Benjamin Tortolani, 'Robust Peacekeeping and Its Limitations', in Bruce Jones (ed.), *Robust Peacekeeping: The Politics of Force* (Centre for International Cooperation, 2009), p. 50.

[26] A. Di Blase, 'The Role of the Host State's Consent with Regard to Non-coercive Actions by the United Nations', in A. Cassese (ed.), *United Nations Peace-Keeping: Legal Essays* (Sijthoff and Noordhoff, 1978), pp. 55–94 at pp. 59–61.

[W]hile it is for the United Nations alone to decide on the composition of military elements sent to a country, the United Nations should, in deciding on composition, take fully into account the view of the host Government as one of the most serious factors which should guide the recruitment of the personnel. Usually, this is likely to mean that serious objections by the host country against participation by a specific contributing country in the United Nations operation will determine the action of the Organization. However, were the United Nations for good reasons to find that course inadvisable, it would remain free to pursue its own line, and any resulting conflict would have to be resolved on a political rather than on a legal basis.[27]

Although this position has been reaffirmed on a number of occasions, one may interrogate its correctness in legal terms in a peace operation not established under Chapter VII of the Charter.

The Security Council explicitly affirmed the position set out above in the resolution establishing the operation in Cyprus, UNFICYP. In Resolution 186 of 1964, the Security Council recommended the creation of a UN peacekeeping force in Cyprus with the consent of the Government of Cyprus, and stated that 'the composition and size of the Force shall be established by the Secretary-General, *in consultation with* the Governments of Cyprus, Greece, Turkey and the United Kingdom of Great Britain and Northern Ireland.'[28] The text of this resolution suggests that consent of the host state is necessary for the establishment of the mission, but that it has a right only to be *consulted* about the composition of the force that will be deployed. That resolution is unusually specific, however.[29]

In regard to ONUC in Congo in 1960, the Status of Forces Agreement between the UN and the Government of Congo affirmed rather forcefully the authority of the UN to determine the composition of the force in a quasi-unilateral fashion. It stated, 'The United Nations shall possess sole competence with respect to decisions concerning the composition of the military units sent to the Congo, it being understood at the same time that the United Nations shall, in determining their composition, give

---

[27] UNSG, 'Summary Study', para. 161. Di Blase, 'Role of Host State Consent', 61, has argued that the 'Secretary-General's declarations and attitudes consistently indicated that the United Nations did not intend to surrender its full discretionary power with regard to matters falling within its competence, such as the composition of one of its subsidiary organs, i.e. the Force ... Instead, it was deemed *convenient* to take into account the host State's demands to a greater or lesser extent ... ' Emphasis added.

[28] UNSC Res 186 (1964), para. 4.

[29] Siekmann, *National Contingents*, p. 73. This is likely due to the fact that the United Kingdom had established bases in Cyprus. See McCoubrey and White, *The Blue Helmets*, pp. 81–82.

every consideration to the opinion of the Government as one of the most important factors to be borne in mind in connexion with recruitment.'[30] In Hammarskjøld's first report on the implementation of Resolution 143 (ONUC), he reiterated the 'general principle' outlined above as being applicable.[31] Siekmann argues that because the Security Council 'commends' the Secretary-General for his First Report on the implementation of UNSC Resolution 143 in UNSC Resolution 145, the Security Council has implicitly approved that principle regarding the composition of the force.[32] He also notes that 'the only thing approved by the General Assembly as a guiding principle for the composition of UNEF "I" was that the consent of the parties ought not to be necessary.'[33]

Siekmann examines the practice in terms of consultation with the host state in a whole series of operations, such as UNDOF, UNIFIL, and UNTAG and also where there is little consultation with the host state. In the end, he concludes that even in practice, host state consent is not required with respect to the composition of the force, although the host state is in 'a position of strength' as long as the forces have not deployed.[34] Furthermore, another scholar asserts that the principle of UN control over the composition of the force extends even to the composition of other bodies that may be created and deployed or sent to a state. Manin cites the example of the Conciliation Commission for the Congo, which the President of Congo objected to on the grounds of its composition (which, from his perspective, included too many representatives of states having expressed public opinions about internal Congolese politics). The Bureau refused to cede, indicating that 'il était impossible de la modifier parce qu'elle relevait exclusivement de l'O.N.U.'[35] In the case of ONUC as well the principle of consent to the presence of a specific individual was raised, testing the composition of the peacekeeping mission to the level of the individual, that is, the Special Representative of the Secretary-General,

---

[30] UN Doc S/5004, 414 UNTS 229, cited in Siekmann, National Contingents, p. 72, who observes that this statement was not made in the UNEF I or UNFICYP SOFA.

[31] UN Secretary-General, 'First Report by the Secretary-General on the Implementation of Security Council Resolution S/4387 of 14 July 1960', UN Doc S/4389 (18 July 1960) at 4.

[32] Siekmann, National Contingents, p. 71.

[33] Ibid., p. 67. As authority, Siekmann points to 'the approval of paragraph 6 of the Second and Final Report in Resolution 1001'.

[34] Ibid., p. 80.

[35] Rapport A/4711 (20 May 1961), cited in Philippe Manin, L'Organisation des Nations Unies et le maintien de la paix: Le respect du consentement de l'état (Paris: Pichon & Durand-Auzias, 1971), p. 178, note 53; see also pp. 176–178. ('It was impossible to modify it because it was exclusively under the UN'; author's translation.)

whom President Kasavubu demanded to be 'recalled'. On that level, however, the Secretary-General relied on Articles 100 and 101 of the UN Charter, and not on the general principle of composition of the force, to refuse the President's demand.[36] A similar situation occurred in Sudan in 2006, when the Sudanese government demanded that Special Representative Jan Pronk be removed from his post. He finished his term but was not reappointed.[37]

On the other hand, Manin argued already in 1971 that the principle has been softened, pointing to examples where the host state's predilections are clearly reflected in the composition of the observer mission or force.[38] Even so, Manin argues that the weakening of the principle goes only so far as to admit an obligation of consultation and, furthermore, that the UN General Assembly or Security Council must settle any conflict in this regard.[39] There is, arguably, no right of veto on the part of a host state.[40] Yet as recently as 2007, deployment of troops to UNAMID was held up due to the Sudanese government's 'reservations about certain non-African units in the force, including the infantry battalion from Thailand, the force reserve/special forces and sector reserve companies from Nepal and the Nordic engineering company'.[41] In that operation, the principle that the members of the force 'should have a predominantly African character and the troops should, as far as possible, be sourced from African countries' was a condition for the consent of the Sudanese government to the operation and figured in the preamble of the Security Council resolution establishing the operation.[42]

An important aspect of the sole competence of the UN in this regard is that the Secretary-General may also refuse to include a contingent from a state even if the host state requests the inclusion of such a contingent in the force.[43] Indeed, states that are 'friendly' to the host state could act in its favour; in this regard, the unilateral right of the

---

[36] See the exchange of letters between President Kasavubu and UN Secretary-General Hammarskjold, UN Doc S/4629 (16 January 1961).

[37] See 'Annan Confirms Pronk Will Serve Out His Term as Top Envoy for Sudan', UN News Centre (27 October 2006), www.un.org/apps/news/story.asp?NewsID=20396&Cr=sudan&Cr1= (accessed 13 August 2013).

[38] Manin, *L'ONU et le maintien de la paix*, pp. 180ff.   [39] Ibid., p. 181.   [40] Ibid., p. 182.

[41] 'Report of the Secretary-General on the Deployment of the African Union–United Nations Hybrid Operation in Darfur', UN Doc S/2007/759 (24 December 2007) para. 18. See also Gray, *Use of Force*, p. 301.

[42] UNSC Res 1769 (2007), preambular paragraph 7. See also Gray, *Use of Force*.

[43] Manin, *L'ONU et le maintien de la paix*, p. 182.

Secretary-General to determine the composition of the force buttresses its impartiality.[44]

As a practical matter, consultation with the host state (and with other interested states) tends to limit the possible pool of troop contributors and slows down the deployment of the mission.[45] At a minimum, this provides a disincentive for the UN Secretary-General to consider that he is legally constrained by consent with respect to the composition of the force. On the other hand, goodwill and full consent may be seen as so vital to the success of the operation in some circumstances that the Secretary-General would be loath to proceed with a force containing contingents to which the host state vehemently objects. In fact, even in UNEF I, Nasser did not allow the troops into Egypt until the compromise on the composition of the force had been reached, leading one writer to take the position that the host state (or at least Egypt in the case of UNEF I) has a de facto veto power over the composition of the force.[46] Siekmann argues, 'It seems that in practice the consultation provision in the enabling resolution resulted in a "right of veto", at least for the host state, vis-à-vis certain countries.'[47]

4.2.2   Transparency and Consent

One may query whether the Secretary-General is required to inform the host state that a part of the peacekeeping force or CIVPOL will be composed of PMSCs. If Manin is correct that there is an obligation of consultation, such transparency would be necessary to make it meaningful.[48] Would a state have to indicate openly that it will supply its contribution via a PMSC? And does the Secretary-General have to inform the host state? In this regard, it is appropriate to recall that all US CIVPOL personnel are recruited, hired, trained and deployed by PMSCs. PMSCs have deployed CIVPOL on behalf of the United States to Haiti, East Timor, Kosovo and Liberia. The UN DPKO indicated in its *Year in Review 2010* report that, contrary to other CIVPOL, who are seconded or loaned by their national governments and who are paid by their national police service (with an additional subsistence allowance paid by the UN), '[w]ithout a national police force, the US government outsources the internal recruitment and

---

[44] Ibid.   [45] Siekmann, *National Contingents*, notes this effect for UNFICYP.
[46] Ibid., p. 69.   [47] Ibid., p. 74.
[48] Laurence Boisson de Chazournes, 'Changing Roles of International Organizations: Global Administrative Law and the Interplay of Legitimacies – Concluding Remarks' (2009) 6 *Intl Org L Rev* 655 at 659–660.

nomination process to private contractors.'[49] However, as discussions with troop- and police-contributing states in the Security Council are held in camera, it is difficult to know through public sources whether this element is openly raised in that forum or with the host state.[50] Furthermore, although the UN has recently reported on its use of PMSCs in peace operations, the degree of transparency in that reporting remains limited. A report by the UN Secretary-General on the use of PMSCs did not indicate which companies are being used nor indeed how many there are.[51] Furthermore, there is confusion in the limited reports that do exist. While a UN General Assembly report indicates that the UN uses armed private security companies in fifteen countries, the UN Department of Safety and Security asserts that they are used in only three.[52]

One of the recent UN policy papers on staffing missions does not mention a requirement to consult the host state, nor a general principle

---

[49] UN DPKO, *United Nations Peace Operations: Year in Review 2010* (2010), p. 21.

[50] It has not always been the case that such discussions were held in camera. Initially, it was not the practice to recruit troop contingents 'in confidence' and make the names of contributing states public only once decisions were finalized. The earlier, more 'open' practice entailed considerable diplomacy, however, especially when it came to rejecting offers of contributions. Siekmann, *National Contingents*, pp. 55 and 21–23. He observes that 'rejection of an offer, even on valid technical or political grounds, would have been embarrassing for the Secretariat.' For UNEF I, offers from states were published. Indeed, the staffing of some operations seems to occur through a kind of horse-trading (ibid., p. 67). Siekmann notes that for UNEF I, Hammarskjøld specifically asked Egypt to make known any of its objections to any of the countries that were going to be participating (which Hammarskjøld had already selected based on what he thought would be non-objectionable choices). Egypt objected to Canada's participation for a number of reasons (formally it stated that it was because of similarities with the United Kingdom and the possibility that the local population would confuse Canadians with Brits and be hostile to them, but likely because Canada had not sufficiently objected to the UK use of force against Egypt prior to the operation). It also objected to NATO countries, New Zealand and Pakistan. In the end, a compromise was reached: 'Egypt gave up the idea of Czech participation, achieved the exclusion of New Zealand, and Pakistan, but had to accept Brazil. Canada was to participate only with logistic units' (footnote omitted) (pp. 65–66). The Secretary-General 'strongly resisted the exclusion of Denmark and Norway, both NATO members, since their non-participation would probably have meant that Sweden and Finland would not supply troops, and without Scandinavian participation it was most probable that no peace-keeping force whatsoever could be dispatched' (p. 66). See also Manin, *L'ONU et le maintien de la paix*, p. 180.

[51] This criticism was made by the UN Working Group on Mercenaries, 'Report of the Working Group on the Use of Mercenaries as a Means of Violating Human Rights and Impeding the Exercise of the Right of Peoples to Self-Determination', UN Doc A/69/338 (21 August 2014), para. 13.

[52] Lou Pingeot, 'The United Nations Guidelines on the Use of Armed Private Security: Towards a Normalisation of UN Use of Security Contractors?' (2014) 16 *ICLR* 461–474 at 462, note 1.

of transparency. The 2009 New Horizons non-paper states only that the Security Council 'must consult meaningfully with troop and police contributing countries in the planning and conduct of individual peacekeeping operations'.[53] Meanwhile, diplomatic efforts are recommended to engage with troop-contributing countries and host states to 'facilitate and sustain the consent of the parties to the conflict, including in addressing the imposition of conditions and restrictions on UN peacekeepers'.[54] This recommendation seems to be aimed towards reducing restrictions on freedom of movement, but it may be broader. Indeed, the only consultation the New Horizons non-paper appears to deem urgent and essential is that between the UN and troop- and police-contributing states, to the complete exclusion of any mention of consultation with the host state in terms of planning a mission.[55] The 2015 High-Level Panel Report takes a similar approach, emphasizing a need to be transparent with troop-contributing countries as to what will be expected of them, apparently without perceiving any need to consult the host state.[56]

On the other hand, states contributing troops and other forces to peace operations may have strong opinions as to the requirement of the host state's consent to the deployment of their armed forces on its territory. Indeed, there may be a sense on behalf of troop-contributing countries that host-state consent extends to the determination of the composition of the force. Siekmann observes that 'Denmark, as a troop-contributing country, had in any case itself laid down the condition of host state consent for its participation'.[57] It is difficult to evaluate how widespread this practice is; however, one may point to the fact that many states are willing to deploy their forces in the absence of a Status of Forces Agreement as evidence that there must be at least some ambivalence.[58]

---

[53] UN DPKO–DFS, 'A New Partnership Agenda: Charting a New Horizon for UN Peacekeeping' (non-paper) (July 2009), 12–13.

[54] Ibid., 12.

[55] Ibid., 12–14. See also Mirko Sossai, 'The Privatisation of "the Core Business of UN Peacekeeping Operations": Any Legal Limit?' (2014) 16 *ICLR* 405–422 at 414–416.

[56] 'Report of the High-Level Independent Panel on Peace Operations on Uniting Our Strengths for Peace: Politics, Partnership and People' (17 June 2015), UN Doc A/70/95; S/2015/446, paras 188–193. The UN Secretary-General's report on implementation likewise makes no mention of consultation with the host state, although it emphasizes the importance of consent and winning the acceptance of the local population: UN Secretary-General, 'The Future of United Nations Peace Operations' (2 September 2015), UN Doc A/70/357-S/2015/682, paras 61–63, 64.

[57] Siekmann, *National Contingents*, p. 74.

[58] That being said, in a discussion of the creation of one of the first stand-by forces, which was composed of Scandinavian forces, Siekmann points out that the Danish Minister of Foreign Affairs published an article setting out the conditions precedent for the deployment of

From the point of view of states contemplating stationing their forces on foreign soil without the express consent of the host state, or even against its will as to their participation (but not the operation as a whole), they may be concerned that their presence could amount to belligerent occupation in the sense of Article 2(2) common to the four Geneva Conventions of 1949.[59] This would mean that consent to a particular nation's participation could be important in terms of the bilateral relationship between the host state and the troop-contributing state but not necessary in terms of the lawfulness of the operation as a whole. If this were correct, however, the absence of consent would change the applicable legal framework for some participating states but not for others within the same mission and mandate, which, although entirely possible, could be cumbersome.

The UN's position clearly reflects its understanding that a host state's lack of consent with respect to a troop contingent from a particular state does not mean that that troop-contributing country is an occupying power in the host state. The concern of some states regarding consent for their presence could be taken as reflecting an abundance of caution, perhaps equally as a means of lessening the probability that their forces will be the object of attack.[60] In any case, the fact that a lack of specific consent could lead to the applicability of the law of belligerent occupation is arguably immaterial to whether such a lack of consent poses a legal impediment to the inclusion of a PMSC contingent in the peacekeeping force. From a *ius ad bellum* perspective, for the UN the issue is: if a PMSC is sent as a state's contribution to a peacekeeping force and the host state does not consent to the presence of the PMSC contingent, does the special regime of peacekeeping and the Secretary-General's inclusion of the PMSC within the force take that act outside the scope of what could normally constitute an act of aggression?[61] There are solid reasons to conclude that it has precisely that effect: peace operations are established by the Security Council in an attempt to fulfil one of the main purposes of the UN: the furtherance

---

the Scandinavian forces. Those conditions included the caveat that '[t]he country in which the forces were to be used must have accepted the UN operation and the Scandinavian participation in it, that is to say that host state consent was necessary for the UN peacekeeping force, and even for the national contingents.' Siekmann, *National Contingents*, pp. 50–51.

[59] According to common Article 2(2), 'The Convention shall also apply to all cases of partial or total occupation of the territory of a High Contracting Party, even if the said occupation meets with no armed resistance.'

[60] In peacekeeping operations deployed in the context of an international armed conflict, this may also stem from a concern to respect obligations under the law of neutrality.

[61] See in particular UNGA Resolution 3314 of 1974, the Definition of Aggression, Annex, Article 3(g).

of international peace and security. The fact that one could nevertheless conclude that the *ius in bello* nevertheless could apply does not influence the *ius ad bellum* analysis.

The position of the UN as outlined above is that the Secretary-General's discretion to determine the composition of the force is not limited in a *legal* sense by the consent of the host state. However, there will be an effort to accommodate the host government's views. Lack of consent on the composition of the force may significantly impede a mission; indeed, the practical utility of consent makes it almost an incontrovertible requirement.[62] For both practical and diplomatic reasons it is probable that a host state that strongly objects to a PMSC as the peace force would hold considerable sway. As well, one can imagine that the UN would not want to be accused of sending in 'mercenaries' and would avoid using them without host-state consent for fear of losing credibility on the international stage.[63] One may even be tempted to surmise that PMSCs would be so qualitatively different from any previous contingents involved in a peace operation that the legal requirement of consent would not allow the Secretary-General to use them without specific consent. However, it is possible to overstate this case, especially considering that the objections of a host state to the presence of another state's forces on its territory due to its serious reservations with regard to that state are no small matter, yet the Secretary-General clearly reserves the legal right to contravene those wishes.

Arguably, the Secretary-General's recent practice in relation to the creation of the static UN guard forces in Somalia, Central African Republic and Libya indicates that the consent of the General Assembly to the use of PMSCs as a guard force via its internal laws will play a role in the decision. While the Secretary-General was transparent about his willingness to consider deploying a PMSC guard force, it is worth noting that he adverted only to the limits set by the General Assembly and did not refer in any way to the consent of the host state – either for the guard force itself or for a PMSC – in such a role.[64]

---

[62] See, for example, the discussion of consent in the Capstone Doctrine, pp. 31–34.

[63] S. Percy, 'The Security Council and the Use of Private Force', in V. Lowe et al. (eds.), *The United Nations Security Council and War* (Oxford: Oxford University Press, 2008), pp. 624–640 at pp. 638–640.

[64] See UN Secretary-General, 'Letter Dated 21 November 2013 from the Secretary-General Addressed to the President of the Security Council', 27 November 2013, UN Doc S/2013/704 (for UNSMIL). See also similar letter dated 29 October 2013 (BINUCA) UN Doc S/2013/636; UN Secretary-General, 'Letter Dated 14 October 2013 from the Secretary-General Addressed to the President of the Security Council', 14 October 2013, UN Doc 2013/606.

When it comes to the use of PMSCs as security guards in existing peace operations, the new UN Guidelines require the UN to *consider* host-country acceptance of PMSCs, but they do not require the UN to obtain the approval or consent of the host state.[65]

4.3 Impartiality

Impartiality is a cornerstone of peace operations[66] – in fact, two authorities identify it as the single most important factor distinguishing robust peace operations from enforcement action.[67] What is impartiality? In his proposal for the first UN peace operation (UNEF), without actually using the word 'impartiality', Secretary-General Hammarskjøld described the essence of the concept thus: 'there is no intent in the establishment of the Force to influence the military balance in the present conflict and, thereby, the political balance affecting efforts to settle the conflict.'[68]

The notion of impartiality seems intuitively linked with the concept of *animus belligerendi*, which Hans Kelsen defined as the 'intention to wage war'.[69] In the early part of the twentieth century, the will of the state was arguably relevant to determining the existence of a war to which international humanitarian law applies.[70] Although today it is widely accepted that the views of states as to whether they believe they are involved in an armed conflict are not relevant to the applicability of IHL if there is in fact an armed conflict,[71] this notion of intending to wage war seems to have pervaded UN thinking and played a role in its long-held (but now fading)

---

[65] UNSMS Security Operations Manual, para. 19.   [66] Capstone Doctrine, p. 33.

[67] Marten Zwanenburg, *Accountability of Peace Support Operations* (Martinus Nijhoff, 2005), pp. 32–33; Mats Berdal, 'Lessons Not Learned: The Use of Force in "Peace Operations" in the 1990s' (2000) 7 *International Peacekeeping* 55–74.

[68] 'Second and Final Report of the Secretary-General on the Plan for an Emergency International United Nations Force Requested in the Resolution Adopted by the General Assembly on 4 November 1956 (A/3276)', UN Doc A/3302 (6 November 1956) para. 8.

[69] Hans Kelsen, *Principles of International Law* (1952), p. 27.

[70] For the debate on the role of *animus belligerendi* already in the 1930s, see J.L. Brierly, 'International Law and Resort to Armed Force' (1932) 4 *Cambridge LJ* 308 at 313; and on the existence of the legal state of war, Elihu Lauterpacht, 'The Legal Irrelevance of the "State of War"' (1968) 62 *Am Soc Intl L Proceedings* 58–68; Richard Baxter, 'The Legal Consequences of the Unlawful Use of Force Under the Charter' (1968) 62 *Am Soc Intl L Proceedings* 68–75, and subsequent discussion, 75–83. See also McDougal and Feliciano, 'The Initiation of Coercion' (1958) 52 *AJIL* 241–259; Christopher Greenwood, 'The Concept of War in Modern International Law' (1987) 36 *ICLQ* 283; Edwin Borchard, '"War" and "Peace"' (Editorial Comment) (1933) 27 *AJIL* 114–117.

[71] Dinstein, *War, Aggression and Self-Defence*, 5th edn (Cambridge: Cambridge University Press, 2011), paras 19 and 22. See also ICRC, *Commentary on the First Geneva Convention,*

position that UN forces are not parties to armed conflicts. In his summary study on UNEF, Secretary-General Hammarskjøld insisted, 'As a matter of course, the United Nations personnel cannot be permitted in any sense to be a party to internal conflicts.'[72] As the determination of whether an armed conflict exists is based on the facts and not on a subjective belligerent intent, however, impartiality cannot be cited as preventing UN peace operations forces from being parties to an armed conflict.

In any case, respect for the principle of impartiality is tricky and requires a sophisticated understanding of the parties and circumstances. Impartiality must not be confused with neutrality, if neutrality is understood to mean passivity.[73] As the Capstone Doctrine states, 'a peacekeeping operation should not condone actions by the parties that violate the undertakings of the peace process or the international norms and principles that a United Nations peacekeeping operation upholds.'[74] Furthermore, while impartiality is often discussed in relation to a use of force in a peace operation, it can in fact apply to a wider scope of actions. Some peacekeepers indicate that, for them, impartiality means that their responsibility is to 'de-escalate' the conflict; another, in a context where peacekeepers support the national armed forces of the host state (thereby already not an impartial force), insisted that impartiality is about honest reporting of crimes committed by such forces.[75] Others indicate that impartiality means protecting civilians from aggression, while yet other peacekeepers and UN doctrine espouse the view that it can mean defending even *armed forces* that have been attacked by those who violate a peace agreement or other accord.[76]

2016, paras 210–216, and J. Pictet (ed.), *The Geneva Conventions of 12 August 1949: Commentary, First Geneva Convention for the Amelioration of the Condition of the Wounded and Sick in Armed Forces in the Field* (ICRC: Geneva, 1952), p. 32 (commentary on Article 2 common to the four Geneva Conventions).

[72] UNSG, 'Summary Study', para. 166.

[73] Dominick Donald points out that UN Secretaries-General, other UN officials and UN reports on peacekeeping have used the terms 'neutrality' and 'impartiality' in confusing and inconsistent ways. See Dominick Donald, 'Neutrality, Impartiality and UN Peacekeeping at the Beginning of the 21st Century' (2002) 9 *International Peacekeeping* 21–38. See also 'Report of the High-Level Independent Panel on Peace Operations on Uniting Our Strengths for Peace: Politics, Partnership and People' (17 June 2015), UN Doc A/70/95; S/2015/446, para. 126.

[74] Capstone Doctrine, p. 33.

[75] These examples are described in Daniel H. Levine, 'Peacekeeper Impartiality: Standards, Processes, and Operations' (2011) 15 *Journal of International Peacekeeping* 422–450 at 429.

[76] Ibid., 428. Levine points out that the Brahimi Report also espoused the aggressor/victim distinction (432).

In simple terms, impartiality would appear to mean that an operation does not take sides.[77] A peacekeeping force with a robust mandate may use military force against an organized armed group in order to enforce its mandate – even if that use of force may lead it to become a party to a conflict. What may arguably allow such uses of force to continue to garner approval as 'impartial' is that they are taken in an effort not to actually defeat a party to a conflict, but rather to enforce a mandate, such as protecting civilians.[78]

In terms of the implications of impartiality for the composition of the force, in its original incarnation, the impartiality principle led to the convention that none of the permanent five members of the Security Council, nor any states neighbouring the host state, was admissible as a member of the peace force. This can be seen as a manifestation of an effort to ensure impartiality in reality and as perceived. The sheer need for troops has meant that those restrictions have been set aside at times when deemed appropriate by the UN Secretary-General, but the requirement of impartiality persists.[79]

Given the relaxation of the application of this principle in regard to the composition of the force, one may enquire whether the principle of impartiality may still affect the substantive establishment of the mission, or whether it is merely a principle governing conduct once the mission exists. I submit that the principle of impartiality nevertheless continues to affect the substantive composition of the force in that, at the very least,

---

[77] This may be a particular problem for non-UN peacekeeping forces. In 2005, for example, Georgian authorities complained that the Commonwealth of Independent States (CIS) peacekeeping force in Abkhazia (which was set up by an agreement between Georgian and Abkhaz authorities and was not a UN-mandated force) was 'rather far from being impartial and [was] often backing Abkhaz separatist paramilitary structures'. See 'Letter Dated 26 January 2005 from the Permanent Representative of Georgia to the United Nations Addressed to the President of the Security Council', UN Doc S/2005/45 (26 January 2005), p. 3.

[78] The operation in Libya by NATO authorized by UN Security Council Resolution 1973 (2011), ostensibly for the protection of civilians and not with the primary goal of ousting Colonel Gaddafi from power, had the potential to skew understandings of impartiality in peace operations. Based on the experience of 'peace enforcement' operations in the 1990s, Berdal, 'Lessons Not Learned', 62, has expressed serious doubts as to whether such a degree of force can be used against a party 'impartially' due to the politicization of the Security Council already in the creation and adoption of mandates.

[79] See UNSG, 'Summary Study', para. 160. This was seen as a manner of ensuring as far as possible that the host states would not object to the composition of the force. McCoubrey and White, The Blue Helmets, pp. 81–82, point to the use of Russian forces in UNPROFOR, in addition to UK troops in Cyprus, as evidence of the relation of the principle of 'non alignment' in the composition of the force as an element of impartiality.

peace forces, including troops and CIVPOL – and arguably also security guards in volatile environments – must be 'outsiders', that is, they must not be nationals of the host state or concerned states. This is an important limitation when it comes to PMSCs: a major way that companies reduce costs is by hiring locals, especially for security duties. In addition, local capacity building is touted as an important goal in peace operations, such that a company may attempt to justify such practices even in the context of a peace operation by paying lip-service to notions of capacity building. But impartiality demands that peacekeeping forces not be locals. If a PMSC force were to adopt that practice in a peace operation, it would contravene the requirement implicit in the principle of impartiality that the troops and police be 'international' – that is, they must be outsiders.[80] The principle in the General Assembly Resolution on outsourcing that any contracting must not compromise the international nature of the organization further buttresses this requirement.[81]

Any contract with a PMSC to provide a force – either troops or CIVPOL – would have to contain a clause prohibiting the PMSC from hiring local nationals to act in either of those roles if the principle of impartiality is to be respected.[82] In my view, this requirement extends also to the provision of security guards, based on the results of the discussion above on the use of force in peacekeeping. The UN Working Group on Mercenaries argues that 'the Organization needs to be mindful of cultural diversity and local political perceptions when hiring private security guards in order to ensure that it is always perceived as an independent and impartial entity.'[83] Furthermore, it has observed that lapses in vetting the security guards that it contracts, in addition to 'subcontracting schemes', raise particular concerns about contracting PMSCs who will be – and be seen to be – independent and impartial.[84] In Afghanistan, the UN has

---

[80] The question whether the obligation that a peace operation must be 'international' also entails that the peacekeeping force must be composed of contingents from state armed forces is a separate issue.

[81] UNGA Res 55/232 'Outsourcing Practices' (23 December 2000) UN Doc A/Res/55/232, para. 4(c).

[82] See, contra, Kovač, 'Legal Issues', 330, who argues, 'If local recruitment [by PMSCs] occurred only exceptionally, one might easily argue that it would not threaten the impartiality of the force.' He does argue, however, that general mass hiring of locals by the UN would impinge on impartiality.

[83] 'Report of the Working Group on the Use of Mercenaries as a Means of Violating Human Rights and Impeding the Exercise of the Right of Peoples to Self-Determination', UN Doc A/69/338 (21 August 2014), para. 21.

[84] Ibid., para. 23.

hired Gurkha security guards – that is, a Nepalese company – to protect UNAMA and other UN agencies, rather than relying on local Afghan private security companies. It does not appear, however, that this has always been the case.

There is, however, no inherent reason why a PMSC forming all or part of a peace operation (except the leadership of a UN operation) could not conduct operations impartially. Some might even argue that PMSCs are likely to be politically disinterested in the outcome of a conflict and that their use therefore ensures that the principle of impartiality is respected. Such a position is likely naïve, however, given that PMSCs' major clients also include the extraction industry, which often has an interest in conflicts. PMSCs may also be vertically integrated into businesses involved in the exploitation of natural resources with particular agendas regarding resource-rich territory.[85]

It should also be recalled that political disinterest in the outcome of a particular conflict does not imply that a firm is apolitical[86] or inherently impartial. PMSCs hailing from a particular region or boasting a predominant number of nationals from a particular state may pose similar problems as interested states to impartiality. States have been known to interfere with UN Command by issuing instructions to their own forces.[87] While PMSCs are not state actors and have the advantage of not being integrated into a national structure and therefore would not necessarily be under a competing legal obligation to obey such orders,[88] the problem highlights a need for a high degree of transparency, in and of itself one of the most problematic aspects of PMSCs. Moreover, in a number of states, PMSCs are owned or controlled by government ministers.[89] While one

---

[85] Peter Singer, *Corporate Warriors* (Ithaca: Cornell University Press, 2003), pp. 104–105; D Avant, *The Market for Force* (Cambridge: Cambridge University Press, 2001), pp. 180–192.

[86] The Chief Executive Officer of a major US PMSC (who has proposed the use of his firm in UN peace operations) even 'issued a corporate newsletter celebrating' the 2004 reelection of former President Bush and, furthermore, demands that his employees swear an oath to the US Constitution. See P. Singer, 'Humanitarian Principles, Private Military Agents: Implications of the Privatized Military Industry for the Humanitarian Community' (2006) 13 *Brown J World Affairs* 105–121 at 113.

[87] See Zwanenburg, *Accountability*, pp. 40–41.

[88] A conclusive answer may depend on articles of incorporation. Furthermore, Kathryn Bolkovac has suggested that employees may be torn between loyalty to the UN and loyalty to the company that hires them. See Kathryn Bolkovac, *The Whistleblower* (Palgrave Macmillan, 2011), passim.

[89] M. de Goede, 'Private and Public Security in Post-war Democratic Republic of Congo', in S. Gumedze (ed.), *The Private Security Sector in Africa*, Monograph 146 (Institute for Security Studies, 2008), pp. 35–68 at p. 45.

would presume that if the UN were contemplating contracting PMSCs as peacekeepers in some way it would attempt to screen out such companies, there may be no fail-safe solution.

In any case, political disinterest is not the lone factor in ensuring impartiality. Implementing a peacekeeping mandate with impartiality entails an element of diplomacy and requires subtle communication skills.[90] Problems with the impartiality of a PMSC may be more a matter of perception; nonetheless, the fact that they are corporate structures as opposed to nation-states should not give rise to a presumption that they will be any more or less impartial than state forces.

4.4   Limited Use of Force

The use of force in self-defence in peacekeeping is complicated first and foremost because self-defence in the context of peace operations has its own meaning, which cannot be assimilated to any other meaning of self-defence, either personal (individual) self-defence or state self-defence. Paul Tavernier argues that the lack of clarity with respect to the meaning of self-defence stems 'not only from the fact that it has been extended beyond its normal meaning, nor that there are uncertainties regarding the limits on it, but is also due to the essentially multiform character of the concept.'[91]

Indeed, the main issue with regard to the principle of limited use of force by peacekeepers and how it may imply limitations for the use of PMSCs as peacekeepers is counterintuitive. The problem is not whether PMSCs are capable of respecting the limits on the use of force (although that may also be a valid concern); rather, it is that the use of force that is actually permitted may go well beyond that which PMSCs should be authorized to use. In order to fully grasp the implications of this principle for the use of PMSCs, a thorough understanding of the contours of the limits on the use of force in peacekeeping is indispensable and is provided below.[92]

In short, there are three distinct ways in which peace operations forces may end up using force in self-defence. First, peacekeeping forces may use

---

[90] Capstone Doctrine, p. 33.
[91] Paul Tavernier, 'La légitime défense du personnel de l'ONU', in Rahim Kherad (ed.), *Légitimes défenses* (Poitiers: LGDJ, 2007), pp. 121–138 at pp. 131–132. (Author's translation of: 'la difficulté d'une définition précise de la légitime défense des personnels des Nations Unies ne trouve pas son origine uniquement dans l'extension de la notion ou dans les incertitudes concernant ses limites, mais aussi dans le caractère essentiellement multiforme de la notion.')
[92] See Chapter 10.

force in self-defence in direct protection of themselves if they are attacked. When such peacekeepers have not already otherwise become parties to a conflict, that kind of a use of force does not entail their becoming engaged in conflict. However, in order for it to remain self-defence in the sense that will not amount to direct participation in hostilities, such uses of force must be limited to what is necessary to protect themselves from the attack.[93] It may not include, for example, an operation against a group responsible for such attacks in order to stop future attacks or even to secure the release of peacekeepers captured in a previous attack without amounting to a participation in hostilities.[94]

Indeed, in the Safety Convention and the Rome Statute, it is an international crime to attack peacekeepers who are not combatants.[95] If the use of force by peacekeepers against an armed group in direct response to such an attack would render them direct participants in hostilities and entail their loss of protection from attack, it could lead to absurd results. For example, imagine a situation where an armed group attacks a group of peacekeepers, failing to kill any but leading the peacekeepers to respond with force. If that response in itself were sufficient for the peacekeepers to become direct participants in an armed conflict against the armed group, it would mean that it would not be a crime to kill peacekeepers once they have begun to respond to an attack to defend themselves. Such an interpretation would seem to rob the prohibition on attacking peacekeepers of any significance, as it would be sufficient for an armed group to fire on

---

[93] This aspect of the distinction between different uses of force is not always clearly indicated in the literature. See, for example, Hans Boddens Hosang, 'Force Protection, Unit Self-Defence, and Extended Self-Defence', in T. Gill and D. Fleck (eds.), *The Handbook of the International Law of Military Operations* (Oxford University Press, 2010), pp. 415–427 at para. 22.04. See, however, Patrick Cammaert and Ben Klappe, 'Application of Force and Rules of Engagement in Peace Operations', in ibid., pp. 151–158 at pp. 154 and 156, who specify that '[d]uring peace operations, use of force beyond personal self-defence may only be used in the circumstances as specified in the ROE', and who describe this as apparently denoting a 'severe limitation on the use of force'. They note, however, that other instructions attenuate the severity of that restriction. See also 'Report of the High-Level Independent Panel on Peace Operations on Uniting Our Strengths for Peace: Politics, Partnership and People' (17 June 2015), UN Doc A/70/95; S/2015/446, para. 128.

[94] See Daphna Shraga, 'The Secretary-General's Bulletin on the Observance by United Nations Forces of International Humanitarian Law: A Decade Later' (2009) 39 *Israel Yearbook on Human Rights* 357–377, at 360–362, for an example of operation in UNPROFOR to rescue captured French troops.

[95] Article 9, Convention on the Safety of United Nations and Associated Personnel, New York, 9 December 1994, in force 15 January 1999, 2051 UNTS 363; Articles 8(2)(b)(iii) and 8(2)(e)(iii), Rome Statute of the International Criminal Court, Rome, 17 July 1998, in force 1 July 2002, 2187 UNTS 3.

peacekeepers in order to draw a response before mounting a larger attack in order for it to be lawful to kill them. This obviously cannot be the case.

In this respect, in addition to what has been argued above, it may be useful to make an analogy with the type of force that can be used by medical and religious personnel in response to attacks made against them.[96] Although they are members of the armed forces, they do not have combatant status and therefore may not be attacked, nor may they attack others.[97] However, if they are attacked or if wounded or sick combatants under their care are attacked, their use of armed force in self-defence does not entail a loss of protected status.[98] The Geneva Conventions and Additional Protocol I anticipate that they may be lightly armed for such purposes.[99] Thus, even if they, as members of the armed forces, fire on enemy combatants of opposing armed forces, if such force has been used only in personal self-defence, it does not make them lose their protected status.

Interpreting peacekeeping in light of that regime, peacekeepers who use force in a first, immediate response to an unlawful attack on themselves do not, by virtue of that use of force, directly participate in hostilities. Using force to protect civilians against a direct attack (assuming those civilians are not already directly participating in hostilities) would also not go beyond such a use of force in self-defence. This means that if PMSCs were to be involved as members of a peacekeeping contingent in such situations, their lack of combatant status would not pose a problem. However, as will be shown below, the broader mandate to protect civilians may involve supporting one party to a conflict against an organized armed group or participating in hostilities against a group that is attacking civilians.[100] It should be recalled, furthermore, that repeated attacks

---

[96] Article 22 of the Convention for the Amelioration of the Condition of the Wounded and Sick in Armed Force in the Field, Geneva, 12 August 1949, in force 21 October 1950 (GC I).

[97] Article 43 of the Protocol Additional to the Geneva Conventions of 12 August 1949, and Relating to the Protection of Victims of International Armed Conflicts (Protocol I) of 8 June 1977, Geneva, in force 7 December 1978, confirms this interpretation (hereafter AP I).

[98] They may not, however, use armed force to prevent a hospital or medical unit from falling under the control of the adversary.

[99] Article 13(2) AP I, Article 22 GC I. Although AP II does not specifically state that medical units may be armed, it does specify that they retain their protection from attack unless they are used to commit hostile acts, outside their humanitarian function (Article 11 AP II). The use of limited force in self-defence is not considered to amount to a hostile act. Protocol Additional to the Geneva Conventions of 12 August 1949, and Relating to the Protection of Victims of Non-International Armed Conflicts (Protocol II) of 8 June 1977, Geneva, in force 7 December 1978.

[100] MONUSCO is the primary example of this.

on peacekeepers leading to repeated uses of force in self-defence can, if sustained, lead a peacekeeping force to become a party to a conflict.[101]

4.4.1 Peacekeepers and Combatant Status

There is a very real concern regarding the capacity of PMSCs to be engaged as peacekeepers given the possibility – even in traditional UN peacekeeping operations – that they will be required to directly participate in hostilities in that capacity. Under international humanitarian law, it makes no difference whether one uses force defensively or offensively: the use of armed force to repel an attack may nevertheless constitute a direct participation in hostilities. Thus, even the minimum force in self-defence permitted, in the most circumscribed conditions, may lead peacekeepers to become direct participants in an armed conflict.[102] In a robust operation such as UN-commanded and -controlled MONUSCO, for example, forces are frequently engaged as combatants. They take on roles providing support to FARDC armed forces in operations against armed groups and may also engage in combat.[103] The reality is that all forces may be

---

[101] Robert Kolb, 'Applicability of International Humanitarian Law to Forces Under the Command of an International Organization', in *Report on the Expert Meeting on Multinational Peace Operations* (Geneva: ICRC, 2004), pp. 61–69: where the attacks by the armed group on the peacekeeping force are of a purely criminal nature or for criminal purposes, however, even repeated attacks may not warrant coming to a conclusion that an armed conflict is occurring between the peacekeepers and the armed group. For example, in Sudan, the JEM attacked an AMIS peacekeeping compound, allegedly for the purpose of looting equipment. See 'Report of the Secretary-General on the Deployment of the African Union–United Nations Hybrid Operation in Darfur', UN Doc S/2007/759 (24 December 2007), para. 45.

[102] The attempt to construe the interpretation of the use of force by ONUC in the early 1960s as respecting the principle of self-defence (i.e., as an exclusively reactive or defensive use of force) has been the subject of much academic writing. James Sloan argues that Hammarskjøld's insistence that ONUC's use of force was commensurate with self-defence was disingenuous; J. Sloan, 'The Use of Offensive Force in U.N. Peacekeeping: A Cycle of Boom and Bust?' (2007) 30 *Hastings Intl & Comp. L Rev* 385 at 402. Oscar Schachter, on the other hand, argues that there was a legal basis for the force used by ONUC; see O. Schachter, 'The Relation of Law, Politics and Action in the United Nations' (1963) 109 *RCADI* 165–256 at 225–228. He points out that ONUC 'did not assert an unlimited right to assume positions and then hold them by military means. Positions were assumed only if required to carry out the functions assigned to the force and in agreement, expressly or under general terms with the government' (227). The use of force in self-defence in order to ensure the freedom of movement of the operation has been a long-standing element of the degree and circumstances of the force to be used.

[103] See UN Doc S/2009/623 at paras 11–13 on the conditions under which MONUC forces will contribute to FARDC operations as well as UN Doc S/2011/20 and UN Doc S/2010/512 for reports describing their involvement in such operations.

called on, without their willing it or intending it, to engage in combat.[104] There would seem to be a definite need for peace force contingents to at least be capable of having combatant status. The question is, then, may the UN Secretary-General create a peacekeeping force made up of individuals who do not have combatant status? Would that violate the 'principles and spirit' of international humanitarian law?

That question is difficult to answer in itself, but it raises a host of other tricky questions. Peace operations may occur in the context of interstate conflicts; in such circumstances, the involvement of a peacekeeping force in the conflict could be an international armed conflict such that the question of combatant status arises.[105] Most peace operations, however, occur in situations of non-international armed conflict. This leads to the question whether, even in non-international armed conflicts, the ability for government or public forces to have combatant status is relevant.[106] While there is probably no obligation on states to use their own armed forces in non-international armed conflicts, they nevertheless remain bound to respect and ensure the respect of IHL. In some respects, combatant status can be a proxy for ensuring that forces distinguish between civilians and combatants and that they are structured in a way that is capable of respecting IHL and with clear disciplinary channels.

For Grotius, state monopoly of the use of force was an essential condition for limited warfare.[107] Although some political scientists point to increasingly privatized violence and the proliferation of the various state and non-state actors akin to that existing prior to the Peace of Westphalia as a form of 'neo-medievalism',[108] it is too categorical to suggest that the principle of limited war in and of itself today prohibits states from using PMSCs in roles in which they may need to use force. Many, including some PMSCs, argue that the conduct of offensive military operations should not

---

[104] In addition, once part of a peacekeeping force is engaged as combatants, arguably the entire force may be considered combatants. PMSCs in UNSOM may be in a similar position to those in MONUSCO. See UN Secretary-General, 'Letter Dated 14 October 2013 from the Secretary-General Addressed to the President of the Security Council' (14 October 2013), UN Doc 2013/606.

[105] This is the ICRC position on the issue; see Tristan Ferraro, 'An ICRC Perspective', in *International Peace Operations and International Humanitarian Law*, Contributions presented at the seminar organized by the International Institute of Humanitarian Law, Rome, 2008, 53–56 at 55.

[106] See also the discussion on implicit limitations in IHL in Lindsey Cameron and Vincent Chetail, *Privatizing War* (Cambridge University Press, 2013), pp. 10–133.

[107] S. Oeter, 'Methods and Means of Combat', in D. Fleck (ed.), *The Handbook of Humanitarian Law in Armed Conflicts* (Oxford: Oxford University Press, 1995), p. 105.

[108] See D. Bederman, 'World Law Transcendent' (2005) 54 *Emory Law Journal* 53 at 68, defining neo-medievalism.

be contracted to the private sector.[109] The difficulty is that even force used in defence may lead to PMSCs conducting hostilities. This raises the question whether IHL prohibits direct participation in hostilities. Nils Melzer points out that none of the statutes of the modern war crimes tribunals has included direct participation in hostilities as an offense in and of itself.[110] Julius Stone wrote that 'unprivileged belligerents, though not *condemned* by international law, are not protected by it, but are left to the discretion of the belligerent threatened by their activities.'[111] That being said, the US prosecuted Omar Khadr for 'Murder in violation of the law of war' on the ground that he allegedly 'did, in Afghanistan... while in the context of and associated with armed conflict and without enjoying combatant immunity, unlawfully and intentionally murder U.S. Army Sergeant First Class Christopher Speer, in violation of the law of war, by throwing a hand grenade at U.S. forces resulting in the death of Sergeant First Class Speer.'[112] Since there is nothing inherently unlawful in the throwing of a grenade at enemy armed forces in the conduct of hostilities according to the circumstances as described, it appears that the 'without enjoying combatant immunity' is what is problematic. While it is unquestionable that a person may be tried for such acts under normal criminal law, it is not at all clear that simply failing to have combatant immunity in carrying out an attack is itself contrary to the 'laws of war'.[113] While IHL does not expressly forbid the direct participation in hostilities by individual civilians, widespread use by states of civilians in roles likely to entail direct

[109] See also R. De Nevers, 'Private Security Companies and the Laws of War' (2009) 40 *Security Dialogue* 169–190, 178.
[110] Nils Melzer, *Targeted Killing in International Law* (Oxford: Oxford University Press, 2008), pp. 330–331, note 128.
[111] Julius Stone, *Legal Controls of International Conflict* (1954), p. 549.
[112] US Department of Defense, 'Memorandum for Detainee Omar Ahmed Khadr 0766, Guantanamo Bay, Cuba: Notification of the Swearing of Charges' (January 2007), para. 25, www.defense.gov/news/d2007Khadr%20-%20Notification%20of%20Sworn%20Charges.pdf.
[113] Michael Schmitt argues that as it is not contrary to the laws of armed conflict to kill a combatant who is not *hors de combat*, the status of the person doing the killing does not affect the lawfulness of the act under the law of armed conflict. It is thus not a war crime for a person without combatant status to kill a combatant. Such a person may, however, be tried under domestic law for murder. See Michael Schmitt, 'Affidavit' 1 November 2004, (in relation to the *Hicks* case), pp. 11–13, www.pegc.us/archive/Rasul_vs_Bush/hicks_mot_for_judgement_20041101_ex_B.pdf (accessed 9 April 2013). David Frakt, 'Direct Participation in Hostilities as a War Crime: America's Failed Effort to Change the Law of War' (2012) 46 *Valparaiso University Law Review* 729–764. See also Derek Jinks, 'The Declining Significance of POW Status' (2004) 45 *Harvard Intl L J* 367–442, 437–439.

participation in hostilities would seem to be at variance with their obligation to ensure the respect of IHL.

Does international law require states to use public armed forces in non-international armed conflicts?[114] And is that requirement transposed to their involvement in peace operations? A serious examination of this issue is essential in order to answer the main question posed here. Consequently, a small digression on the types of forces governments may or must use in non-international armed conflicts is warranted.

To the knowledge of the author, only one attempt has been made to address this question.[115] Sean Watts canvasses the black letter law applying in non-international armed conflicts and observes, 'States thus appear to be free from international regulation of the status or nature of government actors they employ against rebels in NIAC.'[116] He goes on, 'In fact, government forces' status in NIAC generally can be said to constitute one of the remaining voids of the international laws of war.'[117] Watts makes a forceful argument that states' resistance to codification of the law that applies to non-international armed conflicts may be interpreted to include also a refusal for the law to regulate which forces it may lawfully employ in a non-international armed conflict.[118]

---

[114] There is no combatant immunity or POW status in non-international armed conflicts. In this regard, it is important to recall that any immunity of government forces for lawful acts in armed conflicts flows in large part through domestic law empowering them to undertake such action.

[115] Other studies examine the status of organized armed groups in non-international armed conflicts, but few or none consider the government side. See generally, for example, Emily Crawford, *The Treatment of Combatants and Insurgents Under the Law of Armed Conflict* (Oxford: Oxford University Press, 2010); Lisbeth Zegveld, *The Accountability of Armed Opposition Groups* (Cambridge: Cambridge University Press, 2002); Lindsay Moir, *The Law of Internal Armed Conflict* (Cambridge: Cambridge University Press, 2002); Anthony Cullen, *The concept of Non-international Armed Conflict in International Humanitarian Law* (Cambridge: Cambridge University Press, 2010); and Sandesh Sivakumaran, *The Law of Non-international Armed Conflict* (Oxford: Oxford University Press, 2012).

[116] Sean Watts, 'Present and Future Conceptions of the Status of Government Forces in Non-international Armed Conflict', in K. Watkin and A. Norris (eds.), *Non-international Armed Conflict in the Twenty-first Century* (88 Naval War College International Law Studies Series 2012), pp. 145–180 at p. 149.

[117] Ibid.

[118] According to the ICRC's study on customary IHL, however, 'For the purposes of the principle of distinction ... members of State armed force may be considered combatants in both international and non-international armed conflicts.' This suggests that under IHL, it is lawful for members of organized armed groups to attack all combatant members of state armed forces in non-international armed conflicts. Jean-Marie Henckaerts and Louise Doswald-Beck, *Customary International Humanitarian Law*, 2 vols. (Cambridge: Cambridge University Press, 2005), vol. I, pp. 11 and 14, commentary to Rules 3 and 4.

Watts suggests that an obligation for states to use government/state armed forces in non-international armed conflicts can be derived from the principle of distinction.[119] He concludes, however, that such a principle is not ideal because it would lead to absurd results. In support of this, he seems to argue that state police forces would be easily distinguishable by the enemy but that it would contravene the purported obligation that a state use government armed forces if it were to use police forces.[120] Thus, he seems to say, the rationale for the obligation evaporates but the state is nevertheless (undesirably) constrained by the principle and the use of police forces would be unlawful. This indeed would be a strange result. The International Commission of Inquiry on Darfur (which Watts does not mention) specifically considered the legality of attacks on Sudanese police by rebel forces. It stated,

> Normally, in an international armed conflict the civil police force does not formally take part in the hostilities and can, at least theoretically, be considered as a non-combatant benefiting from the safeguards and protections against attack. However, in the particular case of the internal conflict in Darfur, the distinction between the police and the armed forces is often blurred. There are strong elements indicating occurrences of the police fighting alongside the Government forces during attacks ... Therefore, the Commission is of the opinion that the 'civilian' status of the police in the context of the conflict in Darfur is questionable.[121]

Importantly, the Commission made no remarks whatsoever as to the propriety (in legal terms) of the Sudanese government in using the police in this way.

Watts furthermore argues that given the type of operations against non-state armed groups, which can be anticipated to involve 'over-the-horizon' attacks (meaning those in which the attacked cannot see their attackers), the requirement that the attackers distinguish themselves in

---

[119] Watts, 'Status of Government Forces', 157–164.

[120] The fact that police forces are widely accepted as part of the armed forces that a state may use in a non-international armed conflict is affirmed by Article 1 AP II, which stipulates that the Protocol applies to conflicts between the armed forces of a state and an organized armed group. The phrase 'armed force' was chosen over 'regular armed forces' to take into account the fact that states may use police forces and national guard forces, inter alia, in non-international armed conflicts. See Y. Sandoz, C. Swinarski and B. Zimmermann (eds.), *Commentary on the Additional Protocols of 8 June 1977 to the Geneva Conventions of 12 August 1949* (Geneva: ICRC, 1987), para. 4462.

[121] 'Report of the International Commission of Inquiry on Darfur to the United Nations Secretary-General' (2005), p. 108, para. 422.

such circumstances by being in uniform 'amounts at least to empty formalism'.[122]

With all due respect, this approach is problematic. Watts chose to use a single principle – that of distinction – as the basis for an obligation that government forces must be used. While the principle of distinction is without a doubt a cardinal principle of IHL, and while it figures in combatant status (the obligation to distinguish oneself or wear a fixed distinctive sign is relevant to combatant immunity and to recognition of a group of fighters as combatants in international armed conflicts), it is far from the only element relevant to combatant status. It is unclear how Watts draws the obligation to use state armed forces from the principle of distinction. At most, from only this principle, one could draw an argument that a state must use clearly identifiable forces when it fights against an armed group. There are a number of ways a state could do so without using regular state armed forces.

Combatant status is indeed linked to distinction but it is also very much the symbol that one is part of a system or a structure that is capable of respecting the laws of armed conflict in its operations.[123] Combatant status is thus more than a mechanism to determine what protections a person is entitled to under IHL. Generations of military authorities, humanitarians and scholars have taken the view that the best way to ensure that a fighter will respect the international obligations of IHL is if he or she is part of an organized group that is subject to authority.[124] The apogee – or at the very least, the epitome – of such organization and command and control is state armed forces, and this can include police forces.

While it may be illogical that a person launching a cyber-attack distinguish himself (i.e. by wearing a military uniform) even though he is by definition unseen by the enemy during the attack, it is far from nonsensical that such a person be subject to military discipline and authority and that he be instructed to carry out his attack in accordance with the laws and customs of war.[125]

---

[122] Watts, 'Status of Government Forces', 160–161.

[123] See the discussion in Cameron and Chetail, *Privatizing War*, pp. 91–113. See also Lindsey Cameron, 'The Use of Private Military and Security Companies in Armed Conflicts and Certain Peace Operations', PhD thesis, University of Geneva, 2015.

[124] See especially GIAD Draper, 'Combatant Status: An Historical Perspective' (1972) 11 *Military L & L War Rev* 135. This is confirmed in the terms of Article 43 AP I.

[125] Here, I do not condone the approach that asserts that Article 4A(1) of GC III combatants must also comply with all of the requirements of Article 4A(2) in order to have combatant status. States are free to set up their armed forces as they wish, and even the regular armed

In my view, the question whether a state is obliged to use government forces in non-international armed conflicts – and, thus, in peace operations that may amount to armed conflicts – must be considered from a number of angles. International law has no black-letter rule obliging states to use government armed forces in non-international armed conflicts or even a rule stating who has a right to act as a combatant in such conflicts. It is true that the benefits of combatant status – in particular, immunity from prosecution for lawful acts of war – are linked directly with distinction, but distinction (despite its fundamental nature) is not the sole factor in combatant status. If one were to attempt to assert an obligation for states to use public forces in non-international armed conflicts, a better source would be the stringent due diligence obligations on a state to respect and ensure respect for IHL.[126] It would be difficult, if not impossible, for a person not integrated into the military chain of command to evaluate properly the proportionality of an attack and to conduct hostilities in conformity with the requirements of IHL. Indeed, there are strong arguments to suppose that a state would fall short of its obligation to respect and ensure respect of the Geneva Conventions and their Additional Protocols if it used forces that are not its own.[127] The requirement to respect and ensure respect of the Conventions also applies to non-international armed conflicts.[128]

One can imagine ways in which a state could attempt to mitigate the nefarious effects of having non-state actors perform such roles. If a state has taken measures such that any shortcomings flowing from not using public forces have been significantly lessened or overcome, then it may well not be a violation by the state to use other forces in non-international armed conflict. The existing black-letter laws leave it open for states to employ forces other than their own armed forces in non-international

---

forces of states whose forces often violate IHL have the right to POW status. Nevertheless, the requirements of organization and distinction are indeed relevant.

[126] In my view these can be police or armed forces; to assert otherwise ignores the fact that there is often no clear moment when a situation of violence can be classified as a non-international armed conflict and states will be using police forces to suppress; see also 'Report of the International Commission of Inquiry on Darfur to the United Nations Secretary-General' (2005), p. 108, para. 422.

[127] See Cameron and Chetail, *Privatizing War*, pp. 93–102.

[128] This conclusion is logical since Article 3 common to the Conventions forms part of the treaty, even though it describes a regime apart. ICRC, *Commentary on the First Geneva Convention*, 2016, paras 125–126. The ICRC's Interpretive Guidance on Direct Participation in Hostilities appears to take for granted that states will use government armed forces in non-international armed conflicts.

armed conflicts.[129] The mercenary conventions are the strongest example of this. However, it is noteworthy that the UN Security Council has recently adopted resolutions condemning the use of mercenaries by governments in power and imploring states to prevent the flow of mercenaries to states involved in non-international armed conflicts.[130]

In addition, one can consider whether there is any 'status' of combatant in non-international armed conflicts for the fighters themselves – and, thus, immunity. In non-international armed conflicts, Additional Protocol II says that states should consider granting amnesty to fighters at the end of a conflict.[131] For the purposes of Article 6(5) AP II, it is important to bear in mind that state and organized armed group roles can change over the course of a conflict, which may be the key to why there is no formal rule in non-international armed conflicts.[132]

There is a further matter to be considered: in non-international armed conflicts, human rights law can play a significant role in constraining the actions of state armed forces. Some even go so far as to say that this factor necessarily disrupts the equality of belligerents in non-international armed conflict.[133] That being said, many states and academic

---

[129] See in particular A. Cassese, 'Mercenaries: Lawful Combatants or War Criminals?' (1980) 40 *ZaöRV* 1–30 at 5–6.

[130] For the recent example, see UNSC Res 1970 (26 February 2011), para. 9 and UNSC Res 1973 (17 March 2011), paras 16 and 18. In this case, however, the world was rapidly beginning to recognize the legitimacy of an alternative government; therefore, while it may not fit entirely within the usual practice of condemning only the use of mercenaries by rebels against governments, it should not necessarily be wielded as an example of a paradigm shift in relation to the meaning of the norm itself. For a discussion of the previous condemnations of the use of mercenaries, see Cassese, 'Mercenaries', at 2–3.

[131] In addition, Waldemar Solf has advocated that this practice be extended to extradition in order to ensure the incentive for non-combatants to comply with IHL. See Solf, 'The Status of Combatants in Non-International Armed Conflicts Under Domestic Law and Transnational Practice' (1983–1984) 33 *Am UL Rev* 53–65.

[132] The existing commentary on the adoption of this provision is laconic. (See the commentary by Sylvie-Stoyanka Junod in Sandoz et al., *Commentary on the Additional Protocols*, paras 4617–4618.) Beyond what Junod states, the Travaux Préparatoires reveal that most states reaffirmed that, at the time of the Diplomatic Conference, they viewed the content of Article 6(5) as merely a recommendation. Spain vociferously opposed even the inclusion as a recommendation, stating, 'Besides its inapplicability in practice, therefore, in as indicated above its application is subject to unforeseeable contingencies which only States can judge, paragraph 7 [now para 5] is out of place in the operative part of a convention.' See CCDH/SR.50 (Vol. 4) 92. Comment by Spain at p. 103. The Cameroonian delegation, on the other hand, approved the provision and the 'humanitarian spirit' it reflected (p. 104), while the delegate from Zaire underlined the non-binding nature of the provision while espousing its 'profound humanitarian considerations' (p. 105).

[133] See in particular Marco Sassòli, 'Introducing a Sliding-Scale of Obligations to Address the Fundamental Inequality Between Armed Groups and States?' (2011) 93 *IRRC* 425.

commentators agree that private companies and private individuals are not bound by international human rights law. This means that a state using a PMSC to fight on its behalf in a non-international armed conflict would be shirking its obligations under international human rights law if it did not take steps to ensure that such forces were also bound by human rights law to the same extent as its own forces would be.

Thus, while there is no black-letter rule requiring states to use their own public forces as combatants, the legal framework displays a strong preference for the use of such forces. When it comes to peace operations, there are several ways the lack of combatant status could arguably be resolved, which could vary depending on the way such a private force is incorporated into the force: first, if a peace operation were to be delegated to a PMSC by the UN Secretary-General, the Security Council mandate setting up the operation could state specifically that they have combatant status. This solution may fail to take into account the fact that combatant status is more than a status, that it is a status that shows that a person is part of a system or structure that is capable of ensuring that that person respects the law in the chaotic situation of war – if it were not accompanied by further checks and a robust structuring of the force.[134] On the other hand, the advantage of this solution is that it would force clarity and transparency at the highest levels.

Second, if states send a PMSC as their troop contingent, their obligation to ensure respect for IHL under the Geneva Conventions and Additional Protocols could mean that they must somehow incorporate such troops into their armed forces and/or otherwise exercise military discipline over them. Via the rules on state responsibility one might be tempted to argue that that contingent must be a de facto organ of the sending state, but this is not the position I take. However, even if it is a de facto organ, it nevertheless is only part of the armed forces of the state if it is incorporated as such under national law.[135] If it is not incorporated into the armed forces under national law, the essential test will be Article 4A(2) of GC III (or possibly Article 43 of AP I).[136]

A third possibility would be for a state to incorporate such a contingent officially via Article 43(3) AP I as paramilitary forces. I have argued elsewhere[137] that for many reasons, states are unlikely to incorporate PMSCs in their armed forces because the reasons for outsourcing go

---

[134] See also Chapter 6, Section 6.3.1, on 'Discipline' below.
[135] The same is true for de jure organs of states.   [136] See Chapters 7 and 12.
[137] See Cameron and Chetail, *Privatizing War*, pp. 391–392.

entirely against that logic. One may question whether the same pressures would apply in this scenario, but arguably they would.

4.4.2   The Use of Force by PMSCs as Security Guards in Peace Operations

When PMSCs are engaged as security guards in peace operations – especially when that peace operation is engaged as a party to a conflict – their interpretation of self-defence must follow the traditional criminal law meaning (but with the IHL exceptions indicated below) and may not be based on the broader peacekeeping understanding of the term.[138] If they do not abide by the narrower definition, then they may be engaged as civilians directly participating in hostilities in an armed conflict occurring in a peace operation.

4.4.3   Conclusion

The principle that force may be used only in self-defence in UN peace operations thus does not act as a brake on the actual force that may be used in such circumstances for the purposes of IHL. Consequently, members of military contingents participating in peace operations should have the ability to have combatant status. At the very least, they must be governed in such a way as to ensure that the concerns protected via that status are addressed – in particular, to preserve the distinction between civilians and combatants and to maintain discipline so as to be able to respect IHL.

4.5   Forces Must Be Supplied by Member States

As indicated above, Marrack Goulding argues that there is a fifth principle of peacekeeping. He argues, 'National armies and police could be the only source for the uniformed personnel the United Nations required.'[139] This principle, according to Goulding, flows from the fact that it 'would not be practicable for the United Nations to maintain a standing army', in acknowledgement of the lack of Article 43 agreements that would have provided the Security Council with troops.[140] Goulding supplies no other clear legal basis in support of this principle. Below, I will discuss the various options that have been suggested for ways in which the UN could

---

[138] See below, Part III.
[139] Goulding, 'Evolution of UN Peacekeeping', 455.   [140] Ibid.

create its own peacekeeping force. In my view, those proposals and the arguments their proponents expound are sufficient to counter this view in terms of the law, even if legitimate policy and legal concerns remain.[141] In addition, in the following chapter I address the issue from the perspective of whether the UN Secretary-General may accept a PMSC troop contingent from states.

4.6 Conclusion

According to the interpretation provided above, the principles of peacekeeping are sufficiently elastic to contemplate a use of PMSCs as peacekeepers that could be in conformity with their requirements. Nevertheless, important constraints should be borne in mind. First, the operations must be under the overall leadership and control of a UN staff member. Second, if we accept that consent to the composition of the force by the host state is not a legal requirement, it would seem that in most cases in practice it would be necessary to ensure the success of the operation. Third, the requirement that a peace operation be impartial implies some limitations on the way PMSCs could recruit forces. Finally, the principle on the limited use of force in peace operations nevertheless creates the possibility that peacekeepers can become involved in armed conflicts as combatants. This situation leads to difficult questions about public forces in non-international armed conflicts and signals that appropriate steps must be taken in order to remedy any potential harmful effects of a lack of combatant status.

One of the key issues relates to the role that discipline plays in ensuring that regular armed forces use force in accordance with the law, as well as in accordance with the myriad policies that help to lessen the impact of violence on civilian lives. Moreover, using non-state actors in situations where the legal framework is already complex, including in respect to the applicability of human rights law, carries the risk of further blurring the picture of applicable rules, again with potentially negative consequences for the inhabitants of the host state.

---

[141] See below, Chapter 5.

5

PMSCs as the Military or Police Component of the Peace Operation

This chapter examines the legal framework governing whether the UN Security Council or UN Secretary-General may accept a PMSC as a military contingent from a state or delegate all or part of a peace operation to a PMSC. It will then consider whether the Security Council has the capacity to create a standing force using PMSCs (in the absence, but also in the vein, of the forces described in Article 43 of the UN Charter).

5.1 Legal Limits on UN Actions Implementing a Security Council Resolution

Analyzing the lawfulness of the incorporation of a PMSC as a military or police contingent in a UN peace operation raises a preliminary, fundamental question: what are the limits on the powers of the UN Security Council?[1] As the Secretary-General in establishing the mission is exercising delegated powers of the Security Council, the limits on those powers are relevant to assessing what he or she may do.[2] Again, throughout this discussion it is assumed that Article 39 has been correctly invoked and that the peace operation is lawful in all other respects. Furthermore, it is presumed that the resolution itself is silent as to the inclusion of a PMSC contingent as part or all of the peacekeeping force.[3]

Most scholarship focuses on the limits of the decision-making powers of the Security Council. Although an analysis of the preparatory work

---

[1] Although peace operations can also be established by the General Assembly, since the vast majority are established by the UN Security Council, the analysis in this section will be limited primarily to restrictions on the powers of the Security Council.

[2] Danesh Sarooshi, *The United Nations and the Development of Collective Security: The Delegation by the UN Security Council of Its Chapter VII Powers* (Oxford: Oxford University Press, 1999), pp. 53–57.

[3] Recently, UNSC Resolutions creating peacekeeping forces have specified that troops from a particular region will play a prominent role in a force, so it is not inconceivable that a resolution could make precise determinations regarding the composition of the force.

of the UN Charter led one scholar to conclude (provocatively) that the drafters of the Charter intended to make the Security Council free of any legal obligations in its decision-making,[4] it is not generally accepted that the Council is *legibus solutus*.[5] As the Security Council has become more active since the end of the Cold War, questions have arisen in regard to the legality of resolutions it has adopted in relation to the imposition of general and targeted sanctions, the removal of peacekeepers from the jurisdiction of the international criminal court and the creation of the international criminal tribunals, to name a few. In relation to each of these, the search for sources of the legal limits on the decision-making power of the UN Security Council has tended to focus on the UN Charter itself,[6] general principles of law, treaty law where applicable and, possibly, customary international law.[7] Some argue, however, that only *jus cogens* can limit the vast decision-making power of the Security Council.[8]

Even if the decision-making powers are extremely broad, does that necessarily mean that the UN is bound only by *jus cogens* when it is taking executive action to implement the decisions that have been adopted?

---

[4] GH Oostenhuizen, 'Playing the Devil's Advocate: The United Nations Security Council Is Unbound by Law' (1999) 12 *Leiden J Intl L* 549.

[5] For a concise overview, see Antonios Tzanakopoulos, *Disobeying the Security Council: Countermeasures Against Wrongful Sanctions* (Oxford: Oxford University Press, 2011), pp. 55–56. See also *Prosecutor v. Tadic* IT-94–1 (2 October 1995), para. 28. Even the Court of First Instance implied that it would have jurisdiction to review (indirectly) a UN Security Council resolution if it contravened *jus cogens*. Case T-315/01, *Kadi v. Council of Europe* [2005] ECR, para. 57 and Case T-306/01 *Yusuf v. Council* [2005] ECR para. 77.

[6] Experts on international institutional law agree that the constitutive instruments of international organizations set the parameters for lawful decisions for the organization. Scholars have argued, based on this, that Security Council decisions must conform to the purposes and principles of the United Nations and respect the right to self-determination (Article 1(2) of the Charter), human rights (Article 1(3)), sovereign equality of states (Article 2(1)), good faith (Article 2(2)) and non-interference in internal affairs (unless relying on Chapter VII). See, e.g., David David Schweigman, *The Authority of the Security Council Under Chapter VII of the UN Charter: Legal Limits and the Role of the International Court of Justice* (Kluwer Law International, 2001), pp. 163–203, especially pp. 167–179 for an overview, with references to additional authors.

[7] It should be noted that much of the thinking in regard to such limits stems from the imposition of sanctions by the Security Council – at first, general sanctions and, more recently, targeted sanctions against individuals. However, more 'invasive' peace operations involving the administration of territory as well as the establishment of the international criminal tribunals sparked interest in discerning the limits on power and legal obligations of the Security Council.

[8] See generally, for example, Alexander Orakhelashvili, 'The Impact of Peremptory Norms on the Interpretation and Application of United Nations Security Council Resolutions' (2005) 16 *EJIL* 59–88.

There is a convincing argument that if the UN Security Council wishes to derogate from the applicable legal framework, it must do so specifically in its resolution. This question arose in relation to the applicability of the law of occupation following the adoption of UNSC Resolution 1483 in 2004.[9]

There are other limits to UN action executing a Security Council resolution as well. The ILC's Draft Articles on the Responsibility of International Organizations affirm that the internal law of the organization can create international legal obligations for the organization itself. In this regard, it should be recalled that the mandates creating the peace operation are UN Security Council resolutions, which are generally accepted as forming part of the legal framework governing the peace operation and may be used to create binding limitations in regard to the use of private forces. General Assembly resolutions on outsourcing may constitute internal law of the organization that amounts to an international obligation.[10] The customary law of the organization itself also is binding on it.[11] Arguably, the principles on peacekeeping form part of the customary law of the United Nations.[12]

These questions are different from those relating to the scope or extent of the powers of the organization beyond what is written in its constitutive instrument. The following pages consider both types of potential limitations on the powers of the Security Council and Secretary-General when composing a force for a peace operation. As Antonios Tzanakopoulos has observed, the fact that there is no mechanism for judicial review within the UN should not be mistaken for an absence of legal limits on the powers or actions of the Security Council.[13] At the same time, it is important

---

[9] See in particular Marco Sassòli, 'Legislation and Maintenance of Public Order and Civil Life by Occupying Powers' (2005) 16 *EJIL* 661–694 at 681, stating that 'any derogation from IHL by the UN Security Council must be explicit.'

[10] See also the remarks by Oscar Schachter (above, Chapter 1, note 13) in regard to the creation of international law by the various offices and organs of the United Nations.

[11] Robert Kolb, Gabriele Porretto and Sylvain Vité, *L'application du droit international humanitaire et des droits de l'homme aux organisations internationales: Forces de paix et administrations civiles transitoires* (Brussels: Bruylant, 2005), pp. 256–260.

[12] The UNSC has reaffirmed these principles in the Capstone Doctrine (United Nations Department of Peacekeeping Operations and Department of Field Support, 'United Nations Peacekeeping Operations: Principles and Guidelines' (18 January 2008) (hereafter Capstone Doctrine)), and also in UNSC Res 2086 (2013), preambular para. 6, but as helpful guarantors of success, not yardsticks of legality.

[13] Tzanakopoulos, *Disobeying the Security Council*, p. 55. On such control, see *inter alia* Jose Alvarez, 'Judging the Security Council' (1996) 90 *AJIL* 1–39; Dapo Akande, 'International Court of Justice and the Security Council: Is There Room for Judicial Control of Decisions of the Political Organs of the United Nations?' (1997) 46 *ICLQ* 303–343.

to recall that experts on international organizations contend that international organizations may well implement decisions they take even when those decisions go against the rules.[14]

5.2   PMSCs as the Sole Contribution of a Member State

This section will canvass the specific legal issues governing the possibility for the inclusion of a PMSC as a state's contribution to a peacekeeping force. As mentioned above, the United States contributes its civilian police via a PMSC. The government of the United Kingdom, however, has stated that it would not send a PMSC as its contingent to a peace operation.[15]

The most common method of establishing a traditional peace operation force is through the solicitation of troop contributions from UN member states and incorporating them into a UN force under UN command and control. UN-commanded and -controlled peace operations are subsidiary organs set up by the UN Security Council under Article 29 of the UN Charter.[16] As such, the Security Council has the authority to determine their composition. The UN Security Council delegates the authority to the Secretary-General to establish the peace force; furthermore, it is generally agreed that this power includes the power to determine the composition of the force.[17] According to the usual custom, the Secretary-General appoints the Commander-in-Chief of the force,[18] who is generally a high-ranking officer from a state's national forces. National contingents are then placed under the command of the UN Commander-in-Chief, while the Secretary-General 'gives the general instructions and exercises general political guidance'.[19] The Commander-in-Chief is responsible for all military activities of the force. There is a clear chain of command from the Security Council through the Secretary-General to the Commander-in-Chief. The chain usually continues down through the national commanders of national contingents, which are placed under the command of the UN pursuant to participating state agreements, be they formal or informal.[20]

---

[14] Chapter 1, Section 1.4.   [15] See Chapter 2, Section 2.2.

[16] There have been a few cases of peace operations set up by the General Assembly, but this is the exception to the rule and not sufficiently current or predominant to warrant further consideration here.

[17] Sarooshi, *The UN and Collective Security; Certain Expenses of the United Nations (Article 17, Paragraph 2 of the Charter)* (Advisory Opinion) [1962] ICJ Rep 151.

[18] Bothe, 'Peacekeeping', in B. Simma (ed.), *The Charter of the United Nations: A Commentary* (Oxford: Oxford University Press, 2002), para. 101.

[19] Ibid.   [20] Ibid., paras 96 and 108–112.

The practice that has evolved by virtue of the fact that the Security Council does not have its own forces is that states propose to contribute their own troops to the operation or mission. As indicated above, this is usually done 'through informal consultations' between the Secretary-General and potential troop contributing states.[21] Agreements are concluded between the UN and each troop contributing state; in addition, a general Status of Forces Agreement for the overall force is usually (but not always) concluded between the UN and the host state.[22] Again, as noted above, the principles guiding the composition of the force set down by then Secretary-General Dag Hammarskjøld in 1956–1958 were that no troops from the permanent five members of the Security Council and no forces from 'any country which, because of its geographical position or for other reasons, might be considered as possibly having a special interest in the situation which has called for the operation' should be included in the force.[23] However, over time Secretaries-General have strayed from these principles and both of those types of troop contributions have been accepted in peace forces. Above, I indicated that it is broadly agreed that the UN Secretary-General enjoys a unilateral power to determine the composition of the force, and this principle is set out in some of the earliest UN doctrine on peacekeeping.[24] Dan Sarooshi argues that the Secretary-General in fact enjoys the discretion to determine the principles guiding the composition of the force.[25] However, when considering the role of PMSCs in UN peace operations, difficult questions arise: is the Secretary-General's discretion completely unfettered? Or is there an implicit principle that they must be state forces or public forces? Could the Secretary-General of his or her own volition turn to a PMSC to staff a peace mandate? Could a state offer as its entire contribution only a PMSC?

---

[21] Zwanenburg, *Accountability*, p. 35. Zwanenburg notes that the Secretary-General also usually consults the Security Council about offers he has received and states that 'if the Council consents, the Secretary-General then concludes an agreement with the participating state. Ibid. The procedure he outlines gives a greater role to the Security Council than others indicate and suggests that the Secretary-General is merely the negotiator.

[22] For a short but helpful discussion, see Zwanenburg, *Accountability*, pp. 30–40. In addition, Bothe indicates that Status of Forces agreements in particular are not always agreed with Middle Eastern states, potentially due to disputed territorial status. See Bothe, 'Peacekeeping', para. 114.

[23] UN Secretary General, 'Summary Study of the Experience Derived from the Establishment and Operation of the Force', UN Doc A/3943 (9 October 1958) (UNSG 'Summary Study'), para. 160.

[24] Ibid., para. 160: 'the United Nations must reserve for itself the authority to decide on the composition of the force.' See also para. 16 of the same document. See also Di Blase, 'Role of Host State Consent'. See also above, Chapter 4. Section 4.2.

[25] Sarooshi, *The UN and Collective Security*, p. 66.

The concerns raised above regarding the general principles of peace-keeping and the ability of PMSCs to satisfy the requirements of consent and impartiality and the rules on the use of force are especially pertinent to this discussion. When the Secretary-General is composing the peace force without the backstop of Chapter VII powers, that is to say, when a peace operation is not clearly mandated under a resolution adopted under Chapter VII of the Charter, he or she must adhere to the principles of peacekeeping outlined above. If a PMSC – whether it be selected by the Secretary-General alone or offered by a state as its contribution – does not satisfy those requirements, then on those grounds alone the Secretary-General should not accept that PMSC as part of the peace force. While all of the peacekeeping principles will play a role, it is likely that the lack of a host state's consent to a PMSC force would be a paramount concern. Nonetheless, as noted above, it must be recalled that the Secretary-General enjoys wide powers of discretion and in rare cases could, if necessary and appropriate, deviate from those requirements.

A further key question is whether there is an unstated requirement that peace forces contributed by states must hail from UN member states or at least be state organs. There are a number of independent elements that could be marshalled in support of this contention. First, in terms of limits flowing from the internal law of the organization, the General Assembly's 1950 Uniting for Peace Resolution recommends that states survey their resources to determine what contribution they may be able to make, which is broad enough to encompass PMSCs, but then 'Recommends to the States Members of the United Nations that each Member maintain within its national armed forces elements so trained, organized and equipped that they could promptly be made available, in accordance with its constitutional processes, for service as a United Nations unit.'[26] This recommendation belies an underlying presumption that forces will come from a state's national armed forces – but it should be recalled that Uniting for Peace dates from 1950 and precedes the type of peacekeeping operations not considered as collective security activity.

The Security Council has recently emphasized 'the importance of Member States taking the necessary and appropriate steps to ensure the capability of their peacekeepers to fulfil the mandates assigned to them', and underlined 'the importance of international cooperation in this regard, including the training of peacekeepers'.[27] That resolution also refers to the duties of member states with respect to training peacekeepers in their

---

[26] 'Uniting for Peace', UNGA Res 377(V) (3 November 1950), paras 7 and 8, respectively.
[27] UNSC Res 1327 (2000) on the reception of the Brahimi report.

national programmes. While these are recommendations or observations rather than obligations, they raise the question: can a member state argue that it is bearing its share of the burden by funding a PMSC as its troop contribution? It should be noted that in the resolution quoted above, there is no explicit reference to *national* armed forces but rather to 'their peace-keepers'. In its most recent general resolution on peacekeeping, the Security Council 'encourages Troop- and Police-Contributing Countries, in the spirit of partnership, to continue to contribute professional military and police personnel with the necessary skills and experience to implement multidimensional peacekeeping mandates'.[28] This begs the question whether 'professional' must be understood as synonymous for 'members of state armed forces'. In any case, the first resolution shows that a contributing state has additional obligations in terms of overseeing – or at a minimum, monitoring – the training of peacekeepers it sends. This would go against any possibility of a state sending an unvetted, untrained PMSC, but it might not impede a state from sending a PMSC that it has properly trained.

When exercising delegated powers of the Security Council under a Chapter VII mandate, however, the Secretary-General is bound only by the limitations that apply to the Security Council when acting under Chapter VII of the Charter.[29] Thus, it is agreed that the Secretary-General does not have the power to compel states to contribute forces to peace operations in the absence of Article 43 agreements.[30] Beyond this limitation, given the broad powers of the Security Council under Chapter VII, arguably, unless it is contrary to *ius cogens* to accept private forces within the peace force, the Secretary-General is not legally prohibited from doing so.[31] There is no *ius cogens* prohibition on the use of private forces.[32]

---

[28] UNSC Res 2086 (2013), para. 11. See also UNSC Res 2185 (2014) focussing on the police component, '*Urges* police-contributing countries to continue to contribute professional police personnel . . .' (para. 3). The manner of contributing such personnel appears to be irrelevant: the fact that the United States contributes its police to UN peace operations via a PMSC must be understood to be accepted.

[29] On the limitations to the powers of the UN Security Council, see Schweigman, *Authority of the Security Council*, pp. 163–203.

[30] Sarooshi, *The UN and Collective Security*, p. 66.

[31] Nico Schrijver characterizes the preamble, Articles 1 and 2 and 55 (*inter alia*) of the UN Charter as 'normative' (but he does not indicate that it is normative for the UN itself). N Schrijver, 'The Future of the Charter of the United Nations' (2006) 10 *Max Planck Yearbook UN Law* 1–34 at 5.

[32] See Cameron and Chetail, *Privatizing War*, pp. 66–80 and 426–429 on mercenaries. See also Buchan et al., 'Externalization of Peacekeeping', 291, who observe that state monopoly on force is a modern phenomenon.

An additional point this scenario raises is related to the question whether states have a right to participate in peace operations. Siekmann offers an extraordinarily detailed account of the first states proposing troops for the first UN peace operation (UNEF I). He notes that Romania asked 'to be invited to participate' and Czechoslovakia 'announced that it would take part'.[33] Providing a detailed account of the diplomatic efforts of early Secretaries-General in the face of such eagerness on the part of troop contributors, Siekmann indicates that it was 'very clear early in the history' of peacekeeping 'that no country had a right to insist upon participating in peace-keeping operations (including observer missions . . .).'[34] A corollary to the fact that states have no right to participate in such missions would logically be that states have no right to furnish whatever troops they wish if their participation has been accepted.

There are additional concerns regarding related legal issues of peace operations that would have to be satisfied or addressed before a PMSC could be incorporated into a peace force, which apply to peace forces no matter how they are established. This scenario may raise issues for the sending state in terms of whether it would be in keeping with its obligation to respect and ensure respect for international humanitarian law – especially in situations where the peace operation has a robust mandate, which have been partially addressed above.[35] For its part, the UN must also respect and ensure respect for IHL even though it is not a party to the Geneva Conventions.[36] The aspect of this scenario that creates the most cause for concern is the potential lack of disciplinary power over such a force that the sending state may have.[37]

5.3   Delegation of a Peace Operation to a PMSC by the UN Security Council

The UN Security Council has the power to delegate the conduct of peace operations to regional organizations and makes increasing use of this power.[38] It has delegated peace operations or specific components or tasks

---

[33] Siekmann, *National Contingents*, pp. 15–19.   [34] Ibid., 21.

[35] Article 1 common to the four Geneva Conventions. On this issue, see Hannah Tonkin, *State Control over Private Military and Security Companies in Armed Conflict* (Cambridge University Press 2011), pp. 124–141.

[36] ICRC, *Commentary on the First Geneva Convention*, 2016, paras 138–142.

[37] See below, Chapter 6, Section 6.3.1.

[38] See Article 53 UN Charter. See also D. Sarooshi, 'The Security Council's Authorization of Regional Arrangements to Use Force: The Case of NATO', in V. Lowe et al. (eds.), *The*

thereof to NATO[39] and the European Union[40] and has also set up a 'hybrid' mission with the participation of the African Union.[41] Can the UN Security Council through a similar process delegate the conduct of a peace operation to a PMSC? To address this question, I will consider the specific legal framework on delegation of the conduct of a peace operation to regional organizations or states, the limits of the implied powers of the organization, and the general rules on delegation of UN Security Council powers.[42]

Article 53(1) of the UN Charter explicitly authorizes the UN Security Council to, 'where appropriate, utilize ... regional arrangements or agencies for enforcement action under its authority'. The enforcement powers referred to are the Chapter VII powers of the Security Council. Consequently, when the UN Security Council authorizes either member states or a regional organization to deploy as part of a peace operation, it tends to state explicitly in the relevant operative paragraphs of the resolution that it is acting under Chapter VII of the UN Charter.[43] There is, thus, a specific authorization in the Charter for the Security Council to delegate its Chapter VII powers to regional organizations. PMSCs, however, are not a regional organization. The UN thus cannot rely solely on Article 53(1) for such authority. The essential question for this study is thus whether the Security Council may delegate its Chapter VII (or Chapter VI½[44]) powers

United Nations Security Council and War: The Evolution of Thought and Practice Since 1945 (Oxford: Oxford University Press, 2008), pp. 226–247.

[39] For example, certain aspects of UNPROFOR, and also IFOR/SFOR and KFOR in the Balkans. See Bothe, 'Peacekeeping', paras 144–149. See also Sarooshi, 'The Security Council's Authorization of Regional Arrangements to Use Force'.

[40] For example, UNSC Res 1778 (2007) UN Doc S/RES/1778, authorizes the European Union to deploy a police operation in Chad under MINURCAT, at para. 6. UNSC Res 1671 (2006) authorized the temporary deployment of an EU force to support the UN mission in DRC during the elections.

[41] For example, UNAMID in Darfur, Sudan, is a hybrid AU/UN operation: UNSC Res 1769 (2007). This 'hybrid' operation may be something less than a straightforward delegation to the AU, but it nevertheless relies on the same legal foundations in the UN Charter.

[42] The UNGA has never authorized other organizations to conduct peace operations that were not under its authority and control; therefore, our discussion will be restricted to the Security Council's powers in this section. See N. Blokker, 'Is the Authorization Authorized? Powers and Practice of the UN Security Council to Authorize the Use of Force by "Coalitions of the Able and Willing"' (2000) 11 *EJIL* 541–568 at 548.

[43] See, e.g., UNSC Res 1778 (2007) UN Doc S/RES/1778, operative para. 6; UNSC Res 1671 (2006), last preambular paragraph.

[44] Chapter VI½ refers to the fact that peace operations lie somewhere between the pacific settlement of disputes (Chapter VI of the UN Charter) and action with respect to threats to the peace, etc. (Chapter VII of the UN Charter).

to entities other than regional organizations, even if that power is not set down in the Charter.

Even the power of the Security Council to delegate enforcement powers under its authority and control to states, as distinct from regional organizations, is not uncontroversial, at least in academic circles.[45] Also, given that not all 'regional' organizations with the capacity to use force are regional organizations within the meaning of the UN Charter, the Security Council has at times had to be creative in its use of language in order to authorize NATO to conduct peace operations under UN auspices.[46] For example, UN Security Council Resolution 836, which was adopted to allow NATO to take military action to protect the 'safe areas' in Bosnia in the mid-1990s, authorized 'Member States, acting nationally or through regional arrangements' to take action 'under the authority of the Security Council and subject to close coordination with the Secretary-General'.[47] The controversy over this practice lies to a certain extent in the lack of an explicit power in the Charter to authorize states to carry out its enforcement actions within peace operations. However, the UN is not limited to the powers strictly set down in the Charter; it is widely considered to possess 'implied powers' in order to fulfil its mandate.[48] Whether one interprets those powers broadly or narrowly, they permit the UN Security Council to authorize states to carry out military enforcement actions under UN auspices. The logic is straightforward: given that the UN has a mandate from states to maintain international peace and security, as well as an explicit power to take military enforcement action, it must have the ability to use the necessary and appropriate means to perform its functions if the means set out in the Charter are unavailable to it.[49] (The means set out in the Charter for enforcement action were the creation of a UN force

---

[45] Blokker, 'Is the Authorization Authorized?', 544–545. While Blokker notes that states have also criticized this practice, the examples he refers to are exclusively those in which the UN retains no control over the operation, such as Iraq in 1991. As these operations are widely considered to fall outside what can be considered peace operations, that practice is not considered relevant to our analysis. Bothe refers to these forces as 'mandated' forces. See Bothe, 'Peacekeeping', paras 144–159. Bothe takes the view that such forces are not peacekeeping forces due to their authorization to use force beyond self-defence.

[46] See Sarooshi, 'Authorization of Regional Arrangements', 230–232.

[47] UNSC Res 836 (1993), para. 10.

[48] *Reparation for Injuries Suffered in the Service of the United Nations* (Advisory Opinion) [1949] ICJ Rep 174 at 180.

[49] This is a 'narrow' interpretation of the implied powers of the UN, which adverts to an explicit power in the Charter to use force. See Blokker, 'Is the Authorization Authorized?', 547, for examples of broad and narrow interpretations of implied powers in this context.

through agreements with states under Article 43 of the Charter, but such agreements have never been concluded.)

It must be recalled that such delegated operations are not considered by the UN to be UN peacekeeping operations, even if they occur under a UN Security Council mandate.[50]

5.3.1   Implied Powers

Do implied powers permit the UN Security Council to authorize not only states, but also a PMSC, to carry out a peace operation in its name under Chapter VII of the Charter? There are a number of limits on the implied powers of the organization.[51] The most relevant for the question whether the Security Council may authorize a PMSC to carry out a peace operation are, first, that the use of the implied powers must be necessary for the organization to perform its functions and, second, that the use of the implied powers may not violate fundamental rules and principles of international law or the Charter.[52] Again, authorizing states to carry out enforcement aspects of peace operations under its authority is considered to fall easily within these limitations.[53]

The question of whether it is 'necessary' – such that it meets the legal test for the exercise of implied powers – for the UN Security Council to authorize a PMSC to carry out a peace operation is a question of fact that will be determined by the Security Council itself.[54] If the UN deemed it necessary to establish a robust peace operation in order to maintain

---

[50] For a discussion of the debates around this issue, including the interpretation by the European Court of Human Rights in *Behrami and Saramati v. France, Germany and Norway*, see below, Chapter 13, Section 13.2.2.

[51] Blokker, 'Is the Authorization Authorized?', 548–549, enumerates four. In addition to the two above, he includes: that the implied power may not change the distribution of powers within the organization and that the existence of explicit powers in the Charter must not prohibit the recourse to the implied powers such as, for example, Article 43 agreements. If the legal basis for peacekeeping is located in the text of the Charter, however, any limitations would also have to be sought in the Charter's text or its interpretation.

[52] The latter principle is considered by Blokker, ibid., 549 and 552–554, to include aspects of the law on delegation; for this analysis, delegation will be considered separately.

[53] Ibid.

[54] This concept of necessity must be distinguished from necessity as a circumstance precluding wrongfulness in the law on responsibility. When it comes to necessity as a defence in the law on international responsibility, the first essential element is that the organization has violated an obligation otherwise owed to a state or another international organization. In the exercise of implied powers, however, the requirement of necessity is not linked to a presumption of a violation that must be excused.

international peace and security, but no states were willing to act under a Security Council authorization or to contribute troops to such an operation, this requirement could be satisfied. In practice, however, this scenario is unlikely to arise since the negotiation for a mandate for a peace operation occurs simultaneously with efforts to drum up troop contributions from states and should thus be tailored to the support it can garner. Put another way, the Security Council will not adopt a resolution calling for a peace operation staffed with 100,000 troops when it knows it will only be able to get states to contribute 2,000.

A more realistic and likely case of necessity can be made for an urgent deployment of forces in an acute situation as an interim solution, when national troop contributions will be slow in getting on the ground in the host state. There have been a number of efforts by the UN to develop rapid reaction forces and to create 'rapid deployment capability',[55] but delay in deployment is a problem that has continued to plague the UN and is a niche PMSCs have sought to exploit.[56] Due to serious efforts on the part of the UN to cover these gaps, necessity on these grounds should not arise, but the possibility of this scenario arising cannot be excluded. The UN Secretary-General maintained a PMSC guard force in Somalia in 2013 due to precisely such a situation.[57] This raises other issues that could be problematic for PMSCs, however, such as the way discipline is exercised over peacekeeping forces and the conclusion of Status of Forces Agreements, which will be discussed below.[58]

The second limitation on implied powers that is especially pertinent is that implied powers must not contravene fundamental rules or principles of international law. This limitation raises the central question whether force authorized by the Security Council must be exercised by states. Put another way, would an authorization of the use of force to a non-state

---

[55] 'Report of the High-Level Independent Panel on Peace Operations on Uniting Our Strengths for Peace: Politics, Partnership and People' (17 June 2015), UN Doc A/70/95; S/2015/446, paras 198ff. The development of this capacity was one of the key recommendations of the 'Report of the Panel on United Nations Peace Operations', UN Doc A/55/305–S/2000/809 (21 August 2000). For more on efforts taken to implement this recommendation, see Report of the Secretary-General, 'Implementation of the Recommendations of the Special Committee on Peacekeeping Operations and the Panel on United Nations Peace Operations' (21 December 2001) UN Doc A/56/732 at paras 23–34.

[56] Discussed in more detail below in relation to PMSC forces that could be established under Article 43 of the UN Charter.

[57] 'Letter Dated 14 October 2013 from the Secretary-General Addressed to the President of the Security Council' (14 October 2013), UN Doc S/2013/606.

[58] See below, Chapter 6, Sections 6.3 and 6.4.

actor by the Security Council contravene fundamental rules of international law?

The notion that military force may only be used by states seems to be embedded in the UN and collective security system. The UN Charter does not regulate the use of force by non-state actors. This may be inferred by the fact that the UN is itself composed of states and is an interstate organization, and states abhor the notion that force may be used legally by non-state actors. The UN Charter only authorizes *states* to use force in self-defence under Article 51 on their own initiative, not non-state armed groups.[59] The regional organizations Article 53 refers to as being susceptible to UN authorizations to carry out enforcement action are likewise composed of states. Indeed, this precept is taken so much for granted that one group cites no legal authority for the assertion that '[o]nly states can provide the military forces and civilian police needed in UN peace operations'.[60]

It is widely considered to be a peremptory principle of international law that states are prohibited from using force against another state, unless in self-defence or authorized by the Security Council. Is there a corollary principle that when force is used legally, it may *only* be states or international organizations (composed of states) that may use it? In this case, of course, it would be the UN that would be using force, via a PMSC.

It is difficult to answer this question for this particular context. The problem is that this question is inextricably bound up with all questions regarding the use of force by non-state actors, including terrorism. The UN High-Level Panel on Threats, Challenges and Change opined, 'The norms governing the use of force by non-State actors have not kept pace with those pertaining to States. This is not so much a legal question as a political one.'[61] The report goes on to discuss conventions and norms

---

[59] This issue is in some ways linked to the problem of the use of force by states against non-state actors in self-defence. If we consider, by analogy, the cases of the *Wall* and *Congo v. Uganda*, we may note that the ICJ tends to be very conservative in its interpretation of the Charter in this regard. See *Legal Consequences of the Construction of a Wall in the Occupied Palestinian Territories* (Advisory Opinion) [2004] ICJ Rep 136; *Armed Activities on the Territory of the Congo (Congo v. Uganda)* (Merits) [2005] ICJ Rep 116.

[60] W.J. Durch, V.K. Holt, C.R. Earle and M.K. Shanahan, 'The Brahimi Report at Thirty (Months): Reviewing the UN's Record of Implementation' (2002) 8 *Intl Peacekeeping: YB Intl Peace Operations* 1–32 at 16. See also W.J. Durch, V.K. Holt, C.R. Earle and M.K. Shanahan, 'The Brahimi Report and the Future of UN Peace Operations' (Stimson Center 2003) at 70, available at www.stimson.org.

[61] Report of the High-Level Panel on Threats, Challenges and Change, 'A More Secure World: Our Shared Responsibility' (4 December 2004), UN Doc A/59/565, para. 159. In fact, the whole discussion occurs under the heading 'Defining Terrorism'.

related to terrorism and the difficulties in arriving at a unanimously agreed definition of terrorism. But this manifestation of non-state actor use of force would seem to have little in common with the use of PMSCs in peace operations under discussion. The Panel appears to be lamenting a lack of *ius ad bellum* framework for non-state actors and the use of force as well as inadequate *ius in bello* rules.[62] It may be that the thrust of the debate on the terrorism definition indicates that if there is a right of non-state actors to use force, that right exists only in relation to self-determination movements.[63] Consequently, any use of force by non-state actors outside that context cannot claim to have colour of law under international law. On the other hand, even if consensus existed, rules on this type of a use of force by non-state actors would seem ill-suited to apply to the PMSC question in the context of peace operations.

Approaching the problem from the perspective of IHL and its implicit limitations may provide a slightly clearer answer. One author attributes the particularly negative view of the use of force by non-state actors to the fact that 'the manageability of violence is dependent on the organizational structure in which it occurs.'[64] That remark is highly relevant, especially considering the fact that discipline within peace operations, whether in Chapter VI or Chapter VII operations, is left to states. Under international humanitarian law, it is not unlawful for non-state actors to use armed force per se, as long as they abide by the rules on the use of force in that body of law. Indeed, there could be no law on non-international armed conflicts if international humanitarian law prohibited outright the use of force by organized armed groups. On the other hand, above, this study has considered whether states have an obligation to use their own armed forces when they are involved in non-international armed conflicts. It concluded that there is no obligation on governments to use only members of the armed forces as long as the principles of distinction and organization are respected.[65] There tends to be a presumption that states will use state armed forces for direct participation in hostilities, however.

International organizations are not states, but they do not fall clearly within the rubric of 'non-state actors' either, as they are created by and composed of states. Indeed, there is no consensus as to what international

---

[62] Ibid., 159–164.   [63] Ibid., para. 160 for a summary of the critical issues.

[64] M. Schmitt, 'The Resort to Force In International Law: Reflections on Positivist and Contextual Approaches' (1994) 37 *Air Force L Rev* 105 at 115. This does not mean that non-state actors are not organized but that they do not usually have courts, etc.

[65] See Chapter 4, notes 123–128 and accompanying text. See also Cameron and Chetail, *Privatizing War*, pp. 91–107.

organizations truly are: 'a short-hand for the collective of their member States, forums for negotiations ... [or] actors in their own right?'[66] Even though there is no clear rule that states must use governmental forces in non-international armed conflicts, is there a presumption that the UN may only delegate its powers to state armed forces? In the context of peace operations, armed conflicts between the peacekeeping force and an organized armed group tend to be classified as non-international in nature; however, situations in which enforcement operations are delegated to other organizations by the Security Council may be international armed conflicts.

There is no customary law prohibition on the use of mercenaries in general;[67] even less so is there a *ius cogens* prohibition that would bind the Security Council.[68] Even so, a Security Council resolution authorizing a peace operation that will be delegated to a PMSC would have to specifically state in the resolution that forces other than state armed forces may be used.

Thus, while there is a strong argument that state forces should be used in peace operations, there appears to be no fundamental international rule prohibiting the Security Council from exercising its implied powers by authorizing a PMSC to carry out a peace operation under its authority, subject to compliance with the rules on delegation and otherwise compliant with international law – and providing that it does not delegate the actual command of the operation. However, it would have to ensure that such forces act in accordance with IHL – in particular with respect to the distinction between civilians and combatants. Concerns on discipline are further outlined below.[69]

Limitations on the use of such a force may be more likely to flow from concerns regarding legitimacy than anything else. Peace operations are complex and multifaceted, yet we have seen that PMSCs exhibit a wide range of technical expertise. A question that remains is whether they also possess the soft skills, patience, and diplomatic acuity necessary for a successful peace operation, and whether such operations are compatible with the business approach of a for-profit company.

---

[66] August Reinisch, 'Editorial: How Necessary Is Necessity for International Organizations?' (2006) 3 *Intl Org L Rev* 177–183 at 181.

[67] See Cameron and Chetail, *Privatizing War*, pp. 72–80.

[68] See J. Frowein and N. Krisch, 'Article 42', in B. Simma (ed.), *The Charter of the United Nations: A Commentary*, 2nd edn (Oxford: Oxford University Press, 2002), p. 711, para. 29 on *ius cogens* as a limit on Security Council powers.

[69] See below, Chapter 6, Section 6.3.1.

5.3.2 The Specific Rules on Delegation

The limits on the power of the Security Council to delegate 'stem either from the Charter or from general legal principles and the object and purpose of the delegation authority'.[70] Some argue that Article 48 of the Charter permits the Security Council to delegate peace operations to states, and that there is no need to refer to a more general law or power of delegation.[71] Since, however, PMSCs are not states and therefore not caught by Article 48, one would have to subscribe to the Security Council's general power to delegate as part of its implied powers.

The legality of the delegation of powers in UN law is first subject to the requirement that the delegating authority must possess the powers being delegated.[72] That the Security Council has the authority to create peace operations is now settled. In addition, '[t]he scope of the delegated powers must be precisely construed and their exercise must be effectively supervised by the Council.'[73] It is generally accepted that the Security Council exercises effective control over UN-commanded and -controlled peace operations; the situation with respect to authorized enforcement actions is much less clear (although these have also been generally accepted as proper delegations).[74] Finally, the entity to whom the power is delegated must 'exercize [sic] the power for the purpose – or even possibly in the way – stipulated by the delegator'.[75] The first two issues are uncontroversial in the case of peacekeeping, and the third is a matter of factual determination should such a delegation arise.

The question as to whether the entity entrusted to carry out the delegated powers must somehow be public in nature is not addressed in the

---

[70] H. Krieger, 'A Credibility Gap: The Behrami and Saramati Decision of the European Court of Human Rights' (2009) 13 *J Intl Peacekeeping* 159–180 at 165–166, citing also Frowein and Krisch, 'Article 42'.

[71] Article 48 UN Charter: '1. The action required to carry out the decisions of the Security Council for the maintenance of international peace and security shall be taken by all the Members of the United Nations or by some of them, as the Security Council may determine. 2. Such decisions shall be carried out by the Members of the United Nations directly and through their action in the appropriate international agencies of which they are members.' See Frowein and Krisch, 'Article 42', 713, para. 32. For such delegations based on a general power and not a specific Charter article, see Sarooshi, *The UN and Collective Security*, pp. 16–18.

[72] Frowein and Krisch, 'Article 42', para. 33; see also Sarooshi, *The UN and Collective Security*, pp. 20–23.

[73] Krieger, 'Credibility Gap', 165–166.

[74] Ibid., 166; see also Blokker, 'Is the Authorization Authorized?'.

[75] Sarooshi, *The UN and Collective Security*, pp. 20–23, passage quoted at 23.

most authoritative study on the delegation by the Security Council of its Chapter VII powers.[76] In fact, that study did not consider the possibility of delegation to a private entity at all, which could suggest that that author believes that such a delegation is not within the scope of powers. On the other hand, it may simply signal that such a delegation is unlikely to occur and was unimaginable at the time of writing. In terms of the quality of the actor to whom the powers are delegated, Sarooshi merely comments, 'the naming of a person to exercize [sic] power by the entity that initially delegates power may involve an implicit assumption that the person was chosen due to particular institutional or other characteristics.'[77]

Are there any other restrictions on the quality of the agent to whom the power is delegated based on general principles or the Charter? A need for state or civilian control over such forces would seem to be unnecessary, since even when delegating to a regional organization, the Secretary-General retains overall authority and control over both the Force Commander and the operation as a whole.[78] However, it should be recalled that in UN-authorized operations, the Secretary-General and/or Security Council tend to exercise a lesser degree of control over specific uses of force. Sarooshi argues that 'the lawfulness of such delegations of power depend[s] on the Council being able to exercise a sufficient degree of authority and control over the exercise of the delegated powers such that it could decide to change at any time the way in which those powers were being exercised.'[79] In this regard, in Sarooshi's estimation, the use of close air support by NATO in Bosnia in the mid-1990s was a lawful exercise of delegated power due to the fact that there was a 'dual-key' approach: that is, both the Secretary-General and NATO had to agree on the use of force in order for it to go ahead, thus preserving UN control over the operation.[80]

However, that level of control has not always been present in what have been recognized as lawful delegations of Security Council powers. In

---

[76] Sarooshi considers delegation to the UN Secretary-General, to UN subsidiary organs, to UN member states and to 'regional arrangements'. Ibid.

[77] Ibid., 23.

[78] Sarooshi, 'Authorization of Regional Arrangements', 236. See also Bothe, 'Peacekeeping', para. 101.

[79] Sarooshi, 'Authorization of Regional Arrangements', 239.

[80] Ibid., 238. Jean-Marie Guéhenno, however, describes this procedure as 'unwieldy', impeding the ability of peace operations to protect civilians. See his 'Robust Peacekeeping: Building Political Consensus and Strengthening Command and Control', in Robust Peacekeeping: The Politics of Force (New York University Center on International Cooperation, 2009), pp. 7–11 at p. 8.

Behrami v. France, the complainants sought redress for killing and maiming by remnants of unexploded cluster bombs in Kosovo.[81] The families sued the sending states of the NATO forces that were part of KFOR, which was authorized as the peace force under UN Security Council resolution 1244 and which were responsible for the areas in which the cluster bombs were located.[82] The European Court of Human Rights held the complaints to be inadmissible since the actions or omissions complained of could not be attributed to the states in question but only to the UN (not even to NATO). In arriving at its controversial conclusion, the Court was satisfied by the fact that NATO/KFOR was required to submit regular reports to the Security Council and that the Security Council could revoke its authorization of the entire operation, in order to find that the Security Council had ultimate authority and control over KFOR.[83] Although it does not affect the legal analysis, the low level of control the Court sought for a valid delegation of Security Council powers acts as a powerful disincentive in terms of policy for supporting the possibility of delegation of a peace operation to a PMSC.

Presumably in the case of a delegation to a PMSC, the Secretary-General would, at a minimum, have to retain a high level of control over the exercise of force. Admittedly, in delegations or authorizations to regional organizations, maintenance of control is sometimes a tricky matter since it must be reconciled with potentially competing provisions in the regional organization's constitution. However, since for a PMSC there is no competing constitutional authority (i.e. to the delegated organization, in the case of NATO), such control should be decisive as to the use of force.[84]

This analysis suggests that the Security Council may have the authority in limited circumstances to delegate the conduct of a peace operation, under the careful control of the Secretary-General and/or Security

---

[81] *Behrami v. France and Saramati v. Norway* (App nos 71412/01 and 78166/01) ECHR 2 May 2007 (Grand Chamber).

[82] To clarify: the complainants were not suing NATO for having dropped the cluster bombs in the first place, but for the fact that once French forces formed part of the peace operation on the ground, they failed to sufficiently warn the local population of their existence and location in the area for which they were responsible.

[83] *Behrami v. France and Saramati v. Norway* (App nos 71412/01 and 78166/01) ECHR 2 May 2007 (Grand Chamber) paras 128–131, 135, 138, 140. For discussion of this controversial conclusion, see Krieger, 'Credibility Gap'; P. Bodeau-Livinec, G. Buzzini and S. Villalpando, Case comment in 'International Decisions' (2008) 102 *AJIL* 323–331, *inter alia*.

[84] This is independent of the adequacy of the Secretary-General's military decision-making capacity.

Council and subject to the respect of the peacekeeping principles discussed above, to a PMSC. Several important caveats to this conclusion are worth mentioning, however. First, the type of peace operations in which states or regional organizations are authorized to use force beyond that required for self-defence remain controversial. In 1995, then Secretary-General Boutros-Ghali expressed his belief that it was 'desirable in the long term that the United Nations develop...a capacity' to engage in UN-commanded and -controlled enforcement actions, even on a limited scale.[85] In the 2000 Brahimi report, the Panel again recommended ensuring a capacity for 'robust' peacekeeping.[86] However, the Secretary-General was at pains to emphasize that even such robust operations were only those that already operated with the consent of the parties, and the powers in question were only meant to deal with spoilers and criminals.[87] The likelihood that the Security Council would delegate or authorize an already controversial form of peacekeeping to an equally controversial non-state actor may thus be regarded as slim.

5.4   Article 43 and/or the Establishment of a Standby UN Force Composed of PMSCs

Under Article 43 of the UN Charter, member states were supposed to conclude agreements with the Security Council allowing their armed forces (or certain elements of them) to be used by the Security Council 'on its call'.[88] That is to say, the Security Council was to have forces at its disposal, forces that it could compel to take action in order to fulfil its obligations with regard to maintaining international peace and security. However, member states never agreed to put their national armed forces at the beck and call of the Security Council; as a consequence, peacekeeping evolved in an ad hoc manner, and, as noted above, enforcement actions have been carried out by states or regional organizations under an authorization by the Security Council.[89] Although standby agreements have

---

[85] UN Secretary-General, 'Supplement to An Agenda for Peace: Position Paper of the Secretary-General on the Occasion of the 50th Anniversary of the United Nations' (3 January 1995), UN Doc A/50/60–S/1995/1, para. 77.

[86] Brahimi Report (above, note 55), paras 48–55.

[87] Durch et al., 'The Brahimi Report at Thirty (Months)', 9.

[88] Under Article 44, the Security Council is obliged to invite member states not already represented on the Security Council to attend meetings and participate in decisions concerning deployment of those states' forces. A Military Staff Committee set up under Article 47 was to oversee operations.

[89] On the latter, Blokker, 'Is the Authorization Authorized?', 541–568. See also A. Roberts, 'Proposals for UN Standing Forces: A Critical History', in V. Lowe et al. (eds.), *The United*

been concluded through various fora in order to improve the cumbersome and slow procedure of putting together peacekeeping forces on an ad hoc and completely voluntary basis, there remains no standing force available to the Security Council.[90] Not surprisingly, therefore, there have been calls to use private military and security companies as the UN Security Council's standing army, in lieu of Article 43 forces.[91] This section will explore whether the establishment of such forces is a legal possibility.

As is evident from the above, the initial intention was that UN forces under Article 43 would be comprised of units of state armed forces. This is indeed the letter of Article 43, which states,

1. All Members of the United Nations, in order to contribute to the maintenance of international peace and security, undertake to make available to the Security Council, on its call and in accordance with a special agreement or agreements, armed forces, assistance, and facilities, including rights of passage, necessary for the purpose of maintaining international peace and security.
2. Such agreement or agreements shall govern the numbers and types of forces, their degree of readiness and general location, and the nature of the facilities and assistance to be provided.
3. ...

The article clearly calls for member state armed forces. However, as early as 1951 and continuing through the 1990s, there have been calls for a standing force composed of 'volunteers' or individually recruited personnel, as opposed to national troop contributions. The first of these was proposed by then Secretary-General Trygve Lie, to be made up of some 50,000 volunteers.[92] Lie had called for (but quickly abandoned) the establishment of a UN Volunteer Reserve force in 1951.[93] Sohn argued in 1958 that

---

Nations Security Council and War (Oxford: Oxford University Press, 2008), pp. 99–130. As a point of interest, under the official document of the repertory of practice of the UN Security Council, discussions and decisions relating to troop contributions to UN peacekeeping operations are described under Article 43.

[90] See Roberts, 'Proposals for UN Standing Forces', for an excellent overview of the proposals through the decades.

[91] The most recent of these is Jared Genser and Clare Garvie, 'Contracting for Stability: The Potential Use of Private Military Contractors as a United Nations Rapid-Reaction Force' (2015) 16 *CJIL* 439–481; see also Malcolm Patterson, 'A Corporate Alternative to United Nations *ad hoc* Military Deployments' (2008) 13 *J Conflict and Security L* 215–231. It should be noted, however, that the UN itself appears to be less enthusiastic about the need to establish standing forces through Article 43 or any other capacity: Roberts, 'Proposals for UN Standing Forces', 120, argues the notion is in decline in comparison with 1995.

[92] Roberts, 'Proposals for UN Standing Forces', 103.   [93] Ibid.

Article 42 of the UN Charter provides a legal basis for the Security Council to establish UN Forces composed of units other than national forces.[94] Yet another force was proposed in 1993 by Sir Brian Urquhart.[95] In 1995, the Netherlands proposed the creation of 'a permanent, rapidly deployable brigade at the service of the Security Council' with 'personnel recruited on an individual basis'.[96] Although convincing criticism may be made of the ultimate utility of any standing force (be it comprised of national forces or volunteers),[97] the crux of the matter for this analysis is whether it is within the powers of the Security Council to establish its own force using exclusively private military and security companies.

The International Court of Justice held in the *Certain Expenses* case that '[t]here is nothing in the text of Article 43 which would limit the discretion of the Security Council in negotiating' Article 43 agreements.[98] The Court focussed in particular on the right of states and the Security Council to insist on and accept various permutations and combinations in terms of bearing the cost of furnishing, transporting and equipping such forces, but arguably the discretionary power – barring contravention of *jus cogens* – is essentially unlimited.[99] The Court's assertion is not necessarily tantamount to saying the Security Council has carte blanche to establish such forces unilaterally, since the negotiation and agreement between states implies a maintenance of a certain check on its powers. Nonetheless, the Court refuses to accept a limitation on the Security Council's power to act in the face of a threat to international peace and security, proclaiming, 'It cannot be said that the Charter has left the Security Council impotent in the face of an emergency situation when agreements under Article 43 have not been concluded.'[100] This affirms the Security Council may indeed be creative when it comes to maintaining international peace and security.

---

[94] L.B. Sohn, 'The Authority of the United Nations to Establish and Maintain a Permanent United Nations Force' (1958) 52 *AJIL* 229–240 at 230.

[95] B. Urquhart, 'For a UN Volunteer Military Force', *New York Review of Books*, vol. 40 (10 June 1993).

[96] Netherlands non-paper for a UN Rapid Deployment Brigade, cited in Roberts 'Proposals for UN Standing Forces', 117.

[97] Roberts, 'Proposals for UN Standing Forces', 125–130. Diehl argues that the creation of a permanent peacekeeping force is not a 'panacea' to solve all problems relating to peacekeeping and its ad hoc methods. P. Diehl, *International Peacekeeping* (Johns Hopkins University Press, 1993), pp. 117–119. See also P. Diehl, *Peace Operations* (Cambridge: Polity, 2008), pp. 92–98. Diehl never canvasses the possibility of a private standing force.

[98] *Certain Expenses* (Advisory Opinion) [1962] ICJ Rep 151 at 166.   [99] Ibid.

[100] *Certain Expenses* (Advisory Opinion) [1962] ICJ Rep 151 at 167.

The implied powers doctrine discussed above affirms that the Security Council is not limited to using only the kinds of forces enumerated in Chapter VII.[101] In that case, what limits, if any, are there on the forces it may create? Sohn argues that 'it seems possible to envisage the establishment and use of a U.N. Force by the Security Council, and the only obstacle to the use of this method is the requirement of unanimity of the permanent members of the Security Council for any such action.'[102] Implicitly, then, according to Sohn, as long as the force could pass muster in the Security Council, the Council is free to compose it as it sees fit. Sohn further argued that the Secretary General could establish a force under Article 97 within the Secretariat, and thought that mechanism to be 'admirably suited to recruitment of volunteers for such a Force'.[103] He envisioned it working as follows:

> If the General Assembly were willing to make the necessary financial appropriations, the Secretary General could recruit as many individuals as the Assembly should authorize, provide for their training as military units of the Secretariat, and send them on such missions as the Assembly might direct.[104]

The only limitations Sohn foresees as to the Secretary-General's recruiting capability are in terms of numbers.

The most comprehensive recent paper (from a legal perspective) proposing the use of PMSCs as a standby force canvasses some of the same possibilities as Sohn[105] but settles on Chapter VII as the ideal source of authority for the Security Council's power to 'raise and maintain a contract force'.[106] Specifically, that paper proposes that the UN Security Council should create a 'Contractor Directorate' as a subsidiary body under Article 29, which would be empowered to assess tenders submitted by PMSCs and also run a to-be-created UN criminal justice system in order to exercise discipline over the contractors.[107] The author argues that

---

[101] *Reparation for Injuries Suffered in the Service of the United Nations* (Advisory Opinion) [1949] ICJ Rep 174 at 180.

[102] Sohn, 'Authority of the UN', 231.   [103] Ibid., 235.

[104] In this regard Sohn was anticipating the General Assembly would act pursuant to the Uniting for Peace Resolution, as he had before him the very recent example of UNEF, which was set up under that procedure. See ibid., at 235.

[105] Patterson, 'A Corporate Alternative', 222. Patterson does not attribute these ideas to Sohn, although he does refer to his article later on.

[106] Ibid., 222–223.

[107] Ibid., 223ff. Patterson (at 227) argues that a UN criminal justice system is necessary because states may wish to distance themselves from their citizens who as individuals participate in risky UN operations.

enabling PMSC employees to participate in UN operations in this manner may provide the same opportunity to those individuals as lauded by Sir Brian Urquhart in his call for volunteers: that it 'could be an "... inspiring new dimension for national military service".[108]

The refrain throughout earlier proposals for such a volunteer force is for recruitment of 'individuals'. This word is used in contradistinction, certainly, to the national 'units' of state armed forces. But does it have any further significance? And does the fact that private military and security companies are for-profit ventures affect their employability in this context, in contrast to individual 'volunteers', who are presumably intending to be paid, but not to be a profitable business? As the creation of a standing UN force as a subsidiary body of the Security Council is the most likely scenario, the following will consider whether there are limits in this respect.

First is the question of the general matter of the UN Security Council's ability to establish its own, non-state-based force. In the 1960s, an early authority on UN peace operations, D.W. Bowett, asserted, 'Nothing in the Charter specifically precludes the establishment of a permanent Force, and, as we have seen, both the Assembly and the Security Council have powers wide enough to enable them to establish a permanent Force as a subsidiary organ for purposes necessary to the maintenance of international peace and security.'[109] The notion that a permanent standing force is both within the purview of the Security Council and desirable has remained present throughout the decades since. The strongest proponents for such a force argue that it could allow the Security Council to act when states are reluctant to put their national forces in harm's way, despite evident catastrophic consequences if nothing is done – for example, in Rwanda.[110] The Security Council could thus fulfil its primary function, maintaining international peace and security. But is the fact that nothing in the Charter specifically precludes it sufficient to find that it is lawful? In this vein, one may enquire whether the notion that the Security Council may, in effect, create its own army somehow contradicts the spirit of the Charter and its need to rely on the cooperation of member states when it comes to enforcement action or peacekeeping. Understanding the reasons for the failure to conclude Article 43 agreements with states could

---

[108] Ibid., 226, note 54.

[109] D.W. Bowett, *United Nations Forces: A Legal Study of United Nations Practice* (London: Stevens, 1964), p. 327.

[110] Roberts, 'Proposals for UN Standing Forces', 113–114; Robert Siekmann, 'Political and Legal Aspects of a Directly Recruited Permanent UN Force' (1995) *Intl Peacekeeping* (July) 91–93.

provide insight for the state–UN balance of power argument. The predominant reason given is that states wish to retain control over how their national forces would be used; another is that states hesitate to give the UN Security Council the means to carry out its enforcement action with a high degree of independence. The technical reason is that the UN Military Staff Committee was unable to come up with terms for the Article 43 agreements acceptable to all five permanent members of the Security Council such that no agreements could be concluded.[111] Areas of disagreement included how many troops each permanent member of the Security Council would have to provide, where the forces would be stationed and what the overall strength of the force would be.[112] Coupled with the fact that some states have supported proposals for a standing force composed of individually recruited members,[113] these rather prosaic reasons for failure to provide the Security Council with its own force do little to reinforce a notion that a standing force must necessarily be comprised of national armed forces.[114] In this regard, the obligation to respect the general principle of good faith would play an important role in guiding the Security Council.

On a more technical legal analysis, the law on subsidiary organs appears to permit the staffing of a stand-by force through recruitment of PMSCs. The UN Charter provides no definition of subsidiary organs. Moreover, subsidiary organs do not necessarily have to be composed exclusively of member states, but may be comprised of individuals 'in their personal capacity'.[115] There are at least four preconditions for the lawful establishment of a subsidiary organ: it must be established and under the control of a UN principal organ; its establishment must 'not violate the delimitation of Charter powers between the principal organs'; and the subsidiary organ must possess 'a certain degree of independence from its principal

---

[111] See Frowein and Krisch, 'Article 42', 762–763, para. 9.   [112] Ibid.

[113] In addition to the Dutch proposal, the Canadian government backed a proposal in the 1990s for a stand-by force that retained the possibility for an individually recruited force. See Roberts 'Proposals for UN Standing Forces', 118–119.

[114] Admittedly, the Brahimi Report laments that '[m]any Member States have argued against the establishment of a standing United Nations army or police force ... ' (above, note 55), para. 85. However, concerns appear to be related to costs, to where the force would be stationed and to what laws would apply to it. See Kofi Annan's statement, cited in Roberts, 'Proposals for UN Standing Forces', 121. See also James Rossman, 'Article 43: Arming the United Nations Security Council' (1994–1995) 27 NYUJILP 227–263, especially at 242ff. ('Is there a political will for a U.N. army?').

[115] Sarooshi, 'The Legal Framework Governing United Nations Subsidiary Organs' (1996) 67 British Ybk Intl L 413–478 at 415–416. Examples include the international criminal tribunals, which are not staffed by contingents sent by states but by individuals hired directly by the tribunal.

organ'.[116] Finally, according to Sarooshi, 'What will... preclude the lawful establishment of a subsidiary organ is if the principal organ does not possess the express or implied power under the Charter to establish a subsidiary organ to perform certain functions in the area.'[117] It is clear that peacekeeping forces are subsidiary organs (usually of the Security Council).[118] Nothing in the foregoing would seem to impede the Security Council from establishing a subsidiary organ comprising a standing force comprised exclusively of PMSCs.

The principle that the principal organ exercises authority and control over its subsidiary bodies entails the consequence that 'the principal organ possesses the competence to determine the membership, structure, mandate and duration of existence of its subsidiary organ'.[119] This means that the Security Council has the power to create a subsidiary body, staffed by either individually hired professionals or units, of either permanent or temporary duration, and to set the terms of reference of such a body.

Again, all of the proposals above refer to the recruitment of individuals, whereas staffing a permanent force with PMSCs would involve the interposition of a corporate structure. This has the potential to weaken the control of the Security Council over the quality of individuals recruited. However, there is no reason why, on purely legal grounds, recruitment of volunteers would necessarily have to occur on an individual basis rather than through a corporate structure. Indeed, some mechanism of 'quality control' for recruiting standards could be agreed with a PMSC. Thus, unpalatable as it may seem for some, there would appear to be no prima facie impediment to the Security Council deciding that a for-profit company is the 'member' of its subsidiary organ.[120] Thus, subject to the discussion above on principles of peacekeeping, and the discussion below on the responsibility to discipline and punish peacekeepers who commit crimes, this analysis suggests that the Security Council has the competence to create a subsidiary organ constituting a standing force comprised of one or more PMSCs.

5.5 'Through the back door'

The final way we may see the UN incorporating PMSCs as peacekeepers is through an ad hoc mechanism such as the creation of a static guard force.

---

[116] Ibid., 416–417.   [117] Ibid., 431.
[118] As widely accepted and noted by Sarooshi, ibid., 436.   [119] Ibid., 448–449.
[120] See the discussion in Cameron and Chetail, *Privatizing War*, pp. 66–80 and 426–429, regarding mercenaries, etc. Member states may quibble with footing a bill for a for-profit company, however.

In the recent cases we have seen, such a guard force has been created by the UN Security Council based on a recommendation by the Secretary-General.[121] At first sight, such a force does not appear to fall within any of the categories discussed above – it is not a 'regular' troop contingent of a state, nor does it seem to be an Article 43 force as the ambit of its activities is limited to security guarding for UN people, places and activities. However, insofar as such security guarding could well be carried out by members of a national troop contingent participating in the peace operation, and given that it is an armed force component of a peace operation created by the Security Council, such guard units could be construed as a manifestation of any of the above.

5.6 Conclusion

This analysis demonstrates that there are no clear impediments in the legal framework governing the UN Security Council and Secretary-General in the exercise of their powers for PMSC personnel to be used as the military contingent in a UN peace operation. It is one step away from the existing arrangement by which the United States sends its CIVPOL via PMSCs. That being said, the issue of combatant status for the military component of the peacekeeping force is a significant cause for concern.

To the extent that PMSCs are used as security guards in peace operations where the force is engaged as combatants, however, the role of acting as part of the military component of a peace operation may already have been conferred on them. In particular, this may be the case at present in MONUSCO with its Intervention Brigade and large PMSC presence. Importantly, PMSCs were not vested with that role via any of the possible methods described above. The manner in which they may nonetheless be de facto peacekeepers – to a certain extent – shows that apparently subtle changes in the UN's policy framework regarding peace operations may have significant and perhaps unintended consequences.

---

[121] See UN Secretary-General, 'Letter Dated 21 November 2013 from the Secretary-General Addressed to the President of the Security Council', 27 November 2013, UN Doc S/2013/704 (for UNSMIL). See also similar letter dated 29 October 2013 (BINUCA) UN Doc S/2013/636; UN Secretary-General, 'Letter Dated 14 October 2013 from the Secretary-General Addressed to the President of the Security Council', 14 October 2013, UN Doc 2013/606.

6

The Law Applicable to Peace Operations

Understandably, much of the early jurisprudence and scholarship on international organizations focused on the *powers* of alternative subjects of international law as opposed to the obligations binding on those subjects.[1] The recent work of the ILC to define the rules for enforcing the responsibility of international organizations presupposes the existence of limits and obligations on those powers but does little to define them.[2] One authority on the law on international organizations contends that 'international organizations are subject to international law, but it remains unclear which international law, and why: there is no plausible theory of obligation.'[3]

This chapter will show that UN peace operations forces may be involved in armed conflict and, if so, international humanitarian law applies to them. Forces involved in peace operations and the UN itself may be bound by international humanitarian law and international human rights law. In peace operations where no armed conflict is occurring, the primary legal framework will be international human rights law. The applicability of these two bodies of law must be taken into account when assessing the implications of using PMSCs in peace operations, especially when they may be called on to use force in those roles.

---

[1] Consider, for example, the doctrine of implied powers to create peacekeeping operations developed by the ICJ in the *Certain Expenses* (Advisory Opinion) [1962] ICJ Rep 151.

[2] ILC, 'Report of the International Law Commission on the Work of Its 63rd Session' (2011) UN Doc A/66/10. The ILC, 'Report of the International Law Commission on the Work of Its Fifty-fifth Session', 5 May–6 June and 7 July–8 August 2003 UN Doc. A/58/10), para. 44 indicates that the responsibility of international organizations was first identified as an issue in 1963. See also International Law Association, *Committee on Accountability of International Organisations, Final Report* (Berlin Conference, 2004), p. 23.

[3] Jan Klabbers, 'The Paradox of International Institutional Law' (2008) 5 *Intl Org L Rev* 151–173 at 165.

6.1 International Humanitarian Law Applies to Peace Operations

In the context of peacekeeping, several factors have led to confusion as to whether peacekeepers may be involved in armed conflicts and when international humanitarian law applies. First, some appear to forget that the strict separation between *ius ad bellum* and *ius in bello* applies also in the context of UN operations. Second, there have been questions as to whether and how the UN and peacekeeping forces can be bound by IHL. In addition, treaty rules designed to protect peacekeepers from attack have caused confusion as to the threshold of the applicability of IHL. This chapter will address each of those issues in turn. The analysis here should be considered in light of the assessment in Chapter 10 on self-defence in peace operations and armed conflict.[4]

6.1.1 Separation of ius ad bellum and ius in bello

Although within the doctrine of peacekeeping itself there may be distinctions between the different types of operations (peacekeeping, peace enforcement, robust peacekeeping, etc.), those categories are immaterial to the factual determination of whether a peacekeeping operation is involved in an armed conflict and subject to IHL. This flows from the strict separation between the *ius ad bellum* and the *ius in bello*, a fundamental principle that underpins the application of IHL. The separation between *ius ad bellum* and *ius in bello* entails that the legal basis for becoming engaged in an armed conflict – i.e., whether the resort to armed force was lawful or not – is completely irrelevant for the application of IHL. Thus, the fact that an entity becomes involved in an armed conflict with the sole aim of maintaining international peace and security does not influence whether a situation may be described as an armed conflict and whether IHL applies to it. It does not matter whether the UN Security Council adopted a mandate under Chapter VII, nor does it matter, for the purposes of determining whether there is an armed conflict, whether the peacekeeping forces were acting in accordance with or beyond the limits of that mandate.[5] What counts are the facts on the ground. This also

---

[4] See below, Chapter 10.

[5] Keiichiro Okimoto points out that the *jus ad bellum* constraints placed on the peacekeeping force in its mandate continue to govern and set limits on its actions during the mission – in other words, what the force may do, in relation to whom, and where. He also points out that IHL sets additional limits on how a force may carry out those obligations. What he neglects to say, however, is that even if a UN (or other) force acts beyond the scope of the mandate set for it by the Security Council, if those acts occur within an armed conflict, IHL will still

extends to the determination of who may be a party to the conflict.[6] That is to say, even though the United Nations does not see itself as warmongering and even though it is supposed to act impartially in peace operations, those factors are extraneous to and not relevant for a determination as to whether it or its forces actually become party to a conflict.

6.1.2   Peacekeeping Forces Are Bound by IHL

An additional factor that has in the past skewed the debate as to whether a peacekeeping force is involved in an armed conflict is the assertion that the UN is not and cannot be bound by IHL (at least as treaty law). This debate may have repercussions when it comes to the possibility of PMSCs as peacekeepers and therefore will be canvassed here. From the outset of peacekeeping operations, there has been resistance on the part of the UN to the notion that peacekeeping forces are bound by international humanitarian law. Indeed, the public debate over this question between the International Committee of the Red Cross (ICRC) and the UN is well documented.[7] For decades, the UN accepted only that its forces were bound by the 'principles and spirit' of IHL, arguing, inter alia, that as the UN could not become a party to the Geneva Conventions, it could not be legally bound by them.[8] In addition, it pointed to practical problems for a non-state body to implement the full complement of obligations, such as the absence of a criminal justice system.[9] The ICRC argued that at the very least, states contributing forces to the operations continued to be bound by

---

govern them. See Okimoto, *The Distinction and Relationship between* Jus ad Bellum *and* Jus in Bello (Oxford: Hart Publishing, 2011), pp. 164–239.

[6] Marten Zwanenburg makes the specific point that the acknowledgement of the strict separation of *ius ad bellum* and *ius in bello* also relates to the acceptance that the UN can in fact become a party to a conflict. See Zwanenburg, 'International Organisations vs Troops Contributing Countries: Which Should Be Considered as the Party to an Armed Conflict During Peace Operations?' (2012) *Collegium* 23–28 at 25.

[7] See for example Antoine Bouvier, '"Convention on the Safety of United Nations and Associated Personnel": Presentation and Analysis' (1995) 35 *IRRC* 638–666; Umesh Palwankar, 'Applicability of International Humanitarian Law to United Nations Peacekeeping Forces' (1993 (May June)) *IRRC* 227–240; Robert Kolb, *Droit humanitaire et operations de paix internationales*, 2nd edn (Brussels: Bruylant, 2006), pp. 7–12; Jean d'Aspremont and Jérôme de Hemptinne, *Droit international humanitaire* (Paris: Pedone, 2012), pp. 157–164; Daphna Shraga, 'The United Nations as an Actor Bound by International Humanitarian Law' (1998) 5 *Intl Peacekeeping* 64–81, especially at 66–67.

[8] Shraga, 'The United Nations as an Actor', 67.

[9] UN Office of Legal Affairs, 'Question of the Possible Accession of Intergovernmental Organizations to the Geneva Conventions for the Protection of War Victims: Memorandum to the Under-Secretary-General for Special Political Affairs' (1972) *UN Juridical YB* (Part II, Chapter VI) 153–154 (15 June 1972).

their own treaty obligations, which, by virtue of Article 1 common to the four Geneva Conventions, they also had to respect in the context of peace-keeping operations involving armed conflicts.[10] The obligation to respect IHL was written into the Model Agreement for troop contributions and also into Status of Forces Agreements (SOFAs), while the UN assumed the obligation to ensure that the force would respect the 'principles and spirit' of IHL.[11]

Meyrowitz points out that the ability of the UN itself to be bound by IHL is particularly relevant to the scenario in which members of the peace-keeping force are individually recruited.[12] He argues that the mere fact that the UN has international legal personality does not mean that it is bound by all the rights and duties in international law; however, he observes that IHL has many rules that are aimed at non-state actors and that are designed to be implementable even without the benefit of a state struc-ture. He argues that the solution comes from within IHL itself, claiming that when a new 'person' under international law participates in an inter-national armed conflict governed by the law of war, it is immediately given the capacity by that law to have rights and obligations under the *ius in bello*. The question as to whether that person is legally or materially organized to carry out all of those rights and obligations is a secondary matter, he concludes.[13] Another scholar argues that the UN is bound by IHL as treaty law via its incorporation into Memoranda of Understanding (MOUs) with state troop contributors and SOFAs with host states. Keiichiro Okimoto construes this practice as evidence of third-party acceptance of interna-tional treaty obligations by an international organization.[14] That is, how-ever, a minority view that the UN does not appear to endorse.

---

[10] See the Memorandum sent by Léopold Boissier, ICRC President, to all state parties to the Geneva Conventions and members of the UN reminding them of their obligations. In the memo, Boissier also indicates that the ICRC drew the UN Secretary-General's attention to the need to ensure the Geneva Conventions were applied by UN forces from the first peace operation in 1956. 'L'Application des Conventions de Genève par les forces armées mises à la disposition des nations unies' (1961) 43 *IRRC* 592–594.

[11] See Okimoto, Jus ad Bellum *and* Jus in Bello, pp. 190–191, for a list of the SOFAs and MOUs with a clause stipulating that the UN will ensure that the force will respect the principles and spirit of IHL, as expressed in the 1949 Geneva Conventions and Additional Protocols.

[12] Henri Meyrowitz, *Le principe de l'égalité des belligérants devant le droit de la guerre* (Paris: Pedone, 1970), p. 238, note 181.

[13] Ibid., p. 240.

[14] Okimoto, Jus ad Bellum *and* Jus in Bello, p. 192. He bases his argument on Articles 35 and 36 of the Vienna Convention on the Law of Treaties between States and International Organizations or between International Organizations.

With the adoption of the Secretary-General's Bulletin in 1999 on the Observance by United Nations forces of international humanitarian law, the UN undertook to respect a number of principles and *rules* of IHL.[15] Most of those rules relate to the conduct of hostilities and to the protection of civilians and other persons who are hors de combat, including basic rules on the treatment of detainees. Many argue, in addition, that the UN is bound by customary IHL on the basis of its international legal personality.[16] Of course, states remain obligated to respect all of their obligations under IHL when their forces are participating in peace operations. However, the notion that the extent of IHL norms applicable directly to the United Nations (or accepted by it) is narrower than the full Geneva Conventions could mean that, were the UN to use PMSCs in a peacekeeping operation as members of the force, PMSCs might be bound by a narrower complement of obligations than their counterparts from national contingents.[17]

The basic issue as to the possibility for UN forces engaged in peacekeeping operations to be bound by IHL is thus now relatively settled on a general level. However, questions remain as to precisely when, where, and

[15] UN Secretary-General's Bulletin on the Observance by United Nations Forces of International Humanitarian Law, UN Doc ST/SGB/1999/13, 6 August 1999. D'Aspremont and de Hemptinne, Droit international humanitaire, p. 162, categorize this document as a unilateral engagement on the part of the UN.

[16] See, for example, d'Aspremont and de Hemptinne, *Droit international humanitaire*, pp. 157 and 163. See also Dietrich Schindler, 'United Nations Forces and International Humanitarian Law', in Christophe Swinarski (ed.), *Studies and Essays on International Humanitarian Law and Red Cross Principles in Honour of Jean Pictet* (The Hague: Martinus Nijhoff, 1984), pp. 521–530, especially at 526: 'It is uncontested that the United Nations is bound by the customary rules of IHL when engaged in hostilities.' Okimoto, Jus ad Bellum *and* Jus in Bello, pp. 188–189; Shraga, 'The Secretary-General's Bulletin', 357–377. Richard Glick, 'Lip Service to the Laws of War: Humanitarian Law and United Nations Armed Forces' (1994–1995) 17 *Michigan J Intl L* 53, especially 55–59; Kolb et al., *L'application du droit international humanitaire et des droits de l'homme aux organisations internationales* (Brussels: Bruylant, 2005), pp. 129–143, arguing that there is a direct applicability of the treaty norms (in an adapted form) to the UN. Nigel D. White, 'Institutional Responsibility for Private Military and Security Companies', in F. Francioni and N. Ronzitti (eds.), *War by Contract* (Oxford: Oxford University Press, 2011), pp. 381–395.

[17] On the possible discrepancy between customary norms and treaty norms applicable in non-international armed conflicts, see Vaios Koutroulis, 'International Organisations Involved in Armed Conflict: Material and Geographical Scope of Application of International Humanitarian Law' (2012) *Collegium* 29–40 at 39–40; and on the potential difference between the IHL obligations of international organizations and states involved in peace operations, see Marten Zwanenburg, 'International Organizations vs Troops Contributing Countries', 23–28. Of course, even for states participating in multinational operations, there is no perfect unity of obligations, as not all states are parties to all IHL treaties.

for how long members of peacekeeping forces become engaged as combatants – and thus, bound by IHL and subject to attack by opposing forces – and lose the protection to which civilians are entitled. In addition, there are questions as to which entity becomes the party to the conflict – i.e. the UN or the troop-contributing states. The fact that this area of law remains unsettled makes it difficult to know when and in what situations PMSCs can be used as security guards or in other functions in peace operations without running the risk that they will be likely to be required to directly participate in hostilities.

6.1.3 The Safety Convention Does Not Alter the Threshold for the Applicability of IHL

The essential question here is whether there is a threshold for a peacekeeping force to become party to an armed conflict (or for IHL to apply to peacekeepers) different from the one that applies to 'other' armed conflicts. Since there is a difference in the threshold for international armed conflicts and non-international armed conflicts,[18] the answer to this question is inextricably linked to the classification of conflicts involving peace operations. That issue itself is not without controversy. In addition, it is linked to the threshold ostensibly set by the UN Convention on the Safety of United Nations and Associated Personnel of 1994,[19] which was adopted in the wake of attacks on peacekeepers that had been engaged in operations with robust mandates.

Article 2(2) of that convention says:

> This Convention shall not apply to a United Nations Operation authorized by the Security Council as an enforcement action under Chapter VII of the Charter of the United Nations in which any of the personnel are engaged as combatants against organized armed forces and to which the law of international armed conflict applies.

This means that, for the purposes of the Safety Convention, it is *not* a criminal offence to attack peacekeepers when those cumulative criteria are met.

---

[18] An international armed conflict occurs as soon as a state uses armed force against another state, whereas a certain threshold of violence must be met for a non-international armed conflict to occur.

[19] Convention on the Safety of United Nations and Associated Personnel, 9 December 1994, 2051 UNTS 363, entered into force 15 January 1999. See also the Optional Protocol to the Convention on the Safety of United Nations and Associated Personnel, 8 December 2005, UN Doc A/60/518, entered into force 19 August 2010, which does not change anything in regard to IHL issues discussed here.

Christopher Greenwood has argued that 'the threshold for the application of international humanitarian law is also the ceiling for the application of the Convention.'[20] Put another way, 'conduct is recognised as "military" only and precisely at the point when it ceases to be criminal.'[21] If Greenwood is correct, that would mean that the UN Safety Convention changes the threshold of the application of IHL since that Convention establishes new and different factors that are extraneous to the simple factual assessment of whether peacekeepers are involved in an armed conflict.[22] Under IHL, it would normally be lawful to attack someone who is fighting on behalf of a party to the conflict, regardless of how the operation is created and whether the law of international or non-international armed conflicts applies. The essential question is thus whether the Safety Convention creates a special regime that supersedes the normal rules of international humanitarian law. Indeed, that is not the case, which will be explained below. It is important to understand this debate because it appears to continue to influence UN thinking on the application of IHL to its peacekeepers. As such, clarity on this question is a precondition for knowing in which situations it would be particularly inappropriate to use PMSCs in peace operations, in particular, armed PMSC security guards.

The fact that the exclusion clause set out in the Safety Convention is poorly drafted is admitted even by senior UN legal advisors. In the introductory text to the treaty on the UN's website, Mahnoush Arsanjani acknowledges that Article 2(2) is confusing.[23] She goes on to say that 'the intention was to exclude the application of the Convention in cases where international humanitarian law is applicable [to the peacekeepers].'[24] It is,

---

[20] Christopher Greenwood, 'Scope of Application of Humanitarian Law', in D. Fleck (ed.), *The Handbook of Humanitarian Law in Armed Conflicts* (Oxford: Oxford University Press, 2008), p. 53.

[21] As submitted by Mr Pannick, QC, in *R. v. Ministry of Defence* Ex parte *Walker* [2000] UKHL 6 April 2000.

[22] See Kolb, *Droit humanitaire et opérations depaix internationales*, pp. 29–39, on the various possible thresholds for finding a situation of armed conflict exists, and pp. 35–36, regarding Greenwood and a higher threshold.

[23] She writes, 'The purport of the exclusion clause in paragraph 2 of article 2, however, is not entirely clear and is open to interpretations which may not have been anticipated at the time of the negotiation of the Convention.' Mahnoush Arsanjani, 'Convention on the Safety of United Nations and Associated Personnel', United Nations Audiovisual Library of International Law, http://untreaty.un.org/cod/avl/pdf/ha/csunap/csunap_e.pdf (accessed 14 May 2012), 4. See also the comments by the UN Secretary-General in his report, which in effect acknowledge one of the problems.

[24] Ibid., p. 4 of the PDF document. See also Ola Engdahl, *Protection of Personnel in Peace Operations: The Role of the 'Safety Convention' Against the Background of General International*

however, difficult to interpret the exclusion clause to cover all such situations given the cumulative conditions set out therein.[25] Engdahl points out that the US delegate to the conference adopting the convention insisted that the requirement that the operation be established under Chapter VII of the UN Charter must not be interpreted rigidly, but should be taken as 'merely a reflection of the fact that only such operations are likely to involve UN forces as combatants in international armed conflicts'.[26]

While that may be true, the fact that it is furthermore limited to *international* armed conflicts raises yet another unnecessary hurdle to the applicability of IHL. The UN Secretary-General, in the 'Scope of Legal Protection Under the [Safety] Convention' report, observes,

> The exclusion from the scope of application of the Convention of Chapter VII United Nations operations carried out in situations of international armed conflict, gives rise to the suggestion that enforcement actions carried out in situations of internal armed conflict (UNOSOM II type of operations), are included within the scope of the Convention and subject to its protective regime. It will eventually be for the practice of States or any of the competent national or international jurisdictions, to clearly delineate the distinction between the mutually exclusive regimes of international humanitarian law and the protective regime of the Convention. In the final analysis, it is not the nature of the conflict which should determine the applicability of international humanitarian law or that of the Convention,

Law (Leiden: Martinus Nijhoff, 2007), p. 236, and references therein, including the work of Daphna Shraga. Arsanjani's assertion is not entirely borne out by the preparatory work, however. Indeed, an alternative was proposed that would clearly indicate that the exclusion should not be limited to international armed conflicts; but, the record notes, 'This suggestion gave rise to objections.' 'Report of the Ad Hoc Committee on the Elaboration of an International Convention Dealing with the Safety and Security of United Nations and Associated Personnel', UN Doc. A/49/22 (23 August 1994) 19, para. 14. See also Report of the Ad Hoc Committee on the Work Carried Out During the Period from 28 March to 8 April 1994', UN Doc. A/AC.242/2 (13 April 1994) para. 169.

[25] In fact, Costa Rica, when it acceded to the Convention on 17 October 2000, entered a reservation to this article, 'to the effect that limiting the scope of application of the Convention is contrary to the pacifist thinking of our country and, accordingly, that, in the event of conflicts with the application of the Convention, Costa Rica will, where necessary, give precedence to humanitarian law'. See http://treaties.un.org/pages/ViewDetails.aspx?src=TREATY&mtdsg_no=XVIII-8&chapter=18&lang=en (accessed 20 May 2012).

[26] In particular, it requires that an operation be mandated under a Resolution adopted under Chapter VII of the UN Charter, thus removing from its scope those operations mandated without a Chapter VII resolution. Moreover, it appears to require that the conflict be an *international* armed conflict, whereas most conflicts between peacekeepers and organized armed groups are more appropriately qualified as non-international armed conflicts. Finally, the reference to 'enforcement' action is unhelpful as peacekeeping – in doctrine and practice – has gone through endless permutations and combinations.

but whether in any type of conflict, members of United Nations peacekeeping operations are actively engaged therein as combatants, or are otherwise entitled to the protection given to civilians under the international law of armed conflict.[27]

Although there may be good reasons to support this interpretation, that is not what the text of the Convention says. It remains to be seen whether it can be changed – or indeed whether it has been changed – by subsequent practice.

At the time of the adoption of the Safety Convention, Antoine Bouvier of the ICRC opined that any conflict involving the use of international peacekeepers 'internationalized' the conflict, such that 'those forces should logically be subject to the rules of international humanitarian law applicable in international armed conflicts'.[28] For several decades, the predominant view among doctrinal writers was that the mere fact that it was the UN and UN forces meant that a conflict between peacekeeping forces and any opposing side – be it governmental forces or an organized armed group – had to be classified as an international armed conflict.[29] While some continue to espouse this approach,[30] recently, the ICRC has publicly stated its preferred view that conflicts between UN forces (or those of another international organization) and organized armed groups should rather be classified as non-international in nature.[31] This approach focuses on the nature of the parties to the conflict. When one of the parties is a non-state actor, then the conflict must be classified as non-international in nature. This assessment, however, conceivably entails two complications: (1) as noted above, on a strict reading, such operations may not fall within the scope of the exclusion clause of the Safety Convention, and (2) arguably, in the case of a new conflict developing between the

---

[27] Report of the Secretary-General, 'Scope of Legal Protection Under the Convention on the Safety of United Nations and Associated Personnel', UN Doc A/55/637 (21 November 2000) 9, note 3.

[28] Bouvier, 'UN Safety Convention', 652. A strong proponent of this view is also Glick, 'Lip Service', 81–97.

[29] See Kolb, 'Applicability of International Humanitarian Law to Forces under the Command of an International Organization', in ICRC, Report on the Expert Meeting on Multinational Peace Operations (2004), especially at 62 and references in note 1.

[30] For example, Jaume Saura, 'Lawful Peacekeeping: Applicability of International Humanitarian Law to United Nations Peacekeeping Operations' (2006–2007) 58 Hastings Law Journal 479; Kolb, Droit humanitaire et opérations de paix internationales, pp. 57ff.

[31] ICRC, Commentary on the First Geneva Convention, 2016, commentary on common Article 3, para. 413. See also McCoubrey and White, The Blue Helmets, p. 172.

peacekeeping force and an organized armed group, the threshold must be that relating to the existence of a non-international armed conflict.

The fact that the Safety Convention must be interpreted in such a way as to be consistent with IHL is evident in the text of the convention itself. Indeed, Article 20(1) of that convention is a savings clause, which stipulates that nothing in the convention affects 'the applicability of international humanitarian law ... or the responsibility of [UN and associated personnel] to respect such law'. As such, Jaume Saura argues convincingly that IHL applies as usual on its own terms including to a conflict involving a UN peacekeeping force. All the Safety Convention does is set up a specific rule on the protection of peacekeepers under certain circumstances.[32] The problem, then, is in relation to the viability of the rule itself in relation to IHL. According to Saura's interpretation, the worst sin of the rule is that it creates (or at least maintains) an inequality of belligerents in that it is unlawful for armed groups to attack peacekeepers against whom they are engaged in an armed conflict but not unlawful for the peacekeepers to attack the members of the armed group (as long as it is according to their mandate).[33] Recent practice fully sustains this interpretation. In particular, the UN Security Council, while mandating all of the forces in MONUSCO to use all necessary measures to neutralize armed groups, has also imposed sanctions on individuals who attack MONUSCO.[34] The Security Council clearly considers attacks on MONUSCO to violate applicable international law, even though it has authorized and encouraged all parts of the force – and not just the Intervention Brigade – to use lethal force against the armed groups.[35] Admittedly, this inequality of belligerents exists anyway in non-international armed conflicts, as it is always the case that it is a domestic crime for a person to kill a member of a state's security forces. A provision in Protocol II has attempted to soften this inequality by making a plea for the widest possible amnesty for fighters who have respected IHL while fighting.[36] Arguably, by making it an international crime to attack peacekeepers, the Safety Convention

---

[32] Saura, 'Lawful Peacekeeping', 518–519.

[33] Saura admits this shortcoming but does not see it as a significant problem. Perhaps this is also due to the fact that his perception of the extent of the gap of acts that would not be excluded from the Safety Convention is narrower than mine as he subscribes to the theory that the involvement of UN peacekeeping forces 'internationalizes' a conflict and therefore IHL of IAC would apply, thereby eliminating another hurdle.

[34] UNSC Resolution 2136 (2014) (30 January 2014), paras 3 and 4(i).

[35] UNSC Resolution 2147(2014) (28 March 2014), paras 2 and 17.

[36] Article 6(5) AP II. Henckaerts and Doswald-Beck consider this rule to be customary and applicable in non-international armed conflicts.

exacerbates the existing imbalance. Saura admits to the inequality of belligerents, but defends it, stating that peacekeepers 'are worthy of special treatment even if they engage in the use of armed force',[37] relying essentially on consent and the limited use of force to justify his interpretation. Implicitly, he also relies on impartiality since he asserts they are not 'warring parties'. These factors, however, relate primarily to *ius ad bellum* issues.[38] That being said, Saura's argument regarding the fact that the Safety Convention does not alter the threshold of applicability of IHL is correct.

In addition, the notion that the regime protecting peacekeepers does not affect the threshold of application of IHL is supported by the crime of attacking peacekeepers as set out in the Rome Statute only four years later. Under that statute, '[i]ntentionally directing attacks against personnel, installations, material, units or vehicles involved in a humanitarian assistance or peacekeeping mission in accordance with the Charter of the United Nations, as long as they are entitled to the protection given to civilians or civilian objects under the international law of armed conflict' is a war crime in both international and non-international armed conflicts.[39] This provision therefore anticipates that peacekeepers may become direct participants in hostilities in armed conflicts in the context of the peacekeeping missions in which they are deployed, and does not set criteria extraneous to IHL for that analysis. The Secretary-General's Bulletin is similar, in that it stipulates that it applies (such that the IHL rules in it apply) 'to United Nations forces when in situations of armed conflict they are actively engaged therein as combatants, to the extent and for the duration of their engagement'.[40] Even so, these formulations leave open the tricky – but essential – question as to when and under what circumstances peacekeepers are entitled to the protection given to civilians. Or, conversely, for the purposes of this analysis, when are they engaged as combatants? This assessment will be provided below in Part III.[41]

International humanitarian law applies to peace operations forces via the obligations of their sending states and based on the law that applies

---

[37] Saura, 'Lawful Peacekeeping', 520.

[38] There is frequently an insidious intermixing of *ius ad bellum* with *ius in bello* when assessing peacekeeping.

[39] Article 8(2)(b)(iii) and 8(2)(e)(iii) of the Rome Statute. This has also been found to be a rule of customary international humanitarian law. See Henckaerts and Doswald-Beck, *Customary IHL*, Rule 33.

[40] UN Secretary General, 'Bulletin on the Observance by United Nations Forces of International Humanitarian Law', UN Doc ST/SGB/1999/13 (6 August 1999), section 1.

[41] See in particular Chapters 9 and 10.

to the UN itself when carrying out such operations. This means that any decision on the use of PMSCs in such operations must take into account the possibility that peacekeepers themselves may be combatants or fighters in an armed conflict.

6.2   International Human Rights Law Binds the UN During Peace Operations

There are a number of theories postulating that international human rights obligations are binding on international organizations and, at the very least, on the United Nations. The most frequently advanced theory is simply that customary law of international human rights binds international organizations.[42] However, there remains a degree of uncertainty over the content of the resulting substantive obligations for international organizations. Furthermore, not all agree that customary international law is equally binding on all subjects. A variation on that theory is the argument that the customary law of the organization itself renders human rights obligations applicable. This argument tends to be fortified by and difficult to distinguish from arguments that the UN Charter itself and/or the constitution of the organization serves as the primary legal basis for human rights obligations binding on the UN.[43] In this vein, in addition to the powers and explicit obligations of the organization set down in its 'constitution', some argue that organizations have implied obligations that go along with their implied powers.[44] Another theory is that international obligations flow from the sheer existence of

---

[42] Kolb et al., *L'application du droit international humanitaire et des droits de l'homme aux organisations internationales*, pp. 250ff. N. White and D. Klaasen, 'An Emerging Legal Regime?', in N. White and D. Klaasen (eds.), *The UN, Human Rights and Post-conflict Situations* (Manchester University Press, 2005), p. 7. While it may be uncontroversial that obligations flowing from customary law or general principle 'can' apply to international organizations, the question is, which ones *do* apply? In which circumstances? White, observing that 'once it is accepted that organizations legitimately exercise a wide range of powers and functions', agrees with Gaja that it is 'likely that the organization will have acquired obligations under international law in relation to those functions'. White, 'Institutional Responsibility', 386. These carefully worded affirmations do not yet answer the question of which obligations apply, or provide a method to determine which ones apply.

[43] Erika de Wet, *The Chapter VII Powers of the United Nations Security Council* (Oxford: Hart Publishing, 2004), pp. 320 and 198–204. Other international organizations administering territory, such as the European Union in Bosnia, obviously cannot be bound by the UN Charter, but may be bound to respect human rights through their own constitutive instruments.

[44] Gugliemo Verdirame, *Who Guards the Guardians?* (Cambridge: Cambridge University Press, 2011), pp. 73–82.

international legal personality.[45] Third, a conscious move away from the subject-centred approach to international law leads a prominent thinker on international human rights law to argue that the human rights obligations binding on an actor on the international plane depend on that actor's *'capacity... to bear those obligations'.*[46] A fourth approach holds that, although international organizations are not parties to international human rights treaties, they are nonetheless bound through the conventional obligations of their member states.[47] Alternatively, one may look to the specific instruments creating the administration/peace operation and the regulations passed by the administration itself where one exists.[48] Finally, some international human rights bodies are of the view that any entity exercising authority over a territory is bound by the obligations existing for that territory and thus by human rights treaties binding the territory.[49] That approach is closely linked to the theory that holds that the acts of civil servants of international organizations are simultaneously the acts of local government authorities and therefore must be bound by the international legal obligations of the organization *and* by at least some laws of the national government.[50] The argument has been made convincingly that the organization must be bound by the laws applicable in the territory – and especially international human rights law – where it in effect replaces the government.[51]

---

[45] Ibid., pp. 70–73.

[46] Andrew Clapham, *Human Rights Obligations of Non-state Actors* (Oxford: Oxford University Press, 2006), pp. 69, 87. Emphasis added.

[47] Kolb et al., *L'application du droit international humanitaire et des droits de l'homme aux organisations internationales*, p. 242. See also Verdirame, *Guardians*, pp. 86–88.

[48] For example, M. Brand, 'Effective Human Rights Protection When the UN "Becomes the State": Lessons from UNMIK', in N. White and D. Klaasen (eds.), *The UN, Human Rights and Post-conflict Situations* (Manchester University Press, 2005), p. 347.

[49] Human Rights Committee, Summary Record of the 2383rd, 2384th, and 2385th meeting (CCPR/C/SR.2383.Add.1, CCPR/C/SR.2384, CCPR/C/SR.2385), 19–20 July 2006.

[50] R. Wilde, 'International Territorial Administration and Human Rights', in White and Klaasen (eds.), *The UN, Human Rights and Post-Conflict Situations*, pp. 167–169. See also Dieter Fleck, 'The Legal Status of Personnel Involved in United Nations Peace Operations' (2013) 95 *IRRC* 613 at 632. However, the Secretary-General's Bulletin on the Observance by UN forces of IHL is at best ambiguous as to whether forces are bound by the national laws other than those of the troop-contributing state. 'The present provisions do not constitute an exhaustive list of principles and rules of international humanitarian law binding upon military personnel, and do not prejudice the application thereof, nor do they replace the national laws by which military personnel remain bound throughout the operation.' Section 2.

[51] Human Rights Committee, 'Concluding Observations' (14 August 2006) CCPR/C/UNK/CO/1; UNMIK, 'Report to the Human Rights Committee' (7 February 2006)

In a 2012 report on the rule of law, the UN Secretary-General accepted that the UN Secretariat is bound by international law. The report stated, 'The Secretary-General fully accepts that relevant international law, notably international human rights, humanitarian and refugee law, is binding on the activities of the United Nations Secretariat, and is committed to complying with the corresponding obligations.'[52] While this statement is welcome, some ambiguity persists. Does the fact that the Secretariat is bound mean that the whole of the UN is bound? And by what rules, precisely? Ideally, the UN Secretary-General should issue a Bulletin stipulating precisely which human rights obligations bind peace operations. This approach has been taken in relation to two other aspects of peacekeeping operations: the applicability of humanitarian law and the accountability of peacekeepers for sexual exploitation and abuse.[53] Those Bulletins are widely referred to and have contributed to more universal agreement on the applicable legal framework.

In addition to the Rules of Engagement that bind the peace operation, I submit that two soft law instruments may be used as a measure of applicable human rights standards. These are the UN Code of Conduct for Law Enforcement Officials[54] and the UN Basic Principles on the Use of Force and Firearms by Law Enforcement Officials.[55] The aim of these instruments is to ensure that the use of force in law enforcement respects human rights law. As far as possible, and *mutatis mutandis*, they should be seen as guiding peacekeepers and especially UN Police (UNPOL) with executive

CCPR/C/UNK/1 paras 123–124. Note, however, that the European Court of Human Rights also rejected an application submitted by the European Roma Rights Centre on behalf of Roma in Mitrovica on the grounds that UNMIK is not a party to the ECHR. On 20 February 2006, the European Roma Rights Centre announced that it had brought a claim against UNMIK on behalf of Roma who lived in a lead-contaminated area. The Court refused the application. Communication from Andi Dobrushi, ERRC legal officer.

[52] UN Secretary-General, 'Delivering Justice: Programme of Action to Strengthen the Rule of Law at the National and International Levels' (16 March 2012) UN Doc A/66/749, para. 11(d).

[53] Secretary-General's Bulletin, Observance by United Nations Forces of International Humanitarian Law (6 August 1999) UN Doc ST/SGB/1999/13 and Secretary-General's Bulletin, Special Measures for Protection from Sexual Exploitation and Sexual Abuse (9 October 2003) UN Doc ST/SGB/2003/13.

[54] UN Code of Conduct for Law Enforcement Officials (17 December 1979) UN Doc A/Res/34/169.

[55] UN Basic Principles on the Use of Force and Firearms by Law Enforcement Officials, adopted by the Eighth United Nations Congress on the Prevention of Crime and the Treatment of Offenders, Havana, Cuba (27 August–7 September 1990).

policing mandates.[56] They would therefore also have to be respected by PMSCs in such roles.

While this provides a more or less satisfactory framework for peace-keepers that can be attributed to the United Nations, there is a gap when it comes to other PMSC activity in peace operations. Indeed, unless private security guards hired by the United Nations in peacekeeping operations can be considered to be attributable to the UN, it is very difficult to sustain an argument that those private actors are legally bound by international human rights law. Attribution is discussed in detail in Part IV, below. Here, suffice it to say that there is very little doubt that PMSCs acting as military troop contingents would be attributable to the UN (or to their sending states), as would PMSCs who are UNPOL (or CIVPOL). It is much more difficult to assert with certainty, however, that all PMSCs acting as security guards in peace operations are attributable to the UN. The potentially nefarious effects of that conclusion are somewhat mitigated, however, by the fact that private security guards tasked with certain key roles may indeed be attributable to the UN as its agents – and, thus, would be bound by human rights law. Even if the PMSCs cannot be attributed to the UN, the organization bears due diligence obligations in order to respect its obligations.

6.3   Possible Related Legal Problems with PMSC as a Peace Force

Although it may legally be possible for a PMSC to serve in a UN peace operation as part of the force, a number of important legal issues would have to be resolved, in addition to the critical issue of combatant status discussed above. These relate to lacunae in respect to mechanisms for enforcing military discipline and criminal prosecution and punishment, which are normally reserved for sending states, and the problem of a lack of a SOFA.

---

[56] Oswald et al. also argue that the Code of Conduct for Law Enforcement Officials 'provide useful guidance to peacekeepers' and that the Basic Principles on the Use of Force 'are very useful for the creation of rules of engagement (ROE) and directives on the use of force' for peacekeepers. They note that other aspects of the instruments are highly relevant for peacekeepers. Oswald et al., *Documents*, pp. 438 and 444. See, however, Nigel D. White, 'Empowering Peace Operations to Protect Civilians: Form over Substance?' (2009) 13 *J Intl Peacekeeping* 327–355, at 353: 'If a contingent does intervene to protect civilians or to confront spoilers it is unlikely to have the resources or mechanisms to protect the human rights of any detainees in accordance with the TCN's [Troop Contributing Nation's] human rights obligations.'

6.3.1 Discipline

The general legal framework that applies to peace operations as agreed in participating state agreements stipulates that the contributing state retains control over military discipline and is responsible for criminal prosecution of its own troops should they be involved in criminal activity. Indeed, the UK Manual of the Law of Armed Conflict specifies that '[r]esponsibility for ensuring compliance with the law of armed conflict by the members of a PSO force is divided between the national authorities of each contingent and the United Nations or other international organization under whose auspices the operation is conducted.'[57] The Manual notes that the UN will issue the rules of engagement. The critical role of the state is explained thus:

> the model agreement between the United Nations and contributor states requires the contributor state to ensure that the contingent which it contributes complies with the law of armed conflict. Since only states possess a criminal jurisdiction, violations of the law of armed conflict can usually be punished only by national courts and disciplinary authorities.[58]

Leslie Green has aptly described the role of military discipline during armed conflict thus: 'During conflict, it has a function whereby it operates to ensure conduct that is in compliance with the laws of armed conflict to secure obedience to orders on pain of sanction. Without some system of order to which compliance must be given, an army would rapidly become an unruly mob.'[59] Many early disciplinary codes set down basic rules during hostilities; others establish a court martial system to enforce discipline; and yet others are a combination of both.[60] The idea behind the rigour of military discipline is that through training, soldiers will internalize the self-restraint they are expected to use in their application of force such that they should not need the threat of penal sanctions to comply with their obligations or with international humanitarian law.[61] According to a retired Canadian colonel,

> Discipline is what permits commanders to control the use of state-sanctioned violence so that the right amount and type of force can be applied in exactly the right time and place. Discipline ensures that in times

[57] UK Ministry of Defence, *Manual on the Law of Armed Conflict* (Oxford University Press, 2004), p. 379, para. 14.8.

[58] Ibid.

[59] Leslie Green, 'The Role of Discipline in the Military' (2004) 42 *Canadian YB Intl L* 385–421 at 385.

[60] Ibid., 386–396.   [61] Ibid., 417–418, citing the Canadian Somalia Enquiry Report.

of great danger, the individual can and will carry out orders, even if his natural instinct for self-preservation tells him otherwise. Discipline ensures
adherence to laws, standards and values of civilian society during combat
or operational deployments.[62]

The most comprehensive work advocating for the use of PMSCs in peace
operations acknowledges the potential problem raised by the lack of disciplinary authority of a state over a contractor military peace force. In order
to address the absence of a legal framework and mechanisms to enforce
such laws, Malcolm Patterson recommends the creation of a disciplinary
unit specifically for PMSCs.[63] In this light, one can consider the recent UN
attempts to develop an international convention on the criminal accountability of United Nations officials and experts on mission.[64] The proposed
convention, which is being revised through various ad hoc committees
and working groups, would apply to UN officials and experts on mission, and, according to the Secretariat, should also cover persons hired as
contractors and consultants.[65] The current drafts anticipate that the host
state will have primary jurisdiction over criminal acts (*not* of peacekeeping troops – these retain immunity and are subject only to their own state's
military and criminal justice systems), followed by the alleged perpetrator's national state. If a PMSC is sent by a state as its sole contribution to a
peace operation, unless that state makes explicit provision for exercising
its military or criminal jurisdiction, that PMSC should not benefit from
immunity. In any case, the use of such forces as 'troops' contributed by a
state is clearly not contemplated by the current proposed convention for
criminal repression.[66]

   Green's discussion of military discipline shows, however, that discipline
is about more than simply having judicial or court-martial jurisdiction

---

[62] Colonel Michel Drapeau, quoted in Leslie Green, ibid., 420 (Michel Drapeau, 'When One
   Is Tortured, Many Are Wounded', *Globe and Mail*, 6 May 2004, p. A17).
[63] Patterson, 'A Corporate Alternative', 223–228.
[64] In 2007, the UN Secretariat expressed its general support for the idea of a convention. Note
   by the Secretariat, 'Criminal Accountability of United Nations Officials and Experts on
   Mission' (11 September 2007) UN Doc A/62/329.
[65] Ibid., paras 34–36. Note that there is a committee in the Fourth Committee (UNGA) and
   also in the Sixth Committee dealing with the same issue. Support for the development
   of an international convention on the issue remains uneven. See UN General Assembly,
   Sixth Committee, 'Agenda Item 80: Criminal Accountability of United Nations Officials
   and Experts on Mission' (28 October 2015) UN Doc A/C.6/70/SR.9, passim.
[66] For a discussion, see Lindsey Cameron, 'The Use of Private Military and Security Companies in Armed Conflicts and Certain Peace Operations', PhD thesis, University of Geneva,
   2015.

in order to be able to enforce the rules. It entails rigorous training that leads to an inculcation of expected behaviour and an ability to exercise self-restraint in the use of force that can be relied on even in dire circumstances. Moreover, he argues convincingly that even when soldiers have internalized the rules such that enforcement should rarely be necessary, if enforcement within the military disciplinary system is lax or non-existent, abuses tend to follow.[67] This means that not only would the UN have to have a disciplinary system available to enforce the law, it would have to use it as often as necessary to produce an environment in which it is understood that breaches of the law will be punished. Finally, such forces must also undergo rigorous training.

6.3.2 Status of Forces Agreements

As noted above, the United Nations concludes a Status of Forces Agreement (SOFA) with the host state for its peacekeeping operations. The UN has a model SOFA that acts as the basis for these agreements, which are concluded between the UN and the host state and which deal in particular with the status, privileges and immunities of the members of the peace force.[68] However, even with the current delays in getting peacekeepers on the ground, it is often the case that a SOFA is not concluded with the host government prior to their arrival.[69] It is therefore necessary to have an interim solution; consequently, the UN Security Council mandate often specifies that the Model SOFA will apply until a SOFA is concluded between the UN and the host state. In addition, some have argued that the UN Model SOFA is customary law.[70] While that solution, albeit not universally accepted, may work for state national troop contingents, it is much less clear whether it could apply to PMSCs – especially since even the existing Model SOFA, which forms the basis for negotiations for the

---

[67] Green, 'Role of Discipline', 416–421.

[68] See Model Status-of-Forces Agreement for Peace-keeping Operations (9 October 1990) UN Doc A/45/594.

[69] Murphy, UN Peacekeeping, p. 110, points out that the peace force UNIFIL in Lebanon was on the ground for almost twenty years without a SOFA and that many other operations deploy without a SOFA having been agreed for periods as long as eighteen months (at p. 111).

[70] In particular, E. Suy, 'Legal Aspects of UN Peace-keeping Operations' (1988) 35 Netherlands Intl L Rev 318 at 320. Ola Engdahl also makes this argument in 'The Legal Status of United Nations and Associated Personnel in Peace Operations and the Legal Regime Protecting Them', in G.L. Beruto, The Application of International Humanitarian Law to Peace Operations: Specific Issues (IIHL, 2008), pp. 126–131.

actual SOFA of a peace operation and which applies provisionally during the start-up phase (and sometimes beyond), does not contain any clauses referring to contractors.[71] It does, however, provide for the hiring of locally recruited personnel and provides that such personnel 'shall enjoy immunities concerning official acts'.[72] Thus, even the application of the Model SOFA via the Security Council resolution likely does not provide a solution for contractors. Each SOFA may be negotiated on its own terms and it may be in the form of an agreement or an exchange of letters, and standard amendments to the Model SOFA are now commonly made in relation to contractors.[73] There is currently a privately run project to revise the Model SOFA that anticipates incorporating standard provisions for contractors.[74]

Above, the use of Status of Forces Agreements was discussed in light of whether they implicitly or explicitly prohibit or allow the use of PMSCs in various roles in peace operations.[75] Many of the details of that discussion are relevant also here. Terry Gill and Dieter Fleck assert, 'In the absence of a status-of-forces or similar agreement granting functional immunity, the status of private contractors is that of foreign civilian workers in the Receiving State.'[76] However, that status as they intend is meant to be appropriate for PMSCs acting as civilians accompanying the armed forces. The issue here is how PMSCs can be covered by a SOFA if they are to be members of a military peacekeeping force. Furthermore, one may ask whether that solution is appropriate for private security contractors. This issue is significant because it affects PMSCs most at precisely the moment when they are held out as being most potentially useful – at the very urgent initial period of a peace operation. Clearly, a SOFA would have to settle issues regarding PMSC status, immunities (if any) and privileges (if any) prior to deployment. Practice regarding contractors to date underscores the necessity of state consent to any immunity to be accorded to them, which may not bode well for the chances that a Security Council resolution setting down the mandate would stipulate that the Model SOFA applies to them (and specifying which type of protection they would enjoy).

---

[71] UN Model SOFA (above, n. 68).   [72] Ibid., sections 22 and 28.

[73] Oswald et al., *Documents*, pp. 34–38. In terms of their significance for immunity and responsibility, specific details of those clauses will be discussed below, in Part IV on responsibility.

[74] See 'UN Peacekeeping and the Model Status of Forces Agreement', United Nations Peacekeeping Reform Project, School of Law, University of Essex (2011).

[75] See Chapter 3, Section 3.2, above.

[76] Terry Gill and Dieter Fleck, 'Private Contractors and Security Companies', in T. Gill and D. Fleck (eds.), *The Handbook of the Law of Military Operations* (Oxford: Oxford University Press, 2010), pp. 489–493 at p. 492, para. 27.03.

6.4   Regional Organizations Conducting Peace Operations and PMSCs

As noted above, under Chapter VIII of the UN Charter, the UN Security Council may authorize regional organizations[77] to carry out enforcement actions.[78] The UN High-Level Panel recommended that all peace operations – and not just enforcement actions – by regional organizations occur only pursuant to Security Council resolutions,[79] but states did not adopt this recommendation in the World Summit Outcome document in 2005.[80] Indeed, regional organizations do not need UN Security Council authorization in order to conduct 'traditional' peace operations without an enforcement component.[81] The Security Council may, however, authorize an enforcement operation to be conducted by a regional organization, under its authority.[82] Nevertheless, even if it may not occur frequently, regional organizations conducting peace operations without a Security Council mandate will have to comply with the fundamental principles of traditional UN peace operations if they are not to contravene the UN Charter.[83] The principles of consent and impartiality are thus the cornerstones of such operations. When it comes to the degree of force that may be used, a regional organization using more robust force in support of the government requesting its presence will likely fail to be impartial and

---

[77] In fact the precise term is 'regional arrangements or agencies', but it is considered to encompass regional organizations. See M. Zwanenburg, 'Regional Organizations and the Maintenance of International Peace and Security: Three Recent Regional African Peace Operations' (2006) 11 *J Conflict and Security L* 483–508, esp. at 488–489. For a comprehensive discussion, see A. Abass, *Regional Organizations and the Development of Collective Security: Beyond Chapter VIII of the UN Charter* (Oxford: Hart, 2004).

[78] See chapter 5, n. 43 and accompanying text.

[79] Report of the High-Level Panel on Threats, Challenges and Change, 'A More Secure World: Our Shared Responsibility' (4 December 2004) UN Doc A/59/565 at para 272(a). The Panel did acknowledge that 'in some urgent situations' the authorization may be sought after the operation has already begun.

[80] R. Durward, 'Security Council Authorization for Regional Peace Operations: A Critical Analysis' (2006) 13 *Intl Peacekeeping* (2006) 350–365. 2005 World Summit Outcome, UNGA Res 60/1 (16 September 2005), UN Doc A/RES/60/1 (24 October 2005).

[81] Article 52 of the UN Charter specifically states, 'Nothing in the present Charter precludes the existence of regional arrangements or agencies for dealing with such matters relating to the maintenance of international peace and security as are appropriate for regional action, provided that' both the agencies and their activities are 'consistent with the Purposes and Principles of the United Nations.' See also Durward, 'Security Council Authorization', 352.

[82] Article 53 of the UN Charter.

[83] For a study on peace operations by three different regional organizations in Africa that did not occur subsequent to UN Security Council authorization, see Zwanenburg, 'Regional Organizations'.

therefore, even if consented to, will not be considered as a traditional peace operation. Used impartially, however, even robust force can conform to peacekeeping principles.[84] Regional organizations delegating aspects of peace operations to PMSCs will thus have to comply with the principles of traditional peace operations discussed above. If the operations are established pursuant to UN Security Council resolutions, the use of PMSCs will furthermore have to comply with the terms of the resolutions.

Any further study of the possibility of regional organizations to delegate aspects of peace operations to PMSCs will be limited by the internal law of the organization in question. For its part, the European Union does not yet have a law or even a public policy on the use of PMSCs, although it is currently under review in a number of subcommittees.[85] The African Union does not have a specific law or policy on PMSCs.[86] In at least some cases, the use of PMSCs by regional organizations has in fact been paid for by governments outside of the organization and the region – for example, the United States paid for transport and logistics by ICI of Oregon to ECOWAS in Liberia.[87]

---

[84] But see Berdal, 'Lessons Not Learned', who questions the extent to which the use of robust force can truly be impartial.

[85] European Parliament, Subcommittee on Human Rights, 'Exchange of Views on the EU's Role in Combating Human Rights Violations by Private Military and Security Companies (PMCs/PSCs)' (9 February 2009), Brussels; European Parliament, Policy Department External Policies, 'The Increasing Role of Private Military and Security Companies' (October 2007) (A. Bailes and C. Holmqvist), www.europarl.europa.eu/meetdocs/2004_2009/documents/dv/droi_090209_313/DROI_090209_313en.pdf. In practice, there is both a military and a civilian component to Common Security and Defence Policy operations. The military component is led by an Operations Commander, who is responsible for awarding contracts with private contractors in that domain. For PMSCs contracted to the civilian component of a peace operation, the mission itself would directly contract the PMSCs, but the Council of the European Union remains responsible for civilian missions. See G. Den Dekker, 'The Regulatory Context of Private Military and Security Contractors at the European Union Level', in Christine Bakker and Mirko Sossai (eds.), *Multilevel Regulation of Military and Security Contractors* (Oxford: Hart, 2011), pp. 31–52. As of 2011, Den Dekker reports, 'there are no specific regulations of the PMS sector today at the EU level.' Ibid., p. 51. Marco Gestri, 'The European Union and Private Military and Security Contractors: Existing Controls and Legal Bases for Further Regulation', in Bakker and Sossai, *Multilevel Regulation*, pp. 53–77, affirms this view. E. Krahmann, 'Regulating Military and Security Services in the European Union', in A. Bryden and M. Caparini (eds.), *Private Actors and Security Governance* (Geneva: LIT & DCAF, 2006), pp. 189–212. See also Nigel White and Sorcha MacLeod, 'EU Operations and Private Military Contractors: Issues of Corporate and Institutional Responsibility' (2008) 19 *EJIL* 956–988.

[86] Indeed, for the AU, the issue is for the moment solely dealt with by the OAU Mercenary Convention.

[87] ICI of Oregon website, www.icioregon.com (accessed 29 July 2009).

6.5   Other Humanitarian Organizations and the Use of PMSCs

There is presently a broad questioning as to whether humanitarian organizations should or may rely on armed protection, be it through armed forces involved in the conflict, local militias or other means.[88] The principal concern is that the use of armed protection may compromise the exclusively impartial, neutral, and independent nature of the work of humanitarian agencies and that this may negatively affect their ability to provide relief. Any inquiry into whether international law has anything to say about whether humanitarian organizations may contract PMSCs to provide armed security for aid delivery in conflict situations is thus part of the wider discussion on civil-military relations and humanitarianism. In order to understand the legal restraints on using PMSCs in this context, I will outline the legal framework of humanitarian aid (under *ius in bello*) and test the use of PMSCs against it. In addition, I will consider the laws of the humanitarian relief organizations and whether they prohibit or constrain the use of PMSCs.[89] This is not a hypothetical investigation; the most detailed and comprehensive study on PMSCs and humanitarian work concluded: 'Though an exceptional practice, contracted armed security has been used at various times by virtually all major international humanitarian actors',[90] including the United Nations and the International Committee of the Red Cross.

6.5.1   IHL, Humanitarian Aid and PMSCs

The principal role of PMSCs with regard to the provision of medical aid and the distribution of the necessities of life to civilians tends to involve

---

[88] J.-C. Rufin, 'The Paradoxes of Armed Protection', in F. Jean (ed.), *Life, Death and Aid: The Médecins sans Frontières Report on World Crisis Intervention* (London: Routledge, 1993), pp. 111–123. C. Buchanan and R. Muggah, 'No Relief: Surveying the Effects of Gun Violence on Humanitarian and Development Personnel' (Humanitarian Dialogue, 2005). On humanitarian aid in conflict situations more generally, see R.A. Stoffels, 'Legal Regulation of Humanitarian Assistance in Armed Conflict: Achievements and Gaps' (2004) 86 *IRRC* 515–546.

[89] The question of 'humanitarian missions' as a type of UN peace operation will not be considered here as it considered globally within the discussion of peace operations.

[90] A. Stoddard, A. Harmer and V. DiDomenico, 'Private Security Providers and Services in Humanitarian Operations' (2008) Humanitarian Policy Group Reports Issue 27, at 12. In this section I will not deal with the allegation that some PMSCs hold themselves out as humanitarian organizations and thus actively contribute to blurring the lines between true non-profit organizations and PMSCs themselves. See Report of the UN Working Group on the Use of Mercenaries as a Means of Violating Human Rights and Impeding the Exercise of the Right of People to Self-Determination (9 January 2008) UN Doc A/HRC/7/7, at 20.

providing security for convoys and personnel. In line with what their name implies, it will usually concern the security aspect of aid provision. I will deal with the implications of PMSCs providing security to humanitarian aid as well as the rules relating to aid itself, should PMSCs become involved as direct providers.

In international armed conflicts, parties to the conflict are obliged to accept medical relief supplies not only for civilians but also for combatants. When it comes to non-medical items, the obligation is narrower: parties must accept food and clothing when they are destined for certain vulnerable civilian groups – in particular, children under fifteen, expectant mothers and, in the rather clumsy wording of Convention IV, 'maternity cases'.[91] Beyond that, parties to the conflict should consent to the provision of humanitarian assistance for the whole civilian population if existing supplies are inadequate and if the relief is provided impartially and without adverse distinction.[92] Occupying powers are responsible for providing food and medical supplies to the civilian population in the occupied territory, but if they are unable to do so, they are under an obligation to accept relief schemes.[93] In non-international armed conflicts, humanitarian and impartial relief actions to provide supplies essential for the survival of the civilian population should be accepted by the parties to the conflict.[94] The crucial element leading to parties being obligated to accept relief is that it must be humanitarian in character, impartial and provided without discrimination.[95] In this case, then, it is not so much a

---

[91] Article 23 of the Convention relative to the Protection of Civilian Persons in Time of War, Geneva, 12 August 1949, in force 21 October 1950 (GC IV).

[92] Article 70(1) of AP I extends the provision of relief to the whole civilian population but subjects it to the consent of the parties. Distinction may be made only on the basis of need, not on any other criteria (such as nationality, etc.). However, it is considered that if the conditions in the Article are met, a party should not withhold its consent. See Jelena Pejic, 'The Right to Food in Situations of Armed Conflict: The Legal Framework' (2001) 83 IRRC 1097–1109 at 1103. Sandoz, Commentary on the Additional Protocols, pp. 815–829.

[93] Articles 55 and 59 of GC IV.

[94] Again, Article 18 AP II subjects the provision of humanitarian assistance to the consent of the High Contracting Party (thus, only the state party to the conflict), but it is considered that such consent may not be refused 'without good grounds' since refusal would be tantamount to using starvation as a method of combat, which violates art 14 AP II. Sandoz, Commentary on the Additional Protocols, para. 4885. The duty to accept humanitarian relief as an obligation, with no mention of consent, was found to be a rule of customary IHL in the ICRC study. See Henckaerts and Doswald-Beck, Customary IHL, Rule 55.

[95] Again, while consent is formally required, there is a sense that parties may not refuse aid provided the conditions of need exist and provided that the aid fulfils these criteria. See, e.g., UNSC Res 1502 (2003).

question as to whether IHL prima facie prohibits aid organizations from using PMSCs to guard its convoys or stocks or to protect persons distributing aid, but whether their use offends the requirements for relief providers such that parties to conflicts would not be obliged to accept such aid. One may also query whether the providers of aid would lose the protection of IHL merely because they have armed guards. In light of this, I will show that the principles of humanitarian aid or relief provision do not function as direct restraints on the use of PMSCs. However, since failure to comply with them would seriously impede such organizations from carrying out their mandates – since IHL only requires parties to accept such aid – it is necessary to enquire whether the use of PMSCs is consonant with those principles.

Assuming that the aid itself is being provided impartially and is not benefiting only one party when needs exist on both sides,[96] the first question is whether the mere fact of having armed guards protecting the convoy, warehouse or distribution points infringes the requirements of impartiality, non-discrimination and humanitarianism. The short answer to this question is that it does not. IHL foresees that medical personnel may be armed or use arms in their own defence or in defence of the wounded in their care and that this does not deprive them of the protection of Convention I (which is that they may in no circumstances be attacked).[97] In addition, medical personnel may be protected by 'sentries or by an escort'.[98] Moreover, the fact that medical and religious personnel must provide care impartially is fundamental to their protected status. There are thus analogies to aid that must be delivered impartially and entitlements to protect it to ensure its delivery to those who need it. Thus, by extension, the presence of armed guards does not in and of itself contravene the legal requirements of the nature and quality of civilian relief such that the aid and its providers lose the protection of the Conventions.

At the next level, consider the hypothetical situation where a convoy is attacked and armed guards of a PMSC fight back: would that constitute

---

[96] Stoffels, 'Legal Regulation of Humanitarian Assistance', 539, cites the 'hijacking' of aid in Somalia by warlords as the clearest example of aid not being provided impartially successfully.

[97] Article 22(1) GC I. These rules are necessary for medical units since they are normally formed out of parts of the armed forces of a party to the conflict and, without such special protection, would be subject to attack as members of the armed forces. However, the provision of humanitarian relief is usually through civilian persons; as such, civilians are protected from attack insofar as they are not directly participating in hostilities.

[98] Article 22(2) GC I.

direct participation in hostilities such that it compromises or threatens the impartiality of the aid?[99] As for all IHL, the answer depends on the specific facts in a given situation. Nonetheless, a few general comments may be made to guide the analysis. First, most attacks on aid providers are committed by criminals, not by armed groups.[100] Defending against criminal attacks by bandits or criminals does not constitute direct participation in hostilities.[101] Second, in order for a person to be directly participating in hostilities, their act must have a 'belligerent nexus' to the conflict.[102] A belligerent nexus means that an act 'must be specifically designed to [inflict harm] in support of a party to an armed conflict and to the detriment of another'.[103] This is the opposite of 'impartial'. There is a clear qualitative difference between using a significant degree of force in self-defence to protect an impartial convoy of food for civilians and to protect mission-essential equipment for the military in, for example, present-day Afghanistan. Deterring an attack on a military objective with force unquestionably fulfils the belligerent nexus criteria. However, when the initial attack itself is criminal because it is against non-combatants or non-military objectives, it does not constitute direct participation in hostilities to use self-defence to defend against that attack.[104] Some argue that even vigorous force in self-defence is acceptable in this context.[105] Humanitarian relief supplies intended purely for civilians and otherwise complying

---

99 This question is essentially raised by B. Perrin in 'Humanitarian Organizations and the Private Security Debate: Implications for International Humanitarian Law', presented at 'On the Edges of Conflict', Vancouver, BC, 29–31 March 2009. While I concur with his answer in the result, our reasoning is different.

100 Buchanan and Muggah, 'No Relief', 19–20.

101 ICRC, Interpretive Guidance on the Notion of Direct Participation in Hostilities Under International Humanitarian Law (May 2009), pp. 60–61.

102 Ibid., pp. 46 and 58–64.   103 Ibid., p. 58.

104 Ibid., p. 61. Note, however, that an attack on a civilian object may constitute direct participation in hostilities for the attacking party. Perrin (note 99) simply argues that the degree of force available for use in self-defence generally is very broad, without distinguishing between protection of military objectives and criminal attacks. Moreover, citing no authority, Perrin insists that Article 49 AP I does not relate to the concept of what types of acts will constitute 'direct participation in hostilities' by a civilian. See his 'Private Security Companies and Humanitarian Organizations: Implications for International Humanitarian Law', in B. Perrin (ed.), Modern Warfare: Armed Groups, Private Militaries, Humanitarian Organizations, and the Law (University of British Columbia Press, 2012), pp. 124–156 at p. 142. Perrin does identify the relationship between personal self-defence and direct participation in hostilities but without the benefit of a more detailed analysis. Ibid. at p. 143.

105 ICRC consultative meetings on Direct Participation in Hostilities, Second Report, www.icrc.org/web/eng/siteeng0.nsf/htmlall/participation-hostilities-ihl-311205?opendocument. 'Second Expert Meeting: Direct Participation in Hostilities Under

with the requirements of such relief are not military objectives by their nature or purpose.

A second threat to impartiality may arise through the hiring of armed PMSCs who have a link to a party to the conflict. This may be especially the case when 'local' PMSCs are used.[106] However, the contracting of a foreign PMSC does not entirely eradicate the problem.[107] This has already been discussed above in relation to the principle of impartiality and peace operations. First, foreign companies often operate by hiring local staff, which is how they reduce their costs. Humanitarian agencies and NGOs, not exactly flush with cash, will not likely be able to afford to force companies to avoid that practice easily. At the very least, it should not be assumed that all will be able to avoid this problem entirely. Second, a single PMSC may have a contract with a government (party to the conflict) as well as with an organization providing aid. As government contracts are often more lucrative, it may be perceived that the government could exert pressure with regard to the humanitarian aid.[108] This problem is in all likelihood more a problem of perception, but it should be recalled that perceived impartiality is crucial to ensuring parties do not object to aid. Finally, even foreign PMSCs may have a vested interest in the conflict due to the fact that they may be part of larger conglomerates with ties to the extraction industry, such that they may not be entirely neutral/impartial.

There is also the principle of humanitarianism itself. This principle has not been investigated in detail elsewhere in discussions of PMSCs and humanitarian aid, but it is implicit in what the International Federation of the Red Cross and others mean when they observe that it would be catastrophic for the entire Red Cross movement if one of their armed guards killed someone. The notion that aid providers, in contradistinction to 'liberators', may never kill through arms in carrying out their mandate underpins the whole notion of humanitarian assistance.

In addition, albeit more rarely, PMSCs (or other armed guards) may be used to provide third-party security in humanitarian operations. For

International Humanitarian Law', co-organized by the ICRC and the TMC Asser Institute, The Hague (25–26 October 2004) at 14, available at www.icrc.org.

[106] The spectre of this problem is raised by Perrin, 'Humanitarian Organizations and Private Security'; J Cockayne, 'Commercial Security in Humanitarian and Post-conflict Settings: An Exploratory Study' (International Peace Institute, 2006), and Stoddard et al., 'PSCs in Humanitarian Operations'.

[107] Cf. Perrin, 'Humanitarian Organizations and Private Security', 18, for a contrary view.

[108] C. Spearin, 'Humanitarian Non-governmental Organizations and International Private Security Companies: The "Humanitarian" Challenges of Moulding a Marketplace' (DCAF Policy Paper 16, 2007).

example, they may be hired to provide security for persons an international agency is mandated to protect, such as refugees in camps.[109] In such instances, the question is whether the use of PMSCs complies with the internal rules of the relevant organization as well as the principles governing the operation.

A second aspect of PMSC involvement in humanitarian aid relates to PMSCs as providers. Indeed, it is not inconceivable that some PMSCs may be contracted to actually provide aid and organize medical transport.[110] While this kind of role would not normally be considered to fall within the definition of private military and security companies, since 'medical personnel' may be a category of persons forming part of the armed forces, and since the provision of aid is an activity that is closely regulated by IHL, the possibility thus merits a few words here.

In order to enjoy the special protected status accorded to certain medical aid providers under the Conventions and Protocols, PMSCs would have to meet certain conditions. Geneva Convention I and Protocol I grant protection to medical personnel of national Red Cross societies *and* to 'other national voluntary aid societies'. Can a PMSC qualify as a 'voluntary aid society'? First of all, despite the everyday connotations of the word, for the purposes of the Convention and Protocol, 'voluntary' 'does not mean that the staff of such societies are necessarily unpaid'. Rather, it means that 'their work is not based on any obligation to the State, but on an engagement accepted of their own free will.'[111] However, other conditions have to be met, including that the society has to be 'duly

---

[109] Cockayne, 'Commercial Security', 7, provides this example, although the arrangement involved a group of 'international military advisers' and Zairian contingents. He also cites the case of UNMIK hiring PMSCs to protect the property restored to minorities in Kosovo. It should be noted that the 'protection' mandate of such agencies is complex and extends far beyond mere physical/security protection. Thus, using PMSCs in this role should not be construed as somehow tantamount to an abdication of protection roles.

[110] They have provided medical support in a number of situations. ICRC, *Study on the Use of the Emblems: Operational and Commercial and Other Non-operational Issues* (Geneva: ICRC, 2011), p. 180, note 269.

[111] J. Pictet (ed.), *The Geneva Conventions of 12 August 1949: Commentary, First Geneva Convention for the Amelioration of the Condition of the Wounded and Sick in Armed Forces in the Field* (Geneva: ICRC 1952), 224–225. Furthermore, the commentary to Article 12 AP I specifically states that the recognition and authorization requirement 'may also concern private medical units, such as private clinics or ambulance services', implying that such private services may fall within the scope of IHL's protection. Sandoz, *Commentary on the Additional Protocols*, p. 168, para. 525. See, *contra*, ICRC, *Study on the Use of the Emblems*, p. 181.

recognized and authorized by a Party to the conflict.[112] These requirements were inserted specifically to avoid abuses and uncertainty. In fact, proposals to allow for the designation (through a fixed sign) of independent doctors or other medical personnel were explicitly rejected by states.[113] In addition, if they are acting as auxiliaries to the medical services of the armed forces, the personnel of such societies must be made subject to the military laws and regulations of the relevant state and protection is only accorded to those who are engaged *exclusively* in the medical duties provided for in Convention I.[114] Other conditions exist as well.[115] Thus, it is open to states to recognize and authorize for-profit companies to provide medical aid; however, if they are not recognized, the individuals do not benefit from the special protection of the Conventions.[116]

In terms of the provision of humanitarian aid for the benefit of the civilian population, PMSCs should be aware that only aid that meets certain requirements enjoys the benefit of protection under IHL. First, aid must be provided impartially and it must be for the benefit of the civilian population only.[117] In addition, aid must have the consent of the parties to the conflict, but in some cases the state must give consent.[118] In order to ensure that the provision of aid does not result in a definite advantage for a party, the relief may cover only basic needs.[119] If PMSCs were to provide

---

[112] Article 26 of GC I refers to such societies as are 'duly recognized and authorized by *their Governments*'. Article 8 of AP I is similar. The nature of incorporation may also play a role. This is implicit in the commentaries but not in articles – it says only that they have to have been 'regularly constituted in accordance with national legislation'. Sandoz, *Commentary on the Additional Protocols*, para. 358.

[113] M. Bothe, K.J. Partsch and W.A. Solf, *New Rules for Victims of Armed Conflict: Commentary on the Two 1977 Protocols Additional to the Geneva Conventions of 1949* (The Hague: Martinus Nijhoff, 1982), p. 99; Sandoz, *Commentary on the Additional Protocols*, p. 108, para. 280 (part II).

[114] Article 26 of GC I; Pictet, *Commentary on GC I*, p. 228; ICRC, *Commentary on the First Geneva Convention*, 2016, paras 2073–2082 – the duties are those listed in Article 24; these rules are not extended to those providing medical aid to civilians under AP I.

[115] For example, aid must be provided without discrimination. See Article 10 of AP I. For those providing aid to the armed forces, states' parties are required to inform other states which societies it has authorized and recognized. Article 26(2) GC I and Pictet, *Commentary GC I*, pp. 228–229.

[116] As such, they also may not avail themselves of the use of the protective emblem.

[117] Article 23 of GC IV; Article 70 of AP I.

[118] However, under certain circumstances, an occupying power is obliged to accept relief. See, for example, Articles 55 and 59 of GC IV. See also Article 70 of AP I.

[119] Commentary to Article 23 of GC IV, J. Pictet (ed.), *The Geneva Conventions of 12 August 1949: Commentary, Convention relative to the treatment of civilian persons in time of war* (Geneva 1958), pp. 182, 183.

aid in a manner that does not comply with these requirements, they would not be in violation of IHL; simply, their actions would not benefit from the special rules applicable to humanitarian assistance.

Finally, the mere fact that a PMSC is engaged in a humanitarian activity does not mean that that PMSC is a 'humanitarian organization' within the meaning of the Geneva Conventions and Protocols. Indeed, for the purposes of those treaties, for an entity to be an impartial international humanitarian organization, 'it is... essential that the organization *itself* has a humanitarian character, and, as such, follows only humanitarian aims. This restriction excludes organizations with a political or commercial character.'[120] Based on this interpretation of Article 9 of Additional Protocol I, a study by the ICRC on the use of the emblems concluded rather categorically, 'PMCs/PSCs are driven by economic dynamics of profit, are not essentially of a humanitarian character and could hardly be considered as impartial. They may not be qualified as "international humanitarian organizations". They may not, therefore, be protected or use the emblem under this qualification.'[121] Again, this does not mean that PMSCs may not provide aid in situations of armed conflict, but it does suggest that the organization that is concerned with use of the protective emblems would not condone their use by PMSCs.

6.5.2 The Law of the Organizations and PMSCs

International organizations engaged in relief work may have their own internal law or policies on the use of PMSCs to provide armed protection for aid operations. The internal laws of international organizations may be considered to form a discrete part of international law and thus, if laws regarding PMSC use exist, would form an international legal framework for the organization in question.[122] These organizations must therefore be distinguished from non-government organizations, the internal policies of which do not constitute international legal obligations.

The United Nations does not have a clear legal rule prohibiting its agencies or subsidiary bodies from contracting PMSCs to protect humanitarian aid.[123] In addition, specific UN agencies may have their own policies.

---

[120] Commentary to Article 9 of AP I, Sandoz, *Commentary on the Additional Protocols*, para. 440.

[121] ICRC, *Study on the Use of the Emblems*, p. 182.

[122] C. Amerasinghe, *Principles of the Institutional Law of International Organizations*, 2nd edn (Cambridge University Press, 2005), pp. 13–20. See also A.J.P. Tammes, 'Decisions of International Organs as a Source of International Law' (1958) 94 *RCADI* 261.

[123] See the discussion above on UN policies on PMSCs, particularly in relation to security guards.

For the United Nations High Commissioner for Refugees (the UN Refugee Agency), for example, the civilian and humanitarian character of assistance is a key principle, leading to considerable reluctance on the part of UNHCR to contract PMSCs to perform various roles in refugee camps.[124] For its part, the ICRC has a general policy against the use of armed protection for any aspects of its work[125] but has used them in exceptional situations.

6.6 Conclusion to Part II

When it comes to PMSCs and peace operations, former UN Secretary-General Kofi Annan is frequently quoted as saying that he once considered the option of hiring a PMSC to help with the Rwanda conflict but decided against it on the grounds that 'the world is not ready to privatize peace'.[126] This statement should be wielded with caution, however. Annan was not plotting to send a PMSC in to fight the Rwandan government or Interahamwe; instead, he considered their use to help separate combatants from civilians in the refugee camps in (then) Zaire. This represents a much more limited, non-combatant use of PMSCs than any of the scenarios discussed above.

Sarah Percy argues that the general demonization of private forces by the General Assembly[127] makes it impossible for the DPKO to have recourse to PMSCs.[128] The two officials she cites in support of this contention, the chief of the Best Practices unit of DPKO and Director of Executive Office of the Secretary-General, indicate that the stigma associated with PMSCs renders their use impossible "'even though their staff might be superior to some of the peacekeeping contingents currently provided to the UN'".[129] It is possible that those officials have not thought through the ramifications of the lack of state input and control on the framework for peace operations. In addition, a recent study has shown that, even without being given an official role in peace operations, PMSCs nevertheless have

---

[124] See in particular UNHCR, Executive Committee of the High Commissioner's Programme Standing Committee, 'The Security, and Civilian and Humanitarian Character of Refugee Camps and Settlements' (14 January 1999) UN Doc EC/49/SC/INF.2, especially at paras 15–17 (reprinted in (2000) 12 *Intl J Refugee L* 505–513).

[125] ICRC, 'Report on the Use of Armed Protection for Humanitarian Assistance', Extract from Working Paper, ICRC and International Federation, Council of Delegates, Geneva, 1–2 December 1995.

[126] UN Secretary-General Kofi Annan, 35th Annual Ditchley Foundation Lecture, 26 June 1998, UN Press Release SG/SM/6613.

[127] See Cameron and Chetail, *Privatizing War*, pp. 66–80.

[128] Percy, 'The Security Council and the Use of Private Force'.   [129] Ibid., 638–639.

been placed in a position to exercise significant influence over how peace operations are conducted.[130] Political concerns aside, there would seem to be few legal impediments within the general peacekeeping law framework to the use of PMSCs as standing forces or as contingents in peace operations.

There are, however, two further elements of peace operations that the Department of Peacekeeping Operations has underscored as essential for success and that are worthy of discussion in this context. These are the legitimacy and credibility of the operation.[131] With respect to legitimacy, the Capstone Doctrine states,

> The uniquely broad representation of Member States who contribute personnel and funding to United Nations operations further strengthens this international legitimacy.[132]

If this is indeed true, staffing a peace operation with private companies rather than state forces could have a significant impact on the overall legitimacy of the operation. The lack of political will of states to put their own forces in harm's way in such a scenario could signal a failure of international solidarity, which could be a severe blow to the institution of peacekeeping.

The current tendency to prefer robust peace operations under a Chapter VII mandate of the UN Security Council arguably imposes an implicit requirement for peace forces to have combatant status, which PMSCs do not tend to have.[133] For this reason, coupled with concerns that resort to private forces may weaken the legitimacy of peacekeeping as an institution, I am not convinced the existing legal framework supports a significant development of their role as a peace force. It may be within the power of the Security Council to adopt terms in its resolutions that address these concerns. However, as the discussion on discipline here shows, combined with implicit limitations from within international humanitarian law and concerns regarding attribution and responsibility discussed below, combatant status requires something more than simply declaring a person to be a combatant. It implies the creation of a much

---

[130] See in particular Østensen, *UN Use of PMSCs*.
[131] Capstone Doctrine (United Nations Department of Peacekeeping Operations and Department of Field Support, 'United Nations Peacekeeping Operations: Principles and Guidelines' (18 January 2008), pp. 36 and 38, respectively.
[132] Ibid., p. 36.
[133] See below, Part III. See also Cameron and Chetail, *Privatizing War*, pp. 386–431, and Cameron, 'The Use of PMSCs in Armed Conflicts and Certain Peace Operations'.

more comprehensive legal structure that would be capable of implementing IHL – of respecting and ensuring respect for that body of law. It is far from certain that the UN would embark on that enterprise; it has been slow to adopt any disciplinary mechanisms. Furthermore, in its policy on the Use of Armed Security Guards, it displayed no clear assumption of responsibility for ensuring respect for humanitarian law and human rights law but rather placed responsibility on the shoulders of private actors – that is, on the companies themselves.

This study shows, however, that recent UN policies accepting the use of PMSCs as armed security guards may mean that the facts on the ground have already bypassed the niceties of legal and political debate. In these circumstances, the legal framework appears to be inadequate. The possible 'through the back door' use of private security companies in roles tantamount to peacekeepers in some cases means that lacunae have not been fully and transparently addressed.

The previous part illustrated that PMSCs already play a considerable role in peacekeeping operations – even without being deployed as the official military force – and that there has been a move towards formalizing and regulating the use of armed private security guards by the United Nations. The following part looks in detail at international humanitarian law and its application in peace operations.

PART III

PMSCs and Direct Participation in Hostilities

International humanitarian law is a pragmatic body of law. This is natural – its starting point is that it applies in a situation that would not exist if another body of law – the *ius ad bellum* – had been fully respected. International humanitarian law thus places limits on the destructiveness of war, protecting civilians and civilian objects and those who do not, or no longer, directly participate in hostilities. It rarely explicitly prescribes who may do what; instead, it accepts a loss of protection from attack for those who do directly participate in hostilities, be they combatants or civilians.

There is no black-letter rule in IHL prohibiting the use of private military and/or security contractors in armed conflicts or peace operations, including in roles in which they might directly participate in hostilities.[1] Implicit limits may, however, be discerned. In any case, there is general acknowledgement on the part of states and within the industry that PMSCs should not be contracted for tasks that will entail a direct participation in hostilities.[2] Given that PMSCs as an industry rely heavily on their right to use force in self-defence in order to carry out their obligations under their contracts, they must be viewed as an actor likely to use force in situations of armed conflict. Chapter 7 will therefore begin

---

[1] ICRC, Interpretive Guidance on the Notion of Direct Participation in Hostilities under International Humanitarian Law (Geneva, 2009).

[2] 'Montreux Document on Pertinent International Legal Obligations and Good Practices for States Related to Operations of Private Military and Security Companies During Armed Conflict' (17 September 2008), Transmitted to the UN General Assembly and Security Council in UN Doc A/63/467-S/2008/636 (6 October 2008), part II, para 1. See also Benjamin Buckland and Anna Marie Burdzy, 'Progress and Opportunities, Five Years On: Challenges and Recommendations for Montreux Document Endorsing States' (Geneva Centre for the Democratic Control of Armed Forces (DCAF), 2013), pp. 17–20; Rebecca DeWinter-Schmitt (ed.), *Montreux Five Years On: An Analysis of State Efforts to Implement Montreux Document Legal Obligations and Good Practices* (Washington, 2013), www.wcl.american.edu/humright/center/resources/publications/documents/YESMontreuxFv31.pdf, pp. 41–49; Cameron and Chetail, *Privatizing War* (Cambridge University Press, 2013); Lindsey Cameron, 'The Use of Private Military and Security Companies in Armed Conflicts and Certain Peace Operations', PhD thesis, University of Geneva, 2015.

by briefly explaining the status of PMSCs under international humanitarian law. Observing that the vast majority of PMSCs are civilians under IHL, Chapter 8 explains the concept of direct participation in hostilities, and Chapters 9 and 10 explore the situations in which the use of force in self-defence by PMSCs, and in particular in peace operations, may in fact amount to a direct participation in hostilities, which, although not unlawful, is highly undesirable. Finally, Chapter 11 looks at human rights law and examines obligations that are especially pertinent for PMSCs acting as civilian police in peace operations.

The key theme of this part is that while it may be easy to agree in principle that, as civilians, PMSCs should not directly participate in hostilities, translating that principle into concrete, practical guidelines on what they may or may not be tasked to do is complex. Due to the increasing complexity of peace operations and their more and more robust mandates, direct participation in hostilities is an essential – and overlooked – question regarding the use of PMSCs in peace operations.

The Status of PMSC Personnel Under IHL

The international humanitarian law of international armed conflicts is deeply concerned with the 'status' of individuals and requires people to be classified as either combatants or civilians. In non-international armed conflicts, the IHL treaty rules do not make such a distinction, but there is a recent tendency in doctrine, expert discussions and jurisprudence to circumscribe a kind of status of fighters with continuous fighting function who do not have the rights of civilians. In international armed conflicts, in any case, civilians and combatants are the two principal categories of persons under IHL, and the vast majority of rights and – to a controversial extent – obligations flow from the ascription of a person to one or the other. It is unlikely that many private military and/or security contractors satisfy the criteria in order to constitute the armed forces of a party to a conflict recognized by IHL. It is important to recall, nevertheless, that civilians and combatants must respect IHL. Unlike other bodies of international law, international humanitarian law imposes obligations directly on individuals, whether they are state actors or not.[1] Thus, no matter their

---

[1] The criminalization of many rules of IHL is a testament to this fact, and was affirmed by the ICTR in *Prosecutor v. Akayesu* (Trial Chamber Judgment) ICTR-96–4-T (2 September 1998) para. 444. The fact that IHL applies to anyone with a capacity to violate it, whether they were state agents/organs or not, is evidenced by Article 9 of the Brussels Declaration of 1874: 'The laws, rights, and duties of war apply not only to armies, but also to militia and volunteer corps fulfilling the following conditions: 1. That they be commanded by a person responsible for his subordinates; 2. That they have a fixed distinctive emblem recognizable at a distance; 3. That they carry arms openly; and 4. That they conduct their operations in accordance with the laws and customs of war' (Project of an International Declaration Concerning the Laws and Customs of War, Brussels, 27 August 1874). While this declaration was never adopted as a treaty, it formed the basis for the development of IHL and may be said to carry persuasive authority. In addition, Geneva Convention I of 1949 imposes an obligation directly on civilians (Article 18(3)) in regard to wounded and sick members of the armed forces. Geneva Convention [I] for the Amelioration of the Condition of the Wounded and Sick in Armed Forces in the Field of 12 August 1949, 75 UNTS 970 (hereafter GC I). On the criminalization of rules of IHL and how they bind individuals, see Marko Milanovic, 'Is

status, PMSCs active in situations of armed conflict are bound by at least the criminalized rules of IHL.

Unlike combatants, civilians may not, with impunity, directly participate in hostilities. While the history of combatant immunity shows that that concept was not developed in order to protect civilians, in effect it helps to preserve the fundamental distinction between civilians and combatants and to diminish the likelihood that civilians will be directly targeted in armed conflicts.[2]

7.1 PMSCs and Combatant or Fighter Status

One of the fundamental principles of the IHL of international armed conflicts is that one must distinguish between civilians and combatants. The principle of distinction is crucial to IHL's ability to protect civilians from the violence of armed conflict, since it is only lawful to target combatants.[3] Civilians are protected from direct attack.[4] In addition, the 'collateral effects' on civilians of attacks on lawful military objectives must be taken into account, which also serves to limit harm caused to civilians in armed conflict.[5] In terms of the rights flowing from status, only combatants may lawfully directly participate in hostilities: this is the 'combatants' privilege'.[6] The fact that combatants may lawfully directly participate in hostilities means that they are immune to prosecution for lawful acts of war – for example, killing enemy soldiers – but they are not immune

---

the Rome Statute Binding on Individuals? (And Why We Should Care)' (2011) 9 *J Intl Crim Justice* 25–52.

[2] For a short history of combatant status and combatant immunity, see G.I.A.D. Draper, 'Combatant Status: An Historical Perspective' (1972) 11 *Military Law and Law of War Review* 135–143.

[3] Article 48 of the Protocol Additional to the Geneva Conventions of 1949 and Relating to the Protection of Victims of International Armed Conflicts of 8 June 1977, 1125 UNTS 3 (AP I). Indeed, two US officers state, 'Compliance with this concept of distinction is the fundamental difference between heroic Soldier and murderer.' See M. Maxwell and R. Meyer, 'The Principle of Distinction: Probing the Limits of Its Customariness' (March 2007) *Army Lawyer* 1–11 at 1.

[4] As long as they are not directly participating in hostilities. See Article 51(3) of the Protocol Additional to the Geneva Conventions of 12 August 1949, and relating to the Protection of Victims of International Armed Conflicts (Protocol I) of 8 June 1977, Geneva, in force 7 December 1978 (AP I).

[5] Articles 51 and 57 (on proportionality and precautions) of AP I. See M. Sassòli and L. Cameron, 'The Protection of Civilian Objects – Current State of the Law and Issues de lege ferenda', in N. Ronzitti and G. Venturini (eds.), *The Law of Air Warfare: Contemporary Issues* (Utrecht: Eleven, 2006), pp. 35–74.

[6] Article 43(2) of AP I.

from prosecution for the commission of violations of IHL.[7] If captured, combatants have the right to be prisoners of war unless they have failed to distinguish themselves from the civilian population while fighting.[8] The flip side to this 'privilege' is that combatants may be directly targeted and killed by opposing enemy combatants. While there are some limits on the type of weapons that may be used against combatants[9] and which circumscribe tactics to some extent (for example, 'ruses' of war are permitted but perfidious attacks are prohibited), traditionally under IHL there is no 'proportionality calculation' between the harm inflicted on the combatant and the military advantage drawn from the attack for combatants.

It is unlikely that PMSC contractors will have the status of combatants in international armed conflicts. This conclusion is based on an overall assessment of PMSCs, rather than flowing from a specific treaty text.[10] In particular, it should be noted that PMSCs are not incorporated into the regular armed forces of a state. Moreover, the criteria of 'belonging' in Article 4A(2) of the Third Geneva Convention implicitly requires that a state accept that a group fights on its behalf. That is to say, an acceptance that a group carries out other activities on behalf of a state (such as catering) would not be sufficient to render the members of that group (or PMSC) combatants via an application of Article 4A(2).

This fact has important repercussions for the rest of the legal framework defining the rights and obligations of these actors, especially in terms of the types of activities that governments and others may contract with them to carry out and the limits within those activities.

The IHL of *non*-international armed conflicts, on the other hand, contains no status or definition of 'combatants'. This is a natural consequence

---

[7] Combatant immunity is not enshrined as such in GC III; however, it is understood as concomitant of POW status. It is an old concept, 'recognized by Belli, Grotius, Pufendorf, and Vattel', and set down in the Lieber Code. See Waldemar Solf, 'The Status of Combatants in Non-international Armed Conflicts Under Domestic Law and Transnational Practice' (1983) 33 *American U L Rev* 53 at 58.

[8] Article 4A of Geneva Convention III defines who has a right to be a prisoner of war, not who has a right to be a combatant. There are a small number of people who have the right to POW status without having combatant status. Article 44(3) of AP I confirms that a person who does not distinguish himself when attacking loses POW status. 'While fighting' used here includes all the possibilities set forth in Article 44(3) – preparatory to an attack, etc.

[9] See, e.g., Protocol on Blinding Laser Weapons (Protocol IV to the 1980 Convention on Prohibitions or Restrictions on the Use of Certain Conventional Weapons) 13 October 1995, 1380 UNTS 370 (entered into force 30 July 1998); Article 35 of AP I (the prohibition on superfluous injury or unnecessary suffering).

[10] Cameron and Chetail, *Privatizing War*, pp. 386–421. See also Cameron, 'The Use of PMSCs in Armed Conflicts and Certain Peace Operations'.

of the fact that combatant status – and its benefits – originally flowed from the state sovereignty.[11] One of the key reasons why the international law relating to non-international armed conflicts differs to that governing international armed conflicts is because states are unwilling to extend the privileges of combatant immunity to persons who take up arms against them.[12] Although there have been calls to extend the entire regime of POW status to fighters in non-international armed conflicts,[13] states have not been receptive to the notion.

In a nutshell, in international armed conflicts, rules on the targeting and treatment of persons are largely status-based, but in non-international armed conflicts they were traditionally seen as conduct-based. This means that in non-international armed conflicts, the rules as to whether a person may be targeted and the protections to which he or she is entitled were determined by the person's own conduct – in particular, the fact that the person does not (or no longer) directly participates in hostilities. Consequently, the concept of 'direct participation in hostilities' is of general importance in non-international armed conflicts. The concept of 'direct participation in hostilities' also applies in international armed conflicts, but it is not the central factor for determining who constitutes the opposing, enemy armed forces. In non-international armed conflicts, recently the idea has appeared that members of armed groups, or some of them, are 'fighters' who may be attacked, like combatants in international armed conflicts, at any time until they surrender or are otherwise hors de combat.[14] This concept nuances the general rule that civilians who are directly participating in hostilities may only be attacked during their direct participation. Thus, a delineation that may be considered 'status-based'

---

[11] Draper, 'Combatant Status'; Allan Rosas, *The Legal Status of Prisoners of War* (Helsinki: Abo Akademi, 1976), p. 222; Solf, 'The Status of Combatants', 53–67.

[12] M. Bothe, K.J. Partsch and W.A. Solf, *New Rules for Victims of Armed Conflict: Commentary on the Two 1977 Protocols Additional to the Geneva Conventions of 1949* (The Hague: Martinus Nijhoff, 1982), p. 244; Marco Sassòli, 'Combatants', in R. Wolfrum (ed.), *Max Planck Encyclopedia of Public International Law* (Oxford University Press, 2013), para. 35.

[13] Emily Crawford, *The Treatment of Combatants and Insurgents Under the Law of Armed Conflict* (Oxford University Press, 2010).

[14] The nature of membership in such a group and the precise function of the individual in question in order for him or her to be a lawful target of attack is a matter of intense debate. I am convinced that simple membership in an armed group is not sufficient to render a person subject to attack at all times and believe that only those members with a fighting function may be attacked at any time, and others only when they are directly participating in hostilities. See M. Sassòli, 'The International Legal Framework for Stability Operations: When May International Forces Attack or Detain Someone in Afghanistan?' (2009) 39 *Israel YB Human Rights* 177–212.

also appears in the IHL of non-international armed conflicts. When dealing with those who regularly participate in hostilities in non-international armed conflicts, I will use the term 'fighters'.

In order to determine whether PMSCs may constitute 'fighters' in non-international armed conflicts, it is necessary to assess whether they are members of armed groups with a role that entails their direct participation in hostilities in such a way as to constitute a continuous combat function. These will inherently be highly factually dependent and, moreover, are intrinsically linked with the more detailed analysis of direct participation in hostilities.[15] The different means of defining who is a 'fighter' in non-international armed conflict raise an important question with respect to PMSCs. In international armed conflicts, the fact that states and PMSCs deny that PMSCs have a fighting function is fundamental to whether PMSCs have combatant status because in order to 'belong' to a party to a conflict and have combatant status, the party must accept that one fights on its behalf.[16] Is the same true for 'fighter' status in non-international armed conflicts? Put another way, do PMSCs who guard military objectives (and therefore could be said to directly participate in hostilities with a continuous combat function) belong to the party to the non-international armed conflict that gave them that role, irrespective of whether the party acknowledges it as a fighting function? The IHL of non-international armed conflicts, especially in regard to distinguishing between non-state 'fighters' and civilians, is even more highly fact-dependent than in international armed conflicts. Moreover, 'fighter status' in non-international armed conflicts carries no implications of 'combatant privilege', since members of organized armed groups are always at risk of prosecution even for lawful acts of war. However, the concept of 'fighting function' does not apply to government armed forces, even in non-international armed conflicts.

The ICRC's Interpretive Guidance on the Notion of Direct Participation in Hostilities suggests that only non-state organized armed groups in non-international armed conflicts are defined and affected by the concept of 'continuous combat function'.[17] One may therefore wonder whether PMSCs contracted by a state party to a non-international armed conflict tasked with guarding a military objective would not have 'fighter' status,

---

[15] See also discussion below on direct participation in hostilities.
[16] For a discussion, see Cameron and Chetail, *Privatizing War*, pp. 393–401. See also Cameron, 'The Use of PMSCs in Armed Conflicts and Certain Peace Operations'.
[17] ICRC, Interpretive Guidance, Recommendation II.

in contrast to PMSCs in the same situation but who were contracted by an organized armed group. If the same rules apply for defining members of state armed forces in international armed conflicts as in non-international armed conflicts, then PMSCs contracted by states would not be considered fighters.[18] This issue is important and tricky. Many PMSCs are contracted by states. Many conflicts, including current ones in which PMSCs are used extensively (such as Iraq and Afghanistan), start as international armed conflicts and evolve into non-international armed conflicts. This would mean that during one phase of the same conflict when contracted by the same party, a PMSC would not be considered a combatant, but during a second phase could be considered a 'fighter' if we accept that state armed forces may also be in part defined or affected by the 'continuous combat function' rule. The main concrete effect of this would be that PMSCs who were lawful targets only for the duration of their direct participation in hostilities would become targetable on a long-term basis, as long as they do not actively take steps to disengage from their role.

Arguments that may favour defining state armed forces according to the same rules as are applicable for non-state armed forces include respect for the principle of equality of belligerents. Why, for example, would the cook of the state armed forces be a lawful target, while the cook of an armed group would not be? While that may seem a valid question, serious doubts abound as to whether one can truly speak of an equality of belligerents in the context of non-international armed conflicts.[19] The illegality of the non-state armed forces activity means that they are always in a more precarious situation than state armed forces, despite the non-existence of POW status (even for state armed forces).[20] There are no signs that the international community is contemplating changing the way state armed forces are defined in non-international armed conflicts. At the present moment, it would seem that such a change could introduce considerable confusion and may even exacerbate the inequality of belligerents in non-international armed conflicts. PMSCs contracted by state armed forces in

---

[18] Ibid., Recommendation III.

[19] Marco Sassòli, 'Introducing a Sliding-Scale of Obligations to Address the Fundamental Inequality Between Armed Groups and States?' (2011) 93 *IRRC* 425.

[20] For example, while rebel fighters may be prosecuted for having participated in hostilities, even if rebel forces were to become the government (having defeated the government side), they could not prosecute government soldiers for having participated in hostilities against them as that would contravene the criminal law principle of nulla poena sine lege, since at the time of the hostilities it would not have been illegal for them to fight.

such conflicts thus do not become fighters when the conflict becomes non-international.

The discussion below in Chapter 10, relating to the degree to which the entire peacekeeping force becomes a party to a conflict when one or several troop-contributing countries are engaged in a conflict with an armed group, finds a similar echo here.

While it is rare that PMSC personnel will have combatant status in international armed conflicts, it may be the case that they will be 'fighters' with a continuous combat function in non-international armed conflicts, so long as they are not contracted by states. Under the binary structure of IHL, if individuals are not combatants, then they must be civilians.

7.2 PMSCs as Civilians Accompanying the Armed Forces

There is a category of civilians who nevertheless may have the status of POWs. These are civilians who accompany the armed forces of a state, and who are authorized to do so. In fact, there is a category of persons provided for in the Geneva Conventions that seems perfectly suited to catch a significant component of PMSCs and their activities: Article 4A(4) of GC III, 'persons accompanying the armed forces without actually being members thereof.' That paragraph provides that the following persons also have the right to POW status:

> Persons who accompany the armed forces without actually being members thereof, such as civilian members of military aircraft crews, war correspondents, supply contractors, members of labour units or of services responsible for the welfare of the armed forces, provided that they have received authorization from the armed forces which they accompany, who shall provide them for that purpose with an identity card...

It must be stressed that such persons have POW status, but not combatant status, combatant immunity, or combatant privileges, and they may not be attacked like combatants. For all purposes other than treatment when fallen into the power of the enemy in an international armed conflict, they are civilians.[21]

---

[21] It is an old category of prisoners of war, having been included in the 1899 and 1907 Hague Regulations and the 1929 Geneva Convention on prisoners of war. See Article 13 of the annex to Hague Convention II, 1899; Article 13 of the annex to Hague Convention IV, 1907; Article 81 of the Geneva Convention relative to the treatment of prisoners of war (27 July 1929). For a longer discussion, including an assessment of the relationship of this category of persons to those who fall under Article 4A(2) of the Convention relative to the Treatment of Prisoners of War, Geneva, 12 August 1949, in force 21 October 1950, see

The drafters of Geneva Convention III did not discuss any limits on the roles they could undertake,[22] and the list of roles contained in the article is illustrative and not exhaustive.[23] However, it is clear that such roles may not include combat activity.[24] States using civilians in such roles consider that they are not combatants.[25] Moreover, the limitation is important to preserving the distinction between what constitutes mere support for the war effort (which is not a combat activity leading to loss of protection from attack) and what is combat activity. To consider that such individuals are in any case combatants due to these roles would obliterate that distinction.

The idea that POW status could be given to persons who do not have combatant status is by no means anomalous in IHL.[26] For individuals such as medics and chaplains, who are even members of the armed forces but who do not have combatant status, the notion that their status would not

Cameron, 'The Use of PMSCs in Armed Conflicts and Certain Peace Operations', 35–49 and 55–57.

[22] Final Record of the Diplomatic Conference of Geneva of 1949, Vol. II-A (Berne 1949), pp. 416–418.

[23] J. Pictet (ed.), The Geneva Conventions of 12 August 1949: Commentary, Third Geneva Convention Relative to the Treatment of Prisoners of War (Geneva, 1960), p. 64 (Commentary GC III).

[24] ICRC, Interpretive Guidance, pp. 36–37. See also D. Rothwell, 'Legal Opinion on the Status of Non-Combatants and Contractors under International Humanitarian Law and Australian Law' (December 2004), available at www.aspi.org.au/pdf/ASPIlegalopinion_contractors.pdf, at para. 8a. See also Anna Köhler, Private Sicherheits-und Militärunternehmen im bewaffneten Konflikt: Eine völkerrechtliche Bewertung (Frankfurt am Main: Kölner Schriften zu Recht und Staat, 2010), p. 99.

[25] See for US DoD Directive 3040.21 (5 October 2005); for Australia, see Rothwell, 'Legal Opinion'. See also Köhler, Private Sicherheits, pp. 98–100. The UK Manual is somewhat more ambiguous, stating that civilians who are authorized to accompany armed forces 'remain non-combatants, though entitled to prisoner of war status, so long as they take no direct part in hostilities'. See UK Ministry of Defence, Manual on the Law of Armed Conflict (Oxford University Press, 2004), p. 40, para. 4.3.7. This sentence could mean that they remain non-combatants so long as they take no direct part in hostilities, or it could be read that they remain entitled to POW status as long as they take no direct part in hostilities. It is unfortunately not a paragon of clarity.

[26] For example, members of medical units and chaplains are members of the armed forces but do not have combatant status: Article 43(2) AP I. Any civilian who is incorporated into the armed forces and who is not a medic or chaplain does, however, have combatant status. See Y. Sandoz, C. Swinarski and B. Zimmermann (eds.), Commentary on the Additional Protocols of 8 June 1977 to the Geneva Conventions of 12 August 1949 (Geneva: ICRC, 1987), p. 515 (Article 43). When POW status was specified for sutlers and contractors in the early conventions (i.e. Hague Regulations of 1899 and 1929 POW Convention), the granting of that status was in an article that, textually, was comparatively far removed from the article concerning combatant status. In my view, this further supports the notion that there has never been a sense that such persons benefit from combatant status.

prevent their being prosecuted for direct participation in hostilities if their actions crossed the line from force used in self-defence to direct participation in hostilities is a logical and necessary consequence of their lack of combatant status – they do not become POWs but are 'retained personnel'. The same logic applies to PMSC civilians accompanying the armed forces. That being said, the proximity of such individuals to the battle zone by virtue of their roles may entail a greater need to have recourse to force in self-defence.[27]

A number of PMSCs fall easily into this category, as foreseen by US Department of Defense Directives and the Status of Forces Agreements of other states.[28] Clearly, based on the text of the article itself, the primary condition is that such PMSCs be *authorized* by the armed forces they accompany to do so. As such, PMSCs hired by NGOs, private companies or even government departments other than defence departments (depending, of course, on internal laws) would not have POW status by virtue of Article 4A(4).[29]

7.3 PMSCs as Civilians

Under international humanitarian law, in international armed conflicts, one is either a combatant or a civilian – there is no third category.[30] Within the broad category of civilians, under Convention IV there is a narrower category of 'protected persons' (based largely on nationality) who benefit from more detailed rules regarding their treatment in the hands of the enemy.[31] Nevertheless, all civilians, including those who are not 'protected

---

[27] The drafters of the Geneva Conventions limited the force that could be used from hospitals for them to retain protected status, and they could have made a similar limitation here for civilians accompanying the armed forces. If they were negotiating this provision today, this would surely be the most crucial issue but at the time it was thought that this category was nearly obsolete.

[28] Department of Defense Instruction 3020.41 (3 October 2005) on 'Contractor Personnel Authorized to Accompany the U.S. Armed Forces'. Australian Status of Forces Agreements provide for liability structures of civilians accompanying the Australian Defence Forces when deployed abroad; see Rothwell, 'Legal Opinion', esp. paras 5 and 23–25.

[29] See also Rothwell, 'Legal Opinion', para. 5.

[30] For a discussion canvassing and dismissing the existence of a category of 'unlawful combatants', see Cameron and Chetail, *Privatizing War*, pp. 423–426.

[31] See Article 4 GC IV for a complete definition of who is a protected person under that Convention. See also *Prosecutor v. Tadic* (Appeals Chamber Judgment) IT-94-1-A (15 July 1999), paras 164–166 (on the notion of 'allegiance'). See also M. Sassòli and L. Olson, 'The Judgment of the ICTY Appeals Chamber on the Merits in the Tadic Case' (2000) 82 *IRRC* 733–769.

persons', are protected against direct and/or indiscriminate attack (and from the effects of hostilities) as long as they do not actively or directly participate in hostilities.[32] The consequence of direct participation in hostilities is a loss of protection from attack, but it does not alter or affect the civilian status of the individual in question. Thus, if PMSCs meet the criteria to be 'protected persons' under Convention IV, they benefit from the relevant and applicable provisions in that Convention. A limited number of derogations are permitted for protected civilians engaged in activities hostile to the security of the state.[33] Even if PMSCs are not 'protected persons' within the meaning of Article 4, they benefit from immunity from attack and from the fundamental guarantees that apply to all (provided they are not participating in hostilities) that are enumerated in Article 3 common to the four Geneva Conventions, Article 75 of Protocol I (which is recognized as customary international law) and customary international law more generally.

There may be some situations in which this either/or qualification seems unsatisfactory, as perhaps is the case with heavily armed PMSC groups.[34] Indeed, in law, hard cases often push at the boundaries of existing legal definitions and lead to strange results. Nevertheless, under the current state of the law, anomalies do not call into question the overall framework for classifying persons under IHL.

7.4   PMSCs as Mercenaries

One often hears the employees of PMSCs being referred to as 'mercenaries'. Under IHL, it is not a violation of the Geneva Conventions or Protocols to be a mercenary, and mercenarism in and of itself does not entail international criminal responsibility.[35] In IHL, the consequence of being a mercenary is identical to that of being a civilian who directly participates in hostilities – no POW status if captured, such that persons may be tried for the simple fact of fighting enemy armed forces. A mercenary as defined under Article 47(2) of Additional Protocol I may therefore be punished for direct participation in hostilities under the internal laws of

---

[32] Article 13 of the Convention Relative to the Protection of Civilian Persons in Time of War, Geneva, 12 August 1949, in force 21 October 1950 (GC IV), Article 50 of AP I; see also discussion on the notion of direct participation in hostilities, below.

[33] Article 5 of GC IV. Note, however, that for persons in occupied territories, the only rights that are forfeited by such persons are 'rights of communication' (Article 5(2) of GC III).

[34] 'Terrorist' groups are another category that some argue pose a challenge to this bifurcated analysis. See M Sassòli, 'Terrorism and War' (2006) 4 J Intl Crim Justice 959 at 974.

[35] See Cameron and Chetail, Privatizing War, pp. 66–80.

the detaining power, but may be prosecuted for simply *being* a mercenary only if that state also has separate laws designating mercenarism as a distinct crime.[36] Mercenary status is relevant under IHL only in international armed conflicts (since combatant status and its privileges exist only in those conflicts), whereas the mercenary conventions may also apply in situations of non-international armed conflict.[37] No sweeping conclusion can be drawn that all PMSC employees are or are not mercenaries under Article 47(2) AP I since the definition requires an individual determination on a case-by-case basis.[38] While it is possible to conclude that some individual employees or contractors may indeed satisfy all criteria and be validly held by a detaining power to be mercenaries, it is unlikely to be the case for the vast majority of PMSC personnel.

7.5 Conclusion

The vast majority of PMSC personnel will have the status of civilians (or 'non-participants') under international humanitarian law, and a number of those may be civilians accompanying armed forces with a right to POW (but not combatant) status.[39] That civilian status means that they may not, with impunity, directly participate in hostilities. In other words, it sets an important limit on the circumstances and degree of force they may use in a situation of armed conflict. The following two chapters will elaborate on the laws comprising the web of rules on the use of force permissible for non-fighters in armed conflicts and show how those rules affect the tasks that may easily be contracted out to private companies. The question at the heart of this inquiry is: what does civilian/non-participant status mean

---

[36] The six criteria of Article 47(2) must be fulfilled cumulatively in order for a person to meet the legal definition of being a mercenary.

[37] See also J.-M. Henckaerts and L. Doswald-Beck, *Customary International Humanitarian Law*, 2 vols. (Cambridge University Press, 2005), vol. 1, p. 395, Rule 108, commentary on non-international armed conflict: 'Mercenaries participating in a non-international armed conflict are not entitled to prisoner-of-war status as no right to that status exists in such situations.'

[38] For a full discussion, see Cameron and Chetail, *Privatizing War*, pp. 426–429. See also Cameron, 'The Use of PMSCs in Armed Conflicts and Certain Peace Operations', 62–67 and 169–181. The former UN Special Rapporteur on the Right of Peoples to Self-Determination consistently argued that private military companies are mercenaries without distinguishing among individuals. See, for example, Enrique Ballasteros, 'Report of the Special Rapporteur' (13 January 1999) UN Doc E/CN.4/1999/11 at para. 45. This approach has evolved and softened with the new Working Group.

[39] In the 'International Code of Conduct for Private Security Providers' (9 November 2010), the Rules on the Use of Force take for granted that PSCs have civilian status. See Rules 30–32. The Code is available at www.icoc-psp.org (accessed 4 March 2011).

for the roles that can be given to PMSCs without infringing the dichotomy between combatants and civilians? The simple answer is that such individuals should not be given combat roles unless they have combatant status because they should not directly participate in hostilities without that status. PMSCs should seek to avoid activities that will lead them to directly participate in hostilities. In addition, they may not be given roles that are explicitly reserved to members of armed forces.[40] On a separate note, if they are given other roles that are closely related to a conflict but do not involve a combat role, states should make sure that they provide any additional explanation required for a person to carry out such tasks in full compliance with the obligations set out in the Conventions.

Of course, there are many roles PMSCs may be contracted to do in the context of armed conflict that do not lead them to directly participate in hostilities or carry out acts that may weaken the principle of distinction between civilians and combatants. States have relied on civilians to provide logistical and catering support and other non-combat assistance to their armed forces for centuries. PMSCs that are of greatest concern when it comes to the use of force in armed conflict are those in security roles. In current conflicts, approximately 10–12 per cent of PMSC personnel are engaged in security provision under contract with the US Department of Defense.[41] While this is a relatively low percentage of the number of total contractors, it nevertheless represents a significant number of individuals and it may not in fact accurately reflect the true numbers.[42] This cohort of PMSC personnel is the main concern in the following two chapters.

---

[40] For example, responsible officers of POW camps. See Article 39 of GC III.

[41] Special Inspector General for Iraq Reconstruction (SIGIR), 'Quarterly Report to US Congress' (30 October 2009) 40. In Afghanistan, the US Department of Defense has more contractors than armed forces. Seven per cent of the more than 74,000 PMSC/contractors were engaged in security tasks for the US Department of Defense in 2009. Moshe Schwartz, 'Department of Defense Contractors in Iraq and Afghanistan: Background and Analysis' (US Congressional Research Service, 21 September 2009) at 10.

[42] The October 2009 SIGIR report indicates that of the 174,000 contractors working in Iraq for the US Department of Defense at that moment, some 13,145, or 11%, were engaged in security functions. However, it is important to underscore that the same report indicates that other US departments known for hiring PMSCs as security personnel had not entered such persons into the relevant database; thus, their numbers, although suspected to be high, are unknown. See ibid., 40–41. The US Department of State uses PMSCs for security of its embassies in Iraq and Afghanistan (see US Department of State, Broadcasting Board of Governors and Office of the Inspector General, 'Performance Audit of the U.S. Training Center Contract for Personal Protective Services in Afghanistan', Report no. MERO-A-09-08 (August 2009)).

The UN is now relying more on PMSCs as security guards in peace operations – including in operations where IHL applies. Similar concerns arise as for PMSCs contracted by states in other armed conflicts. Indeed, as the discussion below will show, it is not always easy or intuitive to know when a use of force crosses the line to constitute an impermissible combat role or direct participation in hostilities, including in a peace operation. In any case, all PMSC personnel should of course be wary of the risks of direct participation in hostilities and the limits of self-defence, and in addition should be aware of any legal obligations flowing from IHL that are related to or govern the tasks with which they are charged.

8

The Impact of Civilian Status on the Rights and Duties of PMSCs

Direct Participation in Hostilities

The primary consequence of direct participation in hostilities is that persons who directly participate in hostilities in either international or non-international armed conflicts lose protection against attack during their participation. That is to say, they may be directly, intentionally targeted by opposing armed forces, and under IHL at least, the possibility to affect them incidentally does not need to be taken into account under the proportionality principle and no precautionary measures have to be taken for their benefit. In addition, they may be prosecuted for having directly participated in hostilities. There are nuances to these consequences, however. First of all, as mentioned above, the Interpretive Guidance indicates that, while it is not universally agreed, there is an emerging consensus that we must distinguish between two categories of direct participants in hostilities to know when they may be attacked. That is to say, there is a difference between the duration of loss of protection for members of armed groups who have a continuous combat function as compared with individuals who are not armed group members with such a function but who nevertheless sometimes (even frequently) directly participate in hostilities. The temporal aspect of loss of protection will thus differ depending on whether a PMSC employee is considered to be an armed group member with a continuous combat function or whether he is simply deemed to be an individual who on his own occasionally directly participates in hostilities.

For individuals, there is a loss of protection from attack, but this lasts *only* for the duration of their direct participation. (Further elements of 'duration' will be outlined in more detail below.[1]) In addition, civilian direct participants may be prosecuted for acts such as killing enemy armed

---

[1] See below, Section 8.2.

forces – acts that would not be unlawful if committed by a member of the armed forces.[2] In this respect, the consequences are the same if PMSC contractors are civilians who directly participate in hostilities and if they are persons who are found to be mercenaries.[3] Members of armed groups with a continuous combat function, on the other hand, lose protection from attack for as long as they maintain that role and do not actively disengage from the armed group.[4] This extensive loss of protection is counterbalanced with an appeal by IHL for states *not* to prosecute such individuals for hostile acts that comply with IHL. Article 6(5) AP II encourages at least amnesty in such cases.[5] Moreover, it is counterbalanced by the principle of military necessity. As such, Article IX of the Interpretive Guidance stipulates:

> In addition to the restraints imposed by international humanitarian law on specific means and methods of warfare, and without prejudice to further restrictions that may arise under other applicable branches of international law, the kind and degree of force which is permissible against persons not entitled to protection against direct attack must not exceed what is actually necessary to accomplish a legitimate military purpose in the prevailing circumstances.

This approach is entirely logical, but it must be admitted that it has been one of the most contentious aspects of the Interpretive Guidance.[6]

There is disagreement among experts as to whether contractors who are civilians accompanying the armed forces and, as such, entitled to POW status (i.e. under Article 4A(4) GC III) are immune from prosecution for committing hostile acts if they directly participate in hostilities. In other

---

[2] Besides chaplains and medical personnel, who are not combatants.

[3] See Article 47(1) of AP I and discussion above.

[4] See above discussion on fighters in non-international armed conflict. Of course, if they are injured, captured or otherwise hors de combat, they are also protected against direct attack.

[5] On the other hand, this plea in itself must be nuanced by the fact that fighters in non-international armed conflicts should not be detained according to the same paradigm as combatants in international armed conflicts and that some judicial or administrative procedure is necessary. See Marco Sassòli, 'The International Legal Framework for Fighting Terrorists According to the Bush and the Obama Administrations: Same or Different, Correct or Incorrect?' (2010) 104 *Am Society Intl L Proceedings* 277–280.

[6] For the most strident criticism, see W. Hays Parks, 'Part IX of the ICRC "Direct Participation in Hostilities" Study: No Mandate, No Expertise, and Legally Incorrect' (2010) 42 *NYUJILP* 769, and the response by Nils Melzer, 'Keeping the Balance Between Military Necessity and Humanity: A Response to Four Critiques of the ICRC's Interpretive Guidance on the Notion of Direct Participation in Hostilities' (2010) 42 *NYUJILP* 831 esp. at 893–912. For other criticism, see Michael Schmitt, 'Military Necessity and Humanity in International Humanitarian Law: Preserving the Delicate Balance' (2010) *Virginia J Intl L* 795–839.

words, there is some controversy as to whether civilians accompanying the armed forces, including PMSCs, constitute a special group when it comes to consequences for direct participation in hostilities. As noted above, it is possible that some PMSCs (companies or individuals) may have the status of civilians accompanying the armed forces, a fact that makes it worthwhile to explore this issue in a little more detail. An earlier draft of the ICRC's Interpretive Guidance note stated that, 'in contradistinction to ordinary civilians, [civilians accompanying the armed forces] are entitled to POW-status upon capture but, nevertheless, lack combatant privilege and may be prosecuted and punished under the domestic law of the capturing state for the mere fact of having directly participated in hostilities.'[7] During the expert meetings, one expert took issue with this statement, insisting that civilians accompanying the armed forces retain all benefits of POW status, including immunity from prosecution, even if they directly participate in hostilities.[8] With respect, I disagree. Although the expert cited one case in which civilians accompanying armed forces who had fought opposing forces with anti-aircraft weapons retained POW status on capture and were not prosecuted for direct participation in hostilities, that example merely indicates that a detaining power is not *obliged* to prosecute such civilians.[9] It does not indicate or prove that a detaining power is prohibited from doing so. That is, it does not prove that Article 4A(4) civilians necessarily or by law must retain all the privileges of POW status even if they directly participate in hostilities. Another expert, in a background paper, cites two further examples from World War II in which civilians accompanying the armed forces who directly participated in hostilities were not prosecuted for those acts, but again, this merely reinforces my conclusion that a detaining power is not obliged to prosecute.[10] Without more, these examples do not indicate that a detaining power

---

[7] ICRC, 'Fourth Expert Meeting on the Notion of Direct Participation in Hostilities: Summary Report' (Geneva, November 2006) (hereafter 'Fourth Expert Meeting' (2006)) at 35 (at page 18 of draft Interpretive Guidance then being circulated).

[8] Ibid., 35–36.   [9] Ibid., 36.

[10] W. Hays Parks, 'Evolution of Policy and Law Concerning the Role of Civilians and Civilian Contractors Accompanying the Armed Forces', Expert Paper for the ICRC's Third Expert Meeting on the Notion of Direct Participation in Hostilities (2005). This seems to reflect the advice the same expert provides to the US Department of Defense, as, in an email to the Chairman of the Joint Chiefs of Staff Office of the Legal Advisor, the same expert wrote, 'A contractor who takes a direct part in hostilities ... remains entitled to prisoner of war status, but may be subject to prosecution *if his or her actions include acts of perfidy*.' Emphasis added. Email from Hays Parks to Col Meier, quoted in G. Corn, 'Unarmed but How Dangerous? Civilian Augmentees, the Law of Armed Conflict, and the Search for a More Effective Test for Permissible Civilian Battlefield Functions' (2008) 2 *J Natl Security L & Policy* 257, 259, note 5.

is prohibited from doing so. The other hypothetical examples cited by another expert in support of his dissenting view refer rather to cases where it is highly debatable that the individual in question was actually directly participating in hostilities and therefore do not influence my conclusion on this issue. For example, the expert argued that a sniper surveying an airbase could determine that the civilian contractor supervising repairs had a most important role and target him directly.[11]

In its final version of the Interpretive Guidance, the ICRC merely states that civilians accompanying armed forces 'were never meant to directly participate in hostilities on behalf of a party to a conflict.'[12] The document makes no comment or recommendation with respect to a prohibition to prosecute such individuals.[13] In my view, the ICRC could have made a stronger statement: the notion that direct participation in hostilities by civilians accompanying armed forces is not *prohibited* by IHL does not necessarily entail that detaining powers are obliged to give those persons immunity from prosecution, just that they are not obliged to prosecute. This debate thus may have consequences for a relatively small but nonetheless important cohort of PMSCs.

Logically, however, if the contractors from such companies directly participate in hostilities on a regular or semi-regular basis, it would be necessary for them to meet the criteria in Article 4A of GC III (or Article 43 of AP I) in order to benefit from combatant privilege and immunity. If

---

[11] ICRC, 'Fourth Expert Meeting' (2006) at 35–36. In fairness, the expert's phrasing of the example is subtle, taking into account that different people may perceive the same situation differently. Nevertheless, if the expert's view is that legally such actions should not be interpreted as constituting direct participation in hostilities, the emphasis should rather be on ensuring that combatants would not make such an error and directly target such civilian contractors.

[12] ICRC, Interpretive Guidance, p. 38. This is commensurate with earlier conventions dealing with POW status. In particular, in the Regulations annexed to Hague Convention IV of 1907, Article 13 is not at all linked to, nor indeed textually close to, the Article setting down who had combatant status. It states, 'Individuals who follow an army without directly belonging to it, such as newspaper correspondents and reporters, sutlers and contractors, who fall into the enemy's hands and whom the latter thinks expedient to detain, are entitled to be treated as prisoners of war', which implies that in many cases it may not be necessary to detain such persons (i.e. in order to weaken the military forces of the enemy) but that if they are detained, they benefit from POW status. Article 13 of the annex to Hague Convention II (1899) was essentially the same. Article 81 of the 1929 Convention on prisoners of war was also virtually the same, and appeared under the heading 'Application of the Convention to Certain Categories of Civilians'. (This was the only article under that heading.)

[13] The reason they had mentioned it was to clarify the difference between 4A(4) GC III participants and regular civilian individuals who directly participate in hostilities – to say precisely that the 4A4 POW status does not entail immunity from prosecution if they directly participate in hostilities as civilians. ICRC, 'Fourth Expert Meeting' (2006), at 36.

this were not the case, it would mean that a party could in effect create an additional fighting force with combatant privilege but without meeting the necessary criteria for that privilege, which cannot be in conformity with international humanitarian law.

The second reason it matters if PMSC personnel directly participate in hostilities is that that participation may be harmful to the principle of distinction. The notion that the state is supposed to control the use of force (monopoly) is one common to political scientists, but it is also reflected in the law.[14] If the principle of distinction is eroded because people who are not state armed forces regularly participate in hostilities, we may see a weakening in protection of civilians. Finally, there is the question whether it is unlawful for states to allow, encourage or contract civilians to directly participate in hostilities. Indeed, there are important questions as to whether it is possible for persons who are outside the chain of command to respect IHL.[15] That discussion is relevant here.

Bearing these concerns in mind, the discussion that follows will outline the concept of direct participation in hostilities in some detail, measuring activities frequently undertaken by PMSCs throughout the analysis in terms of the standards set out in the Interpretive Guidance. Despite the distinctions noted in terms of consequences for the individuals themselves, the key elements of the concept and the types of acts that typically constitute direct participation in hostilities nevertheless remain the same for all groups.

8.1   Concept, Elements and Time Frame of Direct Participation in Hostilities: What Counts Are Specific Acts

The Interpretive Guidance of the ICRC is formulated as ten recommendations with an accompanying commentary. The commentaries provide further definitions of important related concepts and flesh out difficult concepts more fully. According to the ICRC's Interpretive Guidance, 'hostilities' are defined as 'the (collective) resort by the parties to the conflict to means and methods of injuring the enemy', and 'participation' 'refers to the

---

[14] Even the European Commission for Democracy Through Law (Venice Commission) has approached the issue from this angle. See Venice Commission, 'Report on Private Military and Security Firms and Erosion of the State Monopoly on the Use of Force' (CDL-AD(2009)038, Study 531/2009) June 2009.

[15] For a discussion of this issue, see Cameron and Chetail, *Privatizing War*, pp. 91–107. See also Cameron, 'The Use of PMSCs in Armed Conflicts and Certain Peace Operations', 193–209.

(individual) involvement of a person in these hostilities'.[16] Direct participation thus focuses on an individual's specific acts rather than on a person's status, function, or affiliation.[17] The ICRC's Interpretive Guidance strongly emphasizes that the focus is on each individual act. The fact that a person has repeatedly directly participated in hostilities – without being a member of an armed group with a continuous combat function – may *not* give rise to a presumption on the part of enemy forces that that person continues to directly participate in hostilities when not carrying out specific hostile acts (inferred on the basis of intent or past behaviour).[18] Focusing on specific acts thus allows the interpretation of the components of direct participation in hostilities to be consistent and to preserve the distinction between temporary loss of protection for individuals and the sustained loss of protection 'due to combatant status or continuous combat function'.[19] Thus, individuals who repeatedly engage in direct participation in hostilities without being armed group members with a continuous combat function cannot slide into the same category as such armed group members on the basis of that repeated participation. As such, the 'specific act' element of the definition of direct participation in hostilities is the same for members of armed groups and individuals.

It may seem neither straightforward nor intuitive to know how to distinguish between such a civilian and an armed group member with a continuous combat function, especially since such a determination will depend immensely on the quality of intelligence and information available to opposing forces.[20] Admittedly, this notion is relevant only in non-international armed conflicts and for those who do not work for the state. In any case, for the sake of argument, it should be noted that the pivotal piece of information will be whether a PMSC or some of its employees constitute an armed group or are members of an armed group. If so,

---

[16] ICRC, Interpretive Guidance, p. 43. In English the Conventions use the words 'actively' and 'directly' interchangeably, whereas in French the word 'directement' is used consistently.
[17] Ibid., p. 44. Recommendation IV, at p. 16.
[18] See also discussion in ICRC, 'Fourth Expert Meeting' (2006), at 29–32 (membership approach) and 37–38.
[19] ICRC, Interpretive Guidance, pp. 44–45.
[20] See in particular comments based on the experience of one of the experts at 30–31, ICRC, 'Fourth Expert Meeting' (2006). See also the ICRC's comments regarding the difficulty of knowing whether a civilian individual has done so on a recurring basis and has the intent to continue doing so at ICRC, Interpretive Guidance, p. 45. It is, however, unclear how, logically, the type of information required to determine whether an individual's function within an armed group involves direct participation on a 'continuous' basis will be different to the type of information the ICRC suggests will be elusive for individuals.

then repeated specific acts of direct participation by an individual are more likely to entail a sustained loss of protection from attack than if the PMSC itself cannot be considered to be an armed group. When applying this analysis to reality, however, it should be recalled that, at present, it is predominantly wealthy states with highly developed militaries that are using PMSCs in the context of conflicts against diffuse and nebulous armed groups. Those groups may have a lesser ability to gather and use intelligence on PMSCs (i.e., as constituting armed group members with a continuous combat function as opposed to merely being individuals) than a highly organized military force is likely to possess. This difficulty is mitigated by the rule in IHL that if a person is not in the act of carrying out a hostile act, he must be presumed to be a civilian and therefore not liable/susceptible to direct attack. It nevertheless underscores the risks posed to the respect of IHL by an increasingly complex legal and physical terrain.

8.2   Constitutive Elements

The crux of the ICRC's Interpretive Guidance on direct participation in hostilities is encompassed in a three-part test consisting of a necessary threshold of harm, a direct causal relationship between the act in question and the expected harm, and the existence of a belligerent nexus of the act with the hostilities. The ICRC sets out the test thus:

In order to qualify as direct participation in hostilities, a specific act must meet the following cumulative criteria:

1. The act must be likely to adversely affect the military operations or military capacity of a party to an armed conflict or, alternatively, to inflict death, injury, or destruction on persons or objects protected against direct attack (threshold of harm), and
2. there must be a direct causal link between the act and the harm likely to result either from that act, or from a coordinated military operation of which that act constitutes an integral part (direct causation), and
3. the act must be specifically designed to directly cause the required threshold of harm in support of a party to the conflict and to the detriment of another (belligerent nexus).[21]

---

[21] ICRC, Interpretive Guidance, Recommendation V, pp. 16–17.

8.2.1 'Threshold of harm'

The ICRC categorizes the first part of the test as a 'threshold of harm' test. A few elements must be emphasized in order to understand how this aspect of the test operates, especially with regard to the activities of PMSCs that may come within its purview. First, similar to other analyses under IHL with respect to the conduct of hostilities, the test is concerned with whether harm is *likely* to have the specified effect on the adversary. Thus, it is not limited to an assessment of what actually occurs, but considers what is likely to occur as a result of the acts in question.[22] This makes it possible for forces to respond during or even prior to an attack, rather than only following one. It should also be emphasized that the choice of the word 'likely' is specifically designed to set an objective test, rather than to incorporate any assessment of subjective intent of the individual in question.[23]

Second, the test not only takes into account attacks against military objectives and personnel (which are more obviously linked to harming the adversary), but also encompasses attacks against civilians who are protected against direct attack. As for the first kind of attack, according to the ICRC commentary, when the attack is directed against something of a 'military nature', 'the threshold requirement will generally be satisfied regardless of quantitative gravity'.[24] The test itself is phrased broadly, incorporating acts affecting 'military operations or military capacity'. The 'harm' against military persons or objects does not necessarily have to constitute physical or material injury or damage.[25] The ICRC's

---

[22] This is, for example, similar to the proportionality analysis under IHL, which measures the *expected* loss of life or injury to civilians against the *anticipated* military advantage, rather than toting up what actually happened after the fact. It is therefore an ex ante calculation, not an ex post. See, e.g., AP I Article 57(2)(b).

[23] ICRC, 'Fifth Informal Expert Meeting: The Notion of Direct Participation in Hostilities Under IHL: Expert Comments and Elements of Response Concerning the Revised Draft of the Interpretive Guidance on the Notion of Direct Participation in Hostilities' (2008), 23–24.

[24] ICRC, Interpretive Guidance, p. 47. The relationship of this part of the test with Article 52(2) AP I is not crystal clear. It is not entirely clear from the commentary whether the ICRC meant the phrase 'military nature' in its commentary to be identical in meaning to the use of the same term in AP I Article 52(2) or whether it encompasses a broader remit of objects. For example, would a 'dual use' object such as a bridge that is being used by the military for military purposes constitute an object that is military in nature for the purposes of this test? For further discussion, see Sassòli and Cameron, 'The Protection of Civilian Objects'.

[25] ICRC, Interpretive Guidance, pp. 47–48; see also ICRC, 'Third Expert Meeting on the Notion of Direct Participation in Hostilities: Summary Report' (2005), 29.

commentary provides examples of the general types of activities that would fall under the remit of this part of the test, a number of which may be pertinent to the typical activities of PMSCs. These include 'denying the adversary the military use of certain objects, equipment and territory, guarding captured military personnel of the adversary to prevent them being forcibly liberated . . . and clearing mines placed by the adversary'.[26] On its face, armed or unarmed guarding of sites and objects could easily amount to 'denying' military use;[27] unfortunately, neither the commentary itself nor the preparatory documents to which it refers spells out in more detail what level of obstruction is necessary to 'deny' use. Thus, while this term may be current in military and operational doctrine, in legal terms it is vague. This vagueness, coupled with the ambiguity as to whether such 'denial' implies the use of armed force, could have a significant impact on PMSCs. In armed conflicts and peace operations, PMSCs conduct an enormous amount of site security. While the fact that only a small percentage of contractors on the whole are armed may assuage fears regarding their ability to harm civilians by inappropriate use of weapons, the mere fact that they are not armed does not in and of itself mean that they will not be perceived as directly participating in hostilities when carrying out such guard duties, if their acts satisfy the rest of the elements of the test.

As a general rule, if PMSC contractors are guarding persons or objects, the key factor that determines whether that activity amounts to direct participation in hostilities is the status of the persons or objects that are being protected. In a nutshell, protecting civilians or civilian objects does not constitute a direct participation in hostilities but protecting military personnel or military objectives does. The fact that they are acting merely in 'defence' is irrelevant: Article 49(1) AP I states, '"Attacks" means acts of violence against the adversary, whether in offence or in defence.' One of the tricky aspects of this fact is that objects become military objectives according to their nature, location, purpose or use.[28] There is no set list of military objectives.[29] Thus, the objects that contractor personnel are guarding may be ambiguous or change during the course of hostilities, leaving the contractor in the position of becoming a direct participant in hostilities if he continues to guard it. In addition, if the attackers are

---

[26] ICRC, Interpretive Guidance, p. 48. Footnotes omitted.
[27] The ICRC's Interpretive Guidance states that activities 'restricting or disturbing deployments, logisticians and communications' meet this threshold regardless of whether it is done by armed or unarmed persons. Ibid., p. 48.
[28] Article 52(2) AP I.
[29] Sassòli and Cameron, 'The Protection of Civilian Objects', pp. 39–41.

members of the forces of a party to the conflict, engaging them normally constitutes direct participation in hostilities. Again, a tricky case arises when the attackers themselves are 'direct participants in hostilities' rather than organized armed groups. However, if the 'attackers' or people using violence are civilians engaged in regular criminal activity, using force against them in self-defence lacks a nexus with hostilities and does not amount to direct participation in hostilities.[30] Such situations are governed by domestic criminal law and human rights law, even if they occur in the context of an armed conflict. Thus, and as will be shown throughout, acting as security guards in situations of armed conflict is one of the most problematic roles PMSCs take on, especially when it comes to direct participation in hostilities.

When it comes to guarding and detaining captives, for present purposes it suffices to note that the Interpretive Guidance focuses on whether the actions or presence of the guards prevents the 'forcible liberation' of the detained fighters, and distinguishes that from merely 'exercising authority over' such detainees, the latter not constituting direct participation in hostilities.[31] On the other hand, capturing, arresting or detaining enemy combatants in an international armed conflict is unquestionably a direct participation in hostilities. Since in non-international armed conflicts there is no combatant status, the situation is a little less clear as arrest and detention of fighters occurs pursuant to a different legal framework (namely, domestic law). Nevertheless, by analogy it would be prudent to consider that detaining (capturing, arresting) members of organized armed groups in non-international armed conflict also amounts to a direct participation in hostilities. The most difficult case is if the persons captured were themselves direct participants in hostilities rather than persons with a clear status as combatants or armed group members under IHL. In my view, it depends on what type of act the direct participant was engaged in. For example, arresting or detaining a person who was directly participating in hostilities by attacking civilians may not amount

---

[30] Schmitt, 'Direct Participation in Hostilities' (Expert paper) at 18–19; and J.-F. Quéguiner, 'Direct Participation in Hostilities Under International Humanitarian Law' (HPCR, 2003) at 12; L. Cameron, 'Private Military Companies: Their Status Under International Humanitarian Law and Its Impact on Their Regulation' (2006) 88 IRRC 573–598, 591–592. Some criminal gangs, however, can be involved in armed conflicts since the goals of the armed group are not determinative for whether the violence amounts to an armed conflict.

[31] ICRC, Interpretive Guidance, p. 48. The ICRC admits that this 'nuanced view' distinguishing the exercise of administrative powers from other aspects of guarding was not discussed during the expert meetings. See note 99 of the Guidance.

to a direct participation in hostilities in itself, while capturing a person who was engaging in sabotage of a military object may well do so.

Another activity in which many PMSCs are involved in mine clearance,[32] as are many other humanitarian groups or organizations that are not PMSCs.[33] Clearing mines can amount to direct participation in hostilities if it is done in order to assist military operations. However, it can also be humanitarian work that in no way involves a direct participation in hostilities.[34] The assessment depends on the context. Whether the body engaging in demining is a PMSC or a humanitarian group is irrelevant to determining whether the activity in question constitutes direct participation in hostilities; it is the purpose of the act that counts.

The commentary to the Interpretive Guidance also specifies that 'electronic interference with military computer networks' could also meet the threshold of harm, thus further removing the need for PMSCs to be armed and on the battlefield in order for their acts to be construed as direct participation in hostilities.[35] When it comes to cyber operations, experts continue to disagree on a few issues. One area of contention is in regard to the definition of an attack.[36] Experts disagree as to whether an operation must cause damage, death or destruction in order to constitute an attack, or whether simply neutralizing something (or aiming to neutralize something) without causing damage or destruction is also sufficient to count as an attack.[37] A second issue in dispute is whether data

---

[32] EG G4S Mine Action, available at www.g4s.com/uk/uk-what_we_do/uk-mine_action.htm (accessed 26 February 2010), EOD Technology, Inc. (Munitions Response section), available at www.eodt.com/munitions_response/index.html (accessed 26 February 2010).

[33] E.g., the Geneva International Centre for Humanitarian Demining, http://gichd.ch/.

[34] Indeed, state parties to Amended Protocol II of the CCW have an obligation to record all mined areas (Article 9) and to 'clear, remove, destroy or maintain' 'all mines, booby-traps, and other devices employed by [them]' (Article 3(2)). See Protocol on Prohibitions or Restrictions on the Use of Mines, Booby-Traps and Other Devices as Amended on 3 May 1996 (entered into force 3 December 1998), UN CCW/CONF.I/16. According to Henckaerts and Doswald-Beck, these obligations constitute customary IHL for states: *Customary IHL*, Rules 82–83, pp. 283–286.

[35] ICRC, Interpretive Guidance, p. 48.

[36] In this regard, I refer only to attack in the sense of Article 49(2) AP I, not in the sense of Article 2(4) of the UN Charter. On cyber-attacks in relation to the latter, see Matthew C. Waxman, 'Cyber Attacks as "Force" Under UN Charter Article 2(4)' (2011) 87 *US NWC Intl L Studies Series* 43–57. Here as for the *ius in bello*, one of the factors that causes concern is the potential lack of a kinetic element to 'force' and its relevance for a use of force.

[37] See Michael Schmitt, 'Cyber Operations and the *Jus in Bello*: Key Issues' (2011) 87 *US NWC Intl L Studies Series* 89–110 esp. at 94–96; Knut Doermann, 'Applicability of the Additional Protocols to Computer Network Attacks', available at www.icrc.org/eng/resources/documents/misc/68lg92.htm. At 95, Schmitt admits that these positions suffer from under-

constitute an object for the purposes of Article 52(2) AP I.[38] The recent publication of a manual by a group of experts may lead to some clarification in the law, but ultimately it will depend on how states interpret and react to cyber operations.[39] For PMSCs, the outcome of these debates will broaden or narrow the scope of activities in which they may engage without directly participating in hostilities.[40] It is generally agreed, however, that 'cyber military intelligence gathering, disrupting enemy cyber networks and manipulating data in the enemy's military systems' would constitute acts that involve a direct participation in hostilities.[41]

The second type of attack set out in the test as a potential means of directly participating in hostilities involves attacks that 'inflict death, injury or destruction on persons or objects protected against direct attack'. The inclusion of attacks on civilians within the definition of direct participation in hostilities may seem obvious, but it is far from it. It is important to bear in mind the fact that a person does not have to be directly participating in hostilities in order to commit a war crime. Thus, if such acts were not construed as direct participation in hostilities, that would have little bearing on whether the perpetrators could be prosecuted.[42] Moreover, law enforcement officers (and military) would likely be fully justified in using force – of course, only under the law enforcement paradigm – to prevent or stop such attacks, thereby attenuating a 'need' for such acts to be classified as direct participation in hostilities as a preventive or law enforcement aid. Since attacks and violence against civilians will not necessarily have a connection to the conflict or affect the adversary's ability to fight, unlike attacks on military persons and objects, the ICRC's Interpretive Guidance asserts that such acts do need to be likely to cause physical effects on

---

and over-inclusiveness, respectively. See also Cordula Droege, 'Get Off My Cloud: Cyber Warfare, International Humanitarian Law, and the Protection of Civilians' (2012) 94 *International Review of the Red Cross* 533–578.

[38] See Schmitt, 'Cyber Operations', 94–96; Doermann, 'Applicability of the Additional Protocols'.

[39] Michael Schmitt (ed.), *Tallinn Manual on the International Law Applicable to Cyber Warfare* (Cambridge University Press, 2013).

[40] See also Sean Watts, 'Combatant Status and Computer Network Attack' (2010) 50 *Virginia J Intl L* 391–447.

[41] Schmitt, 'Cyber Operations', 101.

[42] Note, however, that ICTY judgements qualified sniping on civilians and bombardment of civilian residential areas as 'attacks' within the meaning of Article 49(1) AP I. See *Prosecutor v. Galic* (Trial Chamber Judgment) IT-98-29-T (5 December 2003) and *Prosecutor v. Strugar* (Appeal Judgment) IT-01-42 (17 July 2008), cited also in ICRC, Interpretive Guidance, p. 49, notes 109 and 110.

protected persons or objects and furthermore emphasizes the need for such acts to have a 'belligerent nexus'.[43]

This aspect of the test immediately brings to mind two well-known incidents involving PMSCs in Iraq – the abuse of prisoners in Abu Ghraib prison and the shooting to death of civilians in Nisoor Square in Baghdad in September 2007. On the basis of this aspect of the test, do either of these incidents amount to direct participation in hostilities by the PMSC contractors involved? Initially, the ICRC's wording referred to inflicting death or other harm on persons 'not under effective control of the acting individual'.[44] This phrasing was expressly designed to exclude activities such as guarding civilian internees from the scope of activities falling within the conduct of hostilities.[45] The mere fact that mistreatment or killing of such internees is prohibited by IHL does not entail that such conduct amounts to direct participation in hostilities that would lead to a loss of protection from direct attack for the guards themselves.[46] During the expert meetings, this position was challenged, and some experts argued that where prisoners were killed 'as part of military operations designed to support one party by harming another', the act of inflicting harm on those individuals, while not done in the heat of battle or direct attack, had a sufficient 'belligerent nexus' to support its inclusion within the scope of direct participation in hostilities.[47] While the wording of the final version of the test and the accompanying commentary are sufficiently ambiguous to allow for either interpretation, it is clear from the expert meeting reports that the ICRC did not relent in its view that such acts do not constitute direct participation in hostilities.[48] Thus, the ICRC would contend (and I agree) that the Abu Ghraib PMSC guards involved in prisoner abuse were not directly participating in hostilities, but this view does not appear to be unanimous.

With regard to the Nisoor Square incident, in which a group of PMSC contractors guarding a convoy through Baghdad opened fire on pedestrians and civilian cars and killed seventeen civilians,[49] the element of direct attack on civilians is much more self-evident. It is important to recall that the intent to inflict harm on civilians is irrelevant to the direct participation assessment, in contrast to an assessment of criminal responsibility

---

[43] ICRC, Interpretive Guidance, pp. 49–50. See also discussions on this in ICRC, 'Fourth Expert Meeting' (2006) at 42–43; ICRC, 'Fifth Expert Meeting' (2008) at 62–63.
[44] ICRC, 'Fifth Expert Meeting' (2008), 61.   [45] Ibid.
[46] Ibid.   [47] Ibid., 62.   [48] Ibid., 63.
[49] The Memorandum Opinion of 31 December 2009 states that fourteen people were killed, but other reports indicate seventeen.

under international criminal law. Thus, no matter whether the Blackwater guards fired on the civilians thinking they were responding to an attack or for other reasons, the fact that the civilians fired on were themselves civilians and not members of an armed group or armed forces is not dispositive of whether the act constituted direct participation in hostilities. This element of the test is closely linked with the 'belligerent nexus' criteria, which must also be fulfilled in order for this conduct to amount to direct participation, and which will be examined more closely below.

8.2.2 'Direct causation'

The second element of the test is the requirement of direct causation. In the words of the ICRC,

> [T]here must be a direct causal link between a specific act and the harm likely to result either from that act, or from a coordinated military operation of which that act constitutes an integral part.[50]

This part of the test reflects a widely accepted and longstanding tenet of IHL, which is that 'there should be a clear distinction between direct participation in hostilities and participation in the war effort.'[51] Participation in the war effort is perhaps best exemplified by munitions factory workers: while these individuals certainly help the war, their activities are not legally considered to constitute direct participation in hostilities. 'War-sustaining activities' such as political, economic, or ideological (propaganda) support of the war have an even weaker link in terms of direct impact and thus also are not classified as direct participation in hostilities.[52]

Many activities carried out by PMSCs, such as support and logistics activities – that is, catering, construction and maintenance of bases – are not direct participation in hostilities. As noted above, Article 4A(4) GC III foresees that civilians will perform tasks such as supplying the armed forces with food and shelter but that those persons maintain their civilian status. Such 'indirect participation', even where the services are indispensable to the armed forces (e.g., providing food), does not cross the threshold

---

[50] ICRC, Interpretive Guidance, Recommendation V(2).

[51] Sandoz, *Commentary on the Additional Protocols*, Commentary to Article 51(3) Protocol I, para. 1944.

[52] Here again one may distinguish between individual criminal responsibility and direct participation in hostilities: 'enabling' may include financial support and thus constitute a form of participation in a war crime, but it does *not* constitute direct participation in hostilities.

to direct participation and thus carries no loss of protection against direct attack.[53] PMSC employees may thus not be construed as directly participating in hostilities merely for performing such services. Here, however, it is important to reiterate that IHL depends on the facts. Therefore, if PMSCs are hired as kitchen staff but at times are left to guard a military base, the assessment as to whether they directly participate in hostilities depends on what they are doing at any given moment, not on their usual role or the terms of their contract.[54]

The Interpretive Guidance provides an even more detailed framework for analysis when it comes to certain activities that are common for PMSCs. First, it states, 'although the recruitment and training of personnel is crucial to the military capacity of a party to the conflict, the general causal link with the harm inflicted on the adversary will generally remain indirect', such that recruitment and training is *not* direct participation in hostilities.[55] This interpretation is consistent with views on such acts in the context of discussions on mercenaries.[56] The Interpretive Guidance goes on to specify that 'only where persons are specifically recruited and trained for the execution of a predetermined hostile act can such activities be regarded as an integral part of that act and, therefore, as direct participation in hostilities.'[57] Some experts argue that 'training armed group members in military matters, for example, the use of weapons, or tactics' should be construed as direct participation in hostilities.[58] Furthermore, one may question whether this is in fact as much of a bright-line test as it first appears. While many PMSCs have contracts to train military personnel (e.g., the new Iraqi and Afghan military and police forces), it is imperative to look in more detail at the nature of that training before

---

[53] ICRC, Interpretive Guidance, p. 54.
[54] See P. Singer, *Corporate Warriors: The Rise of the Privatized Military Industry* (Cornell University Press, 2003), 163, for evidence of the military's reliance on 'support troops' for combat assistance in certain situations.
[55] ICRC, Interpretive Guidance, p. 53.
[56] Recall that the definition of 'mercenary' under IHL requires that the individual actually take a direct part in hostilities. See Sandoz, *Commentary on the Additional Protocols*, p. 579, para. 1806, on Article 47(2). Note, however, that such activities may nevertheless lead to criminal responsibility of PMSCs under international criminal law.
[57] ICRC, Interpretive Guidance, p. 53.
[58] APV Rogers, 'Direct Participation in Hostilities: Some Personal Reflections' (2009) 48 *Military Law and the Law of War Rev* 143–163 at 157. Within this debate is also the question of training such forces to produce improvised explosive devices. With all due respect, I cannot see why weapons production would amount to a direct participation in hostilities in non-international armed conflicts when it is virtually universally accepted that it does not in international armed conflicts.

concluding that 'training' is not direct participation in hostilities. In places where there is an ongoing armed conflict, at least some PMSCs 'train' by *leading* new forces in military or combat operations.[59] When 'training' involves leaving the classroom and charging into battle, as it were, that particular aspect of what some PMSCs may consider to be merely an integral part of 'training' most certainly constitutes direct participation in hostilities.

While the production of weapons and ammunition unquestionably does not constitute direct participation in hostilities (including, for example, manufacturing IEDs), direct action by civilians operating weapons and/or weapons systems may be.[60] As weapons systems become more sophisticated, it is not uncommon for a manufacturer to supply a civilian contractor with the weapon. The responsibilities of that contractor may involve performing maintenance but may also be linked to programming the weapon.[61] One of the problems with this type of activity is that it is often listed as 'contractor support', making it difficult to know what such a role entails. For example, one expert states that 'other contract technicians supported Predator unmanned aerial vehicles (UAV) and the data links they used to transmit information'.[62] Another is less ambiguous, indicating that such 'support' crosses the threshold of harm, stating: 'Contractors even operate some military systems. Contractors flew on targeting and surveillance aircraft and operated Global Hawk and Predator UAVs in Afghanistan and Iraq.'[63] There is little doubt that such personnel are in fact directly participating in hostilities if their work includes programming and operating the weapon systems to mount specific attacks, rather than simply allowing them to function. If, however, they are merely there to maintain the systems in good order, then arguably they are not directly participating in hostilities.[64]

---

[59] This is a common modus operandi, at least in some companies.

[60] See ICRC, 'Fourth Expert Meeting' (2006) at 49, for a brief overview of certain nuances within this debate. For a view that production of IEDs does constitute direct participation in hostilities, see Schmitt, 'Military Necessity', 834. See also Sassòli and Cameron, 'The Protection of Civilian Objects'.

[61] J. Ricou Heaton, 'Civilians at War: Re-examining the Status of Civilians Accompanying the Armed Forces' (2005) 57 *Air Force L Rev* 155–208, 189–191.

[62] D. Isenberg, 'A Government in Search of Cover: Private Military Companies in Iraq', in S. Chesterman and C. Lehnardt (eds.), *From Mercenaries to Market* (Oxford University Press, 2007), p. 83.

[63] Ricou Heaton, 'Civilians at War', 190.

[64] Watts, 'Combatant Status', 428, states that the United States 'has traditionally evinced a broad view of what constitutes direct participation in hostilities'. He goes on, 'In 1999, the

Some of these acts will not in and of themselves in isolation cause direct harm to the adversary, such as ongoing maintenance of such weapons systems. However, it should be noted that the Interpretive Guidance states that 'where a specific act does not on its own directly cause the required threshold of harm, the requirement of direct causation would still be fulfilled where the act constitutes an integral part of a concrete and coordinated tactical operation that directly causes such harm.'[65]

PMSCs also drive and guard a lot of convoys. One of the more contentious questions of IHL relates to the proverbial ammunition truck driver: is he directly participating in hostilities or not? The answer seems to be that if the driver is transporting ammunition directly to the front lines or to fighters requiring it for immediate use in battle, that truck driver is directly participating in hostilities. If, on the other hand, the ammunition is being transported to a weapons depot, then the same driver is not, in that instance, directly participating in hostilities.[66] Nevertheless, the ammunition itself, being a legitimate military objective, may be directly targeted; thus, even though the driver himself may not be directly targeted in the second example, his proximity to a legitimate military objective makes him vulnerable to the effects of attack. This distinction, although fine, is nevertheless important in the context of PMSCs. While forces able to attack ammunition trucks (not headed to the front lines) through aerial bombardment may in all likelihood consider the likely death of the driver as a proportionate loss relative to the destruction of the supply in question, forces whose activities are, due to the nature of their capacity and organization, limited to ground attacks with light weapons may not lawfully directly target convoy drivers as a means of neutralizing or capturing the ammunition in question since those drivers are not, at the time in question, directly participating in hostilities.[67]

Without question, if PMSC contractors are engaged in the assassination (or targeted killings) of persons who are somehow deemed to be enemy combatants in the context of an armed conflict, as emerging reports

---

U.S. Department of the Army observed that "[e]ntering the theatre of operations in support or operation of sensitive, high Value equipment, such as a weapon system," may constitute active participation in hostilities.' Ibid.

[65] ICRC, Interpretive Guidance, pp. 54–55.   [66] Ibid., p. 56.

[67] As such, the hue and cry over asymmetrical warfare and the inappropriate use of civilians by certain armed groups may be slightly exaggerated, as the practice may not be as one-sided as some commentators make out. On the other hand, such drivers may have to accept that they face the risk of being mistaken for members of the armed forces, which may somewhat muddy the culpability for direct attacks.

suggest, then those attacks, although carried out via collaboration with intelligence agencies, constitute direct participation in hostilities.[68] Great caution must be exercised in assessing such acts, however, since not all such killings are in fact against combatants/fighters in the context of an armed conflict, notwithstanding declarations by governments involved.

An issue that arises with respect to the element of direct causation of harm is the vexed question of human shields in situations of armed conflict. The position of the ICRC in the Interpretive Guidance is that '[w]here civilians voluntarily and deliberately position themselves to create a physical obstacle to the military operations of a party to the conflict, they could directly cause the threshold of harm required for a qualification as direct participation in hostilities.'[69] On the other hand, persons whose presence near a legitimate military objective would affect the balance or tip the scales in the calculation as to the proportionality of an attack (usually aerial or using heavy weapons) – even if they are present voluntarily – are not considered to be directly participating in hostilities.[70] The reason for this conclusion is that such civilians pose only a legal impediment to attack, which is too indirect to meet the necessary standard.[71] Moreover, concluding that such civilians directly participate in hostilities and lose protection from attack by virtue of their presence and will to influence proportionality leads to an absurdity – it is only because they are civilians protected against attack that they influence the proportionality calculation at all; if they are construed as direct participants by virtue of their mere presence, they pose no legal impediment to attack because direct participants may be attacked and their loss does not need to be taken into account during the proportionality calculation.[72] Although this is the position I take, I acknowledge that it is not universally accepted.[73]

To the best of my knowledge, states do not seek to use PMSCs in order to make targets immune from attack due to the presence of PMSC civilians. However, if PMSCs actively intervene in hostilities, such as providing cover for combatants or physically blocking an attack, they are directly participating in hostilities, just as any other civilian would be in such

---

[68] A. Ciralsky, 'Tycoon, Soldier, Spy', *Vanity Fair*, January 2010.
[69] ICRC, Interpretive Guidance, p. 56. [70] Ibid., p. 57.
[71] Ibid. ICRC, 'Fourth Expert Meeting' (2006) at 45–46.
[72] Marco Sassòli, 'Human Shields and International Humanitarian Law', in A. Fischer-Lescano et al. (eds.), *Peace in Liberty, Festschrift für Michael Bothe zum 70. Geburstag* (Baden-Baden: Nomos, 2008), pp. 567–578, 573.
[73] See, e.g., M. Schmitt, 'Human Shields in International Humanitarian Law' (2009) 47 *Columbia J Transntl L* 292 at 317–319.

circumstances.[74] When faced with persons who might be human shields, on the other hand, PMSCs who are participating in hostilities, either as combatants or without such status, must respect IHL. Given that there is some debate, it would be wise to follow the standard that is least likely to lead them to be held to be in conflict with IHL, which, in my view, is the position outlined above. Since PMSCs may be operating remotely-controlled weapons fired from drones where the issue of human shields in aerial bombardment may be relevant, PMSCs should be made aware, in their training, of the fact that civilians present near a military objective, whether they are there voluntarily or not, should not be taken to be direct participants in hostilities.

8.2.3   'Belligerent nexus'

Not only must an act cross the requisite threshold of harm and directly cause the harm in question, but that act 'must be specifically designed to directly cause' that harm *in support of one party and to the detriment of another*. This is the element of a 'belligerent nexus'. It is important to underline, however, that this analysis has nothing to do with the subjective intent of the individual, but focuses rather on the 'objective purpose of the act'.[75] The Interpretive Guidance explains, 'That purpose is expressed in the design of the act or operation and does not depend on the mindset of every participating individual.'[76] The mental state of an individual is relevant only in exceptional circumstances;[77] as such, at issue is not whether individual PMSC contractors want or seek to support or harm one side or the other in a conflict, but whether their actions may be reasonably perceived by a person reacting to that act as being aimed at harming or supporting one side or the other.[78]

Applying this to the Nisoor Square incident discussed above leads to the (somewhat unsatisfactory) conclusion that whether the PMSCs who shot at the civilians were directly participating in hostilities by dint of those acts depends to a large extent on whether they were hired by a party to the conflict. If they were hired by a party (which was the case), the

---

[74] These are the examples given in the Interpretive Guidance. See ICRC, Interpretive Guidance, pp. 56–57.

[75] Ibid., p. 59.   [76] Ibid.

[77] The ICRC's Interpretive Guidance provides the example of 'involuntary human shields physically coerced into providing cover in close combat' at p. 60.

[78] ICRC, 'Fourth Expert Meeting' (2006) at 50, clarification of the concept by the organizers/drafters.

belligerent nexus is more apparent than if they were hired by, for example, a completely neutral NGO. If contracted by a party to the conflict, the connection between their actions and benefit to the party is easier to draw. The line between the acts in the incident and acts taken in self-defence, however, is not always easy to distinguish.

The ICRC Interpretive Guidance asserts that the exercise of individual self-defence against prohibited violence (e.g., rape, murder) lacks the requisite belligerent nexus even if it causes harm to the adversary because 'its purpose clearly is not to support a party to the conflict against another'.[79] Thus, under normal circumstances, the use of violence to repel prohibited attacks does not constitute direct participation in hostilities. This 'exception' to what acts of violence directed against an adversary constitute direct participation in hostilities is logical and appropriate when it comes to regular individuals who may be the victims of unlawful attacks, but it presents a challenge and potential loophole with regard to the ways states may use private military and security companies. With all due respect, the ICRC's dismissal of the possibility that the infliction of violence through individual self-defence may constitute direct participation in hostilities may be too hasty when it comes to the way in which the right to self-defence is exploited by PMSCs. Indeed, this relationship is not explored at all in the Interpretive Guidance. It is, however, imperative to enquire whether the fact that individuals are contracted on the basis that they will exploit the right to self-defence (including the right to use violence in defence of property) demands a more nuanced analysis of the relationship between self-defence and direct participation in hostilities, which I will develop below.[80]

Finally, for the sake of completeness, it should be noted that other types of acts, such as hostage-taking, were considered in considerable detail by the experts at the expert meetings with a view to establishing a position as to whether such acts constitute direct participation in hostilities. Since PMSCs tend rather to be the victims of hostage-taking rather than taking hostages themselves, it is unnecessary to go into this debate.

---

[79] ICRC, Interpretive Guidance, p. 61.

[80] The fact that the service contracts awarded to PMSCs contain clauses requiring or at least anticipating that they will exercise their right to self-defence in defence of military goods their convoys protect is well-known. Moreover, the Defense Federal Acquisition Supplement implicitly confirms this in its extensive discussion of the limits that could or should be placed on the use of force in self-defence. There is a general appeal in the Interpretive Guidance to read and use the document in good faith. In this light, my analysis below may be read as pointing towards a good-faith interpretation of self-defence.

8.3   Beginning and End of Direct Participation in Hostilities

The ICRC Interpretative Guidance states:

> Measures preparatory to the execution of a specific act of direct partici-
> pation in hostilities, as well as the deployment to and the return from the
> location of its execution, constitute an integral part of that act.[81]

The Commentary to this recommendation provides some specific examples of the types of preparatory measures that do fall within the rubric
of direct participation in hostilities and distinguishes those from more
remote measures that do not amount to such participation. For example,
loading bombs onto a plane for an attack on military objectives counts
as direct participation even if the actual flight and bombing raid will
occur only the following day and the specific targets are not yet selected.[82]
Transferring weapons to storehouses, however, does not (similar to the
case of the driver of the ammunition supply truck according to where
the truck is headed). The degree of specificity of the future attack plays
a key role in interpreting whether the acts in question amount to direct
participation.[83] Thus, PMSCs whose support role includes carrying out
activities that involve taking steps to prepare a specific and concrete operation may amount to direct participation in hostilities. The commentary
further provides that,

> if carried out with a view to the execution of a specific hostile act, all of the
> following would almost certainly constitute preparatory measures amount-
> ing to direct participation in hostilities: equipment, instruction and trans-
> port of personnel; gathering of intelligence; and preparation, transport, and
> positioning of weapons and equipment.[84]

The Interpretive Guidance distinguishes between general recruitment and
training of troops and instruction regarding a specific operation, the former not being a form of direct participation.[85] As noted above, it depends
what training entails, but from the perspective of timing, classroom
instruction or true exercises would not constitute direct participation as
some form of preparation of an attack. Certain intelligence activities of

---

[81] ICRC, Interpretive Guidance, Recommendation VI at p. 17.   [82] Ibid., p. 66.
[83] This notion was reiterated in the 2006 discussion, ICRC, 'Fourth Expert Meeting' (2006),
54–57.
[84] ICRC, Interpretive Guidance, p. 66.   [85] Ibid., pp. 66–67.

PMSCs may also entail their being direct participants in hostilities.[86] It is relevant to recall that intelligence activities such as the gathering and analysis of information regarding persons who seek to target US military 'personnel, resources and facilities' in a theatre of armed conflict[87] may also constitute direct participation in hostilities based on the 'preparatory measures' theory.

Furthermore, the commentary specifies that for modes of participation in an attack where geographical proximity is not a factor (e.g., remotely programming or controlling drones, etc.), the time of participation in the attack is limited to 'the immediate execution of the act and preparatory measures forming an integral part of that act'.[88] In addition, as discussed above, the temporal scope of loss of protection changes according to whether a person is a member of an armed group or whether one is simply an individual who directly participates without being part of a group.

This analysis has shown that many of the activities in which PMSC personnel are contracted to engage may lead to or outright entail their direct participation in hostilities. That being said, this observation must be nuanced, in certain circumstances, by additional applicable legal frameworks: the right to use force in self-defence – including in peace operations – and the use of force in law enforcement operations. Consequently, to complete – and, perhaps, to complicate – the legal picture, I turn now to a detailed discussion of those subjects.

---

[86] See Armin Krishnan, 'The Future of U.S. Intelligence Outsourcing' (2011) 18 *Brown J World Affairs* 195–211. At 202, Krishnan cites a source who affirms that 'Lockheed Martin is providing intelligence in Pakistan to "locate people and do *Predator* strikes"'.

[87] S. Fainaru and A. Klein, 'In Iraq, a Private Realm of Intelligence-Gathering; Firm Extends U.S. Government's Reach', *Washington Post*, 1 July 2007, p. A1. That article shows that the company in question not only provides general intelligence assessments, but also relates specific incidents of intelligence-gathering leading the US military to act directly on tips.

[88] ICRC, Interpretive Guidance, p. 68.

The Use of Force by PMSC Personnel in Self-Defence

Domestic and international private security industries rely on the ability of an individual to use force in self-defence as a means of fulfilling the terms of contracts requiring the use of violence without having the benefit of state-conferred powers of arrest, detention and capacity to use force. In order to generate a more complete picture of what PMSCs may legally do in situations of armed conflict, we therefore need to understand the rules on the use of force in personal self-defence and in defence of property and, moreover, to consider how those rules interact with and must be interpreted in relation to international humanitarian law. This analysis will show that transposing the normal modus operandi of PMSCs (of exploiting of the use of force in self-defence) from a domestic, internal security context to a situation of armed conflict may create some thorny problems.[1] In particular, it may not be as straightforward as one may surmise to distinguish force used in self-defence from a use of force that constitutes an (impermissible) direct participation in hostilities. Both may actually overlap. In addition, even without actions amounting to direct participation in hostilities, certain acts taken in ostensible self-defence in a situation of armed conflict can nevertheless seriously erode the strict separation between civilians and combatants, which can lead to a weakening in the ability of IHL to protect civilians generally. That being said, there are many acts that PMSCs may undertake that will not test the boundaries

---

[1] For descriptions of PMSCs reliance on self-defence in a domestic context, see, for example, D. Sklansky, 'The Private Police' (1999) 46 *UCLA L Rev* 1165–1287; E. Joh, 'Conceptualizing the Private Police' (2005) *Utah L Rev* 573; E. Joh, 'The Paradox of Private Policing' (2004) 95 *J Crim L & Criminology* 49–131; and E. Joh, 'The Forgotten Threat: Private Policing and the State' (2006) 13 *Indiana J Global Legal Studies* 357–389. The only other scholarly consideration of self-defence and PMSCs, similar in some respects and different in others to the analysis here, is by G. Den Dekker and E.P.J. Myjer, 'The Right to Life and Self-Defence of Private Military and Security Contractors in Armed Conflict', in F. Francioni and N. Ronzitti (eds.), *War by Contract* (Oxford University Press, 2011), 171–193.

of direct participation in hostilities and for which self-defence will serve as an adequate basis for action. Thus, the rules on self-defence, which flow primarily from domestic criminal law systems, will play a significant role in setting the parameters of the circumstances in which civilian PMSC personnel may use force and the degree of force that may be used such that it is important to be aware of the basic contours of the justification of self-defence in domestic criminal law.[2]

The following discussion begins with a brief consideration of the legal characterization of self-defence – is it a right or merely a justification? Starting at the international level, this chapter will briefly consider whether there is an international legal standard that sets or influences the specific necessary elements of self-defence when it comes to private persons such that we may describe a detailed universal norm. It will conclude that there is not. The bulk of the discussion will then assess the main elements of the criminal defence as it has emerged from domestic law and that are generally shared across legal systems around the world, on the understanding that in any given case the exact parameters will have to be nuanced by a detailed understanding of the criminal law provisions of the territorial state related to self-defence. Indeed, the applicable domestic law to an act of self-defence by civilians will – independently of issues of jurisdiction and immunities – generally be that of the state where the act occurs, and not that of the contracting state or the home state. The only exceptions are possibly legislation introduced for security reasons by an occupying power or, in case of criminal trial in the contracting state, the home state, or any other state based on universal jurisdiction, the *lex mitior* of the *lex fori*. The discussion will also consider the use of force in self-defence in defence of property, on which there may be less common ground between domestic jurisdictions. Again, the problems discussed here pertain in particular to PMSC personnel tasked with or exercising security functions. The specific case of PMSCs using force in self-defence in peace operations will be examined in Chapter 10. The analysis that follows here underpins that in Chapter 10.

---

[2] Self-defence is frequently construed as a 'justification' for otherwise criminal behaviour in both common law and civil law systems. For common law debates on self-defence as justification or excuse, see in particular work by George Fletcher; for the observation that it is 'always' construed as a justification in civil law systems, see J. Hermida, 'Convergence of Civil Law and Common Law in the Criminal Theory Realm' (2005) 13 *U Miami Intl & Comp L Rev* 163, 189. K. Ambos, 'Toward a Universal System of Crime: Comments on George Fletcher's Grammar of Criminal Law' (2007) 28 *Cardozo L Rev* 2647 at 2669.

9.1   The Right to Life Does Not Entail an Unqualified Right to Self-Defence

Personal self-defence has been described as 'an inherent right of every human being.'[3] But even though we commonly speak of a 'right' of self-defence, it does not fit exactly within the realm of human rights as such. The view that self-defence is not an express human right was argued by Special Rapporteur to the United Nations Human Rights Council, Barbara Frey, in a 2006 report concerning small firearms and the right to life, where she opined that, although 'the principle of self-defence has an important place in international human rights law', '[n]o international human right of self-defence is expressly set forth in the primary sources of international law: treaties, customary law, or general principles.'[4] Even though self-defence is recognized in the European Convention on Human Rights, it is not there as a 'right' but 'simply to remove from the scope of application of article 2 (1) killings necessary to defend against unlawful violence. It does not provide a right that must be secured by the State.'[5] On the other hand, the European Court of Justice has held that self-defence is a general principle of law.[6]

---

[3] D.B. Kopel, P. Gallant and J.D. Eisen, 'The Human Right of Self-Defense', (2007) 22 *Brigham Young U J Public Law* 43–178, also take this view. It should be noted that the debate as to whether there is a free-standing human right to use force in personal self-defence is inextricably linked, in many US discussions, to the 'right to bear arms' enshrined in the US Constitution and therefore subject to the vagaries of heated debates on gun control in that country. On whether states have an obligation to extend a legal right to self-defence to individuals, see C.O. Finkelstein, 'On the Obligation of the State to Extend a Right of Self-Defense to Its Citizens' (1999) 147 *Univ Penn L Rev* 1361–1402.

[4] Final Report Submitted by Barbara Frey, Special Rapporteur: Prevention of Human Rights Violations Committed with Small Arms and Light Weapons, 27 July 2006, UN Doc A/HRC/Sub.1/58/27 (Frey Report).

[5] Ibid., at 9, para. 21, citing prepublication work of John Cerone, subsequently published as 'A Human Right of Self-Defense?' (2006) 2 *J L Economics & Policy* 319. The Frey Report goes on to observe that some individual members of the Human Rights Committee have argued that states are required to 'recognize and evaluate a plea of self-defence as part of the due process rights of criminal defendants'. Para. 24. See HRC Comm No. 806/1998, *Thompson v. St Vincent and the Grenadines*, CCPR/C/70/D/806/1998 (5 December 2000), dissenting opinion of Lord Colville, and HRC Comm No. 1077/2002, *Jaime Carpo v. Philippines*, CCPR/C/77/D/1077/2002 (15 May 2003), dissenting opinion of Nisuke Ando.

[6] The ECJ referred to the concept as 'legitimate self-protection'. See Joined Cases 154, 205, 206, 226 to 228, 263 and 264/78, 39, 31, 83 and 85/79, *Valsabbia et al. v. Commission of the European Union* [1980] ECR at 1021, para. 138. As such, although it frequently applies only to individuals taking action to protect their lives or bodily integrity, the ECJ acknowledged that corporate enterprises may also rely on it in certain circumstances: see G. Dannecker, 'Justification and Excuses in the European Community – Adjudication of the Court of

The 'right' to use force in personal self-defence is a justification or excuse in domestic criminal law for an act – up to and including the use of lethal force – that would otherwise be criminal. Isolating a principled theoretical explanation for why we may in fact kill in self-defence, even on the basis of the human rights theory, however, is not an easy task.[7] The contours of the right as expressed in various jurisdictions will be explored below in detail. Generally, the use of force is permitted in self-defence against an unlawful attack, as long as the force used in response is necessary and proportionate. As such, individuals are not expected to rely exclusively on the state to defend their right to life; they may take action that infringes the right to life of another person in certain limited circumstances. The extent to which the right to life of the (unprovoked) attacking party must be taken into account is a source of controversy among theorists and influences interpretations of the appropriate content, in the abstract, of the elements of self-defence – in particular the question whether the victim of an attack has a right to stand fast and fight, or whether he must retreat if possible and use force only when truly necessary.[8] In addition, it is important to note that self-defence operates as a justification or excuse not only in regard to killing, but also in regard to other acts that would normally be an offence in domestic criminal law.[9]

For private individuals, the specific content of the defence is not defined in international human rights law. One can infer that necessity and proportionality are necessary elements due to the right to life of the perpetrator and the balancing act of human rights law, but the specific details are not elaborated in case law. Rather, when individuals have tried to bring cases before international human rights tribunals, usually as a right to fair trial complaint on how their plea of self-defence was put to a jury or considered by a national court, the international tribunals have consistently

Justice of the European Community and Tendencies of the National Legal Systems as a Basis for a Supranational Regulation' (1993) 1 *Eur J Crime, Crim L & Crim Justice* 230, 237–238.

[7] See A. Grabczynska and K. Kessler Ferzan, 'Justifying Killing in Self-Defence' (2009) 99 *J Crim L and Criminology* 235–253.

[8] See A. Ashworth, 'Self-Defence and the Right to Life' (1975) 34 *Cambridge L J* 282, 289–290; Grabczynska and Kessler Ferzan, 'Justifying Killing', 240; Leverick, *Killing in Self-Defence* (Oxford University Press, 2006). At the domestic law level, there is a discussion as to whether one 'forfeits' one's right to life as soon as one commits an unprovoked violent act. If accepted, this would seriously diminish the proportionality response as far as it stems from the right to life as a requirement.

[9] Some states' legislation uses the general term 'offence'; others circumscribe the availability of the defence only to acts that would constitute assault or homicide.

and categorically refused to look into the details of the plea.[10] They have insisted that they will not consider errors of fact or law of national courts unless such errors betray a separate fault, such as a lack of impartiality.[11] In the absence of an international norm of self-defence comprising a detailed content for private individuals, it is thus necessary to consider the elements as spelled out in domestic criminal law.

9.2   Elements of Self-Defence from Domestic Criminal Law, Interpreted in the Light of IHL

When it comes to private individuals, most acts relating to the use of force will fall within the domestic criminal jurisdiction, even during an armed conflict. In contradistinction to a state's regular armed forces deployed abroad, PMSC personnel are normally subject to local laws and would therefore be subject to the criminal law of the state in which they are working.[12] Thus, constraints on the use of force flow from the normal criminal laws. It is not necessary to provide an exhaustive study in comparative criminal law of the elements of self-defence in order to gain a sense of how that law will govern the use of force by PMSC personnel in armed conflicts. Rather, the aim is to provide a general outline of the most common elements of the defence.

As a general rule, force may be used by individuals in self-defence or in defence of others if it meets three conditions: (1) it must be used against an unlawful attack; (2) the use of force in response to the attack must be necessary; and (3) the force used in response must be proportionate to the original threat.[13] While the details of different legal systems may add

---

[10] HRC, *Gordon v. Jamaica*, Comm No. 237/1987, UN Doc CCPR/C/46/D/237/1987 (1992) para. 6.4; *Cabała v. Poland* (App no. 23042/02) (Judgment) ECHR 8 August 2006 at paras 39–41; *Samokhvalov v. Russia* (App no 3891/03) (Judgment) ECHR 12 February 2009. In the latter case, the ECtHR held that the fact that the accused (complainant) was not able to be present at his trial, which raised questions of law and fact on the ground of his self-defence plea, violated section 6(1) of the ECHR.

[11] Ibid. (all cases).

[12] In certain cases, such as in Iraq in 2003–2008, PMSCs may have immunity from local laws (based on a specific law introduced by the occupying powers and subsequently accepted by the Iraqi government for a limited time), but they do not enjoy a general, total immunity. If for some reason they are not subject to the laws of the state in whose territory they are operating, they are subject to the laws of their national state or, possibly, of the contracting state. Nevertheless, the fact that it is domestic criminal law that is paramount remains the same in any of these scenarios.

[13] These elements are incorporated in the following provisions: see, e.g., France, Code pénal, art 122–5; Spain, Ley Orgánica 10/1995, de 23 de noviembre, del Còdigo Penal, articolo

to these requirements or nuance them in some way, in general they may be said to be common to virtually all criminal laws in states around the world. However, all of these elements must be interpreted with particular care in the context of armed conflict.

As noted in the discussion above, the use of force in self-defence does not constitute direct participation in hostilities.[14] That statement may seem unproblematic at first glance; however, this section will show that the line between self-defence and direct participation in hostilities is not as obvious as one may think, especially when it comes to security personnel. The following discussion will show how the self-defence elements must be interpreted in the context of an armed conflict if they are to be consistent with IHL. In the domestic context, if the unlawfulness of the original attack and the necessity and proportionality of the response are not made out, a plea of self-defence will either be rejected and the person found guilty of the crime charged; the crime charged may be qualified; or the sentence may be reduced.[15] International humanitarian law adds a fourth dimension, modifying the way in which various elements of the defence must be interpreted, which is that in the context of armed conflict, the act must lack a belligerent nexus. Self-defence is rather an act that is not covered by the cumulative conditions for an act to constitute direct participation in hostilities, because it does not fulfil the condition of the existence of a belligerent nexus.[16] Indeed, the purpose of the use of force in self-defence is clearly not to support one party against another.

20(4); Germany, Strafgesetzbuch, Titel 4, §32; Switzerland, RS 311.0 Code pénal suisse, art 15; Canada, *Criminal Code*, sections 34 and 37; Botswana, Penal Code, s 16; Ghana, Criminal Code, s 37; Southern Nigerian Criminal Code, s 286. The Sudanese Penal Code allows for self-defence against acts that would be an offence and also for acts that would 'otherwise be a certain offence' but are not due to the youth, unsoundness of mind, etc. of the perpetrator of the act. See Sudanese Penal Code, ss 56 and 57. Relevant excerpts from the Botswanan, Ghanian, Southern Nigerian and Sudanese Penal Codes can be found in S. Yeo, 'Anglo-African Perspectives on Self-Defence' (2009) 17 *African J Intl & Comp L* 118–135. The element of unlawfulness of the primary attack/offence is an element of English criminal law. See *R v. Williams (Gladstone)* (1984) 78 Cr App R 276. See also Hermida, 'Convergence', 189–190, Dannecker, 'Justification and Excuses'. See also entries on self-defence from all states in F. Verbruggen (ed.), *International Encyclopaedia of Laws: Criminal Law* (various dates).

[14] ICRC, Interpretive Guidance, p. 61.

[15] J. Pradel, *Droit pénal comparé*, 3rd edn (Paris: Dalloz, 2008), p. 140, §102. Admittedly, however, one may ask what country's criminal law system will punish a civilian who uses force to defend against an enemy invader whose acts threaten civilians.

[16] ICRC, Interpretive Guidance, p. 61.

9.2.1   Defence of Self, Defence of Others, Defence of Property

Virtually all states' criminal laws permit an individual to use force in defence of him- or herself as well as in defence of others. In the context of an armed conflict, using violence in the defence of oneself poses no problems (combatants simply do not need the criminal law of self-defence to justify attacks against enemy combatants, as combatant privilege implies a right to use force beyond that); however, it is imperative that the defence of others not be read so as to allow an individual to act in self-defence in defence of combatants (or fighters). Defending combatants is unquestionably an act that aids one party to the detriment of another. Allowing 'combatants' to fall within the 'others' who may be defended would unacceptably undermine (or negate) the requirement that the force used in defence lack a belligerent nexus. This will become clear through the examples provided in subsequent sections.

The extent to which force may be used to defend against offences against property varies significantly in domestic criminal laws throughout the world. The self-defence provisions of some criminal codes suggest that force may never be used in defence of property.[17] Many self-defence laws do not allow for the use of deadly force in defence of any and all property,[18] but do allow for a certain degree of force to be used.[19] Some jurisdictions permit the use of deadly force in defence of one's home, which is the most widely accepted exception to a prohibition to use force – especially lethal force – in defence of property, but by no means do all states' criminal laws permit it.[20] PMSCs in a foreign state guarding locations other than their

---

[17] For example, the Canadian Criminal Code states that a person may not 'strike or cause bodily harm' in defence against a trespasser against property. C-46, *Canadian Criminal Code* s 38.

[18] See J. Getzler, 'Use of Force in Protecting Property' (2006) 7 *Theoretical Inquiries in Law* 131–166, for a comparative law discussion regarding Germany, Italy, the United Kingdom, Australia and the United States. See also, e.g., France, Code Pénal, Art 122–5 para. 2, which specifically states that lethal force may not be used in defence of property. The ICC Statute does allow for the use of force in defence of property 'which is essential for the survival of the person or another person or property which is essential for accomplishing a military mission' (31(1)(c)). The inclusion of self-defence in defence of property was very controversial during the negotiation of the Rome Statute. See Kai Ambos, 'Other Grounds for Excluding Criminal Responsibility', in A. Cassese, P. Gaeta and J. Jones (eds.), *The Rome Statute of the International Criminal Court: A Commentary* (Oxford University Press, 2002), pp. 1003–1048, at pp. 1032–1033. However, that defence will apply only if a PMSC finds himself before the ICC on charges of war crimes. Otherwise, domestic legislation will apply.

[19] Pradel, *Droit pénal comparé*, §102 at 138–140.

[20] Getzler, 'Protecting Property', esp. at 142–155.

homes may therefore not be able to rely on this defence.[21] This would seem to severely limit a PMSC guard's ability to defend an object if the PMSC himself (or other proximate civilians) is not attacked during the seizure of the property. However, strict limitations on the degree of force that may be used to defend property may be somewhat illusory, in that if the thieves (or whomever) use force to resist attempts by a defender to stop their actions, *that* force may give rise to a right to use force in self-defence because the attack rises to a level endangering the person. In addition, especially in armed conflicts, it is often not unreasonable to fear that an attacker will attack not only property, but also persons present in that property or linked to that property. Thus, the proportionality of the use of force and the consequence of the use of excessive force on a court's reception of a self-defence plea with regard to property becomes the central issue.

In terms of the impact of IHL on the interpretation of property that may be defended (if national laws allow it), the conclusion is similar to that for 'others': it is imperative that the property being defended is not a military objective. Thus, PMSC personnel may use force in self-defence against an attack on a civilian object if the PMSC personnel themselves are directly targeted (because guarding civilian objects is itself not direct participation in hostilities) or if the attack threatens the life or limb of other civilians in or near that civilian object. Again, this will become clear through the examples and analysis below.

9.2.2 The Attack Being Defended Against Must Have Been Unlawful

According to domestic criminal law, force may be used in self-defence only against unlawful attacks.[22] Thus, the line between direct participation and self-defence must be drawn based on the use of violence in response to an imminent or ongoing use of *unlawful* violence. Although this is a common if not universal aspect of self-defence law, it is rarely discussed in doctrine because it is relatively unproblematic in a domestic context in times of peace.[23] In the domestic context, 'the unlawfulness requirement

---

[21] A specific exception to this rule is Chile, whose criminal laws create a presumption of self-defence when a person resists a night-time intrusion into a commercial or industrial establishment, no matter the damage caused to the assailants. See S.I. Politoff, F.A.J. Koopmans and M.C. Ramirez, 'Chile' (2003), in Verbruggen, *Criminal Law*, at para. 139.

[22] The provisions establishing the defence of self-defence all refer to the unlawfulness of the primary attack as an element.

[23] Where it tends to arise in some jurisdictions is in the context of a consensual fight where the accused is charged with assault. (D. Paciocco, 'Applying the Law of Self-Defence' (2007)

ensures that force cannot be used justifiably against those who have a legal right to interfere with the physical integrity of the accused, such as during a lawful arrest.'[24] In the context of an armed conflict, however, it is necessary and appropriate to measure the (un)lawfulness of the initial attack in light of international humanitarian law.[25] In a situation of armed conflict, due to the complexity of IHL and the factual situations often prevailing on the ground, it may often be very difficult to make a determination about the lawfulness of imminent violence, such that security personnel ostensibly using force only in self-defence may (inadvertently) cross the line into direct participation in hostilities. Furthermore, even where force used in self-defence may not be a clear-cut case of direct participation, it may nevertheless erode the vital distinction between civilians and combatants, leading to a weakening of the ability of IHL to protect civilians. It is thus crucial for PMSCs relying on their ability to use force in self-defence to be able to identify what would constitute an unlawful attack for this purpose.

There are a number of bases under IHL on which an attack or act of violence may be considered to be 'unlawful'. As such, IHL adds an extra dimension in terms of what is unlawful that could be seen to broaden the scope of acts that can be undertaken without crossing over into direct participation in hostilities. However, for reasons that will be explained below, the mere fact that some element of an attack or act may be unlawful would not necessarily be sufficient to distinguish a violent response to such an attack from acts that constitute direct participation in hostilities.[26] The

12 *Canadian Crim L Rev* 25 at 54.) In English jurisprudence, it surfaces as an issue in discussions as to whether the belief in the existence of the unlawful attack must be reasonable or merely honest. See, e.g., *R v. Williams (Gladstone)* (1984) 78 Cr App R 276. In yet other jurisdictions, it arises when the perpetrators of the unlawful attack are, for other legal reasons, not criminally liable. Yeo argues that the 'unlawful' criterion should not be allowed to exclude the use of force in self-defence against 'cases where the assailant's conduct was lawful only because of some legal defence available to him or her, such as where the assailant was a child or insane'. Yeo, 'Anglo-African Perspectives', 126.

[24] Paciocco, 'Applying the Law', 51.

[25] The International Court of Justice has indicated that this is the correct approach in terms of assessing whether a deprivation of the right to life is arbitrary in human rights law in the context of armed conflict. *Legality of the Threat or Use of Nuclear Weapons* (Advisory Opinion) [1996] ICJ Rep 226 at para. 25. Reaffirmed *Legal Consequences of the Construction of a Wall in the Occupied Palestinian Territories* (Advisory Opinion) [2004] ICJ Rep 136 and *Armed Activities on the Territory of the Congo (Congo v. Uganda)* (Merits) [2005] ICJ Rep 168.

[26] Even in the context of the ICC Statute and the 'unlawfulness' element of self-defence, which applies precisely to situations of armed conflict, there is very little in-depth discussion of the content of the requirement. See Ambos, 'Other Grounds for Excluding Criminal Responsibility', pp. 1031–1035.

central question is whether the unlawfulness is sufficient to mean that a responding use of violence lacks a belligerent nexus. The reason for this enquiry is that, when all other requirements of self-defence are met, this is the test that will distinguish force used in self-defence from that which would constitute direct participation in hostilities.

In order to develop an understanding of how 'unlawfulness' should be interpreted in an IHL context, I propose a multipart analysis. First, I will consider the different bases for the unlawfulness of an attack in IHL and assess whether action taken in response to that unlawfulness lacks a belligerent nexus so as to satisfy the IHL standard for distinguishing direct participation in hostilities from self-defence. I will then test whether that technical legal approach leads to realistic and reasonable results in practice. Finally, I will propose a single rule as an optimal solution to the problem (or at least as a guiding rule to be adopted).

For the first part of the analysis, I will group the type of 'unlawfulness' under three broad categories: (1) unlawful due to what is being attacked, (2) unlawful due to who is attacking and (3) unlawful due to means and methods of attacking.

Unlawfulness and the Objective of the Attack

The simplest case arises when an imminent attack/act is unlawful because it is an attack (including murder, rape, torture, assault) on civilians or (destruction of) civilian objects. International humanitarian law prohibits attacks on civilians and civilian objects. Perhaps it is with this kind of attack in mind that the Interpretive Guidance observes that using force to defend oneself or others against 'violence prohibited under IHL lacks belligerent nexus'.[27] Indeed, the purpose of the use of force in defence of such attacks is clearly not to support one party against another.

However, even this clear-cut case has its pitfalls in the PMSC context. First, obviously, the simple fact that PMSC personnel themselves are civilians and are in the vicinity of an object being attacked does not mean that the attack is an unlawful attack on civilians. Moreover, it must be recalled that if PMSC personnel are guarding an object that is a legitimate military objective, such as a convoy of ammunition destined for combatants, they are directly participating in hostilities and it is not unlawful for an opposing party to attack them directly. As the discussion above on direct participation showed, such persons retain their civilian status, but IHL does

---

[27] ICRC, Interpretive Guidance, p. 61.

not prohibit a direct attack on them. Therefore, for PMSCs, it is important to bear in mind that it is not their mere qualification as civilians that determines the lawfulness of a direct attack on them and, furthermore, that their civilian status cannot be used as a pretext to legitimize their use of force in repelling an attack on a military objective. One must also take into account the particular role they have and whether they are already directly participating in hostilities.

Second, when it comes to civilian objects, there is no set list of objects that are *always* civilian and protected from attack. Instead, even objects that are a priori civilian in nature can become legitimate military objectives through their purpose, location or use.[28] This means that a PMSC guard cannot take for granted that the building he is guarding is always a civilian object and that any use of force against it will always be an unlawful attack on a civilian object.

A further wrinkle to guarding objects is linked not to the unlawfulness of the attack on the object but to the specifics of the applicable self-defence regime with regard to property as discussed above. It should thus be borne in mind that, while under international humanitarian law it is prohibited to attack civilian objects and an attack on such objects would ostensibly satisfy the 'unlawfulness' criterion, one must be careful jumping to a conclusion that PMSCs may use force in self-defence of such objects.

The Concept of Attack Justifying Self-Defence Modified by IHL

There is another important distinction added by IHL when it comes to the lawfulness of the objective of an attack, which involves the definition of what action constitutes an 'attack'. IHL narrows the scope of acts against which a person may exercise his right to self-defence: some acts that under criminal law in a purely peacetime framework may give rise to a right to exercise one's self-defence are perfectly lawful and may not be defended against under IHL. For example, under IHL, it is lawful in certain circumstances for a party to seek to take control over persons, places or objects without intending to destroy them. If, for example, a building is located in a place of strategic importance for a party, that party may have no intent to destroy it, but may wish to occupy and use it. The armed forces of that party may thus enter and take control of the building, using violence only

---

[28] Article 52(2) AP I; see also Sassòli and Cameron, 'The Protection of Civilian Objects'. Objects may also be legitimate military objectives by their nature, but these, such as tanks or barracks, are clearly not civilian objects and therefore should never be guarded by civilians.

if they encounter resistance. The same is true for a village, house or other location. This action is not an attack under IHL.[29] Under ordinary criminal law, however, one may defend one's property either against destruction by another or against theft. For PMSCs guarding a building, for example, it would thus be relevant to know whether an armed group seeks merely to take control of that building or whether it seeks to attack it (and those inside). In addition, property may be requisitioned by enemy armed forces under IHL. As long as the requisition conforms to the requirements set out under IHL, it would be unlawful for a person to use force in self-defence to resist complying with the requisition, even though it may seem as though property is being taken against a person's will.[30]

When it comes to actions involving taking persons into custody, a similar nuance is required. As noted above, some states' laws on self-defence permit the use of force in response to 'an offence', which may entail a broad spectrum of acts.[31] For example, if a person detains another, in many states such an act may consist of an offence such as 'unlawful confinement'. While a use of deadly force is often not permitted unless the attack itself poses a lethal threat, criminal laws permitting self-defence against any offence would normally permit one to use at least some degree of violence to prevent or resist being put under the physical control of another individual. However, under IHL, there may be many justifications for a party to take control over persons and it may be inappropriate under the laws of self-defence to use force to repel such an exercise of control. This situation is analogous to the force that law enforcement officers may use to carry out a lawful arrest, but it may be more difficult for the person being detained to understand and recognize the lawfulness of the exercise of control over him under IHL. IHL may thus render lawful certain acts – thereby removing them from the realm of what constitutes an 'unlawful attack' – against which, in peacetime, a person may use his right to self-defence to impede. While it may be difficult to know in advance whether approaching forces are intending to take control of a person or object (again, using force only if they encounter resistance) or whether they anticipate using unlawful violence, these scenarios indicate that persons believing they need to use force in self-defence should not be the first to use violence.

---

[29] Article 49(1) AP I. If, however, the attack is part of a campaign of ethnic cleansing, with or without a use of violence, it would be an unlawful attack under IHL and would give rise to a right to use force in self-defence.

[30] See, e.g., Article 52 of the Hague Regulations for the rules on requisitioning property. Hague Convention IV of 1907, Annex.

[31] See above (note 9).

These caveats aside, these are the clearest cases in which force may be used in self-defence against attacks that are unlawful under IHL, such that PMSCs may rely on that legal basis to carry out their contractual obligations to protect such persons or objects (subject to the limitations indicated in the discussion below). Recall, however, that self-defence is a defence to a criminal charge; it does not necessarily entail some kind of preemptive exoneration of behaviour but may need to be pleaded in response to criminal charges.[32]

Unlawfulness and the Identity, Status or Other Characteristics of the Attackers

There is some controversy as to whether it is unlawful under IHL for a non-combatant to directly participate in hostilities. According to some states' interpretation of IHL, it is, such that any attack by a person without combatant status would be an 'unlawful' attack.[33] This is not the case for all states, however. In my view it is not a direct violation of IHL by an individual for that individual to directly participate in hostilities, even though, as I argue above, states should not take steps that encourage or lead non-combatants to directly participate in hostilities in order to avoid compromising the obligation to ensure the respect of IHL. Consequently, if the test, as I propose it must be, is whether an 'unlawful' attack must be an attack that is 'unlawful' under IHL, the fact that attackers do not have combatant status but are committing acts of hostilities does not, in itself, mean that the attack is 'unlawful' so as to satisfy this requirement under the law of self-defence in the context of armed conflict. Thus, the fact that it is an imperfectly constituted armed group (in international armed conflicts) or outlawed armed group (in non-international armed conflicts) that is attacking a legitimate military objective in a way that otherwise respects humanitarian law does not make it 'unlawful' merely due to the faulty status of the attackers, leaving it open to PMSCs to defend against such an attack (even if directed against a combatant or military objective) on the grounds of 'self-defence'. What is paramount is the rest of the attack

---

[32] See J. Markon, 'Two Defense Contractors Indicted in Shooting of Afghans', *Washington Post*, 8 January 2010, p. A3. The lawyer defending the PMSC contractors accused of murder for having shot and killed civilians protested that the contractors should never even have been charged with a crime since they were acting in self-defence.

[33] For the most comprehensive discussion of the notion to date, see generally David Frakt, 'Direct Participation in Hostilities as a War Crime: America's Failed Efforts to Change the Law of War' (2012) 46 *Valparaiso U L Rev* 729–764. See also the *Khadr* case discussed in Chapter 4, Section 4.4.1.

(on a legitimate military objective) and whether it is an engagement in hostilities by the attacking party.

However, I acknowledge that this analysis has its limits in practice. What, in the fluidity and chaos of armed conflict, may be the apparent differences between an imperfectly constituted armed group mounting an attack on an oil pipeline and a criminal gang (whose same acts would not amount to hostilities and therefore it would not constitute direct participation in hostilities on the part of PMSCs to use force in defence against such acts)? How are PMSCs, sometimes hastily constituted forces themselves, often with intelligence capabilities that are sorely inadequate, supposed to differentiate between the two in the heat of such an attack? An additional complicating factor in this example is the ambiguity of the oil pipeline itself as a legitimate military objective. It is an object that could certainly be a military objective, but it is not necessarily so in nature. War-sustaining material does not constitute, without more, a military objective. Moreover, in unstable situations, it is just as likely to be attacked by criminal gangs seeking to loot petrol as by armed groups for military reasons. There is, thus, a high degree of ambiguity in both the identity of the attackers and the lawfulness of the military objective itself.

This, in a sense, is the heart of the matter. If there were not quasi-criminal, quasi-armed group elements active in theatres of armed conflict today, there would likely be far less reliance on PMSCs as security guards. For the PMSCs in question, acting in a manner that ensures that the essential distinction between civilians and combatants is not further weakened by the increased participation of various non-combatants in hostilities demands a sophisticated understanding of IHL. In my view, the only solution to the complex legal problems introduced by a scenario such as that above is the development of policies regarding the use of PMSC guards that significantly limit the likelihood that they will be placed in situations where they will be called on to distinguish between and respond to such attacks.

Unlawfulness and the Means and/or Methods of the Attackers

Under IHL, an attack may be unlawful because it is disproportionate or indiscriminate.[34] Certain weapons are unlawful as they have been specifically banned by treaty.[35] It is also unlawful to attack 'treacherously' or

---

[34] Article 51(5)(b) and 51(4) AP I.

[35] See, for example, Protocol for the Prohibition of the Use of Asphyxiating, Poisonous or Other Gases, and of Bacteriological Methods of Warfare, Geneva, 17 June 1925, in force

perfidiously.[36] In addition, a combatant who makes an attack on a legitimate military objective but who fails to distinguish himself from the civilian population loses POW status.[37] Do all of these scenarios, and others
like them, amount to 'unlawful' attacks such that PMSCs may exercise
force in self-defence without such acts crossing the line to amount to direct
participation in hostilities? Another way of phrasing the question, as the
Interpretive Guidance puts it, may be: do these acts amount to 'violence
that is prohibited by IHL'? Some clearly do, but using force in ostensible self-defence to protect others against such acts may not, contrary to
what the Interpretive Guidance seems to indicate, in fact lack a belligerent
nexus so as to remove such action from the remit of direct participation
in hostilities.

For example, a PMSC employee who spots an individual who is pre-
tending to be a wounded civilian but who (the PMSC realizes) is in fact a
combatant about to mount an attack on a group of opposing combatants
nearby would be directly participating in hostilities if he were to attack the
(feigning) 'wounded civilian' in order to protect the combatants. Feigning
to be a wounded person to use the protection IHL accords such persons in
order to then attack combatants constitutes perfidy, and perfidy is a use of
'violence that is prohibited under IHL'. It is unlawful. However, the PMSC
employee's acts are clearly designed to protect the combatants and cause
injury to the other side, such that we may not conclude that a belligerent
nexus is missing. The fact that the perfidious conduct is itself unlawful
cannot remove this act from the scope of direct participation in hostilities
and place it within the exclusive realm of self-defence. What matters in
this case is that the PMSC is using force to defend combatants. This example illustrates that IHL imposes a limitation on the general right to act in
defence of self or in defence of others: in the context of an armed conflict
and against a party to an armed conflict, combatants must be excluded
from the 'others' who may be defended in self-defence.

What of disproportionate attacks? May a PMSC guard use force
in self-defence against an imminent attack that he considers will be

---

8 February 1928, 94 LNTS 65; Convention on Prohibitions or Restrictions on the Use of
Certain Conventional Weapons Which May Be Deemed to Be Excessively Injurious or to
Have Indiscriminate Effects, Geneva, 10 October 1980, in force 2 December 1983, 1342
UNTS 137, 19 ILM 1524 (and its protocols); Convention on the Prohibition of the Use,
Stockpiling, Production and Transfer of Anti-Personnel Mines and on Their Destruction,
Ottawa, 18 September 1997, in force 1 March 1999, 2056 UNTS 211; Convention on Cluster
Munitions, Dublin, 30 May 2008, in force 1 August 2010, 2688 UNTS 39.

[36] Article 37 AP I.   [37] Article 44(4) AP I.

disproportionate and, thus, unlawful? In my view, for a number of reasons, the answer is no. A disproportionate attack is one that

> may be expected to cause incidental loss of civilian life, injury to civilians, damage to civilian objects, or a combination thereof, which would be excessive in relation to the concrete and direct military advantage anticipated.[38]

As such, determining the proportionality of an attack requires an ex ante analysis of what is likely to occur. It is predicated not just on the injury or damage it will likely cause, but on a careful balancing of that damage against the concrete and direct military advantage anticipated.[39] It thus reflects the fundamental structure and balancing act of IHL. A PMSC staffer will only be in a position to see the damage or injury he expects from the attack. Not having all the facts available to the planners, and thus unable to know or weigh the concrete and direct military advantage expected from the attack, a PMSC employee cannot (or only in rare cases) presume to know that an attack will be disproportionate. Thus, the 'unlawful' aspect cannot be determined in the circumstances in which PMSCs are relying on self-defence to ground their right to use force.[40]

Testing a violent repulsion of a potentially disproportionate attack against the belligerent nexus criterion strengthens the conclusion above, but it also illustrates that the 'unlawful violence' test to distinguish between direct participation and self-defence is not wholly satisfactory when it comes to the roles in which PMSCs are placed. A hypothetical example helps to flesh out the problem. Consider a PMSC security guard standing in front of a daycare centre. He is tasked with protecting the children in the centre due to general insecurity in the zone (an armed conflict is ongoing). The centre happens to be situated next to a military arsenal. The PMSC guard sees that the arsenal is about to be targeted by opposing forces. The PMSC guard knows about the arsenal and fears that the explosions likely to result from the attack will injure or kill the children in the centre he is responsible for protecting. In his view, the harm likely to result from the attack is disproportionate (therefore unlawful), and he fires on the attackers. The belligerent nexus criterion to test whether an act

---

[38] Article 51(5)(b) AP I; Article 57(2)(c) AP I. This is also a rule of customary international law: see Henckaerts and Doswald-Beck, *Customary IHL*, Rule 14.

[39] For further discussion, see, generally, Sassòli and Cameron, 'The Protection of Civilian Objects'.

[40] There is discussion in the doctrine as to whether mistake regarding the unlawfulness of the conduct is sufficient to justify a use of force in self-defence, including whether such mistake must be honest, reasonable or not permissible at all.

constitutes direct participation in hostilities requires us to examine whether the act of the PMSC guard is specifically designed to injure the enemy in support of one party and to the detriment of another. At the same time, we are told not to look for 'hostile intent' and not to consider the subjective motives of a particular individual. The belligerent nexus, the Interpretive Guidance says, 'relates to the objective purpose of the act'. The objective purpose of the act in this scenario is to prevent such an attack from being carried out. But is the attacking party 'the adversary' of the PMSC in this instance? That is to say, are his actions designed to be to the detriment of the attacking party? The answer to that question may depend heavily on who the PMSC guard is contracted by – whether it be a government or party to the conflict or simply an NGO in the area. A reasonable reading of the Interpretive Guidance indicates that if the PMSC guard's actions in substance prevent an attack on a military arsenal, no matter his motivation for doing so, that action will be to the detriment of the attacking party. On this reasoning also, the PMSC guard's action would constitute direct participation in hostilities, even though the attack is in some way unlawful. This conclusion is not, however, intuitive and may not sit well with a non-specialist in IHL: many would consider the PMSC guard's actions as heroic and not something that should be discouraged or punished. But IHL does not want civilians to be put in positions where they will engage in heroic acts against opposing forces.

If an attack is unlawful because the attacking party is using an indiscriminate weapon, does that unlawfulness give rise to a right for a PMSC to respond in self-defence? If the nature of the weapon or attack is such that the PMSC himself or civilians around him are in the direct line of fire, it would be absurd to argue that he could not defend himself or the civilians from such an attack. On the other hand, if a PMSC observes that a party is using an indiscriminate weapon to attack a military objective and fears potential consequences, does the mere potential for error or harm to civilians make the attack unlawful such that it would negate the belligerent nexus of the PMSC's attack on opposing forces and sustain a defence of self-defence? The second scenario is perhaps best limited by a consideration of whether it is necessary to use force in self-defence in such circumstances. However, in terms of the capacity of the bare unlawfulness of the indiscriminate nature of the attack as sufficient to negate a belligerent nexus in the PMSC's response using force to repel the attack, I have serious reservations. In limited circumstances, then, the unlawfulness of an indiscriminate attack may remove a violent response from the remit of direct participation in hostilities.

A similar analysis may be made in terms of unlawful weapons. If a weapon is unlawful on the grounds that it may cause superfluous injury to those against whom it is directed, but it is directed only against combatants, the unlawfulness of the weapon does not give rise to a right for a PMSC to use force against the attackers in defence of the combatants. Again, this is because under IHL, self-defence in defence of others may never be used in defence of combatants. Such uses of force will always constitute direct participation in hostilities.[41] But may, for example, PMSC security guards directly target individuals who are planting mines in a state that is a party to the land mines ban treaty? As with the scenario above, whether a plea of self-defence may be sustained will likely turn on the question of necessity to take such action in the circumstances. Another tricky scenario is if the unlawful weapon is, for example, a chemical weapon that is being used against combatants but whose effects will harm civilians. In such cases, the problem is muddy. The objective of the attack is a legitimate military target such that interfering with such an attack will satisfy the belligerent nexus criteria of supporting one side against another. Yet it is understandable that a civilian person charged specially with protecting civilians will see the danger in the attack and in good faith want to protect those civilians.

The Complexity of Self-Defence in Practice

These examples of factors that may make attacks 'unlawful' raise difficult and disturbing questions, and the responses are not wholly satisfactory. What about an attack on a military objective that may be unlawful on more than one of the above grounds? Does the fact that it is mostly likely to be disproportionate outweigh other factors? But, what is more, can we honestly expect a person who is placed in the role of guarding civilian persons or objects to make a complicated analysis of the factors leading him to qualify an attack as unlawful in the split second in which he needs to determine his response? Is it reasonable and realistic for the law to demand this kind of analysis before responding? Moreover, how important is it to avoid direct participation in hostilities compared with saving civilian lives? For many, such scenarios may seem exceptional and worthy of being construed as legitimate conduct, regardless of whether it is frowned on by IHL.

---

[41] Assuming that the combatants in question are not wounded or otherwise hors de combat, of course.

This discussion illustrates that it is vital to determine whether self-defence should be construed broadly or narrowly in the context of armed conflict. There are principled reasons to support both positions, but the only conclusion commensurate with IHL is that it must be construed narrowly. If one considers that IHL seeks to protect individuals, one may arrive at the conclusion that self-defence must be interpreted in such a way that it allows civilians to defend against an attack whose effects would put them (or other vulnerable civilians around them) in danger. Commenting on the provision on self-defence in the ICC Statute, Kai Ambos states, 'The use of force is "unlawful" if not legally justified. Given this broad definition, only the "danger" implied by the use of force can restrict the scope of application of self-defence. Certainly, danger must imply a serious risk for the life or physical integrity of a person...'[42]

With all due respect, this construction of what is 'unlawful' is unhelpful. 'Danger' to civilians cannot be used to give content to the concept of what is 'unlawful' in a situation of armed conflict because, unlike in peacetime, a perfectly lawful military operation that satisfies all the requirements of being proportionate and discriminate may nonetheless result in the loss of civilian lives. That is to say, even lawful acts in armed conflict may put civilian lives in danger. In situations of armed conflict, one cannot easily draw a straight line between what is dangerous and what is unlawful; plenty of lawful acts are also dangerous for civilians. Indeed, protecting civilians is only one part of humanitarian law – in order to be viable, it requires balancing protection against military necessity.

In fact, widening the scope of self-defence to take up arms on the basis of self-defence in this way disrupts the structure of IHL. While it seems counterintuitive to argue that civilians may not take up arms in their own defence in such circumstances in order to increase the protection IHL offers them, this is the philosophy of IHL. Otherwise, combatants would begin attacking civilians on grounds that civilians may try to defend against (even lawful) attacks on such grounds. If we were to accept that there is a right to use force in self-defence against attacks on military objectives that may in some way be unlawful, that interpretation would threaten the essential separation between combatants and civilians. Indeed, the solution of IHL for situations where civilians are in proximity to military objectives and therefore whose lives are in danger due to the likelihood of attack is not that such civilians may take up arms against attacks on the objectives close to them. It is rather to urge states to keep military

---

[42] Ambos, 'Other Grounds for Excluding Criminal Responsibility', pp. 1032–1033.

objectives as far as possible away from civilian centres and to separate civilians and/or civilian objects from military personnel and objectives.

Proposed Guiding Rule

Reducing complex legal questions to single rules will not always produce entirely satisfactory solutions, but it is necessary and helpful to identify a touchstone principle that takes into account the overarching concerns and fundamental principles of both self-defence and international humanitarian law. In order to arrive at a practical, workable interpretation of 'unlawful' attack for IHL and self-defence, I propose the following guiding rule: if an attack is directed at a military objective or at combatants, even if some element of that attack is unlawful, a civilian PMSC contractor or security guard may not interfere. Similarly, a civilian PMSC may not interfere if it may be expected that persons belonging to the enemy do not want (absent resistance by the defenders) to kill, injure or destroy, but rather to arrest persons or to obtain control over objects.

This conclusion has repercussions for an appropriate regulatory framework: if, as I argue is the case, it is the question whether an object is a military objective that is the key factor making an attack unlawful, this leads to a conclusion that PMSCs should not be responsible for guarding things that are military in nature, are highly likely to become so due to their nature (i.e. dual-use objects) or are located in places where operations are ongoing.

The Interpretive Guidance suggests that the 'one' rule is violence that is 'unlawful' under IHL that gives rise to self-defence that would lack a belligerent nexus. I believe the actual rule is more nuanced than that. Many of the unlawful attacks listed above even count as grave breaches of the Geneva Conventions and are the epitome of unlawful violence under IHL, but, as this analysis has shown, not every defence against them will lack a belligerent nexus. This conclusion will inform the examination of the final two elements of self-defence – necessity and proportionality – with particular consequences for the interpretation of necessity.

9.2.3 The Use of Force in Response Must Be Necessary

A universal element of the defence of self-defence is that the use of force to defend oneself must be necessary.[43] Determining the content of what

---

[43] One can even say that it must be required in order for a state's criminal laws to be in line with its obligation to protect the right to life.

it means that force be necessary, is, however, not a straightforward exercise. In particular, there is much doctrinal dispute around the appropriate manner of interpreting the two key elements of imminence and the 'duty to retreat'. The context of armed conflict affects the manner in which these elements must be interpreted in light of IHL.

It is important to recall that IHL already contains a principle of necessity. However, for the rules on self-defence, we must consider the relevant elements of necessity in that paradigm and its relationship to armed conflict.

Imminence of the Threat

By and large, domestic criminal law demands that a threat be imminent or so immediate as to leave no other option than to respond by force in order to sustain a plea of self-defence.[44] This requirement is not necessarily listed in all criminal codes as an element of the defence, but commentators argue that its existence is nevertheless present or understood.[45] In some jurisdictions, the imminence requirement is considered to be part and parcel of the inquiry into whether the use of force was necessary or reasonable; in others, it is a stand-alone requirement.[46] There is one very limited exception to the requirement that the threat of harm be imminent, recognized in common law systems, which is that in very circumscribed circumstances, some jurisdictions permit battered women to kill their batterers in self-defence even when the batterer was not about to attack them at that particular instance.[47] It is highly unlikely that PMSCs will be in a position to avail themselves of this narrow exception to the imminence requirement. It is thus important to underscore that the existence of a prior threat from a particular individual does not, in the absence of a new, specific and immediate threat from that same person, satisfy the requirement that a threat be imminent.[48] This is important to bear in mind in an armed

---

[44] Hermida, 'Convergence', 210–213. Hermida makes extensive references to civil codes and to US jurisprudence. In China, the attack must have begun and/or be ongoing in order to sustain a defence of self-defence. See M. Zhou and S. Wang, 'China' (2001) in Verbruggen, *Criminal Law*, at paras 163–164.

[45] Yeo, 'Anglo-African Perspectives', 126–127.

[46] Paciocco, 'Applying the Law', 51–52; Leverick, *Killing in Self-Defence*, in particular chapter 5, 'Imminence of Harm', pp. 87–108 at p. 88. This is the case with UK criminal law. See Ashworth, 'Self-Defence', 284; J. Slater, 'Making Sense of Self-Defence' (1996) 5 *Nottingham LJ* 140, 142–143.

[47] See Hermida, 'Convergence', 211–212. Hermida indicates that this exception is limited to common law jurisdictions.

[48] Paciocco, 'Applying the Law', 52. He notes that while a prior attack may give reason to fear someone, it does not satisfy the necessity of attacking in the absence of another attack. See also Grabczynska and Kessler Ferzan, 'Justifying Killing', 240.

conflict context. PMSCs may thus not rely on self-defence to attack, in the absence of an imminent threat, persons whom they have observed previously engaging in violent or threatening activities simply on the basis of those prior acts.

Duty to Retreat

Many criminal laws allow for the use of force that is 'reasonably necessary', which may allow a defendant slightly more leeway in the choice of means of response than a standard of strict necessity.[49] On the other hand, when there is an option to retreat (thus causing no harm), states and theorists are divided as to whether defendants are obliged to take it. There are at least two circumstances in which it is generally acknowledged that there is no obligation to retreat, but neither of these applies to the situation of PMSCs working as security guards in conflict areas.[50] The position of some common law states is that having no option to retreat is not a 'formal prerequisite' of self-defence but that it is a factor in determining whether the use of force by the would-be victim was reasonable and necessary.[51] In some civil law jurisdictions there is a duty to retreat if possible,[52] whereas in others there is no obligation to retreat.[53]

A human rights approach to self-defence, which would also take into account the right to life of the attacking party, may mean that a defendant may not stand his ground and fight back regardless of an opportunity to protect himself by retreating.[54] The extent to which the right to life of an attacking party needs to be taken into account in a situation of armed conflict is perhaps even less straightforward than in a purely domestic criminal law context.[55] This is because combatants may be attacked (by

---

[49] See, for example, Yeo, 'Anglo-African Perspectives', 129, comparing the Sudanese Penal Code (strict necessity test) with other African codes.

[50] One is people with battered women's syndrome and the other is people who are protecting their own homes from home invasions. See Paciocco, 'Applying the Law', 57.

[51] Ibid., 56–57; this is also the case in Ghana, Kenya, Botswana and Sudan. See Yeo, 'Anglo-African Perspectives', 129. While there is no uniform rule in the United States, a majority of US jurisdictions do not impose an obligation to retreat on a defendant. See V.F. Nourse, 'Self-Defense and Subjectivity' (2001) 68 *Univ Chicago L Rev* 1235 at 1237 and note 10.

[52] For example, in Belgium. See L. Dupont and C. Fijnaut, 'Belgium' (1993), in Verbruggen, *Criminal Law*, at para. 163.

[53] For example, Denmark. See L.B. Langsted, P. Garde and V. Greve, 'Denmark', in Verbruggen, *Criminal Law*, at para. 117. In Chile, the existence of a possibility to flee will not in and of itself render a use of force in self-defence 'disproportionate'. See Politoff et al., 'Chile', in Verbruggen, *Criminal Law*, para. 136.

[54] Ashworth, 'Self-Defence', 289–290, 293 (citing case *R. v. Julien*).

[55] See Leverick, *Killing in Self-Defence*, and Grabczynska and Kessler Ferzan, 'Justifying Killing', for debates.

other combatants) with impunity under IHL. As such, their right to life is already altered by the IHL framework.[56]

Under English common law and the law of some US states, this aspect of the necessity requirement does not entail that a person must *leave* a place where he is even if he has been warned that people are coming to attack him (unlawfully). Rather, the obligation to limit the harm that his self-defence may cause the attackers arises only once their actual attack is imminent or ongoing.[57] Such an interpretation does not sit entirely well with the rules on the conduct of hostilities in IHL, however. Under IHL, armed forces are encouraged to give warnings prior to attack where feasible as a precautionary measure to reduce civilian losses.[58] The logic behind this rule is that civilians can then move away from a legitimate military objective and their lives will be spared. It goes against the grain of IHL to interpret the right to self-defence in such a way that a properly given warning of attack would give rise to a right to civilians to stand their ground and fight such an attack (on the grounds of some presumable unlawfulness of some aspect of the attack) without such action being construed as direct participation in hostilities. At the same time, in a peri-conflict situation, the importance of not obliging law-abiding civilians to leave a place to avoid confrontation when an unlawful attack is announced can be crucial to protect against ethnic cleansing. Indeed, in peacetime, one of the key values that is arguably protected by interpreting 'necessity' as comprising no duty to retreat is the preservation of the freedom of movement of the law-abiding person threatened with attack.[59] Although freedom of movement is a derogable right in situations of emergency such as those prevailing in armed conflict, it nevertheless remains extremely important in such situations as it is integrally linked with limiting internal displacement and, on the other hand, enabling civilians to seek safe havens. It is therefore important to understand how the duty to retreat rule must operate in light of IHL in a situation of armed conflict. The following examples will clarify the interaction between the concepts of self-defence, human shields and direct participation in hostilities in light of the 'duty to retreat' and unlawfulness elements of self-defence.

---

[56] For the right to life of fighters in non-international armed conflicts, see M. Sassòli and L. Olson, 'The Relationship Between International Humanitarian and Human Rights Law Where It Matters: Admissible Killing and the Internment of Fighters in Non-international Armed Conflicts' (2008) 90 *IRRC* 599–627, and L. Doswald-Beck, 'The Right to Life in Armed Conflict: Does International Humanitarian Law Provide All the Answers?' (2006) 88 *IRRC* 881–904.

[57] Ashworth, 'Self-Defence', 295 (citing English and US jurisprudence).

[58] AP I Article 57(2)(c).   [59] Ashworth, 'Self-Defence', 295–296.

In an armed conflict – and especially in the context of ethnic cleansing – whether it is soldiers or run-of-the-mill criminals who try to kill, rape or ill-treat, the individuals defending themselves against such attacks will not be directly participating in hostilities. Under the pure criminal law standard of a duty to retreat[60] and under the duty to retreat as it operates in light of IHL in armed conflict, a person who stands his ground and fights an attack, even when he knows that such tactics may be used or has warning of such attack, will in all likelihood meet the test of necessity for self-defence.

If, however, an armed force has an aggressive policy of attacking apartment buildings where fighters (even low-level foot soldiers) are hiding and they announce an attack on an apartment building that will clearly be disproportionate (and, thus, unlawful), the residents of that building may not rely on a 'no duty to retreat' rule to mount a defence. While the warning given does not give rise to an *obligation* on the part of the residents to leave the building, the only thing self-defence permits them to do in such a case is to remain peacefully present. This is the nub of the intersection of the three concepts: the fact that the civilians remain present in the building after a warning of attack has been given does not mean that they are directly participating in hostilities as human shields by the fact of their very presence on a military objective. However, those civilians (or for that matter PMSCs responsible for protecting the building) cannot rely on the fact that they did not retreat after the warning was given to put themselves into a situation where it is necessary to use force such that their counterattack is removed from the realm of direct participation in hostilities.

With regard to the belligerent nexus of the attack, this example betrays no clearer will or intent on the part of the civilians seeking to protect their homes of a belligerent nexus than does the PMSC security guard in front of the daycare centre. The civilians may even wish that the fighters would leave their building and have absolutely no wish to somehow protect the fighters by their presence, but also do not wish to suffer the consequences of having their homes destroyed if military forces bomb the building. Nevertheless, if they mount a defence against the disproportionate attack on their building, they will be directly participating in hostilities. Moreover, those who argue that people who remain at or near a military objective so as to affect the proportionality of the attack are human shields and thereby directly participate in hostilities must conclude that in IHL, there is a strong duty-to-retreat requirement for self-defence. To be consistent and preserve the integrity of their arguments, they should apply such

---

[60] In many jurisdictions, in any case.

reasoning to all civilians in all situations, such that PMSCs are also under a duty to retreat when attacks begin.

This analysis reinforces the logic of the proposed guiding rule above: if we reduce the above example to the single most important factor delineating the boundary between self-defence and direct participation in hostilities, we again are left with the fact that the attack was on a legitimate military objective.

9.2.4   The Use of Force Must Be Proportionate

Under many domestic criminal laws, a person may use deadly force only against deadly attacks.[61] Some criminal codes broaden the scope of attacks against which lethal force may be used in self-defence to include offences such as rape or other attacks that severely compromise physical integrity.[62] For the most part, courts will weigh whether the force used was reasonable; in general, the urgency of conditions culminating in a use of force in self-defence suggest that one cannot impose a 'least harmful means' obligation on defendants.[63] Nevertheless, the proportionality analysis sets important limits on the scope of the defence: according to Chinese self-defence law, 'it is commonly agreed that the defence should stop as long as the attacker is being controlled or has lost the ability to continue the attack.'[64]

Where the unlawful attack put the defender's life in danger or seriously threatened his physical integrity, most courts will find the use of deadly force in response to be completely proportionate.[65] Proportionality is a more significant factor in cases of defence of property. Where the force used in response to an unlawful attack was excessive, by and large, courts follow one of three possible avenues: (1) the sentence is reduced, such that the self-defence plea is considered to be a mitigating circumstance rather than a justification; (2) they may change the 'qualification' of the offence charged; or (3) self-defence is not accepted and there is no reduction in sentence.[66]

---

[61] Hermida, 'Convergence', 210–211.
[62] Yeo, 'Anglo-African Perspectives', 122 and 132.   [63] Ibid., 129.
[64] M. Zhou and S. Wang, 'China' (2001), in Verbruggen, *Criminal Law*, at para. 166.
[65] Some jurisdictions use a standard of what is 'reasonable' in the circumstances. See Pradel, *Droit pénal comparé*, p. 139, citing in particular the United Kingdom but observing that this standard 'est constant dans divers droits'.
[66] Pradel, ibid.

For the sake of completeness, it should be noted that in domestic criminal law, the innocence of the defender is an important element for the success of a self-defence plea. That is to say, the person using force in self-defence must not have provoked the initial attack. In my view this aspect of the defence needs no specific modification in light of IHL but should be borne in mind by those anticipating relying on the defence in the course of their daily work.

9.3 Conclusion

In conclusion, in a situation where there is a group that seeks to exploit the right to use force in self-defence as a means of commercial profit, it is reasonable to surmise that they may push for a broad interpretation of what is 'violence prohibited by IHL' so as to enlarge the scope of activity in which they may lawfully engage. In this respect, the phrase 'violence prohibited by IHL' in the Interpretive Guidance is unfortunately vague and overbroad, and perhaps does not perfectly encapsulate what the experts had in mind when they affirmed that force used in self-defence does not constitute direct participation in hostilities. Indeed, in the reports of expert meetings, the language used to describe the expert opinion reflects a more circumspect right of self-defence than the wording the Interpretive Guidance could arguably be construed to allow if IHL is not read into it. According to one report, 'All the experts who spoke on the subject stressed that individual civilians using a proportionate amount of force in response to an unlawful and imminent attack against themselves or their property should not be considered as directly participating in hostilities.'[67] In particular, this description of self-defence does not include the defence of others, despite the fact that that aspect is common to most national criminal laws, which perhaps explains one reason why the experts were not alert to a need to carefully describe the contours of self-defence in the context of armed conflict and in light of IHL. The examples provided in the Interpretive Guidance include 'looting, rape, and murder by marauding soldiers', but these are preceded by the more general term 'unlawful attack', which is listed as an alternative.[68]

---

[67] ICRC, 'Direct Participation in Hostilities Under International Humanitarian Law: Summary Report' (2003) at 6.

[68] ICRC, Interpretive Guidance, p. 61: 'For example, although the use of force by civilians to defend themselves against unlawful attack or looting, rape, or murder by marauding soldiers may cause the required threshold of harm, its purpose clearly is not to support a party to the conflict against another. If *individual* self-defence against prohibited violence were

Part of the problem is that it is not entirely reasonable to expect people not to react when the role they are tasked with is protecting people
or objects and they or others around them are threatened with direct violence. It would almost be asking them to contravene human instinct to
require them to step aside and let attacks go on if they suspect they are
lawful attacks under IHL – especially because it is a group of civilians,
who (theoretically) are not necessarily inculcated with an instinct for IHL
or laws of armed conflict. Indeed, Andrew Ashworth, quoting Thomas
Hobbes, argues that 'the instinct towards self-preservation is so strong and
basic to human nature that "no law can oblige a man to abandon" it.'[69] This
is the crux of the matter with PMSC security guards – both they and the
states contracting them insist that they are civilians, but their role in hostile environments and the near impossibility of responding to an attack
in a manner that contravenes human instinct means that their use in this
context almost inevitably disrupts the structure of IHL.

Even though US directives and policies direct that PMSCs should
be used 'cautiously' in areas where there are major ongoing combat
operations,[70] in today's theatres of conflict, which often lack a predictable
front line, this admonition may be insufficient.[71] Indeed, where a state
adopts a regulation or law stipulating that contractors may use force only
in self-defence, yet at the same time puts out calls for tenders for the same
contractors to bid on contracts to provide security for forward-operating
bases in Afghanistan, the exploitation of the use of force in self-defence
is flagrant. While such a 'restriction' to use force only in self-defence may
be meaningful in terms of domestic laws on outsourcing,[72] it does not
dispose of the question as to whether such conduct constitutes direct participation in hostilities.

As an additional note, PMSCs recruited to work in different states may
be surprised to learn that same principles are not applied in exactly the

---

to entail loss of protection against direct attack, this would have the absurd consequence
of legitimizing a previously unlawful attack.' Again, part of the problem with the phrasing
of this rather categorical statement is the assumption that self-defence will be used only in
defence of oneself.

[69] Ashworth, 'Self-Defence', p. 282 (citing a passage from *Leviathan*).

[70] DoD Instruction 3020.41 3 October 2005, section 4.4.2.

[71] DoD Instruction 3020.41 3 October 2005 is in the process of being revised and, according
to US government officials, 'contains significant changes to the existing instruction'.

[72] US Federal Regulation, Title 32, National Defense, A.I.F (Security), Part 159, Private Security Contractors Operating in Contingency Operations, 17 July 2009, ss 159.3(1) and
accompanying footnote is phrased as restricting the use of force to self-defence so as to
comply with the prohibition against outsourcing inherently governmental functions.

same manner everywhere. Thus, companies using PMSCs in security roles where it will be anticipated that they will rely on the defence of self-defence should inform recruits of the legal framework applicable in the relevant state. Again, it must be recalled that this basis for using force applies in defence to criminal charges, thus there is a certain degree of vulnerability on the part of those who must use it no matter how well they know the law.

The Use of Force in Self-Defence in Peace Operations

When it comes to the use of force in self-defence in the context of peace operations, it is necessary to carry out a separate analysis in order to understand when peacekeeping forces or PMSCs may end up directly participating in hostilities. This is because the meaning of 'self-defence' for peace operations is not the same as that in international or domestic criminal law, nor is it the same as that in the international law *ius ad bellum* sense of the term. In peace operations, self-defence can mean the limited amount of force used to protect oneself from an unlawful attack, but it can also mean force used in order to implement or defend the mandate of the peacekeeping force.[1] Some situations may, however, overlap with those described above for 'regular' PMSCs in armed conflicts.

It is important to bear in mind that a 'normal' armed conflict may also be classified by some as a peace operation – but for UN *authorized* peace operations (also sometimes referred to as peace enforcement), the peacekeeping framework does not generally apply. The following analysis applies to those peace operations under a UN mandate, and under UN command and control, where troops have been contributed to the peace operation by states and in which there may or may not be PMSC members of a troop contingent.[2] It will also assess the situation of PMSCs acting as security guards providing protection in accordance with the UN Policy and Guidelines on the use of armed private security companies.

10.1 Limited Use of Force

The use of force in peacekeeping is a complex topic. Since the interpretation of the acceptable degree of force and the circumstances in which

---

[1] See below, Section 10.1.
[2] See the explanation of the various types of peace operations in United Nations Department of Peacekeeping Operations and Department of Field Support, 'United Nations Peacekeeping Operations: Principles and Guidelines' (18 January 2008) 18–25 (Capstone Doctrine).

it may be used has changed over time, the use of force has become one of the thorniest questions of peacekeeping.[3] Indeed, it goes to the heart of the institution of peacekeeping, as some question whether an operation is a 'true peacekeeping operation' if a peacekeeping mission uses force beyond simply in self-defence, such as in the Congo in the 1960s.[4] Concerns regarding the broadening of the permitted use of force also relate to the 'institution of peacekeeping' and its capacity to accomplish the goals for which it has been created.[5] The line between peacekeeping and peace 'enforcement' has long been acknowledged as blurry; the significance of the line in legal terms is difficult to grasp. For the purposes of the application of international humanitarian law, it is irrelevant whether an operation is classified as peacekeeping or peace enforcement – what matters are the facts on the ground.

There are at least four issues in relation to it that have ramifications for this study. First, the use of force is intrinsically related to the issue as to when peacekeepers are engaged in an armed conflict as combatants – that is to say, it is linked to the applicability of IHL to the peace operation. For PMSCs as peacekeepers and security guards, this may be the most important issue. Second (and related to the first point) is that it affects when peacekeepers are entitled to protection against attack (e.g., under the UN Safety Convention and ICC Statute). These issues are discussed below. In general, however, the analysis in this section proceeds on the assumption that UN peacekeeping forces can be involved in armed conflicts to which

---

[3] Trevor Findlay, *The Use of Force in UN Peace Operations* (Oxford University Press, 2002); D. Shraga, 'The United Nations as an Actor Bound by International Humanitarian Law', in L. Condorelli, A.M. La Rosa and S. Scherrer (eds.), *Les Nations Unies et le droit international humanitaire – The United Nations and International Humanitarian Law: actes du colloque international à l'occasion du cinquantième anniversaire de l'ONU (Genève 19, 20, 21 octobre 1995)* (Paris: Pedone, 1996); M. Berdal, 'Lessons Not Learned: The Use of Force in "Peace Operations" in the 1990s' (2000) 7 *International Peacekeeping* 55–74; A. Adebajo and C.L. Sriram (eds.), *Managing Armed Conflicts in the 21st Century* (New York: Frank Cass, 2001); K. Cox, 'Beyond Self-Defense: United Nations Peacekeeping Operations and the Use of Force' (1999) 27 *Denver J Intl L and Policy* 239–273; S. Chesterman, 'External Study: The Use of Force in UN Peace Operations' (UN DPKO Best Practices Unit, undated).

[4] See for example H. McCoubrey and N. White, *The Blue Helmets: Legal Regulation of United Nations Military Operations* (Aldershot: Dartmouth, 1996), p. 88, where they argue that '[i]t is very difficult to see ONUC as a true peacekeeping operation in that it was authorized to use force beyond that necessary for strict self-defence.' However, they also point out that ONUC 'was not impartial in the conflict' and the formal consent of the government was blighted by the fact that 'there was no real government in the Congo' for a certain period.

[5] See generally James Sloan, *The Militarization of Peacekeeping in the Twenty-first Century* (Oxford: Hart Publishing, 2011).

IHL applies. Third, acts of peacekeepers involving the use of force will be measured against the principle of limited use of force to check whether they have remained within the ambit of their mandate. That inquiry is not directly relevant for the present study, but it sometimes causes confusion when evaluating the use of force by peace operations. Finally, an examination of this principle of peacekeeping brings up the question as to which acts involving a use of force in self-defence by security guards in the context of a peacekeeping operation may in fact constitute direct participation in hostilities. This issue is especially tricky and is closely linked to the first issue. Security guarding and direct participation in hostilities in 'normal' armed conflicts have been examined above; the analysis below will provide some additional elements for interpretation in the context of peacekeeping operations.

A further complicating factor is that, even within peace operations and among them, the broad definition of self-defence unique to peacekeeping is not static. Each mandate of each operation is different.[6] The Rules of Engagement set by the UN for each operation also likely differ, introducing yet further fluidity in the definition – but these are not often made public so it is difficult to know for certain.[7] Moreover, as national troop contributions are at some levels under national command, each state may also have its own rules of engagement, such that within a single mission there are many different interpretations.[8]

10.1.1   Meaning and Evolution of the Concept of Self-Defence in Peacekeeping

Early peacekeeping doctrine held that force was to be used only in self-defence by traditional 'interposition' forces.[9] This is most akin to a personal self-defence model. The notion that force may be used only in limited self-defence was first expressed by then Secretary-General Hammarskjøld, who argued that strict limitations on the use of force were

---

[6] Paul Tavernier, 'La légitime défense du personnel de l'ONU', in Rahim Kherad (ed.), *Légitimes défenses* (Poitiers: LGDJ 2007), pp. 121–138 at p. 132.

[7] Ibid. at pp. 132ff. See also Ray Murphy, *UN Peacekeeping in Lebanon, Somalia and Kosovo: Operational and Legal Issues in Practice* (Cambridge University Press, 2007). That being said, Trevor Findlay published a number of Rules of Engagement in appendix 2 of his *The Use of Force in UN Peace Operations*, pp. 411–424, from the UN archives.

[8] Tavernier, 'La légitime défense', 132.

[9] UN Secretary-General, 'Summary Study of the Experience Derived from the Establishment and Operation of the Force' (9 October 1958) UN Doc A/3943 paras 178–180 (hereafter Secretary-General, 'Summary Study').

necessary to maintain the distinction between peacekeeping action and enforcement action (which would require a Security Council resolution under Chapter VII).[10] He stated that for UNEF I, which was established by the UN General Assembly, the executive authority delegated to the Secretary-General to determine how the units provided by states could be used, 'that in the types of operation with which this report is concerned this could never include combat activity'.[11] Interpreting the 'margin of freedom for judgement' on the 'extent and nature of the arming of the units and of their right of self-defence' was, in the case of UNEF, '[r]esolved in consultation with the contributing Governments and with the host Government'.[12]

In 1958, UN Secretary-General Hammarskjøld wrote,

> A reasonable definition seems to have been established in the case of UNEF, where the rule is applied that men engaged in the operation may never take the initiative in the use of armed force, but are entitled to respond with force to an attack with arms, including attempts to use force to make them withdraw from positions which they occupy under orders from the Commander, acting under the authority of the Assembly and within the scope of its resolutions. The basic element is clearly the prohibition against any initiative in the use of armed force. This definition of the limit between self-defence, as permissible for United Nations elements of the kind discussed, and offensive action, which is beyond the competence of such elements, should be approved for future guidance.[13]

The type of limited use of force the Secretary-General described as being appropriate in self-defence in those early days of peacekeeping is strongly reminiscent of the type of force described by the former US Secretary of Defense Donald Rumsfeld in relation to the use of force by PMSCs in Iraq.[14] Governments using PMSCs have insisted that they are restricted to using force only in self-defence; indeed, as shown above, self-defence

---

[10] Ibid., para. 179: 'a wide interpretation of the right of self-defence might well blur the distinction between operations of the character discussed in this report and combat operations, which would require a decision under Chapter VII of the Charter and an explicit, more far-reaching delegation of authority to the Secretary-General than would be required for any of the operations discussed here.'

[11] Ibid., para. 178.

[12] Ibid., para. 178. The Secretary-General made special mention of the 'Advisory Committee on UNEF' established by the UN General Assembly as having been particularly useful in regard to these issues.

[13] Ibid., para. 179. Emphasis in original.

[14] See, e.g., the Reply of Secretary of Defense Donald Rumsfeld to the Honorable Ike Skelton of 4 May 2004, available at www.house.gov/skelton/5-4-04_Rumsfeld_letter_on_contractors .pdf (accessed 1 October 2006).

often forms the basis for the rules on the use of force for PMSCs. As self-defence is the basis on which PMSCs resort to force, they may seem well suited to the job of peacekeeping. There is, however, much more to self-defence when it comes to UN peacekeeping. Moreover, even this incarnation of self-defence in its most limited form would not necessarily exclude the possibility that peacekeepers can directly participate in hostilities in an armed conflict.

The scope of the use of force in self-defence was quickly broadened to include a right for peacekeepers to use force in response to circumstances beyond those traditionally understood to be comprised in the normal rules of self-defence. For example, Secretary-General U Thant set out the parameters of self-defence for the UN Peacekeeping Force in Cyprus largely as above, adding the following:

> Examples in which troops may be authorized to use force include attempts by force to compel them to withdraw from a position which they occupy under orders from their commanders, attempts by force to disarm them, *and attempts by force to prevent them from carrying out their responsibilities as ordered by their commanders.*[15]

As such, the notion that self-defence encompassed an ability to use force in 'defence of the mandate' was adopted early in the history of peacekeeping.[16] This interpretation of the contours of self-defence 'has been stipulated for each peacekeeping force since 1973'.[17]

More recently, the UN High-Level Panel on Threats, Challenges and Change in 2004 observed that in situations in which peacekeepers are deployed, 'even the most benign environment can turn sour – when spoilers emerge to undermine a peace agreement and put civilians at risk – and that it is desirable for there to be complete certainty about the mission's capacity to respond with force, if necessary.'[18] Even though it expressed approval of the practice of establishing peacekeeping operations under a Chapter VII mandate of the Security Council, the High-Level Panel opined that in terms of the actual force that may be used, 'the difference

---

[15] UN Secretary-General, 'Report of the Secretary-General on the Deployment of U.N. Forces in Cyprus', UN Doc S/5960 (10 September 1964) at para 7(c), quoted in James Sloan, 'The Use of Offensive Force in U.N. Peacekeeping: A Cycle of Boom and Bust?' (2007) 30 *Hastings Intl & Comp L Rev* 385 at 403. Emphasis added.

[16] Sloan, ibid., 403–404.

[17] Ibid., 404. Sloan notes that this concept was entrenched in a Security Council resolution in 1978 with the establishment of UNIFIL. See 405.

[18] Report of the Secretary-General's High-Level Panel on Threats, Challenges and Change, 'A More Secure World: Our Shared Responsibility' (4 December 2004) UN Doc A/59/565 para. 213.

between Chapter VI and VII mandates can be exaggerated: there is little doubt that peacekeeping missions operating under Chapter VI (and thus operating without enforcement powers) have the right to use force in self-defence – and this right is widely understood to extend to "defence of the mission".[19] As such, the Panel affirmed the broad interpretation of the degree and circumstance in which force may be used even in traditional peace operations.

The most recent official restatement on the use of force in UN peace operations can be found in the Capstone Doctrine: 'it is widely understood that they may use force at the tactical level, with the authorization of the Security Council, if acting in self-defense and defense of the mandate.'[20] The Doctrine goes on to say:

> A United Nations peacekeeping operation should only use force as a measure of last resort, when other methods of persuasion have been exhausted, and an operation must always exercise restraint when doing so. The ultimate aim of the use of force is to influence and deter spoilers working against the peace process or seeking to harm civilians; *and not to seek their military defeat.* The use of force by a United Nations peacekeeping operation should always be calibrated in a precise, proportional and appropriate manner, within the principle of the minimum force necessary to achieve the desired effect, while sustaining consent for the mission and its mandate. In its use of force, a United Nations peacekeeping operation should always be mindful of the need for an early de-escalation of violence and a return to non-violent means of persuasion.[21]

Combined with the fact that peacekeeping operations are deployed in areas where peace is fragile or non-existent and that mandates are routinely broadened to include active protection of civilians, it is plain to see that the scope for the use of force has been significantly expanded.

10.1.2   The Existence of an Armed Conflict and Direct Participation in Hostilities Depends on the Facts

For the purposes of this study, from the perspective of international humanitarian law, the relevant question is whether respect for the principle of the use of force only in self-defence would mean the members of the peace operation may nevertheless be engaged as combatants

---

[19] Ibid.
[20] Capstone Doctrine, p. 34. It should be noted that the degree of force permitted in 'traditional' peace operations has been the subject of great controversy, not least because it has fluctuated considerably in practice and doctrine over time.
[21] Ibid., p. 35. Emphasis added.

in an armed conflict.[22] Clearly, this is the case. Here, it should be recalled that a non-international armed conflict occurs when there is armed violence of a sufficient intensity occurring between organized armed groups or between an organized armed group and a state. The reason for that violence and/or the goals of the armed groups are irrelevant to determining the existence of a conflict.[23] Thus, even though peacekeepers may be impartial vis-à-vis the parties to the initial conflict, they may be drawn into a conflict over the implementation of their own mandate. In addition, if their mandate requires them to provide support to one side in an existing conflict, that can lead them to become a party to the original conflict itself. These scenarios will be explored in more detail below.

10.1.3 Drawing the Line Between Self-Defence and Armed Conflict in Peacekeeping

Almost everyone agrees that force used by peacekeepers in individual (personal) self-defence does not entail their being engaged as combatants.[24] This is indeed commensurate with the Interpretive Guidance

---

[22] For the UN, the importance of distinguishing between peacekeeping and enforcement action is primarily based in a concern to assert that peacekeeping is something other than 'war'. See also Alexander Orakhelashvili, *Collective Security* (Oxford University Press, 2011), p. 288. However, it may also be linked to the failure of the intended mechanism to supply the Security Council with forces in order for it to carry out enforcement actions under Article 42 of the UN Charter. According to the system set up under the Charter, such enforcement action was to be taken by the UN using the forces provided to it by states through the procedure established in Article 43 (discussed in more detail below). In the *Certain Expenses* case, the ICJ opined that the expenses generated by the two peace operations under scrutiny – UNEF and ONUC – were legitimate expenses because even though they were not established using Article 43 forces (which did not and do not exist) they did not arise through a procedure or exercise of power that was somehow *ultra vires*. (*Certain Expenses of the United Nations (Article 17, paragraph 2, of the Charter)* Advisory Opinion of 20 July 1962 [1962] ICJ Rep 151. Summing up the Advisory Opinion, the office of Legal Affairs wrote in a note to the Under-Secretary-General for Political Affairs in 1982, 'The Court thus excluded the peace-keeping operations of the United Nations from the applicability of Article 43. It further confirmed that the United Nations is not precluded from the use of military forces through procedures other than those envisaged in Article 43 of the Charter *for purposes other than enforcement action*.' UN Juridical Yearbook, 1982, Part Two, Chapter VI, 183–185 at 184 (21 October 1982). Emphasis added. This note could be read as suggesting that Article 43 agreements could be necessary in order for UN enforcement action to be lawful. This would be why the UN then outsources 'authorized' enforcement actions to states and organizations rather than carrying them out itself.

[23] ICRC, *Commentary on the First Geneva Convention*, 2016, commentary on common Article 3, paras 447–451. See also Sylvain Vité, 'Typology of Armed Conflicts in International Humanitarian Law: Legal Concepts and Actual Situations' (2009) 91 *IRRC* 69 at 78.

[24] Not all do, however. Some contend that the Secretary-General's Bulletin on IHL can be interpreted to mean that when peacekeepers use force in self-defence, the principles and

on Direct Participation in Hostilities and is in line with the standard interpretation of international criminal law regarding unlawful attacks on peacekeepers.[25] The fact that there is no bright-line test to distinguish a use of force in personal self-defence from becoming engaged in combat has been pointed out by commentators.[26] Robert Kolb has outlined some key questions in this regard:

> [F]or example, what happens if the multinational forces under the command of an international organization, acting in self defence, reply to an attack? To the extent that the illegal attacks suffered are merely sporadic, it does not seem warranted to consider the forces as being caught up in an armed conflict. The members of the forces remain civilians, and the attack on them is a crime. Conversely, if the attacks degenerate into a general pattern and the forces start conducting military operations on their own so as to respond to the acts of war of the other side, we would find ourselves in the context of an armed conflict, and the mere fact of attacking a member of the forces would no longer be a crime in itself. Or, if taken captive, could members of the forces again be considered to be civilians or would they then be considered combatants ... ? Or would it be possible to adopt the view that the regime applicable to such personnel is not immutable, i.e. that they could temporarily lose their protected status and obtain it back soon after?[27]

In this regard, the factual situation described in *Sesay* is a useful case for analysis. In that case, peacekeepers deployed in Sierra Leone had a

rules of IHL apply to such actions. ICRC, 'Report on the Expert Meeting on Multinational Peace Operations' (2004) 10. Some states, on the other hand, have argued that a peacekeeping force will become a party to a conflict depending on the mandate it is given, in particular if that mandate can clearly be read as in support of one of the parties. This was the case of China's reaction to the establishment of the Rapid Reaction Force in the former Yugoslavia in the 1990s. See Christine Gray, *International Law and the Use of Force*, 3rd edn (Oxford University Press, 2008), p. 284. This is also undoubtedly the case with respect to the mandate given to the 'Intervention Brigade' of MONUSCO in UNSC Res 2098 (2013).

[25] ICRC, Interpretive Guidance; Knut Dörmann, 'Art. 8(2)(b)(iii)' and 'Art. 8(2)(e)(iii)', in K. Dörmann, *Elements of War Crimes Under the Rome Statute of the International Criminal Court: Sources and Commentary* (Cambridge University Press, 2005), pp. 153–160 and 452–457, at pp. 159 and 455–456, respectively. See also Michael Cottier, 'Article 8(iii)', in O. Triffterer (ed.), *Commentary on the Rome Statute of the International Criminal Court: Observers Notes, Article by Article*, 2nd edn (Nomos, 2008), pp. 330–338 especially at p. 336 (para. 53).

[26] Cottier, ibid. Robert Kolb, 'Applicability of International Humanitarian Law to Forces Under the Command of an International Organization', in ICRC, 'Report on the Expert Meeting on Multinational Peace Operations' (2004) 68.

[27] Kolb, ibid., 68–69.

mandate to conduct disarmament, demobilization and reintegration (DDR) of the various armed groups, including the RUF. The RUF began attacking peacekeeping bases and detaining peacekeepers, and subsequently a number of persons were tried for the crime of attacking peacekeepers. The trial chamber thus had the task of determining whether the peacekeepers were, at the time of the attacks, entitled to the protection of civilians.

The trial chamber stated the legal test as follows:

> In the Chamber's view, common sense dictates that peacekeepers are considered to be civilians only insofar as they fall within the definition of civilians laid down for non-combatants in customary international law and under Additional Protocol II ... – namely, that they do not take a direct part in hostilities. It is also the Chamber's view that by force of logic, personnel of peacekeeping missions are entitled to protection as long as they are not taking a direct part in the hostilities – and thus have become combatants – at the time of the alleged offence. Where peacekeepers become combatants, they can be legitimate targets for the extent of their participation in accordance with international humanitarian law. As with all civilians, their protection would not cease if the personnel use armed force only in exercising their right to individual self-defence.[28]

---

[28] *Prosecutor v. Sesay, Kallon and Gbao* (Trial Judgement) Case no. SCSL-04–15-T, (25 February 2009/2 March 2009), para. 233. The peacekeeping operation in Sierra Leone in the relevant time was one of the first UN peacekeeping missions with a mandate to protect civilians. See UNSC Res 1270 (1999), para. 14. National courts have had to consider the question as well. The UK House of Lords held that UK forces were not involved or engaged as 'enemy' forces in the peacekeeping operation in Bosnia in 1994–1995 in respect to the circumstances at bar in that case. See *R v. Minister of Defence* ex parte *Walker* [2000] UKHL 5 April 2000. In a more controversial ruling on that point, Canadian courts have held that the peacekeeping operation in Somalia in 1992 under UN Security Council Resolution 794 was not an armed conflict and that therefore IHL was not applicable to the peacekeepers, whereas a Canadian Commission of Inquiry into the same events came to the opposite conclusion: *R v. Brocklebank* CMAC-383 (2 April 1996). This finding of the Court Martial Appeal Court of Canada appears, however, to be based on a flagrant error in understanding the law on the applicability of the Geneva Conventions. See in particular the text accompanying footnote 33. http://decisions.cmac-cacm.ca/decisia-cmac-cacm/cmac-cacm/cmac-cacm/en/96/1/document.do (accessed 19 May 2012). For commentary, see Katia Boustany, 'A Questionable Decision of the Court Martial Appeal Court of Canada' (1998) 1 *YB Intl Humanitarian L* 371–374. Canada, Department of National Defence and the Canadian Forces, 'Report of the Somalia Commission of Inquiry' (1997), which found that 'Operation Cordon obliged Canada to carry out peacekeeping under Chapter VI of the UN Charter, but Operation Deliverance [pursuant to UNSC Res 794] required Canada to engage in peace enforcement under Chapter VII. Ideally, the drafters should have tailored the ROE to reflect the mission and tasks involved, as well as the dangers they would encounter there.' See Volume 2 of the report. See also the ILA Report on the Use of Force (2010), pp. 16–17, for other examples.

Up to here, the chamber has perfectly stated the law. However, it improperly mixed *ius ad bellum* into its analysis and was incorrect in its final assessment of the test when it stated,

> Likewise, the Chambers opines that the use of force by peacekeepers in self-defence in the discharge of their mandate, provided that it is limited to such use, would not alter or diminish the protection afforded to peacekeepers.[29]

This statement of the law is problematic as it affirms that using force in the discharge of their mandate would still fall within self-defence that warrants protection as a civilian.

The Chamber furthermore held,

> In determining whether the peacekeeping personnel or objects of a peacekeeping mission are entitled to civilian protection, the Chamber must consider the totality of the circumstances existing at the time of the alleged offence, including, *inter alia*, the relevant Security Council resolutions for the operation, the specific operational mandates, the role and practices actually adopted by the peacekeeping mission during the particular conflict, their rules of engagement and operational orders, the nature of the arms and equipment used by the peacekeeping force, the interaction between the peacekeeping force and the parties involved in the conflict, the nature and frequency of such force and the conduct of the alleged victim(s) and their fellow personnel.[30]

The factors the court identifies are indeed relevant. For example, UN SC Resolution 2098 of 28 March 2013 clearly provides a mandate for a peacekeeping force that entails that that force is a party to an armed conflict.[31] In addition, some of the other factors the court lists are the same as those set out in the jurisprudence of the international criminal tribunals in order to evaluate whether violence has reached the threshold of a non-international armed conflict.[32] When it comes to peacekeeping, there is a sense that it would be unfair to consider the peacekeepers as having become party to a conflict if they are lightly armed (i.e., with small arms). However, the UN Office for Disarmament Affairs indicates that '[m]ost

---

[29] *Prosecutor v. Sesay, Kallon and Gbao.* See also *Prosecutor v. Abu Garda* ICC-02/05–02/09, Confirmation of the Charges (8 February 2010), para. 83.

[30] *Sesay*, para. 234.

[31] UNSC Res 2098 (2013) created an 'Intervention Brigade' for MONUSCO in order to combat the armed group M23.

[32] See, for example, *Prosecutor v. Haradinaj, Balaj and Brahimaj* (First Trial Judgment) IT-04–84-T (3 April 2008), para. 49. See also *Prosecutor v. Boskoski and Tarculovski* (Trial Judgment) IT-04–82-T (10 July 2008), para. 177, further elaborating on these criteria.

present-day conflicts are fought mainly with small arms.'[33] Thus, this factor should not be permitted to predominate in an analysis.

The tricky question is, what are the limits of personal self-defence when it comes to attacks on a peacekeeping force by an organized armed group? At what point does a use of force used to repel an attack on a peacekeeping base entail the participation of peacekeepers in combat? What is difficult is the fact that a use of force in self-defence by peacekeepers will likely occur in response to a relatively large-scale attack on something resembling a military base or a convoy of peacekeepers. It is a very different situation to that of an individual in a private context being personally unlawfully attacked. It looks different and is different in scale. Thus, although most may agree that the use of force in personal self-defence by a peacekeeper does not entail the application of IHL, not everyone may have the same scenario in mind. The same may be the case for PMSCs protecting things that have become military objectives.

The facts in *Sesay* help to elucidate these concepts. In particular, the absurdity of confusing the mandate and concepts of self-defence is clearly demonstrated in the following reasoning by the trial chamber:

> 1928. The peacekeepers responded to the attacks on their bases at Makump DDR camp and the Islamic Centre in Magburaka with the use of force. However, the Chamber is satisfied that this response was proportionate and entirely justified in self-defence. Groups of RUF fighters were assembled outside the Makump DDR camp on the morning of 2 May 2000, blocking the road and creating a hostile environment culminating in the attack in which peacekeepers were killed and injured. The evidence that Private Yusif was shot at point blank range indicates that the RUF fighters were acting offensively. Similarly, we find that it was RUF fighters who opened fire on the Islamic Centre in an attempt to capture the UNAMSIL post and its occupants.
>
> 1929. In relation to the attack on the DDR camp at Waterworks, the Chamber recalls that following the arrival at RUF fighters at the camp, the peacekeepers attempted to flee and RUF fighters shot at a retreating armoured vehicle and abducted three peacekeepers. This evidence establishes that RUF forces were the offensive party. Although the evidence is unclear as to whether the UNAMSIL peacekeepers responded with force to the encirclement of their camp, the Chamber is of the view that such conduct would be well within their mandate in these circumstances.

---

[33] United Nations Office for Disarmament Affairs, Small Arms page, www.un.org/disarmament/convarms/SALW/ (accessed 25 February 2013).

1930. We therefore find that the peacekeepers did not resort to the use
of force in response to the nine attacks directed against them on 1 and 2
May 2000.[34]

While the analysis regarding some of the attacks described is commensurate with the rules on self-defence described above (proportionate and
necessary), the reasoning in respect to the encirclement of the camp is
problematic. It is patently illogical to affirm that the evidence shows that
the peacekeepers responded with force to attacks on them (while they were
not directly participating in hostilities prior to those attacks) and to conclude that 'the peacekeepers did not resort to the use of force' – unless by
'resort to' the court meant only 'initiate'.[35] Furthermore, the trial chamber
failed to assess the significance of the fact that Zambatt was organized as a
'combat-ready' force subsequent to the attacks on UNAMSIL on 1–2 May
2000 in terms of whether that shift entailed that the peacekeepers could
now be viewed as understanding that they were participating in hostilities
or involved in an armed conflict. Instead, the Chamber was of the view
that 'this action was appropriate in the context of the eruption of violence
in the previous two days and in light of the information then received that
the RUF had established roadblocks.'[36] With all due respect, it was not up
to the Chamber to determine whether the organization of Zambatt was
'appropriate' – which relates to *ius ad bellum* and whether the force was
acting in accordance with its mandate – but to use that fact in order to
determine whether the peacekeeping force had become a party to a conflict with the RUF. In that context, it may have been correct if it had concluded that although it was organized as such, its reticence to use force
in practice when ambushed may indicate that it had not yet crossed that
threshold. On the other hand, the evidence suggests that it may have been
a tactical decision not to become engaged in a firefight when they were
clearly outnumbered. Either way, it appears that the court failed to ask the
correct question and therefore may have arrived at an incorrect result.[37]
It must be recalled that attacks under IHL are defined as a use of violence

---

[34] *Sesay*, paras 1928–1930. Emphasis added.

[35] If the chamber meant that the peacekeepers did not initiate the use of force, that is a different matter. But according to IHL, a use of force constitutes an attack, whether in offence or
in defence.

[36] *Sesay*, para. 1931.

[37] Daphna Shraga merely notes (seemingly with approval) of the holding of the court on
this issue, suggesting that the UN Office of Legal Affairs shares this view. See Shraga, 'The
Secretary-General's Bulletin on the Observance by United Nations Forces of International
Humanitarian Law: A Decade Later' (2009) 39 *Israel YB Human Rights* 357–377.

against the adversary whether in offence or in defence.[38] Thus, if the force has already been drawn into a conflict, it does not matter whether it is responding with force only in defence. What matters is the existence of a conflict itself.

The Chamber did assess some uses of force on a personal self-defence basis, for example, holding that '[w]hile the ZAMBATT peacekeepers employed force in an unsuccessful attempt to repel the RUF attack on their positions at Lunsar, the Chamber is satisfied that the peacekeepers were then acting defensively *to protect their own lives and that this was a necessary and proportionate response* in the circumstances.'[39] In my view, all uses of force in self-defence should have been assessed on this basis in order to determine whether the peacekeepers were participating in hostilities or entitled to protection, assuming that the entire force has not already been drawn into conflict with the RUF. However, this analysis raises an additional question, which is whether a use of force to repel an attack on their position can truly constitute personal self-defence. Or do they have to cede their positions, and as soon as they try to hold them, they become participants in an armed conflict? Again, this question is related to the issues discussed above as to whether a person may stand and fight or whether he must have taken all possible means to avoid violent confrontation where possible in order to rely on the defence of personal self-defence.

Arguably, international law in relation to peacekeeping has tried to set up a standard that makes the base of peacekeepers (and possibly other installations) something analogous to one's home in national law, where it is lawful to defend against a home invasion using deadly force. As such, peacekeepers are entitled to use deadly force to defend against an attempt to invade their 'home' base, without that use of force being construed as a direct participation in hostilities under IHL, as long as such defence conforms to the requirements of necessity and proportionality for self-defence.[40] This interpretation has the benefit of reconciling the object and

---

[38] Article 49(1) AP I.   [39] *Sesay*, para. 1932. Emphasis added.

[40] Christopher Penny, 'Drop That or I'll Shoot . . . Maybe': International Law and the Use of Deadly Force to Defend Property in UN Peace Operations' (2007) 14 *Intl Peacekeeping* 353–367, argues that it is necessary to take into account the character of the property that force is being used to defend in order to know whether lethal force may be used. Thus, he argues that deadly force may be used to defend against hostile acts in regard to inherently dangerous property, such as weapons or ammunition, as well as in regard to 'mission essential' property. In addition, he argues it can be used to protect humanitarian aid when delivering aid is part of the mission. He argues that the infringement of the right to life of the

purpose of the law protecting peacekeepers with IHL. Indeed, interpreting IHL to mean that peacekeepers must abandon their positions and/or their base at the first attack if they did not want to lose the protection from attack would seriously undermine the institution of peacekeeping but with no great gain for the integrity of IHL or the respect for the principle of equality of belligerents. That being said, the vigour of the defence must be carefully evaluated for a single attack. Moreover, when a series of attacks on bases are repelled, and when, as occurred in Sierra Leone according to the facts in *Sesay*, peacekeepers begin to prepare 'combat ready' battalions, even such uses of force in self-defence may lead them to be drawn into armed conflict, even against their will.

Indeed, the court missed this point in *Sesay*, as it interpreted the expansion of the mandate to use force by UNAMSIL 'as further evidence that the actions of RUF fighters in the various attacks constituted a threat to the safety of UNAMSIL personnel to which their limited use of force in response in self-defence was both necessary and well within their mandate.'[41] Indeed, the question whether the RUF was acting offensively is relevant (but not decisive) for the issue as to whether the peacekeepers may have been acting in personal self-defence. But it does not settle the issue of whether they may have been engaged as combatants. Moreover, although rules of engagement may provide for a limited use of force, that approach represents a chosen strategy and does not affect whether an armed conflict is occurring. In other contexts, indeed, the fact that armed forces took steps to limit the effects of their use of force in order to 'win hearts and minds' in no way altered the understanding of their engagement as being part of an armed conflict.

Turning to a case from a national jurisdiction helps us to further understand the scope of self-defence in peace operations. In a British case in which persons who had been shot by UK members of KFOR sued the UK Ministry of Defence for assault or battery, the High Court judge first examined whether the soldiers could rely on self-defence as a defence. Although the legal test is slightly different in a civil claim than in a criminal case,[42]

---

attackers is 'justified by the grave and imminent threat posed to civilians by the underlying humanitarian situation' (361). See also above, Chapter 6, Section 6.1.3, for additional discussion of the Safety Convention and criminalization of attacks against peacekeepers and their property.

[41] *Sesay*, para. 1935.

[42] In particular, the belief in the fact that one was about to be attacked must have been honest *and* reasonable in a civil claim, whereas in a criminal claim it must simply have been honest. See *Bici and Bici v. Ministry of Defence* [2004] EWHC 786 (QB), para. 42.

the standard takes into account the perspective of a reasonable soldier. That is,

> in assessing his conduct and judging the action of the reasonable soldier, it is important to recognise that his action 'is not taken in the calm analytical atmosphere of the court room after counsel with the benefit of hindsight have expounded at length the reasons for and against the kind and degree of force that was used by the accused, but in the brief second or two which the accused had to decide whether to shoot or not and under all the stresses to which he was exposed.'[43]

The Court went on to hold that the rights and duties of members of the armed forces in peacekeeping operations – and in particular the duty of care owed to civilians not to harm them or their property – are 'no more than those of an ordinary citizen in uniform'.[44] As such, then, this case may be taken in support of the notion that it may not warp the legal framework to employ PMSCs in peacekeeping operations in which a limited use of force, confined purely to personal self-defence, can be expected.

Where, however, does one draw the line between a use of force necessary to stop an unlawful attack on one's own person in self-defence and force that crosses over into a direct participation in hostilities? In my view, at one end of the spectrum is the force used immediately after an initial attack in order to repel that attack and protect the lives of the peacekeepers. At the other end of the spectrum is an operation mounted after a time delay in order to eliminate the source of the attack – i.e., an operation to take control of or destroy a nearby base of an armed group to prevent future attacks.

How does one categorize a response by peacekeepers to an initial attack by an armed group that becomes a long-drawn-out battle? Can such a battle remain a use of force in self-defence that does not become participation in an armed conflict? In such circumstances, in my view, it is appropriate to have recourse to the criteria for establishing the outbreak of a non-international armed conflict. If the attack is by an organized armed group (and not by one individual who may or may not have ties to that group), we can take for granted that both parties are organized (peacekeepers and organized armed group) such that the relevant criterion may be the intensity of the fighting.[45] The criteria set out by the ICTY in the

---

[43] Ibid., para. 46, quoting Lord Diplock in *Attorney General for Northern Ireland's Reference no 1 of 1975* [1997] AC 105 at 138.

[44] Ibid., para. 104.

[45] *Haradinaj*, para. 49. See *Boskoski*, para. 177, further elaborating on these criteria.

Haradinaj case to determine whether the intensity threshold is met are: 'the number, duration and intensity of individual confrontations; the type of weapons and other military equipment used; the number and calibre of munitions fired; the number of persons and type of forces partaking in the fighting; the number of casualties; the extent of material destruction; and the number of civilians fleeing combat zones'.[46] In *Boskoski*, the Tribunal furthermore added that the way the government interprets the right to life in its use of armed force is also indicative of whether it is operating in an armed conflict paradigm or a law enforcement paradigm.[47] While this factor may be helpful for identifying an evolution in a situation of violence, it is important to bear in mind that even in armed conflict situations – and especially non-international armed conflicts – government authorities must continue to use force according to the rules applicable to law enforcement where the circumstances so require.[48] Peacekeeping forces operate on a slightly different framework than government forces as they will respond according to their mandate and the Rules of Engagement that have been established for the mission.[49] As the Rules of Engagement tend to provide for a graduated use of force in response to attacks showing hostile intent,[50] it is reasonable to apply a similar analysis for peacekeeping forces as for governments, *mutatis mutandis* and with the same caveat as expressed above. Globally, then, these criteria can be usefully applied to a peacekeeping operation in order to determine whether (and when) it crosses the line from a pure self-defence or law enforcement paradigm to participation in an armed conflict.

When it comes to the protection of civilians, which can be a distinct justification for a use of force in self-defence in the context of peacekeeping, the analysis is different. Even if UN-commanded and -controlled operations are usually limited to a *reactive* use of force to implement their mandate (as opposed to UN-authorized operations under Chapter VII, which may use force without such a limitation),[51] the use of force

---

[46] *Haradinaj*, ibid.   [47] *Boskoski*, para. 178.

[48] Sassòli and Olson, 'The Relationship Between IHL and Human Rights Law'.

[49] Patrick Cammaert and Ben Klappe, 'Application of Force and Rules of Engagement in Peace Operations', in T. Gill and D. Fleck (eds.), *The Handbook of the International Law of Military Operations* (Oxford University Press, 2010), pp. 151–158, especially at pp. 154–156.

[50] Ibid.

[51] Hans Boddens Hosang, 'Force Protection, Unit Self-Defence, and Extended Self-Defence', in Gill and Fleck, *The Handbook of the International Law of Military Operations*, pp. 415–427 at p. 419. The exception to this general rule is the Intervention Brigade created within MONUSCO by UNSC Res 2098 (2013), para. 9, 'with the responsibility of neutralizing armed groups'.

on that basis can nonetheless entail the direct participation in hostilities of the peacekeeping force – or indeed, the force becoming a party to the armed conflict. The exercise of the use of force in defence of others who are victims of an unlawful attack can be a lawful use of force under national laws. When such cases are restricted only to an immediate use of force in direct response to an attack, that may also fall under the schema outlined above. However, those situations must be distinguished from a mandate to protect civilians entailing a general right for peacekeepers to use robust force in defence of that mandate and in which peacekeepers engage in military operations against armed groups in pursuit of that mandate.

There is often a great deal of confusion as to how peacekeeping mandates are to be interpreted; moreover, '[d]ecisions to use force will often have to be taken at the lowest tactical level, sometimes by individual soldiers'.[52] The mandate for MONUC appeared to restrict the circumstances in which force may be used to little more than traditional self-defence: 'to ensure the protection of civilians, including humanitarian personnel, under imminent threat of physical violence'.[53] That has proven to be an operation in which peacekeepers use force in support of government forces, however, even before the creation of the Intervention Brigade. On the other hand, the requirement that a threat to civilians be imminent is not present in the mandate of UNAMID: 'UNAMID is authorised to take the necessary action, in the areas of deployment of its forces and as it deems within its capabilities in order to . . . protect civilians.'[54] These different mandates seem to belie the force that will be used by the peacekeeping force to implement the mandate and are subject to the interpretation of the various parties responsible for implementing them. Even within the same operation, the Force Commander in theatre and UN headquarters in New York may not agree on the degree of force that should be used when confronted with armed group activity.[55] For PMSCs, as indicated above, if in a given mandate it can be anticipated that force beyond 'classic', personal self-defence will be necessary, they should have combatant status, as their exercise of force within the scope of the mandate can be expected to lead them to directly participate in hostilities.

---

[52] Cammaert and Klappe, 'Application of Force', 155.
[53] UNSC Res 1565 (1 October 2004) para. 4(b).
[54] UNSC Res 1769 (31 July 2007) para. 15(a).
[55] See the description of the MONUC's approach to Nkunda in 2004 in Cammaert and Klappe, 'Application of Force', 155.

The ICTY in *Haradinaj* and *Boskoski* also referred to the attention of the UN Security Council as a factor that may indicate a situation has intensified to a situation of armed conflict.[56] When it comes to UN peace-keeping operations, the Security Council is almost inevitably involved. Therefore, Security Council attention cannot be taken as an a priori indicator that the intensity criterion is met for the peace operation forces themselves. That being said, the mandate may give excellent clues in advance as to whether it can be anticipated that such forces will be drawn into an armed conflict.

10.1.4 Debates as to the Extent of the Force Engaged as Combatants in Time and Space

The former principal legal officer of the UN Office of Legal Affairs has argued that when UN peacekeepers are engaged as combatants, it is not the entire force that loses protection for the duration of the mission, but only certain members and for a limited time.[57] Daphna Shraga has argued, for example, that it is only for such time as a particular unit is carrying out a military operation or is engaged in combat that IHL applies to the peace-keepers and that it extends only to that national contingent (for example, the French forces in Bosnia).[58] This argument essentially amounts to saying that peacekeeping forces do not become parties to a conflict; rather, the actions of a particular national troop contingent may be governed by IHL purely on a model of occasional (*ponctuelle*) direct participation in hostilities. As such, most of the time they are protected against attack by the international criminal rules. One has to wonder whether, according to Shraga, peacekeeping forces could ever assume a 'continuous combat function', in the sense defined by the ICRC's Interpretive Guidance on the Notion of Direct Participation in Hostilities, and consequently be tanta-mount to an organized armed group participating in an armed conflict.[59] This view privileges the protection of peacekeepers and is understandable from a policy perspective.

It is perfectly in conformity with IHL to argue that sporadic attacks and self-defence do not amount to an armed conflict but, if sustained, can rise to that level. Indeed, this approach puts peacekeeping forces on the

---

[56] *Haradinaj*, para. 49, and *Boskoski*, para. 177.
[57] Shraga, 'Secretary-General's Bulletin', generally.   [58] Ibid., especially at 361–362.
[59] Shraga does acknowledge, however, that UNOSOM II forces were engaged as a party to the conflict following the attack on the Pakistani contingent and after 5 June 1993. Ibid., 363.

same footing with other entities that can be involved in non-international armed conflict in terms of determining when violent interaction between them reaches the threshold of an armed conflict in itself. It is not entirely clear that Shraga's approach would allow for this interpretation. The desire to protect peacekeepers against criminal attacks – and in so doing, ensure the supply of peacekeepers from jittery states – arises from valid concerns and is indisputably legitimate; however, the narrow interpretation does not sit well with established principles of international humanitarian law. Moreover, attempting to strengthen the protective regime in this way could backfire, if it gives a sense that an unequal advantage is given to peacekeepers who are regularly engaging in combat or military operations. In the context of a peacekeeping operation, the UN position appears to be that it is only the portion of a group that has a continuous combat function that is involved in an armed conflict with the organized armed group or groups that become combatants within the meaning of the Safety Convention. Another approach, which appears to be the one that the ICRC takes, is rather that the entire peacekeeping force should be assimilated to government forces, all of whom, under international humanitarian law, are subject to lawful attack once they have become party to a conflict.[60]

Either interpretation is sustainable in law and the crux of the problem comes down to their vexed dual (but not simultaneously dual) status of civilians and combatants. In order to understand and properly conceptualize this debate, it is helpful to take a step back and see what the relevant actors are trying to do. It is very much linked with the odd (sui generis) nature of peacekeepers. Although they are members of state armed forces, they are entitled to the protection to which civilians are entitled as long as they are not directly participating in hostilities or as long as the force has not become a party to the conflict. Normally, as indicated above, a person does not change from one status to another. A combatant who is wounded or ceases to fight is hors de combat and may not be attacked, but he does not become a civilian on account of his wounds. By the same token, a civilian who directly participates in hostilities does not become a combatant while he does so, even though for such time as he participates he loses the protection to which civilians are entitled. How far does the notion of being entitled to the protection of civilians extend for peacekeepers, given their nature and role?

---

[60] Tristan Ferraro, 'Applicability/Application of IHL to International Organisations (IO) Involved in Peace Operations' (2012) *Collegium* 15–22, at 22.

Adding another layer of complication, we come to fighters in non-international armed conflicts. According to the ICRC's Interpretive Guidance, members of organized armed groups have a continuous combat function and lose the protection to which civilians are entitled for the duration of the conflict or until they actively disengage from the armed group. A slightly different approach to the issue is to contemplate that there can be many persons who form a group but that the functions of only some members of the group involve a continuous combat function. Only those members of the organized armed group with a continuous combat function lose the protection to which civilians are entitled, but not other members of that same group. Persons who are members of the same group who do not have a continuous combat function are not 'fighters' and remain protected as civilians as long as they do not directly participate in hostilities. According to the ICRC's Interpretive Guidance on the notion of direct participation in hostilities, what counts are specific acts, and they may be targeted only for such time as they are committing such acts.[61] Arguably, an example of a 'group' with distinct fighter (armed) and non-fighter (not armed) functions is Hamas.[62]

On the other hand, the Interpretive Guidance does not indicate that members of armed groups fighting against state forces may target only those forces that are deployed against them. Instead, it would seem that the entire state force becomes a party to the conflict, presumably because it can all be relatively easily mobilized against the armed group. As indicated above, most conflicts involving peacekeeping forces are non-international armed conflicts, since peacekeeping forces are engaged in conflict with organized armed groups and not against states. Given the sui generis 'status' of peacekeeping forces – members of state armed forces entitled to the protection of civilians as long as they are not directly participating in hostilities – the question is whether one should apply the state paradigm to them or the paradigm applicable to armed groups. It would appear that the ICRC treats them as it treats state armed forces. The UN, on the other hand, seems to plead for the application of the paradigm for armed groups, such that only the members of the force with a continuous combat function could be deemed to be members of an organized armed group. While

---

[61] ICRC, Interpretive Guidance, p. 44.
[62] However, under the ICRC's interpretation, it is apparently only the members of the armed wing of Hamas that are members of an organized armed group, no matter the structure of the group or its method of determining its wider membership. This is logical in that the others are not 'armed'.

it must be true that when IHL applies, it applies in the whole of the territory as between the parties and until the end of hostilities, the UN's view is understandable from its policy perspective. Indeed, if only one national troop contingent in a particular region becomes involved in combat with an organized armed group, why should the rest of the peacekeeping force lose the protection against attack offered by international law? It seems to be true that in many cases peacekeeping troops have strict rules of engagement to use only graduated force and only in situations of self-defence or immediate protection of civilians. But this approach raises many problems. Would it mean, for example, that one cannot group together attacks against different contingents to measure the intensity of violence in order to determine whether a peacekeeping force has become a party to a conflict? Here, it is appropriate to recall that the circumstances in Sierra Leone involved attacks against a number of national contingents.

In my view, since UN peacekeeping forces come from government armed forces, they should be subject to a similar regime that applies to government armed forces, with some modifications. How should an armed group know whether a peacekeeper is from GreekBatt or UrBatt if both are operating in the same area? Granted, they may have little flags on their arms, but that would not likely be sufficient to distinguish them from one another. In this respect, it would seem more logical that all of the peacekeeping forces operating in a region or area where armed groups are active and actively opposed to the peacekeeping forces are subject to IHL once one part of the force has lost the protection to which civilians are entitled. By the same token, if members of a peacekeeping force far away from the zone in which combat between armed groups and the force are occurring take action – including arrests – against members of that organized armed group, then such actions are also governed by IHL.[63] However, contingents of a peacekeeping force that are in an area in which no hostilities are occurring and which take no action against members of an organized armed group could be deemed not to have a continuous combat function and, thus, entitled to the protection of civilians.

This approach may seem logical and straightforward and could work if the only way in which UN forces involved in peace operations became

---

[63] This seems to be in line with the position that states take in multinational operations – e.g. as outlined by Ola Engdahl re Afghanistan/NATO. See Ola Engdahl, 'Multinational Peace Operations Forces Involved in Armed Conflict: Who Are the Parties?', in K. Mujezinovic Larsen, C. Gudahl Cooper and G. Nystuen (eds.), *Searching for a 'Principle of Humanity' in International Humanitarian Law* (Cambridge University Press, 2012), pp. 233–271.

parties to an armed conflict were due to being drawn in through a use of force in self-defence. However, as the section at the beginning of this chapter shows, peace operations forces can also become parties to an armed conflict through the mandate in the Security Council Resolution. In this regard, it is worthy of note that the UN Secretary-General, in his report on MONUSCO and the Intervention Brigade, clearly supported the position that *all* of MONUSCO had an obligation to engage in armed operations against armed groups. He stated,

> MONUSCO's framework brigades must also play a more active role in protecting civilians by deterring and, if necessary, preventing and stopping armed groups from inflicting violence on the population. Measures will be taken to prepare troop-contributing countries to conduct operations aimed at mitigating the threat from armed groups and protecting civilians, including through the use of lethal force.[64]

One cannot expect armed groups engaged in a conflict with a peace operations force to distinguish between whether all of that force or only parts of it have become party to the conflict based on the way in which the peace operations force initially became a party to that conflict. In this light, the only solution may be to determine that once part of the force has become engaged as a party to a conflict, the whole force is so engaged.

One final note: a common element of peacekeeping mandates raises an important question – do disarmament and demobilization activities entail direct participation in hostilities? Normally, they would not. It will depend on the types of acts that the peace operations force undertakes in order to carry out this obligation under its mandate. If it is simply organizing a place and circumstances for forces to voluntarily hand in weapons and helping ex-combatants find alternative sources of employment, then such activities do not amount to direct participation even in regard to members of the same group that is elsewhere engaged in hostilities against the force.[65]

---

[64] UN Secretary-General, 'Report of the Secretary-General on the United Nations Organization Stabilization Mission in the Democratic Republic of the Congo Submitted Pursuant to Paragraph 39 of Security Council Resolution 2147' (2014), 30 December 2014, UN Doc. S/2014/957, para. 52.

[65] Note, however, that in international armed conflicts, enticing members of opposing forces to disband voluntarily is a tactic that is used and that would lead to the general weakening of the forces of the other side.

10.1.5   Self-Defence and Security Guards in UN Peace Operations

As noted above, for peace operations that are authorized by the United Nations and not under UN command and control, the assessment as to whether security guards active in that operation are directly participating in hostilities will be the same as that provided above for armed conflicts. But what about the situation in which armed private security companies providing security services repel an attack by an armed group on forces in a peace operation under UN command and control? The United Nations' recently adopted Policy and Guidelines on the use of armed private security guards permits their use for such purposes and in such circumstances.[66] The policy states that

8. The objective of armed security services from a private security company is to provide a visible deterrent to potential attackers and *an armed response to repel any attack* in a manner consistent with the United Nations 'Use of Force Policy', the respective host country legislation and international law.
9. Armed security services from a private security company may not be contracted, except on an exceptional basis and then only for the following purposes:
   a. To protect United Nations personnel, premises and property.
   b. To provide mobile protection for United Nations personnel and property.[67]

The force they may use in such instances is limited to the force permitted in the UN rules on the use of force. A determination as to whether the use of force by PMSCs in such scenarios amounts to participation in a conflict may thus hinge to some extent on the specifics of those rules (which are not publicly available). Where a peacekeeping force has not become a party to an armed conflict or is not itself directly participating in hostilities, the use of force in their defence should not result in the private security guards themselves becoming direct participants in hostilities.

Where a peacekeeping force has become a party to an armed conflict, on the other hand, the use of force by security guards in their defence may amount to a direct participation in hostilities. The current UN-commanded and -controlled operation in Congo is a challenging case in point. The UN has hired significant numbers of armed international

---

[66] 'Chapter IV: Security Management. Section I: Armed Private Security Companies', in United Nations Security Management System, *Security Policy Manual*, November 2012.
[67] Ibid., paras 8 and 9, emphasis added.

security guards for MONUSCO and the Security Council has recently created an Intervention Brigade clearly mandated to use force against an armed group.[68] This scenario raises difficult questions in this regard in light of the discussion above.

In particular, there appears to be little consensus among states as to whether the creation of the Intervention Brigade within MONUSCO leads to all of the forces participating in that operation becoming involved in an armed conflict against M23 and other organized armed groups, or whether it is only the Brigade itself. The statements by representatives of several states explaining their vote during the meeting of the Security Council when the resolution creating the Intervention Brigade was adopted indicate that impact of the Brigade on the status of the whole force was a cause for concern.[69] The representative of Rwanda considered that creation of an enforcement component within MONUSCO did not alter the status of the rest of the force, stating,

> By deploying the Intervention Brigade, we underscore the need to ensure that the impartiality of the military component of MONUSCO and the protection of Blue Helmets not be endangered at any cost. We reiterate the importance of a clear separation between the role of the Intervention Brigade and that of the regular forces of MONUSCO, whose main purpose is to protect civilians ... [70]

The representative from Guatemala, however, was not so sure, indicating that Guatemala 'would have preferred ... that the Brigade, mandated with offensive capabilities, be defined as a self-contained unit with specific responsibilities, clearly distinguishable from the mandates of the other MONUSCO brigades, which would then be entrusted with the more conventional duties of robust peacekeeping operations, including the protection of civilians.' He went on, 'We are concerned that the entire MONUSCO runs the risk of indirectly becoming a peace enforcement mission. That would raise many conceptual, operational and legal considerations that, in our view, have not been adequately explored.'[71]

---

[68] UN Advisory Committee on Administrative and Budgetary Questions, 'Reports on the Department of Safety and Security and on the Use of Private Security' (7 December 2012) UN Doc A/67/624, Annexes I and II; UNSC Res 2098 (28 March 2013), para. 9.
[69] See UN Doc S/PV.6943 (28 March 2013). See also UN Secretary-General, 'Special Report of the Secretary-General on the Democratic Republic of the Congo and the Great Lakes Region', UN Doc S/2013/119 (27 February 2013), recommending the establishment of the intervention brigade, paras 60ff.
[70] UN Doc S/PV.6943 (28 March 2013).   [71] Ibid.

The representative from the United Kingdom clearly indicates a view that the entire force is implicated in the conflict by the creation of the Intervention Brigade. He heartily approved of the approach and stated,

> For it to succeed, it will be important for the whole Mission, including all its troop contingents, whether they are part of the Intervention Brigade or not, to be willing and able to fully implement the whole of the Mission's mandate. It is one Mission with one mandate, one Special Representative and one Force Commander.[72]

If it were only the Intervention Brigade itself that is a party to the conflict, then, arguably, providing armed protection for other components of the peace operation force in the territory might not amount to direct participation in hostilities on the part of the security guards. Notwithstanding the position of the representatives of Rwanda and Guatemala, however, in this case the entire force is arguably already a party to the conflict given that MONUSCO was already providing support to the Congolese government in its armed conflict against M23 and other organized armed groups.[73] This would mean that private security guards using force against attacks by organized armed groups on peacekeepers or UN property (in line with the UN policy above) would in fact be directly participating in hostilities. Some reports indicate that MONUSCO uses unarmed private security guards, which may diminish the risk that they would become direct participants in hostilities.[74] However, if the UN were to use armed guards, the risk would be significant. Furthermore, the discussion above indicates that it is not only armed persons who become direct participants in hostilities, such that acts by unarmed PMSCs could also entail direct participation in hostilities.

If one were to accept the approach proposed above that only the components of the peace operation who are located in an area of hostilities or carrying out acts such as arrests against the armed group in other areas are

---

[72] Ibid. The statement of the representative from Luxembourg appears to go in the same direction.

[73] It should be recalled that peacekeeping forces may be carrying out activities within the scope of their mandate that do not involve an obvious use of force but that nevertheless constitute direct participation in hostilities (an example is reconnaissance operations). Armed security guards using force to repel an attack on such peacekeeping forces would, on the basis of the analysis above, likely be directly participating in hostilities.

[74] 'Report of the Working Group on the Use of Mercenaries as a Means of Violating Human Rights and Impeding the Exercise of the Right of Peoples to Self-Determination', UN Doc A/69/338 (21 August 2014), para. 11, note 5. Others suggest that it uses only unarmed guards.

members of the UN force with a continuous combat function and subject to attack, theoretically, private security guards could protect some UN personnel and property against armed attack without becoming direct participants in hostilities.[75] However, we have seen that such an approach, while theoretically possible, poses some problems when applied to facts on the ground.

At the same time, it must be recalled that modern peace operations are multifaceted and often have a large civilian component. Not all persons and objects in a peace operation would be military objectives, such that using armed security guards to protect the civilian component of a peace operation would occur according to the same paradigm as that outlined above for regular armed conflicts and the analysis would be the same. Thus, if private security guards were deployed in Congo to protect only the civilian components of the mission and ideally in areas located far away from hostilities, the likelihood of their being drawn into direct participation in hostilities would be slim. Intuitively, however, it seems likely that armed security guards for the civilian component of the mission would be necessary for precisely those areas where security is fragile and/or hostilities are ongoing.

10.1.6 Self-Defence and Security Guards in Special Political Missions

The use of private security guards to protect UN personnel and property in special political missions such as the United Nations Assistance Mission in Afghanistan (UNAMA) and the United Nations Assistance Mission for Iraq (UNAMI) raises further questions. According to the High-Level Panel on Peacekeeping, in 2015, 'More than 90 per cent of personnel in political missions... are deployed in situations of ongoing armed conflict.'[76] The key question is, when special political missions are deployed alongside a UN-authorized peace operation (i.e. such that forces are involved in an armed conflict against organized armed groups in the

---

[75] This scenario raises an additional complication, however, which is whether the threshold for bringing other parts of the force into the armed conflict occurs according to the paradigm of creating a new non-international armed conflict or whether an attack by an armed group immediately expands the conflict to that other component of the peace operation. See especially Tristan Ferraro, 'The Application of International Humanitarian Law to Multinational Forces' (2013) 95 *IRRC* 561–612.

[76] 'Report of the High-Level Independent Panel on Peace Operations on Uniting Our Strengths for Peace: Politics, Partnership and People' (17 June 2015), UN Doc A/70/95; S/2015/446, para. 296.

same host state territory), can the political mission – which does not have its own armed forces – become a party to the conflict?

In my view, there are two possible ways that a political mission could become a party to an armed conflict. The first is if it exercises a sufficient degree of control over the armed forces that are present in the territory for the actions of those forces to be attributable to it. This is an application of the regime identified in the *Nicaragua* case (effective control test) and applied by the ICTY in *Tadic* (overall control test). A variation of this test was applied in the context of peace operations by the European Court of Human Rights in *Behrami*. Without wishing to go into detail as to the different levels of control necessary to satisfy each test, as well as the correctness of the standards in those tests, it must be pointed out that the ECtHR was widely criticized for concluding that the NATO forces conducting the mission in Kosovo could be attributed to the United Nations on the grounds that the UN Security Council maintained overall authority and control via the reporting process and the fact that it could stop the mission by adopting a resolution. Suffice it to say here that at the very least, arguably, operational command and control over the armed component of the mission would have to vest in the same person or office responsible for the political mission in order to find that the whole mission has become a party to the conflict. Even then, the civilian components of the mission remain civilian. As such, a use of force in defence of them would constitute direct participation in hostilities according to the same framework as outlined above.

The second way that a political mission could become a party to an armed conflict might be if the security guard forces that it contracts could become its de facto armed forces. In such a situation, the existence of an armed conflict would depend on the normal criteria for a non-international armed conflict – that is, the intensity of the violence and the organization of the parties. Here, one may suppose that unlike in the case of regular peacekeeping forces, the organization of the security guards may not be such that it satisfies the standard for an armed group; however, it will depend on the facts. The situation of Nepali private security guards defending against a mob attack on a UN compound clearly falls short of the threshold for a non-international armed conflict.[77] Nevertheless, it is not impossible to imagine that the threshold could be met. If so, there may be an additional factor as well: in order to consider that a conflict has arisen between the UN political mission and an armed group

---

[77] See above, Chapter 1, Section 1.3.

due to violence that meets the criteria for a non-international armed conflict, the security guard force (or its actions) would somehow have to be attributable to the UN mission itself. That is to say, one has to be able to distinguish between a conflict arising between a group of private security guards and an organized armed group and a conflict between an organized armed group and a UN political mission, via the actions of the guards that it hires. Although such a situation has yet to arise, I submit that analysis of whether it would result in the UN being a party to an armed conflict should use the criteria for attribution for international organizations.[78]

This argument may seem far-fetched. However, looking at the situations in which private security contractors are authorized to use force by the United Nations in its recent policy, one is struck by the fact that the authorization is very similar to that granted to the first peacekeeping forces. In this light, one may ask whether the UN has not already privatized peacekeeping to a much greater degree than one might suspect at first glance.

10.2   The Cumulative Effect of the Two Concepts of Self-Defence for PMSCs in Peace Operations

Both concepts of self-defence must be considered together to understand their significance for the use of PMSCs in peace operations in various roles – that explored in Chapter 9 and that discussed here. Often, the limitation of the use of force to self-defence or the principle of a limited use of force in peace operations may mean that a peace operation does not become a party to an armed conflict, even if it is deployed in a territory in which a conflict is occurring. In such situations, the military contingents of peace operations retain the protection of civilians. In such situations, the use of force in self-defence by PMSCs contracted as security guards, including to protect the peacekeeping forces themselves, would not amount to a direct participation in hostilities.

However, the principle of a limited use of force is sufficiently elastic to allow for a significant use of force in practice, which may entail that (all or part of) a peace operation does become a party to a conflict. Alternatively, a peace operation may be drawn into becoming a party to a conflict, depending on the intensity of the violence, through cumulative responses in self-defence to attacks against it by an organized armed group. The repercussions of this conclusion in relation to the possibility of using PMSCs as the military contingent of a peacekeeping force were explored

---

[78] See Part IV below.

in Chapter 4. However, when it comes to PMSCs as security guards in a peace operation that has become a party to a conflict, it means that uses of force in self-defence can entail direct participation in hostilities according to the same paradigm as that set out above for PMSCs in 'regular' armed conflicts.

11

Human Rights Law

Even in armed conflicts, the use of force by the authorities is not governed exclusively by international humanitarian law. Where their activities involve law enforcement, they are governed by the law applicable – in peacetime and during armed conflicts – to such activities, which includes human rights law.[1] The exact relationship between IHL and IHRL depends on the situation and on whether the armed conflict is international or non-international, as the latter is regulated in less detail under IHL regarding the use of force.[2] In peace operations deployed in situations where there is no armed conflict, it is a fortiori the case that operations of the forces are not governed by IHL. When it comes to PMSCs as private actors in armed conflicts and peace operations, however, there is an

---

[1] The applicability of human rights law in times of armed conflict is affirmed by the ICJ in Legality of the Threat or Use of Nuclear Weapons (Advisory Opinion) [1996] ICJ Rep 226, para. 25, and subsequently in Legal Consequences of the Construction of a Wall in the Occupied Palestinian Territory (Advisory Opinion) [2004] ICJ Rep 136, para. 106. See also HRC, 'General Comment No. 31: Nature of the General Legal Obligation Imposed on States Parties to the Covenant', UN Doc CCPR/C/21/Rev.1/Add.13, 2004. Françoise Hampson argues that even though the United States and Israel have consistently disputed the simultaneous applicability of IHRL with IHL, 'it appears unlikely that they can claim to be "persistent objectors".' See Hampson, 'Direct Participation in Hostilities and the Interoperability of the Law of Armed Conflict and Human Rights Law', in R. Pedrozo and D. Wollschlaeger (eds.), International Law and the Changing Character of War (87 Naval War College International Law Series 2011), pp. 187–216 at p. 188.

[2] Willliam Abresch, 'A Human Rights Law of Internal Armed Conflict: The European Court of Human Rights in Chechnya' (2005) 16 EJIL 741–767; John Cerone, 'Human Dignity in the Line of Fire: The Application of International Human Rights Law During Armed Conflict, Occupation, and Peace Operations' (2006) 39 Vanderbilt J Transnational L 1447; Cordula Droege, 'The Interplay Between International Humanitarian Law and International Human Rights Law in Situations of Armed Conflict' (2007) 40 Israel Law Review 347; Heike Krieger, 'A Conflict of Norms: The Relationship Between Humanitarian Law and Human Rights Law in the ICRC Customary Law Study' (2006) 11 J Conflict and Security L 265–291; Sassòli and Olson, 'The Relationship Between IHL and Human Rights Law'; M Sassòli, 'Le droit international humanitaire, une lex specialis par rapport aux droits humains?' in A. Auer, Y. Flückiger, M. Hottelier (eds.), Les droits de l'homme et la constitution, Etudes en l'honneur du Professeur Giorgio Malinverni (Geneva: Schulthess, 2007), pp. 375–395.

additional hurdle to identifying the relevant obligations.[3] This is because, in contrast to international humanitarian law, which applies to members of the armed forces and to civilians, human rights law applies to states. This means that it should not be lightly assumed that PMSCs (as non-state actors) are bound by human rights law in armed conflicts. When it comes to peace operations, the way in which the United Nations (and the people it uses in peace operations) is bound by this body of law has been examined above, in Chapter 6. This section will therefore focus on the basis on which PMSCs and international organizations carrying out peace operations may be bound by human rights law.

11.1 PMSCs and Human Rights Law

When it comes to PMSCs used in law enforcement roles on behalf of states in armed conflict situations that are not peace operations, a preliminary question that arises is how a private, non-state actor may be bound by human rights law. In armed conflicts, this issue also arises for organized armed groups, and some conclude that there is an inequality of belligerents based on an understanding that such groups are not bound by human rights law.[4] Part of the concern is that such rules would be unrealistic for some armed groups to comply with, such that they result in a situation where people may be less protected than if IHRL did not apply at all.[5] It is, therefore, not an issue that is specific to PMSCs. It is distinct, however, in that it is generally states that use PMSCs in the context of non-international armed conflicts. If PMSCs are engaged in a law enforcement

---

[3] A further complication is the fact that some states contest the extra-territorial application of human rights law. See notes 1 and 2, above.

[4] See Jann Kleffner, 'The Applicability of International Humanitarian Law to Organized Armed Groups' (2011) 93 *IRRC* 443–461, for a review of the theories and literature. See also Lindsay Moir, *The Law of Internal Armed Conflict* (Cambridge University Press, 2002), pp. 44–45, stating that IHL has 'no binding force for the insurgents'; Liesbeth Zegveld, *The Accountability of Armed Opposition Groups* (Cambridge University Press, 2002), pp. 38–55 (reviewing theories). See also Sandesh Sivakumaran, *The Law of Non-international Armed Conflict* (Oxford University Press, 2012), pp. 93–99, especially at p. 97, where he argues, 'There is a fair amount of practice to suggest that, at least in certain limited situations, armed groups have obligations pursuant to international human rights law.'

[5] Marco Sassòli, 'Introducing a Sliding-Scale of Obligations to Address the Fundamental Inequality Between Armed Groups and States?' (2011) 93 *IRRC* 425 at 430. For example, if insurgents were to conclude that they could not lawfully detain government soldiers, they might simply decide to kill them.

role by states in non-international armed conflicts, the fact that they operate in conjunction with the state means either that their conduct can be attributed to the state and therefore must be subject to the obligations binding the state or that one cannot presume that it would be unrealistic for them to comply with those obligations. In addition, where human rights violations would amount to international crimes, such as torture, PMSCs may be bound by the human rights norm via international criminal law.[6] Of course, where the right to life is concerned, private actors have no power to use lethal force except in situations of self-defence, as outlined above. But where they have been specifically tasked with law enforcement functions by a state, due diligence obligations entail that the state must ensure that there are checks on their power at least equivalent to those that apply to state forces.[7] I will now turn to a discussion of PMSCs and law enforcement under IHL and IHRL, particularly in regard to the use of force and detention activities – including in peace operations.

11.2   Law Enforcement Rules Under IHL and IHRL

There are few rules in IHL on how law enforcement operations must be conducted, but IHL does make clear that even in international armed conflicts, not all situations are governed by IHL rules on the conduct of hostilities when it comes to the use of force. In some cases, the use of force permitted under IHL will more closely resemble the standards of law enforcement rules than those on the conduct of hostilities.[8] In armed conflicts – especially in non-international armed conflicts, but also in situations of occupation and peace operations – it is crucial to distinguish between military operations and law enforcement.

For the purposes of this study, for PMSCs in armed conflicts, it is important to understand that some activities that look like law enforcement in fact entail directly participating in hostilities. When it comes to peace support operations, I have argued above that in circumstances where the

---

[6] Andrew Clapham makes this argument in 'Human Rights Obligations of Non-state Actors in Conflict Situations' (2006) 88 *IRRC* 491–523 at 518.

[7] Clapham refers to the Voluntary Principles on Security and Human Rights as the 'voluntary code model which is currently most influential' (ibid., 521). In my view, voluntary codes and other self-regulatory mechanisms are insufficient to conclude that PMSCs are subject to 'binding' obligations.

[8] ICRC, Interpretive Guidance, Recommendation IX.

peacekeepers are fighting an armed group, even PMSC peacekeepers must in any case have combatant status.

In non-international armed conflicts, government armed forces seeking to use force against or to detain fighters operate on the cusp of a law-enforcement paradigm.[9] However, even though human rights rules may significantly inform the acts armed forces may take against fighters in non-international armed conflicts, in both international and non-international armed conflicts, the use of force, arrest and detention of enemy armed forces, fighters or members of armed groups remains an act of hostilities. Consequently, if such acts were to be conducted by non-members of armed forces, such as PMSCs, those acts would constitute direct participation in hostilities.

In a peaceful, domestic context, it is not unusual to see private security guards exercising quasi-law-enforcement activities such as patrolling specific zones, conducting preventive surveillance by monitoring data transmitted by security cameras, and organizing security measures to 'police' public events.[10] When transposed to a situation where armed conflict is occurring, some of those activities, although carried out in a spirit of law enforcement, may lead the security personnel in question to directly participate in hostilities. While I understand the vital need for security in conflict situations for the civilian population, and while I acknowledge the role PMSCs may help to play in ensuring that security, I believe that it nonetheless remains crucial that the activities of PMSC personnel do not cross the line into direct participation in hostilities. Accordingly, identifying the relevant factors distinguishing law enforcement from military operations under IHL is key.

The line between what constitutes a use of force constituting a military operation versus that which is a police operation (or law enforcement) is much easier to draw in the context of international armed conflicts than in non-international armed conflicts. In IHL of international armed conflicts, any use of force against the adversary's combatants is perforce a military operation and subject to the rules on the conduct of hostilities. Uses of force against civilians, unless those civilians are directly participating

---

[9] Sassòli and Olson, 'The Relationship Between IHL and Human Rights Law'; Doswald-Beck, 'The Right to Life in Armed Conflict'; Abresch, 'A Human Rights Law', 741–767. The ICRC considers that this flows from obligations under IHL and not from human rights law. See ICRC, Interpretive Guidance, Recommendation IX and accompanying commentary; ICRC, *Commentary on the First Geneva Convention* (2016), para. 463.

[10] For a detailed description of such activities in the United States, see Joh, 'Paradox of Private Policing', 73–83.

in hostilities, may occur only in the context of law enforcement, either on the party's own territory or in situations of occupation. As noted above, specific, detailed rules on the use of force in law enforcement operations carried out against civilians on a belligerent's own territory[11] or on occupied territory, beyond prohibitions against torture, cruel treatment, murder and physical or moral coercion, are not set out in the Geneva Conventions or Additional Protocol I.[12] One can, however, deduce some rules on law enforcement for occupying powers from the existing rules of IHL – in particular, via a combination of Article 43 of the Hague Regulations requiring the occupying power to 'restore and ensure . . . public order and safety' and Article 64 of GC IV regarding the power to legislate in order to 'maintain orderly government of the territory'.

In non-international armed conflicts, force used in the context of an arrest of members of an armed group may legitimately be construed as either a military operation or a law enforcement operation, depending on the circumstances. In peacekeeping operations where the peacekeeping force is engaged in an armed conflict against an armed group, the same reasoning applies. Human rights tribunals, and in particular the ECtHR, do not always clarify whether they conceive a use of force to be a military operation or a police operation.[13] As such, it can be difficult to determine with absolute clarity whether, in their view, different rules on the use of force apply according to whether it is a military operation or a law enforcement operation.[14] In some tribunals, IHL and its rules on the conduct of hostilities supersede any human rights principles on proportionality in the use of force when operations involve armed groups.[15] This would imply that such actions against armed group members (in a clearly hostile situation) are not law-enforcement activities. Cases from the European Court of Human Rights, however, are less clear. For example, the Court has

---

[11] For example, the internment of civilians of enemy nationality during World War II in North America. At that time, no international humanitarian law treaty dealt with the treatment of civilians, but even now, the Fourth Geneva Convention prescribes detailed rules on internment conditions but no rules on how an arrest may be effected beyond the absolute prohibitions listed above.

[12] See Articles 27, 31, 32 GC IV and Article 3 common to the four Geneva Conventions.

[13] See, for example, ECHR, *Isayeva v. Russia* (App no 57950/00) Judgment 24 February 2005, paras 175–176; ECHR, *Khatsiyeva v. Russia* (App no 5108/02) Judgment 17 January 2008; ECHR, *Mansuroğlu v. Turkey* (App no 43443/98) (Judgment) 26 February 2008, paras 86–89; ECHR, *Pad v. Turkey* (App no 60167/00 (28 June 2007) (Admissibility).

[14] Sassòli and Olson, 'The Relationship Between IHL and Human Rights Law', 612.

[15] This is what the Inter-American Commission on Human Rights held in *Abella v. Argentina*, Case no 11.137, Report no 55/97, 18 November 1997, para. 178.

suggested that even in a case where the facts regarding the degree of hostile action were contested between the parties, but where it was admitted that at least some of the persons killed were members of an armed group, the government forces should have respected the requirements for the use of force normally applicable to a law enforcement paradigm and been prepared with non-lethal means to subdue the individuals in question.[16] Whether this is the standard also expected by IHL in such a context is a somewhat unsettled question.

In situations in which armed group members are not engaged in hostile action, a law enforcement operation using force based on the principles drawn from international human rights law is required.[17] However, the qualification of such an act as a law enforcement operation calling for a human rights law paradigm does not settle the question as to whether such acts entail direct participation in hostilities. In my view, because such acts occur against armed groups in the context of armed conflict, they involve hostilities. Thus, PMSCs may not be charged with law enforcement roles that would entail their conducting 'police' operations against armed group members.

This principle may not be easy to grasp. Armed groups may be outlawed in domestic law in the territory in which they are operating and therefore also treated as criminal (or 'terrorist') in nature. Nevertheless, operations against them may thus easily cross the boundary between what is mere law enforcement and what constitutes direct participation in hostilities. This can especially be a problem when PMSCs are patrolling unstable environments as part of the overall security 'forces' in a non-international armed conflict. If such PMSC patrols encounter violence by armed groups in non-international armed conflicts, since in any case they should not take action that would lead them to directly participate in hostilities, it would be wise to limit their responses to what is permitted under a self-defence framework, which is in turn in line with law enforcement and human rights law standards, governed by the cornerstone principles of necessity and proportionality. Ideally, PMSC guards should not be contracted to patrol areas subject to attack by armed groups. The problem is that this may be precisely the kind of place where they are used in an effort to enhance stability or security. A trickier situation, however, is one where

---

[16] ECHR, *Mansuroğlu v. Turkey* (App no 43443/98) (Judgment) 26 February 2008, paras 86–89.

[17] Human Rights Committee, *Suarez de Guerrero v. Colombia*, Comm no. R.11/45 (31 March 1982) UN Doc Supp no. 40 (A37/40).

PMSC security guards are faced with civilians who are directly participating in hostilities but who are not members of armed groups. Would a use of force on the part of PMSCs against such individuals constitute in itself a direct participation in hostilities or would it be merely law enforcement?

When it comes to what are unquestionably law enforcement operations involving a use of force against civilians who are not directly participating in hostilities and not armed group members with a continuous combat function, IHL has little to say beyond fundamental guarantees such as the prohibition of summary execution and torture. Thus, such actions will be governed by domestic law and international human rights law.

In peace operations, the rules of engagement for the force and the mandate will provide the legal basis and framework for such activities.[18] Some argue also that the rules on the use of force in military occupation should be applied on a de facto basis for peacekeeping.[19] As a graduated use of force tends to be required in peace operations, the appropriate response to a use of force by an armed group will be more in line with that of police in law enforcement situations than that for combatants operating in an armed conflict paradigm.[20] When it comes to detention activities, the mandate and relevant documents can specify different procedures to those set down in human rights law.[21] The Secretary-General's Bulletin on IHL also sets down specific obligations with respect to the treatment

---

[18] On the rules of engagement, see Cammaert and Klappe, 'Application of Force', 154–157. See also Marten Zwanenburg, 'Pieces of the Puzzle: Peace Operations, Occupation and the Use of Force' (2006) 45 *Military Law and Law of War Rev* 239–248.

[19] Zwanenburg, ibid., at 244.

[20] Cammaert and Klappe, 'Application of Force', 155, write, 'In a case of hostile intent, Rules of Engagement will authorize an incremental escalation of force to counter the threat.' The rule they articulate, however, indicates that '[i]n some circumstances operational urgency may dictate the immediate use of deadly force.' Ibid., 154.

[21] For example, the SOFA for UNFICYP authorized 'UN military police' to detain 'any Cypriot citizen committing an offence or causing a disturbance on [UN] premises . . . without subjecting them to the ordinary routine of arrest, in order to immediately hand him to the nearest appropriate Cypriot authorities . . .' Exchange of Letters Constituting and Agreement Concerning the Status of the United Nations Peacekeeping Force in Cyprus, 492 UNTS 57 (para. 14) (31 March 1964), cited in B. Oswald, 'The Law on Military Occupation: Answering the Challenges of Detention During Contemporary Peace Operations?' (2007) 8 *Melbourne J Intl L* 311–326 at 314, note 14 and accompanying text. See also Frederik Naert, 'Detention in Peace Operations: The Legal Framework and Main Categories of Detainees' (2006) 45 *Military Law and Law of War Rev* 51–78, 53. Naert asserts that international human rights law may form part of the applicable law, but he does not specify on what basis that law applies to UN peace operations – or indeed, if it applies to UN peace operations. See also B. Oswald, 'Detention by United Nations Peacekeepers: Searching for Definition and Categorisation' (2011) 15 *J Intl Peacekeeping* 119–151.

of detained persons.[22] If the forces of the peace operation are engaged in an armed conflict, IHL rules on detention may also apply.[23]

As for the specific content of the applicable rules, since there is no change in the way they must be applied by PMSCs (on the theory that PMSCs are indeed somehow bound by such obligations), it is not necessary to explain the rules in further detail here. Where the rules in peacekeeping operations are vastly different (due to the mandate, etc.) to the normally applicable law, it will be important to ensure that PMSCs are well informed and trained to apply such rules in a manner that conforms to the general international law framework.

11.3   Conclusion to Part III

If international humanitarian law is to protect the greatest number of people in dire situations, it must not be overly complicated to understand or respect. If everyone in situations of armed conflict would abide by its most basic prohibitions not to murder, rape and torture, it would already go a long way to protecting civilians and other vulnerable persons. But some rules of international humanitarian law are perhaps less intuitive due to the fact that are a product of the fundamental tension of IHL, which is to balance the principle of humanity against military necessity. International humanitarian law allows for significant numbers of individuals to use force against and to kill others lawfully and with impunity. It is an extraordinary law for extraordinary circumstances, but which is recognized and accepted by all states. In this, the principle of distinction plays a central role in keeping armed conflict from descending into murderous total war.

This part has discussed the ways in which private military and security contractors can be drawn into hostilities as direct participants. This occurs in part due to the nature of the tasks that states sometimes contract them to perform, and in part due to an evident willingness on the part of the

---

[22] UN Secretary-General, Observance by United Nations Forces of International Humanitarian Law, 6 August 1999, UN Doc ST/SGB/1999/13, section 8.

[23] In this regard, the Copenhagen Process Principles and Guidelines may provide a useful framework: the Copenhagen Process on the Handling of Detainees in International Military Operations, October 2012: http://um.dk/da/~/media/UM/Danish-site/Documents/ Politik-og-diplomati/Nyheder_udenrigspolitik/2012/Copenhangen%20Process %20Principles%20and%20Guidelines.pdf. These guidelines have been criticized, however, and it is not clear that they are meant to apply to UN peace operations.

industry to exploit the individual right to use force in self-defence order to fulfil their contractual duties.

Any concerns with this tendency may seem overwrought to some. Certainly, industry representatives sigh in exasperation any time mention is made of concerns about direct participation in hostilities by PMSCs. They scoff that apparent worries over whether PMSCs would have prisoner-of-war status are rooted in a complete lack of understanding of contemporary conflicts, in which PMSCs legitimately have more reason to fear being kidnapped and beheaded than tried by a detaining power for unlawfully participating in hostilities.

I am not impervious to the validity of the sentiment behind such statements; in my view, however, they miss the point. I agree that a probable lack of POW status may not be a paramount concern for the average PMSC. But I do think that some might be interested to know that the nature of some of their tasks and acts means that, under IHL at least, it may be lawful for opposing forces to target them directly, even if only for a limited time. Moreover, my concerns regarding the increasing use of persons who are neither combatants nor fighters in situations of armed conflict in roles implicating them in hostilities centre on the likelihood that such participation inevitably contributes to a weakening of the principle of distinction. When it is not clear who may be lawfully targeted in war, the danger is that everyone becomes a potential target.

In increasingly complex peace operations, where even a UN-commanded and -controlled 'peacekeeping' force may be involved in an armed conflict against an armed group, similar problems arise. These are rendered even more complicated by the controversy surrounding the status and protection of peacekeepers under international humanitarian law.

Also, recommendations made with the goal of reducing the proliferation of the use of PMSCs in peace operations may be at odds with the conclusions drawn from the analysis presented here. Elke Krahmann, for example, for very good reasons recommends that the UN should identify 'new minimum threat levels, which are established by the UN's regular threat assessments, *above which* the use of unarmed and armed security guards may be considered. Such a rule would prevent that guards are used to assess perceived vulnerabilities where the probability of harm is low.'[24] Krahmann's recommendation is highly logical if one's main goal is to

---

[24] Elke Krahmann, 'The UN Guidelines on the Use of Armed Guards', (2014) 16 *International Community Law Review* 475–491 at 483. Emphasis added.

control the proliferation of security guards by the UN, which for many reasons is a very sensible goal. However, obliging the UN to use armed guards only above a certain threat level means that such guards are more likely to be deployed only in situations in which they may be more likely to be drawn into direct participation in hostilities, unless it is solely to protect in an environment subject to high levels of pure criminality or banditry. That recommendation would therefore not seem to be a fail-safe solution for the concerns raised here and could even exacerbate the problem. The conclusions here would suggest the reverse approach would be more appropriate in circumstances in which the peace operation is deployed in a situation of ongoing armed conflict, that is, that recourse should be had to PMSCs only where the level of threat is very low.

PART IV

Responsibility

The legal concept of responsibility entails the set of legal rules that apply when an international obligation is breached. Responsibility in this sense is seen as the corollary to international legal personality: the ability to enjoy rights and possess obligations under international law entails 'the capacity to bear international responsibility'.[1] Although the notion that international organizations could bear international responsibility was accepted already in 1949 by the International Court of Justice,[2] many publicists had a difficult time imagining the context in which an organization could violate an obligation such that responsibility would accrue, which meant that the issue was not studied seriously or in depth until the 1980s.[3] Furthermore, the nature of international organizations means that writers consistently begin by enumerating the types of legal obligations incumbent on organizations to show that they do indeed have such obligations, and then proceed to their view on the rules on responsibility.[4] Pierre Klein writes, 'l'étude de la responsabilité des organisations internationales en droit des gens impose donc un – relativement long – détour par le domaine des obligations « primaires », puisqu'elle suppose avant toute chose que soient délimitées avec précision les « obligations en vigueur » à l'égard de l'organisation.'[5] The implementation of the responsibility of international

---

[1] Moshe Hirsch, *The Responsibility of International Organizations Toward Third Parties: Some Basic Principles* (Martinus Nijhoff, 1995), p. 8. Hirsch describes this as 'one of the derivative features' of international legal personality.

[2] *Reparation for Injuries Suffered in the Service of the United Nations* (Advisory Opinion) [1949] ICJ Rep 174.

[3] See Klabbers, *An Introduction to International Institutional Law* (Cambridge University Press, 2002), p. 301.

[4] See, for example, Hirsch, *Responsibility of International Organizations*, first chapters; Amerasinghe, *Principles of the Institutional Law of International Organizations*, 2nd edn (Cambridge University Press, 2005), pp. 399–406.

[5] Pierre Klein, *La Responsabilité des organisations internationales* (Brussels: Bruylant, 1998), p. 313.

organizations is, likewise, less developed on the formal plane in comparison to states.

When discussing the responsibility of states and international organizations for the acts of private military and security companies, there are two distinct, equally important aspects to consider. First, there is the question whether the acts of a PMSC are attributable to a state and/or an international organization. When it comes to PMSCs in peace operations, this analysis requires a fresh look at an already complicated (and still unsettled) area of the law on responsibility. The normal starting point for determining whether the acts of a peacekeeping contingent are attributable to the sending state or to the international organization takes for granted that the contingent is unquestionably prima facie attributable to both, in that it has the necessary legal relationship with both.[6] When it comes to PMSCs as the troop contingent, however, one cannot presume the existence of that relationship and therefore may not start from the same point. In addition, there has as yet been very little discussion on the attribution of acts of civilian police to states or international organizations – even with the increasing use of formed police units. Finally, the attribution of security guards poses its own challenges.

Second, there is the issue of how that responsibility can be implemented, taking into account the obstacles of state immunity and the immunity of international organizations. In addition to immunity, there is a general lack of forum for individual proceedings against international organizations, although in peace operations there are some claims commissions. The question whether an actionable right is vested in individuals for violations of IHL also poses a challenge that will not be discussed in detail here.[7]

Some of the questions and issues related to responsibility can become circular or tangled. For example, the question of whether an act can be attributed to a given state is often closely related to a determination of

---

[6] The ILC points this out in its commentary to the final version of the Draft Articles on the Responsibility of International Organizations; ILC, 'Report of the International Law Commission on the Work of Its 63rd Session' (2011) UN Doc A/66/10, para. 5 of the Commentary to Art 7, p. 88 (hereafter ILC, 'DARIO with Commentaries'). Tom Dannenbaum, 'Translating the Standard of Effective Control into a System of Effective Accountability: How Liability Should Be Apportioned for Violations of Human Rights by Member State Troop Contingents Serving as United Nations Peacekeepers' (2010) 51 *Harvard Intl LJ* 113–192.

[7] See ICJ, *Jurisdictional Immunities of the State (Germany v. Italy: Greece Intervening)* (Judgment) [2012] ICJ Rep 99; see also L. Cameron and V. Chetail, *Privatizing War* (Cambridge University Press, 2013), pp. 546–563.

whether a court has jurisdiction over the events in question.[8] When it comes to individual responsibility and state responsibility, the overlap has been nicely summarized as follows:

> Traditionally, international law attributes acts of individuals who act as state organs exclusively to the state. Although in factual terms states act through individuals, in legal terms state responsibility is born not out of an act of an individual but out of an act of the state. State responsibility neither depends on nor implies the legal responsibility of individuals.[9]

This may be especially the case when it comes to attributing the acts of private individuals – who may not individually be bound via international law other than by international criminal law by a particular obligation – to states. Moreover, the question of whether an individual, state, or organization is bound by an international obligation must be distinguished from how or whether any responsibility flowing from a breach of that obligation may be implemented. These concepts may be closely interlinked, but the focus here is exclusively on the issue of whether the state or the organization itself bore an obligation at the time of the impugned conduct.

Chapter 12 will briefly outline the regime of state responsibility – and in particular, attribution – for the acts of private military and security companies. Chapter 13 will outline the framework for the responsibility of international organizations, focussing on the key articles for attribution of conduct in the context of peace operations. Chapter 13 furthermore takes a case-by-case approach to analyzing the attribution of troop contingents, civilian police and security guards to states and international organizations in peace operations. Although the case for PMSCs as a troop contingent is speculative, the rest is not. This analysis also has the benefit of enabling the identification of new questions in the law on responsibility of states and international organizations. Chapter 14 addresses questions of implementing international responsibility. Aspects of criminal responsibility for civilian personnel in peacekeeping operations are beyond the scope of this work.[10]

---

[8] This has in particular been the case in the way the European Court of Human Rights has dealt with cases involving peace operations. See in particular *Behrami and Behrami v. France* and *Saramati v. France, Germany and Norway* (App nos 71424/01 and 78166/01) Decision on Admissibility (GC) ECHR 31 May 2007, discussed below.

[9] André Nollkaemper, 'Concurrence Between Individual Responsibility and State Responsibility in International Law' (2003) 52 *ICLQ* 615–640 at 616, footnotes omitted.

[10] For an overview, see Lindsey Cameron, 'Private Military and Security Companies in Armed Conflicts and Certain Peace Operations', thesis, University of Geneva, 2015, pp. 465–471.

12

Attribution of the Actions of PMSCs Active in Peace Operations to States

The general framework on state responsibility is more familiar than that for international organizations. By virtue of that fact, this chapter will provide a focused analysis applying the rules set down by the ILC in its Articles on State Responsibility to PMSCs. Although these articles are not a treaty, they are widely accepted as essentially codifying international law in this area.[1] The key articles for attribution of conduct to states when it comes to PMSCs are Articles 4 (state organs), 5 (delegation of governmental authority) and 8 (entities acting on the instructions, direction or control of states).

12.1 Article 4 ASR

12.1.1 De jure State Organs

According to Article 4 of the ASR, 'the conduct of any State organ shall be considered an act of that State under international law', no matter its functions, the position it holds in the State, or whether it is part of the central government or a territorial government. Article 4(2) goes on to say, 'An organ includes any person or entity which has that status in accordance with the internal law of the State.'

The starting point is thus whether a PMSC has been designated as a state organ by domestic law. In most situations, this is not the case, but it can happen. For example, a PMSC was contracted by the government of the United Arab Emirates to form a Security Support Group (SSG), which

---

[1] ILC, 'Draft Articles for Responsibility of States for Internationally Wrongful Acts with Commentaries', in 'Report of the International Law Commission on the Work of Its Fifty-third Session', UN Doc A/56/10 (2001) (hereafter ILC, 'ASR with Commentaries'). See also J. Crawford and S. Olleson, 'The Continuing Debate on a UN Convention on State Responsibility' (2005) 54 *ICLQ* 959–972; D. Bodansky, J. Crook and D. Caron, 'The ILC Articles on State Responsibility: The Paradoxical Relationship Between Form and Authority' (2002) 96 *AJIL* 857.

is, in effect a military unit.[2] In an annex that forms part of the contract, an introductory statement regarding the arrangement says:

> The Client [UAE] has determined that a need exists to provide an independent unit for security support operations internal to the country of the United Arab Emirates (UAE). This unit will be staffed by expatriate personnel trained and mentored by expatriate Contractors and will be directly subordinate to the Military Intelligence (MI) section of the Client.[3]

The fact that the battalion is 'directly subordinate to the Military Intelligence section' of the UAE and the fact that the troops are outfitted in Emirati military uniforms[4] suggest that it is incorporated into the UAE armed forces as a state organ. It is relevant to note, however, that according to the contract, it is the PMSC that 'undertakes that all the individuals included in this Contract shall abide by the UAE and Armed Forces laws, regulations and by laws'.[5] It would be helpful to look closely at UAE legislation to know what status the forces are given in Emirati law. It is possible that one could argue that individuals are recruited and supplied by a private company but that they are integrated into the armed forces by some other process – but one cannot make that assumption based on the evidence here. The two other situations where this occurred that are generally cited by authorities include Sandline in Papua New Guinea in 1997 (who were apparently enrolled as special constables in state forces) and Executive Outcomes in Sierra Leone in 2000. This type of situation is rare, however, such that it is necessary to explore other ways in which PMSCs can be attributed to states – including as state organs.

12.1.2   De facto State Organs

By and large, international law leaves it to states to determine what constitute state organs and agents for the purposes of attribution. Nevertheless,

---

[2] This raises the question whether a 'contract' can form part of domestic law for the purpose of determining whether an entity is a state organ.

[3] Contract no. 346/4 for the Provision of Services to the Armed Forces Units, Dated 13 July 2010, Abu Dhabi, Between the GHQ Armed Forces of the United Arab Emirates and Reflex Responses Management Consultancy LLC, 31–32 (Addendum G). (Note: the numeral '4' in the 346 is handwritten and almost illegible and may be a different number.) Available at http://graphics8.nytimes.com/packages/pdf/CONTRACT.pdf?ref=middleeast (accessed 10 September 2012).

[4] Mark Mazzetti and Emily B. Hager, 'Secret Desert Force Set Up by Blackwater's Founder', *New York Times*, 15 May 2011, p. A1.

[5] Contract no. 346/4 for the Provision of Services to the Armed Forces Units, section 2-3-3.

the Articles on State Responsibility leave open the possibility for an entity to be deemed a 'de facto' state organ.[6] The notion that there may be 'de facto' state organs under international law has developed only recently. The idea that states are responsible for the acts of entities that they effectively control has been clearly identified for some time, but the concept that international law may actually designate an entity as a state organ in and of itself has only been distinguished in the past few years.[7]

The ICJ has articulated a test for such 'de facto state organs' and has applied it to the facts before it in three cases, but it has never in fact reached a finding that an entity is a de facto organ.[8] While the implications in terms of state responsibility may seem self-evident, arguably, the way in which a determination that an entity is a de facto state organ affects the legal rights and duties of that organ has not entirely been fleshed out. Of particular interest to this study is whether a finding that an entity contracted by a Department or Ministry of Defence constitutes a 'de facto state organ' by virtue of its complete dependence on the state must entail a corresponding conclusion that that entity necessarily forms part of the armed forces of that contracting state. In my view, the answer is no. The quality of the organ in terms of its rights and duties under international law must be determined according to the relevant international legal rules governing that specific entity – in this case, international humanitarian law. Moreover, as I will show, the very stringent requirements for the test as to whether an entity is a 'de facto state organ' mean that in most cases PMSCs are not likely to be 'de facto organs.'[9]

---

[6] Article 4(2) of the ASR defines state organs as follows: 'An organ includes any person or entity which has that status in accordance with the internal law of the State.' According to the Commentary, '[I]t is not sufficient to refer to internal law for the status of State organs. In some systems the status and functions of various entities are determined not only by law but also by practice, and reference exclusively to internal law would be misleading.' ILC, 'ASR with Commentaries', para. 11 of the Commentary to Article 4.

[7] Stefan Talmon points out that academic literature and 'decisions of other international courts, with very few exceptions, refer only to one test in connection with the ICJ – the effective control test. The ICJ, however, has in fact applied two different "tests . . . of control" in the two leading cases on the subject.' S. Talmon, 'Responsibility of Outside Powers for Acts of Secessionist Entities' (2009) 58 *ICLQ* 493–517 at 497, footnotes omitted, emphasis in original.

[8] *Case Concerning the Application of the Convention on the Prevention and Punishment of the Crime of Genocide (Bosnia and Herzegovina v. Serbia and Montenegro)* (Merits) [2007] ICJ Rep 43; *Military and Paramilitary Activities in and Against Nicaragua (Nicaragua v. United States of America)* (Merits) [1986] ICJ Rep 14; *Armed Activities on the Territory of the Congo (Congo v. Uganda)* (Merits) [2005] ICJ Rep 168.

[9] The ILC's Commentary to Article 4 indicates that it was principally referring to potential idiosyncrasies in the way states define, name and categorize their own organs and entities

The test set out by the International Court of Justice for classifying an entity as a de facto state organ has been labelled the 'strict control' test[10] (as distinct from the 'effective control' test relevant for attribution under Article 8 of the ASR) and is characterized by a relationship of 'complete dependence'. According to Stefan Talmon, citing from the ICJ decisions in the *Nicaragua* and *Bosnian Genocide* cases, 'complete dependence means that the ... entity is "lacking any real autonomy" and is "merely an instrument" or "agent" of the outside power.'[11] According to the analysis, '[c]ommon objectives may make the ... entity an ally, albeit a highly dependent ally, of the outside power, but not necessarily its organ. In no case does the maintenance of some unspecified "ties" or a "general level of coordination" between the outside power and the ... entity, or the notion of "organic unity" between the two, suffice.'[12]

Talmon further elaborates on the factors and elements of the 'strict control' test, in particular in light of secessionist movements. He argues,

> The fact that the outside power conceived, created and organized the secessionist entity ... seems to establish a strong presumption that the secessionist entity – as its creature – is completely dependent on the outside power and is nothing more than its instrument or agent. However, it is not sufficient that the outside power merely took advantage of the existence of a separatist movement and incorporated this fact into its policies vis-à-vis the parent State. Complete dependence on the outside power is also demonstrated if the multifarious forms of assistance (financial assistance, logistic support, supply of intelligence) provided by it are crucial to the pursuit of the secessionist entity's activities. The secessionist entity is completely dependent upon the outside power if it cannot conduct its activities without the multi-faceted support of the outside power and if the cessation of aid results, or would result, in the end of these activities.[13]

for their own internal legal purposes when it used the word 'includes' in the definition of state organs. It states that 'the internal law of a State may not classify, exhaustively or at all, which entities have the status of "organs". In such cases, while the powers of an entity and its relation to other bodies under internal law will be relevant to its classification as an "organ", internal law will not itself perform the task of classification. Even if it does so, the term "organ" used in internal law may have a special meaning, and not the very broad meaning it has under article 4. For example, under some legal systems the term "government" refers only to bodies at the highest level such as the Head of State and the cabinet of ministers. In others, the police have a special status, independent of the executive; this cannot mean that for international law purposes they are not organs of the State. Accordingly, a State cannot avoid responsibility for the conduct of a body which does in truth act as one of its organs merely by denying it that status under its own law.' ILC, 'ASR with Commentaries', para. 11 of the Commentary to Article 4. Footnotes omitted.

[10] Talmon, 'Responsibility of Outside Powers', 498.
[11] Ibid., 499.   [12] Ibid. Footnotes omitted.   [13] Ibid., 499–500.

He goes on, 'Secondly, this complete dependence must extend to "all fields" of the secessionist entity's activity.'[14] Indeed, if an entity has 'some qualified, but real, margin of independence',[15] it is not completely dependent on an outside entity. The ICJ went so far as to hold that even the fact that the entity in question 'could not have "conduct[ed] its crucial or most significant ... activities"' without the 'very important support given' by the state did not 'signify a total dependence' of the entity on the state.[16]

The ICJ itself warns that 'to equate persons or entities with State organs when they do not have that status under internal law must be exceptional'.[17] Would this caveat apply also when it comes to commercial partners of states, or is it designed to take into account sensitive and highly thorny questions (such as relationships between states and armed groups) in international relations? Here we would do well to recall that the manner in which a state chooses to organize itself internally has also been a highly sensitive matter in international relations. When it comes to PMSCs providing services such as logistics and catering to the government armed forces, even when states give themselves a fair degree of control over the actions of those companies, the test for a de facto organ is too stringent to capture most commercial relationships.[18]

In situations of international armed conflict, an additional issue arises due to the way in which international humanitarian law provides for resistance fighters who 'belong' to a party to a conflict to be granted prisoner-of-war status if captured. One way of conceiving the interplay between IHL and the law on international responsibility is to assert that the test for 'belonging' in Article 4A(2) of the Third Convention must satisfy the complete dependence test (or at least the effective control or overall control tests) under the law of responsibility since a state will be responsible for the acts of those forces in the same way as for the members of its armed forces. I reject that approach as, in my view, IHL must be the *lex specialis*; it will be more protective for captured resistance fighters if a looser, factual standard is adopted.[19] Is it possible that Article 4A(2) GC III sets up a

---

[14] Ibid., 500.   [15] *Bosnia v. Serbia*, para. 394.
[16] Ibid. The ICJ cites its own holding from *Nicaragua* within the quotation itself.
[17] *Bosnia v. Serbia*, para. 393.
[18] For an extensive discussion, see Cameron and Chetail, *Privatizing War*, pp. 142–158.
[19] See Lindsey Cameron, 'The Use of Private Military and Security Companies in Armed Conflicts and Certain Peace Operations', PhD thesis, University of Geneva, 2015, pp. 35–43.

special rule for the recognition of an 'organ' in the meaning of Article 4(2) ASR? The logical answer is 'no'. The conduct of such forces is better attributed to states on the basis of Article 5 ASR as an act of the governmental authority. When an organized armed group or volunteer or militia force fights on behalf of a state – which is central to the concept of 'belonging' in 4A(2) GC III – it indisputably exercises an element of the governmental authority. Alternatively, when a state accepts that a group fights on its behalf it may in essence adopt that behaviour as its own. In such cases, Article 11 ASR provides a hook for the attribution of conduct to the state. There is thus no need for a state to exercise the same level of control that would be required under Article 4 or 8 of the ASR over such groups in order for their actions to be attributable to it.

In addition, the Montreux Document rather takes the approach of affirming that the type of forces recognized in Article 43 AP I ('organized armed forces, groups and units which are under a command responsible to that Party for the conduct of its subordinates') may be a de facto organ for the purposes of attribution.[20]

In the hypothetical scenario that a state sends a PMSC as its contribution to a UN-commanded and -controlled peace operations force, does the mere fact that the force is participating in an international endeavour on behalf of a state render it somehow a 'de facto' state organ? Here again it is important to recall that the test for a 'de facto state organ' relates to the degree of control the state exercises over the entity and not to the type of function. Thus, on that ground alone, it would not suffice. Above, I noted that the exercise of discipline over such forces is key to ensuring that a state respects its obligations under IHL (where a peace operations force is deployed in a territory in which IHL applies); that being said, it is far from clear that discipline and training would meet the level of control required to find it is a de facto organ under Article 4(2) ASR. At most, it might be considered as an element of the exercise of effective control for Article 8 ASR. Thus, unless a state were to create a PMSC exclusively to participate in a peace operation, exercise discipline and control to the point of putting all of the PMSC's operations under the direct control of one of the state's own military officers, and dissolve it at the end of the mission, in my view it is unlikely that such a PMSC force would be attributable to a state as a de facto organ under Article 4 ASR on the basis of participation as a contingent in a peace operation alone.

[20] See below, note 48 and accompanying text. See also Cameron, ibid., chapter 2, note 14.

12.2   Article 5 ASR

Article 5 of the ASR states,

> The conduct of a person or entity which is not an organ of the State under article 4 but which is empowered by the law of that State to exercise elements of the governmental authority shall be considered an act of the State under international law, provided the person or entity is acting in that capacity in the particular instance.

The logic of this article is clear: states should not be able to escape their international legal obligations by outsourcing tasks to private entities. In this regard it appears perfectly suited to capturing the acts of PMSCs. It may indeed be the best hook by which to ensure the attribution of the conduct of some PMSCs to states; especially as policing, justice and military activity are generally considered to be exercises of governmental authority. Elsewhere, I have argued that a number of activities are core state functions that should not be outsourced.[21] Even if those activities are outsourced by a state, however, the conduct of the persons or entities carrying them out would be attributable to a state based on Article 5.[22] However, the apparent simplicity of the article is marred by disagreement and uncertainty as to what exactly constitute 'elements of the governmental authority'.[23] It is important to recall that PMSCs carry out a wide variety of tasks, from mundane catering services to programming of high-tech weapons systems. Consequently, it is necessary to carry out the analysis for the wide variety of tasks for which PMSCs are contracted by states.

In its commentary on Article 5, the ILC acknowledged the lack of a definition and demurred,

> Beyond a certain limit, what is regarded as 'governmental' depends on the particular society, its history and traditions. Of particular importance will be not just the content of the powers, but the way they are conferred on an entity, the purposes for which they are to be exercised and the extent to which the entity is accountable to government for their exercise.[24]

---

[21] Cameron, 'The Use of PMSCs in Armed Conflicts and Certain Peace Operations', chapter 3 and especially pp. 219–233; Cameron and Chetail, *Privatizing War*, chapter 1.

[22] Cameron, 'The Use of PMSCs in Armed Conflicts and Certain Peace Operations', chapter 3 and especially pp. 219–233; Cameron and Chetail, *Privatizing War*, chapter 1.

[23] While other issues such as 'empowered by law' and 'acting in that capacity' may also be relevant, they do not pose additional problems when it comes to PMSCs. This section will thus focus exclusively on the question of what the elements of the governmental authority are.

[24] ILC 'ASR with Commentaries', para. 5 of the commentary to Article 5.

The first sentence is problematic because it appears to propose a 'relativistic' application of the rule, which ILC debates suggest is the exact opposite of the purpose of the rule in the first place.[25]

If one relies on the decisions of the European Court of Justice, providing security services is generally not an act involving an exercise of the governmental authority;[26] however, in my view, it is in situations where it involves direct participation in hostilities.[27] Also, when the security services being contracted are to be performed extra-territorially – that is, in another state – in the context of a military operation being conducted by a state abroad, however, does that context in itself change the nature of the act of providing security into an act of governmental authority? There are good arguments to suggest that it does, at least for those providing security for government facilities or headquarters in the territory in which the military operation is occurring. It is more difficult to sustain such an argument for security contractors protecting construction sites prone to attack, however, even if those projects are financed by the government in question as part of its overall operation.

Furthermore, it is important to point out that, while acts involving direct participation in hostilities by PMSCs contracted by states are attributable to the state on the basis of Article 5 ASR, other acts that do not entail direct participation in hostilities may also be attributable as an exercise of the governmental authority. One such example may be guarding regular prisoners in a conflict zone; another may be carrying out arrests related to criminal activity (when it does not involve arresting members of armed groups).[28]

---

[25] See the comments of Roberto Ago: 'If the same public function were performed in one State by organs of the State proper and in another by para-State institutions, it would indeed be absurd if the international responsibility of the State were engaged in one case and not in the other.' (1974) 1 *Yearbook of the International Law Commission* 8, para. 17.

[26] Case C-465/05, *Re Private Security Guards: EC v. Italy* [2008] 2 CMLR 3, para. 33 and similar cases.

[27] Cameron and Chetail, *Privatizing War*, pp. 201–203. Hannah Tonkin arrives at a similar conclusion, without specifically discussing the term 'direct participation in hostilities'. See Tonkin, *State Control over Private Military and Security Companies in Armed Conflict* (Cambridge University Press, 2011), pp. 107–108.

[28] Nigel White gives the example of guarding prisoners as an exercise of the governmental authority: 'Institutional Responsibility for Private Military and Security Companies', in F. Francioni and N. Ronzitti (eds.), *War by Contract: Human Rights, Humanitarian Law, and Private Contractors* (Oxford University Press, 2011), pp. 381–395 at p. 390. Guarding prisoners of war would constitute direct participation in hostilities and be attributable on that basis, but in any case IHL requires POWs to be guarded by members of the regular armed forces. See Article 39 of GC III.

An additional question for this study is whether sending PMSCs as civilian police or even as a troop contribution to participate in a peace operation is automatically or highly likely to be an exercise of an element of the governmental authority. In my view, it is. The framework described in Part I as to how states contribute police and or troops to peace operations shows that the forces are sent by the state to participate in the operation on behalf of that state. To perform the functions of international police or troops in the context of a peacekeeping operation epitomizes one of the functions of government in the international sphere. Here, one can ponder whether peacekeeping forces act as representatives of a state on the international stage, a role that must devolve from an exercise of governmental authority. A statement on the US Department of State web page on civilian police suggests as much: 'A U.S. CIVPOL assignment represents a great opportunity to serve America – while serving overseas.'[29] At the same time, the actions of both of these types of units or forces may also be attributable to the international organization using them, pursuant to the rules outlined below.

On the other hand, where the action is limited to financing or contracting a PMSC to provide logistical or training support for an operation in lieu of the state participating itself – or, indeed, for a peace operation delegated to a regional organization – the fact that the activity is performed for an international purpose does not transform that actor into an entity exercising elements of the governmental authority. Such activities are not reflective of an exercise of 'governmental authority'.

12.3   Article 8 ASR

Article 8 of the ASR provides a test for attributing the acts of private groups or individuals to a state under certain circumstances. The article states,

> The conduct of a person or group of persons shall be considered as an act of a State under international law if the person or group of persons is in fact acting on the instructions of, or under the direction or control of, that State in carrying out the conduct.

The ILC commentary points out that 'most commonly cases of this kind will arise where State organs supplement their own action by recruiting

---

[29] US Department of State, 'Office of Criminal Justice Assistance and Partnership: Civilian Police', www.state.gov/j/inl/civ/c27153.htm.

or instigating private persons or groups who act as "auxiliaries" while remaining outside the official structure of the State.'[30] Although on the face of it, this description appears very close to a description of PMSCs, the crucial factor is that for the conduct of a private entity, according to the ICJ,

> it has to be proved that they acted in accordance with that State's instructions or under its 'effective control'. It must however be shown that this 'effective control' was exercised, or that the State's instructions were given, in respect of each operation in which the alleged violations occurred, not generally in respect of the overall actions taken by the persons or groups of persons having committed the violations.[31]

Scholars familiar with PMSCs have raised interesting points as to the contours of this requirement. Hannah Tonkin argues that 'an instruction to a private security guard to shoot anyone who comes near the protected object would effectively authorise a violation, since it authorises the contractor to shoot indiscriminately without prior warning and without considering whether the person might be an innocent civilian.'[32] As such, she also cites Carsten Hoppe, who has argued that a command to a PMSC 'to get the prisoner to talk by any means necessary' would constitute an unlawful instruction because it essentially authorizes violations of IHL or IHRL.[33]

These examples may seem compelling, but they do not convincingly square with the ILC's interpretation of 'instructions'. Indeed, the ILC states, 'In general a State, in giving lawful instructions to persons who are not its organs, does not assume the risk that the instructions will be carried out in an internationally unlawful way.'[34] The ILC refers to auxiliaries 'sent' to 'neighbouring countries, or who are instructed to carry out particular missions abroad'.[35] De Frouville indicates that Paul Reuter did not mince words at the ILC when it came to the type of activity this article

---

[30] ILC Commentary to Article 8 ASR, para. 2. This explanation has remained essentially identical since 1974: see ILC Yearbook 1974, Vol. II(1), p. 283, para. 2, also cited in Olivier de Frouville, 'Attribution of Conduct to the State: Private Individuals', in J. Crawford, A. Pellet and S. Olleson (eds.), *The Law of International Responsibility* (Oxford University Press, 2010), pp. 257–280 at p. 266.

[31] *Bosnia v. Serbia*, para. 400.   [32] Tonkin, *State Control*, p. 115.   [33] Ibid.

[34] ILC, 'ASR with Commentaries', commentary to Article 8, para. 8. This remark is made in the context of the commentary on 'Directions and control', but there is no reason not to apply it here. See also Emanuela-Chiara Gillard, 'Business Goes to War: Private Military/Security Companies and International Humanitarian Law' (2006) 88 *IRRC* 525–572 at 555.

[35] ILC, 'ASR with Commentaries', commentary to Article 8, para. 2.

was aimed at capturing: "'the lower work of the State: spying, provocation, sabotage, etc.'".[36] This suggests that the state is in fact instructing the private actor to do something that is itself a violation of its obligations. That is, there is no way to do lawfully what it is being instructed to do: one cannot sabotage or invade foreign territory in full respect of the law. In the examples Tonkin and Hoppe give, on the other hand, theoretically, it would be possible for a PMSC to carry out the essence of its task but only within the limits of the law. Thus, there is a degree of ambiguity in these examples (which Tonkin admits). In addition, a PMSC is more likely to be given a contract stipulating that its task is to 'protect' a given object or person and not a contract stating it should shoot anyone who comes near a particular person or thing.[37] If that supposition is correct, if one were to interpret the four corners of such a contract (assuming it were to state nothing else) as consisting of the entire extent of obligations on that PMSC and that it is exonerated from the rest of the general legal framework that is normally applicable, then one would place an extremely high burden on states contracting private firms to incorporate by reference the entire law of the state in the contract – and not just for PMSCs, but for all actors with which states contract. The ILC anticipates that otherwise lawful instructions may give rise to state responsibility for the manner in which they are carried out if the 'unlawful or unauthorized conduct was really incidental to the mission or clearly went beyond it'.[38] This is a matter of appreciation. I am not convinced that the ILC (or international law) anticipates that states should be responsible for individuals taking instructions such as those indicated by Tonkin and Hoppe literally and to mean that it is not necessary to also respect the normal legal framework that applies to such activities.

In any case, one can nevertheless only agree wholeheartedly with Tonkin that the best way for a state to be sure that it cannot be found responsible for unlawful acts of PMSCs based on its instructions is to issue clear and detailed instructions that comply with IHL (and international human rights law), in addition to giving further instructions and taking precautions on the ground.[39]

---

[36] De Frouville, 'Attribution of Conduct', p. 266.

[37] Contracts with PMSCs can run to hundreds of pages in length, but they do not appear to incorporate extensive human rights obligations. Laura Dickinson, 'Contract as a Tool for Regulating Private Military Companies', in Simon Chesterman and Chia Lehnardt (eds.), *From Mercenaries to Market* (Oxford University Press, 2007), pp. 217–238 at p. 221.

[38] ILC, 'ASR with Commentaries', commentary to Article 8, para. 8.

[39] Tonkin, *State Control*, pp. 116–117.

Aside from via unlawful instructions, the acts of private actors can be attributed to a state if they were under the direction or control of that state. The degree of control required in order for the conduct of private persons or groups to be attributed to a state, according to the ICJ, is high. In *Nicaragua*, the Court held that 'United States participation, even if preponderant or decisive, in the financing, organizing, training, supplying and equipping of the *contras*, the selection of its military or paramilitary targets, and the planning of the whole of its operation, is still insufficient in itself, on the basis of the evidence in the possession of the Court, for the purpose of attributing to the United States the acts committed by the *contras*...'[40] The Court went on,

> All the forms of...participation mentioned above, and even the general control by the respondent State over a force with a high degree of dependency on it, would not in themselves mean...that the United States directed or enforced the perpetration of the acts contrary to human rights and humanitarian law...For this conduct to give rise to legal responsibility of the United States, it would in principle have to be proved that the State had *effective control of the military or paramilitary operations in the course of which the alleged violations were committed.*[41]

The Court reaffirmed this test in *Bosnia v. Serbia*, rejecting the lower standard of 'overall control' developed by the ICTY in *Tadic* relating to the classification of the conflict when it comes to state responsibility.[42] At the same time, it should be noted that these passages and others related to the relationship of the United States with the Contras have also been used in setting out the 'complete dependence' test described above for Article 4(2).

In any case, the fact that states establish licensing systems for PMSCs clearly does not meet the standard sought in this test. Beyond licensing, states that rely heavily on PMSCs have taken steps to increase their operational command over the acts of contractors in theatre. In this regard, a DoD Instruction on Determining Workforce Mix observes, 'Commanders often cannot compel DoD civilians or contractor employees to perform work or assume risks that were not agreed upon under the terms of their contract. In emergency situations, a military commander may direct DoD civilians to take lawful actions.'[43] Thus, in general, the military

[40] *Nicaragua* case, para. 115.   [41] Ibid. Emphasis added.
[42] *Bosnia v. Serbia*, paras 402–406.
[43] See for example DoD Instruction 1100.22, 'Policy and Procedures for Determining Workforce Mix', 12 April 2010, Enclosure 5 2.d.(3)(a) (at pp. 50–51), www.dtic.mil/whs/directives/corres/pdf/110022p.pdf.

commander does not have control over the contractors, but in certain circumstances it does. However, the Instruction goes on: 'Generally, contractor employees (unlike U.S. and foreign national civilian and military personnel) are not under the direct supervision of the military commander. The contracting officer, or designee, serves as the liaison between the commander and the defense contractor for directing or controlling the contractor's performance.'[44] In terms of being able to ensure that contractors continue to carry out their jobs and stay in theatre and do not simply quit or run away in the face of the enemy, the Instruction notes that the prohibition of desertion applies only to members of the armed forces under the Uniform Code of Military Justice.[45]

For the most part, these policies amount to a general control, which would not appear to meet the requirement of a specific control over the operation in which the violation occurred. However, in the case that a military commander directs contractors to take actions or takes control of an operation, that situation would likely give rise to effective control over the PMSC personnel. It is entirely possible that this degree of control will be exercised over contractors; everything depends on the facts of a given situation. For other states, it will depend also on the specifics of their legislation or regulations.

When it comes to the degree of control states may exercise over contractors in peace operations where the contractors are not accompanying the forces of the state in question, the situation may be a little less clear. According to the contractor that provided air support in Sierra Leone, 'ICI was contracted by the [US Department of State] to provide 2 helicopters and crew. All flight taskings originate[d] directly from the U.S. Embassy in Sierra Leone. Area of operations include[d] Sierra Leone and Guinea.'[46] The air support it conducted included transport of personnel, food and other items and providing 'limited heli-borne surveillance to facilitate the monitoring of any movement of armed rebels'.[47] Flight taskings may be interpreted as 'instructions', but, based on the discussion above, lawful instructions would not give rise to attribution of unlawful conduct to the state unless the unlawful conduct was truly incidental to the mission. Without more, the degree of control described here would not amount to effective control over the contractor.

---

[44] Ibid., and para. 5 2.d.(3)(b).   [45] Ibid., para. 5 2.d.(1) and (2).
[46] ICI of Oregon website, www.icioregon.com/SierraLeone2.htm (accessed 1 October 2011).
[47] Ibid.

Finally, I note that according to the Montreux Document, the conduct of PMSCs is attributable to contracting states if the PMSCs are:

a) incorporated by the State into its regular armed forces in accordance with its domestic legislation;
b) members of organised armed forces, groups or units under a command responsible to the State;
c) empowered to exercise elements of governmental authority if they are acting in that capacity (i.e. are formally authorized by law or regulation to carry out functions normally conducted by organs of the State); or
d) in fact acting on the instructions of the State (i.e. the State has specifically instructed the private actor's conduct) or under its direction or control (i.e. actual exercise of effective control by the State over a private actor's conduct).[48]

Perhaps tellingly, there are no statements on the attribution of the conduct of PMSCs in the Montreux Document for territorial or home states. This is, as can be expected, a fairly conservative restatement of the law on attribution. Although one may quibble with the Document's characterization of 'elements of governmental authority', the restatement is not incorrect in law as the law currently stands. Furthermore, the Document affirms the attributability of conduct of PMSCs who are incorporated into a state's armed forces along the lines set out in Article 43 AP I as a state organ.

12.4 Responsibility Arising from Due Diligence Obligations

Due diligence obligations may arise for states in relation to the acts of a private individual even when that individual's actions are not directly attributable to the state. As due diligence obligations arise directly from the primary rules of international law, the ILC's Articles on State Responsibility do not deal with them.[49] Given the potentially significant obstacles

---

[48] 'Montreux Document on Pertinent International Legal Obligations and Good Practices for States Related to Operations of Private Military and Security Companies During Armed Conflict' (17 September 2008), Transmitted to the UN General Assembly and Security Council in UN Doc A/63/467-S/2008/636 (6 October 2008) (Montreux Document) Part I, Article 7.

[49] ILC, 'Report of the International Law Commission on the Work of Its Fifty-first Session', UN Doc A/54/10 (1999), para. 420: 'Defining the precise nature of due diligence could not be done in the context of the draft articles without spending many more years on the

to attributing the conduct of PMSCs – as companies or as individuals – to states via the available rules under the law of state responsibility, the obligation to exercise due diligence to prevent harm by private individuals is an important means to ensure that states respect their obligations when PMSCs are involved. As Riccardo Pisillo-Mazzeschi explained, states have an obligation under general international law to have an administrative and law enforcement system to enable them to fulfil their international legal obligations. The obligation to exercise due diligence is not to have such a system in place, but to *use* it.[50]

Given the nature of due diligence obligations and the fact that they arise depending on the primary obligation, there is no universal list of such obligations. Clear due diligence obligations in international humanitarian law flow from Article 27 GC IV and Article 13 GC III, which stipulate that women and POWs must be protected from harm by others.[51] In addition, Article 43 of the Hague Regulations prescribes that an occupying power must 'take all the measures in his power to restore, and ensure, as far as possible, public order and safety . . .'. The Montreux Document makes reference to this obligation in Part I, restating existing legal obligations.[52] The International Court of Justice has held that Article 43 of the Hague Regulations 'comprise[s] the duty to secure respect for the applicable rules of international human rights law and international humanitarian law, to protect the inhabitants of the occupied territory against acts of violence, and not to tolerate such violence by any third party'.[53] In this way, the court found that an occupying power has due diligence obligations to protect

---

topic and, even if the problem were resolved, that would in effect be based on the presumption that any primary rule, or a certain class of primary rules, contained a qualification of due diligence.' See also Timo Koivurova, 'Due Diligence', in R. Wolfrum (ed.), *Max Planck Encyclopedia of Public International Law* (Oxford University Press, 2008–), paras 4–27.

[50] Riccardo Pisillo-Mazzeschi, 'The Due Diligence Rule and the Nature of the International Responsibility of States' (1992) 35 *German YB Intl L* 9–51 at 27–28.

[51] Article 27(2) of the Convention Relative to the Protection of Civilian Persons in Time of War, Geneva, 12 August 1949, in force 21 October 1950 (GC IV): 'Women shall be especially protected against any attack on their honour, in particular against rape, enforced prostitution, or any form of indecent assault.' Article 13(2) of the Convention Relative to the Treatment of Prisoners of War, Geneva, 12 August 1949, in force 21 October 1950 (GC III): 'prisoners of war must at all times be protected, particularly against acts of violence or intimidation and against insults and public curiosity.'

[52] Montreux Document, Part I, Article 1: 'If [contracting states] are occupying powers, they have an obligation to take all measures in their power to restore, and ensure, as far as possible, public order and safety, i.e. exercise vigilance in preventing violations of international humanitarian law and human rights law.'

[53] *Congo v. Uganda*, para. 178.

human rights via its obligations under IHL. In my view, the use of PMSCs in the context of occupation may be construed as a means to enhance security in an unstable environment; on the other hand, if acts of violence by PMSCs go unchecked, that may represent a state failing to meet its obligations of due diligence in this regard.[54]

Article 1 common to the four Geneva Conventions and Additional Protocol I requires states to 'respect and to ensure respect for the present Convention in all circumstances'.[55] Clearly and uncontroversially, this means that states must ensure the respect of the Conventions by those whose conduct is attributable to it under international law.[56] The wording of the Article was intended to underscore that 'it would not, for example, be enough for a State to give orders or directives to a few civilian or military authorities, leaving it to them to arrange as they pleased for the details of their execution.'[57]

In Part I restating existing obligations under international law, the Montreux Document specifically refers to due diligence obligations of contracting, territorial and home states in relation to PMSCs. In this regard, it states that each type of state has 'an obligation, within [its] power, to ensure respect for international humanitarian law by PMSCs [they contract/on their territory/of their nationality]'.[58] The Montreux Document is calibrated to take into account the degree of influence and control that states in various roles can be expected to have over PMSCs.[59] As such, contracting states have the obligation 'to ensure that PMSCs that they contract and their personnel are aware of their obligations and trained accordingly', whereas territorial and home states are obliged only to 'disseminate, as widely as possible, the text of the Geneva Conventions and other relevant norms of international humanitarian law among PMSCs and their

---

[54] I have explored the specific nature of this obligation in respect to PMSCs in Cameron and Chetail, *Privatizing War*, pp. 236–240.

[55] The wording in Protocol I is adapted to the Protocol but identical in substance.

[56] Affirming that the obligation applies in non-international armed conflicts and that it extends to an obligation on states not parties to a conflict to take steps to bring state parties to conflict back into compliance with IHL, see ICRC, *Commentary on the First Geneva Convention* (Cambridge University Press, 2016), commentary on common Article 1. See also L. Boisson de Chazournes and L. Condorelli, 'Common Article 1 of the Geneva Conventions Revisited: Protecting Collective Interests' (2000) 82 *IRRC* 67–87, inter alia.

[57] J. Pictet (ed.), *The Geneva Conventions of 12 August 1949: Commentary, First Geneva Convention for the Amelioration of the Condition of the Wounded and Sick in Armed Forces in the Field* (Geneva: ICRC 1952), 26.

[58] Montreux Document, Part I, paras 3, 9 and 14.

[59] Pisillo-Mazzeschi, 'Due Diligence', affirms that the degree of influence a state has over an actor affects the nature or degree of due diligence owed in regard to the acts of that actor.

personnel'. In addition, contracting states are expected to use military regulations to suppress violations of IHL in addition to the other administrative, regulatory or judicial sanctions that apply for other states. Finally, the document specifies that 'All other States have an obligation, within their power, to ensure respect for international humanitarian law. They have an obligation to refrain from encouraging or assisting in violations of international law by any party to an armed conflict.'[60] This may be taken as a restatement and interpretation of Article 1 common to the four Geneva Conventions. In addition, the document affirms that all states must implement their obligations under human rights law.[61] More than this general restatement of obligations, when it comes to PMSCs, the good practices set out in the Montreux Document provide, in my view, an excellent starting point to understand how states may effectively fulfil their due diligence obligations.[62]

---

[60] Montreux Document, Part I, para. 18.   [61] Ibid., paras 4, 10, 15, 19.

[62] Hannah Tonkin does not mention the Montreux Document but takes a similar approach in 'Common Article I: A Minimum Yardstick for Regulating Private Military and Security Companies' (2009) 22 Leiden J Intl L 779–799.

13

Responsibility of International Organizations

In 2011, the International Law Commission adopted the Draft Articles on the Responsibility of International Organizations and their commentaries following the second reading of the articles.[1] In contrast to the Articles on State Responsibility, which were developed over a period of fifty years and under the leadership of five Special Rapporteurs, the DARIO were developed and adopted in a little over a decade under the leadership of Special Rapporteur Georgio Gaja.[2] The Drafting Committee leaned heavily on the ASR for the structure and substance of the DARIO – a decision for which it was greatly criticized by some. In particular, José Alvarez stated bluntly, 'From my perspective, the ILC's decision to undertake this topic and to use as its model its prior Articles of State Responsibility (ASR) was, from the start, a miscalculation', calling the project overly ambitious.[3] Just prior to the adoption of the Draft Articles, he argued that the General Assembly should scrap the whole project and replace it with a more focused study.[4] Blanca Montejo observes that the 'methodology [basing itself on the ASR], together with the absence of practice, has generated a great deal of controversy with respect to certain provisions, to the extent it has been argued that international organizations are characterized, unlike

---

[1] ILC, 'Report of the ILC on the Work of Its Sixty-third Session', UN Doc A/66/10 (2011), paras 82 and 87.

[2] The recommendation to begin the project can be found in the ILC, 'Report of the ILC on the Work of Its 52nd Session, Annex, Syllabuses on Topics Recommended for Inclusion in the Long-Term Programme of Work of the Commission', UN Doc A/55/10 (2000) 135–140 (Alain Pellet). It was included in the programme of work in 2002, in the fifty-fourth session of the ILC: 'Report of the Work of the International Law Commission on the Work of its Fifty-fourth Session', UN Doc A/57/10 (2002) 228–236.

[3] One of the most scathing general criticisms comes from José Alvarez, 'Revisiting the ILC's Draft Rules on International Organization Responsibility' (2011) 105 *Am Soc Intl L Proceedings* 344–348, 344. This criticism dates from before the second reading of the articles and the changes introduced, but changes made between the first and second readings would not seem to alleviate most of Alvarez's concerns.

[4] Ibid., 347.

states, by the principle of speciality and that a "one size fits all approach" was ill-suited for international organizations.'[5] From the point of view of the UN Secretariat, Daphna Shraga echoed a similar form of criticism, stating, 'In the Secretariat's critique of the Draft Articles, it took issue not with the Commission's heavy reliance on the Articles on State Responsibility, but with its reliance on them too often with too little regard to the specificities of international organizations.'[6] These statements may be compared with that of Jean d'Aspremont, who proclaims, 'The adoption of the Articles on the Responsibility of International Organizations (ARIO) should certainly be celebrated with enthusiasm by our professional community', although he acknowledges that 'the ARIO fell short, in the view of – almost all – observers, of meeting the conceptual consistency which legal scholars expect from such a set of secondary rules'.[7] Some states have also voiced their support for the work and approach of the ILC in this area and have called the criticism 'unfounded'; others are more ambivalent.[8]

In its commentary, the ILC openly acknowledges that the fact that the Draft Articles 'are based on limited practice moves the border between codification and progressive development in the direction of the latter'.[9] It goes on to say, 'It may occur that a provision in the articles on State responsibility could be regarded as representing codification, while the corresponding provision on the responsibility of international organizations is more in the nature of progressive development.'[10] However, the commentary accompanying the Draft Articles fails to specify which of the articles it considers to be 'progressive development' and which reflect the *lege lata*. It then goes on to say that 'their authority will depend on their reception by those to whom they are addressed'.[11]

Despite this criticism, this chapter will use the DARIO as a framework for analyzing the potential responsibility of international organizations in

---

[5] Blanca Montejo, 'The Roles and Responsibilities of International Organizations: Introductory Remarks' (2011) 105 *Am Soc Intl L Proceedings* 343–344 at 343.

[6] Daphna Shraga, 'The ILC Draft Articles on Responsibility of International Organizations: The Interplay Between the Practice and the Rule' (2011) 105 *Am Soc Intl L Proceedings* 351–353 at 353.

[7] Jean d'Aspremont, 'The Articles on the Responsibility of International Organizations: Magnifying the Fissures in the Law of International Responsibility' (2012) 9 *Intl Org L Rev* 15–28 at 16.

[8] See for example the comments of the Netherlands in UN Doc A/CN.4/636/Add.1 (2011) 7, para. 4; see also the comments of Mexico (ibid.) 5, para. 3; Germany: UN Doc A/CN.4/636 (2011) 7. More ambivalent about the success of the approach of using the ASR as a starting point and relying heavily on them is Austria (UN Doc A/CN.4/636 (2011) 6–7, para. 7. Clearly critical is Portugal: UN Doc A/CN.4/636 (2011) 8.

[9] ILC 'DARIO with Commentaries', General Commentary, para. 5 (p. 70).

[10] Ibid.   [11] Ibid.

regard to PMSCs. The scope of that analysis will be limited to international organizations engaged in peace operations. However, due to the difference with the Articles on State Responsibility in terms of the level of acceptance of the principles and rules set down in the DARIO, the analysis will also serve as a means to test the robustness of the rules themselves as proposed by the ILC.

13.1 Basic Concepts

Draft Article 4 DARIO defines internationally wrongful acts as 'conduct consisting of an action or omission' that '(a) is attributable to that international organization under international law' and that '(b) constitutes a breach of an international obligation of that organization'.[12] In addition, the drafters perceived a need to stipulate that the 'characterization of an act of an international organization as internationally wrongful is governed by international law'.[13] This article is designed to take into account the fact that the rules of an organization, unlike the internal law of a state, may form part of international law. As such, the DARIO could not stipulate that an organization's internal law may not be invoked to justify a violation, as the ASR does with respect to states. This is because the internal 'law' of international organizations may form part and parcel of international law and may be directly relevant to ascertaining the existence of a breach of an obligation of that organization.[14]

Buttressing this affirmation, in the chapter on the existence of a breach of an international obligation (Chapter III), Draft Article 10 provides:

1. There is a breach of an international obligation by an international organization when an act of that international organization is not in conformity with what is required of it by that obligation, regardless of the origin and character of the obligation concerned.
2. Paragraph 1 includes the breach of an international obligation that may arise for an international organization towards its members under the rules of the organization.

Article 10 thus implicitly forces the following question: what is required of a given international organization under international law in the circumstances at the time of the alleged violation?[15] Indeed, for many, there

---

[12] Klabbers, *Introduction to International Institutional Law*, pp. 310–311. See also Amerasinghe, *Principles*, pp. 400–401.
[13] ILC, 'DARIO with Commentaries', Article 5, at 82.
[14] Ibid., Commentary to Article 5, paras 2 and 3, at 82.
[15] See also Alvarez, 'Revisiting the ILC's Draft Rules', 346.

remain 'uncertainties about which primary rules (e.g., which part of the human rights covenants?) apply to international organizations'.[16] For the purposes of this study, peace operations in particular raise the question: is the United Nations bound by international human rights law? By international humanitarian law? These questions have been addressed and answered affirmatively.[17]

In terms of circumstances precluding wrongfulness, after considerable debate, the Special Rapporteur argued that essentially the same grounds apply for international organizations as for states.[18] Thus, he posited that international organizations may claim that an act was not wrongful because there was consent to the act, because it was carried out in self-defence or because the act arose due to force majeure, distress or necessity. In the early phases, the discussion of whether an international organization may resort to countermeasures was left for discussion at a later date, as it was extremely controversial.[19] In the end, a circumscribed version of the taking of countermeasures was included as a circumstance precluding wrongfulness for international organizations, although many continue to express having difficulty imagining what sort of countermeasures an organization could take.[20] As for the other bases, necessity gave rise to the greatest controversy, but was accepted by the ILC. The conditions giving rise to these circumstances are most often those prevailing in peace operations or humanitarian emergencies.[21] Obviously, such circumstances cannot excuse any infringement of peremptory norms.[22]

For the purposes of this analysis, the most pertinent of these circumstances may be self-defence. Article 21 DARIO stipulates, 'The wrongfulness of an act of an international organization is precluded if and to the

---

[16] Ibid. See also Jan Klabbers, 'The Paradox of International Institutional Law' (2008) 5 *Intl Org L Rev* 151–173 at 165.

[17] See above, Chapter 6.

[18] See Special Rapporteur Gaja, 'Fourth Report on Responsibility of International Organizations', UN Doc A/CN.4/564 (28 February 2006) paras 5–46.

[19] This was finally dealt with in the Special Rapporteur's sixth report and in the ILC's 2008 session, but as it does not affect the issues addressed here, it will be left aside.

[20] ILC, 'DARIO with Commentaries', Article 22, p. 114.

[21] Self-defence and necessity are always discussed in relation to a peace operation being able to respond if attacked and to distinguish between general necessity and military or operational necessity (which the UN anyway insists is a basis for excluding responsibility). Moreover, the example for how an organization could infringe international law out of 'distress' was given by Pierre Klein (cited by the Special Rapporteur) as e.g. an organization needing to cross an international border in order to save the lives of refugees. See Gaja, 'Fourth Report', para. 33, note 40.

[22] ILC, 'DARIO with Commentaries', Article 26, p. 120.

extent that the act constitutes a lawful measure of self-defence under international law.' The ILC commentary indicates that this article was designed to replicate Article 21 ASR on self-defence; however, the DARIO article refers to international law rather than the UN Charter since international organizations are not parties to the Charter.[23] The ILC Commentary on Article 21 DARIO is not entirely clear as to whether it limits the concept of self-defence for international organizations as strictly analogous to that for states. It starts by saying 'For reasons of coherency, the concept of self-defence which has thus been elaborated with regard to States should also be used with regard to international organizations' even though it will rarely be relevant.[24] Adverting to the situation of peacekeeping and the interpretation of self-defence in that context, it goes on, 'While these references to "self-defence" confirm that self-defence represents a circumstance precluding wrongfulness of conduct by an international organization, the term is given a meaning that encompasses cases other than those in which a State or an international organization responds to an armed attack by a State. At any event, the question of the extent to which United Nations forces are entitled to resort to force depends on the primary rules concerning the scope of the mission and need not be discussed here.'[25]

With all due respect, this superficial treatment of an essential question is unsatisfactory. First of all, it does not state clearly that self-defence has both meanings: that of states and that accepted for peacekeeping when it comes to international organizations. One is left to wonder whether it is a backwards attempt to express that the latter understanding of self-defence is recognized *de lege lata* or whether it is not applicable for the purposes of the Draft Articles. In addition, the ILC failed to engage with the essential question as to whether, in the event that a UN peace operation used force in a manner that was *not* within its mandate but claimed it did so in self-defence, it can claim this circumstance precluding wrongfulness. Here, it would seem to be inadequate to rely solely on the reasoning and logic of the ASR.[26] These general points highlight some of the questions the DARIO raise. The main focus in this chapter, however, will be on its approach to attribution.

---

[23] ILC, 'DARIO with Commentaries', para. 5 of the Commentary to Article 21, p. 114.
[24] Ibid., para. 2 of the Commentary to Article 21, p. 113.
[25] Ibid., para. 3 of the Commentary to Article 21, pp. 113–114.
[26] See also Paolo Palchetti, 'Armed Attack Against the Military Force of an International Organization and Use of Force in Self-Defence by a Troop Contributing State: A Tentative Legal Assessment of an Unlikely Scenario' (2010) 7 *Intl Org L Rev* 241–260.

There are two rules that have been set out by the ILC on the attribution of conduct to an international organization and both are relevant to the potential use of PMSCs – especially those involved in peace operations. Article 6 DARIO addresses the attribution of conduct of the agents or organs of the organization itself, while Article 7 sets down the rule in respect to the conduct of agents or organs of a state or another international organization that are placed at the disposal of an international organization. As each article raises different issues for PMSCs and their various potential roles in peace operations, each head of attribution will be discussed separately in relation to the role most closely linked to it.

13.2   Attribution Under Article 7 DARIO – Troop Contingents

The rule to determine the attribution of conduct of national troop contingents in peace operations is set down in Article 7 DARIO. The key question is whether the acts of such troops should be attributed to the contributing states or to the international organization that is ostensibly carrying out the peace operation, bearing in mind that dual attribution is possible.[27] Article 7 places the focus of the analysis for attribution of conduct on the question of *control* over the impugned act or incident. Entitled 'Conduct of organs of a State or organs or agents of an international organization placed at the disposal of another international organization', it states:

> The conduct of an organ of a State or an organ or agent of an international organization that is placed at the disposal of another international organization shall be considered under international law an act of the latter organization if the organization exercises effective control over that conduct.

The rule clearly indicates that the standard to apply is 'effective control'. In addition, it is useful to highlight that the rule refers to control over conduct, not control over the organ or agent more generally. The bulk of the

---

[27] In the introduction to the chapter on attribution of the DARIO, the ILC Commentary states: '(4) Although it may not frequently occur in practice, dual or even multiple attribution of conduct cannot be excluded. Thus, attribution of a certain conduct to an international organization does not imply that the same conduct cannot be attributed to a State, nor does attribution of conduct to a State rule out attribution of the same conduct to an international organization. One could also envisage conduct being simultaneously attributed to two or more international organizations, for instance when they establish a joint organ and act through that organ.' ILC, 'DARIO with Commentaries', Chapter II, Commentary, p. 83, para. 4. The same remark was made in ILC, 'Report of the International Law Commission on the Work of Its 61st Session', UN Doc A/64/10 (2009) 56.

discussion to date has focused on the interpretation of 'effective control'. While that is an important issue, both elements of the rule must be considered in order to fully understand and assess the application of the rule and the surrounding controversies.

13.2.1   Article 7 – Lex lata *or a New Development?*

Before turning to a discussion of the content of the article, however, it is appropriate to consider the pedigree of the rule itself. Indeed, although the ways in which the rule has been applied have been contested, the rule itself does not seem to have been openly disputed often by states.[28] This leads to the question whether this rule can be considered to codify the *lex lata*, or whether it represents a new development. While states commenting on this rule during the drafting of the articles tended to support it as a relatively accurate representation of their understanding of the appropriate rule, the same cannot be said for international organizations.[29] The ILC specifically requested governments to provide their views to the Committee on 'the extent to which the conduct of peacekeeping forces is attributable to the contributing State and the extent to which it is attributable to the United Nations'.[30] In 2004, only two states responded directly to this question, and both indicated their belief that further study of the matter is required.[31]

There appears to be debate on two aspects of the rule: first, does this rule apply at all to UN-commanded and -controlled operations? This question can imply an assertion of a *lex specialis* for UN operations not reflected in the general rule, or an expression by a persistent objector that the general rule, as expressed, does not apply to the UN. Second, other practice raises

---

[28] See the controversial decision by the ECHR in *Behrami and Behrami v. France* and *Saramati v. France, Germany and Norway* (App nos 71424/01 and 78166/01) Decision on Admissibility (GC) ECHR 31 May 2007.

[29] In addition to the specific positions set out below, it should be pointed out that other organizations voiced some concerns that the rule as expressed did not accurately reflect the practice of international organizations when it comes to seconding or loaning individuals from one organization to another. Although those comments may be less relevant in terms of peace operations and PMSCs, they provide further evidence that the rule is far from unassailable from many points of view.

[30] ILC, 'Report of the International Law Commission on the Work of Its 58th Session', UN Doc A/58/10 (2003) para. 27. Note that only Mexico, Poland, Austria and Italy submitted comments and observations in response to this request.

[31] See ILC, 'Comments and Observations Received from Governments', UN Doc. A/CN.4/547 (6 August 2004). Only Mexico and Poland answered this question directly, and both rather called for 'further study' by the Commission on the issue.

the question whether the content of the rule reflects the standard states have understood as applicable when it comes to attribution of this kind of activity (i.e. military operations) even when not UN peace operations.

On the first question, for its part, the United Nations Secretariat insists that, while this rule may be appropriate generally speaking, when it comes to the division of responsibility between the UN and troop-contributing countries, only the UN understanding must prevail. It asserts that UN responsibility for the actions of troops in UN-commanded and -controlled operations (and a concomitant lack thereof for UN-authorized operations) is a long-standing principle that cannot be displaced by this rule.[32] It proclaims, 'In the practice of the United Nations, therefore, the test of "effective control" within the meaning of draft article 6 [now Article 7] has *never been used* to determine the division of responsibilities for damage caused in the course of any given operation between the United Nations and any of its troop-contributing States.'[33] It went on to say, 'This position continued to obtain even in cases – such as UNOSOM II in Somalia – where the United Nations command and control structure had broken down.'[34]

Another important international organization questioned the accuracy of the rule as stated by the ILC. In its comments on the penultimate version of the Draft Articles, the European Commission, after pointing to the controversy between the ECtHR and others, remarked,

> Regardless of the merits of the disagreements, the question must be asked whether the international practice is presently clear enough and whether there is identifiable *opinio juris* that would allow for the proposed standard of the International Law Commission (with thus far has not been followed by the European Court of Human Rights) to be codified in the current draft. There is no doubt that this remains a controversial area of international law . . . [35]

That statement represents a marked departure from its original position, where, in response to the question posed in 2004 on the extent to which the conduct of peacekeeping forces is attributable to the sending state or to the United Nations, the European Commission answered, 'The European

---

[32] ILC, 'Comments and Observations Received from International Organizations', UN Doc A/CN.4/637/Add.1 (17 February 2011), 13.
[33] Ibid., 13–14, para 3. Emphasis added.   [34] Ibid.
[35] ILC, 'Comments and Observations Received from International Organizations', UN Doc A/CN.4/637 (14 February 2011), 22. For its part, the ILO commented that the rule as expressed does not fully reflect the difference between agents on 'loan' and agents 'seconded' to an international organization. Ibid., p. 23.

Community does not take a position on [the question] as it does not relate to Community law.'[36] The change in perspective may be linked to the fact that the European Union began participating in peace operations in the intervening period. It may also reflect a view that the correct standard is that set by ECtHR's decision in *Behrami* – to which it alludes – in spite of the fact that that decision has been widely criticized (see below).

Additional state practice regarding states' sense of the attribution of responsibility between states and international organizations can be gleaned through their submissions to the ICJ in the *Legality of the Use of Force* cases. Indeed, even prior to the landmark cases of *Behrami* or *Al Jedda*, and before the ILC took up the project to draft articles on the subject, submissions by states regarding attribution of responsibility regarding the actions of states participating in the NATO Operation Allied Force in the pleadings on the *Legality of the Use of Force* cases addressed the issue. There is a certain ambiguity as to whether that practice supports the rule as adopted by the ILC.

First, some pleadings regarding the actions of the Kosovo Force (KFOR) mandated by UN SC Resolution 1244 (1999) indicate state support for the notion that the actions of troop contingents in peace operations authorized by the UN Security Council in which command and control was delegated to a different organization are attributable to the United Nations. For example, Philippe Kirsch, who drafted the pleadings for Canada, argued that, regarding the actions of KFOR in Kosovo,[37] a key party – the United Nations – had not been included among the defendants. Thus, Kirsch argued that, based on the *Monetary Gold* principle, those claims should be regarded as inadmissible. Significantly, Canada pleaded that KFOR's 'structure, mandate and activities are under the jurisdiction of the Security Council'. Citing the obligation to report to the Security Council as indicative of the fact that the 'Security Council did not create KFOR and then relinquish its authority', the pleadings assert, 'It is a Security Council activity, not a Canadian activity, that is the essential target of the inadmissible new claims.'[38] While this situation can be distinguished from *Behrami* in that the Yugoslav claim was made in regard to actions in

---

[36] ILC, 'Comments and Observations Received from International Organizations', UN Doc A/CN.4/545 (25 June 2004), 16.
[37] This was a new element Yugoslavia attempted to add to the proceedings.
[38] *Case Concerning Legality of Use of Force (Yugoslavia v. Canada)*, Preliminary Objections of Canada (July 2000), 56, paras 199–200. Germany and the United Kingdom raised a preliminary objection along the same lines: see *Case Concerning Legality of the Use of Force (Yugoslavia v. Germany)*, Preliminary Objections of the Federal Republic of Germany

Kosovo generally and not to one specific act or omission, it shows that the kernel of the notion of attribution of the actions of KFOR to the United Nations was discernible in international pleadings already in 2000. For its part, France argued that the setup of KFOR 'create[d] a "double veil" between the acts committed by KFOR and the responsibility which the FRY [Federal Republic of Yugoslavia] seeks to impute to France'.[39] At a minimum, all states in the *Legality of the Use of Force* cases argued that the actions of KFOR were attributable to NATO or to the UN and not to them.

Curiously, however, not all of the NATO participating states argued in the *Legality of the Use of Force* cases that their actions during the March–June 1999 bombing campaign – as opposed to the activities of KFOR following the adoption of Resolution 1244 by the UN Security Council – were attributable to NATO. Instead, the United Kingdom and Canada argued that key members of NATO participating states (i.e., the United States) that had played a significant role in the campaign were not and could not be parties before the dispute. As such, they argued, the case could not be heard on the basis of the *Monetary Gold* principle.[40] Despite having formulated an attribution argument in respect of another part of the case (KFOR), these states steered clear of making the same submission when it came to Operation Allied Force.

On the other hand, Italy and Portugal argued strongly that NATO itself should have been included as a party also in respect to Operation Allied Force on the grounds that their actions should have been attributable to NATO.[41] Italy appears to base its grounds for such attribution in the fact that it merely 'took part in the action decided within NATO' and emphasized NATO's decision-making role.[42] Portugal argued, 'As FRY recognizes throughout its Memorial . . . the acts which are the subject of the present proceedings are acts of NATO. Hence the references to "NATO aviation" or "acts of Nato". Indeed, all the political and military decisions were taken by NATO bodies, respectively its Council, its

---

(5 July 2000), paras 3.63–3.67; Preliminary Objections of the United Kingdom, paras 6.23–6.27.

[39] *Case Concerning the Legality of the Use of Force (Yugoslavia v. France)*, Preliminary Objections of France (July 2000), para. 27.

[40] Preliminary Objections of Canada, paras 189ff.; Preliminary Objections of the United Kingdom, paras 6.9–6.23.

[41] *Case Concerning Legality of the Use of Force (Yugoslavia v. Italy)* Preliminary Objections of the Italian Republic (3 July 2000), 19. *Case Concerning Legality of the Use of Force (Yugoslavia v. Portugal)*, Preliminary Objections of the Portuguese Republic (5 July 2000), paras 130–141.

[42] Preliminary Objections of Italy (ibid.), 19.

Secretary-General and its military authorities.'[43] For those two states, at least, the decision-making power of NATO was central to a determination of where attribution should lie. There is no mention of *control* as a factor in relation to a determination of attribution. In a similar vein, the French argument combines the *Monetary Gold* principle objection (that not all NATO states nor NATO itself were included in the pleadings) with a submission that 'Operation "Allied Force" was devised, decided and carried out by NATO as such and France never acted individually or autonomously.'[44] For its part, Belgium did not argue specifically that NATO should have been a party to the proceedings, but instead submitted that FRY had not made out a specific case as to how NATO's actions could be imputed to Belgium, thus, in a sense, reversing the starting point.[45]

These pleadings, together with the responses of governments and international organizations to the principle of attribution of responsibility as articulated by the ILC in the Draft Articles, support the notion that such acts can be attributed to international organizations rather than to states. However, they would seem to do little to clarify the basis of the contours of a test to determine that attribution. Three states appear to consider that the power to decide an action – including the power to make 'military decisions' – is a sufficient basis for attribution. That would appear to be a much looser basis than an 'effective control' standard; however, it does leave room for attribution to participating states in the event that states retained decision-making power within an operation. France's insistence that it 'never acted . . . autonomously' provides support for that view. Insofar as decision-making power is emblematic of effective control, the pleadings could be counted as state practice in support of the ILC's articulation of the rule. However, in order to determine whether control is truly effective, it is submitted that one needs much more detail on the scope of that decision-making power. Italy and Portugal appear to argue that the mere fact that NATO decided to undertake the operation as a whole means that every action within that operation must be attributable only to NATO. In my view, that practice does not support the ILC's rule as articulated. It does go some way to supporting the UN's view of the rule, however. France's position allows for a more nuanced view and could therefore potentially support the rule as expressed by the ILC.

---

[43] Preliminary Objections of Portugal, 38, para. 130. Footnotes omitted.
[44] Preliminary Objections of France, paras 41, 46–47.
[45] *Case Concerning Legality of the Use of Force (Yugoslavia v. Belgium)*, Preliminary Objections of the Kingdom of Belgium (5 July 2000), paras 468–478 esp. at 475.

This survey of prior practice and responses to the articulation of the rule seem to suggest that the ILC is on somewhat shaky ground in proposing this rule as a general rule also for the context of peace operations. Moreover, it should be pointed out that a number of other organizations also objected to the rule in other contexts. Some courts have begun applying the rule, however, meaning that new practice is being generated. Thus, while the ILC certainly did not codify an existing rule, it remains possible that states and international organizations will adopt the rule as expressed.

13.2.2   Effective Control, Troop-Contributing Countries and Peace Operations

Setting aside concerns that the rule expressed in Article 7 DARIO may be more *de lege ferenda* (if accepted) than a reflection of the *lex lata*, the analysis turns now to the specific content of the rule. The question that has been most debated in regard to this rule as expressed by the ILC is: what does effective control mean in this context? In particular, does it have the same meaning as 'effective control' for the purpose of Article 8 of the Articles on State Responsibility? Switzerland, in its comments to the ILC on this Draft Article, specifically requested clarification of the appropriate standard,[46] but the ILC did not clarify what the test means. It has been argued by academics that the standard is not the same as that for Article 8 ASR.[47] If one goes by the reasoning of the ECtHR in *Behrami*, 'effective control' indeed has a very different meaning than the same term for the ASR, as in that case the court was satisfied on the basis of a very loose 'ultimate authority and control' test.

As this rule has remained unchanged in substance from the time it was first proposed,[48] it is relevant to consider how courts have used the draft rule in its earlier iterations to interpret the final version. This exercise demands a look at case law from the ECtHR (*Behrami, Saramati* and *Al Jedda*) as well as national case law and comments by academic observers. At present, it appears that the meaning of 'effective control' for the

---

[46] See A/CN.4/636/Add.1 (13 April 2011), 11.

[47] In particular, Dannenbaum, 'Translating the Standard', but also Christopher Leck, 'International Responsibility in United Nations Peacekeeping Operations: Command and Control Arrangements and the Attribution of Conduct' (2009) 10 *Melbourne J Intl L* 346.

[48] See ILC, 'Report of the International Law Commission on the Work of Its 59th Session', UN Doc A/59/10 (2004), 109 (formerly Article 5). The only change from the first iteration to the final is the removal of the words 'that is placed at the disposal of another international organization'. These words remain only in the title of the draft article.

purposes of the DARIO is still in a state of flux. There are essentially two competing interpretations, which will be set out below.

Behrami and *Saramati v. France, Germany and Norway* and *Al Jedda v. United Kingdom*

In *Behrami*, the ECtHR was faced with a claim by the relatives of children in Kosovo who had been killed and injured by cluster bombs that had not been cleared following the conflict in 1999.[49] The claim was brought against France since the bombs were located in French KFOR's area of operations. The Court did not get to the merits of the case as it focused exclusively on admissibility, which it decided by determining whether the actions of French forces participating in KFOR were attributable to France. If the actions were not attributable to France, the court reasoned, the ECtHR would not have jurisdiction over the impugned conduct. In coming to the conclusion that the actions of French troops in KFOR were attributable to the United Nations (not even to NATO!), the Court came up with an all new standard of 'overall authority and control', even though it was ostensibly applying the relevant ILC Draft Article, which set the standard as effective control. Having acknowledged Draft Article 7 (at that time Draft Article 5), the ECtHR said, 'The Court considers that the key question is whether the UNSC retained *ultimate authority and control* so that *operational command only* was delegated.'[50] Oddly, the Court then purported to examine whether the method of delegation to set up the operation in Kosovo satisfied UN law, thereby entirely sidestepping the crucial issue of who or which entity actually had effective control over the impugned events.[51]

The ECtHR has been widely criticized for this decision and the judicial sleight of hand.[52] The International Law Commission responded critically to the ECtHR's analysis in a subsequent report on the Draft Articles, saying, 'One may note that, when applying the criterion of effective

---

[49] *Saramati* was a joined case relating to the lawfulness of an arrest by KFOR.

[50] *Behrami* and *Saramati*, para. 133. Emphasis added. Linos-Alexandre Sicilianos observes, 'Or, poser la question en ces termes c'était y répondre.' Linos-Alexandre Sicilianos, 'Entre multilatéralisme et unilatéralisme: l'autorisation par le conseil de sécurité de recourir à la force' (2008) 339 *RCADI* 9–436, 377–378. He points out that the Court was very much encouraged to take such an approach by the states appearing before it.

[51] See *Behrami* and *Saramati*, paras 134–141.

[52] The ILC (2009) report lists this criticism in note 102: P. Bodeau-Livinec, G. Buzzini and S. Villalpando, Case comment in 'International Decisions' (2008) 102 *AJIL* 323–331; K. Larsen, 'Attribution of Conduct in Peace Operations: The "Ultimate Authority and Control" Test' (2008) 19 *EJIL* 509 at 521–522; M. Milanovic and T. Papic, 'As Bad as It Gets: The

control, "operational" control would seem more significant than "ulti-mate" control, since the latter hardly implies a role in the act in question.'[53] In the commentary to the final version of the DARIO, the ILC repeated that statement and added that 'it is therefore not surprising that in his report of June 2008 on the United Nations Interim Administration Mission in Kosovo, the United Nations Secretary-General distanced himself from the latter criterion and stated: "It is understood that the international responsibility of the United Nations will be limited in the extent of its effective operational control."'[54] The ILC furthermore listed the extensive academic commentary criticizing the *Behrami* decision on this point.[55] Interestingly – and perhaps tellingly – it did not list the pleadings of the state parties to *Behrami* (and the state intervenors) that had led and encouraged the ECtHR to adopt its approach in the first place. However, it is equally important to note that some states, in their comments on the Draft Articles of the ILC, voiced their approval of ILC's rejection of the ECtHR's approach in *Behrami*.[56]

In this light, it is worth pointing out that the applicants in *Behrami* provided fairly detailed arguments regarding the control by NATO's KFOR in Kosovo and more specifically on the control in the area in question by 'French KFOR'. They argued that as the 'lead nation' in the region from June 1999 onward, French KFOR exercised overall control over the region, localized control over the specific area and control over the persons (*ratione personae*).[57] In terms of control over the area, the applicants

---

European Court of Human Rights *Behrami* and *Saramati* Decision and General International Law' (2009) 58 *ICLQ* 267 at 283–286; A. Sari, 'Jurisdiction and International Responsibility in Peace Support Operations: The *Behrami* and *Saramati* Cases' (2008) 8 *Human Rights L Rev* 151 at 164. See also Amina Maneggia, '"Controllo effetiva" e imputabilità della condotta nella decisione Behrami/Saramati della Corte europei del diritto dell'uomo', in C. Focarelli (ed.), *Le nuove frontiere del diritto internazionale* (Perugia: Morlacchi Editore, 2008), pp. 191–210 at pp. 197ff., calling the Court's approach 'incoherent' (p. 198).

53 ILC, 'Report of the International Law Commission on the Work of Its 61st Session' (2009), UN Doc A/64/10, 67.

54 ILC, 'DARIO with Commentaries', para. 10 of the Commentary to Article 7, p. 91, quoting UN Doc S/2008/354, para. 16.

55 Ibid., note 115.

56 See Belgium's remarks in UN Doc A/CN.4/636 (14 February 2011), 13–14. For its part, Germany took note of the ILC's interpretation on this point. See ibid., 14. Mexico also approved the ILC's approach in contrast to 'recent jurisprudence'. See UN Doc A/CN.4/636/Add.1 (13 April 2011), 11.

57 Parties' Observations: *Behrami and Behrami v. France* App no. 71412/01; *Saramati v. Germany, Norway and France* App no. 78166/01: Applicants' submissions as to admissibility prepared under the Practice Direction on Written pleadings issued in accordance with Rule 32 of the Rules of the Court of 1 Nov 2003 (as amended) and the Court's questions of 10 June 2006 (on file with author).

pointed out that '[t]he UNMIK police report annexed to the application and referred to in the Court's statement of facts makes it clear that not even the Belgian soldier accompanying the UNMIK CIVPOL officers considered that he could proceed further towards the scene of the events without the permission or presence of a senior French KFOR officer.'[58] This (albeit anecdotal) evidence strongly supports the notion that NATO command over KFOR cannot be viewed holistically, contrary to the Court's preferred approach. Otherwise, another NATO member of KFOR would not likely hesitate to enter an area of responsibility. It would indeed seem to be indicative of a high degree of operational control residing in the regional commands assigned to lead nations.

Moreover, in support of their claim that French KFOR had the authority to exclude Kosovar civilians from specific areas on account of security, the applicants pointed to the fact that the 'Commander of French KFOR created security exclusion zones ... on a number of occasions including in February 2000, one month before the incidents occurred.'[59] After the incident, it emerged that French KFOR had been aware for months that the site in question was contaminated but that it had not fenced it off because taking such action '"wasn't a high priority on their list"', as avowed by a French captain.[60] This candid response suggests that French KFOR had the freedom to determine its priorities and actions within its mandate – but it would have been highly relevant to know in more detail who or which entity set priorities within the mandate.[61] In the cases discussed below, it is apparent that national courts put stock in whether national contingents were taking orders from the UN commander or from their national departments of defence. Indeed, in *Nuhanovic v. the Netherlands,* the Dutch Court of Appeal held that in making a determination of effective control, 'significance should be given to the question whether that

---

[58] Ibid. Emphasis in original.   [59] Ibid.
[60] Ibid. Quotation from the report to the UNMIK police investigator, para. 12 of responses regarding the Violation of Article 2.
[61] Indeed, France, in its pleadings on the Preliminary Objections in the *Case Concerning the Legality of the Use of Force,* argued in July 2000, 'For its part, France participates actively in KFOR, but under operational control by NATO's SACEUR (Supreme Allied Commander Europe) and political control by the NAC (North Atlantic Council)' (para. 44). It continued, 'On the international level, responsibility for events having occurred after 10 June 1999 ... therefore lies primarily with NATO and to a lesser extent with the United Nations, which authorized KFOR's deployment and receives regular reports on its activities, but not with their member States, which do not enjoy freedom of action in Kosovo and which act under unified command and control. Accordingly, all acts by the French contingent or its members were carried out in the name of NATO, to whose power of direction and control they are subject).' Ibid., para. 45.

conduct constituted the execution of a specific instruction, issued by the UN or the State, *but also the question whether, if there was no such specific instruction*, the UN or the State had the power to prevent the conduct concerned.'[62] In *Behrami*, it was a question not of competing command or orders in regard to an incident (although responsibility for mines was shared between UNMIK and KFOR) but rather of the freedom to choose priorities within a broad mandate.

The ECtHR, in attributing the actions of French KFOR to the UN based on the correctness of the delegation of authority within UN law, completely sidestepped this analysis. This is unfortunate, as it would have been useful to have the court's opinion on whether freedom to choose priorities within a mandate (if indeed such existed) and within a multinational operation is sufficient to denote effective control over an act or omission. Indeed, freedom to choose (coupled with the actual exercise of that choice) would seem to reflect a certain degree of operational control, such that the conduct of the contingents should be attributable to the sending state for that conduct rather than to NATO or the UN, where such choices are the primary reason for the violation. In this case, the ECtHR found that NATO had operational control, which is an equally logical conclusion, but it did not deem 'operational control' to meet the necessary standard. Indeed, had the court found that NATO had operational control and declared that operational control was tantamount to 'effective control' for the purposes of Article 7 (then Article 5) DARIO, it is likely that few would have found significant fault with that decision. Moreover, as responsibility would have rested at the level of an organization, it might have gone some way to allaying fears about discouraging troop contributions (see below). Unfortunately, the Court did not take that path and instead came up with its convoluted scheme. The ECtHR has continued to apply the standard of ultimate authority and control in a series of other cases dealing with peace operations, such as *Beric v. Bosnia*,[63] *Kasumaj v. Greece*[64] and *Gajic v. Germany*.[65]

---

[62] *Nuhanovic v. the Netherlands*, BR 5388 Gerechtshof 's-Gravenhage 200.020.174/01 (5 July 2011), para. 5.8. Emphasis added (English version).

[63] *Beric and Others v. Bosnia and Herzegovina* (App nos 36357/04, 36360/04, 38346/04, 41705/04, 45190/04 . . .) Decision on Admissibility ECHR 16 October 2007.

[64] *Kasumaj v. Greece* (App no. 6974/05) Decision on Admissibility ECHR 5 July 2007.

[65] *Gajic v. Germany* (App no. 31446/02) Decision on Admissibility ECHR 28 August 2007. In another case dealing with the actions of a French soldier in UNIFIL, it has determined *propriu moto* that the case was inadmissible based on the rule that a case must be brought within six months. It came to the astonishing conclusion – considering that neither party presented evidence on this point – that the complainants should have realized that the investigations they had launched would never lead to any result and therefore brought

Recently, however, the ECtHR purported to distinguish from *Behrami* – on the facts – in a case involving an Iraqi national detained by UK forces participating in the Multi-National Force in Iraq.[66] In *Al Jedda v. UK*, the UK government – basing itself on the ECtHR's decision in *Behrami* – argued that UK forces in Iraq at the time of Mr Al Jedda's detention were operating pursuant to UNSC Resolution 1511 (2003) and that therefore the acts and omissions of British forces were solely attributable to the United Nations.[67] The European Court acknowledged that UNSC Resolution 1511 authorized a 'multinational force under unified command' and that '[t]he United States, on behalf of the multinational force, was requested periodically to report on the efforts and progress of the force' to the UN Security Council.[68] It coordinated with the UN civilian mission on the ground, the UN Assistance Mission in Iraq (UNAMI). Despite the similarity of this setup to the situation in *Behrami*, the Court refused to accept that 'as a result of the authorisation contained in Resolution 1511, the acts of soldiers within the Multi-National Force became attributable to the United Nations or – more importantly, for the purposes of this case – ceased to be attributable to the troop-contributing nations.'[69] In support of its conclusion distinguishing *Behrami* on the facts, the Court insisted on the fact that the Multi-National Force had already been present on the ground in Iraq at the time of the adoption of the resolution and that '[t]he unified command structure over the force, established from the start of the invasion by the United States and United Kingdom, was not changed as a result of Resolution 1511.'[70]

The Court's attempt to distinguish the two situations on the facts is so specious as to be almost laughable, were it not such a serious matter. In this light, it is important to recall that, although there was no *land* invasion of Serbia (or Kosovo) prior to the arrival of KFOR troops under UNSC Resolution 1244, that peace operation was preceded by a NATO-led

---

a case before the Court much sooner. *Atallah v. France* (App no. 51987/07) Decision on Admissibility ECHR 30 August 2011.

[66] *Al Jedda v. UK* (App no 27021/08) ECHR GC Judgment, 7 July 2011.

[67] Ibid., paras 64–68. Lord Rodger's separate opinion in the UK House of Lords decision specifically notes that the United Kingdom pleaded this aspect only subsequent to the ECtHR's decision in *Behrami*. See para. 49: 'First . . . counsel submitted that the acts of the British forces in detaining the appellant were to be attributed to the United Nations in international law. The [ECtHR] would accordingly be incompetent ratione personae to consider any application by him in respect of those acts. The point was not, and could not have been, argued in the courts below since it is based on the subsequent decision of the Grand Chamber of the [ECtHR] in *Behrami v France*.'

[68] Ibid., para. 79.   [69] Ibid., para. 80.   [70] Ibid.

bombing campaign that lasted three months. Given that UNSC Resolution 1244 specified that there should be 'substantial North Atlantic Treaty Organization participation' in KFOR and that it 'must be deployed under unified command and control' – which the ECtHR itself points out in its incomprehensible attempt to distinguish the two cases – one has to question the sincerity of the Court and the significance of the *Al Jedda* decision.[71] Indeed, Lord Rodger argued convincingly in his separate opinion in *Al Jedda* when it was before the House of Lords that the factual scenarios in *Behrami* and *Al Jedda* were virtually indistinguishable when it came to UN authorization and control over operations and, therefore, following the ECtHR's lead in *Behrami*, held that the actions of UK forces in Iraq were not attributable to the United Kingdom.[72] He even found that in certain respects, UNSC Resolution 1546 gave the UN Security Council more control over the operations in Iraq than UNSC Resolution 1244 gave it in Kosovo.[73]

One thing is for certain – in *Al Jedda* the European Court made no effort to shed new light on the relevant test for the purposes of Article 7 DARIO. It reaffirmed that the parties agreed that Article 7 DARIO was the appropriate test; however, it also repeated the standard it had invented for *Behrami* alongside the ILC's test. That is, it concluded, 'For the reasons set out above, the Court considers that the United Nations Security Council had neither effective control *nor ultimate authority and control* over the acts and omissions of troops within the Multi-National Force and

---

[71] See also Linos-Alexandre Sicilianos, 'Le Conseil de sécurité, la responsabilité des Etats et la Cour européenne des droits de l'homme: vers une approche intégrée?' (2015) 119 *Revue général de droit international public* 779–795, at 783. Sicilianos, a judge at the ECtHR, asserts that the Court corrected its approach in *Al Jedda* and acknowledges that the facts of the two cases are rather similar. At least one scholar argues that in *Al Jedda* the ECtHR has in effect overturned *Behrami*: see Francesco Messineo, 'Things Could Only Get Better: *Al-Jedda* Beyond *Behrami*' (2011) 50 *Military L and L War Rev* 321; given the series of cases that follow *Behrami* and the fact that the Court in *Al Jedda* rather appeared to restate its original position and assert that it was following *Behrami*, it remains to be seen. Moreover, in other cases where the Court has overturned itself, it has clearly stated the shortcomings of its prior approach. See, for example, *Vilho Eskelinen v. Finland* (App no. 63235/99) ECHR 17 April 2007, para. 52, overturning *Pellegrin v. France* (App no. 28541/95) ECHR 1999-VIII, para. 65.

[72] *R on the Application of Al Jedda v. Secretary of State for Defence* [2007] UKHL 58, Lord Rodger of Earlsferry, paras 87–91. Compare with that of Lord Bingham at para. 24, who asserts, 'The analogy with the situation in Kosovo breaks down, in my opinion, at almost every point.'

[73] Ibid. See esp. paras 97 and 99–101.

that the applicant's detention was not, therefore, attributable to the United Nations.[74] It thus neither disavowed its highly criticized test nor did it illuminate the content of that test or provide a convincing basis for distinguishing the situations on the facts. The reasons it set out did little to distinguish the facts in *Al Jedda* from those in *Behrami* and the court continued to gloss over the fact that ILC reports marshalling the evidence of state practice indicated that the actions of states during UN-*authorized* operations – even if they are peacekeeping operations – are not attributable to the UN due to the absence of UN command and control.[75] In addition, it failed to delve into the nitty-gritty details of effective control over the specific, impugned facts.[76]

Based on these two cases, in addition to those in which it followed its decision in *Behrami*, the ECtHR can be seen as seeking to take a 'holistic' approach to attribution: it classifies an entire operation as attributable to individual states partaking in that operation or not. The line the court purports to draw remains difficult to understand given that both operations in the two cases discussed here could be classified as UN-authorized operations on the facts. At the very least, this represents a blatant disregard for the UN's position on the matter. Nevertheless, it is important to observe that the Court applies the 'effective control' test (or the 'ultimate authority and control test', which it apparently seeks to keep alive) at a macro level.

This approach is questionable on several levels aside from the dubious factual basis for its findings, but on the face of it, it would seem consistent with the pleadings of some states in the *Legality of the Use of Force* cases discussed above. The macro-level approach means that the court does not concern itself with the reality of which actor actually had control over the situation at the time. While in the result the notion that the acts are attributable to the United Kingdom in *Al Jedda* may be satisfactory, the criteria the court used to arrive at that conclusion – still relying on its specious test – are not. Indeed, if the purpose of responsibility is to ensure that states and international organizations take the necessary steps to

---

[74] Ibid., para. 84. Emphasis added.

[75] For a useful summary, see Sicilianos, 'Entre multilatéralisme et unilatéralisme', especially at 370–375. The Court did acknowledge a possibility of dual attribution but failed to indicate what might be the basis for such a finding.

[76] It remains to be seen how the Court's approach in *Jaloud v. Netherlands* (App No. 47708/08) Judgment, 20 November 2014, paras 112–154, might affect the assessment of the existence of jurisdiction in cases involving a peace operation.

protect the human rights of those their actions affect, it only makes sense that the finding of control be realistic so as to demonstrate convincingly that the demands placed on them are also realistic.[77]

Commentators do not agree as to the correct approach. Laurence Boisson de Chazournes argues convincingly that a nuanced approach is required for this analysis. She points out that it is necessary to examine the specific facts in a given situation since the UN may maintain an important role for itself even in 'authorized' operations (she gives the example of the 'double key' test in Bosnia) and that even in UN-commanded and -controlled operations, states retain control over certain aspects of their forces.[78] She thus rejects the macro-level approach to effective control of the ECtHR. Others take an approach that is similar to the macro-level assessment outlined above, stating the rule thus:

> The question, whether the conduct of a peacekeeping force can be attributed to the international organization or to troop contributing States is determined by the legal status of the Force and agreements between the international organization and the contributing States.[79]

When it comes to equating 'command' and control with effective control, the distinct manner in which the United Nations has understood and exercised 'command' over peacekeeping forces can lead to confusion in the assessment of the existence of effective control.[80] As such, Alexander Orakhelashvili asserts, 'Even where strategic command is performed by the UN, all pertinent activities on the ground relating to the conduct of operations were effectively performed by national authorities' who transmit orders and 'prepar[e] contingents for duty'.[81] This approach may

---

[77] This conception of responsibility is apparent also in the ILC's discussion in plenary of what became Draft Article 7, the *Behrami* decision, and what to do about it. See in particular the comments of Ms Escarameia UN Doc A/CN.4/SR.2999 (18 May 2009), 10.

[78] Laurence Boisson de Chazournes, 'Les relations entre organisations régionales et organisations universelles' (2010) 347 *RCADI* 79–406 esp. at 317–320.

[79] Boris Kondoch, 'The Responsibility of Peacekeepers, Their Sending States, and International Organizations', in T. Gill and D. Fleck (eds.), *The Handbook of the International Law of Military Operations* (Oxford University Press, 2010), pp. 515–534, 519, para. 30.03.

[80] Kondoch explains that UN command is more like operational command than full command of armed forces. See ibid., 521, para. 30.04. See also Patrick Cammaert and Ben Klappe, 'Authority, Command, and Control in United Nations–Led Peace Operations', in Gill and Fleck, *The Handbook of the International Law of Military Operations*, pp. 159–162. See also Nigel White and Nicholas Tsagourias, *Collective Security: Theory, Law and Practice* (Cambridge University Press, 2013), pp. 368ff.

[81] Alexander Orakhelashvili, *Collective Security* (Oxford University Press, 2011), 327. This statement was not made in relation to the exercise of command for responsibility.

confuse command and control with the implementation of orders – while it is true that UN commanders may not be the ones giving the detailed orders to national troops, they usually determine priorities. In the cases discussed below, national courts suggest that that level of control would satisfy the text for 'effective control'. Nevertheless, Orakhelashvili's warning may serve to highlight some of the potential pitfalls of moving beyond a 'holistic' assessment of control. Yet another expert, Marten Zwanenburg, argues that the test to answer the question as to which entity (i.e. the troop-contributing state or the international organization) should be considered *a party to the conflict* – if indeed peacekeeping troops are involved in a conflict during the mission – should be the same as the test for responsibility.[82] This approach would again seem to suggest a 'holistic' approach à la *Behrami* rather than a more detailed consideration of which entity actually exercised control over the impugned acts or omissions. Indeed, it may be a factor but not the sole 'litmus' test. Even if the international organization is a party to the conflict, if within that operation a state were to go its own way, there may be room for attribution of the acts of its troops to the state rather than to the UN. Encouragingly, a judge of the European Court of Human Rights has recently expressed the view that the Court should delve more deeply into the details of each situation and take a case-by-case approach.[83]

In my view, the 'holistic' approach goes against the wording of the Draft Article. Draft Article 7 says that conduct may be attributed to whichever entity has effective control *over that conduct*. It refers not to effective control generally over the organ – in this case, the forces in the peace operation – but to specific control over the conduct. This speaks in favour of looking in detail at the circumstances of the impugned act or omission. In all fairness, however, it is important to recall that the Draft Articles are not a treaty – such that one may question whether they should be subject to regular rules of treaty interpretation – and that the ILC itself acknowledged that some of the rules are more *de lege ferenda* than *lex lata*, without specifying which rules or parts of rules may, in its estimation, be concerned.[84] It would indeed seem that this part of the rule, in addition

---

[82] Marten Zwanenburg, 'International Organisations vs Troops Contributing Countries: Which Should Be Considered as the Party to an Armed Conflict During Peace Operations?' (2012) 42 *Collegium* 23–28 at 26–27.

[83] Linos-Alexandre Sicilianos, 'Le Conseil de sécurité', 787.

[84] Vienna Convention on the Law of Treaties, Vienna, 23 May 1969, in force 27 January 1980, 1155 UNTS 331, Article 31(1). For the ILC's comment on this point, see ILC, 'DARIO with Commentaries', para. 5 of the General Commentary, p. 70.

to the way 'effective control' is to be interpreted, is still a matter of some controversy.

One commentator argues that the ECtHR's attempt to distinguish *Al Jedda* from *Behrami* on the facts may have been done in the guise of essentially overturning *Behrami* without openly saying so.[85] This may be an overly rosy view, but only time will tell. It is important to bear in mind that, while the approach of the ECtHR is important as an example of a regional court passing judgement on these issues, it is far from the only instance that can interpret and apply this law. Other international courts can apply it, as can national courts. The ECtHR does not have the last word on how Article 7 DARIO should be interpreted. Nonetheless, the fact that the UK government pleaded a lack of effective control over its forces in *Al Jedda* following the *Behrami* decision (whereas prior to that it had accepted that it was in control of its forces in UN-authorized operations) is indicative of how states may be likely to follow the Court's decisions – especially when it tends to absolve them of responsibility.

13.2.3   National Courts

National courts have decided cases involving questions of attribution and effective control in peace operations. Those courts have shown themselves to be willing to distinguish cases before them from *Behrami*. This includes a decision on admissibility by a Belgian court of first instance and a pair of jointly decided cases from the Netherlands. Two post-*Behrami* decisions from the Netherlands Court of Appeal approach the Article 7 DARIO analysis by looking into the details of the specific factual situation. By virtue of that approach, they attributed the conduct of the peacekeepers in question to the sending states rather than to the UN, even though the operations were UN commanded and controlled. This is indeed a far cry from the ECtHR's approach in *Behrami*. Although these cases arise from extraordinary facts, they strongly support the contention of Boisson de Chazournes that a nuanced analysis is essential and that one cannot presume that all conduct even in a UN-commanded and -controlled operation will be attributable to the UN. For that matter, nor can one assume that all conduct in UN-authorized operations is necessarily attributable to contributing states.[86] I will now turn to a more detailed discussion of the three cases.

---

[85] Messineo, 'Things Could Only Get Better', 323.
[86] As Messineo does, accepting entirely the UN's position and even asserting that Article 7 DARIO is not applicable at all to UN-authorized operations. Ibid., 336.

Mukeshimana-Ngulinzira v. Belgium

In *Mukeshimana-Ngulinzira v. Belgium*, the Belgian court of first instance had to decide the admissibility of a complaint by Rwandan nationals against the state of Belgium in regard to actions and omissions of Belgian troops during the genocide in 1994.[87] Belgium argued that the court had no jurisdiction over the case because a judgement necessarily implied the responsibility of the United Nations, which has immunity, and that of other states.[88] The court rejected that argument and also rejected the notion that the case bore any similarity to *Behrami* and *Saramati*.[89] In finding that it did have jurisdiction, the Court highlighted the fact that Belgium had put pressure on the UN in order to be able to withdraw its troops from UNAMIR following the attacks against Belgian forces.[90] That act is an exercise of the 'full control' that troop-contributing countries always retain in peace operations. It also appeared to consider relevant the fact that Belgium's highest priority was evacuating all Belgian nationals from Rwanda as quickly as possible.[91] The Court agreed with the claimants, who argued that the control over the troops in question had been withdrawn from UNAMIR and put under the exclusive responsibility of the Belgian state.[92]

Prior to agreement being given by the UN for the withdrawal of the Belgian contingent from UNAMIR, some Belgian forces were sequestered in the Ecole Technique Officielle (ETO) in Kigali, where 2,000 moderate Hutus and Tutsis had also taken refuge. When the Belgian forces left the ETO, the Rwandans remaining there were massacred within hours. In its preliminary statement of the facts, the court found that the Belgian forces, their Belgian commander and his superiors were aware of the dangers and the threat posed to the Rwandans and that no steps were taken to ensure the protection of the persons who had taken refuge there. Furthermore, the husband of Mme Mukeshimana, having participated in the negotiation of the Arusha accords, was specifically under UNAMIR protection but was left to fend for himself when the Belgian troops left the ETO.[93] He was killed when they left.

---

[87] *Mukeshimana-Ngulinzira v. Belgium* R.G. no. 04/4807/A and 07/15547/A, Tribunal de première instance, Bruxelles, Jugement avant dire droit (projection du film), 8 December 2010.

[88] Ibid., para. 25.

[89] The court did not reject the case in so many words, but it stated, 'On ne se trouve pas dans les conditions de la jurisprudence citée par l'ETAT BELGE où il était reproché à celui-ci d'avoir consenti *au sein* de l'OTAN, à une opération militaire, au Kosovo, décidée par l'OTAN, et d'y avoir apporté un soutien opérationnel.' Ibid., para. 26.

[90] Ibid., para. 14. This is the 'full control' that troop-contributing countries always maintain over their forces.

[91] Ibid., para. 15.   [92] Ibid., para. 25.   [93] Ibid., paras 15, 16 and 21.

Significantly, in light of the arguments made above regarding *Behrami*, the court found, 'Il n'y avait pas d'empêchement absolu, inhérent au mandat de la MINUAR ou aux circonstances de fait, que les soldats cantonnés à l'ETO y demeurent au-delà du 11 avril 1994 et continuent à faire bénéficier les réfugiés de l'ETO de leur presence.'[94] Thus, while the court's argument is not extensive, it supports the notion that where a state participating in a peace operation has the leeway to make decisions regarding its course of action and can set its own priorities, it can be responsible for its actions and omissions. In this case, it was sufficient even in the context of a UN-commanded and -controlled operation given that the Belgian government had withdrawn the force from UNAMIR. The court observed that neither the mandate nor the circumstances would have prevented Belgian forces from deciding to remain as a protective force. It held that it had jurisdiction, saying, '[L]es faits reprochés à l'Etat belge ne relevant pas de son action en qualité d'Etat participant à la MINUAR . . . '[95] This suggests that the mere fact that the troops were on the ground as part of the UNAMIR force did not mean that all of their actions are automatically attributable to the UN.

It should be pointed out that at this stage of the proceedings, in determining whether the actions of Belgian troops should be attributed to Belgium or to the UN, the Belgian court of first instance did not use the word 'attribution', although it did discuss 'exclusive responsibility' for the forces in question.[96] While 'responsabilité exclusive' is not the same as 'effective control', it is arguably more in line with that standard rather than a looser test of 'overall authority and control'. Furthermore, it should be noted that the court did not openly consider or apply the Draft Articles on the Responsibility of International Organizations – nor the Articles on State Responsibility, for that matter. It seems that the Belgian court looked both at the effective control over the Belgian troops in general and at the specific circumstances surrounding the evacuation of forces from the ETO. It is distinct from *Behrami*, however, in that it did not rely on the general legal structure of the operation to arrive at its conclusion regarding

---

[94] Ibid., para. 23. Author's translation: 'There was no absolute impediment, either inherent in the mandate or in the factual circumstances, for the soldiers stationed in the ETO to remain there beyond 11 April 1994 and to allow the refugees in the ETO to benefit from their presence.'

[95] Ibid., para. 26. Author's translation: 'as the facts for which the State of Belgium is reproached do not come under its action as a State participating in UNAMIR . . . '

[96] Ibid. The court approved the claimants' contention that the troops were under the 'responsabilité exclusive' of Belgium.

effective control over the forces, but it looked at the facts. In my view, this is already a step in the right direction.

Nuhanovic v. Netherlands and Mustafic v. Netherlands

In *Nuhanovic v. Netherlands* and in *Mustafic v. Netherlands*, the Dutch Court of Appeal and Dutch Supreme Court were faced with claims that the Dutch forces present in Potocari, Bosnia, in 1995 failed to do what they could to protect members of the Nuhanovic and Mustafic families. The Dutch forces were participating members of UNPROFOR. Both Nuhanovic and Mustafic were working for the Dutch contingent of UNPROFOR; they themselves were evacuated but members of their families were not and were killed by Bosnian Serb forces. The lucidity of the judgement in these cases makes it worthwhile to quote rather extensively as it helps to illuminate a number of important aspects of the 'effective control' test and the state–UN relationship in peace operations.[97]

The claimants were appealing the decision of the District Court, which had held, in part, that

> there could be a reason for attribution of Dutchbat's conduct to the State in case the State had violated the UN command structure, if Dutchbat had been instructed by the Dutch authorities to ignore UN orders or to go against them and Dutchbat had behaved in accordance with this instruction from the Netherlands, or if Dutchbat to a greater or lesser extent had backed out of the structure of UN command, with the consent of those in charge in the Netherlands, and considered or demonstrated themselves for that part as exclusively under the command of the competent authorities in the Netherlands; however, there are insufficient grounds for attribution to the State in case of parallel instructions . . . [98]

The court of first instance thus set up a non-cumulative test to determine which entity had effective control over the troops, essentially looking factually at which entity was giving orders to the forces during the events in question. Significantly, parallel instructions were not sufficient.

On appeal, the claimants attempted to take a different tack and argued that the issue of attribution should be governed by Bosnian law.[99] The

---

[97] The decisions share an identical analysis in terms of the state–UN relationship and the question of effective control; however, they are distinct in the facts surrounding each of the claimants.

[98] As summarized by the Dutch Court of Appeal, *Nuhanovic v. Netherlands*, para. 3.8(ix). It may be noted that the notion that a contingent that has 'backed out of UN command' resonates with the Belgian court's finding in *Mukeshimana-Ngulinzira*, quoted above.

[99] *Nuhanovic*, para. 5.2.

Court of Appeal disagreed and reframed the question as solely one of international law, stating:

> The question here is not whether the Dutchbat troops acted wrongfully with respect to Nuhanovic, but whether, based on an agreement concluded or not between the State and the UN ... for the deployment of troops, the actions of these troops that are placed at the disposal of the UN should be attributed to the State, the UN or possibly to both.[100]

Nuhanovic specifically pleaded that, in the context of a Chapter VII peace-keeping mission, "'command and control' can only be transferred by an explicit act based on an agreement' and claimed that there was no such agreement.[101] The Court disagreed with that contention and insisted, 'No special procedural requirements are applicable to this kind of agreement', but that such agreement could be inferred by the facts.[102] The Court held that Dutchbat had indeed been placed under UN command but, crucially, went on to say:

> Whether this also implies that 'command and control' had been transferred to the UN, and what this actually means, can remain an open question because, as will appear hereafter, Nuhanovic is right in asserting that the decisive criterion for attribution is not who exercised 'command and control' but who actually was in possession of 'effective control'.[103]

The Court thus rejected the UN's preferred approach. It went on to cite the relevant Draft Article of the ILC on the matter (Article 6 at the time) and clarified:

> Although strictly speaking this provision only mentions 'effective control' in relation to attribution to the 'hiring' international organization, it is assumed that the same criterion applies to the question whether the conduct of troops should be attributed to the State who places these troops at the disposal of that other international organization.[104]

As I pointed out above, Article 7 DARIO refers to effective control over *conduct*, a fact that was not lost on the Dutch Court. It said,

> Moreover, the Court adopts as a starting point that the possibility that more than one party has 'effective control' is generally accepted, which means that it cannot be ruled out that the application of this criterion results in the possibility of attribution to more than one party. For this reason the

---

[100] Ibid., para. 5.3. The Court of Appeal's approach was not challenged on appeal and was upheld by the Supreme Court, *State of the Netherlands v. Nuhanovic*, First Chamber, 12/03324, 6 September 2013, para. 3.6.2.

[101] Ibid., para. 5.6.   [102] Ibid., para. 5.7.   [103] Ibid.   [104] Ibid., para. 5.8.

Court will only examine if the State exercised 'effective control' *over the alleged conduct* and will not answer the question whether the UN also had 'effective control'.[105]

The Court specified that it 'attaches importance to the fact that the context in which the alleged conduct of Dutchbat took place differs in a significant degree from the situation in which troops placed under the command of the UN normally operate', as was the case in *Behrami* and *Saramati*.[106] In this regard, it considered the unique circumstance that the mission had failed and that Dutchbat was pulling out of the area, similar to the circumstances above in *Mukeshimana-Ngulinzira*. It was thus easily able to escape having to point out that *Behrami* was also not a case in which troops were placed under UN command and control. In *Nuhanovic*, the fact that the Dutch government participated in decision-making regarding the actions of the force 'at the highest level' and issued orders to its commanders on the ground regarding the withdrawal of Dutchbat were important to the court's finding.[107]

The Dutch Supreme Court added an important element to this analysis. First, it emphasized the possibility of dual attribution provided for in Article 48 of the DARIO and in the commentaries to the Draft Articles.[108] Furthermore, it affirmed that the forces a state contributes to a peace operation should be examined under Article 7 of the DARIO.[109] Finally, the Supreme Court analyzed the facts closely, confirming that a state does not have to go against or override the orders given by the UN commander in order to be considered to exercise effective control.[110] Relying on the ILC's commentary to Article 7 of the DARIO, the Court held that 'the attribution of conduct to the seconding State or the international organization is based on the factual control over the *specific conduct*, in which all factual circumstances and the special context of the case must be taken into account.'[111] The Dutch Supreme Court thus upheld the analytical approach of the Court of Appeal.

The difference in the approach of the national courts as compared with the ECtHR is a move away from relying solely on the formal (legal)

---

[105] Ibid., para. 5.9, emphasis added.
[106] Ibid., para. 5.10. This was patent lip-service to the ECtHR as the Dutch Court would have been fully aware that KFOR troops were not under UN command but under NATO command.
[107] Ibid., paras 5.12, 5.13, 5.18.
[108] Dutch Supreme Court, *State of the Netherlands v. Nuhanovic*, First Chamber, 12/03324, 6 September 2013, paras 3.9.4 and 3.11.2.
[109] Ibid., paras 3.10.1–3.10.2.   [110] Ibid., para. 3.11.3.   [111] Ibid. Emphasis added.

structure of the relationships toward an assessment of how they played out in reality and in particular in relation to the facts related to the complaints. As such, they do not clearly articulate an alternative test for control, and studiously distinguish their approach from that of the ECtHR in *Behrami* ostensibly on the facts. They do, however, display an encouraging willingness not to hide behind facile, formal constructions of the relationships at issue.

While the Dutch court clearly reserved to itself the right to find that in a 'normal' situation of peacekeeping, it could base its analysis on the formal relationship (insofar as it affirmed the legitimacy of the approach in *Behrami* given a different set of facts), it is worth pointing out that pre-*Behrami*, the UK government did not contest that the conduct of the troops it had contributed to KFOR should be attributed to the United Kingdom. In the 2004 case *Bici v. Ministry of Defence*, a UK court dealt with a complaint regarding an incident in which British soldiers in KFOR in Pristina shot and killed two men and injured two others during a nighttime demonstration in 1999, allegedly in self-defence. The key point here is that the judge summed up the UK government's position as follows:

> The defendant has conceded that it is vicariously liable for any wrongs committed by any of the soldiers. The Crown retained command of the British forces notwithstanding that they were acting under the auspices of the U.N.[112]

That is, pre-*Behrami*, the UK government did not contest that, as it had command of the UK forces in Kosovo under KFOR, it bore responsibility for any wrongful acts of those forces.[113] Indeed, the ECtHR's decision and approach in *Behrami* are even more astonishing in light of this case. Furthermore, KFOR was under NATO – not UN – command and control, which may imply an even looser relationship in *Bici* than that alluded to by the Dutch court in *Nuhanovic*. Nevertheless, the UK government's concession in *Bici* confirms the correctness of a fact-based approach to attribution rather than an abstract 'legal framework' approach.

In its commentary to Article 7 DARIO, the ILC confirms the correctness of a fact-based approach. It says,

---

[112] *Bici and Bici v. Minister of Defence*, High Court of Justice, Queen's Bench, Leeds (7 April 2004), para. 2.

[113] In the case in question, the Crown argued that the soldiers acted in personal self-defence and therefore the acts were not wrongful.

> The criterion for attribution of conduct either to the contributing State or organization or to the receiving organization is based according to article 7 on the factual control that is exercised over the specific conduct taken by the organ or agent...[114]

It cites with approval a comment by the United Kingdom that this analysis needs to consider the "'full factual circumstances and particular context'".[115] This would seem to allow for the nuanced approach recommended by Boisson de Chazournes, recognizing that there can be blurring across the lines.

Such an approach is, however, rejected out of hand by the United Nations. It insists that the effective control test may indeed apply, but that it may only be interpreted as distinguishing UN-commanded and -controlled operations (for which the conduct of forces must be attributed to the UN) and UN-authorized operations (for which no such attribution is possible).[116] The Secretariat insisted,

> It has been the long-established position of the United Nations... that forces placed at the disposal of the [UN] are 'transformed' into a United Nations subsidiary organ and, as such, entail the responsibility of the Organization, just like any other subsidiary organ, regardless of whether the control exercised over all aspects of the operation was, in fact, 'effective'. In the practice of the United Nations, therefore, the test of 'effective control' within the meaning of draft article 6 has never been used to determine the division of responsibilities for damage caused in the course of any given operation between the United Nations and any of its troop-contributing States.[117]

With all due respect, the UN's position suffers from the same fault of relying on formal structures to determine results in the abstract as plagues the much-criticized *Behrami* decision.[118] What the ILC's draft article calls for is a more detailed assessment of the facts on the ground in order to settle the question as to which entity exercised effective control over the conduct in question. As Boisson de Chazournes and others argue, the analysis must not be limited to a determination as to whether the acts occurred

---

[114] ILC, 'DARIO with Commentaries', para. 4 of the Commentary to Article 7, pp. 87–88.
[115] Ibid., citing UK comments from A/C.6/64/SR.16, para. 23.
[116] ILC, 'Comments and Observations Received from International Organizations', UN Doc A/CN.4/637/Add.1 (17 February 2011), 13.
[117] Ibid., 13–14.
[118] Messineo, 'Things Could Only Get Better', 336, falls into the trap of accepting the UN assertion of uniform practice, which neglects the case law cited here (and to which Messineo makes passing reference).

in the context of a UN-commanded and -controlled operation or a UN-authorized operation.

In my view, the classification of an operation as a UN-commanded and -controlled operation or other does no more than set up a rebuttable presumption: in operations under UN command, a Court may start from the premise that acts of national contingents are attributable to the UN, but, on careful analysis of all of the evidence and the facts, it may find that conduct should in fact be attributed to a state or another international organization. In UN-authorized operations, the presumption may be reversed, that attribution would prima facie seem to be to the international organization commanding the operation (e.g., NATO) or to individual participating states and not to the UN, but again here, that presumption could be refuted depending on the facts.

The Rwanda and Srebrenica cases arose out of extraordinary sets of facts that – I fervently hope – will not be repeated. But the fact that such scenarios are unlikely to recur does not mean that we can simply take a holistic approach from now on. Indeed, there are many reasons to support the test proposed by Dannenbaum, 'control most likely to be effective in preventing the wrong in question'.[119] Alternatively, even if one accepts the pure dichotomy insisted on by the United Nations, the effects of that position can be appropriately nuanced by recognizing the dual responsibility of the state.[120]

One may question, however, how far the nuanced approach can go. The test asserted by the complainants in *Behrami* and apparently endorsed by the Dutch court in *Nuhanovic* creates the potential for almost always attributing conduct – and especially omissions – to troop-contributing states since it demands a look at whether a state had the leeway to act in order to prevent a violation. In the case of *Nuhanovic* and *Mustafic* and again in the case of *Mukeshimana-Ngulinzira*, the scope of that responsibility was limited in that the obligation was construed by the courts as being owed to specific individuals whose individual cases were well known by the state authorities in question. It did not extend to an overall obligation to act vis-à-vis an entire population whose life was under threat. This is a key issue in light of the development of the doctrine of the responsibility to protect and especially the protection of civilians in peacekeeping

---

[119] See Dannenbaum, 'Translating the Standard', 114 and 156–183. See also Leck, 'International Responsibility in UN PKOs', 346–364.

[120] This appears to be the approach of Kondoch, 'Responsibility of Peacekeepers', para. 30.07: 'Sending States are responsible for all acts performed by peacekeepers on their behalf.'

operations. The Dutch Court at the level of first instance set up a higher standard of competing orders – that only when national troops contravened or strayed from UN orders would the state be responsible. Yet in a case of parallel orders, it held, no attribution was to lie with the state. And what about a case of 'no orders' at all in respect of a particular situation? Kondoch argues, 'In regard to omissions, States are responsible, if there was a duty to act.'[121] This of course leads to a questioning of how the primary and secondary obligations fit together.

The UN and many troop-contributing countries may prefer to have a more simplistic reading as it may seem to create more certainty at the moment when the UN is attempting to staff missions and to dispel fears related to future costs and lawsuits. Indeed, the ECtHR clearly telegraphed its results-based reasoning in *Behrami* and *Saramati*. The ECtHR repeated all of the state parties' public policy arguments that a finding of state responsibility for such action would have 'serious repercussions' on the ability of the UN to acquire troop contributions from responsible states.[122] The Court heard those arguments loud and clear, holding that

> the Convention cannot be interpreted in a manner which would subject the acts and omissions of Contracting Parties which are covered by UNSC Resolutions and occur prior to or in the course of such missions, to the scrutiny of the Court. To do so would be to interfere with the fulfilment of the UN's key mission in this field including, as argued by certain parties, with the effective conduct of its operations.[123]

With all due respect, it is a weak court indeed that would find that obliging states to protect human rights while carrying out actions in the name of international peace and security as determined by the UN Security Council would undermine the effectiveness of such operations. It is extraordinary that a human rights court would bow to the pressure – especially in a post-9/11 security climate – that protecting international peace and security would be hampered if one had also to respect one's human rights obligations.

Furthermore, there may be a concern that extensive litigation along these lines can be expensive for all – and the impossibility of suing the UN in national courts or anywhere else may push people to try to sue states. The ILC in its commentary stated that the Draft Articles do not state when

---

[121] Ibid.
[122] *Behrami and Behrami*, paras 90 (Norway), 94 (France and Norway), 108 (Germany), 111 (Poland), 115 (UK).
[123] Ibid., para. 149.

an act is not attributable to international organizations, preferring to focus on the positive rules of attribution. Thus, it says, 'the articles do not say, *but only imply*, that the conduct of military forces of States or international organizations is not attributable to the United Nations when the Security Council authorizes States or international organizations to take necessary measures outside a chain of command linking those forces to the United Nations.'[124] That interpretation is affirmed in standard works on the subject.[125] This statement can be found in the introductory section to the articles on attribution, rather than in the specific commentary on Article 7 DARIO.[126]

As for the EU position on responsibility for the actions of peacekeepers in the course of peace operations under EU command and control, according to Gert-Jan van Hegelsom, the contributing state (whether it be an EU state or a third state) 'is responsible for the settlement of claims caused by its personnel as well as for the conduct of disciplinary and/or judicial proceedings against the personnel of that State'.[127]

13.2.4   Responsibility in the Hypothetical Situation of PMSCs as a Troop Contingent

We have seen that the allocation of responsibility for conduct of troops participating in a UN-mandated peace operation, despite the ILC's draft articles, remains a relatively unsettled area of law. Although there is agreement on the broad principles that responsibility of states and international organizations may be engaged, the devil is in the details. For the purposes of this study, the next issue is, what additional complications or questions would the use of a PMSC as a state troop contribution raise? We note that the use of private actors in peace operations was present in the minds of at least one state during the drafting of the DARIO: Austria, which in its comments and observations to the ILC on the penultimate draft regretted that the DARIO did not deal with private actors in this context.[128] There

---

[124] ILC, 'DARIO with Commentaries', para. 5 of General Commentary on Part II, Attribution, p. 83.

[125] See in particular, Kondoch, 'Responsibility of Peacekeepers', paras 30.04 and 30.06.

[126] ILC, 'DARIO with Commentaries', para. 5 of General Commentary on Part II, Attribution, p. 83.

[127] Gert-Jan van Hegelsom, 'Command and Control Structure in Peace Operations: The Concrete Relationship Between the International Organization and Its Troops Contributing Countries' (2011) *Collegium* 77–82 at 81.

[128] ILC, 'Comments and Observations Received from Governments', UN Doc A/CN.4/636 (14 February 2011), 13, para. 2 of Austria's comments on Draft Article 7.

may indeed seem to be a significant question when it comes to PMSCs used as a troop contribution.

As pointed out above, Article 7 DARIO deals with attribution when a state sends an *organ* to an international organization. However, I have argued that PMSCs as troop contingents would be a state organ only if they were attributable de jure or de facto under Article 4 ASR, and it is generally accepted that this is unlikely to be the case given the high threshold international courts and tribunals have set for attribution on this head. If it were the case that PMSCs were attributable as a state organ, in any case many of the issues related to the PMSC question as a whole fall away because we are no longer dealing with a private actor.[129] But if the conduct of PMSCs participating in a peace operation is not attributable to states under Article 4 ASR, that would raise the following important question: given that Article 7 DARIO is arguably based on the premise that the conduct of organs lent from a state to an international organization is prima facie automatically attributable to both (due to the clear legal relationship with both), can that Article provide the framework of reference for PMSC troop contingents that may be attributable to the sending state under a different head of attribution?

It appears that the ILC anticipated such a scenario. The commentary to Article 7 DARIO specifically states that for this article, the definition of a state organ would be wide enough to encompass the conduct of persons or entities that is attributable to states on the basis of Articles 5 or 8 ASR.[130] The ILC provides no support for this rule of interpretation, which it introduces in light of the fact that Article 7 DARIO mentions only 'organs' and not 'agents' or individuals, but which goes far beyond that problem.

If, as is persuasively argued by Dannenbaum and as generally accepted here based on the analysis of the cases from national courts above, the proper way to interpret the 'effective control' test for Article 7 DARIO is to place responsibility with the entity in possession of 'control most likely to be effective in preventing the wrong in question', as that test demands an approach wholly based on the detailed facts of the situation, it will yield an odd result. One could surmise that the conduct of a PMSC troop

---

[129] With the important exception of the question whether the staff of the PMSC have combatant status or are members of the armed forces of the state, which may not be the case even if they are an organ of the state.

[130] ILC, 'DARIO with Commentaries', para. 2 of the Commentary to Article 7, p. 87. The Commentary states, 'the term "organ", with reference to a State, has to be understood in a wide sense, as comprising those entities and persons whose conduct is attributable to a State according to articles 5 and 8 [ASR]'.

contingent that would be attributable to a state based on Article 8 ASR would likely remain attributable to that state under Article 7 DARIO if the nuanced test of effective control is applied. If the approach of the UN secretariat (and the ECtHR) is followed, however, and if the alleged violation occurred in the context of a UN-commanded and -controlled operation, we would find ourselves in the extraordinary situation in which conduct that would be attributable to a state based on a high degree of control – including, according to some views, control over the violation itself – would be attributable not to the state but to the UN. Although legally such a construction is perfectly possible, it is illogical if the purpose of responsibility is to ensure that the entity with the capacity to act to prevent or suppress a violation of international law will actually take steps to do so.

If, on the other hand, the conduct of PMSCs participating in a peace operation under UN command and control is attributable to the sending state on the basis of Article 5 ASR, the sending state is not likely to exercise a high level of control over that conduct (although it will always be necessary to examine the facts in question). If the standard asserted by the UN is applied, then attributing the actions of such PMSC 'troops' to UN-commanded and -controlled operations is likely to produce a logical result in that the degree of control exercised by the UN will be commensurate with its responsibility. If a more detailed, case-by-case test for effective control is applied, it can be surmised that in most cases, the conduct of Article 5 ASR PMSCs will be attributable to the UN and not to the sending state. On the other hand, the flow of attribution of conduct when a PMSC is delegated the task of performing the role of troop contingent in a peace operation (i.e. Article 5 ASR attribution) may provide a disincentive for a state to take the initiative to fulfil its due diligence obligations to ensure the respect of IHL and IHRL by such forces if such action would entail exercising greater control over the PMSC. From a policy perspective, this may produce an undesirable result.

13.3   Attribution Under Article 6 DARIO – Agents and Organs: CIVPOL? Security Guards?

Article 6 DARIO reads,

1. The conduct of an organ or agent of an international organization in the performance of functions of that organ or agent shall be considered an act of that organization under international law, whatever position the organ or agent holds in respect of the organization.

2. The rules of the organization shall apply in the determination of the functions of its organs and agents.

On its face, this rule requires what would appear to be a straightforward analysis as to whether PMSCs may be considered the organs or agents of international organizations, as well as an assessment as to whether the act occurred 'in the performance of functions of that organ'. If their conduct is attributable to the organization, and if that conduct constitutes a breach of an international obligation in force for that organization, then the organization is responsible for the PMSC's act.[131]

13.3.1 General Comments on Article 6 DARIO – Lex lata or de lege ferenda?

Article 6 DARIO cannot be considered in isolation, however, as it is closely linked to other concepts defined in the draft articles. In particular, the draft articles provide a definition of the term 'agent' in Article 2(d): "'agent of an international organization'" means an official or other person or entity, other than an organ, who is charged by the organization with carrying out, or helping to carry out, one of its functions, and thus through whom the organization acts.'[132] This is a change from the definition proposed in the Articles for the first reading, which stated, "'Agent' includes officials and other persons or entities through whom the organization acts.'[133] The new version is designed to reflect the International Court of Justice's definition in the *Reparation for Injuries* case.[134] In its commentary, the ILC cited the opinion of the ICJ in *Reparation for Injuries* in order to flesh out the definition of an 'agent':

> the Court understands the word 'agent' in the most liberal sense, that is to say, any person who, whether a paid official or not, and whether permanently employed or not, has been charged by an organ of the organization

---

[131] Article 4 DARIO stipulates these two requirements as elements of an internationally wrongful act of an international organization.

[132] Article 2(d) DARIO, ILC, 'DARIO with Commentaries', p. 73.

[133] Article 2(c) in the DARIO set out in ILC, 'Report of the International Law Commission on the Work of Its 64th Session' (2009), UN Doc A/64/10. This definition was previously a part of the article on attribution that became Article 5, but (along with the definition of rules of the organization) was moved from that article to Article 2 as a more general definition.

[134] ILC, 'Eighth Report on Responsibility of International Organizations' (Special Rapporteur Gaja), UN Doc A/CN.4/640 (14 March 2011), para. 21.

with carrying out, or helping to carry out, one of its functions – in short, any person through whom it acts.[135]

Articles 6 and 2(d) DARIO clearly represent, in part, a codified version of the ICJ's definition of an 'agent'.

The reference to 'entities' is intended to take into account the fact that '[i]nternational organizations do not act only through natural persons, whether officials or not.'[136] This formulation allows for the actions of legal persons, such as the NGO implementing partners of UN agencies, to be attributable to the UN[137] and could be highly relevant for private companies such as PMSCs. It is also important to observe that the first definition was phrased in an inclusive, rather than an exhaustive manner, whereas the final version has dropped the term 'includes' but remains broad.

Furthermore, paragraph 6(2) DARIO identifies the 'rules of the organization' as one of the means to determine the functions of the organization and its agents, but the ILC insists in its commentary that the 'wording of paragraph 2 is intended to leave the possibility open that, in exceptional circumstances, functions may be considered as given to an organ or agent *even if this could not be said to be based on the rules of the organization*'.[138] In separate comments to the ILC on a previous version of the Draft Articles, both the ILO and UNESCO argued that 'it remains unclear what such "exceptional circumstances" could be' and requested that the ILC provide examples.[139] In the final version, the ILC has maintained the argument

---

[135] ICJ Rep [1949] 177, cited in ILC, 'DARIO with Commentaries', para. 23 of the Commentary to Article 2, p. 79. Pierre Klein points to the very same definition: P. Klein, 'The Attribution of Acts to International Organizations', in J. Crawford, A. Pellet and S. Olleson (eds.), *The Law of International Responsibility* (Oxford: Oxford University Press, 2010), pp. 297–315 at p. 298.

[136] Commentary to Art 2 DARIO (para. 19), UN Doc A/64/10 (2009), p. 51; repeated in final commentary: ILC, 'DARIO with Commentaries', para. 25 of the Commentary to Article 2, p. 79.

[137] Klein, 'Attribution', p. 301, referring to the relations between UNHCR and its implementing partners, at note 20 (arguing on the basis of effective control, but the fact that NGOs are legal persons is no less important).

[138] ILC, 'DARIO with Commentaries', para. 9 of the Commentary to Article 6, p. 86. Emphasis added. The same remark was made in an earlier version of the Commentary to the Draft Articles before adoption: see para. 9 of the Commentary to Article 5, ILC, 'Report of the 64th session', UN Doc A/64/10 (2009), 61. Similarly, the ASR specify that international law will not always follow domestic law of states in terms of determining what or who is a state organ for the purposes of attribution for state responsibility. See para. 11 of the ILC's Commentary to Article 4 ASR.

[139] Quotation from the comments of the ILO, A/CN.4/568/Add.1 (12 May 2006) at 10; see also 11 for UNESCO's comments.

and no such examples have been forthcoming. The 'rules of the organization' themselves are defined in Article 2(b) and mean 'in particular, the constituent instruments, decisions, resolutions and other acts of the international organization adopted in accordance with those instruments, and established practice of the organization'.[140]

Prior to considering how Article 6 DARIO may apply to PMSCs as CIVPOL or security guards in peace operations, or in other roles, it is worth taking a moment to assess whether the rule as expressed represents a codification of an existing principle of international law, reflects customary law, or whether it somehow deviates from or builds on an identifiable existing rule.

Special Rapporteur Gaja has acknowledged that that article is meant to be an amalgamation of Articles 5 and 8 of the ASR – that is, 'persons or entities exercising elements of the governmental authority' and persons or a group 'acting on the instructions of, or under the direction and control of' a state.[141] The ILO stated its concern that this approach rendered the article overly broad.[142] Furthermore, it argued that the rule does not reflect current practice.[143] UNESCO specifically raised the issue of the attributability of private contractors in this regard. Taking issue with the penultimate definition of 'agent' encompassing 'other persons or entities through whom the organization acts', UNESCO pointed to the following clause, which it inserts in contracts between it and its private contractors:

> Neither the contractor, nor anyone whom the contractor employs to carry out the work is to be considered as an agent or member of the staff of UNESCO and, except as otherwise provided herein, they shall not be entitled to any privileges, immunities, compensation or reimbursements, nor are they authorized to commit UNESCO to any expenditure or other obligations.[144]

UNESCO went on to say,

> Although the same types of activity [as are contracted out] could be carried out by UNESCO officials, in the case of contractors UNESCO is of the view that acts performed by the latter may not be considered as acts of the

---

[140] See ILC, 'DARIO with Commentaries', paras 16–19 of the Commentary on Article 2 for further detail on this definition (pp. 78–79).
[141] UN Doc A/CN.4/610 (27 March 2009) 8, para. 228.
[142] UN Doc A/CN.4/568/Add.1 (12 May 2006) 9, note 17.
[143] UN Doc A/CN.4/637, para. 2, p. 17. It also railed against this in 2006, UN Doc A/CN.4/568/Add.1.
[144] UN Doc A/CN.4/568/Add.1 (12 May 2006), 10.

organization, since the rules of the organization clearly exclude this possibility. Furthermore, the contracts in question only impose on contractors
an obligation of result (for instance, the execution of a project in the field),
while the organization has no direction or control over their actions nor
may it exercise disciplinary powers on them.[145]

Although the ILC changed the definition in the final version, the articles,
taken together, still do not prima facie remedy the problem identified by
UNESCO or exclude the attribution of contractors. UNESCO seems to be
arguing that non-officials charged with one of the functions of the organization must be controlled by that organization, perhaps along the lines
of that required by Article 8 of the ASR in order for the conduct of that
person to be attributable. Thus, the two conditions are merged and must
be fulfilled cumulatively. There is some logic to narrowing the scope of
the article: if 'functions of the organization' replaces 'elements of governmental authority', it could encompass much more than even the perenni-
ally nebulous and undefinable 'elements of governmental authority'. For
example, government (or public) functions are widely acknowledged to
be much broader than 'governmental authority', but here, it is not evident
how 'functions of the organization' circumscribes responsibility to a limited set of delegated acts. A closer parallel might be 'core functions' of the
organization. Moreover, the UN's position on peace operations themselves
(discussed below) strongly suggests that control is integral to attribution
for entities charged with carrying out 'one of the functions' of the organizations – peace operations being emblematic of the UN's responsibility
to maintain international peace and security. Pierre Klein also argues that
once one goes beyond the 'formal links' of an individual with an organization, 'the criterion of effective control by an organization . . . then becomes
predominant'.[146]

There is no indication that Special Rapporteur Gaja perceives the conditions as cumulative, however. Rather, he seems to consider the definition
of an 'agent' to encompass the acts of a person that would be attributable
based on the control exercised by the organization; thus, an organization
acts through one it controls.[147] A person or entity charged with carrying
out the functions of the organization would thus be a separate basis for
attribution, which would also be encompassed by the term 'agent'. Since

---

[145] UN Doc A/CN.4/568/Add.1 (12 May 2006), 11.   [146] Klein, 'Attribution', p. 299.

[147] Gaja notes that Austria 'suggested that the case of "a private person acting under the effective control of the organization" should also be considered. As was noted . . . such a person
would come within the definition of agent in article 4, paragraph 2 [now Article 2(c) definition of agent as cited above]'. See UN Doc A/CN.4/610 (27 March 2009) 8, note 26.

Special Rapporteur Gaja states that 'the connection of officials to the organization is generally specified in a formal act (personnel regulations or similar documents)', it would seem that a contract for 'outsourced services' would not fall under what he considers as 'formal links'.[148] This may mean they would not be 'officials', but it does not settle the question as to whether they may nevertheless be 'agents' of the organization based on other criteria.[149]

In its comments on the draft articles, the UN Secretariat fought back against the broad scope of attribution permitted by Articles 2(d) and 6 of the DARIO as expressed in their earlier incarnation.[150] Taking issue with the earlier definition of 'agent' as a person 'through whom the organization acts', the UN objected to the rule specifically in relation to the use of private contractors in peace operations.[151] Like UNESCO, it pointed out the fact that it acts in part through contractors to carry out its functions and quoted the clause that it includes in contracts to the effect that the conduct of contractors cannot be attributed to the UN. As such, the UN has openly acknowledged that it acts through its contractors and that they help in carrying out the functions of the organization.[152] However, it has strongly voiced its opposition to the possibility of their conduct being attributable to it. Although the ILC modified the definition of 'agents' in the final version of the draft articles, it did little to take into account the UN's view that the nature of those functions is also relevant.[153] If the draft articles are supposed to be a codification of the principle of attribution of the conduct of agents to international organizations, the reaction of the UN secretariat and other UN agencies strongly suggests that the detail of the rule does not reflect the practice or *opinio juris* of those organizations.

---

[148] Klein, 'Attribution', p. 298.

[149] The ICJ in *Mazilu* distinguished between appointed officials and others, who were given functions and tasks and had the status of 'experts on mission' but who were not UN 'officials'. *Applicability of Article VI, Section 22, of the Convention on the Privileges and Immunities of the United Nations* (Advisory Opinion) [1989] ICJ Rep 177 See para. 48 (*Mazilu*).

[150] A/CN.4/637/Add. 1.   [151] A/CN.4/637/Add. 1, paras 7–9, pp. 7–8.   [152] Ibid., para. 9.

[153] On the nature of the functions, see ibid., paras 8–10. In its review of the comments by states and international organizations, the ILC adverts to this issue but merely states that 'these elements may be considered as implied in the requirement that agents of an international organization are "persons or entities through whom the organization acts".' Putting perhaps too much stake into the potential authority of a commentary, even with the changes made to the rule, Gaja states, 'This point could usefully be developed in the commentary.' See ILC, 'Eighth Report on the Responsibility of International Organizations', UN Doc A/CN.4/640 (14 March 2011), para. 22.

The reason for the UN Secretariat's objection to the rule is the following:

> It is the view of the Secretariat that the broad definition adopted by the International Law Commission could expose international organizations to unreasonable responsibility and should thus be revised. In the practice of the Organization, a necessary element in the determination of whether a person or entity is an 'agent' of the Organization depends on whether such person or entity performs the *functions* of the Organization. However, while the performance of mandated functions is a crucial element, it may not be conclusive and should be considered on a case-by-case basis. Other factors, such as the status of the person or entity, the relationship and the degree of control that exists between the Organization and any such person or entity, would also be relevant. As indicated above, even persons and entities who perform functions that are also performed by the Organization, may not be regarded as 'agents' by the Organization, but rather as partners who assist the Organization in achieving a common goal.[154]

Thus, even though the ILC modified the definition of 'agent' to specify that it is a person who carries out the functions of the organization and is not just someone through whom the organization acts, it did not include an element of control as an essential part of the test. The UN's proposed factors capture the nuances in the persons through which it may act. Thus, one can imagine that it need not exercise demonstrable control over a Special Rapporteur, but that the status of that office would suffice to make the Rapporteur's official conduct attributable to the UN. On the other hand, persons given tasks with less stature (e.g., more technical functions) would need to be under a greater degree of UN control in order for their conduct to be attributable as that of agents of the organization. The ILC's decision to adopt a rule to which a variety of international organizations have expressed their strong opposition would seem to indicate a refusal to adopt a narrower rule that might reflect the *lex lata* (from the perspective of international organizations) and appears to move this rule into the realm of the law as the ILC thinks it should be.

There is a close parallel with the rules on defining state organs in the ASR, as discussed above. Domestic law is one of the ways state organs may be identified, but it does not have the final word.[155] In the same way, the rules of the organization may define agents and organs, but a court may not feel it is bound by that. In my view, however, this is one area where the parallel approach breaks down. While it is accepted that domestic law cannot be a reason for violating international obligations and is not a part

---

[154] P. 9 A/CN.4/637/Add. 1, para. 12.
[155] Article 4(2) ASR and accompanying commentary.

of international law, the same cannot be said for the rules of international organizations.[156] It is acknowledged that some of the rules of international organizations form part and parcel of international law, although there may be a hierarchy of norms and competing obligations. The ILC draft articles seem to assert that the rules of the organization should in some respects be treated like domestic law of states – as a fact. Yet if an organization has contracted an entity according to its rules because it has to do it that way, arguably the fact that that flows from international law leads to a different result than would be the case for a state.

The accuracy of the rule set up in Articles 6 and 2 DARIO in the view of states is difficult to determine. Most states did not comment on it; those that did were divided in their opinion of the broadness of the rule. Belgium remarked, 'Belgium notes that the definition of the term "agent" is imprecise and could lead to a proliferation of cases in which the responsibility of an international organization could be invoked for acts performed, for example, by a subcontractor.'[157] It went on, 'Belgium ventures to suggest to the Commission that it either redraft this provision, on the lines of the articles pertaining to the responsibility of States for internationally wrongful acts and, more particularly, articles 5 and 8; or that it specifies and limits the notion of "agent" by providing a commentary on the draft article or by amending paragraph (c) as follows: *"'Agent' includes officials and other persons or entities through whom the organization acts directly and in accordance with its internal operating rules."*'[158] Portugal, on the other hand, preferred a broad definition.[159]

Indeed, Belgium's remarks clearly reflect a demand that the test be a cumulative assessment of the principles established in Articles 5 and 8 ASR (i.e. including control, instructions, etc. as well as carrying out a function). That interpretation is echoed by the World Bank in its comments, in which it argues that a purely functional approach is insufficient.[160] It said,

---

[156] In its comments on the penultimate version of the Draft Articles, the UN Secretariat criticized the transposition of 'the definition of the "rules" from the 1986 Vienna Convention . . . to the field of international responsibility. It is furthermore of the view that the broad definition of the "rules of the organization" which includes instruments extending far beyond the constituent instruments of the organization, not only increases greatly the breadth of potential breaches of "international law" obligations for which the organization may be held responsible, but also, and more importantly . . . could extend them to breaches of internal rules as well.' See ILC, 'Comments and Observations Received from International Organizations', UN Doc A/CN.4/637/Add.1 (17 February 2011), 6, comments on Draft Article 2.

[157] UN Doc A/CN.4/636 (14 Feb 2011), 10.   [158] Ibid.
[159] Ibid., 11.   [160] UN Doc A/CN.4/637, 22.

'[O]ne may question whether something more is not, in practice, required for attribution, namely that the agent has not only factually performed functions of the organization but that it has also acted on the instruction and under the control of the organization in question.'[161]

The requirement of control is not self-evident in the pure wording of the text of the Draft Articles. Nevertheless, there are good reasons to consider it to be an important element – in particular, in situations where the acts in question are carried out by a person who, according to the rules of the organization, is not an official or an expert on mission.

13.3.2   Only Official and ultra vires Conduct Is Attributable

It is generally accepted that not all conduct of state agents is attributable to the state. According to the ILC's Draft Articles, the same principle for attribution of conduct applies for the acts of agents of international organizations: conduct must have occurred in the exercise of official duties (even *ultra vires*) and not in a private capacity in order to be imputable. This is affirmed in Article 6(1) DARIO ('in the performance of functions of that organ or agent') and Article 8 DARIO, which affirms the applicability of the principle of *ultra vires*:

> The conduct of an organ or agent of an international organization shall be considered an act of that organization under international law if the organ or agent acts in an official capacity and within the overall functions of that organization, even if the conduct exceeds the authority of that organ or agent or contravenes instructions.[162]

Here, again, international organizations contested the transposition of this principle to a different context.[163] In addition to that criticism, I submit

---

[161] Ibid. In terms of the level of control necessary, Corinna Seiberth argues that the overall control standard would be appropriate. Corinna Seiberth, *Private Military and Security Companies in International Law* (Intersentia, 2014).

[162] See also ILC, 'DARIO with Commentaries', para. 7 of the Commentary to Article 6, p. 86.

[163] Joint Submission of the Comprehensive Nuclear-Test-Ban Treaty Organization, the International Civil Aviation Organization, the International Fund for Agricultural Development, the International Labour Organization, the International Maritime Organization, the International Organization for Migration, the International Telecommunication Union, UNESCO, UN World Tourism Association, the WHO, WIPO, WMO and WTO on Draft Article 7 [now Article 8], in ILC, 'Comments and Observations Received from International Organizations', UN Doc A/CN.4/637 (14 February 2011), 24. Contesting the automatic transposition of the rule, the organizations argued, 'At least, a better balance should be struck... between attribution of ultra vires acts and the protection of third parties who rely on the good faith of agents or organs acting beyond their mandate, and... on

that the way in which the ILC defined agents of an organization introduces a certain level of complication. The key issue is the fact that the ILC apparently broadened the notion of who may be an agent of an international organization such that a finding that a person carries out or helps to carry out one of the functions of the organization may be construed as an agent of that organization even if this is contrary to the rules of the organization. This alleged possibility makes it difficult to know how to discern what conduct has been carried out 'in an official capacity *and* within the overall functions' of the organization.[164] Indeed, there is the added complication that, unlike the fact that it is necessary that there be a legal basis for delegation of elements of the governmental authority in Article 5 ASR (although this is slightly questionable), 'in exceptional circumstances, functions may be considered as given to an organ or agent even if this could not be said to be based on the rules of the organization.'[165] It may be difficult indeed to determine the 'official functions' of an 'agent' attributed to an international organization even in contravention of the rules of the organization – and when the conduct in question was also *ultra vires*.[166] It is difficult to understand, on a plain reading, how an unappointed person can be acting in an official capacity when that itself is contrary to the rules of the organization. This may be a trickier issue when it comes to PMSCs as private security guards in peace operations than for CIVPOL, who unquestionably operate according to a mandate.[167] For Article 8 DARIO, unlike in Articles 2 and 6 DARIO, the test is cumulative. It appears that the requirement to act in an 'official' capacity was added in light of the comments by the UN on the previous version of the Article.[168]

A further perplexing factor is that the 'official conduct, including *ultra vires* acts', rule does not apply to the conduct of persons or entities

---

the principle of speciality and the fact that an agent or organ acting ultra vires operate [*sic*] beyond the mandate and functions entrusted to an international organization by its members. Due account should be taken in this respect of internal mechanisms and rules.'

[164] Emphasis added.

[165] ILC, 'DARIO with Commentaries', para. 9 of the Commentary to Article 6, p. 86.

[166] Although the ILC appears to attempt to address this issue in its commentary, its solution is not satisfactory and fails to fill the gaps. See ILC, 'DARIO with Commentaries', para. 2 of the Commentary to Article 8, p. 94.

[167] See the hypothetical examples provided by Oswald and Bates regarding *ultra vires* acts of UNPOL based on the mandate. Bruce Oswald and Adrian Bates, 'Privileges and Immunities of United Nations Police' (2010) 14 *J Intl Peacekeeping* 375–402 at 393–394.

[168] See 'Comments and Observations Received from International Organizations', UN Doc A/CN.4/637/Add. 1 (17 February 2011), 15, para. 3: 'the Secretariat recommends that the word "official" be inserted to make it clear that the organ or agent must be acting in an official rather than a private capacity.'

attributable to a state based on Article 8 ASR (attribution of conduct based on instructions, directions or control of private persons by the state). However, the ILC seems to be applying it to Article 6 DARIO, which the ILC openly admits is meant to be an amalgamation – but on a non-cumulative basis – of Articles 5 and 8 of the ASR. This already gives one pause, as according to the usual interpretation of Article 8 ASR, the state has to have effective control over the operation in which the unlawful conduct occurred, which does not reflect a sense that *ultra vires* conduct may be attributable.[169] Regarding the attribution of conduct that is incidental to instructions given, in my view two interpretations are plausible: that this would include the attribution of *ultra vires* conduct, or that it is similar to but different from *ultra vires*.[170] This analysis suggests that Article 6 DARIO is actually more like an amalgamation of Articles 5 and 4(2) ASR, as both of those heads of attribution would entail attribution of *ultra vires* conduct.

As the flip side of the 'attributability' of such conduct to the UN can be a concomitant immunity of the individual from prosecution, it is relevant to consider the way the UN perceives acts carried out as an official function for the purposes of maintaining immunity (discussed in more detail below). Indeed, the ILC also refers to this practice in its commentary on Article 8 DARIO. The ILC (among others) refers to an opinion of the UN Secretariat from 1986 to distinguish between 'on-duty' and 'off-duty' (i.e. official and private) acts.[171] In that opinion, which the ILC quotes at length, the Secretariat declared,

> We consider the primary factor in determining an 'off-duty' situation to be whether the member of a peacekeeping mission was acting in a nonofficial/non-operational capacity when the incident occurred and *not* whether he/she was in military or civilian attire at the time of the incident or whether the incident occurred inside or outside the area of operation.[172]

The opinion went on to emphasize that each situation would be determined on a case-by-case basis. The UN, however, in its comments on the penultimate version of Article 8 DARIO and its accompanying

---

169 *Bosnia v. Serbia*, paras 399–400, affirming its holding in *Nicaragua*, para. 115.
170 The ICTY Appeals Chamber in *Tadic* held that when a person is acting on the instructions of the state, the state would also be responsible for *ultra vires* conduct. *Prosecutor v. Tadic* (Appeals Chamber Judgment) 94–1-T (15 July 1999), para. 119. See also para. 121.
171 ILC, 'DARIO with Commentaries', para. 9 of the Commentary to Article 8, p. 96. See also Oswald and Bates, 'Privileges and Immunities', 393.
172 (1986) UN Juridical YB 300, quoted in ILC, 'DARIO with Commentaries', ibid.

commentary, insisted that that 1986 opinion 'does not reflect the consistent practice of the Organization'[173] and recommended that the ILC not include the excerpt in its Commentary.[174] The UN referred to earlier practice relating to an opinion regarding a Claims Review Board for UNEF dealing with 'tortious acts committed during the Force members' off-duty periods'. The Office of the Legal Advisor in that case had

> advised that 'there may well be situations involving actions by Force members off duty which the United Nations could appropriately recognize as engaging its responsibility', and made a distinction between off-duty acts of Force members in circumstances closely related to the functions of the Force member (i.e., the use of a Government-issued weapon), and actions entirely unrelated to the force member's status as such.[175]

Consequently, according to the UN, 'the test for the attribution of the act was whether it was related to the functions of the Organization, irrespective of whether the Force member was on or off duty at the time'.[176] That approach is interesting, since, under the law of state responsibility, it is generally considered that the unlawful use of a state-issued weapon by a law enforcement officer would not render that act attributable to the state if in all other respects it was private. The example given by the UN above thus appears to diverge from that approach. This may bring it slightly closer to the scope of state responsibility for both the on- and off-duty acts of members of state armed forces in international armed conflicts as understood and articulated in Article 91 AP I.[177] The ILC in its commentary maintained the original quote regarding on-duty and off-duty activity but nuanced it with an acknowledgement that the UN may sometimes have a different approach.[178]

13.4 PMSCs as 'Agents' of an International Organization Under Art 6 DARIO

With this theoretical background in mind, it is useful to turn now to a case-by-case study regarding the attribution of the conduct of PMSCs in peace operations on the basis of these rules. Given the fact that the rules

---

[173] ILC, 'Comments and Observations Received from International Organizations', UN Doc A/CN.4/637/Add.1 (17 February 2011), 15, para. 4. Emphasis added.

[174] Ibid., 16, para. 6.   [175] Ibid.   [176] Ibid.

[177] Marco Sassòli, 'State Responsibility for Violations of International Humanitarian Law' (2002) 84 *IRRC* 401; Article 91 AP I.

[178] ILC, 'DARIO with Commentaries', paras 9–10 of the Commentary to Article 8, p. 96.

cannot, in my view, be taken as an expression of entirely settled law, the analysis will consider the issues from various perspectives. Above, I noted the different capacities in which the UN may contract PMSCs to participate in peace operations. This section will canvass the possible attribution of the conduct of PMSCs in those various roles to the United Nations.

13.4.1   CIVPOL/UNPOL

The clearest case for attribution of PMSCs under Article 6 DARIO in many respects is that of civilian police recruited, selected and deployed by a PMSC and seconded to an international organization as a state's contribution to a peace operation. As a preliminary matter, it is worth noting that Article 7 DARIO does not apply to police contributions by states to UN operations – even when states contribute formed police units. For individual CIVPOL, they are not necessarily police officers on active service within their own forces; they may be retired or no longer on active duty. Therefore, the premise for Article 7 does not apply automatically here. For formed police units, while such units are more likely to be composed of active duty police, the consensus is that they are entirely under the control of the UN police commissioner.

It is perhaps easiest to start with the case of a normal (non-PMSC) civilian police officer working in a peace operation. As a legal officer in the UN Office of Legal Affairs writes, 'UN police are considered "agents" of the Organization' in terms of Article 6 of the DARIO.[179] This is the case for individual UNPOL as well as for formed police units.[180] The question is, what is the effect (if any) of the interposition of a private company

---

[179] Katarina Grenfell, 'Accountability in International Policing' (2011) 15 J Intl Peacekeeping 92–117 at 115.

[180] This result is logical: while police officers must be 'sworn' and have had a minimum number of years of experience, unlike military contingents, they may be retired, or need not be on active duty. They may not have been retired for more than nine years, however. Once seconded to the peace operation, however, even for formed police units the sending state retains no control over the unit – not even the disciplinary control retained for military troop contingents. This remains true despite recent initiatives to improve sending state accountability for the criminal acts of UNPOL by encouraging criminal prosecution, etc. State practice appears to support this interpretation. For example, when the Human Rights Committee asked Austria to provide further information on the acts of its CIVPOL allegedly in violation of human rights, Austria responded to most queries of the HRC but not this one. UN HRC, 'List of Issues to Be Taken Up in Connection with the Consideration of the Fourth Periodic Report of Austria', UN Doc CCPR/C/AUT/Q/4 (9 May 2007) para. 9.

recruiting, selecting and deploying the civilian police – that is, when civilian police are hired and deployed by a PMSC – on the attribution of the civilian police's actions to the UN or to another international organization? On one reading, it must be the function with which the individual is tasked by the UN (or other international organization) that matters, and not the way the person is hired. This interpretation would seem to be in line with the UN's assertion of its view of the rule and in particular its concerns regarding the *nature* of the functions involved. The functions of UNPOL are of a nature to warrant designation as an agent of the organization, no matter how a person is hired or the formalities surrounding the contract, as long as those formalities indicate that such are indeed the functions of the individual.[181]

This is supported by practice and legal opinions of the UN – in other words, with the rules of the organization. In a 1993 opinion issued by the UN Office of Legal Affairs in relation to contractors working for UNPROFOR in Bosnia, the Secretariat applied a 1985 administrative instruction to the effect that '[a]gents or employees of the contractor shall not be considered in any respect as being officials or staff members of the United Nations.'[182] This nevertheless leaves open the possibility that a contractor can be an expert on mission – who would be an agent of the organization – because one defining element of an expert on mission is that he or she is *not* an official or staff member of the organization.[183] Other opinions of the OLA in respect of contractors (many of whom will be employees of companies such as PMSCs) suggest that some may be experts on mission.[184] UN Police tend to be designated as 'experts on mission' in the Status of Forces Agreement;[185] the fact that PMSCs/contractors are capable of having that status despite their being employees of a company affirms the possibility of this arrangement in legal terms.

[181] This view is buttressed by the fact that the tasks of UNPOL are set down in the UN Security Council resolution establishing the mandate of the peacekeeping operation.

[182] OLA, 'Memorandum to the Deputy Director, Field Operations Division, Status of Internationally Contracted Personnel Provided by Civilian Contractors in the Context of United Nations Peacekeeping Operations – Understanding of the Term "Experts on Missions"' (1993) UN Juridical YB 400–401 (11 February 1993) (hereafter OLA, 'Status of Civilian Contractors' 1993).

[183] Convention on Privileges and Immunities of the United Nations, New York, 13 February 1946, in force 17 September 1946, 1 UNTS 15 and 90 UNTS 327 (corrigendum), Article VI, Section 22.

[184] OLA, 'Status of Civilian Contractors' 1993, 400–401.

[185] UN Model Status of Forces Agreement, UN Doc A/ 45/594 (9 October 1990), Annex, para. 26.

According to the available practice and an analysis of the legal regime, there is no reason to doubt that the conduct of UNPOL recruited and deployed by a PMSC on behalf of a state may be attributable to the UN. The best-known case is of course the United States, which uses PMSCs to recruit and deploy its contribution to UNPOL in the absence of a national police service. It appears that the PMSC contractors that the United States sends as its UNPOL contribution assume the normal functions of UNPOL according to the mandate and are placed under UN command. From the available evidence, they are seconded to the UN by the United States, but their contract is with a private company.[186]

In addition to the nature of the functions, it may be important to consider the level of control that the UN has over such contractors, in case the exercise of control over the acts is accepted as an additional requirement for designation as an agent. In this regard, the relevant question is whether the existence or actions of the PMSC itself serve to attenuate that control in a way that would warrant not attributing conduct of PMSC civilian police to the UN.

Case Studies

Three short case studies help to illustrate the attribution of the conduct CIVPOL to international organizations, including PMSC CIVPOL. In addition to the nature of the functions and the purported requirement of control, these case studies help to flesh out the concept that only conduct that occurred in the function of official duties is attributable to the international organization.

The most scrutinized use of PMSCs as CIVPOL is that in Bosnia, where US contractors working as UN CIVPOL were implicated in trafficking in human beings and sexual slavery.[187] In assessing the control the UN exercised over the PMSCs involved, there is no question that the PMSCs were

---

[186] It is not entirely clear; according to Grenfell, 'Accountability in International Policing', 99, they sign a contract with the UN. However, other UN documents seem to indicate that while some UN police are UN staff members on contracts directly with the UN, most are merely seconded to the UN. See, for example, 'New Procedures for Assessing Individual Police Officers', in *UN Police Magazine* (July 2012), 14–15. In addition, reports on the trafficking and sex slavery that occurred in Bosnia describe the significant compensation packages offered by the private companies to the officers.

[187] At least one report also indicates that contractors working for UNMIK police in Kosovo may have also been implicated in trafficking in women and girls. See Amnesty International, 'Kosovo (Serbia and Montenegro): "So does it mean that we have the rights?" Protecting the Human Rights of Women and Girls Trafficked for Forced Prostitution in Kosovo', (5 May 2004) EUR 70/010/2004, text accompanying notes 273–275.

subject to the same chain of command as other civilian police active in the mission.

What may complicate the issue is that UNPOL contracted through a PMSC may be in leadership roles in that chain of command, thus blurring the line between company control and UN control. One account of that situation in Bosnia indicates that some individuals – and particularly those in managerial positions or at higher levels – may have been in a position of dual, conflicting loyalties to the UN and to the company itself.[188] For example, a superior may be hesitant to openly address misconduct of fellow employees on the grounds that exposure may harm the company's reputation, with all of the financial ramification that entails. Such potentially conflicting loyalties may seem to attenuate the control by the organization over the conduct of PMSC UNPOL further down the chain of command. Nevertheless, the company remains plugged in to the general chain of command and under the direct authority of the organization. Here, unlike in Article 7 DARIO situations, there is no weighing of which entity exercised effective control, but rather an examination of whether the persons in question are acting as 'agents' of an international organization.

In another respect, Kathryn Bolkovac also stated that DynCorp employees in Bosnia were subject to much less supervision by the company in comparison to that exercised by states such as Germany over the CIVPOL they had contributed.[189] While that may be a cause for concern for other reasons, this lack of supervision could also be interpreted as a tendency not to exercise control over conduct that might conflict with that demanded by the UN. Moreover, if even the national control exercised by some states does not interfere with the designation of CIVPOL – and even those hailing from formed police units – as agents of the organization under Article 6 DARIO, one can surmise it would require a fair amount of control by a company to oust or offset the control of the UN.[190]

There is no evidence to suggest that the United Nations or NATO ever attempted to argue that the American members of the International Police Task Force (IPTF) in Bosnia who were deployed by a PMSC and who were implicated in trafficking in persons and/or the purchasing of women as sexual slaves were somehow not UN CIVPOL.[191] In one case, NATO

---

[188] See generally, Kathryn Bolkovac, *The Whistleblower* (Palgrave Macmillan, 2011).
[189] Ibid. [190] See below, discussion on Romanian CIVPOL in Kosovo.
[191] In this regard, Ban Ki-Moon reportedly displayed great reluctance and displeasure at the screening at the UN of a film based on Kathryn Bolkovac's *The Whistleblower*, but to my knowledge, no statement was made to suggest that the contractors were not part of the mission. That being said, I was not able to identify any record of compensation being paid

declined to waive the immunity of an SFOR contractor in Bosnia who had allegedly 'purchased' two women.[192] While that situation was not related to the acts of a civilian police officer, it serves to remind us that if an organization asserts immunity for an individual, there are strong arguments to be made that it is accepting that that individual is an agent of the organization and that it must accept responsibility for the conduct of the individual.[193] In the case of the UN, it will be seen below that an explicit connection is made in the Convention on Immunities between the assertion of immunity and the resulting responsibility of the organization in relation to that conduct.

It is a little murky whether the alleged violations occurred in the course of official duty or in a private capacity. While some evidence suggests that the contractors acted in a purely private manner, it is not inconceivable that others used their position as civilian police in the course of their unlawful acts.[194] To the best of my knowledge, there have never been any proceedings brought against the UN for these acts, such that there has never been a determination as to whether they were attributable to the UN. The UN has acknowledged the incidents as being 'in clear breach of the UN peacekeeper's "code of conduct" and, in some cases, were illegal'.[195] However, it has focused on trying to ensure individual accountability for those acts rather than asserting its own responsibility. Indeed, the discussion rarely – if ever – centres on whether the acts can be attributed to the UN itself. As indicated above, NATO maintained immunity for a contractor implicated in trafficking, but I have unearthed no correlative

to the victims of that trafficking – on behalf of either the contractors or the rest of the mission staff.

[192] Human Rights Watch, 'Hopes Betrayed: Trafficking of Women and Girls to Post-Conflict Bosnia and Herzegovina for Forced Prostitution' (November 2002), 67. Shortly thereafter, the contractor reportedly left Bosnia for Croatia. 'SFOR' was the Stabilization Force in Bosnia and Herzegovina.

[193] Gerhard Hafner of the ILC made the connection between the assertion of state immunity and an act of governmental authority. See 'Summary Record of the 2554th Meeting', (1998) 1 YBILC 234 at 237, para. 35 in the context of the discussion on the Draft Articles on State Responsibility. On the other hand, the ILC affirmed the distinction for the concept of acts *de jure imperii* 'for the purposes of the law of State immunities and the acts of the State for the purposes of State responsibility'. Ibid., para. 30.

[194] See in particular Human Rights Watch, 'Hopes Betrayed', 62–68.

[195] Comments of UN Under-Secretary-General for Communications and Public Information, Kiyo Akasaka, at the UN screening of the film *The Whistleblower*, 14 October 2011. See UN News Centre, 'At Film Screening, Ban Reaffirms Zero Tolerance for Sexual Abuse' (14 October 2011), available at www.un.org/apps/news/story.asp?NewsID=40065&Cr=sexual+abuse&Cr1#.UKj-vWdNITA.

expression of an assumption of responsibility on the part of NATO towards the victim in that case.

For its part, the UN has taken a number of steps over the past decade in the face of this and many other cases of sexual exploitation and abuse during peacekeeping operations by military and civilian personnel in order to put a stop to such abuse in general, which is a welcome response. Arguably, it could reflect a sense of a due diligence obligation. The UN has not made a recommendation that states should avoid using PMSCs to recruit and deploy UNPOL. This may be due to the fact that sexual exploitation and abuse is, regrettably, a widespread problem and the violations by the PMSCs in Bosnia were but one manifestation of abuse in that operation.[196] Without a direct assumption of responsibility and transparent compensation to the victims, however, these acts appear to be more in line with a sense of due diligence obligations than with responsibility of the organization for such acts. Given the potential use of one's status and powers as a police officer in the territory to perpetuate or take advantage of the system in which trafficking occurred, it is certainly possible that such acts could be construed as committed in the course of official duties, even though they would obviously be *ultra vires*.[197]

A second case does not involve PMSC civilian police but is nevertheless helpful to underline the attribution of acts of civilian police to the UN. In Kosovo in 2007, the actions of CIVPOL during the course of their official duties allegedly violated human rights and led to the responsibility of the UN. Members of UNMIK police fired rubber bullets during a demonstration, killing two protestors and wounding several others.[198] The UN paid compensation to the families of the victims and 'apologised to them on behalf of the UN', thereby essentially accepting responsibility for the acts of the CIVPOL.[199] The CIVPOL in question were members of a formed police unit from Romania and were using outdated rubber bullets (supplied by Romania) that had been banned by the UN Police Commissioner

---

[196] See Human Rights Watch, 'Hopes Betrayed'.
[197] See in particular *Estate of Jean-Baptiste Caire (France) v. United Mexican States* V RIAA 516–534 (7 June 1929) 530.
[198] Case No. 04/07 *Kadri Balaj (on behalf of Mon Balaj), Shaban Xheladini (on behalf of Arben Xheladini), Zenel Zeneli and Mustafa Nerjovaj v. UNMIK*, Human Rights Advisory Panel, Decision (31 March 2010), paras 2–5 (*Mon Balaj v. UNMIK* 2010).
[199] Ibid., para. 7; See also the decision reopening the case before the Human Rights Advisory Panel: Case No. 04/07 *Kadri Balaj (on behalf of Mon Balaj), Shaban Xheladini (on behalf of Arben Xheladini), Zenel Zeneli and Mustafa Nerjovaj v. UNMIK*, Human Rights Advisory Panel Decision (11 May 2012), paras 27–28 (*Mon Balaj v. UNMIK* 2012).

due to their lethality[200] and the officers were repatriated to Romania before they could be investigated in Kosovo.[201] This case is important because it shows that the acts of UNPOL are attributable to the UN as they are under UN command, but that the actions of the sending state can be pertinent to the occurrence of a violation. In this case, the Police Commissioner had 'directed that [the expired rubber bullets] be either sent home or destroyed'.[202] Furthermore, considering the importance of an investigation into a death as an essential component of the human right to life, the removal of the officers from Kosovo by Romania may be viewed as having contributed to a continuing violation.[203] In fact, the special prosecutor who first investigated the incident 'recommended UNMIK, the United Nations *and the Government of Romania* to consider initiating appropriate procedures for compensation'.[204] Some reports indicated that Romanian UN police contingents were known for an excessive use of force, especially in riot control situations,[205] which could lead to questions as to the UN Police Commissioner's responsibility for his decision to deploy them in such situations.

The Human Rights Advisory Panel in Kosovo – to which a complaint was made – accepted jurisdiction over the matter (twice) after acknowledging that its mandate is limited to 'acts and omissions that are attributable to UNMIK'.[206] At no point during the admissibility proceedings did UNMIK argue that the actions of the Romanian UNPOL contingent could not be attributed to UNMIK. Indeed, the UN can be viewed in some respects as having assumed responsibility by providing compensation through an alternative process.[207] Finally, the fact that

---

[200] Matt Robinson, 'Hardened Rubber Bullets Killed Kosovo Protesters', Reuters, 18 April 2007, available at www.reuters.com/article/2007/04/18/idUSL18289584.

[201] Krenar Gashi, 'Romanian UN Officers Blamed for Pristina Deaths', Balkan Insight, 19 April 2007.

[202] Robinson, 'Hardened Rubber Bullets'.

[203] See *McCann v. UK* (App no. 18984/91) ECHR 29 September 1995; *Anguelova v. Bulgaria* (App no. 38361/97) ECHR 13 June 2002, para. 137; *Jasinskis v. Latvia* (App no. 45744/08) ECHR 21 December 2010, para. 72, among others.

[204] *Mon Balaj v. UNMIK* 2010, para. 4. Emphasis added.

[205] Jeta Xharra, Krenar Gashi and Marian Chiriac, 'Investigation: Romanian Police Blamed for Kosovo Protest Carnage', Balkan Insight, 23 February 2007.

[206] *Mon Balaj v. UNMIK* 2012, para. 89.

[207] Of course, the UN has also issued an apology for its failure to act in Srebrenica and Rwanda, which can also be construed as an assumption of responsibility, in spite of the specific role played by state troop contributions in those events. However, that is consistent with UN dogma that it is responsible for all acts in UN-commanded and -controlled operations, which both were at the time.

the violation clearly occurred in the course of duty or as part of official functions is uncontroversial, even if the officers contravened the instructions of the UN by using the outdated rubber bullets allegedly supplied by the sending state. It is not apparent from any official documents that the UN construed Romania's actions as attenuating the UN's own responsibility.[208] This is, then, a relatively straightforward case of an example of UN responsibility for the official conduct of CIVPOL.[209]

Finally, two complainants brought a case against Spain before the UN Human Rights Committee based on the alleged conduct of Spanish police officers acting as part of UNMIK police. The authors of the complaint had attempted to file complaints in Kosovo against the UNMIK police, but, due to the jurisdictional obstacles they encountered, filed a complaint against Spain for the conduct of its officers. They alleged broadly that Spain exercised control over its officers even when they were acting extra-territorially.[210] The government of Spain argued that the impugned conduct occurred in the course of duty of the police acting within UNMIK and that, consequently, 'the entity ultimately responsible was UNMIK'.[211] The Human Rights Committee held that the complainants had not exhausted domestic remedies – in addition by attempting to launch a proceeding in Spain – and that the complaint was inadmissible on that basis. Without wishing to read too much into that decision, it would undoubtedly be in bad faith for the HRC to expect the complainants to pursue a remedy in Spain if it considered a priori that claims against civilian police participating in peace operations can never be attributable to the sending state. There would thus appear to be room for dual attribution (to the state and to the international organization) depending on the facts, but this possibility is raised only in relation to Article 7 DARIO. While this case does not go far in illuminating further issues regarding PMSCs as UNPOL and the possibility of attributing their acts to states or international organizations, it does provide further

---

[208] Here it is relevant to recall that the principle of dual attribution is recognized as potentially applicable in cases where Article 7 DARIO would apply; however, its relevance in an Article 6 DARIO situation when it comes to Formed Police Units could be appropriate.

[209] For the victims, implementing that responsibility has been considerably less straightforward, and I will return to the case below in the discussion on implementation of the responsibility of an international organization.

[210] *Azem Kurbogaj and Ghevdet Kurbogaj v. Spain*, Comm No. 1374/2005, UN Doc CCPR/C/87/D/1374/2005 (2006), para. 3.2.

[211] Ibid., para. 4.1.

evidence that states consider that civilian police are uniquely attributable to the organization to which they are seconded.

Based on the above, there do not seem to be any additional issues with regard to PMSCs when it comes to attributing the acts of UNPOL to an international organization. Issues that may arise are in relation to the possibility of a state exercising extra-territorial criminal jurisdiction, as the state may perceive the link as less strong (and indeed the facts in the Bosnia case show the steps it took were limited even though there was strong evidence of trafficking). This is an issue for individual responsibility but it is equally relevant in terms of state responsibility at a due diligence level.

13.4.2 Private Security Guards and Attribution

The second area in which it is known that the UN has recourse to PMSCs is for the provision of security in peace operations and other operations.[212] Private security contractors are an important cohort in missions because they may be tasked with roles that require them to use force, albeit only on the basis of self-defence.[213] The relationship of the use of force in self-defence with IHL has been explored in detail in Chapters 9 and 10; here, the analysis is concerned with the attribution to an international organization of the conduct of private security guards in case of a violation of an international legal obligation. Again, this discussion does not seek to condemn or condone the use of private security guards in peace operations, nor does it seek to sensationalize potential risks. Instead, it simply attempts to determine how accountability flows from their acts.[214]

Can the acts of private security guards contracted by the United Nations to provide security in peace operations be attributed to the UN as acts of agents of the organization? On the basis of the wording of the ILC's Draft Article 6 and Article 2(d), a plain-meaning reading might lead to the conclusion that they could. Given the centrality of a secure environment to the accomplishment of mandates, those who act to enhance security would most certainly be helping to carry out a function of the organization. Recall that Article 2(d) defines 'agent of an international organization' as 'an official or other person or entity…who is charged by the organization with carrying out, or helping to carry out, one of its functions, and thus through whom the organization acts'. The crux of the

---

212 See the discussion and evidence presented in Chapter 1.
213 See Chapter 1, Section 1.3, and Chapters 9 and 10.
214 For a somewhat alarmist view, see Lou Pingeot, *Dangerous Partnership: Private Military and Security Companies and the UN.*

matter is whether providing security within a peace operation falls within the definition of a 'function of the organization', and whether contracting a PMSC to provide security is tantamount to conferring that function on the contractors.[215]

As noted above, the UN asserts that it is contrary to the rules of the organization to consider contractors as agents. That may be true, but it begs the question: contrary to which rules? When it comes to applying Articles 6 and 2 DARIO, how does one reconcile potentially competing rules from an organization? Is there a hierarchy? The analysis below will develop this point. The ILC insists that in certain circumstances, there may be attribution even when it is contrary to the rules of the organization.[216] The ILC did not provide many clues as to what the appropriate test would be when it comes to international organizations. This will also be developed below. Finally, the ICJ has accepted a similar rule in principle when it comes to attributing conduct to states on the basis of the actors in question constituting de facto state organs, even when not so defined by internal law. However, it has insisted that it will only be very rarely that such a finding will be made, and it has never made such a finding to date.[217] The test for coming to a conclusion that an entity is a de facto organ is the 'complete dependence' test for states. No test for attribution on this basis has been articulated for international organizations.

First, it may help to unpack the ILC's proposed rule. If we use Article 5 ASR by analogy, being mandated a function may be the equivalent of being delegated a power through a law.[218] This requirement is clearly echoed in the need for a mandated function based on the rules of the organization. In addition, the task being delegated must be an element of the governmental authority. While that concept remains somewhat fuzzy, there is some agreement on what it entails. That aspect of the Article 5 ASR test leads to the conclusion that, in the context of agents of international organizations, it is not only how a function is conferred on a person or entity that matters, but also the qualitative nature of the function itself that is relevant. Thus, the closer an outsourced activity is to the heart of the functions and purpose of an international organization itself, the more it should be susceptible to lead to attribution of conduct of the persons carrying it out. Put

---

[215] See ILC, 'DARIO with Commentaries', para. 3 of the Commentary to Article 6, p. 85.
[216] Ibid., para. 9 of the Commentary to Article 6, p. 89.
[217] *Bosnia v. Serbia*, paras 392–393.
[218] Article 5 ASR stipulates that the person or entity must be 'empowered by law' of the delegating state. This requirement is not without its critics, however.

another way, at a minimum, or at least when it may somehow be said to contravene some of the rules of an international organization, the conduct of a person charged with carrying out a *core function* of an international organization may be attributable to the organization.

Second, while the ILC's draft articles do not mention control as an element of defining an agent or when an agent's conduct is attributable to an organization, it does appear as a factor in the commentary. In fact, the commentary alludes to Article 8 ASR as an avenue of attribution. Astonishingly, in light of the absence of an article specifying as much, the commentary to Article 6 DARIO proclaims, 'Should persons or groups of persons act under the instructions, or the direction or control, of an international organization, they would have to be regarded as agents according to the definition given in subparagraph (d) of article 2.'[219] It thus appears to incorporate by reference Article 8 ASR into the DARIO through the commentaries on the rules. It then goes on, rather cryptically and laconically, 'As was noted above in paragraph (9) of the present commentary, in exceptional cases, a person or entity would be considered, for the purpose of attribution of conduct, as entrusted with the functions of the organization, even if this was not pursuant to the rules of the organization.'[220] As this is the last sentence of the commentary to Article 6, there is no further discussion as to whether the same standard would apply to define 'instructions, direction or control' as has evolved in the context of state responsibility. Nor is it entirely clear whether the two tests must be met cumulatively. This is furthermore a slightly odd amalgam as it appears to incorporate rather the notion of Article 4 ASR 'de facto organs' (exceptional circumstances when not defined by internal law as an organ) but on the basis of Article 8 ASR. As the two standards are already somewhat blurred, the ILC's use of them here is perplexing.

However, the UN proposed further elements for a test, which the ILC did not completely incorporate into the draft article or its accompanying commentary. The UN argued that the performance of 'mandated functions' is a 'crucial element' but that attribution must be made on a case-by-case basis, taking into account other factors, 'such as the status of the person or entity, the relationship and the degree of control that exists between the Organization and any such person or entity'.[221] The UN commented in passing that the ILC did not consider the nature of the functions. While

---

[219] ILC, 'DARIO with Commentaries', para. 11 of the Commentary to Article 6, p. 86.
[220] Ibid.
[221] UN Doc A/CN.4/637/Add. 1 (February 2011), 8–9, quotation from para. 12.

it did not develop this point to indicate any qualitative factors that would help to define which functions of which nature may make the conduct of the actors performing them more susceptible to attribution, it does express a preference for 'mandated functions'.[222] In UN speak when it comes to peacekeeping operations, that means someone who has been given a task in the resolution establishing the mission (or possibly in the UNSG report forming the basis of the resolution, taken together with the resolution itself). The final version of the ILC's draft articles does however take into account some of the UN's concerns in that the focus must be placed on the *functions* of the person or entity and not a looser standard of merely any person through 'whom the organization acts'.

The key questions would thus seem to be: are PMSCs carrying out security work in peace operations mandated to perform that function? How much control does the UN exercise over PMSCs as they carry out their functions? Applying the test, I will begin with an examination of the rules of the organization and then proceed to the control aspect. Indeed, we know that the UN accepts in general that contractors carry out functions of the organization. Thus, a priori, it may be possible to assume that this part of the test is met. The core of their argument is that attribution of the conduct of such persons as agents is contrary to the rules of the organization. This raises the question, to which rules in particular does it rely on in making this assertion?

Even in the early years of the United Nations, many eminent scholars considered that internal rules of an international organization may constitute international obligations.[223] In addition, the Commentary to the Draft Articles affirms that internal rules of the organization form part of international law. In indicating why Article 4 (setting out the elements of an internationally wrongful act of an international organization) does not refer to 'internal law' (in contrast to the Draft Articles on State Responsibility), the Special Rapporteur explained during the drafting process that

> the internal law of an international organization cannot be sharply differentiated from international law. At least the constituent instrument of the international organization is a treaty or another instrument governed by

---

[222] UN Doc A/CN.4/637/Add. 1 (February 2011), para. 13.

[223] A.J.P. Tammes, 'Decisions of International Organs as a Source of International Law' (1958) 94 *RCADI* 261. Oscar Schachter, 'The Development of International Law Through the Legal Opinions of the United Nations Secretariat' (1948) 5 *British YB Intl L* 91–133. See also José E. Alvarez, *International Organizations as Law-Makers* (Oxford University Press, 2005).

international law; some further parts of the internal law of the organization may be viewed as belonging to international law.[224]

International organizations that offered comments on the Draft Articles appear to agree. The International Criminal Police Organization, expressing its support for the idea that the ILC should somehow include the rules of international organizations in its works, distinguished those rules from the internal law of states. It stated, 'Issues implicating the organic principles or internal governance of international organizations are governed by international law. The obligations resting upon international organizations by virtue of their constituent instruments *and the secondary law of international organizations* are international legal norms.'[225] That organization went on to argue that, 'unlike when States breach their own domestic law, any breach of its own rules by an international organization is by definition a breach of an international obligation of the organization.'[226] The UN Secretariat unfortunately refused to express an opinion on this matter.[227]

Security Council resolutions are an excellent example of rules of the UN organization that also form part of international law. They are the primary way peace operations are mandated and staffed. The Security Council resolution establishing MONUSCO provides the basis for an interesting case study, since MONUSCO is an operation in which it is known that significant numbers of PMSCs are contracted to provide security.[228] First, looking at the terms of the mandate itself, we observe that the resolution states, 'MONUSCO shall comprise, in addition to the appropriate civilian, judiciary and correction components, a maximum

---

[224] ILC, 'Report of the International Law Commission on the Work of Its 64th Session', UN Doc A/64/10 (2010), Commentary to Draft Article 4, para. 5 (see also 2003 ILC report, Commentary to Draft Article 3, para. 9).

[225] ILC, 'Comments and Observations Received from Governments and International Organizations', UN Doc A/CN.4/556 (12 May 2005) at 30. Emphasis in original.

[226] Ibid., 31. Note that the International Monetary Fund stated that 'it would be inappropriate to treat the rules of an international organization as equivalent either to domestic law or as subordinate to general rules of it.' See p. 38.

[227] Ibid., 39. The Secretariat defended its refusal to take a position thus: 'in the absence of any indication as to the nature of the obligations breached by an international organization – other than its treaty obligations – this office is not in a position to express an opinion on whether the Commission should study the question [of internal rules], or what weight should be given to it in the general framework of its study on responsibility of international organizations.'

[228] The high value of the contracts awarded to private security companies from 2010 to 2012 are indicative of the numbers of security personnel. See www.un.org/depts/ptd/11_field_po_others.htm for 2011 amounts.

of 19,815 military personnel, 760 military observers, 391 police personnel and 1,050 personnel of formed police units.'[229] Thus, PMSCs working as private security guards do not appear to be a component of MONUSCO. In itself, this could constitute the rule of the organization stipulating that PMSCs (or PSCs) are not members of the peace operation or agents of the organization.

However, if one construes the resolution more broadly, it might be possible to arrive at the opposite conclusion. In the preamble of the resolution, for example, it states, '*Stressing* the significant security challenges' and affirms that the Security Council is '*determined* to avoid a security vacuum that could trigger renewed instability in the country'.[230] These, among many other statements, highlight the importance of a secure environment to the success of the mission. Depending on where and how they are supplied, therefore, security services could play a key role. Moreover, at least one element of the mandate of MONUSCO itself can be surmised to be carried out in part by private security companies: 'Ensur[ing] the protection of United Nations personnel, facilities, installations and equipment'.[231] Stephen Mathias, UN Assistant Secretary-General for Legal Affairs affirmed,

> Almost all UN operations use private security companies for some purpose. For the most part, these are unarmed local contractors who provide static access control at UN premises and at the residences of staff in field locations. However, over the last 10 years, the use of private security companies has expanded in a few cases to include mobile security of relief and humanitarian convoys.[232]

The recently adopted UN policy on the use of armed security guards provides that they may be used in order to act as a deterrent to potential attacks, but also may use force to repel attacks when necessary.[233] There may be a gulf between 'static access control' – i.e., checking identification badges, etc. – and what is meant to be encompassed by 'ensuring the protection of' personnel, facilities and so forth. However, arguably, providing mobile security of relief convoys is much closer to a function set out in the

---

[229] UNSC Resolution 1925 (2010), operative para. 2.
[230] UNSC Res 1925 (2010), preambular para. 5.   [231] UNSC Res 1925 (2010), para. 12(b)
[232] Stephan Mathias, 'Regulating and Monitoring Private Military and Security Companies in United Nations Peacekeeping Operations', International Institute for Humanitarian Law, Roundtable, San Remo, September 2012.
[233] 'Chapter IV: Security Management. Section I: Armed Private Security Companies', in United Nations Security Management System, *Security Policy Manual*, November 2012, paras 8 and 9.

mandate. Indeed, one can deduce that they are being used in such roles in the absence of sufficient numbers of troops to cover such duties. Such PMSCs may thus be considered to be implicitly mandated to perform a function of the organization.

As pointed out above, the UN does not deny that contractors carry out or help to carry out the functions of the organization. However, it strenuously argues that such persons cannot be construed as agents of the organization against its own rules. The ILC nevertheless retained this option in the final version of the DARIO. In the case described above, the essential questions are thus: (1) Can one interpret the UN Security Council resolution as one of the 'rules of the organization' that has implicitly conferred a function on PSCs, thereby making them agents of the organization? (2) If not, might the use of PSCs in such roles warrant attributing their conduct to the UN even if that contravenes another rule of the organization?

As is often the case with law, especially in the absence of a particular, concrete set of facts, the answer to the broad question is: it depends. This in itself is, however, an important conclusion. At the very least, it suggests that the UN's position that contractors are never attributable to it must be nuanced. While we may start from a presumption that they are not attributable to it since they do not fall into one of the categories of persons who are mandated with carrying out the mission, in some limited circumstances, they may well be attributable as agents of the organization because they are implicitly tasked to perform a given function.

Mathias argues that the use of PSCs in providing mobile security for convoys is a 'last resort' and this is indeed the approach taken in the UN policy. The policy stipulates, 'The fundamental principle in guiding when to use armed security services from a private security company is that this may be considered only when there is no possible provision of adequate and appropriate armed security, alternate member State(s), or internal United Nations system resources' such as the UN's own security officers recruited directly.[234] In addition, the policy states that PSCs will be used only 'on an exceptional basis to meet its obligations . . . when threat conditions and programme need warrant it'.[235] Without wishing to read too much into these statements, they are indeed revealing. The approach

---

[234] Ibid., para. 3.
[235] 'Chapter IV: Security Management. Section I: Armed Private Security Companies', in United Nations Security Management System, *Security Policy Manual*, November 2012, para. 2. See Elke Krahmann, 'The UN Guidelines on the Use of Armed Guards' (2014) 16 *ICLR* 475–491 at 481–483 for criticism on the 'last resort' criterion.

suggests that there are no other options but that the security being provided is essential to implementing other aspects of the mandate. In other words, but for the security contractors, the UN could not implement its essential tasks. The limited circumstances in which such companies may be used indeed speaks to the fact that they are central to a core function at the heart of the UN.

There is other evidence of the importance of the role of such contractors, including the sheer price of the contracts for security. While contracts for security in many current missions run in the tens or hundreds of thousands of dollars per year, those for MONUSCO and UNAMA can be over $5 million.[236] In the case of UNAMA, there can be no doubt that the need for extensive security contracting is related to the fact that it is a political mission (i.e. without UN peacekeeping forces on the ground) in a highly unstable environment. There are, therefore, no UN forces under UN command and control available to provide any security for anything UNAMA does. The dependence of the mission on private security companies is thus a logical consequence of that fact. This is not to argue, however, that contract price is a certain indicator of whether the function a person is performing should be attributable to the organization. Indeed, these prices fluctuate over the years, apparently in relation to the security situation in a given operation. They may also be correlated with an increase or decrease in mission size or an evolution in a mandate.[237] However, the size of the contracts provides a rough indication of the number of PSCs active in a given operation at a given time. As such, it may help to be an indicator of where PSCs are in fact being used in roles that would previously have been filled by troop contingents. As it is notoriously difficult to attract sufficient troop contributions from member states, using PSCs where possible to in effect stand in for troops in certain roles may mean that, in fact, the security activity of PSCs should be read into the mandate for the troop levels – especially where the number of forces actually deployed is below the number authorized in the mandate. In this respect, the UN policy setting out

---

[236] Information taken from the UN Procurement Division website: www.un.org/depts/ptd/12_field_po_others.htm. For example, in February 2012, IDG Security (Afghanistan Ltd) won a contract worth $2,381,300 for security services. In April of that year, in addition to several smaller contracts, it was awarded a contract worth $5,454,120 to provide such services. In 2011, contracts for security services for MONUSCO also ran to the millions of dollars; www.un.org/depts/ptd/11_field_po_others.htm. In 2008–2009, such multi-million-dollar contracts were awarded for companies providing security for UNMIL in Liberia.

[237] For example, see the contracts for UNMIL in Liberia at the time when the number of troops deployed was shrinking.

the restricted circumstances in which armed PSCs should be used affirms the reasonable nature of this approach. More transparency on how and when PSCs are used in such roles is urgently necessary.

13.4.3   PMSC Trainers and Security Sector Reformers

Similar arguments can be made to those above in respect of PMSCs tasked with training the police, security, or armed forces of the host state in which a peace operation is occurring. The importance of security sector reform and training of armed forces is often a central component of peace operations. This is also work commonly performed by PMSCs.[238]

13.5   PMSCs and the Instructions, Direction and Control of the Organization

In terms of instructions, the tasks of the PSC will be set out in the contract, as is the case when PMSCs are contracted by states.[239] More specifically, however, the UN policy on the Use of Armed Private Security Companies, which has only recently been adopted and made publicly available, allows a more in-depth assessment of the level of control the UN requires itself to exercise over PMSCs (in particular PSCs) that it contracts. The UN published its policy in November 2012 as part of its Security Policy Manual. This section will focus exclusively on the elements in that policy relating to instructions, direction and control by the UN over the companies that are set out in that manual and its accompanying guidelines.

It is important to recall that Article 8 ASR (or its equivalent) is not formally part of the DARIO. Instead, the ILC appears to incorporate the article by reference in the commentary, leaving the question as to whether the test is meant to be identical completely without answer. It is therefore very difficult to evaluate with any certainty whether the degree of control the UN exercises over the PMSCs it hires would satisfy this purported requirement. As such, the most that can be done in the following analysis is to identify and make a preliminary assessment in the abstract of the elements of control in UN policies.

---

[238] See Chapter 1. See also Åse Gilje Østensen, 'Implementers or Governors? The Expanding Role for Private Military and Security Companies Within the Peace Operations Network' (2014) 15 *ICLR* 423–442 at 427ff.

[239] Here again, arguably, the UN Security Council mandate establishing a peace operation may contain instructions that will be applicable to the activities of a PMSC contracted by the UN to provide security.

On a general level, the UN policy stipulates that the private security company itself must come up with its own policy on the use of force, which must conform to the UN policy on the use of force.[240] It must also develop its own weapons policy and its own standard operating procedures for the implementation of the contract.[241] Although these tasks must be done by the company itself, they must either conform to or be more restrictive than UN policies and, in the case of the standard operating procedures, must be developed 'in consultation with the United Nations Security Management organization involved'.[242] In addition, the guidelines accompanying the policy stipulate that 'All Standard Operating Procedures may be reviewed by the UN [Security Management System] organization in question. The UNSMS organization in question has the authority to direct the [armed private security company] to change the Standard Operating Procedures.'[243] The policy and guidelines thus walk a fine line in terms of instructions. By requiring the companies themselves to come up with their own rules on the use of force, etc., the UN may seem to avoid providing instructions to the companies directly. On the other hand, by reserving to UN security management personnel the authority to oblige a company to change the method it has said it will use to carry out its assigned tasks, it essentially retains the power to instruct companies on a very operational and concrete level. While such instructions would not satisfy a 'complete dependence' test (if the tests from the rules on state responsibility are applied *mutatis mutandis*), they may come close to amounting to 'acting on the instructions of . . .', along the lines of an Article 8 ASR standard (which remains speculative as a litmus test). Further elements of control over the companies set out in the policy may reinforce this conclusion.

There are a number of layers of oversight (i.e., control) over the activities of PSCs set down in the UN policy and guidelines. First, as is the case with states, contract officers are responsible for overseeing the performance of the contract.[244] Here, as in the case with states, this level of control alone would not likely be sufficient to bring the companies within

---

[240] 'Chapter IV: Security Management. Section I: Armed Private Security Companies', in United Nations Security Management System, *Security Policy Manual*, November 2012, para. 24(a).

[241] Ibid., para. 24(b) and (c).   [242] Ibid., para. 24(c).

[243] UN Security Management System, Security Management Operations Manual, *Guidelines on the Use of Armed Security Services from Private Security Companies*, November 2012, para. 37.

[244] 'Chapter IV: Security Management. Section I: Armed Private Security Companies', in United Nations Security Management System, *Security Policy Manual*, November 2012, para. 27; *Guidelines*, ibid., para. 42.

an Article 8 standard or its equivalent. However, an additional level of much closer oversight is also set down in the policy and guidelines. According to those documents, the UN security management officer on site (or his or her delegate) is required to conduct a daily inspection of the private security company.[245] The guidelines state,

> The Daily Operations Review of the performance of the APSC should include, as a minimum, an inspection of the following:
>
> a. safe handling and storage of firearms and ammunition
> b. required equipment is being carried
> c. equipment is functional
> d. physical condition of security posts/stations
> e. personal appearance and condition of the security force
> f. continuity of APSC personnel
> g. availability of all required personnel
> h. that the conduct and demeanor of APSC personnel reflects United Nations requirements
> i. quality of response to spot test training questions and readiness drills
> j. quality of response to actual situations arising during the day/shift
> k. review of the security log as maintained by the on-duty APSC security supervisor for accuracy and completeness
> l. explore concerns raised by the recipients of the services of the APSC.

This daily inspection amounts to a review of the companies' daily activities and oversight of its capability to perform its functions, presumably to the standard agreed on in the contract. Whether it also amounts to a control of their activities is a little more difficult to judge. It is noteworthy that it is described as an 'inspection'. It does not appear to amount to the type of control that is entailed in planning and supervising specific operations, for example. In addition to this inspection, there is a monthly review, for which the UN DSS Chief Security Adviser is accountable. That review 'should include' an assessment of all incident reports, all reports on the use of force (including armed and non-lethal) made by the PSC, all convoy protection reports to high-risk areas, selected daily situation reports, other threat assessments and risk analyses, training programme documents, individual performance reports and contract compliance.[246] Similarly, the policy and guidelines require PSCs to be signatories of the International Code of Conduct for Private Security Providers, which has its own reporting requirements.[247]

---

[245] *Guidelines*, ibid., paras 44–50.   [246] Ibid., para. 53.
[247] International Code of Conduct for Private Security Providers (9 November 2010), www.icoc-psp.org. This Code and its oversight mechanism are the result of a 'multistakeholder

Taken together, do reporting requirements and inspections amount to a significant degree of control exercised by the entity to which those reports are given or which is carrying out the inspections? Is such control 'effective control', if one were to use the standard from Article 8 ASR? There seems to be a qualitative difference in 'reporting' control and control over how an entity is made to carry out a task in a specific way at a given moment.[248] Indeed, states have to report on how they meet their human rights obligations under the ICCPR to the Human Rights Committee, but the Committee's review of those reports and issuing of conclusions does not mean that it exercises effective control over the reporting states. States and the HRC would likely view such a proposition as preposterous.

This means that it is likely that the key question is whether the UN control over standard operating procedures may in fact amount to having control over the companies.[249] For Article 7 DARIO, in order to determine whether the acts of an organ should be attributed to the lending state (or international organization) or to the UN, the test is who has effective control over the conduct. Logically, when imputing the conduct of an entity as an agent of an international organization against the rules of the organization, the organization must also exercise a high degree of control over that conduct. While it is virtually impossible to determine whether such control is exercised in the abstract, in my view, the case can be made that in the policies and guidelines it has developed for the use of PMSCs, the UN has given itself the tools and the possibility to exercise such control should it wish to do so. One cannot determine categorically that all private security contractors in peace operations are attributable as agents to the United Nations (or other organization) based on control. By the same token, it is not possible to conclude that they will never be attributable. A determination as to whether such control is in fact exercised can only be made with due consideration to all of the concrete facts in a given situation. Nevertheless, it is important to recognize that that possibility does in fact exist.

---

initiative convened by the Swiss government' (ICOC website). It was drafted by representatives of the industry working with NGOs and supported largely by the British and Swiss governments. See Krahmann, 'The UN Guidelines', for relevant criticism of the guidelines.

[248] Consider the statement by Lord Bingham in *Al Jedda*: 'it is one thing to receive reports, another to exercise effective command and control', *R (on the application of Al Jedda) (FC) v. Secretary of State for Defence* [2007] UKHL 58, para. 24.

[249] In addition, the companies are not placed under the direct control of a military commander in a peace operation involving deployed armed forces.

13.6   'Experts on mission' and Article 6 Attribution

Finally, if one argues from the perspective of attribution as a counterpart to immunity, it makes sense to look at whether PMSCs carrying out security can be considered 'experts on mission'. According to the Convention on the Privileges and Immunities of the United Nations, 'experts on mission' enjoy functional immunity.[250] The term itself is not defined in the Convention on Immunities beyond indicating that experts are not 'officials' and that they are 'performing missions for the United Nations'.[251]

Anthony Miller, a former Principal Legal Officer of the UN Office of Legal Affairs has defined them as 'persons retained under a variety of arrangements by which they agree to perform specific tasks, usually within a specific period',[252] although he recognizes that there is an 'immense difficulty of formulating a definition of experts on mission, other than in terms of an expert being a person so classified by the UN'.[253] Although he states that experts on mission is a concept that is defined by a 'deliberately broad formulation' possibly 'to ensure that it would be a flexible "catch all" that could encompass every agent of the UN who needed protection and who was not an official',[254] Miller implies that contractors are not experts on mission. He lists as examples of 'other persons engaged in helping the United Nations (UN) discharge its mandates' 'individual contractors, employees of corporate contractors and members of national contingents serving in UN peacekeeping operations', clearly distinguishing such actors from the category of persons comprising 'experts on mission'.[255]

In a legal opinion, the OLA has offered a definition that it proposed specifically in the context of contractors in peace operations. In its view, the term 'experts on mission' 'is understood to apply to persons who are charged with specific and important functions and tasks for the United Nations'.[256] Can private security guards (PMSCs) be considered 'experts on mission' in light of the definition provided by the OLA and despite the

---

[250] UN Convention on the Privileges and Immunities, Article VI, section 22.

[251] Ibid. Miller points out that the distinction between officials and experts remains ambiguous and poses problems for states due to the different privileges and immunities each status entails. See Anthony J. Miller, 'United Nations Experts on Mission and Their Privileges and Immunities' (2007) 4 *Intl Org L Rev* 11–56 at 20–21.

[252] Anthony J. Miller, 'United Nations Experts on Mission and Their Privileges and Immunities' (2007) 4 *Intl Org L Rev* 11–56 at 12.

[253] Ibid., 24.   [254] Ibid., 25.   [255] Ibid., 12.

[256] OLA, 'Privileges and Immunities and Facilities for Contractors Supplying Goods and Services in Support of United Nations Peacekeeping Operations' (1995) UN Juridical YB, Part Two, Chapter VI (23 June 1995), 407–408, 407, para. 3.

negative response implied by Miller's interpretation of the concept? The OLA specified that tasks that are *not* specific or important include those that are 'commercial in nature' or that 'range from the procurement of goods and the supply of services to construction and catering services'.[257] I have argued extensively elsewhere that the provision of security generally has been considered by some courts as a commercial service rather than an act of governmental authority.[258] However, here it is relevant to ask whether context matters. What if it is a commercially provided service that is part of a mandate and that is fundamental to the accomplishment of that mandate?

In addition, one may further inquire whether the term 'expert' implies a specific definition or somehow limits the type of missions that can fall within this category. Indeed, Miller notes that, early on, one of the features helping to define experts on mission was precisely that of expertise.[259] That is, does the mission itself assigned to the individual require technical skill or 'professional expertise'?[260] Although that aspect of the definition was intended to help distinguish between officials and experts on mission, it may also be relevant to circumscribing or delimiting the category of persons who are experts on mission. In an Advisory Opinion in which the definition of an 'expert on mission' was important, the ICJ concluded, 'The essence of the matter lies not in their administrative position but in the *nature* of their mission.'[261] The Secretary-General, in his submissions related to the concept in that matter, having enumerated a number of areas for which the UN frequently relies on experts on mission, stated, 'Many of these tasks *can only be fulfilled by highly qualified and specialized experts* who cannot always be found among the staffs of these organizations.'[262] In the context of peacekeeping, the experts the Secretary-General identified in his submissions in *Mazilu* included the military observers in UNTSO and UNMOGIP and the Commander's Headquarters Staff in UNEF and Cyprus.[263]

---

[257] Ibid., 407, para. 4.

[258] See, for example, the decisions of the European Court of Justice, *Commission of the European Communities v. Italy* (C-283/99) (ECJ (5th Chamber)) European Court of Justice (Fifth Chamber) 31 May 2001, [2001] ECR I-4363; *EC Commission v. Spain* (Case C-114/97) [1999] 2 CMLR 701; *EC Commission v. Belgium* (Case C-355/98) [2000] 2 CMLR 357; *Re Private Security Guards: Commission of the European Communities v. Italy* (Case C-465/05) [2008] 2 CMLR 3.

[259] Miller, 'UN Experts on Mission', 21–22. [260] Ibid., 28.

[261] *Mazilu* case, para. 46, emphasis added.

[262] See the Written Statement Submitted on Behalf of the Secretary-General of the United Nations in *Mazilu*, p. 173 at 187, para. 60. Emphasis added.

[263] Ibid., Annex I, p. 196.

The OLA also quoted the ICJ's Advisory Opinion in *Mazilu* to help round out its definition of 'experts on mission', in particular the fact that such persons, who are not UN officials, conduct mediation and investigative work. That, coupled with its opinion that persons providing commercial services are not experts on mission, would suggest a limitation to a type of activity perhaps somewhat in line with what one could consider akin to acts of a governmental authority. It is important to note that the Advisory Opinion could be seen as much broader in scope than that, as it also indicated that 'experts on mission' may encompass persons who 'have participated in certain peacekeeping forces, technical assistance work, and a multitude of other activities.'[264]

However, in one of its legal opinions, the UN Office of Legal Affairs, while affirming the general correctness of the ICJ's opinion in *Mazilu*, stated that persons performing 'functions such as those of vehicles mechanics [*sic*], dispatchers, drivers, electricians, carpenters and plumbers' in peacekeeping missions do not fall within the scope of the UN concept of 'experts on mission'.[265] It appeared to base this conclusion largely on the 'specific and important functions' aspect of the definition.[266]

For the purposes of this study, it is reasonable to surmise that basic security guarding activities are likely to be considered as falling within the same category as those enumerated – i.e. as not 'specific or important'. While some security providers may provide an expert service in terms of security analysis, much of the work of security guarding is not considered to require training to the level of an expert. If this criterion is significant or even decisive in limiting who is an expert on mission – and this would seem to jive with the UN's argument that the nature of an agent's task is relevant to whether a person can be considered as an agent of the organization for the purposes of attribution – then it would mean that very few security personnel would be experts on mission for the United Nations.[267]

---

[264] *Mazilu* case, p. 194, para. 48. While the Court was particularly concerned with the status of a special rapporteur and focused on that type of work, it nonetheless concluded, 'In all these cases, the practice of the United Nations shows that the persons so appointed ... have been regarded as experts on missions within the meaning of Section 22.'

[265] OLA, Memorandum to the Deputy Director, Field Operations Division, 'Status of Internationally Contracted Personnel Provided by Civilian Contractors in the Context of United Nations Peacekeeping Operations – Understanding of the Term "Experts on Missions"' (1993) UN Juridical YB 400–401 (11 February 1993).

[266] Ibid.

[267] It is worthwhile noting that the word 'mission' is not particularly significant for the definition. See Miller, 'UN Experts on Mission', 27.

The counterargument is of course that helping to create and preserve a secure environment in which the rest of the mandate may be carried out is a very important function or task.

Furthermore, arguably, the relationship between the individual who will have status as an expert on mission and the United Nations must be direct.[268] The UN OLA has stated that a person employed by a company contracted by the UN cannot have the status of an official or staff member of the UN.[269] If the interposition of a contracting company furnishing personnel indeed severs the necessary link between the UN and the individual who may be considered to be an expert on mission, then that would impede PMSC employees from having that status.[270]

Arguably, the terms of a Status of Forces Agreement providing for functional immunity for private security contractors may be sufficient to find that they are experts on mission, and their acts (official and *ultra vires*) would be attributable to the organization. This interpretation is supported by the fact that the OLA would not object to immunity being granted to contractors in the SOFA with the consent of the state on an ad hoc basis.[271] While the interposition of a company means a contractor employed by a company may not be an official or staff member of the United Nations,[272] the immunity consented to by the state in question would be intrinsically linked to the relationship of the contractor with the UN.[273]

The official UN position regarding the private security guards it contracts is that 'the personnel employed by private security companies do not enjoy the privileges and immunities afforded to United Nations personnel and that private security companies are accountable for the actions of their personnel.'[274] Furthermore, 'In cases of misconduct or illegal acts,

---

[268] Ibid., 29.

[269] Administrative Instruction ST/AI/327 of 23 January 1985, quoted in OLA, on the Draft Agreement on the status of the United Nations Operation in Mozambique – 'Proposal That Internationally Contracted Personnel Provided by Civilian Contractors in the Context of United Nations Peacekeeping Operations Be Accorded Privileges and Immunities such as Those Accorded to United Nations Officials' (1993) UN Juridical YB 396–400, 399 (3 February 1993) (hereafter OLA, 'Mozambique Memo 1993'), para. 11.

[270] Miller implies that this criterion has been asserted by the ICJ in *Mazilu*. See Miller, 'UN Experts on Mission', 24.

[271] OLA, 'Mozambique Memo 1993', para. 12.   [272] Ibid., 399, para. 11.

[273] See also Miller, 'UN Experts on Mission', 28–29.

[274] UN Advisory Committee on Administrative and Budgetary Questions, 'Reports on the Department of Safety and Security and on the Use of Private Security', UN Doc A/67/624 (7 December 2012), para. 28.

the personnel of private security companies are subject to the national law of the country in which they operate.'[275]

In my view, one cannot consider private security personnel in all peace operations as a whole in determining whether they may or may not have the status of experts on mission. Where private security personnel are contracted to fulfil roles that have traditionally been carried out by members of state troop contingents (such as convoy security), and especially where they involve the use of armed force, there is a strong argument in favour of finding that they are tasked with a specific and important function amenable to falling within the scope of functions performed by 'experts on mission'. Where such contractors have been accorded immunity in a Status of Forces Agreement, the argument would be strengthened even further. Where, on the other hand, they are performing very basic security guarding functions and benefit from no special treatment in the SOFA, they are unlikely to be considered as experts on mission.

The reasoning that applies in light of the 'expert on mission' analysis is commensurate with the discussion above regarding other ways in which the conduct of PMSCs engaged as private security guards may be attributable to the UN as the acts of agents of the organization. The nature of certain security functions – in particular, providing security for convoys, or activities that entail or are likely to entail a use of force to repel an attack by an armed group – are such that conduct in carrying out those tasks entails attribution to the United Nations. For many security tasks, however, that may not be the case.[276]

13.7   Applying Article 6 DARIO

13.7.1   PMSC Force

As the possibility was considered above,[277] it is relevant to affirm here that if the UN were to create a peacekeeping force using PMSCs, they would be agents of the organization according to this rule – either as its own organ or as individual agents.[278] This is so for a number of reasons. Such a force

---

[275] Ibid.
[276] This conclusion may have important policy implications: in particular, it implies that guards would not be easily transferable from one role to another, or at least transferable only within a circumscribed set of tasks. In addition, the certainty of status should be established.
[277] See Chapter 5.
[278] Organs are defined in Article 2(c) DARIO as 'any person or entity which has that status in accordance with the rules of the organization' – thus, a more limited category than agents.

would meet the criteria for attribution under Article 6 even if the most stringent version of the test is applied. This is because it would undoubtedly be carrying out a function of the organization and, given the argument above that in order to be a UN peacekeeping mission, it would have to be under the command and control of the UN, the criterion of control would also be met.[279]

13.7.2 Logistics

When it comes to logistics services, the OLA opinion from 1995 stating that services that are clearly commercial in nature do not entail immunity for those who perform those services provides a clear indication that persons performing such services are not experts on mission.[280] In addition, a 1993 opinion said that vehicle mechanics, dispatchers, drivers, electricians, carpenters and plumbers – in other words, many of the jobs done by PMSCs in terms of logistics work, including base support and maintenance, do not qualify for 'expert on mission' status.[281] Insofar as I have argued that experts on mission are attributable as agents of the organization, the fact that this category of PMSCs does not benefit from that status leads logically to the conclusion that their conduct is very unlikely to be attributable to the organization.

In Kosovo, KFOR contractors were given immunity in a regulation promulgated by the Special Representative of the Secretary-General at the head of the interim civilian administration of the territory. UNMIK Regulation 2000/47, On the Status, Privileges and Immunities of KFOR and UNMIK and Their Personnel in Kosovo, granted immunity to UNMIK and KFOR contractors.[282] That regulation stipulated that 'KFOR contractors, their employees and subcontractors shall be immune from legal process within Kosovo in respect of acts performed by them within their official activities.'[283] In my view, even though that immunity was not granted via a Status of Forces Agreement, the simple fact that functional immunity was accorded to contractors may be sufficient to deem such contractors experts on mission, such that their wrongful conduct may be

---

[279] Chapter 4, Section 4.1.

[280] OLA, 'Privileges and Immunities and Facilities for Contractors', 408.

[281] OLA, 'Status of Internationally Contracted Personnel', 400–401.

[282] UNMIK Regulation 2000/47, On the Status, Privileges and Immunities of KFOR and UNMIK and Their Personnel in Kosovo, section 4.

[283] Ibid., section 4.2.

attributable to the United Nations.[284] The immunity granted in this case goes far beyond the contractor facilities (visas, freedom of movement, etc.) normally accorded to contractors in a SOFA. In other words, if the UN has determined that a person requires functional immunity in order to be able to carry out their assigned tasks satisfactorily, then the UN must assume responsibility for any wrongs committed in the exercise of those functions.[285]

In Part I, I noted that even prosaic logistical tasks such as waste management can have severe repercussions on the local population in the host state of a peacekeeping operation – for example, the cholera epidemic in Haiti that was allegedly in part triggered by poor waste management by the contractor for the peacekeeping forces. It would seem unsatisfactory to suggest that the organization has no responsibility for such events on the grounds that the activity is not directly attributable to it. But, indeed, that is not the case, as it would be highly relevant to examine whether the obligations of due diligence in regard to the contractors have been met.

13.7.3   Observer Force

PMSCs have acted as an observer force in certain peace operations, or even in circumstances close to such operations (as noted in Chapter 1). The types of tasks such observers are given include monitoring, investigating and reporting. Those tasks were singled out by the ICJ in the *Mazilu* Advisory Opinion as representative of the kinds of activities performed by experts on mission. The Court observed that experts on mission 'have been entrusted with mediation, with preparing reports, preparing studies, investigations or finding and establishing facts'.[286] Thus, PMSCs conducting observer missions would be experts on mission, and their conduct, on

---

[284] In this case the legal construction is complex because the regulation was promulgated by a Special Representative of the Secretary-General of the UN in respect to NATO contractors.

[285] A KFOR contractor suspected of infringing the prohibition on knowingly using the services of a trafficked person was arrested in Kosovo in 2003 but was never prosecuted in Kosovo or in his home state. Again, depending on the function of the individual, such acts may, although *ultra vires*, occur within the framework of official functions of the individual. If immunity is not waived, then the organization must assume responsibility for those acts. For the case, see Amnesty International, 'Kosovo (Serbia and Montenegro): "So does it mean that we have the rights?" Protecting the Human Rights of Women and Girls Trafficked for Forced Prostitution in Kosovo' (5 May 2004), EUR 70/010/2004, text accompanying note 150 (pages not numbered).

[286] *Mazilu* case, p. 194, para. 48.

the basis that the conduct of UNPOL as experts on mission is considered to be attributable to the UN, would likewise be so attributable.

13.8 Due Diligence

The fact that states retain obligations of due diligence when international organizations operate on their territory is well known.[287] The due diligence obligations of international organizations themselves, however, have not been explored in much detail. The reason for this is fairly self-evident: due diligence obligations arise out of primary obligations in respect of persons or entities who were not otherwise attributable to the state or the international organization.[288] When it comes to PMSCs, I submit that many of the 'Good Practices' set down in the Montreux Document represent good ways for states to meet their due diligence obligations even when PMSC conduct is not directly attributable to them. For international organizations, however, some may question the existence of due diligence obligations based on the fact that it remains unclear what primary obligations bind international organizations.[289]

In the context of peace operations, without it being articulated in so many words, this question is at the heart of the debate about robust operations with a protection of civilians mandate. Indeed, if UN forces are responsible for taking steps to stop violations by other groups in territories where a peace operation is established, that is tantamount to saying that the UN has a due diligence obligation to prevent human rights abuses by armed groups (or others) against civilians. For various reasons, many of them political, states and organizations themselves are uncomfortable with the notion that the UN could be under a legal obligation to act in such situations.

For states, the due diligence obligation to protect the right to life arises in respect to specific threats to known individuals, where states could have taken steps to protect the person and failed to do so.[290] Indeed, the case

---

[287] In particular, the line of cases from the ECtHR including *Waite and Kennedy v. Germany* (App no. 26083/94) ECHR 18 February 1999 make this point.

[288] IACtHR, *Velasquez Rodriguez v. Honduras*, Judgment, Series C, no. 4 (29 July 1988), paras 172 and 174; ECtHR, *Osman v. UK* (App no 23452/94) (GC) ECHR 1998-VIII, para. 115.

[289] In addition, some argue that the obligation to exercise due diligence represents the obligation to use the administrative and legal infrastructure that states must have under general international law. One can ask whether there is a similar principle that international organizations must have a certain legal or administrative infrastructure in order to respect their international obligations.

[290] *Osman* case, para. 115.

law explored above relating to state responsibility in peace operations falls very much along this line of reasoning, without explicitly saying as much. The Dutch and Belgian courts were careful to find that the states owed a duty of care to protect specific, known individuals from the genocidaires in Srebrenica and Rwanda. They did not find that the forces had a general duty to protect all civilians at risk within their area of operations or responsibility.

In the context of peace operations, arguably, the burning question is no longer whether the UN is bound by human rights obligations, but rather, what is the extent of the scope of those obligations? Very few would today contest the notion that the UN must not violate the right to life via its own agents in peace operations – that is, UN agents must not engage in arbitrary killing.[291] But the question is whether its obligations go beyond that to protecting people. Siobhan Wills has pointed out the problematic institutional reaction of the UN DPKO with regard to the catastrophe in Rwanda – the DPKO thought that its error was in not explaining better that it was not there to protect people so as not to get their hopes up that it would actually do something while they were being massacred.[292] Indeed, in *Behrami*, the obligation on French troops in Kosovo would have been one of due diligence to do more to protect people from unexploded ordnance in their area of responsibility. When it comes to due diligence regarding human rights obligations for extra-territorial acts, courts have accepted that it is only reasonable to expect states to exercise due diligence where they have a certain degree of territorial control.[293]

The argument was made in Part II that international human rights law applies to the UN. In addition, via the Secretary-General's Bulletin, it has arguably accepted that it is bound by IHL. For IHRL, the due diligence obligations of international organizations may be similar to those that have been identified for states acting extra-territorially: where the organization exercises a high level of control over territory (for example, in the case of international administrations such as in UNMIK and UNTAET), it is also bound by the full gamut of due diligence obligations in respect to human rights. When, on the other hand, it does not control territory

---

[291] The *Mon Balaj* case discussed above goes some way to supporting this principle, but the weak mechanisms and constant stonewalling by the UN in having an open process and investigation stymie a conclusion that it considers itself fully bound by the same obligations that apply to states in such situations.

[292] Siobhan Wills, *Protecting Civilians* (Oxford University Press, 2010), pp. 39–40.

[293] *Congo v. Uganda*, para. 179. In that case, Uganda was responsible for not exercising due diligence in relation to the acts of armed groups in the territory it occupied.

but has deployed a peace operation, it can be expected to exercise due diligence in proportion to the influence it enjoys over entities capable of abusing human rights.[294]

When it comes to the UN using PMSCs in peace operations, given the strong arguments that the UN is bound by human rights law as well as by the IHL set down in the Secretary-General's bulletin, there are good reasons to conclude that the UN also has obligations of due diligence in respect to the PMSCs it contracts. It has an enormous potential to influence how the companies execute their obligations under the contract. In this light, it is worth noting that the European Union has signed the Montreux Document. Moreover, the UN's new policies on PMSCs very much reflect a sense of due diligence obligations, including reporting, oversight and training, and making sure they have the appropriate tools for the job.

---

[294] *Bosnia v. Serbia*, para. 430. The Court made this finding in respect of the obligation to prevent genocide, however, which some may argue is distinct from the obligation to prevent other violations of international law.

14

Implementation of Responsibility

14.1 States

The impediments to enforcing state responsibility are well known. States enjoy immunity in the courts of other states[1] and can be brought before the International Court of Justice only by other states, and only if they have already consented to the jurisdiction of the Court in a treaty or by a declaration.[2] Furthermore, arbitration, a common method of settling disputes between private parties and states, is not likely to be a viable mechanism for enforcing state responsibility for violations of international law by PMSCs for the simple reason that the legal basis for arbitration is an agreement between the two parties. It generally does not provide rights for third parties.[3] The fact that one is seeking to implement the responsibility of a state for the acts of PMSCs that are attributable to it – as opposed to some other state agent or actor – does not give rise to particular or additional legal difficulties.[4]

Given the fact that, on the whole, no new problems arise when it comes to implementing state responsibility for PMSC conduct, here it is sufficient to point out areas where differences may exist. In this respect, it is conceivable that seeking to enforce state responsibility for the acts of PMSCs that are attributable to a state but that are not considered members of its armed forces is in fact legally easier than when armed forces are involved in one respect.

---

[1] *Jurisdictional Immunities of the State (Germany v. Italy, Greece intervening)*, Judgment, ICJ Reports 2012, p. 99, represents the most recent affirmation of this principle.

[2] Article 36(2) of the Statute of the International Court of Justice allows states to declare that they accept the jurisdiction of the Court. For a recent reaffirmation of the principle of state immunity in the domestic courts of other states, see *Germany v. Italy*.

[3] Stavros L. Brekoulakis, 'The Relevance of the Interests of Third Parties in Arbitration: Taking a Closer Look at the Elephant in the Room' (2009) 113 *Penn State L Rev* 1165–1188, 1169–1170 and 1187.

[4] For a more detailed discussion, see Cameron and Chetail, *Privatizing War*, pp. 539–570.

There is an exception to the law of state immunity where the impugned act arises in the form of a 'territorial tort'. The UN Convention on Jurisdictional Immunities states this principle as follows:

> Unless otherwise agreed between the States concerned, a State cannot invoke immunity from jurisdiction before a court of another State which is otherwise competent in a proceeding which relates to pecuniary compensation for death or injury to the person, or damage to or loss of tangible property, caused by an act or omission which is alleged to be attributable to the State, if the act or omission occurred in whole or in part in the territory of that other State and if the author of the act or omission was present in that territory at the time of the act or omission.[5]

A similar provision articulating that principle in the European Convention on State Immunity is tempered by an article stipulating that, where such acts are committed by the armed forces, the 'territorial tort' exception to state immunity does not apply.[6] In addition, the commentary on the UN Convention specifies that, although it is not stated in the text of Article 12, the article does not apply in situations of armed conflict.[7] The ICJ dealt with this question specifically in the *Germany v. Italy* case and held that relevant state practice and *opinio juris* support the existence of a customary rule upholding state immunity in domestic courts for the acts of a state's armed forces.[8] While that holding may be open to criticism, for the purposes of this study, the consequences are distinct. If the conduct of PMSCs during an armed conflict can be attributed to a state, but if, as I have argued, the contractors do not form part of the armed forces of the state, a state would not be able to claim state immunity on the basis of the 'armed forces' exception to the 'territorial tort' exception to state immunity. As the 'acts of armed forces' exception can apply for visiting armed forces where there is no armed conflict as well as in situations of armed conflict, the exclusion of PMSCs from the armed forces can be important.[9]

On a separate note, national courts have accepted jurisdiction over the acts of their forces participating in peace operations abroad. In particular,

---

[5] Article 12, UN Convention on Jurisdictional Immunities of States and Their Property (2004) (not in force).

[6] See Article 11 of the European Convention on State Immunity (14 May 1972) 1495 UNTS 182, for the general principle of territorial tort exception, and Article 31 for the exclusion from the exception of the acts of the armed forces.

[7] In fact, the ILC commentary was made for the 1991 version of the Convention as Draft Articles but is commonly used as an interpretive tool for the Convention itself. See (1991) YBILC Vol II (2), 46, para. 10. See also *Germany v. Italy*, para. 69.

[8] *Germany v. Italy*, paras 77–78.   [9] Ibid., especially at paras 70–72.

we have seen this in *Bici v. UK, Nuhanovic v. Netherlands* and *Mukeshimana v. Belgium*. As those cases have been discussed above, it is not necessary to add much more here. All of those cases were heard in the courts of the same nationality as the troop contingent that had allegedly committed the impugned acts. This factor limits the accessibility of this option for many, if not most, potential claimants.

It is relevant to note, furthermore, that it is questionable whether state courts would accept responsibility for all human rights violations allegedly committed by their forces in the context of peace operations, including 'positive' obligations.

14.2   International Organizations

International organizations are, by and large, immune from suit in the territory of states. While this may be beginning to wane, it remains the predominant situation.[10] This immunity means that individuals cannot sue an international organization before state courts. On the international plane, international organizations cannot be parties to contentious disputes before the international court of justice.[11] Arbitration is the 'classic' tool for dispute resolution with international organizations, but is not generally accessible for individuals.[12] As a consequence of the increasing power and activity of international organizations and the rising sense of frustration that any potential legal complaints against them run into a brick wall, the accountability of international organizations for all of the actions they take, including regarding individuals, is a burgeoning field of research and international debate. As the International Court of Justice affirmed in *Cumaraswamy*, immunity from legal process does not absolve the organization from responsibility for

---

[10] See August Reinisch, 'The Immunity of International Organizations and the Jurisdiction of Their Administrative Tribunals', IILJ Working Paper 2007/11 (Global Administrative Law Series), who argues that national courts apply immunity less and less, relying on *Waite and Kennedy v. Germany* (App. no 26083/94) ECHR 18 February 1999.

[11] ICJ statute, Article 34(1): 'Only States may be parties in cases before the Court.' See also Kirsten Schmalenbach, 'International Organizations or Institutions: Legal Remedies Against Acts of Organs', in R. Wolfrum (ed.), *Max Planck Encyclopedia of Public International Law* (Oxford University Press 2008–), para. 8, on how access to the ICJ may occur through indirect means regarding the UN Convention on Privileges and Immunities.

[12] Michael Bothe, 'Security Council's Targeted Sanctions Against Presumed Terrorists: The Need to Comply with Human Rights Standards' (2008) 6 J Intl Crim Justice 541 at 542, noting it is particularly the case for contractual disputes, which generally does not mean employment contracts with individuals, but contracts based on 'international agreements'.

unlawful acts.[13] The question, then, is how to put that responsibility into effect.

One impediment to formal implementation of responsibility of international organizations is a lack of forum. International organizations cannot be parties to cases brought before the International Court of Justice.[14] Moreover, the DARIO do not include persons as falling within the actors who are able to invoke the responsibility of international organizations.[15] The ILC recognized the implications of the limitations of the DARIO and set down in Article 33(2) that the limitation of the scope of responsibility to states and international organizations 'is without prejudice to any right, arising from the international responsibility of an international organization, which may accrue directly to any person or entity other than a State or an international organization'. No state or international organization objected to this limitation during the final rounds of comments on the penultimate version of the Draft Articles.

The choice to limit the scope of responsibility to international organizations and states was clearly stated by the Special Rapporteur as being based purely on expedience. In the commentary regarding this article in his Fifth Report, Gaja states that the limitation

> would not only be a way of following the general pattern provided by the articles on State responsibility, *it would also avoid the complications that would no doubt arise* if one widened the scope of obligations here considered in order to include those existing towards subjects of international law other than States or international organizations.[16]

That comment was not reiterated in the final commentary accompanying the Draft Articles as adopted in 2011. In respect to same limitation in the Articles on State Responsibility, Edith Brown Weiss lamented in 2002 that the ILC 'should have done more to recognize the expanded universe of participants in the international system entitled to invoke state responsibility'.[17] Brown Weiss observes that the ILC left the invocation of

---

[13] *Difference Relating to Immunity from Legal Process of a Special Rapporteur of the Commission on Human Rights* (Advisory Opinion) [1999] ICJ Rep 62, para. 66 (*Cumaraswamy*).

[14] ICJ Statute, Article 34(1): 'Only States may be parties in cases before the Court.'

[15] Article 43 DARIO provides for the invocation of responsibility by an injured state or international organization. ILC, 'DARIO with Commentaries', p. 136. See also Article 49, which is equally limited to states or international organizations, but other than the injured party.

[16] ILC, 'Fifth Report of the Special Rapporteur Giorgio Gaja', UN Doc A/CN.4/583 (2007), para. 37, emphasis added.

[17] Edith Brown Weiss, 'Invoking State Responsibility in the Twenty-first Century' (2002) 96 *AJIL* 798 at 809

state responsibility by individuals to the *lex specialis* in the regimes that already provided for that possibility, rather than identifying a generalized rule.[18] Arguably, the same is true here. In its commentary, the ILC acknowledged two 'significant area[s] in which rights accrue to persons other than States or organizations': employment and peacekeeping.[19] The ILC stated, 'The consequences of these breaches with regard to individuals ... are not covered by the present draft articles.'[20] The fact that the responsibility regime vis-à-vis individuals harmed in peacekeeping operations constitutes its own *lex specialis* warrants limiting the scope of the study here to that regime.

As will be shown below, most frequently, claims brought against the UN for injury or damage in the course of peace operations have been brought by individuals through claims commissions.[21] The Special Rapporteur, however, has highlighted the few instances where reparation for injury and damages arising in a peace operation has been dealt with through traditional dispute resolution mechanisms between a state and an international organization (exchanges of letters).[22]

In the context of peace operations, moreover, there is precedent to suggest that it may not be entirely straightforward for a host state to take up the claim of (one of) its nationals against an international organization. Kirsten Schmalenbach, through research in the UN archives, has unearthed an Egyptian espousal of claims of its citizens toward UNEF and a letter in response by a UN official stating that

> The Egyptian Government is not an interested party in any claim by a private individual, so that I trust that there is no implication that UNEF and the Egyptian Government represent opposite sides in a dispute. While your Liaison Headquarters may serve as a channel for claims in appropriate instances, and in helping us to arrive at disinterested estimates of any case, it would be a serious matter if it were to take a partisan stand in pressing claims against us.[23]

[18] Ibid., 815. Brown Weiss canvassed the regimes of human rights law, environmental protection, investor claims and others to support her argument.

[19] ILC, 'DARIO with Commentaries', para. 5 of the Commentary to Article 33, p. 127.

[20] Ibid.

[21] Ibid., 14, but note that he also relies on the statements by the UN Secretary General on Rwanda and Srebrenica as examples of 'satisfaction' (therefore, as an assumption of responsibility). Marten Zwanenburg, *Accountability of Peace Support Operations* (Leiden: Martinus Nijhoff, 2005), discusses the international nature of the claims.

[22] This was the case in Congo in the 1960s with respect to ONUC.

[23] Kirsten Schmalenbach, 'Third Party Liability of International Organizations: A Study on Claim Settlement in the Course of Military Operations and International Administrations' (2005) 10 *Intl Peacekeeping* 33–51 (this quotation at 41).

This would appear to be a clear rejection of a possibility for Egypt to exercise diplomatic protection in this context.[24] Indeed, the tone at the end of the passage is almost threatening. In the case of ONUC, claims that were dealt with between governments and the UN were those relating to third-state nationals – i.e., Belgians, Swiss, Luxembourgeois.[25] It is not unreasonable to understand the UN official's comments above as saying that a host state may not take up the claims of its own nationals against the organization conducting the peace operation or that those kinds of obligations do not amount to international obligations giving rise to diplomatic protection. However, in the 2008 ILC report on the Third Part of the Draft Articles, namely with respect to invocation of international responsibility, the ILC (perhaps honestly) completely ignores this precedent and asserts, in its commentary:

> [D]iplomatic protection could be exercised by a State also towards an international organization, for instance when an organization deploys forces on the territory of a State and the conduct of those forces leads to a breach of an obligation under international law concerning the treatment of individuals.[26]

It may be that the legal position has changed since the first peace operation. Indeed, international organizations other than the United Nations engaging in peace operations allow the host state of the operation to forward claims on behalf of its citizens and to engage in full diplomacy. The Status of Forces Agreements for the EU Force in Chad and in the Central African Republic provide for a range of options, starting with the host state forwarding claims on behalf of their nationals to EUFOR for an 'amicable settlement', progressing to an arbitral claims commission and, if all else fails to achieve a satisfactory settlement, diplomatic means and arbitration between EU representatives and host state representatives.[27]

---

[24] For a general discussion of a state exercising diplomatic protection against an organization, see Karel Wellens, *Remedies Against International Organisations* (Cambridge University Press, 2002), pp. 73–78.

[25] Zwanenburg, 'UN Peace Operations Between Independence and Accountability' (2008) 5 *Intl Org L Rev* 23 at 40.

[26] ILC, 'Report of the International Law Commission on the Work of Its 63rd Session', UN Doc A/63/10 (2008) 286, para. 2 of the commentary to Draft Article 48.

[27] 'Accord entre l'Union européenne et la République du Tchad relatif au statut des forces placées sous la direction de l'Union européenne dans la République du Tchad', Official J EU, Doc L 83/40 (26 March 2008) Article 15; 'Accord entre l'Union européenne et la République centrafricaine relatif au statut des forces placées sous la direction de l'Union européenne dans la République centrafricaine', Official J EU, Doc L 146/36 (24 May 2008) Article 15. Note that for the European Union military operation in Democratic Republic of the Congo

It is therefore logical to proceed to the special regime that has evolved governing the responsibility of the UN for violations of international law arising in peacekeeping operations. Broadly speaking, there are three main ways in which the UN has been held accountable for actions during peace operations: through in situ claims commissions accessed by individuals, via international inquiries and apologies in the face of large scale failure and, finally, in some cases, by settling claims with states on behalf of affected nationals. For this study, the first is the most relevant.

Peace operations are subsidiary organs of the United Nations and therefore engage the responsibility of the UN as a whole. Beginning with UNEF in 1958 and then in Congo (ONUC) in the 1960s, Regulations and Status Agreements with respect to those operations established methods of dealing with claims against UN forces.[28] In the mid-1990s, at the height of large-scale and ambitious peace operations, the UN took a number of actions regarding its liability and responsibility in peace operations. Initially, the UN undertook to create a 'standing claims commission' to handle claims for damages arising from its actions in peace operations; furthermore, arbitral tribunals were to be set up to hear appeals from that commission.[29] However, the standing claims commission has never been established.[30] Instead, ad hoc commissions or review boards are created, but not on a systematic basis and not for every peace operation.[31] These

---

(DRC) in 2006 in support of the election, the enabling Security Council Resolution urged the European Union Force (EUFOR) (Althea) to conclude a SOFA with the DRC (which would set out privileges and immunities) but specified that until such time the SOFA agreed for MONUC in May 2000 would apply *mutatis mutandis*. There is no public record of such a SOFA, and the provision in the relevant EU Council Joint Action stipulates that privileges and immunities 'will be determined in accordance with the relevant provisions' of UNSC Resolution 1671 (2006). See Article 12 of 'Council Joint Action 2006/319/CFSP of 26 April 2006 on the European Union Military Operation in Support of the United Nations Organisation Mission in the Democratic Republic of the Congo (MONUC) During the Election Process', Official J EU, Doc L 116/98 (29 April 2006).

[28] Finn Seyersted, 'United Nations Forces: Some Legal Problems' (1961) 37 *British YB Intl L* 351 at 420–421.

[29] Model SOFA 'Draft Model Status-of-Forces Agreement Between the United Nations and Host Countries', Annex to the Report of the Secretary-General, UN Doc A/45/594 (9 October 1990) (UN Model SOFA), para. 51.

[30] Ibid. See also Daphna Shraga, 'UN Peacekeeping Operations: Applicability of International Humanitarian Law and Responsibility for Operations-Related Damage' (2000) 94 *AJIL* 406 at 409; Zwanenburg, 'UN Peace Operations', 28, and J.M. Sorel, 'La responsabilité des Nations Unies dans les opérations de maintien de la paix' (2001) 3 *International Law Forum* 127.

[31] Shraga, ibid., and Sorel, ibid. (for criticism). For example, no claims commission was created for MINUSTAH, despite severe criticism of its use of force and the destructiveness of

'local' claims commissions are composed entirely of mission staff and do not include an adjudicator/member appointed by the host state, as the standing commissions outlined in the Model SOFA would have it.[32]

The UN has also limited its financial liability in terms of the amount that can be claimed and the circumstances or conditions under which it would be liable.[33] For instance, the UN Secretary-General prescribed that the UN is not responsible for damages arising from 'operational necessity'.[34] Responsibility for compensating individuals for such damages falls to the host state. While some commentators have expressed important concerns with this limitation,[35] a legal opinion issued by the Office of Legal Affairs of the UN Secretariat has argued that in peace operations deployed where there is no functioning government capable of compensating its citizens (and residents), the UN should assume responsibility for such compensation.[36]

---

some of its operations. See Matt Halling and Blaine Bookey, 'Peacekeeping in Name Alone: Accountability for the United Nations in Haiti' (2008) Hastings Intl and Comparative L Rev 461–486.

[32] Zwanenburg, 'UN Peace Operations', 28; Sorel, 'La responsabilité des Nations Unies'; Frédéric Mégret, 'The Vicarious Responsibility of the United Nations for "Unintended Consequences" of Peacekeeping Operations', in Chiyuki Aoi, Cedric de Cooning and Ramesh Thakur (eds.), The 'Unintended Consequences' of Peace Operations (Tokyo, UN University Press, 2007), pp. 250–267; Schmalenbach, 'Third Party Liability', 41. Note also that in the Parliamentary Assembly of the Council of Europe Resolution 1417 (2005) it recommended that independent members be appointed at least at the appeal level for the KFOR and UNMIK claims review boards.

[33] Shraga, 'UN Peacekeeping Operations', 409–410.

[34] Report of the Secretary-General, 'Financing of the United Nations Protection Force', UN Doc A/51/389 (20 September 1996) Part II, B2.

[35] Zwanenburg, 'UN Peace Operations', 32, points out that often peace operations occur in states that are not capable of or likely to compensate people, so people end up with nothing. He also points out that this limitation on the responsibility of the international organization is not commensurate with the permissible 'circumstances precluding wrongfulness' of the ILC draft articles. However, this argument seems, on the face of it, to be misplaced – under international law, if an operation complies with the requirements of military necessity, it by definition does not infringe international law and therefore the question of circumstances precluding wrongfulness does not even arise. Amerasinghe would appear to be in agreement with this assessment. See Amerasingh, Principles, p. 402.

[36] OLA, 'Claim for Rental Payment for the Use of a Compound by United Nations Mission in Somalia (UNOSOM II)' (1994), UN Juridical YB 403–406. In that case, the claim was with respect to Somalia. However, in Kosovo, a provision in Regulation 2000/47 stipulated that damages to be addressed by UN and NATO claims commissions would be limited to those not arising out of operational necessity (see para. 7), thereby leaving residents without recourse for the much more likely damages that occur due to the normal operations of the mission. Arguably, however, on the basis of the Somalia precedent, in situations of territorial administration, that limitation should not apply.

The Secretary-General also suggested that the amount of compensation available should be limited and the UN General Assembly has accepted these limitations, which have been incorporated into Status of Forces agreements for recent missions.[37] Finally, as noted above, the UN does not accept responsibility for private acts (as distinct from *ultra vires* acts) of its peacekeeping personnel, but there is precedent for the UN to provide compensation for damage caused by a shooting by a peacekeeper 'where no official function or superior order required him to shoot'.[38] In addition to these limitations, claims must be brought within six months of the date of the event giving rise to the claim (or from the moment when the person could be aware of the basis for a claim). This limited and ad hoc method of addressing claims arising out of peace operations has been criticized,[39] but considering that states ultimately bear the financial burden generated by compensation claims, the will to create a more robust system has been lacking.

In terms of other means of addressing or assuming international responsibility for large-scale failure, commissions of inquiry have been set up and quasi-apologies issued. These have occurred following the cases of inaction or failure to protect in Rwanda in 1994 and Srebrenica in 1995.[40] Under the international law of responsibility, such actions may constitute satisfaction.[41] Some, however, have criticized these reports and the official statements surrounding them, observing that the words 'I apologize' were never used, and arguing that 'even if a proper apology had been offered

---

[37] General Assembly Resolution 52/247, 'Third Party Liability: Temporal and Financial Limitations', UN Doc A/RES/52/247 (17 July 1998); Zwanenburg, 'UN Peace Operations', 35, cites the Sudan mission agreement.

[38] Amerasinghe, *Principles*, p. 402.

[39] In particular, Klein, *La Responsabilité*, p. 189 and more generally pp. 184–191.

[40] See 'Letter Dated 15 December 1999 from the Secretary-General Addressed to the President of the Security Council' (Enclosure: Report of the Independent Inquiry into the Actions of the United Nations During the 1994 Genocide in Rwanda), UN Doc S/1999/1257 (15 December 1999) and 'Report of the Secretary-General Pursuant to General Assembly Resolution 53/35: The Fall of Srebrenica', UN Doc A/54/549 (15 November 1999). The UN Security Council accepted responsibility on presentation of the Rwanda report on 14 April 2000 (see UN Press Release SC/6843 14 April 2000). Considerable regret and responsibility was expressed by the Secretary-General at the time of the reception and presentation of the reports. Some have acknowledged that this marks progress in the UN accepting fallibility and responsibility, but still criticized it, arguing that it 'falls short of issuing a real apology and taking responsibility for the wrong committed'. See Jean-Marc Coicaud and Jibecke Jönsson, 'Elements of a Road Map for a Politics of Apology', in M. Gibney, R. Howard-Hassmann, J.-M. Coicaud and N. Steiner (eds.), *The Age of Apology: Facing Up to the Past* (University of Pennsylvania Press, 2008), pp. 77–91, p. 90.

[41] Zwanenburg suggests it may be; but see Coicaud and Jönsson, 'Elements of a Road Map'.

to the victims of Srebrenica and Rwanda, one has to admit that it would have represented a rather meagre form of overall accountability for the UN (and its member states).'[42]

Above, I noted that the UN offered compensation to the families of the protesters who were killed by UNMIK civilian police.[43] With respect to implementation of the responsibility of the UN, in that case, the families pursued a number of avenues for redress and compensation. They filed a claim against UNMIK through a unique body that was set up in Kosovo, the Human Rights Advisory Panel,[44] which initially declared the claim admissible.[45] The hearing before the Human Rights Advisory Panel was postponed due to UNMIK's expression of concerns that it could not guarantee security for a public hearing (and the complainant's insistence that the hearing be public). In the intervening time, the Special Representative of the Secretary-General issued an administrative direction whose effect, if lawful and applicable, would be to render the initial complaint inadmissible if the complainants had also filed a claim for compensation via the UN Third Party Claims Process.[46] The families had indeed also sought compensation via the UNMIK Claims Review Board, which was offered to them,[47] and on that basis the Panel declared the claim inadmissible.[48] The families ultimately accepted the compensation offered by the Third Party Claims mechanism.[49] However, the Human Rights Advisory Panel reopened the proceedings, giving apparent weight to the argument of the complainants that receiving the UN Third Party Claims Process did not address all of the issues they raised, including 'the right to life, the right to freedom from torture..., the right to a fair trial, the right to freedom of assembly and the right to an effective remedy.'[50] In arriving at this decision, the Panel determined that waivers the parties had signed could not prevent these claims from going forward.[51]

---

[42] Coicaud and Jönsson, 'Elements of a Road Map', p. 90.

[43] See Chapter 13, notes 198–209 and accompanying text.

[44] Case No. 04/07 Kadri Balaj (on behalf of Mon Balaj), Shaban Xheladini (on behalf of Arben Xheladini), Zenel Zemeli and Mustafa Nerjovaj v. UNMIK, Human Rights Advisory Panel, Decision (6 June 2008).

[45] Ibid. [46] Mon Balaj v. UNMIK 2010, paras 32–36.

[47] The details of that claim are provided in the second Human Rights Advisory Panel decision adopted in the case, ibid., paras 6 and 7.

[48] Ibid., paras 52–53.

[49] The third decision of the Human Rights Advisory Panel in the case affirms that compensation was accepted. See Mon Balaj v. UNMIK 2012.

[50] Ibid., paras 87 and 93. [51] Ibid., para. 82.

This case is illustrative of the hurdles complainants may face in attempting to implement the responsibility of the UN for wrongful acts during peacekeeping operations. Indeed, the mechanism is far from being straightforward and easily accessible by the injured parties: the complainants in this case are represented by barristers from chambers in London.[52]

As noted above, in this case, the least complicated matter was the fact that the Human Rights Advisory Panel and the UN accepted that the acts of the Romanian UNPOL were attributable to it. Having to prove attribution of PMSCs to an international organization can thus only be anticipated to complicate matters further in such proceedings. On the other hand, the fact that the Advisory Panel was willing to reopen the proceedings despite the fact that the parties had received compensation and signed waivers sends an important signal. That is, compensatory claims commissions may not be sufficiently well rounded to handle all aspects of the responsibility of an international organization. In Kosovo, the Human Rights Advisory Panel was only belatedly established and it is not a feature of other peace operations. Certainly, the wide powers of an international organization administering territory warrant the creation of a robust and independent mechanism to enforce human rights; one may wonder whether the same need will be perceived to arise in other peace operations where the powers are narrower in scope.

The case *Mothers of Srebrenica v. Netherlands and UN* provides a further illustration of the quasi-impossibility of enforcing the international legal obligations of the United Nations in national courts. The complainants brought a claim against the Netherlands and against the United Nations for the failure of UNPROFOR and Dutchbat to protect the Bosnian Muslims in the Srebrenica enclave. The UN refused to waive its own immunity and did not appear in any of the proceedings before Dutch courts, at any level.[53] All three levels of Dutch courts upheld the United Nations' immunity.[54] The European Court of Human Rights found a complaint in relation to these decisions inadmissible, holding that they did not violate

---

[52] Paul Troop and Jude Bunting from Tooks Chambers, London.

[53] A summary of the proceedings is provided in *Mothers of Srebrenica v. Netherlands and United Nations*, final appeal judgement, Netherlands Supreme Court (13 April 2012) LJN: BW1999; ILDC 1760 (NL 2012), Oxford Reports on International Law in Domestic Courts. See also the District Court decision: *Mothers of Srebrenica et al. v. the Netherlands and the United Nations*, Case number 295247/HA ZA 07/2973 (10 July 2008); for the UN's invocation of its own immunity, see para. 5.13.

[54] District Court decision, ibid., para. 6.1; Appeal court decision: BL8979, 30 March 2010.

the Netherlands' obligations under Article 6 of the ECHR.[55] That immunity is based on Article 105 of the UN Charter and Article II(2) of the Convention on the Privileges and Immunities of the United Nations.[56]

Furthermore, cases brought in US courts against the UN regarding the cholera epidemic in Haiti allegedly caused by inadequate handling of sewerage by private contractors have run up against the wall of UN immunity.[57] The fact that the UN has invoked immunity in this case has given rise to much consternation, including from within the UN itself.[58] Four Special Rapporteurs and one Independent Expert of the UN Human Rights Council even went so far as to write an open letter to the UN Secretary-General criticizing the fact that the victims remain unable to access an effective remedy.[59]

The International Court of Justice has held that 'any such claims [for damage arising out of acts of agents or officials for whom immunity is not waived] against the United Nations *shall not be dealt with* by national courts.'[60] Thus, although there is a process by which immunity of individuals within the organization may be waived, there is no such process by which the immunity of the organization itself may be waived. Instead, the organization is bound to 'make provisions for appropriate modes of settlement of: ... (b) Disputes involving any official of the United Nations who by reason of his official position enjoys immunity, if immunity has not been waived by the Secretary-General.'[61] In effect, then, the UN is under an obligation to provide 'reasonable alternative means' to

---

[55] *Stichting Mothers of Srebrenica and others v. the Netherlands* (App No. 65542/12) Decision on admissibility, 11 June 2013.

[56] Article 105 of the Charter reads (in relevant part), 'The Organization shall enjoy in the territory of each of its Members such privileges and immunities as are necessary for the fulfilment of its purposes.' Article II(2) of the Immunities Convention states, 'The United Nations, its property and assets wherever located and by whomsoever held, shall enjoy immunity from every form of legal process except insofar as in any particular case it has expressly waived its immunity. It is, however, understood that no waiver of immunity shall extend to any measure of execution.' Convention on the Privileges and Immunities of the United Nations, 13 February 1946, 1946-1947 UNTS 16-32, entered into force 17 September 1946.

[57] *Delama Georges et al. v. United Nations et al.*, US District Court (Southern District New York), C1:13-cv-07146-JPO, 9 January 2015, finding that the UN has absolute immunity.

[58] See also Kristen Boon, 'The United Nations as Good Samaritan: Immunity and Responsibility' (2016) 16 *Chicago J IL* 341–385.

[59] UN Office of the High Commissioner for Human Rights, Letter from Leilani Farha, Phillip Alston, Gustavo Galln, Dainius Puras, Léo Heller to UN Secretary-General, 23 October 2015.

[60] *Cumaraswamy*, para. 66. Emphasis added.   [61] 'Immunities Convention', section 29.

individuals seeking redress, but, unlike in the ECHR cases, there is no entity that is endowed with the capacity to determine whether the means provided actually fulfil that obligation.[62] Indeed, a state upon whose territory an international organization operates with immunity nonetheless cannot avoid its obligation to provide a remedy for the persons within its jurisdiction despite the immunity of the organization.

The problem with immunity of international organizations for states is that it puts them in a situation of having to deal with two conflicting obligations: on the one hand, to provide access to justice for persons under their jurisdiction; on the other, to honour the obligation to provide immunity to certain organizations on its territory.[63] The major ECtHR cases dealing with immunity of international organizations do not seek to consider the appropriateness of that immunity, but rather examine whether the state in which the organization operates and enjoys immunity violated its human rights obligation to provide access to justice.[64]

In *Waite and Kennedy v. Germany* and *Beer and Regan v. Germany*, the ECtHR set out a test to determine whether Germany's decision not to waive immunity for the European Space Agency (when its former employees sought to sue it in German courts) complied with the European Convention. Affirming that the right of access to courts is not absolute, the ECtHR went on to define criteria that would respect that right even if immunity were upheld. First, the Court must 'be satisfied that the limitations applied do not restrict or reduce the access left to the individual in such a way or to such an extent that the very essence of the right is impaired'.[65] In addition, the limitation (on access to court, i.e. upholding immunity) must pursue a legitimate aim and there must be 'a reasonable relationship of proportionality between the means employed and the aim sought to be achieved'.[66] In a crucial passage, the ECtHR insisted that the state is not absolved of its obligation to protect human rights simply because it has granted immunity to an international organization.[67] The final 'material factor' for the European Court as to whether a grant of immunity from local jurisdiction is permissible is whether there were 'reasonable alternative means' for the applicants to protect effectively their rights under the Convention.[68]

---

[62] As, for example, the ECHR may do for other organizations.

[63] August Reinisch, *International Organizations Before National Courts* (Cambridge University Press, 2000), pp. 278ff., makes this observation, while Dan Sarooshi, *International Organizations and Their Exercise of Sovereign Powers* (Oxford University Press, 2005), comments that states rarely seem to see this as directly conflicting.

[64] *Waite and Kennedy v. Germany* (App no. 26083/94) ECHR 18 February 1999.

[65] Ibid., para. 59.   [66] Ibid.   [67] Ibid., para. 67.   [68] Ibid., para. 68.

In the *Waite and Kennedy* case, the Court was relatively easily satisfied that the immunity had a legitimate objective because it is 'an essential means of ensuring the proper functioning of such organisations free from unilateral interference by individual governments'.[69] This finding is consonant with the traditional justification for granting immunity to international organizations.[70] Some authors argue that the UN cannot possibly need to protect itself from unilateral interference by governments when it *is* the government, such that this justification cannot apply in that context.[71] Historically, states also benefited from sovereign immunity, but over time this has eroded to some extent.[72] Some academic critics are now proclaiming that the time is right to begin the same slow process of erosion of immunity for international organizations.[73]

The Dutch Supreme Court however considered that the *Waite and Kennedy* test did not even necessarily apply to the United Nations. It cited the ECtHR's controversial decision in *Behrami* and *Saramati v. France and Norway* to support its assertion that the UN (and in particular the Security Council) has a special place in the international legal system.[74] Furthermore, it held that, due to Article 103 of the UN Charter, which asserts the paramountcy of obligations under the Charter over other obligations, UN immunity is absolute, even in the face of conflicting obligations.[75] This appears also to follow the ICJ's decision in *Cumaraswamy* to the effect that national courts shall not deal with immunity claims.

Thus, the Dutch Supreme Court has held that a state does not even have to consider whether there are alternative means available for the complainants when it upholds the immunity of the UN. Thus, not even

[69] Ibid., para. 63.
[70] Emmanuel Gaillard and Isabelle Pingel-Lenuzza, 'International Organisations and Immunity from Jurisdiction: To Restrict or to Bypass' (2002) 51 *ICLQ* 1–15.
[71] Especially Frederick Rawski, 'To Waive or Not to Waive: Immunity and Accountability in U.N. Peacekeeping Operations' (2002) 18 *Conn J Intl L* 103 at 123–124.
[72] Gaillard and Pingel-Lenuzza, 'International Organisations and Immunity'.
[73] See, for example, Guido den Dekker and Jessica Schechinger, 'The Immunity of the United Nations Before the Dutch Courts Revisited' (May 2010) Hague Justice Portal; generally, Wellens, *Remedies Against International Organizations*.
[74] *Mothers of Srebrenica v. Netherlands and United Nations*, Final appeal judgement, Netherlands Supreme Court (13 April 2012) LJN: BW1999, para. 4.3.4 (in Dutch): 'De VN (Veiligheidsraad) neemt in de internationale rechtsgemeenschap een bijzondere plaats in...'
[75] Ibid., para. 4.3.6: 'Die immuniteit ist absoluut. Het handhaven daarvan behoort bovendien tot de verplichtingen van de leden van de VN die, zoals ook het EHRM in Behrami, Behrami en Saramanti [sic] in aanmerking heeft genomen, ingevolge art. 103 Handvest VN in geval van strijdigheid voorrang hebben boven verplichtingen krachtens andere internationale overeenkomsten.'

the weak standard of equivalent justice is required. States (or their courts) do not have to satisfy themselves that claims processes are available when refusing admissibility of cases against the United Nations. In addition, the court relied on the ICJ's decision in *Germany v. Italy* to find that the immunity of international organizations cannot be displaced on the basis of the gravity of the acts or omissions alleged. In *Germany v. Italy*, it was war crimes for which Germany admitted the facts (and responsibility). In *Mothers of Srebrenica*, the allegations centred around the obligation to prevent genocide.

The European Court of Human Rights held the applicant's claim that the Dutch court decisions resulted in a violation of Article 6 of the ECHR to be inadmissible. Canvassing its jurisprudence on the immunity of international organizations, it reiterated its previous decisions and arguably went beyond them. It acknowledged that the nature of the claim in Mothers of Srebrenica, as third parties (i.e., not employees) directly against the organization (i.e. and not against a state party carrying out a resolution of the organization) was qualitatively different to any of its previous cases.[76] However, it found no reason to stray from its previous decisions affirming that 'since operations established by United Nations Security Council resolutions under Chapter VII of the United Nations Charter are fundamental to the mission of the United Nations to secure international peace and security, the Convention cannot be interpreted in a manner which would subject the acts and omissions of the Security Council to domestic jurisdiction without the accord of the United Nations.'[77] What is more, the Court held that even though in *Waite and Kennedy* it had held the existence of an alternative mechanism allowing access to a remedy to be a '"material factor"... in determining whether granting an international organisation immunity from domestic jurisdiction was permissible under the Convention', and even though it was obvious that no such alternative existed, the fact that the UN had not done so was 'not imputable to the Netherlands'.[78] With all due respect, in the other cases, the failure (or provision) of an alternative remedy was neither imputable to nor within the power of the host state either, but that factor is immaterial to whether the alternative remedy existed. Obviously, it is not within the power of the Netherlands to force the UN to create a claims tribunal or some other remedy in a specific peace operation. Even so, the Court insisted that

---

[76] *Mothers of Srebrenica and Others v. the Netherlands* (App No. 65542/12) Decision on admissibility, 11 June 2013, para. 152.

[77] Ibid., para. 154.   [78] Ibid., para. 165.

'the present case is fundamentally different from earlier cases in which the Court has had to consider the immunity from domestic jurisdiction enjoyed by international organisations, and the nature of the applicants' claims did not compel the Netherlands to provide a remedy against the United Nations in its own courts.'[79] In conclusion, it held that 'in the present case the grant of immunity to the United Nations served a legitimate purpose and was not disproportionate'.[80] Leaving one to imagine exactly what is being balanced in its calculation of proportionality, the ECtHR does not give any reason to believe there are chinks in the UN's armour of immunity.

All this leads rather to the conclusion that, although it may seem desirable to be able to assert that the conduct of PMSCs may be attributed to the UN such that it must be responsible for that conduct, the sheer impossibility of enforcing such responsibility in any court means that successfully asserting attribution to the UN is far from a panacea. In fact, it may be the opposite. If immunity is upheld for the individuals by the organization (which has been the case even in the case of a NATO contractor involved in sex trafficking), there may be no way for an individual to obtain satisfaction other than through the processes which the UN sets up (and controls) itself.

Françoise Hampson has advocated the creation and adoption of an additional protocol to the ICCPR specifically allowing claims to be brought against states for the actions of their nationals participating in UN peace operations alleged to violate human rights – including civilian police.[81] In her view, ideally, such a mechanism could have reporting requirements and a possibility for individual petitions.[82] This is an excellent idea. This would inevitably entail affirming the extra-territorial human rights obligations of states under the ICCPR – including when states are not in control of the actor specifically. It should also provide for jurisdiction over any civilian national a state contributes to a peace operation, including PMSCs. However, while this solution provides redress in some form, it still does not get at the responsibility of the UN itself.

In all missions, in response to sexual exploitation and abuse scandals, a number of reforms designed to address that issue have been implemented.

---

[79] Ibid.   [80] Ibid., para. 169.
[81] Françoise Hampson, 'Fora for Effectuating International Responsibility in Relation to Wrongful Acts Committed in the Course of Peace Operations, or, Where Can You Sue?: International Organisations' Involvement in Peace Operations: Applicable Legal Framework and the Issue of Responsibility' (2012) 42 *Collegium* 111–117, especially at 117.
[82] Ibid.

For example, telephone hotlines to report abuse have been set up and 'focal points' where abuse can be reported in person have been established.[83] These may assist in triggering investigations of misconduct or criminal activity, an accountability mechanism that will be discussed below, but in and of themselves they are not sufficient to be considered accountability mechanisms. Rather, they orient the victims towards medical, psychosocial and legal assistance available in the area.[84] Nonetheless, facilitating reports of abuse and addressing the impact on victims is integral to developing accountability.

This assessment shows that the existing ways of implementing the responsibility of the United Nations for wrongful conduct that may be attributable to it – or even of its due diligence obligations – remain weak. The fact that they essentially remain subject to the control of the organization itself in terms of their appreciation and decisions to waive immunity creates a situation in which the UN is arguably above the law. This observation makes the organization's efforts to promote the rule of law in states ring hollow. Moreover, when it comes to PMSCs, it suggests that being able to attribute their conduct to the UN is only half the battle in enforcing responsibility. The work of the Human Rights Advisory Panel in Kosovo, in particular in relation to the *Mon Balaj* case, illustrates that an independent court for peace operations helps to ensure that the organization cannot escape full responsibility for human rights (and IHL) violations by changing the applicable rules or demanding waivers in exchange for unilaterally decided compensation packages. Pressure should be put on the UN to create such courts in all peace operations, and the ability to make claims must be extended to the local population also in respect of the acts of contractor activity. For those PMSCs such as CIVPOL and some security guards whose conduct may be attributable as that of agents of the organization, such 'jurisdiction' is a given. However, where the UN is employing vast numbers of contractors in such situations, local nationals must also be able to enforce the UN's due diligence obligations in respect of such actors.

14.3   Conclusion

The United Nations does not have a good record of accepting responsibility for its failings – or for alleged violations of its obligations under international law – in peace operations. As this part has shown, the law

---

[83] Report of the Secretary-General, 'Measures to Strengthen Accountability at the United Nations', UN Doc A/60/312 (30 August 2005), para. 48.
[84] Ibid.

on responsibility of international organizations is still in a relatively early phase of its formal development. National courts have begun using the ILC's Draft Articles on the Responsibility of International Organizations and appear to accept that actions of peacekeepers may be attributed to the troop-contributing country and to the organization itself.

National courts have shown themselves to be willing to accept dual attribution even in situations for which the United Nations' legal reading would absolve the state of responsibility. While this may go a long way to palliate the wrongs done to victims of violations of international law, these same courts have allowed the UN to hide behind its immunity and, thus, to remain above the law.

It remains to be seen, however, how responsibility for the actions of a PMSC in a peace operation may be implemented. Even if the wrongful conduct of a PMSC could be attributed to the United Nations, or if it can be shown that the UN failed to meet its obligations of due diligence, it remains difficult, if not impossible, to enforce the responsibility of the organization in court. At the same time, the international political climate seems to be becoming less tolerant of immunity than it has been in the past, giving reason to hope.

~

General Conclusion

The recent proliferation of private military and security companies profoundly challenges commonly held notions of the necessary degree of state control over the use of armed force, especially in armed conflicts. For this reason alone, the industry has garnered a great deal of attention in recent years. Efforts to control the industry and to reaffirm the responsibility of states using private military and security contractors have flourished. For its part, the industry itself has aggressively engaged in the creation of highly visible mechanisms of self-regulation.

At its heart, the fundamental question raised by this study is whether even perfectly implemented regulations can be sufficient to control and constrain PMSCs in situations of armed conflict and in peace operations. The strange character of international humanitarian law – as a law that seeks to regulate a situation that, in an ideal world, should not exist – provides the first clue. Indeed, IHL is designed to regulate a situation that most people would wish to do away with entirely. While general international law prohibits a first resort to armed force and strives to avert the outbreak of armed conflict, it nevertheless accepts that armed conflict occurs, and IHL seeks to regulate it. Within this context, pragmatic efforts to regulate a newly predominant actor, rather than seeking to prohibit it entirely, make sense.

Regulatory efforts nevertheless raise important questions. The most obvious question is: what must such regulations contain? To date, regulatory efforts have mainly focused on the proper vetting of candidates, training and oversight. While the Montreux Document reminds all states of their obligation to disseminate and ensure respect for IHL, the main concern raised by this study is that a key aspect of international humanitarian law for PMSCs – the complex question of the relationship between self-defence and direct participation in hostilities – has not yet been sufficiently taken into account. Of course, the law of armed conflict does not directly prohibit civilians from directly participating in hostilities and it does not prohibit mercenarism. That being said, in international armed conflicts, combatants may directly participate in hostilities under IHL and retain all the protection of that law for people of their status, while civilians may not. The notion that combatants may directly participate in hostilities and retain the protection that IHL offers for their normal status denotes a clear preference built into the law.

Most private military and security contractors have the status of civilians under international humanitarian law. One important consequence of that status is that PMSCs should not be used in roles in which they will directly participate in hostilities. Although that limitation is widely acknowledged, its significance for the ways in which PMSCs may be used is not generally well understood, mainly due to the fact that the concept of direct participation in hostilities is itself complex. The International Committee of the Red Cross has published an Interpretive Guidance that provides a generally helpful framework for analysis. According to the ICRC's Interpretive Guidance, force used in self-defence against an unlawful attack lacks a belligerent nexus and therefore does not constitute direct participation in hostilities. This study has shown, however, that not all force used in self-defence in a situation of armed conflict will necessarily lack a belligerent nexus. In national legal systems, a person may use force in self-defence against an unlawful attack. Civilians who are otherwise not directly participating in hostilities may unquestionably use force in self-defence against direct attacks against themselves or other civilians without becoming direct participants in hostilities on that basis. However, for PMSCs, as an industry that seeks to exploit the right to use force in self-defence in order to carry out its contractual obligations in situations of armed conflict, it is imperative to understand that using force to defend against an unlawful attack on a combatant or on a military objective in fact may entail direct participation in hostilities. Indeed, there are many types of attacks that are unlawful under IHL, but the mere fact that some element of an attack is unlawful does not necessarily mean that defending against it lacks a belligerent nexus. This conclusion has repercussions for private military and security contractors who perform security services – in particular, it means that precautions should be taken to make sure that PMSCs are not tasked with guarding military objectives or combatants. Ideally, they should also not be used in places in which hostilities are likely to occur due to the fact that there is no static definition of what is a military objective. Admittedly, however, it may be in precisely such unstable areas in which recourse to private security contractors may be most appealing from the point of view of some of those who use them. Regulators will need to find a way to resolve this inherent tension.

In this regard, the admonition in the Montreux Document that contracting states should carefully determine the services for which PMSCs may be contracted and 'take into account... whether a particular service could cause PMSC personnel to become involved in direct participation in hostilities' is an important starting point.[1] However, this study has shown that such an analysis can prove complex. Moreover, similar limitations in laws regulating PMSCs in the states in which they are registered present difficult logistical challenges for those who must implement such laws.[2] Studies on the implementation of the Montreux Document emphasize as a key weakness that states have not yet adopted clear and precise laws specifying what functions PMSCs may or may not perform, in particular in relation to direct participation in hostilities.[3]

Under international humanitarian law, the principal reason why it is so important that PMSCs not be used in roles in which they directly participate in hostilities is to ensure respect for the principle of distinction, which is a cardinal principle of this body of law. There is reason to fear that the prohibition in IHL against directly attacking civilians will be eroded if states continue to use civilians in roles in which they are likely to participate directly in hostilities. When it is not clear who is a lawful target in war, everyone may become a potential target.

At the same time, on a broader level, the notion of who may directly participate in hostilities on behalf of a state is closely linked with the concept of whether some acts must remain solely within the preserve of the state, to be carried out exclusively by state organs or agents. Current international law imposes other limits on the tasks or activities that states may outsource to PMSCs. States may not outsource the capacity to take a decision to use force against another state. The entire Westphalian system is designed to protect the sovereign equality of states, such that outsourcing that decision-making power would constitute an abdication of the

---

[1] Montreux Document on Pertinent International Legal Obligations and Good Practices for States Related to Operations of Private Military and Security Companies During Armed Conflict' (17 September 2008), Transmitted to the UN General Assembly and Security Council in UN Doc A/63/467-S/2008/636 (6 October 2008), Part II, para. 1.

[2] See for example the recent Swiss bill, which stipulates that PMSCs registered in Switzerland will not be permitted to provide services in places in which they will be likely to directly participate in hostilities. See 'Loi fédérale sur les prestations de sécurité privées fournies à l'étranger', Feuille fédérale (2012) 1651.

[3] Benjamin Buckland and Anna Marie Burdzy, 'Progress and Opportunities, Five Years On: Challenges and Recommendations for Montreux Document Endorsing States', DCAF, 2013, pp. 17–20; Rebecca DeWinter-Schmitt (ed.), 'Montreux Five Years On: An Analysis of State Efforts to Implement Montreux Document Legal Obligations and Good Practices', 2013, pp. 41–49.

essence of the sovereign powers at the heart of the system. In this light, it is important to recall that PMSC personnel operate drones and may possess some of the technical expertise necessary for computer network attack. A drone strike against a group or individual in the territory of a foreign state may give rise to an international armed conflict if the state in which the targeted person or group does not consent to such operations. Allowing a PMSC drone operator to decide whether to carry out a strike on foreign soil would thus involve an impermissible delegation of the power to decide to use force against another state. The same analysis applies for computer network attacks, especially when those attacks may amount to armed conflicts.

It is hoped that the existing limits in international law that have been identified here may provide a helpful background or starting point in regard to efforts to implement the Montreux Document and its Good Practices. These limits may also inform the recent efforts by the UN Working Group to develop a Draft Convention on PMSCs that may contain a clause prohibiting potential state parties from outsourcing specific tasks or activities that some contend are inherently governmental.

Private military and security companies have long been engaged in peace operations. However, their scope of activity is becoming broader, raising important issues. In peace operations, the concept of self-defence plays a role on two levels. First, the interpretation of the force that peacekeeping forces may use in self-defence has evolved over time to include the defence of the mandate. In effect, this broad understanding of the notion of self-defence allows peacekeepers to respond with a robust use of force against 'spoilers' and armed groups, yet remain within their mandate. In practice, it means that even peacekeeping forces in UN-commanded and -controlled operations can become involved as participants in an armed conflict. Since the creation of the Intervention Brigade in MONUSCO in spring 2013, which is a brigade mandated to neutralize armed groups, operating within a UN-commanded and -controlled peace operation, that role has become even more evident.[4] A more robust use of force, including in self-defence, is a significant factor in the growing complexity of peace operations.

In addition, PMSCs contracted to provide security services in peace operations rely on the use of force in self-defence to meet their contractual obligations, just as PMSCs do in other situations. It is striking that the United Nations' policy on the use of armed security guards permits such guards to use force essentially to the same degree and in the same

---

[4] UNSC Res 2098 (28 March 2013) para. 9.

circumstances as the first UN peacekeepers. That is, armed security guards may use force to defend and repel attacks on UN property and personnel, including to provide mobile protection.[5] One of the questions this study has sought to answer is whether the UN may legally use a PMSC as the military force in a peace operation. Arguably, in light of the recent policy, it has already done so. This crucial observation means that the dialogue needs to shift. The essential question is no longer 'should we go down this path?' Rather, attention and efforts must focus on determining whether the existing regulatory framework is adequate – and this study suggests that it is not – and on making it fit for reality.

Peace operations may be tasked with protecting civilians in unstable environments. In such cases – and in other situations – this study has shown that peacekeepers may be drawn into armed conflict with armed groups. This may be the case even in so-called traditional UN peacekeeping. In such cases, the personnel in the military contingent of peace operations should have combatant status. Recently, some have called for the use of PMSCs as peacekeepers in relation to the attacks on civilians in Darfur, Sudan, which one government characterized as a genocide. If the existing legal framework appears not to prohibit the use of PMSCs as peacekeepers, as this study has shown, what is the significance of their lack of combatant status in such circumstances? In other words, in the face of extreme situations, does it really matter whether PMSCs have combatant status? After all, this work has concluded that, while there is an implicit obligation to use state armed forces, including in non-international armed conflicts, that obligation may not be a peremptory norm of international law.

Indeed, situations in which there is a great deal of violence perpetrated against civilians might seem to warrant exceptional measures, and a lack of combatant status on the part of the members of a peacekeeping force might not seem like a serious impediment. This study has also suggested that there may be ways that the UN Security Council could remedy that lacuna. However, even the force used to suppress genocidal or any other criminal acts may not and must not be unbound by law. In dire circumstances, could the UN policies and rules for armed security guards or other such rules make up for the fact that PMSCs are not members of state armed forces? In this regard, it is imperative to recall that combatant status is much more than a status. Between states, combatant status emblemizes membership in a system that is designed to respect and implement

---

[5] UN Department of Safety and Security, Chapter IV: Security Management, Section I – Armed Private Security Companies', in UNSMS Security Policy Manual (November 2012) paras 8 and 9.

international humanitarian law. Via their integration into a chain of command, combatants (and especially their commanding officers) are able to evaluate the proportionality of an attack or operation and thereby ensure that it is carried out in a way that respects IHL. In addition, the discipline that is so central to armed forces is more than the simple existence of an enforcement mechanism for violations of the law. It is what keeps an army from becoming 'an unruly mob' and ensures that soldiers are able to exercise self-restraint.[6] Such discipline is all the more essential in the face of cataclysmic events such as genocide, crimes against humanity, or other serious attacks on a civilian population. Thus, without wishing to disparage the integrity of PMSCs, the analysis presented here has indicated that the Security Council would need to do more than simply declare that all members of a PMSC peacekeeping force have combatant status in order to fully compensate for the fact that they are not members of state armed forces.

Finally, this study has examined how states and international organizations may be responsible for the wrongful conduct of PMSCs. The focus of the analysis was on international organizations due to fact that the responsibility of international organizations has received much less attention than that of states and because this work focuses on peace operations. The recent adoption of the Draft Articles on the Responsibility of International Organizations by the International Law Commission provided the framework for analysis, even though the detailed study also carried out herein revealed that it is not evident that the Draft Articles codify existing customary law. Debate in this area primarily centres on the degree of control an international organization must exercise over a state's troop contribution for the conduct of those troops to be attributable to the United Nations. Perhaps even more salient in light of the current extensive use of PMSCs as security guards in peace operations is the rule on the attribution of conduct of organs or agents of an international organization.[7] A key finding of this study is that although it is the position of the United Nations Secretariat (and other UN bodies) that contractors are not agents of the organization, in some circumstances, armed private security guards may be tasked with performing a core function of the organization. Thus, the wrongful conduct of such armed guards may be attributable to the United

---

[6] Leslie Green, 'The Role of Discipline in the Military' (2004) 42 *Canadian YB Intl L* 385–421 at 385, 417–418.

[7] Article 6 DARIO, ILC, 'Report of the International Law Commission on the Work of Its 63rd Session' (2011) UN Doc A/66/10, p. 84.

Nations, even if it goes against the rules of the organization to consider those guards as agents of the organization.

There are, of course, no guarantees that public forces will always act in perfect conformity with international humanitarian law or human rights law in armed conflicts or peace operations. Indeed, there are plenty of examples to show they do not always do so. There is, however, some consolation in the fact that if public forces do not respect the law, there is a system in place, albeit imperfect, to hold states responsible where they have failed to uphold their obligations. Where there is a risk of being held responsible for wrongful acts, one expects to see diligence in attempting to meet the requirements of obligations, thereby raising the standard of expected behaviour. At present, the international system does not have a mechanism for regulating the use of force by private actors, nor of ensuring accountability or responsibility in case of wrongful acts. However, it is not just the missing accountability mechanisms that make the use of private force seem maladapted to the international system at the present time. In theory, private forces could respect the key prohibitions and obligations in international humanitarian law and human rights law, but it is difficult to get around the fact that the system was not set up for them to be using force in the first place. Indeed, the state monopoly on the use of force is somehow part of the foundation of international humanitarian law and to some extent in international human rights law. Broadening the cohort of actors who may use force, while preserving the gains made via the adoption of international rules, requires more than just tweaking the system in small ways.

The ability to deploy a peacekeeping force has been an important tool for the international community and will continue to be so for the foreseeable future. Some privatization of peacekeeping would seem to be unavoidable, as it is inevitable that the increased use of private military and security contractors more broadly will affect the composition of the forces on the ground in peace operations. However, more transparency in regard to their use in UN peace operations is urgently needed. Clear and enforceable legal obligations on all actors in peace operations can only help to increase their legitimacy and success. It is hoped that this work provides the foundation for earnest and open debate on appropriate regulation of the use of private military and security contractors in peace operations.

BIBLIOGRAPHY

Abraham, E., 'The Sins of the Savior: Holding the United Nations Accountable to International Human Rights Standards for Executive Order Detention in Its Mission in Kosovo' (2003) 52 *Am U L Rev* 1291

Abresch, William, 'A Human Rights Law of Internal Armed Conflict: The European Court of Human Rights in Chechnya' (2005) 16 *EJIL* 741–767

Akande, Dapo, 'International Court of Justice and the Security Council: Is There Room for Judicial Control of Decisions of the Political Organs of the United Nations?' (1997) 46 *ICLQ* 303–343

Alvarez, José, *International Organizations as Law-Makers* (Oxford: Oxford University Press, 2005)

'Revisiting the ILC's Draft Rules on International Organization Responsibility' (2011) 105 *Am Soc Intl L Proceedings* 344–348

Ambos, Kai, 'Other Grounds for Excluding Criminal Responsibility', in A. Cassese, P. Gaeta and J. Jones (eds.), *The Rome Statute of the International Criminal Court: A Commentary* (Oxford: Oxford University Press, 2002), 1003–1048

'Toward a Universal System of Crime: Comments on George Fletcher's Grammar of Criminal Law' (2007) 28 *Cardozo L Rev* 2647

Amerasinghe, Chittaranjan, *Principles of the Institutional Law of International Organizations* (Cambridge University Press, 1996)

Principles of the Institutional Law of International Organizations, 2nd edn (Cambridge University Press, 2005)

Antonyshyn, D., J. Grofe and D. Hubert, 'Beyond the Law? The Regulation of Canadian Private Military and Security Companies Operating Abroad', in Christine Bakker and Mirko Sossai (eds.), *Multilevel Regulation of Military and Security Contractors* (Oxford: Hart, 2011), 381–409

Ashworth, Andrew, 'Self-Defence and the Right to Life' (1975) 34 *Cambridge L J* 282

d'Aspremont, Jean, 'The Articles on the Responsibility of International Organizations: Magnifying the Fissures in the Law of International Responsibility' (2012) 9 *Intl Org L Rev* 15–28

d'Aspremont, Jean, and Jérôme de Hemptinne, *Droit international humanitaire* (Paris: Pedone, 2012)

377

Avant, Deborah, *The Market for Force* (Cambridge University Press, 2001)

'Think Again: Mercenaries' *Foreign Policy*, 1 July 2004

'The Implications of Marketized Security for IR Theory: The Democratic Peace, Late State Building, and the Nature and Frequency of Conflict' (2006) 4 *Perspectives on Politics* 507–528

Barbour, S., and Z. Salzman, '"The Tangled Web": The Right of Self-Defense Against Non-State Actors in the *Armed Activities* Case' (2008) 40 *NY U J Intl L & Politics* 53

Baxter, Richard, 'The Legal Consequences of the Unlawful Use of Force Under the Charter' (1968) 62 *Am Soc Intl L Proceedings* 68–75

Bederman, David, 'World Law Transcendant' (2005) 54 *Emory Law J* 53

Bellamy, Alex J., and Paul D. Williams, *Understanding Peacekeeping*, 2nd edn (Cambridge: Polity Press, 2010)

Berdal, Mats, 'Lessons Not Learned: The Use of Force in "Peace Operations" in the 1990s', in A. Adebajo and C.L. Sriram (eds.), *Managing Armed Conflicts in the 21st Century* (New York: Frank Cass, 2001)

Blokker, Niels, 'Is the Authorization Authorized? Powers and Practice of the UN Security Council to Authorize the Use of Force by "Coalitions of the Able and Willing"' (2000) 11 *EJIL* 541–568

Bodansky, D., J. Crook and D. Caron, 'The ILC Articles on State Responsibility: The Paradoxical Relationship Between Form and Authority' (2002) 96 *AJIL* 857

Boddens Hosang, Hans, 'Force Protection, Unit Self-Defence, and Extended Self-Defence', in T. Gill and D. Fleck (eds.), *The Handbook of the International Law of Military Operations* (Oxford University Press, 2010), 415–427

Bodeau-Livinec, P., G. Buzzini and S. Villalpando, Case Comment in 'International Decisions' (2008) 102 *AJIL* 323–331

Boissier, Léopold, 'L'Application des Conventions de Genève par les forces armées mises à la disposition des nations unies' (1961) 43 *IRRC* 592–594

Boisson de Chazournes, Laurence, 'Changing Roles of International Organizations: Global Administrative Law and the Interplay of Legitimacies – Concluding Remarks' (2009) 6 *Intl Org L Rev* 655

'Les relations entre organisations régionales et organisations universelles' (2010) 347 *RCADI* 79–406

Boldt, Nikki, 'Outsourcing War: Private Military Companies and International Humanitarian Law' (2004) 47 *German YB Intl L* 502–544

Bolkovac, Kathryn, *The Whistleblower* (Palgrave Macmillan, 2011)

Bongiorno, Carla, 'A Culture of Impunity: Applying International Human Rights Law to the United Nations in East Timor' (2001–2002) 33 *Columbia Human Rights L Rev* 623

Boothby, Bill, '"And for such time as": The Time Dimension to Direct Participation in Hostilities' (2010) 42 *NYU J Intl L & Politics* 741

Bothe, Michael, 'Security Council's Targeted Sanctions Against Presumed Terrorists: The Need to Comply with Human Rights Standards' (2008) 6 *J Intl Crim Justice* 541

Bothe, Michael, and T. Marauhn, 'The United Nations in Kosovo and East Timor – Problems of a Trusteeship Administration' (2000) *Intl Peacekeeping* 152

Bothe, Michael, K.J. Partsch and W.A. Solf, *New Rules for Victims of Armed Conflict: Commentary on the Two 1977 Protocols Additional to the Geneva Conventions of 1949* (The Hague: Martinus Nijhoff, 1982)

Boustany, Katia, 'A Questionable Decision of the Court Martial Appeal Court of Canada' (1998) 1 *YB Intl Humanitarian L* 371–374

Bouvier, Antoine, '"Convention on the Safety of United Nations and Associated Personnel": Presentation and Analysis' (1995) 35 *IRRC* 638–666

Bower G., and H. Bellot, 'The Law of Capture at Sea: The Peace of Utrecht to the Declaration of Paris' (1918) 3 *Intl L Notes* 181

Bowett, D.W., *United Nations Forces: A Legal Study of United Nations Practice* (London: Stevens, 1964)

Brand, Marcus, 'Effective Human Rights Protection When the UN "Becomes the State": Lessons from UNMIK', in N. White and D. Klaasen (eds.), *The UN, Human Rights and Post-Conflict Situations* (Manchester University Press, 2005)

Brekoulakis, Stavros L, 'The Relevance of the Interests of Third Parties in Arbitration: Taking a Closer Look at the Elephant in the Room' (2009) 113 *Penn State L Rev* 1165–1188

Brierly, J.L., 'International Law and Resort to Armed Force' (1932) 4 *Cambridge LJ* 308

Brooke-Holland, Louisa, 'Unmanned Aerial Vehicles (Drones): An Introduction', UK House of Commons Library Report, Standard Note SN06493 (25 April 2013)

Brooks, Doug, 'Messiahs or Mercenaries? The Future of International Private Military Services' (2000) 7 *Intl Peacekeeping* 129–144

'Private Military Service Providers: Africa's Welcome Pariahs', in *Nouveaux Mondes – Guerres d'Afrique* (Spring 2002) 69–86 (special issue edited by Laurent Bachelor)

Brown Weiss, Edith, 'Invoking State Responsibility in the Twenty-first Century' (2002) 96 *AJIL* 798

Browne, Marjorie Ann, 'United Nations Peacekeeping: Issues for Congress', CRS Report (updated 13 November 2008)

'United Nations Peacekeeping: Issues for Congress', CRS Report (13 August 2010)

Buchan, Russell, Henry Jones and Nigel White, 'The Externalization of Peacekeeping: Policy, Responsibility, and Accountability' (2011) 15 *J Intl Peacekeeping* 281–315

Buchanan, C., and R. Muggah, 'No Relief: Surveying the Effects of Gun Violence on Humanitarian and Development Personnel' (Centre for Humanitarian Dialogue, 2005)

Bures, Oldrich, 'Private Military Companies: A Second Best Peacekeeping Option?' (2005) 12 *Intl Peacekeeping* 533–546

Burmester, H.C., 'The Recruitment and Use of Mercenaries in Armed Conflicts' (1978) 72 *AJIL* 37–56

Buzzini, Gionata, 'La théorie des sources face au droit international général' (2002) 106 *Revue général du droit international public* 582

Cameron, Lindsey, 'Private Military Companies: Their Status Under International Humanitarian Law and Its Impact on Their Regulation' (2006) 88 *IRRC* 573
'New Standards for and by Private Military Companies?', in A. Peters et al. (eds.), *Non-State Actors as Standard Setters* (Cambridge University Press, 2009), 113–145
'The Use of Private Military and Security Companies in Armed Conflicts and Certain Peace Operations', PhD thesis, University of Geneva (2015)

Cammaert, Patrick, and Ben Klappe, 'Application of Force and Rules of Engagement in Peace Operations', in T. Gill and D. Fleck (eds.), *The Handbook of the International Law of Military Operations* (Oxford University Press, 2010)

Canada, Department of National Defence and the Canadian Forces, 'Report of the Somalia Commission of Inquiry' (1997)

Canny, N., 'A Mercenary World: A Legal Analysis of the International Problem of Mercenarism' (2003) 3 *U College Dublin L Rev* 33–56

Cassese, Antonio, 'Mercenaries: Lawful Combatants or War Criminals?' (1980) 40 *ZaöRV* 1–30
'Terrorism Is Also Disrupting Some Crucial Legal Categories of International Law' (2001) 12 *EJIL* 993

Cerone, John, 'Human Dignity in the Line of Fire: The Application of International Human Rights Law During Armed Conflict, Occupation, and Peace Operations' (2006) 39 *Vanderbilt J Transnational L* 1447

Chesterman, Simon, 'We Can't Spy ... If We Can't Buy!' (2008) 19 *EJIL* 1055–1074
'Lawyers, Guns and Money: The Governance of Business Activities in Conflict Zones' (2011) 11 *Chicago J Intl L* 321
'External Study: The Use of Force in UN Peace Operations' (UN DPKO Best Practices Unit, undated)

Chesterman, Simon, and Chia Lehnardt (eds.), *From Mercenaries to Market* (Oxford University Press, 2007)

Clapham, Andrew, *Human Rights Obligations of Non-State Actors* (Oxford University Press, 2006)
'Human Rights Obligations of Non-State Actors in Conflict Situations' (2006) 88 *IRRC* 491–523

Clarke, M.H.F., T. Glynn and A.P.V. Rogers, 'Combatant and POW Status', in M.A. Meyer (ed.), *Armed Conflict and the New Law* (1991), 107–135

Cockayne, James, 'Commercial Security in Humanitarian and Post-Conflict Settings: An Exploratory Study' (International Peace Institute, 2006)

Cockayne, James, and David Malone, 'The Ralph Bunche Centennial: Peace Operations Then and Now' (2005) 11 *Global Governance* 331–350

Cockayne, James, and Daniel Pfister, 'Peace Operations and Organised Crime' (Geneva Centre for Security Policy and IPI, 2008)

Coicaud, Jean-Marc, and Jibecke Jönsson, 'Elements of a Road Map for a Politics of Apology', in M. Gibney, R. Howard-Hassmann, J.-M. Coicaud and N. Steiner (eds.), *The Age of Apology: Facing Up to the Past* (University of Pennsylvania Press, 2008), 77–91

Corn, Geoff, 'Unarmed but How Dangerous? Civilian Augmentees, the Law of Armed Conflict, and the Search for a More Effective Test for Permissible Civilian Battlefield Functions' (2008) 2 *J Natl Security L & Policy* 257

Cottier, Michael, 'Article 8(iii)', in O. Triffterer (ed.), *Commentary on the Rome Statute of the International Criminal Court: Observers Notes, Article by Article*, 2nd edn (Nomos, 2008), 330–338

Cotton, Sarah, et al., *Hired Guns: Views About Armed Contractors in Operation Iraqi Freedom* (RAND Corporation, 2010)

Cox, Katherine, 'Beyond Self-Defense: United Nations Peacekeeping Operations and the Use of Force' (1999) 27 *Denver J Intl L and Policy* 239–273

Crawford, Emily, *The Treatment of Combatants and Insurgents Under the Law of Armed Conflict* (Oxford University Press, 2010)

Crawford, James, *The International Law Commission's Articles on State Responsibility: Introduction, Text and Commentaries* (Cambridge University Press, 2002)

Crawford, James, and Simon Olleson, 'The Continuing Debate on a UN Convention on State Responsibility' (2005) 54 *ICLQ* 959–972

Cullen, Anthony, *The Concept of Non-International Armed Conflict in International Humanitarian Law* (Cambridge University Press, 2010)

Dannecker, G., 'Justification and Excuses in the European Community – Adjudication of the Court of Justice of the European Community and Tendencies of the National Legal Systems as a Basis for a Supranational Regulation' (1993) 1 *European J Crime, Criminal L & Crim Justice* 230

Dannenbaum, Tom, 'Translating the Standard of Effective Control into a System of Effective Accountability: How Liability Should Be Apportioned for Violations of Human Rights by Member State Troop Contingents Serving as United Nations Peacekeepers' (2010) 51 *Harvard Intl LJ* 113–192

David, Eric, *Mercenaires et volontaires internationaux en droit des gens* (Brussels: Bruylant, 1978)

Principes de droit des conflits armés, 4th edn (Brussels: Bruylant, 2008)

De Nevers, Renee, 'Private Security Companies and the Laws of War' (2009) 40 *Security Dialogue* 169–190

Del Mar, Katherine, 'The Requirement of 'Belonging' Under International Humanitarian Law' (2010) 21 *EJIL* 105–124

Den Dekker, G., 'The Regulatory Context of Private Military and Security Contractors at the European Union Level', in Christine Bakker and Mirko Sossai (eds.), *Multilevel Regulation of Military and Security Contractors* (Oxford: Hart, 2011) 31–52

Den Dekker, G., and E.P.J. Myjer, 'The Right to Life and Self-Defence of Private Military and Security Contractors in Armed Conflict', in Francesco Francioni and Natalino Ronzitti (eds.), *War by Contract* (Oxford University Press, 2011), 171–193

Di Blase, Antonia, 'The Role of the Host State's Consent with Regard to Non-coercive Actions by the United Nations', in A. Cassese (ed.), *United Nations Peace-Keeping: Legal Essays* (Sijthoff and Noordhoff, 1978), 55–94

Dickinson, Laura, 'Contract as a Tool for Regulating Private Military Companies', in Simon Chesterman and Chia Lehnardt (eds.), *From Mercenaries to Market* (Oxford University Press, 2007), 217–238

Outsourcing War and Peace: Foreign Relations in a Privatized World (New Haven: Yale University Press, 2011)

Diehl, Paul, *International Peacekeeping* (Baltimore: Johns Hopkins University Press, 1993)

Peace Operations (Cambridge: Polity, 2008)

Dinstein, Yoram, *War, Aggression and Self-Defence*, 3rd edn (Cambridge University Press, 2001)

War, Aggression and Self-Defence, 5th edn (Cambridge University Press, 2011)

Domb, Fania, 'The Privatisation of Prisons Case: H.C. (High Court) 2605/05, Human Rights Division et al. v. Minister of Finance et al.' (2010) 40 *Israel YB Human Rights* 307–331

Donald, Dominick, 'Neutrality, Impartiality and UN Peacekeeping at the Beginning of the 21st Century' (2002) 9 *Intl Peacekeeping* 21–38

Dörmann, Knut, 'Art. 8(2)(b)(iii)' and 'Art. 8(2)(e)(iii)', in K. Dörmann (ed.), *Elements of War Crimes Under the Rome Statute of the International Criminal Court: Sources and Commentary* (Cambridge University Press, 2002)

'The Legal Situation of "Unlawful/Unprivileged Combatants"' (2003) 85 *Intl Rev Red Cross* 45–74

'Applicability of the Additional Protocols to Computer Network Attacks', www.icrc.org/eng/resources/documents/misc/68lg92.htm

Doswald-Beck, Louise, 'The Right to Life in Armed Conflict: Does International Humanitarian Law Provide All the Answers?' (2006) 88 *IRRC* 881–904

'Private Military Companies Under International Humanitarian Law', in S. Chesterman and C. Lehnardt (eds.), *From Mercenaries to Market: The Rise and Regulation of Private Military Companies* (Oxford University Press, 2007)

Draper, G.I.A.D. 'Combatant Status: An Historical Perspective' (1972) 11 *Military L & L War Rev* 135–143

Droege, Cordula, 'The Interplay Between International Humanitarian Law and International Human Rights Law in Situations of Armed Conflict' (2007) 40 *Israel L Rev* 347

Dunigan, Molly, *Victory for Hire: Private Security Companies' Impact on Military Effectiveness* (Stanford: Stanford University Press, 2011)

Dupont, L., and C. Fijnaut, 'Belgium', in F. Verbruggen (ed.), *International Encyclopaedia of Laws: Criminal Law* (1993)

Durch, William, and Tobias Berkman, *Who Should Keep the Peace? Providing Security for Twenty-first Century Peace Operations* (Henry Stimson Center, 2006)

Durch, W.J., V.K. Holt, C.R. Earle and M.K. Shanahan, 'The Brahimi Report at Thirty (Months): Reviewing the UN's Record of Implementation' (2002) 8 *Intl Peacekeeping: YB Intl Peace Operations* 1–32

Durward, R, 'Security Council Authorization for Regional Peace Operations: A Critical Analysis' (2006) 13 *Intl Peacekeeping* (2006) 350–365

Dwan, Renata (ed.), *Executive Policing: Enforcing the Law in Peace Operations*, SIPRI Research Report No. 16 (Oxford University Press, 2002)

Elsea, Jennifer, and Nina Serafino, *Private Security Contractors in Iraq: Background, Legal Status, and Other Issues* (CRS Report for Congress) (21 June 2007)

Engdahl, Ola, *Protection of Personnel in Peace Operations: The Role of the 'Safety Convention' Against the Background of General International Law* (Leiden: Martinus Nijhoff, 2007)

Ferraro, Tristan, 'Applicability/Application of IHL to International Organisations (IO) involved in Peace Operations' (2012) *Collegium* 15–22

'The Applicability and Application of International Humanitarian Law to Multinational Forces' (2013) 95 *IRRC* 561–612

Findlay, Trevor, *The Use of Force in UN Peace Operations* (Oxford: SIPRI and Oxford University Press, 2002)

Finkelman, Andrew, 'Suing the Hired Guns: An Analysis of Two Federal Defenses to Tort Lawsuits Against Military Contractors' (2009) 34 *Brooklyn J Intl Law* 395

Finkelstein, C.O., 'On the Obligation of the State to Extend a Right of Self-Defense to Its Citizens' (1999) 147 *U Penn L Rev* 1361–1402

Fountain, F., 'A Call for "Mercy-naries": Private Forces for International Policing' (2004) 13 *Michigan State U J Intl L* 227–261

Frakt, David, 'Direct Participation in Hostilities as a War Crime: America's Failed Efforts to Change the Law of War' (2012) 46 *Valparaiso U L Rev* 729–764

Franklin, Sarah, 'South African and International Attempts to Regulates Mercenaries and Private Military Companies' (2008) 17 *Transnatl L & Contemporary Problems* 239

de Frouville, Olivier, 'Attribution of Conduct to the State: Private Individuals', in J. Crawford, A. Pellet and S. Olleson (eds.), *The Law of International Responsibility* (Oxford University Press, 2010), 257–280

Frowein, Jochen, and N. Krisch, 'Article 42', in B. Simma (ed.), *The Charter of the United Nations: A Commentary*, 2nd edn (Oxford University Press, 2002), 711

Gaillard, Emmanuel, and Isabelle Pingel-Lenuzza, 'International Organisations and Immunity from Jurisdiction: to Restrict or to Bypass' (2002) 51 *ICLQ* 1–15

Garvey, Jack, 'United Nations Peacekeeping and Host-State Consent' (1970) 64 *AJIL* 241–269

Gaultier, L., et al., 'The Mercenary Issue at the UN Commission on Human Rights: The Need for a New Approach', *International Alert* (undated)

Gazzini, Tarcisio, *The Changing Rules on the Use of Force in International Law* (Manchester: Juris, 2005)

Gestri, Marco, 'The European Union and Private Military and Security Contractors: Existing Controls and Legal Bases for Further Regulation', in Christine Bakker and Mirko Sossai (eds.), *Multilevel Regulation of Military and Security Contractors* (Oxford: Hart, 2011), 53–77

Getzler, J., 'Use of Force in Protecting Property' (2006) 7 *Theoretical Inquiries in Law* 131–166

Ghebali, Victor-Yves, 'The United Nations and the Dilemma of Outsourcing Peacekeeping Operations', in Alan Bryden and Marina Caparini (eds.), *Private Actors and Security Governance* (Geneva: DCAF, 2006), 213–230

Gichanga, Margaret, 'Fusing Privatisation of Security with Peace and Security Initiatives' (2010) ISS Paper 219

Gill, Terry, and Dieter Fleck, 'Private Contractors and Security Companies', in T. Gill and D. Fleck (eds.), *The Handbook of the Law of Military Operations* (Oxford University Press, 2010), 489–493

Gillard, Emanuela-Chiara, 'Business Goes to War: Private Military/Security Companies and International Humanitarian Law' (2006) 88 *IRRC* 525–572

Glick, Richard, 'Lip Service to the Laws of War: Humanitarian Law and United Nations Armed Forces' (1994–1995) 17 *Michigan J Intl L* 53

de Goede, M., 'Private and Public Security in Post-War Democratic Republic of Congo', in S. Gumedze (ed.), *The Private Security Sector in Africa* (Monograph 146) (Institute for Security Studies, 2008), 35–68

Gomez del Prado, Jose, 'Private Military and Security Companies and the UN Working Group on the Use of Mercenaries' (2008) 13 *J Conflict & Security L* 429–450

Goulding, M, 'The Evolution of United Nations Peacekeeping' (1993) 69 *Intl Peacekeeping* 453

Gowan, Richard, and Benjamin Tortolani, 'Robust Peacekeeping and Its Limitations', in Bruce Jones (ed.), *Robust Peacekeeping: The Politics of Force* (Centre for International Cooperation, 2009)

Grabczynska, A., and K. Kessler Ferzan, 'Justifying Killing in Self-Defence' (2009) 99 *J Crim L and Criminology* 235–253

Gray, Christine, 'The Charter Limitations on the Use of Force: Theory and Practice', in V. Lowe et al. (eds.), *The United Nations Security Council and War: The Evolution of Thought and Practice Since 1945* (Oxford University Press, 2008), 86–98

  International Law and the Use of Force, 3rd edn (Oxford University Press, 2008)

Green, James, *The International Court of Justice and Self-Defence in International Law* (Oxford: Hart, 2009)

Green, Leslie, 'The Role of Discipline in the Military' (2004) 42 *Canadian YB Intl L* 385–421

Greenwood, Christopher, 'The Concept of War in Modern International Law' (1987) 36 *ICLQ* 283

  'Scope of Application of Humanitarian Law', in D. Fleck (ed.), *The Handbook of Humanitarian Law in Armed Conflicts* (Oxford University Press, 2008)

Grenfell, Katarina, 'Accountability in International Policing' (2011) 15 *J Intl Peacekeeping* 92–117

Guéhenno, Jean-Marie, 'Robust Peacekeeping: Building Political Consensus and Strengthening Command and Control', in Bruce Jones (ed.), *Robust Peacekeeping: The Politics of Force* (New York University Center on International Cooperation, 2009)

Guillory, Michael, 'Civilianizing the Force: Is the United States Crossing the Rubicon?' (2001) 51 *Air Force L Rev* 111

Gumedze, Sabalo (ed.), *The Private Security Sector in Africa Country Series* (Monograph 146, Institute for Security Studies, 2008).

Hallo de Woolf, A, 'Modern Condottieri in Iraq: Privatizing War from the Perspective of International and Human Rights Law' (2006) 13 *Indiana J Global Legal Studies* 315

Hampson, Françoise, 'Mercenaries: Diagnosis Before Proscription' (1991) 22 *Netherlands YB Intl L* 3–38

  'Direct Participation in Hostilities and the Interoperability of the Law of Armed Conflict and Human Rights Law', in R. Pedrozo and D. Wollschlaeger (eds.), *International Law and the Changing Character of War* (Naval War College International Law Series, vol. 87, 2011), 187–216

  'Fora for Effectuating International Responsibility in Relation to Wrongful Acts Committed in the Course of Peace Operations, or, Where Can You Sue?' (2012) 42 *Collegium* 111–117

Hansen, Annika, *From Congo to Kosovo: Civilian Police in Peace Operations* (Oxford University Press, International Institute for Strategic Studies, 2002)

Heaton, J. Ricou, 'Civilians at War: Re-examining the Status of Civilians Accompanying the Armed Forces' (2005) 57 *Air Force L Rev* 155–208

van Hegelsom, Gert-Jan, 'Command and Control Structure in Peace Operations: The Concrete Relationship Between the International Organization and Its Troops [*sic*] Contributing Countries' (2011) 41 *Collegium* 77–82

Heintschel von Heinegg, Wolff, 'The Law of Armed Conflict at Sea', in D. Fleck (ed.), *The Handbook of Humanitarian Law in Armed Conflicts* (Oxford University Press, 1995)

Henckaerts, Jean-Marie, 'Customary International Humanitarian Law: A Response to US Comments' (2007) 89 *IRRC* 473

Henckaerts, Jean-Marie, and Louise Doswald-Beck, *Customary International Humanitarian Law*, 2 vols. (Cambridge University Press, 2005)

Hermida, J, 'Convergence of Civil Law and Common Law in the Criminal Theory Realm' (2005) 13 *Univ Miami Intl & Comp Law Rev* 163

Hirsch, Moshe, *The Responsibility of International Organizations Toward Third Parties: Some Basic Principles* (Dordrecht: Martinus Nijhoff, 1995)

Holt, Victoria, Glyn Taylor and Max Kelly, *Protecting Civilians in the Context of UN Peacekeeping Operations* (Independent study jointly commissioned by the Department of Peacekeeping Operations and the Office for the Coordination of Humanitarian Affairs, 2009)

Hoppe, Carsten, 'Passing the Buck: State Responsibility for Private Military Companies' (2008) 19 *EJIL* 989–1014

Hough, Leslie, 'A Study of Peacekeeping, Peace-Enforcement and Private Military Companies in Sierra Leone' (2007) 16.4 *African Security Review (Institute for Security Studies)* 8–21

Howland, T, 'Peacekeeping and Conformity with Human Rights Law: How MINUSTAH Falls Short in Haiti' (2006) 13 *Intl Peacekeeping* 462–476

ICRC, *International Humanitarian Law and the Challenges of Contemporary Armed Conflicts* (2011)

Study on the Use of the Emblems: Operational and Commercial and Other Non-operational Issues (Geneva: ICRC, 2011)

Ipsen, Knut, 'Combatants and Non-combatants', in D. Fleck (ed.), *The Handbook of Humanitarian Law in Armed Conflicts* (Oxford University Press, 1995)

Isenberg, David, 'A Government in Search of Cover: Private Military Companies in Iraq', in S. Chesterman and C. Lehnardt (eds.), *From Mercenaries to Market* (Oxford University Press, 2007)

Jinks, Derek, 'The Declining Significance of POW Status' (2004) 45 *Harvard Intl L J* 367–442

Joh, Elisabeth, 'The Paradox of Private Policing' (2004) 95 *J Crim L & Criminology* 49–131

'Conceptualizing the Private Police' (2005) *Utah L Rev* 573

'The Forgotten Threat: Private Policing and the State' (2006) 13 *Indiana J Global Legal Studies* 357–389

Johnstone, Ian, 'Managing Consent in Contemporary Peacekeeping Operations' (2011) 18 *J Intl Peacekeeping* 168–182

Jones, B., R. Gowan and J. Sherman, 'Building on Brahimi: Peacekeeping in an Era of Strategic Uncertainty' (Center on International Cooperation, April 2009)

Juma, Laurence, 'Privatisation, Human Rights and Security: Reflections on the Draft International Convention on Regulation, Oversight and Monitoring of Private Military and Security Companies' (2011) 15 *Law, Democracy & Development*

Karis, Daniel, 'A Comparative Study of Two Peacekeeping Training Programs: The African Crisis Response Initiative (ACRI) and the African Contingency Operations Training Assistance Program (ACOTA)', thesis (2009), www .peaceopstraining.org/theses/karis.pdf

Kestian, Matthew, 'Civilian Contractors: Forgotten Veterans of the War on Terror' (2008) 39 *U Toledo L Rev* 887

Klabbers, Jan, *An Introduction to International Institutional Law* (Cambridge University Press, 2002)

'The Paradox of International Institutional Law' (2008) 5 *Intl Org L Rev* 151–173

Kleffner, Jann, 'From "Belligerents" to "Fighters" and Civilians Directly Participating in Hostilities – On the Principle of Distinction in Non-international Armed Conflicts One Hundred Years After the Second Hague Peace Conference' (2007) *Netherlands Intl L Rev* 315–336

'The Applicability of International Humanitarian Law to Organized Armed Groups' (2011) 93 *IRRC* 443–461

Klein, Pierre, *La Responsabilité des organisations internationales* (Brussels: Bruylant, 1998)

'The Attribution of Acts to International Organizations', in J. Crawford, A. Pellet and S. Olleson (eds.), *The Law of International Responsibility* (Oxford University Press, 2010), 297–315

Köhler, Anna, *Private Sicherheits-und Militärunternehmen im bewaffneten Konflikt: Eine völkerrechtliche Bewertung* (Frankfurt am Main: Kölner Schriften zu Recht und Staat, 2010)

Koivurova, Timo, 'Due Diligence', in R. Wolfrum (ed.), *Max Planck Encyclopedia of Public International Law* (Oxford University Press, 2008–)

Kolb, Robert, *Ius contra bellum* (Basel/Brussels: Helbing & Lichtenhahn/Bruylant, 2003)

'Applicability of International Humanitarian Law to Forces Under the Command of an International Organization', in ICRC, *Report on the Expert Meeting on Multinational Peace Operations* (2004)

Droit humanitaire et opérations de paix internationales, 2nd edn (Brussels: Bruylant, 2006)

Kolb, Robert, Gabriele Porretto and Sylvain Vité, *L'application du droit international humanitaire et des droits de l'homme aux organisations internationales: Forces de paix et administrations civiles transitoires* (Brussels: Bruylant, 2005)

Kondoch, Boris, 'The Responsibility of Peacekeepers, Their Sending States, and International Organizations', in T. Gill and D. Fleck (eds.), *The Handbook of the International Law of Military Operations* (Oxford University Press, 2010), 515–534

Kontos, A.P., '"Private" Security Guards: Privatized Force and State Responsibility Under International Human Rights Law' (2004) 4 *Non-State Actors & Intl L* 199–238

Kopel, D.B., P. Gallant and J.D. Eisen, 'The Human Right of Self-Defense' (2007) 22 *Brigham Young U J Public L* 43–178

Kotzur, M, 'Good Faith (Bona fide)', in R. Wolfrum (ed.), *Max Planck Encyclopedia of Public International Law* (Oxford University Press, 2008–)

Koutroulis, Vaios, 'International Organisations Involved in Armed Conflict: Material and Geographical Scope of Application of International Humanitarian Law' (2012) 42 *Collegium* 29–40

Kovač, Matija, 'Legal Issues Arising from the Possible Inclusion of Private Military Companies in UN Peacekeeping' (2009) 13 *Max Planck YB UN Law* 307–374

Krahmann, Elke, 'Regulating Military and Security Services in the European Union', in A. Bryden and M. Caparini (eds.), *Private Actors and Security Governance* (Geneva: LIT & DCAF, 2006), 189–212

States, Citizens and the Privatization of Security (Cambridge University Press, 2010)

'The UN Guidelines on the Use of Armed Guards: Recommendations for Improvement' (2014) 16 *ICLR* 475–491

Krieger, Heike, 'A Conflict of Norms: The Relationship Between Humanitarian Law and Human Rights Law in the ICRC Customary Law Study' (2006) 11 *J Conflict & Security L* 265–291

Kuhl, Corinna, 'The Evolution of Peace Operations, from Interposition to Integrated Missions', in Gian Luca Beruto (ed.), *International Humanitarian Law, Human Rights and Peace Operations* (31st Round Table, San Remo, 2008), 70–76

La Rosa, Anne-Marie, and C. Wuerzner, 'Armed Groups, Sanctions and the Implementation of International Humanitarian Law' (2008) 90 *IRRC* 327–341

Langsted, L.B., P. Garde, V. Greve, 'Denmark', in F. Verbruggen (ed.), *International Encyclopaedia of Laws: Criminal Law* (Netherlands: Kluwer Law International, 2003)

Lauterpacht, Elihu, 'The Legal Irrelevance of the "State of War"' (1968) 62 *Am Soc Intl L Proceedings* 58–68

Leander, Anna, and Rens van Munster, 'Private Security Contractors in the Debate About Darfur: Reflecting and Re-inforcing Neo-Liberal Governmentality' (2007) 21 *Intl Relations* 201–216

Leck, Christopher, 'International Responsibility in United Nations Peacekeeping Operations: Command and Control Arrangements and the Attribution of Conduct' (2009) 10 *Melbourne J Intl L* 346

Lehnardt, Chia, 'Peacekeeping', in Simon Chesterman and Angelina Fischer (eds.), *Private Security, Public Order: The Outsourcing of Public Services and Its Limits* (Oxford University Press, 2009), 205–221

Private Militärfirmen und völkerrechtliche Verantwortlichkeit (Tübigen: Mohr Siebeck, 2011)

Levie, Howard, 'The Employment of Prisoners of War' (1963) 57 *AJIL* 313–353

Prisoners of War (International Law Studies Series Naval War College, 1977)

Levine, Daniel H., 'Peacekeeper Impartiality: Standards, Processes, and Operations' (2011) 15 *J Intl Peacekeeping* 422–450

Lewis, Michael, 'Is President Obama's Use of Predator Strikes in Afghanistan and Pakistan Consistent with International Law and International Standards?' (2010–2011) 37 *William Mitchell Law Review* 5021–5033

Maffai, Margaret, 'Accountability for Private Military and Security Company Employees That Engage in Sex Trafficking and Related Abuses While Under Contract with the United States Overseas' (2008–2009) 26 *Wisconsin Intl L J* 1095–1139

Malkin, H.W., 'The Inner History of the Declaration of Paris' (1927) 8 *British Ybk Intl L* 1–43

Mani, K., 'Latin America's Hidden War in Iraq' *Foreign Policy* (11 October 2007)

Manin, Philippe, *L'Organisation des Nations Unies et le maintien de la paix: le respect du consentement de l'état* (Paris: Pichon & Durand-Auzias, 1971)

Martin, J.S., 'Fighting Piracy with Private Security Measures: When Contract Law Should Tell Parties to Walk the Plank' (2010) 59 *American U L Rev* 1363–1398

Matheson, M.J., 'Remarks', in 'Session One: The United States' Position on the Relation of Customary International Law to the 1977 Protocols Additional to the 1949 Geneva Conventions' (1987) 2 *Am U J Intl L & Policy* 419

Mathias, Stephan, 'Regulating and Monitoring Private Military and Security Companies in United Nations Peacekeeping Operations', IIHL Roundtable, San Remo, September 2012

Maxwell, M., and R. Meyer, 'The Principle of Distinction: Probing the Limits of its Customariness' (March 2007) *Army Lawyer* 1–11

McCoubrey, Hilaire, and Nigel White, *The Blue Helmets: Legal Regulation of United Nations Military Operations* (Aldershot: Dartmouth, 1996)

McDougal, M., and F.P. Feliciano, 'The Initiation of Coercion' (1958) 52 *AJIL* 241–259

Mégret, Frédéric, 'The Vicarious Responsibility of the United Nations for "Unintended Consequences" of Peacekeeping Operations', in Chiyuki Aoi, Cedric de Cooning and Ramesh Thakur (eds.), *The 'Unintended Consequences' of Peace Operations* (Tokyo: UN University Press, 2007), 250–267

Melzer, Nils, *Targeted Killing in International Law* (Oxford University Press, 2008)
'Keeping the Balance Between Military Necessity and Humanity: A Response to Four Critiques of the ICRC's Interpretive Guidance on the Notion of Direct Participation in Hostilities' (2010) 42 *NYUJILP* 831

Messineo, Francesco, 'Things Could Only Get Better: *Al-Jedda* Beyond *Behrami*' (2011) 50 *Military L and L War Rev* 321

Meyrowitz, Henri, *Le principe de l'égalité des belligérants devant le droit de la guerre* (Paris: Pedone, 1970)

Milanovic, Marko, *Extraterritorial Application of Human Rights Treaties: Law, Principles, and Policy* (Oxford University Press, 2011)
'Is the Rome Statute Binding on Individuals (And Why We Should Care)' (2011) 9 *J Intl Criminal Justice* 25–52

Milanovic, Marko, and Tania Papic, 'As Bad as It Gets: The European Court of Human Rights *Behrami* and *Saramati* Decision and General International Law' (2009) 58 *ICLQ* 267

Miller, Anthony J, 'United Nations Experts on Mission and Their Privileges and Immunities' (2007) 4 *Intl Org L Rev* 11–56

Milliard, Todd, 'Overcoming Post-Colonial Myopia: A Call to Recognize and Regulate the Companies' (2003) 176 *Military L Rev* 1–95

Mineau, M.L., 'Pirates, Blackwater and Maritime Security: The Rise of Private Navies in Response to Modern Piracy' (2010) 9 *J Intl Business & L* 63–78

Mkutu, K., and K. Sabala, 'Private Security Companies in Kenya and Dilemmas for Security' (2007) 25 *J Contemporary African Studies* 391–416

Modirzadeh, Naz (Moderator), 'Targeting with Drone Technology: Humanitarian Law Implications' (2011) 105 *Am Society Intl L Proceedings* 233–252 (panelists Chris Jenks and Nils Melzer)

Moir, Lindsay, *The Law of Internal Armed Conflict* (Cambridge University Press, 2002)

Montejo, Blanca, 'The Roles and Responsibilities of International Organizations: Introductory Remarks' (2011) 105 *Am Soc Intl L Proceedings* 343–344

Moskos, Charles C., *Peace Soldiers: The Sociology of a United Nations Military Force* (Chicago and London: University of Chicago Press, 1976)

Mujezinovic Larsen, Kjetil, 'Attribution of Conduct in Peace Operations: The "Ultimate Authority and Control" Test' (2008) 19 *EJIL* 509
The Human Rights Treaty Obligations of Peacekeepers (Cambridge University Press, 2012)

Murphy, Ray, *UN Peacekeeping in Lebanon, Somalia and Kosovo: Operational and Legal Issues in Practice* (Cambridge University Press, 2007)

Murphy, Sean, 'Self-Defense and the Israeli *Wall* Advisory Opinion: An *Ipse Dixit* from the ICJ?' (2005) 99 *AJIL* 62–76

Naert, Frederik, 'Detention in Peace Operations: The Legal Framework and Main Categories of Detainees' (2006) 45 *Military L & L War Rev* 51–78

Naqvi, Yasmin, 'Doubtful Prisoner-of-War Status' (2002) 84 *IRRC* 571–594

Nasu, Hitoshi, *International Law on Peacekeeping: A Study of Article 40 of the UN Charter* (Leiden: Martinus Nijhoff, 2009)

Nollkaemper, André, 'Concurrence Between Individual Responsibility and State Responsibility in International Law' (2003) 52 *ICLQ* 615–640

Nourse, VF, 'Self-Defense and Subjectivity' (2001) 68 *U Chicago L Rev* 1235

Oeter, Stefan, 'Methods and Means of Combat', in D. Fleck (ed.), *The Handbook of Humanitarian Law in Armed Conflicts* (Oxford University Press, 1995)

Okimoto, Keiichiro, *The Distinction and Relationship Between Jus ad Bellum and Jus in Bello* (Oxford: Hart Publishing, 2011)

Oostenhuizen, G.H., 'Playing the Devil's Advocate: The United Nations Security Council Is Unbound by Law' (1999) 12 *Leiden J Intl L* 549

Oppenheim, International Law – A Treatise, Vol II: *Disputes, War and Neutrality*, 7th edn, H. Lauterpacht (ed.) (London: Longman, 1952)

Orakhelashvili, Alexander, 'The Legal Basis for Peacekeeping' (2003) 43 *Vanderbilt JIL* 485

'The Impact of Peremptory Norms on the Interpretation and Application of United Nations Security Council Resolutions' (2005) 16 *EJIL* 59–88

Collective Security (Oxford University Press, 2011)

Østensen, Åse Gilje, *UN Use of Private Military and Security Companies: Practices and Policies* (Geneva: DCAF, 2011)

'In the Business of Peace: The Political Influence of Private Military and Security Companies on UN Peacekeeping' (2013) 20 *Intl Peacekeeping* 33–47

'Implementers or Governors? The Expanding Role for Private Military and Security Companies Within the Peace Operations Network' (2014) 16 *ICLR* 423–442

Oswald, Bruce, 'The Law on Military Occupation: Answering the Challenges of Detention During Contemporary Peace Operations?' (2007) 8 *Melbourne J Intl L* 311–326

'Detention by United Nations Peacekeepers: Searching for Definition and Categorisation' (2011) 15 *J Intl Peacekeeping* 119–151

Oswald, Bruce, and Adrian Bates, 'Privileges and Immunities of United Nations Police' (2010) 14 *J Intl Peacekeeping* 375–402

Oswald, Bruce, Helen Durham and Adrian Bates, *Documents on the Law of UN Peace Operations* (Oxford University Press, 2010)

Paciocco, David, 'Applying the Law of Self-Defence' (2007) 12 *Canadian Crim L Rev* 25

Palchetti, Paolo, 'Armed Attack Against the Military Force of an International Organization and Use of Force in Self-Defence by a Troop Contributing State: A Tentative Legal Assessment of an Unlikely Scenario' (2010) 7 *Intl Org L Rev* 241–260

Palwankar, Umesh, 'Applicability of International Humanitarian Law to United Nations Peacekeeping Forces' (1993) *IRRC* 227–240

Parks, W Hays, 'Part IX of the ICRC "Direct Participation in Hostilities Study": No Mandate, No Expertise, and Legally Incorrect' (2010) 42 *NYUJILP* 769

Parodi, Florence, 'Les sociétés militaires et de sécurité privées en droit international et droit comparé', thesis, Université Paris I Panthéon-Sorbonne (2009)

Parrillo, Nicholas, 'The De-privatization of American Warfare: How the U.S. Government Used, Regulated, and Ultimately Abandoned Privateering in the Nineteenth Century' (2007) 19 *Yale J L & Humanities* 1–95

Patterson, Malcolm, 'A Corporate Alternative to United Nations *ad hoc* Military Deployments' (2008) 13 *J Conflict and Security L* 215–231

Privatising Peace: A Corporate Adjunct to United Nations Peacekeeping and Humanitarian Operations (Palgrave Macmillan, 2009)

Pattison, James, 'Outsourcing the Responsibility to Protect: Humanitarian Intervention and Private Military and Security Companies' (2010) 2 *Intl Theory* 1–31

Paust, J, 'Self-Defense Targetings of Non-State Actors and Permissibility of U.S. Use of Drones in Pakistan' (2010) 19 *J Transnational L and Policy* 237

Pejic, Jelena, 'The Right to Food in Situations of Armed Conflict: The Legal Framework' (2001) 83 *IRRC* 1097–1109

Penny, Christopher, '"Drop That or I'll Shoot ... Maybe": International Law and the Use of Deadly Force to Defend Property in UN Peace Operations' (2007) 14 *Intl Peacekeeping* 353–367

Percy, Sarah, 'Mercenaries: Strong Norm, Weak Law' (2007) 61 *Intl Org* 367

Mercenaries: The History of a Norm in International Relations (Oxford University Press, 2008)

'The Security Council and the Use of Private Force', in V. Lowe et al. (eds.), *The United Nations Security Council and War* (Oxford University Press, 2008), 624–640

Pfanner, Toni, 'Military Uniforms and the Law of War' (2004) 86 *IRRC* 93

Pictet, Jean (ed.), *The Geneva Conventions of 12 August 1949: Commentary, First Geneva Convention for the Amelioration of the Condition of the Wounded and Sick in Armed Forces in the Field* (ICRC: Geneva, 1952)

(ed.), *The Geneva Conventions of 12 August 1949: Commentary, Fourth Geneva Convention Relative to the Protection of Civilian Persons in Time of War* (Geneva: ICRC, 1958)

(ed.), *The Geneva Conventions of 12 August 1949: Commentary, Third Geneva Convention Relative to the Treatment of Prisoners of War* (ICRC: Geneva, 1960)

Pingeot, Lou, *Dangerous Partnership: Private Military and Security Companies and the UN* (Global Policy Forum and Rosa Luxemburg Foundation, 2012)

Pisillo-Mazzeschi, Riccardo, 'The Due Diligence Rule and the Nature of the International Responsibility of States' (1992) 35 *German YB Intl L* 9–51

Politoff, S.I., F.A.J. Koopmans and M.C. Ramirez, 'Chile', in F. Verbruggen (ed.), *International Encyclopaedia of Laws: Criminal Law* (Netherlands: Kluwer Law International, 2003)

Pradel, J, *Droit pénal comparé*, 3rd edn (Paris: Dalloz, 2008)

Pratt, F.T. (ed.), *Notes on the Principles and Practices of Prize Courts by the Late Judge Storey* (London: William Benning et al., 1854)

Primosch, Edmund, 'The Roles of United Nations Civilian Police (UNCIVPOL) within United Nations Peace-Keeping Operations' (1994) 43 *ICLQ* 425–431

Quéguiner, J.F., 'Direct Participation in Hostilities under International Humanitarian Law' (HPCR, 2003)

Rawski, Frederick, 'To Waive or Not to Waive: Immunity and Accountability in U.N. Peacekeeping Operations' (2002) 18 *Conn J Intl L* 103

Reinisch, August, *International Organizations Before National Courts* (Cambridge University Press, 2000)

'Editorial: How Necessary Is Necessity for International Organizations?' (2006) 3 *Intl Org L Rev* 177–183

'The Immunity of International Organizations and the Jurisdiction of their Administrative Tribunals', IILJ Working Paper 2007/11 (Global Administrative Law Series)

Renault, Louis, 'War and the Law of Nations in the Twentieth Century' (1915) 9 *AJIL* 1–16

Renaut, Céline, 'The Impact of Military Disciplinary Sanctions on Compliance with International Humanitarian Law' (2008) 90 *IRRC* 319–326

Roberts, A., 'Proposals for UN Standing Forces: A Critical History', in V. Lowe et al. (eds.), *The United Nations Security Council and War* (Oxford University Press, 2008), 99–130

Roberts, A., and R. Guelff (eds.), *Documents on the Laws of War*, 3rd edn (Oxford University Press, 2000)

Rochester, Christopher, 'White Paper: A Private Alternative to a Standing United Nations Peacekeeping Force' (Peace Operations Institute, 2007)

Rogers, A.P.V., 'Combatant Status', in E. Wilmshurst and S. Breau (eds.), *Perspectives on the ICRC Study on Customary International Humanitarian Law* (Cambridge University Press, 2007), 101–27

'Direct Participation in Hostilities: Some Personal Reflections' (2009) 48 *Military L & L War Rev* 143–163

Ronzitti, N., 'The Use of Private Contractors in the Fights Against Piracy: Policy Options', in F. Francioni and N. Ronzitti (eds.), *War by Contract: Human*

Rights, Humanitarian Law, and Private Contractors (Oxford University Press, 2011), 37–51

Rosas, Allan, *The Legal Status of Prisoners of War* (Finland: Abo Akademi, 1976)

Rossman, James, 'Article 43: Arming the United Nations Security Council' (1994–1995) 27 *NYUJILP* 227–263

Ruffert, M, 'The Administration of Kosovo and East-Timor by the International Community' (2001) 50 *ICLQ* 613

Rufin, J.-C., 'The Paradoxes of Armed Protection', in F. Jean (ed.), *Life, Death and Aid: The Médecins Sans Frontières Report on World Crisis Intervention* (London: Routledge, 1993), 111–123

Salmon, J., 'Article 26 – Convention de 1969', in Olivier Corten and Pierre Klein (eds.), *Les Conventions de Vienne sur le Droit des Traités: Commentaire article par article*, vol. 2 (Brussels: Bruylant, 2008), 1075–1115

Salzman, Z., 'Private Military Contractors and the Taint of a Mercenary Reputation' (2008) 40 *NYUJILP* 853–892

San Remo Manual on International Law Applicable to Armed Conflicts at Sea (adopted June 1994)

Sandoz, Y., C. Swinarski and B. Zimmermann (eds.), *Commentary on the Additional Protocols of 8 June 1977 to the Geneva Conventions of 12 August 1949* (Geneva: ICRC, 1987)

Sands, Philippe, and Pierre Klein, *Bowett's Law of International Institutions*, 6th edn (London: Sweet and Maxwell, 2009)

Sari, Aurel, 'Jurisdiction and International Responsibility in Peace Support Operations: The *Behrami* and *Saramati Cases*' (2008) 8 *Human Rights L Rev* 151

Sarooshi, Danesh, 'The Legal Framework Governing United Nations Subsidiary Organs' (1996) 67 *British Ybk Intl L* 413–478

    The United Nations and the Development of Collective Security: The Delegation by the UN Security Council of Its Chapter VII Powers (Oxford University Press, 1999)

    International Organizations and Their Exercise of Sovereign Powers (Oxford University Press, 2005)

    'The Security Council's Authorization of Regional Arrangements to Use Force: The Case of NATO', in V. Lowe et al. (eds.), *The United Nations Security Council and War: The Evolution of Thought and Practice Since 1945* (Oxford University Press, 2008), 226–247

Sassòli, Marco, 'State Responsibility for Violations of International Humanitarian Law' (2002) 84 *IRRC* 401

    'Legislation and Maintenance of Public Order and Civil Life by Occupying Powers' (2005) 16 *EJIL* 661

    'Terrorism and War' (2006) 4 *JICJ* 959

    'Le droit international humanitaire, une lex specialis par rapport aux droits humains?', in Andreas Auer, Alexandre Flückiger and Michel Hottelier (eds.),

Les droits de l'homme et la constitution, Etudes en l'honneur du Professeur Giorgio Malinverni (Geneva: Schulthess, 2007) 375–395

'Combatants', in R. Wolfrum (ed.), *Max Planck Encyclopaedia of International Law* (Oxford University Press, 2008–)

'The International Legal Framework for Stability Operations: When May International Forces Attack or Detain Someone in Afghanistan?' (2009) 39 *Israel YB Human Rights* 177–212

'Introducing a Sliding-Scale of Obligations to Address the Fundamental Inequality Between Armed Groups and States?' (2011) 93 *IRRC* 425

Sassòli, M., and L. Cameron, 'The Protection of Civilian Objects – Current State of the Law and Issues *de lege ferenda*', in N. Ronzitti and G. Venturini (eds.), *The Law of Air Warfare: Contemporary Issues* (Utrecht: Eleven, 2006), 35–74

Sassòli, M., and L. Olson, 'The Judgment of the ICTY Appeals Chamber on the Merits in the *Tadic* Case' (2000) 82 *IRRC* 733–769

'The Relationship Between International Humanitarian and Human Rights Law Where It Matters: Admissible Killing and the Internment of Fighters in Non-international Armed Conflicts' (2008) 90 *IRRC* 599–627

Saura, Jaume, 'Lawful Peacekeeping: Applicability of International Humanitarian Law to United Nations Peacekeeping Operations' (2006–2007) 58 *Hastings LJ* 479

Schachter, Oscar, 'The Development of International Law Through the Legal Opinions of the United Nations Secretariat' (1948) 5 *British YB Intl L* 91–133

'The Relation of Law, Politics and Action in the United Nations' (1963) 109 *RCADI* 165–256

International Law in Theory and Practice (Dordrecht: Martinus Nijhoff, 1991)

Schermers, Henry, and Niels Blokker, *International Institutional Law*, 5th revised edn (Dordrecht: Martinus Nijhoff, 2011)

Schindler, Dietrich, 'United Nations Forces and International Humanitarian Law', in Christophe Swinarski (ed.), *Studies and Essays on International Humanitarian Law and Red Cross Principles in Honour of Jean Pictet* (The Hague: Martinus Nijhoff, 1984), 521–530

Schindler, Dietrich, and Jiri Toman, *The Laws of Armed Conflict*, 4th edn (Leiden: Martinus Nijhoff, 2004)

Schmalenbach, Kirsten, 'Third Party Liability of International Organizations: A Study on Claim Settlement in the Course of Military Operations and International Administrations' (2005) 10 *Intl Peacekeeping* 33–51

'International Organizations or Institutions: Legal Remedies Against Acts of Organs', in R. Wolfrum (ed.), *Max Planck Encyclopedia of Public International Law* (Oxford University Press, 2008–)

Schmidl, Erwin, 'Police Functions in Peace Operations: An Historical Overview', in Robert Oakley, Michael Dziedzic and Eliot Goldberg (eds.), *Policing the New*

World Disorder: Peace Operations and Public Security (University Press of the Pacific, 1998), 19–40

Schmitt, Michael, 'The Resort to Force in International Law: Reflections on Positivist and Contextual Approaches' (1994) 37 *Air Force L Rev* 105

'Humanitarian Law and Direct Participation in Hostilities by Private Contractors or Civilian Employees', expert paper (2004)

'Humanitarian Law and Direct Participation in Hostilities by Private Contractors or Civilian Employees' (2005) 5 *Chicago J Intl L* 511–546

'Human Shields in International Humanitarian Law' (2009) 47 *Columbia J Transnational L* 292

'Deconstruction Direct Participation in Hostilities: The Constitutive Elements' (2010) 42 *NYUJILP* 697

'Military Necessity and Humanity in International Humanitarian Law: Preserving the Delicate Balance' (2010) *Virginia J Intl L* 795–839

'Cyber Operations and the *Jus in Bello*: Key Issues' (2011) 87 *International Law Studies Series, US Naval War College*, 89–110

'The Status of Opposition Fighters in a Non-international Armed Conflict' (2012) 88 *International Law Studies Series US Naval War College* 119–144

Schmitt, Michael (ed.), *Tallinn Manual on the International Law Applicable to Cyber Warfare* (Cambridge University Press, 2013)

Schwartz, Moshe, 'Department of Defense Contractors in Iraq and Afghanistan: Background and Analysis' (Congressional Research Service Report) 21 September 2009

Schwarzenberger, Georg, 'The Fundamental Principles of International Law' (1955) 87 *RCADI* 195–385

Schweigman, David, *The Authority of the Security Council Under Chapter VII of the UN Charter: Legal Limits and the Role of the International Court of Justice* (The Hague: Kluwer Law International, 2001)

Seyersted, Finn, 'United Nations Forces: Some Legal Problems' (1961) 37 *British YB Intl L* 351

Shaw, Malcolm, *International Law*, 5th edn (Cambridge University Press, 2003)

Shraga, Daphna, 'The United Nations as an Actor Bound by International Humanitarian Law', in L. Condorelli, A.M. La Rosa and S. Scherrer (eds.), *Les Nations Unies et le droit international humanitaire – The United Nations and international humanitarian law: actes du colloque international à l'occasion du cinquantième anniversaire de l'ONU (Genève 19, 20, 21 octobre 1995)* (Paris: Pedone, 1996)

'The United Nations as an Actor Bound by International Humanitarian Law' (1998) 5 *Intl Peacekeeping* 64–81

'UN Peacekeeping Operations: Applicability of International Humanitarian Law and Responsibility for Operations-Related Damage' (2000) 94 *AJIL* 406

'The Secretary-General's Bulletin on the Observance by United Nations Forces of International Humanitarian Law: A Decade Later' (2009) 39 *Israel YB Human Rights* 357–377

'The ILC Draft Articles on Responsibility of International Organizations: The Interplay Between the Practice and the Rule' (2011) 105 *Am Soc Intl L Proceedings* 351–353

Sicilianos, Linos-Alexandre 'Entre multilatéralisme et unilatéralisme: l'autorisation par le conseil de sécurité de recourir à la force' (2008) 339 *RCADI* 9–436

Siekmann, Robert, *National Contingents in United Nations Peace-Keeping Forces* (Dordrecht: Martinus Nijhoff, 1991)

Simma, Bruno, 'Commentary to Article 2(2)', in B. Simma (ed.), *The Charter of the United Nations: A Commentary* (1995)

Singer, Peter, *Corporate Warriors: The Rise of the Privatized Military Industry* (Ithaca: Cornell University Press, 2003)

'Humanitarian Principles, Private Military Agents: Implications of the Privatized Military Industry for the Humanitarian Community' (2006) 13 *Brown J World Affairs* 105–121

Sivakumaran, Sandesh, *The Law of Non-international Armed Conflict* (Oxford University Press, 2012)

Sklansky, David, 'The Private Police' (1999) 46 *UCLA L Rev* 1165–1287

Slater, J, 'Making Sense of Self-Defence' (1996) 5 *Nottingham L J* 140

Sloan, James, 'The Use of Offensive Force in U.N. Peacekeeping: A Cycle of Boom and Bust?' (2007) 30 *Hastings Intl & Comp L Rev* 385

The Militarization of Peacekeeping in the Twenty-first Century (Oxford: Hart Publishing, 2011)

Smith, H.A., 'Le développement moderne des lois de la guerre maritime' (1938) 63 *Recueil des Cours de l'Académie de Droit International* 603–719

Sohn, L.B., 'The Authority of the United Nations to Establish and Maintain a Permanent United Nations Force' (1958) 52 *AJIL* 229–240

Solf, Waldemar, 'The Status of Combatants in Non-international Armed Conflicts Under Domestic Law and Transnational Practice' (1983) 33 *American U Law Rev* 53

Sorel, J.M., 'La responsabilité des Nations Unies dans les opérations de maintien de la paix' (2001) 3 *International Law Forum* 127

Spearin, C., 'Humanitarian Non-Governmental Organizations and International Private Security Companies: The "Humanitarian" Challenges of Moulding a Marketplace' (DCAF Policy Paper 16, 2007)

Stahn, Carsten, *The Law and Practice of International Territorial Administration: Versailles to Iraq and Beyond* (Cambridge University Press, 2008)

Stanger, Allison, *One Nation Under Contract: The Outsourcing of American Power and the Future of Foreign Policy* (New Haven: Yale University Press, 2011)

Stoddard, Abby, Adele Harmer and Victoria DiDomenico, 'Private Security Providers and Services in Humanitarian Operations' (2008) *Humanitarian Policy Group Reports Issue* 27

Stoffels, R.A., 'Legal Regulation of Humanitarian Assistance in Armed Conflict: Achievements and Gaps' (2004) 86 *Intl Rev Red Cross* 515–546

Stone, J., *Legal Controls of International Conflict* (London: Stevens & Sons, 1954)

Suy, E., 'Legal Aspects of UN Peace-Keeping Operations' (1988) 35 *Netherlands Intl L Rev* 318

Swisspeace, *Private Security Companies and Local Populations: An Exploratory Study of Afghanistan and Angola* (2007)

Tabarrok, A., 'The Rise, Fall, and Rise Again of Privateers' (2007) 11 *The Independent Review* 565–577

Talmon, Stefan, 'Responsibility of Outside Powers for Acts of Secessionist Entities' (2009) 58 *ICLQ* 493–517

Tammes, A.J.P., 'Decisions of International Organs as a Source of International Law' (1958) 94 *Recueil des Cours de l'Académie de Droit International* 261

Tavernier, Paul, 'La légitime défense du personnel de l'ONU', in Rahim Kherad (ed.), *Légitimes défenses* (Poitiers: LGDJ, 2007), 121–138

Thomson, J.E., 'State Practices, International Norms and the Decline of Mercenarism' (1990) 34 *Intl Studies Quarterly* 23–47

Mercenaries, Pirates, and Sovereigns: State-Building and Extraterritorial Violence in Early Modern Europe (Princeton: Princeton University Press, 1994)

Thurnher, J.S., 'Drowning in Blackwater: How Weak Accountability over Private Security Contractors Significantly Undermines Counterinsurgency Efforts' (July 2008) *Army Lawyer* 64–90

Tomuschat, Christian, *International Law: Ensuring the Survival of Mankind on the Eve of a New Century, General Course on Public International Law 134* (The Hague: Martinus Nijhoff, 2001)

Tonkin, Hannah, *State Control over Private Military and Security Companies in Armed Conflict* (Cambridge University Press, 2011)

Tougas, Marie-Louise, *Droit international, societes militaires privées et conflit armé: entre incertitudes et responsabilités* (Brussels: Bruylant, 2012)

Tzanakopoulos, Antonios, *Disobeying the Security Council: Countermeasures Against Wrongful Sanctions* (Oxford University Press, 2011)

UK Ministry of Defence, *Manual of the Law of Armed Conflict* (Oxford University Press, 2004)

Urquhart, B., ' For a UN Volunteer Military Force' *New York Review of Books* 40 (10 June 1993)

Van Deventer, H.W., 'Mercenaries at Geneva' (1976) 70 *AJIL* 811

Verbruggen, F. (ed.), *International Encyclopaedia of Laws: Criminal Law* (various dates)

Verdirame, Gugliemo, *Who Guards the Guardians?* (Cambridge University Press, 2011)

Verkuil, Paul, *Outsourcing Sovereignty: Why Privatization of Government Functions Threatens Democracy and What We Can Do About It* (Cambridge University Press, 2007)

Vierucci, Luisa, 'Prisoners of War or Protected Persons *qua* Unlawful Combatants? The Judicial Safeguards to Which Guantánamo Bay Detainees Are Entitled' (2003) 1 *JICJ* 288–314

Virally, M, 'Review Essay: Good Faith in Public International Law' (1983) 77 *AJIL* 130–134

Walker, Clive, and D Whyte, 'Contracting Out War?: Private Military Companies, Law and Regulation in the United Kingdom' (2005) 54 *ICLQ* 651–690

Watkin, Kenneth, 'Warriors Without Rights? Combatants, Unprivileged Belligerents, and the Struggle over Legitimacy' (2005) 2 *Harvard Program on Humanitarian Policy and Conflict Research, Occasional Papers*

'Opportunity Lost: Organized Armed Groups and the ICRC "Direct Participation in Hostilities" Interpretive Guidance' (2010) 42 *NYUJILP* 641

Watson, James, Mark Fitzpatrick and James Ellis, 'The Legal Basis for Bilateral and Multilateral Police Deployments' (2011) 15 *J Intl Peacekeeping* 7–38

Watts, Sean, 'Combatant Status and Computer Network Attack' (2010) 50 *Virginia J Intl L* 391–447

'Status of Government Forces in Non-international Armed Conflict', in K. Watkin and A. Norris (eds.), *Non-international Armed Conflict in the Twenty-first Century* (NWC Bluebook Series Vol. 88, 2012), 145–180

Waxman, Matthew C., 'Cyber Attacks as "Force" Under UN Charter Article 2(4)' (2011) 87 *International Law Studies Series US Naval War College* 43–57

Wedgwood, Ruth, 'The ICJ Advisory Opinion on the Israeli Security Fence and the Limits of Self-Defense' (2005) 99 *AJIL* 52–61

Wellens, Karel, *Remedies Against International Organisations* (Cambridge University Press, 2002)

de Wet, Erika, 'The Direct Administration of Territories by the United Nations and Its Member States in the Post Cold War Era: Legal Bases and Implications for National Law' (2004) 8 *Max Planck UN YB* 291

The Chapter VII Powers of the United Nations Security Council (Oxford: Hart Publishing, 2004)

White, Hugh, 'Civilian Immunity in the Precision-Guidance Age', in Igor Primoratz (ed.), *Civilian Immunity in War* (Oxford University Press, 2007), 182–200

White, Nigel D., *Democracy Goes to War: British Military Deployments Under International Law* (Oxford University Press, 2009)

'Empowering Peace Operations to Protect Civilians: Form over Substance?' (2009) 13 *J Intl Peacekeeping* 327–355

'Institutional Responsibility for Private Military and Security Companies', in F. Francioni and N. Ronzitti (eds.), *War by Contract* (Oxford University Press, 2011), 381–395

'The Privatisation of Military and Security Functions and Human Rights: Comments on the UN Working Group's Draft Convention' (2011) 11 *Human Rights L Rev* 133–151

White, Nigel, and Dirk Klaasen, 'An Emerging Legal Regime?', in N. White and D. Klaasen (eds.), *The UN, Human Rights and Post-conflict Situations* (Manchester University Press, 2005)

White, Nigel, and Sorcha MacLeod, 'EU Operations and Private Military Contractors: Issues of Corporate and Institutional Responsibility' (2008) 19 *EJIL* 956–988

Wilde, Ralph, 'Quis Custodiet Ipsos Custodes' (1998) 1 *Yale Human Rights & Development LJ* 119–120

'International Territorial Administration and Human Rights', in N. White and D. Klaasen (eds.), *The UN, Human Rights and Post-conflict Situations* (Manchester University Press, 2005)

Wills, Siobhan, *Protecting Civilians* (Oxford University Press, 2010)

Winthrop, W., 'The United States and the Declaration of Paris' (1894) 3 *Yale L J* 116–118

Woolsey, T.S., 'The United States and the Declaration of Paris' (1894) 3 *Yale L J* 77–81

Wulf, Herbert, *Internationalizing and Privatizing War and Peace* (Basingstoke: Palgrave Macmillan, 2005)

Yeo, S., 'Anglo-African Perspectives on Self-Defence' (2009) 17 *African J Intl & Comp L* 118–135

Zegveld, Liesbeth, *The Accountability of Armed Opposition Groups* (Cambridge University Press, 2002)

Zhou, M., and S. Wang, 'China', in F. Verbruggen (ed.), *International Encyclopaedia of Laws: Criminal Law* (2001)

Zwanenburg, Marten, *Accountability of Peace Support Operations* (Leiden: Martinus Nijhoff, 2005)

'Pieces of the Puzzle: Peace Operations, Occupation and the Use of Force' (2006) 45 *Military L & L War Rev* 239–248

'Regional Organizations and the Maintenance of International Peace and Security: Three Recent Regional African Peace Operations' (2006) 11 *J Conflict & Security L* 483–508

'International Organisations vs Troops Contributing Countries: Which Should Be Considered as the Party to an Armed Conflict During Peace Operations?' (2012) *Collegium* 23–28

INDEX